CASES AND MATERIALS ON THE
INCOME TAXATION OF TRUSTS, ESTATES, GRANTORS AND BENEFICIARIES

By

Jeffrey N. Pennell
Professor of Law
Emory University School of Law

AMERICAN CASEBOOK SERIES

WEST PUBLISHING CO.
ST. PAUL, MINN., 1987

610 Opperman Drive
P.O. Box 64526
St. Paul, MN 55164–0526

Printed in the United States of America

Library of Congress Cataloging-in-Publication Data

Pennell, Jeffery N., 1949–
Cases and materials on the income taxation of trusts, estates, grantors, and beneficiaries.
(American casebook series)
Includes index.
1. Trusts and trustees—Taxation—United States—Cases. 2. Decedents' estates—Taxation—United States—Cases. I. Title. II. Series.
KF6443.A7P46 1987 343.7305'264 87–10563
347.3035264

ISBN 0–314–42565–9

Pennell, Income Taxation ACB
1st Reprint–1996

TEXT IS PRINTED ON 10% POST CONSUMER RECYCLED PAPER

To J. S. P.

*

Preface

The collection of cases and materials and the writing and editing of this casebook has been a singularly solitary task, for good reason: there just aren't many people engaged in the process of teaching, or even learning, Subchapter J of the Internal Revenue Code. Nevertheless, this book is largely the product of a strong, and growing, belief that the income taxation of trusts, estates, grantors and beneficiaries will eclipse the wealth transfer taxes in importance. With increases in the unified credit (and a corresponding decline in the number of estate and gift tax returns filed) and with the new generation-skipping tax exemption, it seems clear that the government can afford to, and already has begun to, devote more of its enforcement resources to the long neglected area of the income taxation of fiduciary entities, their creators and their beneficiaries.

Unfortunately, when I first recommended to our curriculum committee that we add a course on this subject, there was simply no classroom text available. Hence, this casebook is also largely the product of necessity. In a sense, that is both its strength and its weakness. I had to learn Subchapter J virtually from scratch, which (I think) makes me aware of what students experience in learning this subject. I hope the book reflects the knowledge gained in that struggle. Because the book is alone in the market, however, it probably suffers from a lack of perspective. It reflects my method of teaching, which may not suit everyone. Fortunately, there is plenty of room for supplementation of these materials with additional reading and problems.

The practice of law in this area is beginning to improve, as are the government's compliance efforts, and it is difficult to discern which is driving the other. Certainly reform has been the reaction to some of the abuses that previously existed when practitioners took advantage of glitches and deficiencies in the law. There have been important recent changes to Subchapter J, particularly in 1984 and 1986. While far more extensive changes had been recommended, it now appears relatively clear that Congress has little stomach for additional major tax reform. It thus seems probable that this area will see major changes only if Congress undertakes a sweeping wealth transfer tax reform and, as part of that process, attempts to integrate the income tax rules with the wealth transfer tax principles. With this expected tranquility in mind, several new resource materials are now in production, the most important including a revision and expansion of the excellent work by Ferguson, Freeland and Stephens and an additional treatise on Subchapter J. Both are well along, under the hands of respected authorities. Frankly, they come along none too soon: this little corner of tax law can use all the help it can get, and there is still a terrible dearth of useful authority and commentary to parse this difficult subject. Therefore, primarily for the assistance of professors who are first learning this subject, there is a Teachers' Manual available to assist in preparing the course.

In the preparation of the book, normal liberties were taken in editing cases and other materials, with omissions (excepting some citations) noted. Most footnotes from reproduced materials are omitted entirely; those that remain carry their original numbers. Section references, when not otherwise identified, are to the Internal Revenue Code of *1986*—and it almost hurts to call it that. The material is up to date as of January 1, 1987.

I am grateful for the assistance that I received over many years as a professor at the University of Oklahoma College of Law. This book began there and my students in Norman suffered the most in its earlier drafts and through my learning process. Students in the Graduate Tax Program and the Graduate Estate Planning Program at the University of Miami and in the Graduate Tax Program here at Emory have been additional sources of support and useful recommendations for improvement of the book. I owe special thanks to former Dean and now Federal District Judge Wayne Alley and to Sylvia Burgess, John Nicholson and Kim Roberson, all of the University of Oklahoma College of Law, and to Dorothy Breen of the University of Miami School of Law, for the roles they played in the development of these materials. An additional not insignificant source of assistance in the preparation of the book were my many colleagues and contacts in professional associations, especially including the American Bar Association Real Property, Probate and Trust Law Section and the American College of Probate Counsel. Tax laws do not work in a vacuum and the insights of leading practitioners in this area have helped me tremendously in knowing what the problem areas of Subchapter J are in the real world.

My penultimate thanks go to Dean David Epstein of Emory University School of Law for his support and assistance. Finally, four individuals have played the major role in influencing the development of my orientation on life, learning and teaching. Vernon Northcutt, A. Judd Davis and Austin Fleming are no longer alive for me to express my gratitude. Fortunately it is the fourth, and most important, who is still with us, and it is to him that I dedicate the book. Thanks Dad.

JEFFREY N. PENNELL

Atlanta, Georgia
July 22, 1987

Summary of Contents

*

Table of Contents

Appendix

*

Table of Cases

References are to Pages

Table of Statutes

References are to Page

UNITED STATES

UNITED STATES CODE ANNOTATED

26 U.S.C.A.—Internal Revenue Code

26 U.S.C.A.—Internal Revenue Code

26 U.S.C.A.—Internal Revenue Code

26 U.S.C.A.—Internal Revenue Code

26 U.S.C.A.—Internal Revenue Code

26 U.S.C.A.—Internal Revenue Code

26 U.S.C.A.—Internal Revenue Code

Sec.	This Work Page
2054 (Cont'd)	32
	189
	190
	191
2055(a)(2)	190
2056	91
	174
2056(a)	172
2056(b)(5)	254
2502	217
2503(b)	254
2503(c)	211
	212
	225
	227
2513	216
2513(d)	217
2514	236
2514(e)	209
	254
2518	258
6072(a)	44
	45
6324(b)	217
6501	32
6621	276
6654	45
7701	26
7701(a)(3)	8
	12
	13
	14
	17
	20
7701(a)(30)	279
7701(a)(31)	279
7701(b)	187

STATUTES AT LARGE

Year	This Work Page
1978, Nov. 6, P.L. 95–600 92 Stat. 2925	176
1986, Oct. 22, P.L. 99–514 100 Stat. 2811	3

POPULAR NAME ACTS

TAX REFORM ACT OF 1986

Sec.	This Work Page
1401(b)	214
1402(c)(2)	214
1806(b)	3

REVISED UNIFORM PRINCIPAL AND INCOME ACT

Sec.	This Work Page
3(b)(4)	40
3(b)(8)	39
	211
6	40
9	29
13(a)(2)	29
14	29

*

Table of Regulations

References are to Page

TREASURY REGULATIONS

TREASURY REGULATIONS

TREASURY REGULATIONS

PROPOSED TREASURY REGULATIONS

TEMPORARY TREASURY REGULATIONS

ESTATE & GIFT TAX REGULATIONS

*

Table of Revenue Rulings

References are to Page

REVENUE RULINGS

*

Table of Letter Rulings

References are to Page

LETTER RULINGS

Rul.	This Work Page
7809057	**116**
8029001	209
8105028	108
8145026	**95**
8307022	266
8324002	40
	108
8429005	107
8431004	106
8447003	**98**
8501011	50
	141
8501084	50
	141
8506005	107
8514017	277
8517052	209
6404234660A	107

*

CASES AND MATERIALS ON THE

INCOME TAXATION OF TRUSTS, ESTATES, GRANTORS AND BENEFICIARIES

*

Chapter One

INTRODUCTION TO THE FEDERAL INCOME TAXATION OF TRUSTS, ESTATES, GRANTORS, AND BENEFICIARIES

Almost since inception of the federal income tax, the common law garden variety trust has been recognized for its tax minimization and income splitting opportunities. Similarly, while probate can often be avoided by proper planning, estates are often desirable entities kept open after the need for administration has ceased, if it ever existed. Because estates and valid trusts are separate taxpayers under the federal income tax, the issue for tax purposes is frequently whether income should be taxed to the estate or trust or, to prohibit tax avoidance, must it be taxed to the grantor of the trust or to the beneficiaries of the trust or estate. Subchapter J of the Internal Revenue Code (of which sections 641 to 691 deal with our subject, most since their original adoption in 1939) is a particularly complex amalgam of rules designed to answer these questions. Relating to the income taxation of trusts, estates, grantors and beneficiaries, it recognizes trusts and estates as legitimate taxpaying entities under certain circumstances, but may require taxation to the grantor or the beneficiaries in other cases.

FUNDAMENTAL PRINCIPLES

The basic feature of the tax rules embodied in Subchapter J is "conduit taxation." Under those rules, one fundamental objective is to tax income to the beneficiaries of a trust or estate as if the legal entity did not intercede between the payor of income and those beneficiaries. Thus, for example, to the extent a trust is either required to or actually does distribute its income, the trust is generally granted a deduction for the amount of that income under section 651(a) or 661(a) and the beneficiaries of the trust are required to include the same amount of income in their gross incomes under section 652(a) or 662(a). Moreover, that income retains the same character in the hands of the beneficiaries (for example, capital gain, ordinary income, items of tax preference or tax exempt) as it had before distribution by the trust or estate, by virtue of sections 59(c), 652(b) and 662(b).

For a number of reasons, however, this conduit tax precept is, at best, only imperfectly instituted. First among those reasons is that certain items of taxable income of a trust or estate are neither required to be nor, in most cases, are they actually distributed. Under the fundamental rules of Subchapter J, these items must consequently be taxed to the entity. This may occur if the trust or estate accumulates income, thus producing neither a deduction for the trust nor inclusion to the beneficiaries. It may also occur by virtue of the definition in section 643(b) of "income," which generally means "fiduciary accounting income" as determined under local law, such as an applicable Principal and Income Act. A troublesome source of misunderstanding in studying Subchapter J is that income for fiduciary accounting purposes and income for tax purposes may differ. For example, under local laws, some items of taxable income, such as capital gains,[1] are fiduciary accounting principal and thus are not covered by those deduction and inclusion rules that refer to the "income" of the trust or estate. In addition, a distribution from corpus, under proper circumstances, may be regarded for Federal income tax purposes as a distribution of taxable income. In the following materials, remember that it is taxable income and income in a tax sense that is relevant (even though that income may initially be defined by reference to income in a fiduciary accounting sense), regardless of the source of the item or the accounting label imposed thereon by virtue of fiduciary principles.

A second reason why the conduit precept works imperfectly is illustrated with respect to income taxed currently to beneficiaries, as to which the time of inclusion under sections 652(c) and 662(c) may differ from that which would apply had the entity not existed. Further affecting the conduit form of taxation are trusts that are "grantor trusts," as determined under Subpart E (sections 671 to 678) of Subchapter J. As we will discover in Chapter Eight, grantor trusts are taxed under principles that regard the grantor as owner of trust income, notwithstanding its actual distribution to other beneficiaries, effectively superseding conduit taxation principles. Treasury Regulation section 1.671–1(a).

In addition to those reasons that make conduit taxation less than perfectly applicable, several principles may make conduit taxation irrelevant because they cause certain trusts to be denied recognition for tax purposes. Do not assume that an estate or trust for purposes of state property or wealth transfer law will be one for tax purposes, or vice versa; while there is a general similarity, it is not absolutely

1. See Revised Uniform Principal and Income Act (RUPIA) § 3(b)(8) (1962), as reproduced in Appendix A.

uniform. This may occur to the extent the trust is utilized as a recipient of income in an invalid assignment of income, such as in the so-called "family" or "constitutional" trusts that uniformly have been rejected as tax avoidance devices.[2] It may also be the result of the trust being regarded as invalid or nonexistent because it has become passive, executed or is otherwise deficient under state trust law principles.[3]

A more significant example involves a "multiple trust" rule that, for tax purposes, may regard several separate but identical trusts as a single entity unable to fragment its aggregate income, thereby frustrating an effort to reduce the overall tax bracket applicable to that total income. For example, a single trust with $100,000 of taxable income might pay tax in a 28 percent bracket but five trusts with income of $5,000 each would pay in a 15 percent bracket because the progressive tax bracket for $5,000 is lower than it is for $100,000. Unless prevented, the saving would be possible just by creating separate trusts. The "multiple trust" rule of section 643(f) establishes the simple proposition that substantially identical separate trusts, created for the purpose of tax minimization through fragmentation of income, will be treated as a single consolidated entity for purposes of Subchapter J. When the multiple trust rule was established only by Regulation,[4] several Tax Court decisions declared it to be invalid.[5] In 1984, the Treasury Department was able to persuade Congress to exact a codification of the rule in section 643(f), limited to trusts created after 1 March 1984.[6]

Because of the multiple trust rule, consolidation of multiple separate trusts may alter the tax effect of actions taken in those separate trusts and thus deny literal conduit treatment to some of them. For example, assume two trusts have equal amounts of income that, if distributed, would be taxed to the beneficiary currently. Instead of making such a distribution from both trusts, one trust accumulates its income while the other distributes all its income, plus principal in an amount equal to the income accumulated in the first trust. Conduit taxation under sections 661 and 662, recognizing the separate existence of the two trusts, would result in the second trust's distributed income being taxed to the beneficiary but the former trust's accumulated

2. See, e.g., Rev.Rul. 75–257, 1975–2 C.B. 251, and cases cited at Stand.Fed.Tax. Rep. (CCH) ¶ 3749.1973 and West keynumbers Internal Revenue 4000, 4017 and 4024–25.

3. See, e.g., Scott, Trusts § 69.2 (4th ed. 1987) and § 334 (3d ed. 1967).

4. Treas.Reg. § 1.641(a)–0(c), declared invalid in Stephenson Trust Co. v. Commissioner, 81 T.C. 283 (1983), and then codified in 1984 as section 643(f). Referred to in the regulations as a "multiple" trust rule, this treatment should be distinguished from section 667(c), which also deals with multiple trusts and which does nothing to consolidate them or disregard their separate vitality. But cf. Treas.Reg. § 1.6012–3(a)(4) (recognizing the existence of multiple trusts for the same beneficiary and created by the same settlor with the same trustee). For a more detailed discussion of the factors considered in identification of multiple trusts, see 9 Mertens, Law of Federal Income Taxation §§ 36.31 to .33 (1986), and Pennell, "Subchapter J: Evolution or Revolution?" 19 U.Miami Inst.Est.Plan. ¶ 804 (1985).

5. Stephenson Trust Co. v. Commissioner, 81 T.C. 283 (1983); Estelle Morris Trusts v. Commissioner, 51 T.C. 20 (1968), aff'd, 427 F.2d 1361 (9th Cir.1970).

6. Tax Reform Act of 1986 § 1806(b), Pub.L. No. 99–514, 100 Stat. 2811 (1986).

income being taxed to that trust. Application of the multiple trust rule would deny recognition of the trusts' separate existence and regard the two trusts as one trust that made distributions not exceeding the total aggregated income, resulting in conduit taxation under section 662 of that combined income to the beneficiary.

To curb a related abuse, estates that are kept "open" for a period longer than necessary for proper administration may be ignored for tax purposes. Treasury Regulation section 1.641(b)–3(a) (penultimate sentence). In addition, certain entities or relationships that are or resemble trusts are denied trust status under Subchapter J. For example, custodianships and guardianships are not regarded as tax entities separate from their wards; thus, application of Subchapter J is unnecessary.[7] Employee benefit trusts and common trust funds are specifically not subject to Subchapter J,[8] nor are charitable remainder trusts, except to the extent of any unrelated business income.[9]

Finally, legitimate trust entities that are created and maintained for essentially business purposes, as a substitute for a corporation or association or other business entity, also may be disregarded under Subchapter J. In the following two cases, consider what tests are utilized to ascertain whether a trust constitutes an association for tax purposes and the factors that tend to bespeak such a business association.[10]

BEDELL v. COMMISSIONER

United States Tax Court, 1986.
86 T.C. 1207.

RAUM, JUDGE:

The issue presented for decision is whether the Estate of Harry M. Bedell, Sr., Trust (the trust or the Bedell Trust) is properly taxable as a trust, or classified as an association taxable as a corporation. The resolution of this one issue will dictate the proper tax treatment to the trust of income earned by it and distributions to beneficiaries made by it in 1980 and 1981. It will also determine whether cash distributions received by Harry M. Bedell, Jr., from the trust in 1981 are taxable as dividends or whether he is to be charged with his share of the trust's income for that year. Additionally, it will determine whether the trust or Harry Bedell, Jr., is entitled to an investment tax credit.

* * *

7. Anastasio v. Commissioner, 67 T.C. 814 (1977), aff'd, 573 F.2d 1287 (2d Cir. 1977); see also Rev.Rul. 56–484, 1956–2 C.B. 23 (custodianship of assets and income treated as ward's own property and income for Federal income tax purposes). But see I.R.C. § 641(a)(2) (income collected by guardian of an infant, to be held or distributed pursuant to court order, subject to tax under section 1(e)).

8. Section 584(b); Treas.Reg. § 1.641(a)–0(a), (b).

9. Section 664(c); Treas.Reg. § 1.664–1(a)(1)(i) (last sentence).

10. For a more detailed discussion, see 2 Nossaman & Wyatt, Trust Administration and Taxation, § 42.23 (rev. 2d ed. 1986).

This residuary estate, which constituted the original res of the trust, included at least the following assets: the remainder interest (after a life estate to his wife) in the family home at 1620 Massachusetts Avenue, a summer home in Chesapeake Beach, Maryland (the Chesapeake Beach house), a filling station in Mt. Rainier, Maryland (the Mt. Rainier property), and the assets of the Bedell Manufacturing Co.

Notwithstanding that the decedent, as noted above, had provided for the conveyance of the residuary estate to his wife and children in trust, he then named as trustees only his three children, Helen Bedell Stamer, Beverly Bedell Shone, and Harry M. Bedell, Jr. He directed that the trustees continue to operate the company "indefinitely or so long as [the trustees] and/or their successors find it advisable and profitable to do so". He also charged them with the following duties: "The Trustees shall hold, and manage the property as a Trust Fund; invest and reinvest the same".

The decedent further instructed the trustees to expend funds and distribute net income [3] in the following manner. He specified that salaries to his son and sons-in-law who devoted their full time and attention to the company would be an operating cost of the company. Further, he directed that after necessary working capital was set aside one-third of the net annual income should be distributed to his wife, Laurel Bedell. However, provision was also made to the effect that such amount might be greater or that principal might even be invaded for her benefit in specified circumstances. Thus, the will provided that if she should prefer to reside in an apartment rather than in the large Massachusetts Avenue home, she might rent an apartment for up to $1,800 a year, and if her one-third share of the income of the trust were insufficient to provide her with funds for such rent and for a $100 monthly drawing account, then she should receive a larger share or a distribution from principal. Further, "upon [her] written request," the trustees could in their discretion withdraw principal from the trust and pay it over to their mother for her "maintenance, comfort and general welfare". In the event that the company showed no profit for a year, the trustees were instructed to "pay Laurel Bedell any amounts that in their judgment shall be necessary for her comfort and care". Any balance after Laurel Bedell was provided for was to be divided among the three children of decedent and Laurel Bedell. On the death of such a child, the surviving issue of that child would share that child's interest. Principal could not be distributed to a grandchild until he or she had reached the age of 21. Finally, the decedent provided that the "Estate may be divided, * * * but not before [the] youngest living grandchild reaches the age of twenty-one years" at which time "the rest and residue of the Trust shall be conveyed to [the] grandchildren, share and share alike".

3. Throughout the will, when the decedent referred to "income" he failed to distinguish clearly between the income of the company and that of the trust. We construe the term to mean income of the entire trust.

The decedent further directed that "if any child or grandchild of mine of the whole blood should unfortunately contract Polio, Muscular Dystrophy, or any crippling disease and is unable financially to bear the expense, then and in that event, the entire estate shall be charged with the expense of treatment". His concern in this respect was attributable to the fact that he had had two brothers who were stricken with a disabling disease and whose assets were presumably largely depleted as a consequence.

While the decedent provided detailed instruction to the trustees with respect to distributions of income and principal, he gave them "exclusive power to determine whether or not money or property coming into their possession shall be treated as principal or income, according as they may deem just and equitable". He also directed that distributions be made out of income net of the level of working capital the trustees and the company accountant determined to be required by the company.

The decedent's will contained no provisions specifically governing the transferability of interests by beneficiaries, the extent of liability on the part of beneficiaries, or the effect of a death of a beneficiary on the continued life of the entity. However, the testator's emphatic efforts in various parts of the will to make sure that the benefits of the estate were to inure only to his blood descendants (and not even to legally adopted grandchildren or to a daughter-in-law) strongly suggest an intention that the beneficial interests therein were to remain within the family. The two trustees who were alive at the time of trial of this case understood their father's intention to be that the beneficial interests were not to be assigned, and would resist any effort by any beneficiary to attempt an assignment.

* * *

In the administration of the trust, the trustees would meet only informally, as at dinner, to discuss or decide matters relating to the trust. No votes were ever taken; there was generally an informal consensus. No minutes were kept. There were no bylaws; unlike a corporation, there was no seal; and no certificates of beneficial interest were ever issued, or even contemplated. The trustees were motivated mainly by the objective of carrying out their father's wishes. Other than as "trustees", no one connected with the trust had an office or title such as president, secretary, treasurer, or the like.

The trust's financial history, as revealed by financial statements of the Bedell Manufacturing Co. and tax returns of the trust, shows income from the following sources: the operations of the Bedell Manufacturing Co., the rental of trust property, and the sale of other trust assets. In the years at issue, 1980 and 1981, net rental income constituted approximately 33 percent and 48 percent, respectively, of total net income.

* * *

Between decedent's death and the time of trial, the trust had disposed of all its major assets except the business premises of the company and the valuable real estate. Sales of assets are recorded as sources of income in the trust's records in 1969, 1970, 1971, and 1973.

Each year the current income beneficiaries of the trust have paid taxes on their full share of trust income. Those shares of income were determined by reference to decedent's will, not in accordance with capital contributions. Until her death in 1973, Laurel Bedell received distributions from the trust each year, receiving distributions totaling less than her share of the year's profits in some years, more than her share in other years (1969, 1972, and 1973), and dipping into the trust principal in 1973.

The other income beneficiaries have taken distributions from the trust when available and "as the need arose". When a beneficiary left a portion of his share of funds undrawn in the trust, that amount would be used by the company as working capital. The beneficiary's balance of undrawn funds would accumulate from year to year and interest would be earned on it. Before her death in 1983 Beverly Shone, who was suffering with cancer, withdrew from the trust more than her accumulated share of income and interest. She did not pay the trust interest on the principal she withdrew. Since Beverly Shone's death, her three children have shared her one-third interest in the trust income, drawing on the cash due them.

In 1980 and 1981, the Harry M. Bedell Trust filed Form 1041 "U.S. Fiduciary Income Tax Return", reporting both as taxable income and as an income distribution deduction the profits from the operations of the Bedell Manufacturing Co. and the rental of the trust's excess warehouse space, figures taken from the "Bedell Manufacturing Company Statement of Operations" for those years. The Commissioner, in his notice of deficiency, increased the trust's taxable income by the full amount of its income with no deduction for the distribution, stating that "It has been determined that the entity known as the Bedell Manufacturing Company, administered by the Estate of Henry [sic] M. Bedell, functions as an association. * * * Accordingly, the entity is considered a corporation which is to be taxed on its net income. Such net income may not be reduced by income distribution deductions". The Commissioner had not previously challenged the classification of the Bedell Trust as a trust for any of the years prior to 1980.

* * *

The principal matter before us is the determination of which side of the shadowy line of separation between trusts and associations the Bedell Trust falls. The starting point for considering whether any particular organization or entity qualifies as an "association" taxable as a corporation is *Morrissey v. Commissioner,* 296 U.S. 344 (1935). The Supreme Court granted certiorari in *Morrissey* (and three companion cases) for the obvious purpose of establishing authoritative guidelines in a field which was then regarded as "seemingly in a hopeless state of confusion", and in which there was a widespread conflict of decisions in the lower courts. 296 U.S. at 347. To be sure, the Court recognized that it was not feasible to draw a hard and fast line between "associations" and other entities like trusts and partnerships. It noted that (p. 356) "it is impossible in the nature of things to translate the statutory concept of 'association' into a particularity of detail that would fix the status of every sort of enterprise or organization which ingenuity may create". It nevertheless proceeded to establish a degree of consistency in this field and give guidance in the attempt to classify a particular entity.

The Court noted that (p. 357) "The inclusion of associations with corporations implies resemblance * * * and not identity", and it set forth six significant criteria or attributes to be taken into account in the process of determining the status of a given entity. These consisted of (i) Associates, (ii) an objective to carry on business and divide the gains therefrom, (iii) continuity of life, (iv) centralization of management, (v) liability for corporate debts limited to corporate property, and (vi) free transferability of beneficial interests. The Court stated that (p. 360) "these attributes make the trust sufficiently analogous to corporate organization to justify the conclusion that Congress intended that the income of the enterprise should be taxed in the same manner as that of corporations". Moreover, apart from the foregoing six criteria, the Court recognized that "the use of corporate forms may furnish persuasive evidence of the existence of an association", but it added that "the absence of particular forms, or of the usual terminology of corporations, cannot be regarded as decisive". (296 U.S. at 358.)

The opinion in *Morrissey* also pointed out with approval that the Treasury Department had authority within permissible bounds of administrative construction to promulgate regulations or supply rules for the "enforcement" of the statute. 296 U.S. at 354–355. The statute in question in *Morrissey* and as subsequently reenacted and now in effect is section 7701(a)(3) of the Code which defines the term "corporation" to include "associations". It was in the exercise of the authority recognized by the Supreme Court that the Treasury promulgated the present regulations modifying and expanding upon prior regulations. The new regulations, as amended, are currently to be found in sections 301.7701–1 through 301.7701–4, Proced. & Admin. Regs. The six tests outlined in *Morrissey* were incorporated in the new regulations, which further provided that "other factors may be found in some cases which may be significant in classifying an organization" and that the classification of an entity will depend on whether the "organization more nearly resembles a corporation than a partnership or trust. See *Morrissey et al v. Commissioner* (1935) 296 U.S. 344". Sec. 301.7701–2(a)(1), Proced. & Admin.Regs.

In respect of both trusts and partnerships the regulations contain the following significant provisions (sec. 301.7701–2(a)(2) and (3)):

(2) * * * Some of the major characteristics of a corporation are common to trusts and corporations, and others are common to partnerships and corporations. *Characteristics common to trusts and corporations are not material in attempting to distinguish between a trust and an association,* and characteristics common to partnerships and corporations are not material in attempting to distinguish between an association and a partnership. For example, since centralization of management, continuity of life, free transferability of interests, and limited liability are generally common to trusts and corporations, *the determination of whether a trust which has such characteristics is to be treated for tax purposes as a trust or as an association depends on whether there are associates and an objective to carry on business and divide the gains therefrom.* On the other hand, since associates and an objective to carry on business and divide the gains therefrom are generally common to both corporations and partnerships, *the determination of whether an organization which has such characteristics is to be treated for tax purposes as a partnership or as an association depends on whether there exists centralization of management, continuity of life, free transferability of interests, and limited liability.*

(3) An unincorporated *organization shall not be classified as an association unless such organization has more corporate characteristics than noncorporate characteristics.* In determining whether an organization has more corporate characteristics than noncorporate characteristics, *all characteristics common to both types of organizations shall not be considered.* * * *

[Emphasis supplied.]

Central to the application of these provisions is the final clause quoted above to the effect that all characteristics common to corporations and trusts or partnerships "shall *not* be considered". (Emphasis supplied.) Thus, the regulations provide that since four of the six criteria are generally characteristic of both trusts and associations, the determinative test depends upon only the two remaining criteria, namely, whether there are "associates *and* an objective to carry on business and divide the gains therefrom." * * *

The governing methodology in dealing with these regulations was established by this Court in *Larson v. Commissioner,* 66 T.C. 159 (1976). That case involved the provisions relating to distinguishing between partnerships and associations. The Court held that under the regulations, an entity could not be classified as an association (as opposed to a partnership) unless it had more than half (i.e., more than two) of the four attributes specified in the regulations in respect of partnerships, assuming that there were no "other factors" in addition to the original six that might be significant. Furthermore, the Court applied a purely mechanical test in which each of the individual four factors were to be given equal weight, and in which it was simply necessary to count the critical factors to see whether they came to at least three. Thus, an entity might fail to be classified as an association rather than a partnership even though considering all four significant attributes as a group under a more flexible approach giving each attribute a different level of significance in the context of the particular case, one might arrive at an opposite conclusion.

In our judgment, this Court's literal reading of the regulations in respect of partnership v. association is equally applicable in the case of trust v. association, dealt with in the same provisions of the regulations. In the case of classifying an entity as an association rather than a trust, the regulations provide that the result depends merely upon the two (not six) critical criteria relating to trusts, i.e., "whether there are associates *and* an objective to carry on business and divide the gains therefrom". (Emphasis supplied.) In short, applying the regulations literally, as was done in *Larson,* the Bedell Trust cannot be classified as an association unless it satisfies both the associates and the business tests. Not only do the regulations refer to both attributes in the conjunctive, but they also specifically require that, after eliminating "all characteristics common to both types of organizations", an organization "shall not be classified as an association unless [it] * * * has *more* corporate characteristics than noncorporate characteristics". (Emphasis supplied.) Sec. 301.7701–2(a)(3), Proced. & Admin.Regs. Thus, in accordance with the latter requirement, since the trust must have "more" than half of the two determinative characteristics to qualify as an "association" rather than a trust, it must fail to qualify as such if it satisfies only one of the tests. So much is plainly called for by the methodology employed in *Larson* that was approved by a majority of the Court.

Turning to the case before us, we must conclude that the Bedell Trust is not an association since we find that it does not have "associates". Failure to satisfy the "associates" test is itself sufficient to prevent it from being classified as an association. * * *

The beneficiaries here have not "plan[ned] a common effort or enter[ed] into a combination for the conduct of a business enterprise". *Morrissey v. Commissioner,* 296 U.S. 344, 357 (1935). Additionally, they did not affirmatively enter into the enterprise by way of a purchase of their beneficial interests. *Elm Street Realty Trust v. Commissioner,* 76 T.C. at 814.

Further, a relevant factor to be taken into account is that it was the decedent's "desire to create an estate for [his] * * * children [and grandchildren] which could not be dissipated by spendthrift operations, a desire which was effectuated by the restriction on the beneficiaries' interests against any anticipatory assignment thereof". *Elm Street Realty Trust v. Commissioner, supra,* 76 T.C. at 815. To be sure, there were no specific provisions against assignment in the decedent's will, but his desire that the beneficial interests in the trust remain within the family comes through loud and clear.

The beneficiaries' interests were too personal to be freely transferable. It was Mr. Bedell's clear intention that the trust income be used only to benefit children and grandchildren of the whole blood—an intention that, in our judgment, would be given effect by any local court construing the will. Only one of those so limited descendants can look to trust funds in case he contracts a "crippling disease and is unable financially to bear the expense". Since a beneficiary cannot confer upon a substitute "all the attributes of his interest" in the trust, such interest is not transferable. *Foster v. Commissioner,* 80 T.C. 34, 190 (1983), affd. on this issue 756 F.2d 1430 (9th Cir.1985). Sec. 301.7701–2(e)(1), Proced. & Admin.Regs. This non-transferability of interests militates against a finding of associates. *Elm Street Realty Trust v. Commissioner, supra* at 815. See *Curt Teich Trust No. One v. Commissioner,* 25 T.C. 884 (1956); *Living Funded Trust of Harry E. Lyman v. Commissioner,* 36 B.T.A. 161 (1937). We cannot find, where one person has created an entity, unilaterally distributed interests in it to others, and then restricted their ability to transfer their interests, that there exists "a voluntary association of individuals for convenience and profit", which characteristic is the very essence of an association. *Blair v. Wilson Syndicate Trust,* 39 F.2d 43, 46 (5th Cir.1930).

Further, the beneficiaries did not, qua beneficiaries, control trust affairs. Only 3 of the original 10 beneficiaries (wife, 3 children, 6 grandchildren) participated in trust affairs as trustees in the years at issue. These trustees, to a large extent, are responsible for the "protection and conservation of property for beneficiaries who cannot share in the discharge of this responsibility", those beneficiaries being the wife and grandchildren. Sec. 301.7701–4(a), Proced. & Admin.Regs. Participation in trust management by so few beneficiaries does not transform all the beneficiaries into associates and the trust into an association. See *United States v. Davidson,* 115 F.2d 799, 800, 801 (6th Cir.1940); *Curt Teich Trust No. One v. Commissioner,* 25 T.C. at 892; *Living Funded Trust of Harry E. Lyman v. Commissioner,* 36 B.T.A. at 166, 168. This conclusion is particularly clear where the non-participating beneficiaries have no right to appoint or control those beneficiaries who do act as trustees.

What we have here is a unique family estate plan, involving a trust characterized by a dominant familial objective. We conclude that the beneficiaries, who neither created nor contributed to the trust, whose interests in the trust are not transferable, and only a few of whom participate in the trust affairs, are not associates and their trust is not an association.

A final note. We wish to emphasize that the result reached herein is based upon this record, and that the case should not be regarded as authority for the conclusion that no testamentary trust can be classified as an association. Nor do we consider any particular element relating to the trust herein as determinative. The result rests upon all the facts taken in the aggregate. We understand that the Government regarded this case as a test case in respect of testamentary trusts and trusts engaged in the conduct of a business, and that high levels in the IRS were active in pressing the matter. It is difficult to imagine a more unsuitable vehicle than this case for any such purpose, and we think it regrettable that extensive misguided efforts were exerted to such a fruitless end in this litigation.

ELM STREET REALTY TRUST v. COMMISSIONER

United States Tax Court, 1981.
76 T.C. 803, acquiescence, 1981–2 C.B. 1.

NIMS, JUDGE: * * * The issue for decision is whether the Elm Street Realty Trust is an association within the meaning of section 7701(a)(3) and thus taxable as a corporation.

* * * On March 1, 1971, the date of the petitioner's creation, Egan and Harvey effected a conveyance of the Elm Street property (which they previously had acquired) to the petitioner. Also on that date, the trustee, Whitfield W. Johnson, executed a lease with Risley on behalf of the trust.

The declaration of trust stated that petitioner was formed "to acquire, hold, improve, manage and deal in real estate." The maximum term of the trust was 11 years, the same duration as the lease term; the trust and the lease were intended to be coterminous. However, the trust could also be terminated.

* * *

Petitioner's original beneficiaries were Egan and Harvey, each of them having a 50–percent beneficial interest.

* * *

One of the reasons Egan and Harvey utilized a trust to hold title to the Elm Street property was to facilitate their estate planning; they desired a form of ownership by which later transfers of beneficial interest to other members of their families would be permitted.

Whitfield W. Johnson, the trustee, is an attorney who has had substantial experience serving as trustee for a number of trusts. Except in his capacity as the attorney for Egan and Harvey, he had no business or professional relations with them. At the time of the trial of this case, he was serving as trustee or cotrustee of approximately 20 other trusts which have assets totaling between 15 and 20 million dollars.

Johnson's understanding with respect to the Elm Street Realty Trust was that it was to be a passive trust; his duties would be to collect the rent from the tenant, pay the mortgage, and distribute the income. The lease was a net lease under which Risley bore all expenses in connection with the property. Moreover, the trust was a "simple" trust which did not allow for any accumulation of income.

It was never suggested to Johnson that the trust purchase additional property. He had no duties with respect to the Elm Street property because they were all assumed by the lessee. He never had occasion to confer with any of the beneficiaries regarding the real estate nor did he ever see the trust real estate.

* * *

There have never been any meetings of beneficiaries of the trust. It has no share certificates evidencing ownership of beneficial interests. It has no seal, bylaws, officers, stationery or printed material, and no place of business. Its affairs required a negligible amount of the trustee's time.

Subsequent to the petitioner's formation, Harvey transferred his 50–percent beneficial interest to his son, Kenneth Harvey, who in turn transferred one-half of his interest to John Belante and the other one-half of his interest to a trust for the benefit of his minor children. Subsequent to the petitioner's formation, Egan transferred his 50–percent beneficial interest to his daughter, Suzanne M. Egan, who in turn transferred her interest to a trust for her benefit.

* * *

Section 7701(a)(3) defines corporations to include associations. The regulations promulgated pursuant to that section indicate that the presence or absence of (i) associates, (ii) an objective to carry on business and divide the gains therefrom, (iii) continuity of life, (iv) centralization of management, (v) liability for corporate debts limited to corporate property, and (vi) free transferability of interests, generally will determine whether an organization is to be classified as an association. Sec. 301.7701–2(a), Proced. & Admin. Regs.

The corporate characteristics which are our chief concern herein are (i) associates and (ii) an objective to carry on a business. Not only are these two characteristics essential to any association classification, they are also usually the only ones that are relevant when it becomes necessary to distinguish between a trust and an association. The primacy of these two characteristics in the case at bar is made clear by the regulations:

> the absence of either of these essential characteristics will cause an arrangement among co-owners of property for the development of such property for the separate profit of each not to be classified as an association. * * * Characteristics common to trusts and corporations are not material in attempting to distinguish between a trust and an association, and characteristics common to partnerships and corporations are not material in attempting to distinguish between an association and a partnership. For example, since centralization of management, continuity of life, free transferability of interests, and limited liability are generally common to trusts and corporations, the determination of whether a trust which has such characteristics is to be treated for tax purposes as a trust or as an association depends on whether there are associates and an objective to carry on business and divide the gains therefrom. * * * [Sec. 301.7701–2(a)(2), Proced. & Admin. Regs.]

Accordingly, our analysis will focus primarily on whether petitioner has associates and the requisite business objective.

Business Objective

Petitioner has directed a major portion of its argument toward the business objective issue. It is contended that the trust was created solely for the purpose of protecting and conserving the Elm Street property for the trust's beneficiaries and that there never was any intent to engage in a business enterprise. Petitioner also avers that a business enterprise was never in fact engaged in since the trustee merely let the property on a net lease basis.

Respondent asserts that a business objective is discernible from the express terms of petitioner's organizing document, the declaration of trust. In particular, respondent characterizes the powers granted to the trustee as being extremely broad and as powers which would allow petitioner to engage in the operation of a business. Thus, the potential to engage in a business, as manifested by the trustee's powers in the declaration of trust, demonstrates a business objective which extends beyond the usual goals of private trusts, namely, the mere preservation and protection of the trust assets for the beneficiaries.

In response, petitioner counters that the powers enumerated in petitioner's declaration of trust are ordinary trust powers which were exercisable solely with a view to keeping the trust res invested. In an effort to negate any suggestion that the trustee's powers were overly broad, Whitfield W. Johnson, the attorney who drafted the trust instrument, testified that these powers were broad in scope in order to avoid any unforeseen circumstances that might arise.

To our mind, it seems reasonably clear that neither the original nor the subsequent beneficiaries ever intended that the trust would engage generally in the operation of a business. Nor can it be said that a business was ever actually conducted. The mere passive receipt of income from one parcel of rental property, particularly in a net lease context, does not constitute an activity which rises to the level of a business operation. Nonetheless, the form of petitioner's governing instrument indicates that petitioner had the potential to operate a business and the courts have consistently given substantial weight to the actual powers contained in an entity's organizing document, particularly where, as in article Sixth, they are of the type or scope which in our judgment go beyond the powers which normally involve the doing only of such business acts as traditionally and generally have been recognized as being incidents in the administration of an "ordinary" (vis-a-vis "business") trust. See *Nee v. Main Street Bank,* 174 F.2d 425, 429 (8th Cir.1949). We therefore agree with respondent that the powers given to petitioner's trustee provided the authority to engage in business activity. The presence of such powers, regardless of their exercise, require a finding of a business objective for purposes of section 7701(a)(3) and the regulations thereunder.

In *Morrissey v. Commissioner,* 296 U.S. 344 (1935), the landmark case which provides the basis for a substantial portion of the current association regulations, all of the business activity (primarily subdivision, construction, and lot sales of realty) occurred prior to the taxable years which were at issue; the trust there under scrutiny merely held stock of a corporation during the years before the Court. The Supreme Court noted that—

> The fact that these sales were made before the beginning of the tax years here in question, and that the remaining property was conveyed to a corporation in exchange for its stock, did not alter the character of the organization. Its character was determined by the terms of the trust instrument. * * * The powers conferred on the trustees continued and could be exercised for such activities as the instrument authorized. [*Morrissey v. Commissioner, supra* at 361.]

Similarly, in *Helvering v. Coleman-Gilbert Associates,* 296 U.S. 369 (1935), one of the three companion cases with *Morrissey,* the Supreme Court emphasized the paramount status which is to be accorded the terms of the organizing document. The First Circuit had ruled in favor of the taxpayer in holding that the trust in question was not an association. Among other things, the court noted that the power to purchase additional property and other broad powers vested in the trustees had never been exercised. In reversing the Circuit Court's judgment, the Supreme Court stated:

> We agree with the Circuit Court of Appeals that weight should be given to the purpose for which the trust was organized, but that purpose is found in the agreement of the parties. * * * The parties are not at liberty to say that their purpose was other or narrower than that which they formally set forth in the instrument under which their activities were conducted. Undoubtedly they wished to avoid partition of the property of which they had been co-owners, but their purpose as declared in their agreement was much broader than that. * * * [*Helvering v. Coleman-Gilbert Associates, supra* at 373–374.]

In the instant case, the organizing document stated that its purpose "shall be to acquire, hold, improve, manage and deal in real estate." In addition, article Sixth specified the various activities in which the trustee was authorized to engage. The specific powers included authorization to buy, sell, and subdivide property; provide drains, sewers, and cables; build roads, bridges, and other structures necessary to develop the land; landscape and develop the land in any way; and erect, improve, remodel, or demolish buildings. If petitioner had, for example, embarked upon a general and continued course of acquiring and improving property and then selling it in lots, we do not doubt that such would have comprised engaging in a business for present purposes.

The facts of the case at hand are similar to those in *Sears v. Hassett,* 111 F.2d 961 (1st Cir.1940). In that case, six parcels of land were conveyed (jointly by the six residual beneficiaries of a will) in 1921 to a trust which contained "the usual broad powers found in Massachusetts real estate trusts." *Sears v. Hassett, supra* at 962. Shortly thereafter, the trustee entered into a long-term lease for one of the parcels. All of the other parcels were sold by 1925; between that time and 1935 and 1936 (the 2 taxable years which were at issue), the trustees merely leased the remaining parcel. Testimony was introduced to the effect that the beneficiaries did not establish the trust for the purpose of engaging in real estate operations as a business, but rather to simplify the holding of legal title and thus facilitate disposition of the remaining parcels. In analyzing whether the trust was created as a joint enterprise for carrying on a business, the First Circuit stated that—

> the character of the trust as an association is not determined by the intentions or expectations of its creators, proved by parol, nor by the extent to which the powers in the trust instrument have actually been exercised, but rather by the purposes and potential activities as disclosed on the face of the trust instrument. * * * [*Sears v. Hassett, supra* at 962–963.]

See also *Nee v. Main Street Bank, supra* at 429.

It is thus apparent that some considerations relevant to the determination of the existence of a business objective include the trustee's discretion to improve and build upon any realty which might be acquired at some future time, as permitted here. In such a case, the trustee is empowered to exercise business judgment for the profit of those associated together (assuming "associates" are present) in the undertaking. In the absence of limiting language contained in the organizing instrument, there is nothing to insure that the trust would not engage in future business activity even though it might initially be confined to function as a passive receptacle for rental or investment income. Compare *Commissioner v. North American Bond Trust,* 122 F.2d 545 (2d Cir.1941), cert. denied 314 U.S. 701 (1942), with *Commissioner v. Chase National Bank,* 122 F.2d 540 (2d Cir.1942). In the case before us, the trustee's powers were in no way limited merely to conserving and protecting the Elm Street property for the trust's beneficiaries. See *White v. Hornblower,* 27 F.2d 777 (1st Cir.1928) (powers in organizing document of a liquidating trust limited by liquidation purpose); *Hugh MacRae Land Trust v. Commissioner,* 1 T.C. 899 (1943) (trustees specifically prohibited from operating a coal business); *Wyman Building Trust v. Commissioner,* 45 B.T.A. 155 (1941) (trust could only deal with one piece of property). Rather, the trustee's powers expressly go beyond those kinds of activities which are generally typified by the usual nonbusiness trust. Accordingly, we hold that petitioner possessed an objective to carry on a business and divide the gains therefrom within the meaning of section 301.7701–2(a), Proced. & Admin. Regs.

Associates

The second fundamental test is the presence of associates. Sec. 301.7701–2(a)(2), Proced. & Admin. Regs. "Associates" refers to those individuals who possess a beneficial interest in the entity. *Morrissey v. Commissioner, supra* at 356–357; *Crocker v. Malley,* 249 U.S. 223, 234 (1919). However, a group's status as beneficiaries of a trust, standing alone, does not resolve the question of whether those within the group are associated together in a common business enterprise. In *Morrissey v. Commissioner, supra* at 357, the Supreme Court suggested that associations generally require some concerted volitional activity on the part of those beneficially interested, noting that the beneficiaries of an ordinary trust "do not ordinarily, and as mere cestuis que trustent, plan a common effort or enter into a combination for the conduct of a business enterprise."

The beneficiaries' role in creating a trust may provide an indication of a planned, common effort. Active participation in establishing the entity evinces a voluntary association for engaging in a joint endeavor. On the other hand, the lack of the current beneficiaries' role in the trust's creation does not mandate a finding that they are not "associates." See *Swanson v. Commissioner,* 296 U.S. 362 (1935); *Roberts-Solomon Trust Estate v. Commissioner,* 34 B.T.A. 723 (1936), affd. 89 F.2d 569 (5th Cir.1937). The absence of Egan and Harvey's continuing interest in petitioner, qua beneficiaries, is not determinative of the issue, since classification as an association can nonetheless result—

> where those who become beneficially interested, either by joining in the plan at the outset, or by later participation according to the terms of the arrangement, seek to share the advantages of a union of their interests in the common enterprise. [*Morrissey v. Commissioner, supra* at 357.]

See also sec. 301.7701–4(b), Proced. & Admin. Regs. As to those cases where the beneficiaries have either not participated in the trust's creation, or affirmatively entered into the enterprise (e.g., by way of a purchase of their beneficial interests), some further voluntary activity may be necessary on their part to satisfy the "associates" requirement. See R. McGee, "Problems of the Unintentional Corporation: The Association Taxable as a Corporation," 29 N.Y.U. Tax Inst. 853, 863 (1971). Where nongrantor beneficiaries receive their beneficial interests gratuitously, without solicitation, it is doubtful that they can be considered associated together in a common enterprise in the absence of some further joint activity (or at least the potential therefor) vis-a-vis the trust.

It is in this context that the beneficiaries' relationship to the organized entity must be considered. Thus, the beneficiaries' influence over the trust's activities may militate in favor of a finding of associates. See *Hynes v. Commissioner,* 74 T.C. 1266, 1280 (1980) (sole beneficiary was similar to a 100–percent shareholder since he could control the trust profits to which he was entitled). The regulations under section 7701(a)(3) speak to this point:

> Generally speaking, an arrangement will be treated as a trust under the Internal Revenue Code if it can be shown that the purpose of the

> arrangement is to vest in trustees responsibility for the protection and conservation of property for beneficiaries *who cannot share in the discharge of this responsibility and, therefore, are not associates in a joint enterprise for the conduct of business for profit.* [Sec. 301.7701–4(a), Proced. & Admin. Regs. Emphasis supplied.]

One commentator has made the following observation regarding the issue of whether beneficiaries constitute associates:

> Thus, the characteristic of associates does not exist where the beneficiaries by taking no part in the creation of the trust are not voluntarily associated at the outset; the nature of their interests is such that no other persons can become voluntarily associated by acquiring their interests; and they have no participation in the conduct of the trust's affairs. But the characteristic of associates can exist even where the trust has not been created by the beneficiaries, if their interests are freely transferable and they have some voice in decisions as to amendments to the trust or its termination, though they have no voice in management. [M. Lyons, "Comments on the New Regulations on Associations," 16 Tax.L.Rev. 441, 454–455 (1961).]

We believe that the above-mentioned factors, particularly the role of beneficiaries in a trust's creation and the extent of their participation in its affairs, provide a helpful framework for ascertaining whether a trust's beneficiaries should be deemed associates. In fact, this framework is suggested by various cases which have considered the issue.

In *Curt Teich Trust No. One v. Commissioner,* 25 T.C. 884 (1956), a husband and wife established a trust in order to create an estate for the benefit of their four children, which contained a spendthrift provision. Nine parcels of realty were transferred to the trustees to hold, manage, invest, and reinvest; collect the gross income and pay expenses; and distribute the balance to the designated beneficiaries. The trustees were given broad powers over the trust estate including power to sell, assign, or transfer any portion thereof, reinvest in other property and erect, repair, and reconstruct improvements. The trustees were expressly authorized to deal with the property as would be lawful for an owner in fee to do. This Court held that the trust was not taxable as an association because the beneficiaries did not associate themselves in any enterprise. Particular emphasis was placed on the grantors' desire to create an estate for their children which could not be dissipated by spendthrift operations, a desire which was effectuated by the restriction on the beneficiaries' interests against any anticipatory assignment thereof. In addition, the Court indicated that the grantors entirely disassociated themselves from the trust property; that the beneficiaries had no previous interest in the property; and that the beneficiaries did not have any certificates or evidences of interest or participation which would make them associates in the operations of the trust. We held that—

> Under the circumstances of this case it is our opinion that it cannot be said that the beneficiaries planned a common effort or

> entered into a combination for the conduct of a business enterprise. It is our view that these beneficiaries are not associates and that the trust should not be considered an association within the meaning of the statute and the regulations and the rule of the *Morrissey* case. * * * [*Curt Teich Trust No. One v. Commissioner, supra* at 891.]

In an earlier case, *Living Funded Trust of Harry E. Lyman v. Commissioner,* 36 B.T.A. 161 (1937), an individual established a trust to provide for the maintenance, welfare, and comfort of his wife, children, and grandchildren. The trustees were given broad authority to manage and deal with the trust property, including the power "to operate any business or interest in business comprised in this trust estate." The beneficiaries were precluded from selling, encumbering, or making any other anticipatory assignments of their interests. The trust did not provide for any stock certificates or certificates of beneficial interest. The Board of Tax Appeals held that the trust was not an association since it was not operated in essential respects in accordance with corporate forms of management. The Board stated that—

> In the case under consideration the beneficiaries did not establish a trust for the management of properties owned by them as tenants in common. They did not associate themselves together for the prosecution of a common enterprise; they did not create an "association" upon the methods and forms used by corporations; they had no part in establishing the trust, and were without power to modify the trust agreement or to terminate the trust. * * * [*Living Funded Trust of Harry E. Lyman v. Commissioner, supra* at 166.]

We are cognizant that both of the cases quoted above, as well as the previously quoted comment by Lyons, stress the importance of any restrictions placed upon the beneficiaries' ability to transfer their interests. Consideration of this factor, in relation to an analysis of the beneficiaries' status as associates, would thus appear to overlap the provisions of section 301.7701–2(e), Proced. & Admin. Regs. (wherein free transferability is listed as one of the four other factors bearing on corporate resemblance). In any event, absence of free transferability, in addition to hindering others from becoming voluntarily "associated" by acquiring the current beneficiaries' interests, bespeaks a form that is inconsistent with that of a quasi-corporate entity and accordingly suggests a nonassociation classification.

Turning to the circumstances of the instant case in light of the above-mentioned considerations, we note that the beneficiaries played no role in petitioner's creation. Egan and Harvey transferred the Elm Street property to petitioner and were the original beneficiaries, but they soon thereafter assigned their interests pursuant to article Sixth of the declaration of trust. It also appears that the subsequent beneficiaries received their interests gratuitously. We think it can be safely said that the individuals who were petitioner's beneficiaries during the years in issue played no active role either in the creation of petitioner or upon their subsequent entrance into a beneficial relationship with the trust.[5]

The interests of the beneficiaries in the trust were transferable only under certain restrictive provisions contained in article Sixth. That article generally prohibited a transfer of the beneficiaries' interests with the exception of testamentary transfers pursuant to the will of a beneficiary and transfers assented to by the trustee and all of the other beneficiaries. The requirement that all other beneficiaries agree to any transfer of a beneficial interest imposes a substantial limitation on free transferability (sec. 301.7701–2(e)(1), Proced. & Admin. Regs.), and thus significantly hinders the ability of the beneficiaries to voluntarily and unilaterally substitute others for themselves as associates.

The beneficiaries' other powers under the trust instrument included the authority to appoint a successor trustee in the event of the trustee's death, inability to serve, or resignation; amend or modify the trust instrument if acknowledged in writing by the trustee and all of the other beneficiaries; and terminate the trust prior to the expiration of the stated 11–year period if all of the beneficiaries notified the trustee in writing, or if any 25–percent (or greater) interest holder notified the trustee, subject to the trustee's absolute discretion to refuse to terminate the trust.

In our view, the ability of the beneficiaries to influence or otherwise participate in the trust's activities is limited in scope by virtue of the conditions attached to the exercise of the relevant powers—either concurrence by all of the beneficiaries or concurrence of the trustee in addition. Although petitioner possessed a business objective, the evidence concerning the trust's creation and its subsequent operations does not indicate that the beneficiaries affirmatively planned or entered into a joint effort for the conduct of a common enterprise. Similarly, the nature of the beneficiaries' interests, including the powers incident thereto, does not suggest that they could effect an unfettered, significant influence on petitioner. We thus conclude that petitioner's form did not afford a medium by which the beneficiaries could conduct income-producing activities through a quasi-corporate entity. The beneficiaries were not associates for purposes of section 7701(a)(3) and the regulations thereunder.

* * *

Questions

Time magazine (September 15, 1980, at 61) reported that a number of Texas oil companies were transferring old oil and gas wells to trusts, in some cases owned by their shareholders, in others with "shares" in the trusts being sold to investors to raise cash for the company.

5. For example, beneficiaries' purchase of beneficial interests would tend to indicate the presence of associates, since the purchase signifies a voluntary and affirmative entrance into the enterprise. See *Second Carey Trust v. Helvering,* 126 F.2d 526 (D.C.Cir.1942), cert. denied 317 U.S. 642 (1942).

1. What income tax consequences do the companies expect? With respect to this form of transaction, see section 386(d).

2. If the two tests for ascertaining whether a trust constitutes an association are whether there are two or more individuals (beneficiaries or associates) who have (1) voluntarily associated in a joint venture (2) for the pursuit of a business objective, which factors would be relevant in determining whether the foregoing transaction qualifies as a trust?

Chapter Two

DISTRIBUTABLE NET INCOME

Read Code sections 642(b), 642(e), 642(g), & 643(a) (except (a)(6)).

Read Regulation sections 1.641(a)–2, 1.641(b)–1, 1.642(b), 1.642(e), 1.642(g), 1.643(a)–0 through 1.643(a)–5, 1.643(b) and 1.643(d)–2.

Skim the Revised Uniform Principal and Income Act (RUPIA) reproduced at Appendix A.

"Distributable Net Income" (DNI) plays a limited but pivotal role in the income taxation of trusts and estates. It serves as a yardstick or measure, placing a limit on the amount of the entity's distribution deduction [1] and on the amount and character of current income that is attributed to the income beneficiaries.[2] It also serves as an element in the section 665 definitions of "undistributed net income" (UNI) and "accumulation distribution" for throwback purposes [3] and is thus an essential aspect in the operation of these dependent operations. Because DNI fills all these roles, and because the definition of DNI is rooted in certain fundamental income tax concepts, a study of DNI makes a good introductory concept to the Federal income taxation of trusts, estates, grantors and beneficiaries.

TAXABLE INCOME

As defined in section 643(a), distributable net income is based on taxable income of the entity, with several modifications. Occasionally the question arises whether income belongs for tax purposes to an estate or trust, or to its beneficiaries. For example, if Decedent owned Blackacre at death and devised it to Beneficiary, is rental income therefrom estate income or does it belong ab initio to Beneficiary? If the asset is subject to administration in Decedent's estate, the income

1. As explored in more detail in Chapter Three, under Code sections 651(a) and 661(a), the distribution deduction is equal to the amount of fiduciary accounting income currently (required to be) distributed, but may not exceed the taxable portion of DNI.

2. Under Code sections 652(a) and 662(a), the amount of income includible to any beneficiary is limited to that beneficiary's pro rata share of the DNI that was actually, or was deemed to have been, distributed.

3. See Chapter Four.

belongs to the estate. Rev.Rul. 75–61, 1975–1 C.B. 180. If, on the other hand, state law specifies that title passes directly from Decedent to Beneficiary, then that income is Beneficiary's liability. See Treasury Regulation section 1.661(a)–2(e). Nevertheless, to the extent Decedent's personal representative is entitled to, and does, use any portion of Blackacre to satisfy claims against or obligations of the estate, income from that portion used is taxable as estate income. Rev.Rul. 59–375, 1959–2 C.B. 161.

Under section 641(b), "taxable income" is essentially the same for a trust or an estate as it is for any individual taxpayer, though it is subject to several modifications under section 642. Most common among those deviations from an individual's computation of taxable income is denial of the section 151 personal exemption. Substituted in its stead is the section 642(b) deduction of $600 annually for an estate, $300 annually for any trust that is required to distribute all its income currently, and $100 for all other trusts. By definition, the $300 deduction applies to "simple" trusts (which we study in Chapter Three). In addition, a "complex" trust (also covered in Chapter Three) may qualify for the $300 deduction if it requires distribution of all income annually and is complex only because it either provides for charity or distributes principal during the current year. Treasury Regulation section 1.642(b)–1. For these and most other purposes, "income" means fiduciary accounting income, as defined under section 643(b).

A second common deviation is attributable to section 67(e), which specifies that the two percent floor on deductibility of miscellaneous itemized deductions for individuals will not apply with respect to "costs which are paid or incurred in connection with the administration of the estate or trust and would not have been incurred if the property were not held in such trust or estate". Some uncertainty exists with respect to the meaning of this provision in the context of items of deduction that are attributable to expenses that would be incurred even if the property were not held in a trust or estate. For example, it seems clear that a fiduciary's costs to prepare a Fiduciary Income Tax Return (Form 1041) are fully deductible, notwithstanding the two percent floor, because this Form is necessary only because the property is held in a fiduciary capacity. But what about the fiduciary's own fees for administration of the entity? For example, suppose the grantor of a trust paid for investment advice prior to creation of the trust, but that the trustee of the trust provides investment counsel with respect to trust assets as part of the services it renders. If the trustee does not account or charge separately for this investment function, will the full fee be deductible, or must the fiduciary somehow allocate its fees in order to identify items of expense that might have been incurred were the property not held in the trust? No guidance yet exists on this practical and important question.

Less common deviations in computing the entity's taxable income include modifications to taxable income under section 642(a), relating to the credits for foreign death taxes and for political contributions (the credit for foreign taxes is allocated under section 901 among the entity and its beneficiaries, and the credit for political contributions is denied entirely), restrictions under sections 642(c), 663(a)(2), and 681, all relating to charitable contributions (the Code and regulation requirements relating to charitable trusts and contributions are considered in Chapter Seven; essentially permitted is a current deduction for complex trusts and estates that distribute amounts of gross income for qualified charitable organizations or purposes), and minor adjustments under section 642(d) and Treasury Regulation section 1.642(d)–1 in computing the net operating loss deduction for businesses operated in a trust or estate (excluded from the net operating loss deduction computation is any charitable or distribution deduction, along with both income and deductions that are governed by the grantor trust rules of Subpart E).

Because DNI is essential to the taxation of income between an entity and its beneficiaries, it is important to identify which taxpayers are "entitled to" or "saddled with" various items (or portions thereof) that enter into the computation of taxable income and, therefore, into the determination of DNI. For example, special rules govern allocation of deductions for depreciation and depletion, under section 642(e). Apportionment of the deduction for both depreciation and depletion is essentially a two step process: if a reserve is established pursuant to local law or the governing instrument, the deduction is allocated to the entity dollar for dollar for any income actually set aside to that reserve. In many states requiring establishment of a depletion reserve, it is presently the case that the full deduction will be thus allocated to the entity because the reserve is set at 27.5 percent of annual receipts from extraction and the available deduction under section 613 is only 15 percent of those receipts.

If there is any excess deduction remaining after this first step (by virtue of a different provision in the governing instrument, or in states that do not require such a large reserve for either depreciation or depletion), that excess is pro rated between the entity and its beneficiaries on the basis of distributions and accumulations of current income. Treasury Regulation sections 1.167(h)–1(b) and 1.611–1(c)(4). If an income beneficiary is a charity or low bracket taxpayer, this allocation would unavoidably fail to maximize use of the deduction, as it did in Lambert Tree Estate v. Commissioner, 38 T.C. 392 (1962) (allocation of deduction to tax exempt charity). While allocated deductions may exceed the amount of income allocated to various beneficiaries, pro ration of the deduction may not be altered to direct a larger portion of the deduction to a beneficiary than the pro rata portion of income distributed to that beneficiary, both as illustrated below.

Similar principles are adopted under section 642(f) for allocation of amortization, and section 48(f) applies for apportionment of the investment credit. In reading the following materials, consider the rationale underlying the various allocation rules applicable in each.

REVENUE RULING 74-530

1974-2 Cumulative Bulletin 188.

Advice has been requested concerning the computation and apportionment of the allowable deductions for depreciation and for depletion between an estate and its heirs, legatees and devisees, and between a trust and its income beneficiaries.

An estate and a trust each own properties that are subject to the deductions for depreciation and depletion.

Section 642(e) of the Internal Revenue Code of [1986], provides that an estate or trust shall be allowed the deduction for depreciation and depletion only to the extent not allowable to beneficiaries under sections 167(h) and 611(b).

Section 643(b) of the Code provides, in part, that the term "income", when not preceded by the words "taxable", "distributable net", "undistributed net", or "gross", means the amount of income of the estate or trust for the taxable year determined under the terms of the governing instrument and applicable local law.

Section 167(h) of the Code, relating to depreciation allowable to life tenants and beneficiaries of trusts and estates, provides, in part, that in the case of an estate, the allowable deduction shall be apportioned between the estate and the heirs, legatees, and devisees on the basis of the income of the estate allocable to each. Section 611(b)(4), relating to depletion of property held by an estate, contains a corresponding provision.

Section 167(h) of the Code also provides that in the case of property held in trust, the allowable deduction shall be apportioned between the income beneficiaries and the trustee in accordance with the pertinent provisions of the instrument creating the trust, or, in the absence of such provisions, on the basis of the trust income allocable to each. Section 611(b)(3), relating to depletion of property held in trust, contains a corresponding provision.

Section 1.167(h)-1(b) of the Income Tax Regulations provides, in part, that if property is held in trust, the allowable deduction is to be apportioned between the income beneficiaries and the trustee on the basis of the trust income allocable to each, unless the governing instrument (or local law) requires or permits the trustee to maintain a reserve for depreciation in any amount. In the latter case, the deduction is first allocated to the trustee to the extent that income is set aside for a depreciation reserve, and any part of the deduction in excess of the income set aside for the reserve shall be apportioned between the income beneficiaries and the trustee on the basis of the trust income (in excess of the income set aside for the reserve) allocable to each.

Section 1.167(h)-1(b) of the regulations illustrates further that, if under the trust instrument or local law the income of a trust computed without regard to depreciation is to be distributed to a named beneficiary, the beneficiary is entitled to the deduction to the exclusion of the trustee. If, under the trust instrument or local law, the income of a trust is to be distributed to a named beneficiary, but the trustee is directed or permitted under the governing instrument to maintain a reserve for depreciation in any amount, the deduction is allowed to the trustee (except to the extent that income set aside for the reserve is less than the allowable deduction). No effect shall be given to any allocation of the depreciation deduction which gives any beneficiary or the trustee a share of such deduction greater than his pro rata share of the trust income, irrespective of any provisions in the trust instrument, except, as provided above, when the trust instrument or local law requires or permits the trustee to maintain a reserve for depreciation. Section 1.611–1(c)(4) contains corresponding provisions relating to depletable mineral or timber property held in trust.

* * *

For purposes of section 167(h) and section 611(b) of the Code the allowable deductions described therein are the depreciation and depletion deductions attributable to properties owned by an estate or a trust. The computation of the allowable deductions is made by the estate or trust in its capacity as a separate taxable person under section 7701.

Accordingly, before apportioning the deduction for depreciation under section 167(h) of the Code and the deduction for depletion under section 611(b), such deductions first must be computed by the estate or trust based on the properties it holds in its capacity as a separate taxable person.

Furthermore, it is possible under section 167(h) and section 611(b) of the Code to allocate depreciation and depletion deductions between an estate and its heirs, legatees, and devisees or between a trust and its beneficiaries in amounts that are greater than their pro rata shares of the income of the estate or income of the trust. This is so because although the depreciation and depletion deductions are apportioned on the basis of the income of the estate or income of the trust allocable to each of the parties (without regard to any depreciation or depletion allocable to them), they are not limited by the amount of such income.

DUSEK v. COMMISSIONER

United States Court of Appeals, Tenth Circuit, 1967.
376 F.2d 410.

BREITENSTEIN, CIRCUIT JUDGE.

Petitioners seek review of a Tax Court decision disallowing deductions claimed on account of depreciation of property held in trust for the benefit of petitioner Velma Dusek.

Raymond Dusek created a trust in favor of Velma, his wife. Raymond was both the grantor of the trust and the trustee. The term of the trust was 10 years and one month. The trust agreement provided that the net income "may be distributed" to Velma when, in the discretion of the trustee, her needs required. Net income was all income from the trust property after payment of "all the necessary costs and expenses incident to the management, maintenance and conservation of this Trust," the compensation of the trustee, and "such adjustments thereto as are permitted and provided for hereinafter in Item (f) of Article V." The latter item relates to the determination of net income and provides, among other things, that "depreciation and depletion shall be reserved out of income." Article V, Item (m), reads:

> "The Trustee is authorized to apportion and allocate between the Trust and the Primary Beneficiary [Velma] all appropriate tax deductions for depletion and depreciation and any other apportionable tax deductions in such manner as he may see fit."

Raymond contributed over $100,000 to the trust. These funds were used for the purchase of rental property. During the three tax years in question, 1959, 1960, and 1961, the net income of the trust before depreciation ranged from $5,100 to $15,800, and in the same period the depreciation ranged from $4,500 to $11,000. In each year, the trustee distributed only $100 to Velma and, at the same time, allocated to her all of the federal income tax deductions for depreciation. In their joint federal income tax returns for each year the taxpayers claimed as a deduction from their gross income the depreciation on the trust property. Although he made no point of the propriety or accuracy of the depreciation computations made by the trustee, the Commissioner disallowed the deductions and assessed deficiencies.

The controlling provisions of the applicable statute, § 167(h) of the Internal Revenue Code of [1986], 26 U.S.C. § 167(h), are:

> "In the case of property held in trust, the allowable deduction shall be apportioned between the income beneficiaries and the trustee in accordance with the pertinent provisions of the instrument creating the trust, or, in the absence of such provisions, on the basis of the trust income allocable to each."

The question is what are the "pertinent provisions" of the trust agreement. The Commissioner says they are those of Article V, Item (f), requiring that depreciation be reserved out of income. The taxpayers say they are those of Article V, Item (m), relating to the allocation of tax deductions for depreciation. The Tax Court adopted the theory of the Commissioner and upheld the deficiency determination.

Section 167(h) is a carry-over from § 23(k) of the Revenue Act of 1928, ch. 852, 45 Stat. 791. Before the enactment of § 23(k) the rule was that the trust as the entity with legal title to the depreciable assets was the only taxpayer entitled to any portion of the depreciation deduction regardless of whether it would derive any tax benefit therefrom. This situation had caused "uncertainty and considerable hardship." An example of the operation of the provisions that became § 23(k) is given thus in the House Conference Report: [4]

4. H.Conf.Rep. No. 1882, 70th Cong., 1st Sess., 1939–1 Cum.Bull. (Part 2) 444, 445.

"* * * if the trust instrument provides that the income of the trust computed without regard to depreciation shall be distributed to a named beneficiary, such beneficiary will be entitled to the depreciation allowance to the exclusion of the trustee, while if the instrument provides that the trustee in determining the distributable income shall first make due allowance for keeping the trust corpus intact by retaining a reasonable amount of the current income for that purpose, the allowable deduction will be granted in full to the trustee."

The taxpayers say that this legislative history is not pertinent because the statute is not ambiguous. The answer is that the statute does not define "pertinent provisions" and the example given in the House Conference Report is significant to show what Congress considered a pertinent provision.

From 1928 until amended in 1956, the applicable regulations stated the substance of the statute and gave the same example as that contained in the House Conference Report. As amended, the pertinent provisions of the regulation are:

> "If property is held in trust, the allowable deduction is to be apportioned between the income beneficiaries and the trustee on the basis of the trust income allocable to each, unless the governing instrument (or local law) requires or permits the trustee to maintain a reserve for depreciation in any amount. In the latter case, the deduction is first allocated to the trustee to the extent that income is set aside for a depreciation reserve, and any part of the deduction in excess of the income set aside for the reserve shall be apportioned between the income beneficiaries and the trustee on the basis of the trust income (in excess of the income set aside for the reserve) allocable to each. For example:
>
> * * *
>
> (2) If under the trust instrument or local law the income of a trust is to be distributed to a named beneficiary, but the trustee is directed to maintain a reserve for depreciation in any amount, the deduction is allowed to the trustee (except to the extent that income set aside for the reserve is less than the allowable deduction). The same result would follow if the trustee sets aside income for a depreciation reserve pursuant to discretionary authority to do so in the governing instrument. * * *"

The taxpayers argue that the amended regulation rewrites the statute because its effect is to say that the only pertinent provision in a trust instrument is one permitting a trustee to set aside from trust income a reserve for depreciation. The argument overlooks what we believe to be the intent of Congress in enacting § 23(k). The purpose was to recognize that the equitable interest of a trust beneficiary, as reflected in the trust income allocable to him, is sufficient to entitle him to claim the depreciation deduction to the extent of the income so allocable. Income set aside in a depreciation reserve is not so allocable.

The treatment of depreciation in the cases of life estates with remainder over and of beneficiaries of estates is covered by the same section as that applying to beneficiaries of trusts. For life tenants, heirs, legatees, and devisees, Congress required that the deduction for depreciation follow the income on the depreciable property. It would be strange indeed to construe the section so as to permit, in the case of a trust beneficiary, a complete separation of the income and the deduction. In Calvin v. United States, 10 Cir., 354 F.2d 202, 204, we held that an income tax deduction may be taken only by the taxpayer who incurs it. The same principle applies here. The depreciation here was incurred by the trustee—not by the beneficiary.

* * *

Questions

1. Consider the effect of RUPIA sections 9, 13(a)(2) and 14, reproduced at Appendix A, under the allocation rules established by Code sections 167(h) and 611(b)(3) and (b)(4).

2. What result did the taxpayer hope to accomplish in *Dusek,* and how might the drafter have achieved that objective? What was the effect of "burying" the deduction in the trust?

3. What results should apply with respect to Code section 168 ACRS depreciation? See Proposed Treasury Regulation section 1.168–1(a) (second sentence).

4. Why was the trust in *Dusek* not ignored in its entirety under sections 674 and 677?

In computing taxable income, special rules also exist to disallow deduction of certain items that are claimed as estate tax deductions. Code section 642(g) requires an election between claiming certain expenditures as either (1) an income tax deduction under section 162, 163, 165, 212, or (on decedent's final income tax return) 213, (2) as a reduction of the selling price in determining gain on the disposition of assets, or (3) as a section 2053 or 2054 estate tax deductible administration expense or loss. The objective is to prevent utilization of the same expenditures to work double duty under either of the estate or income taxes. Nevertheless, it is common to claim the same amount on Forms 706 and 1041 both and later waive or amend one of them when enough facts are ascertained to know which is preferable (sometime prior to final audit of the proper return). By Proposed Treasury Regulation section 1.642(g)–1, this "double" deduction is permissible only if the amendment or waiver is filed at least 180 days before the estate tax statute of limitations expires, thus permitting the IRS sufficient time to disallow the deduction on the estate tax return before allowing the deduction for income tax purposes, or vice versa. In this fashion the Service hopes to curb the prior abuse of filing the waiver or amendment at such a late date that audit of the return on which improperly claimed is no longer feasible. It is still permissible to split the deductions, claiming a portion on each Form.

In reading the following ruling, consider why deductions in respect of a decedent are not subject to the special rule of section 642(g).

REVENUE RULING 76–498

1976–2 Cumulative Bulletin 199.

In January 1970 the decedent, *A*, a resident of the State of New York, created a trust, the corpus of which consisted of income producing assets and certain real property not held for the production of income. Under the terms of the trust agreement, the trustees were directed to hold the properties of the trust, invest and reinvest the same, collect the income therefrom, and pay the entire net income, plus any principal as they might deem advisable, to or for the benefit of *A*. Upon *A* 's death, the trustees were directed to distribute the principal of the trust to such persons as *A* might direct or appoint by will or, in default of such appointment, to the legal representative of the decedent's estate. Thus, *A* was treated as the owner of the trust under section 677 of the Code, and under section 671 all items of income, deductions, and credits against tax of the trust were included in computing the taxable income and credits of *A* to the extent that such items would be taken into account in computing taxable income or credits against tax of an individual. *A* used the cash receipts and disbursements method of accounting.

A died on July 1, 1974, and exercised the power of appointment by will over the trust corpus, directing that the income producing assets of the trust be paid to the executors of *A* 's estate and that the real property be conveyed absolutely to *A* 's children. In addition *A* directed that all *A* 's just debts be paid out of the estate.

After *A* 's death, the trustees of the trust liquidated the income producing assets of the trust, filed their final account under the applicable provisions of New York law, and thereafter delivered the corpus of the trust to the parties entitled to it under the will.

Under New York law, Civil Practice Law and Rules section 8005 (McKinney 1975), which refers to the Surrogate's Court Procedure Act section 2309 (McKinney 1967), the trustee of a trust is entitled to: (1) annual commissions at certain statutory rates; and (2) on the settlement of the trustee's account, reasonable and necessary expenses actually paid by the trustee, in addition to a commission from principal (at the rate of one percent) for paying out all sums of money that are principal. This statutory schedule of compensation, including the paying out commission, has been interpreted by New York courts as an effort to compensate trustees for the reasonable value of all services performed during the trust period, not merely the specific acts to which the statute refers. *See Matter of Roth,* 53 Misc.2d 1066, 281 N.Y.S.2d 225 (1967).

The estate paid all the annual commissions due, and all the expenses and paying out commissions due at the termination of the trust. The payment of such claims was allowable under New York law.

Section 691(b) of the Code provides that the amount of any deduction specified in section 212, in respect of a decedent, that is not properly allowable to the decedent for the taxable period in which falls the date of death, or a prior period, shall be allowed to the estate of the decedent in the taxable year when paid, or, if the estate of the decedent is not liable to discharge the obligation to which the deduction relates, the deduction shall be allowed to the person who by reason of the death of the decedent or by bequest, devise, or inheritance acquires, subject to such obligation, from the decedent an interest in property of the decedent.

Section 1.691(b)–1(a) of the Income Tax Regulations provides that the expenses described in section 212 of the Code that are deductible under section 691(b) are those for which the decedent was liable but which were not properly allowable as a deduction in the decedent's last taxable years or any prior taxable year.

Section 212 of the Code provides that in the case of an individual, there shall be allowed as a deduction all the ordinary and necessary expenses paid or incurred during the taxable year for the production or collection of income, or for the management, conservation, or maintenance of property held for the production of income. Trustee's fees are deductible under section 212, if they are ordinary and necessary and paid during the taxable year. *See Trust of Bingham v. Commissioner,* 325 U.S. 365 (1945), 1945 C.B. 103.

Since *A* was treated as owner of the trust, *A* would have been treated as being liable for the commissions, if *A* had lived, to the extent that the commissions were for services rendered by the trustees prior to *A* 's death. If *A* had lived and paid the commissions and expenses *A* would have been allowed a deduction under section 212 of the Code for the commissions and expenses to the extent that they were attributable to the management of the income producing assets. Since the real property in the trust was not held for the production of income, the portion of the statutory commissions and expenses attributable to it would not have been deductible by *A*.

Accordingly, to the extent that the statutory commissions and expenses are attributable to the income producing assets of the trust and represent a fee for services rendered through July 1, 1974, the date of the decedent's death, the commissions and expenses paid by the estate to the trustee may be deducted under section 691(b) of the Code for income tax purposes. *See* Rev.Rul. 71–423, 1971–2 C.B. 255. The statutory commissions and expenses paid by the estate to the trustees for services rendered after *A* 's death on July 1, 1974, are not deductible under section 691(b). An allocation of the commissions between the period before and after death is therefore necessary. Commissions that represent compensation for the services made necessary by *A* 's death cannot be deducted under section 691(b). Such services include activities in terminating the trust and making a final distribution and accounting. Under New York law the trustees are entitled to the reasonable value of such services, limited by the statutory amount. *In re Barnett's Will,* 231 N.Y.S.2d 471 (1962).

Section 642(g) of the Code and section 1.642(g)–2 of the regulations provide, in part, that amounts allowable under section 2053 or 2054 as a deduction in computing the taxable estate of a decedent shall not be allowed as a deduction in computing the taxable income of the estate or any other person, but that this provision shall not apply with respect to deductions allowed under section 691.

Under section 2053(a)(3) of the Code, claims against the estate can be deducted from the gross estate to determine the taxable estate, to the extent that such claims are allowable by the laws of the jurisdiction under which the estate is being administered.

The portion of all the commissions and expenses that is allocable to services performed by the trustees prior to *A* 's death should be treated as a personal obligation of the decedent. Accordingly, the statutory commissions and expenses accrued prior to *A* 's death but paid by the estate are deductible for estate tax purposes under section 2053(a)(3) of the Code as claims against the estate. Also, under section 642(g), the deduction of such commissions and expenses under section 691(b) for income tax purposes (to the extent attributable to the income producing assets) is not precluded by the same deduction under section 2053 for estate tax purposes. *See* Rev.Rul. 71–422, 1971–2 C.B. 255.

Under section 2053(a)(2) of the Code, administration expenses of the estate can be deducted from the gross estate in the same manner as claims against the estate. In addition, under section 2053(b), and section 20.2053–8 of the Estate and Gift Tax Regulations, amounts representing expenses incurred in administering property not subject to claims that is included in the gross estate can be deducted, in determining the taxable estate, to the same extent such amounts would be allowable as a deduction under subsection (a) if such property were subject to claims, and such amounts are paid before the expiration of the period of limitation for assessment provided in section 6501.

Since *A* directed that the income producing assets be turned over to the estate, those assets are property subject to claims, that is, property includible in the gross estate that, under applicable state law, would bear the burden of the payment of deductions in the final adjustment and settlement of the decedent's estate. See section 20.2053–1(c) of the regulations. However, although the value of the real property is includible in *A* 's estate under section 2036 of the Code, it is not subject to claims because title passes to the designated beneficiaries as remaindermen of the trust. *See In re Rolston's Estate,* 170 Misc. 548, 10 N.Y.S.2d 660 (1939); and *Chase National Bank of City of New York v. Central Hanover Bank & Trust Co.,* 265 App.Div. 434, 39 N.Y.S.2d 541 (1943).

Accordingly, the statutory commissions and expenses that are allocable to services performed by the trustees after *A* 's death and that were paid by the estate are deductible by the estate under section 2053 of the Code as administration expenses. The commissions and expenses attributable to the income producing assets turned over to the estate are deductible under section 2053(a)(2), and the commissions and expenses attributable to the real property are deductible under section 2053(b) and section 20.2053–8 of the regulations. *See* Rev.Rul. 69–402, 1969–2 C.B. 176. However, since such commissions and expenses of the estate attributable to the income producing assets and to the real property are not deductible under section 691(b), their deduction by the estate under section 2053 for estate tax purposes would preclude their deduction by the estate for income tax purposes. See section 642(g).

DISTRIBUTABLE NET INCOME

Distributable net income is determined by making several adjustments to taxable income. First is to perform the section 643(a)(2) "add back" of the amount of the deduction in lieu of the personal exemption, allowed under section 642(b) in computing taxable income. By this increase, distributable net income is larger, meaning that (1) a larger distribution deduction is available to the entity for current income distributions and (2) a larger amount is subject to inclusion to beneficiaries of the trust or estate who received distributions, in each case because distributable net income is a cap on each.

Question

What is the rationale for the section 643(a)(2) adjustment, and why is the deduction in lieu of the personal exemption granted in the first instance if this adjustment, in essence, takes it back away? See H.Rep. No. 1860, 75th Cong., 3d Sess. (1938), reprinted in 1939–1 C.B. (part 2) 728, 761.

An additional add back, with a similar effect on DNI, is dictated under section 643(a)(5) for section 103 tax exempt income. By increasing DNI, and thus increasing both the distribution deduction and the amount subject to inclusion at the beneficiary level, the add back serves to permit this form of tax favored income to pass through to the beneficiaries. If distributed currently, the character pass through rules of the conduit system of taxation, under sections 652(b) and 662(b), permit the beneficiaries to enjoy the special status of income items that trigger this adjustment. However, because sections 652(b) and 662(b) dictate a pro rata allocation of the character of all items included in DNI, distributions that generate deductions for the entity are also pro rated to various items of taxable and tax favored or exempt income, under Treasury Regulation sections 1.643(a)–5(b), 1.652(c)–4, 1.661(b)–2 and 1.661(c)–2(d). Care must be exercised to assure proper allocation of these items to the proper beneficiaries. Otherwise the IRS may attempt to allocate deductions to tax exempt income, which essentially wastes the deduction (the income and deductions balancing out) while the taxpayer attempts to allocate deductibles to receipt of taxable income to maximize their utility. In reading the following materials, consider how the taxpayer sought to improve the allocation of deductible expenses in trusts producing tax exempt income.

REVENUE RULING 77-355

1977-2 Cumulative Bulletin 82.

Advice has been requested whether, under the circumstances described below, a simple trust that does not distribute capital gains, because they are allocable to corpus under the trust instrument or applicable local law, may include, for purposes of computing its distributable net income under section 643(a) of the Internal Revenue Code of [1986], capital gains in the formula for allocating indirect expenses to tax-exempt income.

In 1975 *A* created a simple trust for the benefit of *A*'s child, *B*. The trust instrument provides that the trustee shall distribute, currently, the entire net income of the trust to *B*. The trust instrument does not authorize distributions of corpus during *B*'s lifetime. Capital gains are allocable to corpus under state law.

For the taxable year 1976 the trust's income consisted of taxable interest, tax-exempt interest, and capital gains. In the trust's U.S. Fiduciary Income Tax Return (Form 1041) for 1976, the trustee in computing distributable net income allocated its compensation between taxable and tax-exempt income on the basis of a formula that included the trust's capital gains.

Section 641(b) of the Code provides that the taxable income of an estate or trust will be computed in the same manner as in the case of an individual, except as otherwise provided.

Section 643(a)(3) of the Code provides, in part, that in computing distributable net income, capital gains are excluded to the extent they are allocable to corpus and are not (A) paid, credited, or required to be distributed to any beneficiary during the taxable year, or (B) paid, permanently set aside, or to be used for the purpose specified in section 642(c).

Section 652(a) of the Code provides for the amount of income for the taxable year required to be distributed currently by a trust described in section 651 to be included in the gross income of the beneficiaries to whom the income is required to be distributed to the extent of their respective shares of distributable net income.

Section 652(b) of the Code provides, in part, that the items of deduction entering into the computation of distributable net income shall be allocated among the items of distributable net income in accordance with regulations prescribed by the Secretary or the Secretary's delegate.

Section 1.652(b)-3(b) of the Income Tax Regulations provides, in part, that deductions that are not directly attributable to a specific class of income may be allocated to any item of income (including capital gains) included in computing distributable net income, but a portion must be allocated to nontaxable income (except dividends excluded under section 116) pursuant to section 265 and the regulations thereunder.

Section 1.652(b)–3(b) of the regulations further indicates that deductions that are not directly attributable to a specific class of income are not to be allocated to capital gains of the trust allocable to corpus since the capital gains are not taken into account in the computation of distributable net income.

With regard to a trust required to distribute all its income currently, section 1.652(c)–4 of the regulations sets forth a comprehensive example showing the application of the allocation rule for deductions not directly allocable to a specific class of income for a trust that has tax-exempt income and capital gains allocable to corpus.

Section 265(1) of the Code provides, in part, that no deduction shall be allowed for any amount otherwise allowable as a deduction that is allocable to one or more classes of income other than interest wholly exempt from tax, or any amount otherwise allowable under section 212 that is allocable to interest wholly exempt from tax.

Section 1.265–1(c) of the regulations provides, in part, that if an expense or amount otherwise allowable is indirectly allocable to both a class of nonexempt income and a class of exempt income, a reasonable proportion thereof determined in light of all the facts and circumstances in each case shall be allocated to each.

Section 265 of the Code governs the allocation of expenses between taxable and tax-exempt income. Section 1.265–1(c) of the regulations requires that allocation of indirect expenses be made "in light of all facts and circumstances in each case." The distributable net income concept is the primary mechanism by which the income of a trust is taxed only once, either to the trust or to its beneficiaries, and should not be disregarded in applying the general allocation provisions of section 265 to the particular problems of trust income. See *Manufacturers Hanover Trust Co. v. United States,* 312 F.2d 785 (Ct.Cl.1963); and *Tucker v. Commissioner,* 322 F.2d 86 (2d Cir.1963).

* * *

In the case of an individual taxpayer there is no division of the taxable income between two or more parties. Therefore, it is proper to allocate expenses under section 212 of the Code to all of the taxable income (including capital gains) of the individual. However, in the case of a simple trust, there may be a division of the taxable income earned by the trust between the trust and its beneficiaries. Therefore, in computing the distributable net income of such trusts, which will determine the amount to be included by the beneficiaries in their gross income, the allocation of indirect expenses must be made only with respect to the income (taxable and tax-exempt) that is to be distributed currently to the beneficiaries by the trust.

In the instant case, the trust's capital gains are not included in the computation of distributable net income under the provisions of section 643(a)(3) of the Code. Therefore, the capital gains may not be included in the formula for allocating indirect expenses to tax-exempt income, and the trustee's allocation was improper.

REVENUE RULING 77-466

1977-2 Cumulative Bulletin 84.

Advice has been requested whether, under the circumstances described below, the method of allocating trustees' commissions is an appropriate method for purposes of section 265 of the Internal Revenue Code of 1954.

In 1960 a taxpayer created a revocable trust by transferring to it municipal bonds and other securities. The interest on the municipal bonds was exempt from Federal income tax under section 103 of the Code and the income derived from the other securities was subject to Federal income tax. During its existence the trust received interest and dividends and made numerous sales of bonds and securities that resulted in capital gains and losses. On January 2, 1975, the trustees sold all of the trust's municipal bonds and purchased taxable securities with the proceeds so that on December 31, 1975, the day on which the trust terminated and its assets were distributed, the entire portfolio of the trust consisted only of taxable securities. The net fair market value of the trust assets distributed included a substantial amount of unrealized capital appreciation in excess of unrealized capital depreciation. Under state law, certain commissions were paid to the trustees on termination of the trust as compensation for receiving, administering, and paying out all amounts and property (which included capital appreciation as well as ordinary and capital gains income) belonging to the trust over its life and not as compensation for any specific act of the trustees. Since there was no tax-exempt income in the year the trust terminated, the full amount of those commissions was allocated to taxable income and deducted as expenses for the production of income under section 212.

Section 265(1) of the Code provides that no deduction is allowed for any amount otherwise allowable as a deduction that is allocable to one or more classes of tax-exempt income other than tax-exempt interest, or any amount otherwise allowable under section 212 that is allocable to tax-exempt interest.

Section 1.265-1(c) of the Income Tax Regulations provides that expenses and amounts otherwise allowable that are directly allocable to any class or classes of exempt income shall be allocated thereto; and expenses and amounts directly allocable to any class or classes of nonexempt income shall be allocated thereto. If an expense or amount otherwise allocable is indirectly allocable to both a class of non-exempt income and a class of exempt income, a reasonable proportion thereof, determined in the light of all the facts and circumstances in each case, shall be allocated to each.

In the instant case, since under state law the trustees' termination commissions were not directly allocable to any particular class of income, but instead were paid for all the activity of the trustees during the trust's lifetime, such commissions are properly allocable to: (1) the trust's ordinary income (including tax-exempt income) realized during its existence, (2) net realized capital gains from its inception to its termination, and (3) any net unrealized capital appreciation of the assets distributed by the trust. However, the method used by the trustees resulted in none of the commissions being allocated to tax-exempt income, even though the trust had realized tax-exempt income during the period of its existence.

Accordingly, since none of the trustees' commissions were allocated to tax-exempt income the method used is not reasonable in the light of all the facts and circumstances and, therefore, is not an appropriate method for purposes of section 265 of the Code. However, in the instant case, a reasonable and appropriate method of allocation would be one based on the ratio of tax-exempt income realized by the trust during its existence to the total of ordinary income (including tax-exempt income) realized by the trust during its existence plus the excess of capital gains realized over capital losses sustained over the life of the trust plus any net unrealized capital appreciation of the assets distributed.

FABENS v. COMMISSIONER

United States Court of Appeals, First Circuit, 1975.
519 F.2d 1310.

McEntee, Circuit Judge.

The parties stipulated that from 1953 to 1969 taxpayer Fabens maintained in a trust account municipal bonds, the income from which was tax-exempt, and other securities the income from which was taxable. The trust also realized capital gains and losses from transactions involving its holdings. Upon termination the fair market value of the trust assets included a considerable amount of unrealized capital appreciation which was reflected in the fiduciary fees paid on termination and computed under local law as a percentage of current market value. Taxpayer deducted the full amount of these commissions as expenses for the production of income under Int.Rev.Code § 212. The Commissioner disallowed a portion of this deduction pursuant to Int. Rev.Code § 265(1) prohibiting the deduction of expenses directly or indirectly allocable to the production of tax-exempt income. The fees were disallowed in the ratio of tax-exempt income over the life of the trust to total income (including net capital gains) realized during that period.[3] In the Tax Court taxpayer argued that this formula was not

3. In allocating a portion of these expenses to the tax-exempt income, the Commissioner first determined the total amount of tax-exempt income earned by

reasonable in the light of all the facts and circumstances, Treas.Reg. § 1.265–1(c), because it did not reflect the unrealized appreciation of the trust assets. The court upheld the Commissioner's allocation and taxpayer appeals.

The Commissioner argues there was no evidence that the trust assets were actually managed for capital appreciation; and that to the extent they were so managed, the Commissioner's inclusion in his allocation formula of net capital gains realized over the life of the trust would reasonably reflect this fact. We disagree on both counts. As an initial matter even if achieving appreciation were not a prime goal of the trustee's management, it would remain unclear how fees created solely because of a rise in the value of taxable investments could be considered "allocable" within the statute to the production of tax exempt income. At any rate, while there is no specific evidence as to the trustee's investment objectives, that appreciation was such an objective is inferable from the facts that the trustee apparently insisted on compensation for appreciation when the trust was established, and that appreciation under the trustee's management comprised more than half of the corpus value at termination. As to the second point, since the trustee's decision to sell securities (thereby realizing capital appreciation) is dictated by considerations other than that of the trust's termination date, there is no necessary reason to suppose that the net capital gains realized over the life of the trust and included in the Commissioner's formula will fairly reflect the trustee's division of labor between exempt and taxable income-production activities in administering the trust.[4] Since the value of the property comprising corpus

the trust between 1953 and 1969 ($211,443), and then computed the total income of the trust for this period ($740,093), which included taxable interest and dividends and capital gains, plus the tax-exempt income. Tax-exempt income was then expressed as a percentage of total income $\frac{(\$740,093}{(\$211,443}$ [sic] = 28.57 percent), and this percentage was applied to the total amount of receiving and paying commissions incurred upon termination of the trust ($50,695) to determine the amount of the termination commissions ($14,484) allocable to tax-exempt income. The Commissioner made a separate allocation with respect to the annual commissions (income and principal commissions) for 1969 in the total amount of $3,241. The Commissioner allocated this commission by computing the total income (taxable and tax exempt) of the trust for 1969 ($24,743), and computing tax-exempt income for 1969 ($9,028), as a percentage of total income $\frac{(\$\ 9,028}{(\$24,743}$ = 36.49 percent). The percentage was applied to the total annual commissions ($3,241) for 1969 to determine the amount ($1,183) allocable to tax-exempt income for that year. The total amount ($15,667) allocable to tax-exempt income ($14,484 of the termination charges, plus $1,183 of the annual commissions) was disallowed as a deduction pursuant to the provisions of Section 265 of the Code. The Commissioner allowed the remaining amounts ($38,269) as deductions for 1969.

4. Here the unrealized appreciation exceeded the net capital gain included in the Commissioner's ratio by a factor of 60. It is not wholly unrealistic to conceive of a trust owning common stock, which experiences enormous appreciation during the trust's existence while paying little or nothing in dividends as growth stocks often do, along with a single municipal bond paying a steady coupon interest. In such a situation the Commissioner's formula would obviously result in a distorted apportionment of termination fees paid for the whole job of administering the trust. *See*

generates the fee, an allocation measure like taxpayer's which somehow reflects that value will seemingly result in a fairer apportionment.[5] See M. Ferguson, J. Freeland & R. Stephens, Federal Income Taxation of Estates and Beneficiaries 492–93, 644 n. 115 (1970). The Tax Court characterized the appreciation as "ephemeral," but the commissions it produced represented an outlay very tangible indeed.

* * *

In sum, we agree that the Commissioner's allocation was proper as to the annual fees but conclude it was not reasonable in light of all the facts and circumstances, including taxpayer's proposed allocation, insofar as the termination fees were concerned.

Questions

1. What was the abuse the taxpayer was attempting to work in Revenue Ruling 77–355 and how did it differ from that in Revenue Ruling 77–466? To really understand these two rulings, you should try to describe the fraction that would apply for allocation purposes. How do the fractions differ as between the two rulings, and can you explain why?

2. Why did the Service allow inclusion of capital gains in determining the proper allocation in Revenue Ruling 77–466 but not in Revenue Ruling 77–355?

In addition to adding back the deduction in lieu of the personal exemption and tax exempt income in computing DNI, three items normally considered in the determination of taxable income are ignored for purposes of computing DNI. First, under section 643(a)(1), ignored is the distribution deduction allowed by sections 651(a) and 661(a). Because that deduction is limited to the taxable portion of DNI, an unavoidable circularity would otherwise develop if DNI were equal to taxable income after allowance of the distribution deduction: the deduction would be limited by DNI and DNI would be dependent for computation on the amount of the deduction.

The second and third items that are ignored are items of taxable income that are allocated to principal and not currently distributed. Thus, for example, under section 643(a)(3) and Treasury Regulation section 1.643(a)–3, capital gains that are allocated to corpus (either under local law[4] or the terms of the document) and not distributed or set aside for charity, along with capital losses used in computing taxable income, are ignored for purposes of computing DNI. The effect

In re Gildersleeve's Estate, 75 Misc.2d 207, 347 N.Y.S.2d 96 (Sur.Ct.1973).

5. [Court's footnote] This may be a special "fact and circumstance" to be considered in making the allocation under Treas. Reg. § 1.265–1(c). M. Ferguson, J. Freeland & R. Stephens, Federal Income Taxation of Estates and Beneficiaries 493 (1970).

4. Unless altered by the governing instrument, gains are typically allocated to principal under state Principal and Income Acts. See RUPIA § 3(b)(8), reproduced in Appendix A.

is to reduce DNI and, correspondingly, to reduce the maximum distribution deduction, thereby causing these gains to be taxed to the entity in years when not distributed to the beneficiaries.[5] Similarly, but applicable only to simple trusts,[6] under section 643(a)(4), taxable extraordinary or stock-on-stock dividends that are allocated to principal under the instrument or local law and are not currently distributed[7] are also excluded from DNI, again reducing the maximum distribution deduction and causing the tax thereon to fall on the entity.

To illustrate the foregoing adjustments in computing DNI, consider the following example.

Assume a simple trust: receipts and disbursements for the year include:

1.	Taxable Dividends, allocable to income	$ 25,000
2.	Taxable Dividends, allocable to principal	$ 12,000
3.	Taxable Interest	$ 15,000
4.	Tax Exempt Interest	$ 10,000
5.	Long Term Capital Gain	$ 7,000
6.	Long Term Capital Loss	$ (2,000)
7.	Fiduciary Fees, charged to income	$ (5,000)
8.	Fiduciary Fees, charged to principal	$ (5,000)

Fiduciary Accounting Income includes the following items:

1.	Taxable Dividends	$ 25,000
3.	Taxable Interest	$ 15,000
4.	Tax Exempt Interest	$ 10,000
7.	Fiduciary Fees	$ (5,000)
	FAI =	$ 45,000

5. Distribution of gains to beneficiaries (1) may be dictated by the instrument, (2) may be deemed to occur if principal distributions regularly equal the amount of sale proceeds realized by the entity (see Treasury Regulation section 1.643(a)–3(d) Ex. (1) and Private Letter Ruling 8324002 (even though trustee distributed exact amount of gains incurred on sale, distribution was not pursuant to a practice of regularly distributing gains because it was the first year of the trust and there could be no established practice at that time)) and (3) will occur in the year of termination of the trust or estate. See Pennell, "Subchapter J: Evolution or Revolution?" 19 U.Miami Inst.Est.Plan. ¶ 903.5 (1985). However, gains realized by an estate upon sale of realty devised to beneficiaries who take title directly from decedent under state law are taxable to those beneficiaries, with the estate being treated essentially as an agent in selling the land to facilitate partition. Rev.Rul. 59–375, 1959–2 C.B. 161. For a complete discussion of the issue when gain is properly includible in DNI, see pages 104–109 infra.

6. Unlike the adjustment for capital gains, which applies to all trusts and estates, this modification does not apply to complex trusts or to estates. The rationale for this disparity relates to the throwback rules that apply to these dividends if ever subsequently distributed. See Treasury Regulation section 1.643(a)–4. Similar treatment is not accorded capital gains that are accumulated and later distributed because the throwback rules no longer apply to capital gains. This adjustment is similarly inapplicable to estates because there is no throwback rule applicable to estate distributions. The accumulation distribution and throwback rules are studied in detail in Chapter Four.

7. See RUPIA §§ 3(b)(4) and 6, reproduced in Appendix A.

Taxable Income includes the following items:

1. Taxable Dividends	$ 25,000	
2. Taxable Dividends	$ 12,000	
3. Taxable Interest	$ 15,000	
5. Long Term Capital Gain	$ 7,000	
6. Long Term Capital Loss	$ (2,000)	
7. 80% of Fiduciary Fees	$ (4,000)	A portion of these
8. 80% of Fiduciary Fees	$ (4,000)}	is lost under § 265
Taxable Income =	$ 49,000*.	

* For ease, this figure has been computed before the section 651(a) distribution deduction, with its section 643(a)(1) adjustment, and before the 642(b) deduction, with its section 643(a)(2) adjustment. The effect is the same.

Distributable Net Income is computed as:

Taxable Income	$ 49,000	adjusted under
Section 643(a)(3)	(5,000)	(for items 5 & 6)
Section 643(a)(4)	(12,000)	(for item 2)
Section 643(a)(5)	8,000	(for 80% of item 4)
DNI =	$ 40,000	

As illustrated by the foregoing example, fiduciary accounting income, taxable income and distributable net income may each differ during any given year. In any year, fiduciary accounting income *could exceed* taxable income if deductible expenses were paid from principal or due to the deduction in lieu of the personal exemption; fiduciary accounting income *could be less than* taxable income if taxable items, such as capital gains or certain dividends, were allocable to principal. Similarly, taxable income *could exceed* DNI because the distribution deduction is ignored or because capital gains or taxable dividends are allocated to principal and thus excluded in computing DNI; taxable income *could be less than* DNI due to tax exempt income or the deduction in lieu of the personal exemption, all of which being considered in computing taxable income but not in determining DNI. Finally, there need be no correlation between fiduciary accounting income and DNI. Consequently, using short-cuts to determine the tax treatment of a trust or estate, by assuming a correlation between any of these three concepts, could be hazardous.

Question

Based on the following facts, determine each of the trust's fiduciary accounting income, taxable income and DNI.

An accumulation trust distributes $1200 in the current year.

It has the following receipts and no expenses or similar deductions:

Taxable Dividends, allocated to income	$ 1000
Taxable Dividends, allocated to principal	750
Long Term Capital Gains	2000
Long Term Capital Losses	(700)
Tax Exempt Interest	500
	3550

Chapter Three

SIMPLE AND COMPLEX TRUSTS

All trusts that are not disregarded for income tax purposes (as discussed in Chapter Eight) are taxed as either a simple, a complex, or a grantor trust. The first two categories are mutually exclusive. By definition, a trust must be one or the other in a given year. However, a trust (but not an estate) may be simple in one year, complex the next, depending on the nature of its distributions. Because the grantor trust rules supersede those applicable to simple or complex trusts and will control for tax purposes, it will be necessary in Chapter Eight to learn about grantor trusts. For the present, however, we will direct our attention to simple and complex trusts on the assumption that the trust involved will be respected for income tax purposes. Before studying the tax consequences that apply to each type of trust, we take a short look at the timing rules that apply to trusts and estates and that partially belie what we will come to know as the fundamental conduit principle of Subchapter J.

TIMING

Read Code sections 642(c)(1) (penultimate sentence), 645, 652(c), 662(c), and 663(b).

Read Regulation sections 1.652(c)–1 through 1.652(c)–3, 1.662(c)–1 through 1.662(c)–3, and 1.663(b)–1(a).

Among Subchapter J's rules governing the income taxation of trusts and estates, the timing aspect does not completely comport with the otherwise pervasive conduit treatment described in Chapter One. Unlike the amount and character of income and deductions, which are meant to eventually pass through the entity to its beneficiaries, essentially as if no trust or estate were an intermediary, the time of inclusion of income and enjoyment of deductions is not necessarily the same as if the entity did not exist. Rather, under sections 652(c) and 662(c), applicable to simple and complex trusts and to estates, income and deductions are returned by the beneficiary in the beneficiary's tax year with which, or within which, the entity's tax year of distribution ends. Indeed, under the so-called "65–day" rule of section 663(b) (which we will study in Chapter 4, applicable to complex trusts), and the special rule of section 642(c)(1) (penultimate sentence, which provides an election to treat distributions to charity as having been made in the prior taxable year of the distributing entity), each section allows the entity to treat distributions as having been made in a prior tax year, making the year for which the entity claims the distribution deduction the proper year for determining the beneficiary's tax consequences thereof.

The special timing rules of sections 652(c) and 662(c) can create problems if the entity and beneficiary's tax years differ, but only with respect to the issue of when certain tax consequences should apply, not whether they should attach or to what extent. For example, in Estate of Petschek v. Commissioner, 738 F.2d 67 (2d Cir.1984), affirming 81 T.C. 260 (1983), taxpayer expatriated during the calendar year and, because he was not subject to U.S. taxation at year end, argued under section 652(c) that no part of trust income for the year of expatriation was taxable to him. The court rejected this argument on the ground that the trust was a conduit for purposes of determining the amount of income the taxpayer should report for the period prior to his expatriation. Thus, income of the trust was pro rated for that year, based on the number of days the taxpayer was a beneficiary prior to his expatriation. In *Petschek,* the trust and taxpayer were both on a calendar year, but the court indicated its decision would have been the same even if that were not the case. Thus, only the time for reporting the income would be affected by that difference, and not the application of the tax nor the amount taxable to the taxpayer.

To illustrate the operation of the timing rule, consider an estate with a fiscal tax year ending on November 30, but with beneficiaries on the calendar year. (A trust is not used in this example because, as discussed below, most trusts must select a calendar year for accounting purposes and the calendar year will be the accounting period used by the beneficiaries as well. Similar problems to those considered in this example may arise, however, if the trust's beneficiaries are not on a calendar year. Because this is not common, it is easier to think here in terms of a calendar year beneficiary and a fiscal year estate). In this example, any distribution made by the estate prior to December 1 of the current year will be reported by the recipient in the recipient's calendar year ending December 31, because distribution would be in the estate's current tax year ending in the recipient's current tax year. However, a distribution after November 30 of the current year will be reported in the recipient's next tax year because December 1 begins a new tax year for the estate, ending in the recipient's next tax year, and the rule requires returning income for the recipient's tax year in which the estate's tax year of distribution ends. Thus, income received by a beneficiary in December of year 1 would be reported on the beneficiary's tax return for year 2 which, under section 6072(a) (time for filing return is the 15th day of the fourth month following close of the tax year), need be filed no sooner than April 15 of year 3.

Also by virtue of section 6072(a), the estate will normally file its return on or before the 15th day of the fourth month following close of its tax year. Since the end of 1986, however, all trusts (and all estates, beginning after their second tax year) are required to make estimated tax payments under section 6654. This will not, however, alter the deferral aspects of the rules above considered to the extent the entity distributes all its income and therefore has no tax to pay in quarterly estimated installments.

In the year of a beneficiary's death (or the year of an artificial entity's termination, if the beneficiary is an entity), what rule should apply to accommodate the fact that there is no tax year of the beneficiary with which or within which the distributing entity's tax year ends (because the distributing entity's tax year will end after the close of the last tax year of the beneficiary—unless the beneficiary happens to die or terminate on the last day of the distributing entity's tax year)? Income paid to a beneficiary's estate or successors in interest after death is taxable to those recipients as income in respect of a decedent (IRD) under section 691(a) (which we study in Chapter Six). But what of income actually paid prior to the beneficiary's death? Consider how the following case answers this question and, in so doing, "recaptures" any tax deferral advantage gained on selection of the distributing entity's prior tax year.

SCHIMBERG v. UNITED STATES

United States Court of Appeals, Seventh Circuit, 1966.
365 F.2d 70.

SWYGERT, CIRCUIT JUDGE.

* * *

The facts were stipulated. Anna H. Collins died on November 29, 1957. The plaintiff, as the executor of the estate, filed an income tax return for the decedent covering the period from January 1, 1957 to the date of death. The decedent was the sole income beneficiary of the Philip Henrici trust, which kept its books and filed its income tax returns for fiscal years beginning February 1 and ending January 31, and a forty per cent income beneficiary of the William M. Collins trust, which kept its books and filed tax returns for fiscal years beginning April 1 and ending March 31. The decedent kept her books and filed tax returns on the cash basis for calendar years.

In the decedent's final income tax return, the plaintiff included the following: (1) the decedent's distributive share of the income of the Henrici and Collins trusts for their fiscal years ending January 31, 1957 and March 31, 1957, respectively; (2) $27,621.69, that portion of the income from the Henrici trust for its fiscal year ending January 31, 1958 which was actually distributed to the decedent prior to her death; (3) $7,041.57, that portion of the income from the Collins trust for its fiscal year ending March 31, 1958 which was actually distributed to the decedent before her death. The plaintiff subsequently sought a refund of the taxes attributable to the inclusion in the return of the amounts distributed to the decedent prior to her death which related to the fiscal years of the trusts ending after her death. The district court held that these amounts were properly included in the decedent's final return and dismissed that part of the claim. Schimberg v. United States, 245 F.Supp. 616 (N.D.Ill.1965).

The general rule that an individual taxpayer must report his income in the year that it is received is different as to income received by the beneficiary of a trust. Section 652(c) of the Internal Revenue Code provides that "[i]f the taxable year of a beneficiary is different from that of the trust, the amount which the beneficiary is required to include in gross income * * * shall be based upon the amount of income of the trust for any taxable year or years of the trust ending within or with his taxable year." The literal language of this "different taxable years" provision has been modified by the regulations in an attempt to resolve the anomaly arising when the death of the trust beneficiary presents a situation in which the taxable year of the trust will not end "within or with" the final taxable year of the beneficiary. In such cases Treasury Regulation section 1.652(c)–2 provides that the "gross income for the last taxable year of a beneficiary on the cash basis includes only income actually distributed to the beneficiary before his death" and that trust income distributed to the beneficiary's estate is to be included in the gross income of the estate as "income in respect of a decedent" under section 691 of the Internal Revenue Code.

The plaintiff * * * argues that the statute permits a beneficiary to be taxed on trust income only when the taxable year of the trust ends within or with the beneficiary's taxable year, that the statute does not authorize a different rule in the event of the death of the beneficiary, and that therefore all trust income attributable to the taxable year of a trust not ending within or with the beneficiary's last taxable year must be reported as income by the beneficiary's estate. We do not agree. The problem resolved by the regulations in question, the treatment of trust income actually received by a cash basis beneficiary prior to his death, is either one not contemplated by the statute or one as to which the application of the statute is unclear, given the general Congressional policy with respect to the time and incidence of income taxation. In such a case the regulations must be sustained unless they are unreasonable. Commissioner of Internal Revenue v. South Texas Lumber Co., 333 U.S. 496, 501, 68 S.Ct. 695, 92 L.Ed. 831 (1948). As the district judge commented, "It is difficult to find oppressive a regulation which attempts only to impose tax liability on income the taxpayer has actually received and enjoyed prior to the taxing date."

The plaintiff maintains that the regulations are unreasonable because they permit "bunching" of more than twelve months' trust income in the decedent's final return. * * * Insofar as a "bunching" hardship may be permitted by the regulations, however, it should be noted that "bunching" generally occurs as a result of the trust having adopted a fiscal tax year, which may well have given the beneficiary the advantage of postponing the reporting of trust income for several months over a period of years. And again, the restriction of "bunching" to trust income actually received prior to the beneficiary's death militates against the alleged hardship. * * *

The decision of the district court is affirmed.

MAJOR, SENIOR CIRCUIT JUDGE (dissenting).

In my judgment, under the plain, unambiguous language of the statutory provisions involved, the taxpayer should prevail. The Treasury Regulations relied upon should not be sustained on the pretext that they are no more than a permissible interpretation or construction of such provisions. The government in its brief states, "Certainly, Congress did not intend any income from a trust should escape taxation unless definitely exempted." The point is that the income in the instant case was by statute "definitely exempted," and it is only by reason of the Treasury Regulations that it was "definitely" required to be reported. The government continues, "Obviously, the trust income herein is not definitely exempted and therefore will have to be reported some place in order that it be subjected to tax." So, based on the premise that it should be reported someplace and being unable to find any place provided by Congress, the Commissioner promulgates the regulations contrary to the statutory provisions. This must be a novel approach in seeking to justify the regulations.

In June 1956, at the time the regulations were proposed, the Section of Taxation of the American Bar Association, through its committee on the Taxation of Estates and Trusts, transmitted to the Commissioner its comments on the proposed regulations. Inasmuch as I thoroughly agree with the views therein expressed, I take the liberty of quoting in part as follows:

> "Sections 652(c) and 662(c) unequivocally provide that, if the taxable year of the beneficiary is different from that of the trust, the amount which the beneficiary includes in gross income 'shall be based upon the amount of income of the trust for any taxable year or years of the trust ending within or with his taxable year.' There are no exceptions in the statute. Thus, since the taxable year of the beneficiary will end with his death, he should include nothing under the statute with respect to any year of the trust which ends after his death. The regulations contain the statement that Sections 652(c) and 662(c) of the Code do not apply to amounts paid to the beneficiary during the taxable year of the trust in which he dies. There is absolutely no statutory justification for this statement."

The same committee included in its comments the further pertinent observation:

"Furthermore, the rule which the regulations purport to set forth with no statutory justification can result in the bunching of income in the final taxable year of the beneficiary. For example, let us assume that the beneficiary is on a calendar year and that the trust is on [a] January 31 fiscal year. The beneficiary dies on December 1, 1956. The regulations would require that the beneficiary's last tax return include all of the income from the trust for its fiscal year 1956, plus the income of the trust payable to the beneficiary for the period from February 1, 1956 to December 1, 1956. This result is most unjust and is completely contrary to the statute."

I would reverse the judgment.

Because of the various consequences of the timing rules, Congress enacted section 645 in 1986, requiring trusts with private beneficiaries to utilize a calendar year for tax purposes. If necessary, to put the trust on the required period, Treasury Regulation section 1.441–1(b)(3) permits the trust's first year to be a short tax year. Under section 645, wholly charitable and other tax exempt trusts, and all estates, are excepted from this rule. For them, only a complete failure to select a tax year will result in automatic calendar year treatment under section 441(b)(2).

Because fiscal years are still allowed for estates, careful attention must be devoted to coordination of the tax year of the estate with the years of its beneficiaries. Selection of tax year is one item of post-mortem tax planning customarily considered by the personal representative, and administration of even a simple, no frills estate can entail time consuming and often difficult details of this type that many planners and most beneficiaries do not recognize or appreciate. Similarly, for both trusts and estates, some discretion exists in selecting when the last year of the entity will end for tax purposes. In this respect, both trusts and estates are deemed to continue to exist for a reasonable period necessary to perform the ordinary duties of administration and thereafter to distribute all but a reasonable reserve for contingent claims. Any attempt to unduly prolong administration (for example, to force termination into a later tax year of the beneficiaries) will be disallowed and the entity will be deemed terminated when that reasonable time for administration has expired.[1]

Question

If decedent's estate pours over into a complex trust (one that may accumulate income) and maximum deferral of tax on estate income is

1. Treasury Regulation sections 1.641(b)–3(a) and 1.641(b)–3(b). With respect to taxation of funded grantor trusts (for example, a Will substitute) after the grantor's death, see Fleming, "Taxation of Income of Grantor Trusts After Death of Grantor and Before Implementation of Successor Trusts or Shares", 63 Ill.B.J. 78 (1974); and Ufford, "Income Taxation of the Funded Revocable Trust After the Death of the Grantor", 30 Tax Lawyer 37, 45–46 (1976).

desired, how should the estate structure its tax year to maximum advantage? Assume both the beneficiary and the accumulation trust are on a calendar year.

SIMPLE TRUSTS

Read Code sections 641, 642(b), 643(a)(3), 643(b), 643(c), 651 and 652.

Read the Regulations to sections 651 and 652.

Under section 651(a), a simple trust, governed by the rules of Subpart B of Subchapter J, must distribute all current income annually, must make no distributions for the year in excess of the amount of current income, and may make no charitable distributions or set asides. The trust must *require* distribution of all income currently, but not all income must actually *be* distributed to qualify. That is, even if income is not currently distributed, the fact that distribution is required will suffice under Treasury Regulation section 1.651(a)–1 to satisfy the all income requirement. A trust might require distribution of income but not actually distribute it (1) whenever the trust's tax year ends with income on hand but not distributable under normal administrative practice until the next periodic income distribution date (monthly, quarterly, semi-annually or whatever), (2) because the beneficiary requested or authorized a delay in distribution of income, or (3) if the trustee is unsure of the identity of the proper beneficiary and seeks instructions while withholding trust income pending a judicial determination.[2] To avoid disqualification as a simple trust in any of these events, the tax rule intentionally does not require actual distribution of all income annually. It also does not require that the entitlement of any given beneficiary be specified. For example, a trust that requires distribution of all income annually among a group of beneficiaries, in whatever proportions the trustee selects, would be a simple trust even though no single beneficiary has a guaranteed entitlement.

As to the requirement for qualification as a simple trust that there be no distribution in excess of current income, the trustee need not be prohibited from distributing amounts in excess of current income. Rather, the trustee must simply insure that only income is distributed in a given year, thus allowing the trust to be taxed as a simple trust. This imposes a burden on the trustee to carefully monitor distributions, because expected tax consequences may be lost due to inadvertent excess distributions. "Inadvertent" might seem to be an inappropriate term because even the most inexperienced trustee ought to be able to tell whether a distribution exceeds income. Here the difference between trust accounting income and income in a tax sense becomes important.

2. See Estate of Bruchmann v. Commissioner, 53 T.C. 403 (1969) (taxpayer taxed on income for seven years during which trustee withheld income pending determination whether taxpayer, as an adopted child, was a proper beneficiary); and Rev. Rul. 62–147, 1962–2 C.B. 151.

For tax purposes, distributions made by a trust are income under section 643(b) to the extent they are not in excess of the amount of the current year's fiduciary accounting income, not to the extent they do not exceed distributable net income. That is, "income" *means* fiduciary accounting income, as determined by the fiduciary in good faith under the governing instrument and applicable local law. Thus, Treasury Regulation section 1.651(a)–2(a) recognizes the validity of reserves to which income may be allocated without constituting failure to distribute all current income annually. See Letter Rulings 8501084 and 8501011 (dealing with the income tax consequences of the type of compensating adjustment that is studied in Chapter Five), but see Treasury Regulation section 1.643(b)–1 (penultimate sentence), which specifies that "[t]rust provisions which depart fundamentally from concepts of local law in the determination of what constitutes income are not recognized * * *."

The *amount* of current income, rather than the actual identity of items received as income, is determinative for simple trust qualification purposes, under section 651(a) (last sentence, referring to "amounts of income" described in section 651(a)(1)), regardless of the source of that distribution for trust accounting purposes. Thus, if a trust has income of $1000 for the current year and is required to distribute all income currently, a distribution of stock held in the trust with a fair market value of $1000 would be regarded as a distribution of income, even though the stock was held as a part of trust corpus on the trust accounting ledger. Distributions not in excess of the current year's fiduciary accounting income are "income" for purposes of applying the simple trust rules, and it is the amount of fiduciary accounting income, not the actual source of the distribution, that the trustee must monitor to insure qualification as a simple trust. Indeed, because fiduciary accounting income may exceed either taxable income or distributable net income, it is possible to distribute amounts of fiduciary accounting income in excess of what would otherwise be taxable to the trust, without losing the status of a simple trust.

If a trust qualifies as a simple trust, the tax consequence is "conduit" treatment. Effected under sections 651(a) and 651(b) through a "distribution deduction," resulting in a tax wash to the trust, distributions of fiduciary accounting income from the trust "carry out" DNI to the recipients thereof under section 652(a) and Treasury Regulation section 1.652(a)–1, and those recipients thereby acquire the liability to pay tax thereon. Thus, in computing its income tax liability for the year, a qualifying simple trust may deduct the amount of income it was required to or did in fact distribute. However, to prevent a deduction larger than the trust's taxable income, which would put the trust in a loss position for tax purposes, under section 651(b) the distribution deduction may not exceed distributable net income, computed for the year without inclusion of the net amount of tax exempt income. Thus, Treasury Regulation section 1.651(b)–1 requires reduction of DNI by the amount specified in section 643(a)(5) (as adjusted by any deductions allocable thereto). The effect of this adjustment is to limit the distribution deduction to the taxable portion of DNI so as not to put the trust in a loss position in computing its taxes for the year. The tax exempt quality of the income is not lost, however, because it carries over to the recipients by virtue of section 652(b).

The tax consequence of qualification as a simple trust to beneficiaries entitled to receive required distributions of income is section 652(a) inclusion in income of the amount allowed as a deduction to the trust, whether the income was actually distributed or only required to be distributed. If distributions exceed the allowable deduction, because fiduciary accounting income is greater than the taxable portion of DNI, each recipient includes a pro rata portion of the amount of the deduction, based on the total distributions made by the trust. So complete is the pass through of tax liability to the beneficiaries that, under section 652(b) and Treasury Regulation section 1.652(b)–1, amounts originally received by the trust retain their tax character (tax exempt income, capital gains, tax preference items and so forth) when distributed to the beneficiaries. Moreover, unless specifically altered by a provision of the governing instrument mandating non pro rata distribution of various classes of income, the character of all amounts included in DNI, both income (including tax exempt income) and deductions, is effectively allocated pro rata to the recipients by section 652(b) and Treasury Regulation section 1.652(b)–2. Discretionary non pro rata distributions of various classes of income will not alter this allocation. Treasury Regulation section 1.652(b)–2(b)(1). The overall effect of both the distribution deduction and the inclusion rules is conduit taxation that generally taxes the beneficiaries as if the trust did not exist as an intermediary.

Questions

1. Assume that a simple trust realized $10,000 of income for the current year, all allocable to the income ledger for trust accounting purposes. It paid $3,000 of deductible section 212 fiduciary fees that were not subject to the 2% floor on deductibility by virtue of section 67(e) and the trustee properly charged these items on its trust ledger to principal. The trustee distributed $5,000 to each of beneficiaries A and B during the year, as required by the terms of the trust. Ignoring the section 642(b) deduction in lieu of the personal exemption, what is the trust's distribution deduction and how much income is taxable to the beneficiaries?

2. If $2,000 of the income in question 1 were tax exempt, how would your answer differ?

ESTATES AND COMPLEX TRUSTS

Read Code sections 661–663.

Read all the Regulations to sections 661–663.

All estates, any trust that is not a simple trust for the year (because it either (1) may accumulate income, (2) provides for charity, or (3) actually made distributions exceeding current income), and all trusts in the year of termination (because principal is, of necessity, distributed), are governed by the complex trust rules of Subpart C (sections 661–664) of Subchapter J. To the extent income of an estate or complex trust is currently distributed or required to be distributed, the tax consequences to the entity and beneficiary are essentially the same as the conduit tax treatment of a simple trust: the entity is entitled to a distribution deduction under section 661(a), the beneficiaries include the deducted amounts under section 662(a), and the character of each item in DNI carries through to the beneficiaries pro rata under sections 661(b) and 662(b) (unless the governing instrument specifically dictates otherwise).

One notable difference between the distribution deduction for a complex trust and that for a simple trust is that, while both deductions cannot exceed the amount of DNI (see section 651(b) and the last sentence of section 661(a)) as reduced by tax exempt income (see the last sentence of section 651(b) and section 661(c)), the amount of DNI will differ by virtue of application only to simple trusts of section 643(b)(4) (exclusion from DNI of taxable dividends allocable to principal). In addition, unlike a simple trust, a complex trust or an estate may make distributions of amounts in excess of the dollar amount of fiduciary accounting income (whether the distributed asset comes from fiduciary accounting income or principal) that are deemed to carry out income to the extent of current DNI (or prior years' accumulations of income, known as "UNI" and defined below), thus generating additional distribution deductions for the trust or estate and requiring inclusion by the recipients thereof under sections 662(a)(2).

To illustrate the difference between simple and complex trusts, assume a trust has $33,000 of fiduciary accounting income for the year, consisting of $24,000 of ordinary income and $9,000 of tax exempt income. The trustee is required to distribute all the income annually to Beneficiary (B). If the trustee actually distributes more than $33,000 for the year the trust would be a complex trust. The distribution would carry out the $33,000 of DNI, of which $9,000 would be tax exempt to B and the trust would be entitled to a $24,000 distribution deduction. In addition, the trust would have made either an accumulation distribution of UNI or a tax free distribution of corpus (or some of each) in the amount in excess of $33,000 that was distributed to B, making the trust complex. No additional distribution deduction would be available to the trust for this excess distribution, and the tax consequence to B would depend on the extent to which the distribution carried out UNI, as explored in detail below. By way of comparison, if the trustee had properly distributed only $22,000 for the year, in this example the amounts distributed would be $^{24}/_{33} \times$ $22,000 of taxable income items and $^{9}/_{33} \times$ $22,000 of tax exempt income and the trust would be complex by virtue of accumulating the income that was not currently distributed. B would include taxable income of 24/33 × $22,000 ($16,000) and report tax exempt income of 9/33 × $22,000 ($6,000), and the trust would deduct the full 24/33 × $22,000 ($16,000) of taxable income that was distributed.

IN–KIND DISTRIBUTIONS AND SPECIFIC BEQUESTS

As explored in detail in Chapter Five, under section 643(e), distributions in kind from a complex trust carry out income (either DNI, UNI or a combination of both) only to the extent of the lesser of the distributed assets' adjusted basis or their fair market value. In addition, by section 663(a)(1), excepted entirely from the income carryout rules applicable to complex trusts are transfers in satisfaction of a specific bequest, devise or legacy, if payable in less than four installments and not required to be satisfied only out of income. To constitute a "specific" disposition, the identity of the property conveyed, or the dollar amount of a pecuniary gift, must be ascertainable as of inception of the trust or estate. "Formula" bequests (for example, a distribution that is tied to a concept such as a decedent's gross estate for Federal estate tax purposes) do not qualify because they are dependent on variables (such as valuation and tax elections) that make them unascertainable until some later time. Treasury Regulation section 1.663(a)–1(b). And, in determining whether payment is to be made in less than four installments, terms of the governing instrument, not actual administration, are determinative under Treasury Regulation section 1.663(a)–1(c)(1).

Questions

1. Decedent's Will calls for distribution to Decedent's surviving spouse of a particular asset, plus an amount of cash or other property necessary to qualify for an "optimum" marital deduction (that amount needed to reduce taxes to the amount protected by Decedent's federal estate tax unified credit). Does this distribution qualify under section 663(a)(1) as a specific bequest?

2. Why are distributions in kind and specific bequests, devises and legacies granted special treatment, why is this treatment limited to complex trusts, and what are the tax consequences to both the trust or estate and to the recipient of a qualified distribution?

ACCUMULATED INCOME

The key difference between the taxation of simple trusts under Subpart B and the taxation of estates or complex trusts under Subpart C is attributable to accumulations of income in the latter. Only gains or other income properly allocable to corpus are taxed to a simple trust. All other income is offset completely by the distribution deduction and is thereby taxed through to the beneficiaries. In a complex trust or an estate, income that is accumulated rather than distributed will be taxed to the trust or estate because the distribution deduction is less than the total income and, thus, does not wash out the full amount of income for the year. By virtue of this essential difference, the entity as a taxpayer permits fragmentation between the beneficiaries and the entity, generating a now very modest reduction in tax rates for all, and necessitating several concepts not applicable to simple trusts. While the beneficiaries are still taxed on income actually distributed and the fiduciary receives a corresponding deduction therefor, it is accumulated income, taxed to the entity, that accomplishes tax minimization. To deal with this factor, Subchapter J creates a new term, "undistributed net income" (UNI), and imposes complex rules known as the accumulation distribution and throwback rules.

UNI is defined under section 665(a) as DNI less both of (1) the distribution deduction, and (2) any taxes paid by the entity that are attributable to DNI. In effect, UNI is what remains after the entity distributes income and pays its tax on accumulated income. It represents the amount available for distribution to beneficiaries in later years. Thus, if a trust had $100,000 of DNI for the year and distributed only $70,000, leaving $30,000 subject to tax after reflecting its distribution deduction, and if the tax on this $30,000 were $10,000, UNI would be the remaining $20,000.

The intent is to identify UNI in order to tax it when finally distributed to beneficiaries in future years, as if it had not been accumulated in the first instance. That is, the accumulation distribution and throwback rules seek to impose a tax on the beneficiaries as if the trust had been a simple trust and the income had been distributed in the year in which it was earned. Without such rules, a trust would accumulate income in years in which its effective tax cost was lower than that of the beneficiary and then make distribution in a later year when the beneficiary's tax cost had dropped to a more desirable level. "Effective tax cost" for these purposes should take into consideration more than just the marginal tax bracket of the entity and the beneficiary. In addition, consideration must be given to whether distribution would cause the beneficiary's section 1(g) gradual adjustments to kick-in (causing the beneficiary to lose the benefit of the 15% bracket or the personal exemption), and also the effect of distribution on items such as the beneficiary's 2% floor on certain deductions, the passive activity rules, and any alternative minimum tax consequences.

Perhaps unrealistically, Congress does not perceive the same degree of tax abuse involving estates, which explains why the throwback rules do not apply to accumulation distributions from an estate. Moreover, when the current tax rates were amended and substantially reduced in 1986, decreasing the benefit of separate trust or estate existence to a maximum of $650 per year (before considering the deduction in lieu of the personal exemption, which can vary from trust to trust and will change as it is indexed for inflation), the need for the accumulation distribution and throwback rules declined. Nevertheless, sufficient benefits remain that Congress has chosen to retain Subpart D, which we study in Chapter Four.

The accumulation distribution and throwback rules provide that distributions from a complex trust first carry out current income (DNI) and then prior years' UNI. Only after exhaustion of both these amounts is a section 102 tax free distribution of principal deemed to occur. DNI is taxed upon distribution as it is in a simple trust. The UNI is then subjected to a complex computation determining (actually by a shortcut method that estimates rather than actually determines) what the recipient would have paid in taxes on that UNI had it been distributed in the year it was accumulated. After application of several credits, the balance of this "throwback tax" is the amount of tax due on the accumulation distribution. Thus, in the prior example, if the trust had $50,000 of DNI in the next year and distributed $80,000, the distribution would carry out all that next year's DNI and all the prior year's UNI before any portion of the distribution would be deemed a tax free distribution of corpus.

A second rule exists to minimize the use of complex trusts to fragment income into multiple separate taxpaying entities, each with its own separate rates and deduction in lieu of the personal exemption. By the "multiple trust" rule of section 643(f), separate trusts created by substantially the same grantor(s), with substantially the same beneficiar(ies) and with a principal purpose to avoid taxes, are regarded as a single taxpaying entity.

A third special rule is a reflection of the fact that it may not be possible to know, as of year end, how much income must be distributed in order to avoid a complex trust accumulation. Thus, the "sixty-five day" rule of section 663(b) permits complex trusts to make distributions within 65 days after year-end while electing to treat those distributions as current distributions of DNI during the year just ended. The rule is applicable only to complex trusts because the object is to avoid accumulations that may subsequently be subject to the accumulation distribution and throwback rules, which do not apply to estates or simple trusts.

THE TIER RULES

A fourth concept, the "tier" rules, is made necessary in complex trusts by the ability to accumulate income for later distribution. The term "tier" is not utilized in the Code or Regulations, but refers to the distinction drawn in sections 661(a)(1) and (2) between amounts of income required to be distributed currently ("Tier 1") and other amounts properly paid, credited or required to be distributed ("Tier 2"). To illustrate the importance of this concept, assume that a complex trust has $50,000 of fiduciary accounting income for the year but DNI of only $40,000 (due to an income tax deduction of expenses charged to principal for fiduciary accounting purposes), that the trustee must currently distribute all income in equal shares to beneficiaries A and B, and that the trustee also makes a discretionary distribution of $50,000 to B. Without the tier rules it would appear that, because A has received $25,000 while B has received $75,000, the $40,000 of DNI ought to be pro rated between them in proportions of $10,000 and $30,000 respectively. However, by virtue of the terms of the trust, it is apparent that A received half the income, not just one-fourth, and should be taxed on half the DNI. The tier rules provide the mechanism for distinguishing between the various distributions to A and B in order to effect this treatment.

The technical definitions under the tier rules relate to distributions made by the trust. Under section 661(a)(1), Tier 1 distributions are required current distributions of income (not in excess of DNI). Under the parenthetical provision in section 661(a)(1) and Treasury Regulation section 1.661(a)–2(b), if a required distribution could have been made from principal (such as an annuity payment or payment of a widow's allowance), it is still a Tier 1 distribution if actually made from income. Thus, in Revenue Ruling 75–124, 1975–1 C.B. 183, a widow's allowance was treated as a section 661(a)(1) Tier 1 distribution to the widow, notwithstanding classification as a distribution in satisfaction of a debt under local law. Moreover, under section 662(a)(1), a required distribution will be treated as having been made for purposes of causing inclusion to the beneficiary, even if the distribution is not actually made.

Under section 661(a)(2) and Treasury Regulation section 1.661(a)–2(c), Tier 2 distributions are all other distributions, whether required or discretionary and whether made from current income, accumulated income or principal. In the example, A and B are equal Tier 1 beneficiaries because the trustee must make current distribution of all income to them. Consequently, the $40,000 of DNI is pro rated equally between them under section 662(a)(1) and Treasury Regulation section 1.662(a)–2(b), rather than $10,000 to A and $30,000 to B. Were there any remaining DNI after satisfaction of all Tier 1 required current distributions of income, that excess DNI would similarly be pro rated under section 662(a)(2)(B) and Treasury Regulation section 1.662(a)–3(c) among the Tier 2 beneficiaries on the basis of their Tier 2 distributions, and the amount of their distributions in excess of any DNI that is includible in their incomes would be either a section 665(b) accumulation distribution of prior years' UNI or a section 102 tax-free distribution of principal.

Finally, if there had been a qualified section 642(c) deductible charitable distribution of income from the trust, it would effectively constitute a so-called "intermediate tier" that may be regarded as falling between Tier 1 and Tier 2, essentially exhausting DNI to the full extent of the charitable distribution after all Tier 1 distributions had been made but before any Tier 2 distributions. By virtue of the parenthetical clause appearing in section 662(a)(1) but not in section

662(a)(2), the charitable deduction is considered only in determining the amount of DNI that remains to be carried out to Tier 2 beneficiaries, but is ignored in determining the amount of DNI available to be taxed to Tier 1 beneficiaries. Thus, DNI effectively goes first to Tier 1 beneficiaries, then to charity, then to Tier 2 beneficiaries, until exhausted. Thus, if the foregoing trust had been required to distribute only $15,000 currently to each of A and B and also distributed $15,000 of income to Charity as well, the Tier 1 amounts would be $15,000 of DNI to each of A and B, with the remaining $10,000 of DNI being regarded as carried out to Charity. The balance of the distributions to all would be UNI (first to Charity, then any excess to A and B) and, once UNI was exhausted, tax free corpus.

In theory, however, this "intermediate" tier is no such thing. Instead, the actual operation of the Code is to simply ignore the section 642(c) deduction in determining the amount of taxable income, and thus DNI, available to be carried out by Tier 1 distributions, but not to ignore the deduction in determining taxable income and DNI for any other purpose. Thus, DNI is not actually "carried out" to charity. It is just reduced by virtue of a smaller amount of taxable income, caused by the section 642(c) deduction.

The final relevant concept under Subpart C is a "separate share rule," applicable under section 663(c) to trusts (but, as illustrated by Treasury Regulation section 1.663(c)–3(f), not to estates), providing that substantially independent and separately administered shares of a single trust will be treated as separate trusts for DNI allocation purposes. Consequently, activity such as accumulations or distributions in one separate share will not affect application of the tier rules or the tax consequences of activity in other shares, regardless of how many beneficiaries there are of any separate share or whether separate books of account are maintained for the separate shares. Treasury Regulation sections 1.663(c)–3(a) and 1.663(c)–3(c).

To summarize, DNI in both simple and complex trusts is carried out to trust beneficiaries by required current income distributions. Any remaining DNI is effectively exhausted by charitable distributions of income, if any, followed by any other distributions made, in that order. Within any class or tier of distribution, DNI is shared pro rata by the recipients thereof, and each item of income in DNI is shared pro rata within each class or tier (unless the governing instrument provides otherwise).

Questions

Apply the foregoing rules of Subparts B and C of Subchapter J in the following situations, in each case ignoring the deduction in lieu of the personal exemption:

1. A trust received $100,000 of fiduciary accounting income that it was required to distribute currently, 60 percent to A and 40 percent to B. How large is the trust's distribution deduction and how much income

should A and B include on their tax returns to represent those distributions? Would your answers differ based on whether the trust were simple or complex?

2. In question 1, if the $100,000 of trust income was $90,000 of taxable items and $10,000 of tax exempt items, how large would the distribution deduction be, and how would the tax consequences to A and B differ?

3. If, in question 1, a third beneficiary, C, were to receive discretionary distributions of $20,000 in addition to the $100,000 of mandatory current distribution of income to A and B, how would the results to A and B differ and what treatment would apply to C's distribution?

4. If, in question 3, A and B were discretionary recipients along with C, receiving distributions of $60,000 and $40,000, respectively, in addition to the $20,000 distributed to C, how would A, B, C and the trust be taxed?

5. In question 4, if $10,000 of the $100,000 of current income were tax exempt, what effect would that have on A, B, C and the trust?

6. If, in question 5, A were a mandatory recipient of income and C were a charity, how would A and B's distributions carry out DNI, what portions would be tax exempt, and how would C's distribution and the trust be taxed?

7. Assume that a different trust received $50,000 of income, of which $10,000 was tax exempt, and that it had $10,000 of deductible expenses. A mandatory distribution of $25,000 of income was made to A. Discretionary income distributions of $15,000 to B and $10,000 to C, a qualified charity, were also made. How large is the trust's distribution deduction and how much income (and of what character) should each of A and B include on their tax returns to represent these distributions?

8. If, in question 7, the distribution to A had been $35,000 and that to B were only $5,000, how would your answer differ?

Chapter Four

ACCUMULATION DISTRIBUTIONS AND THROWBACK

Read Code sections 665(a), 665(b), 665(d)(1), 665(e), 666, and 667(a) through 667(c).

The regulations to Subpart D antedate the 1976 changes to the throwback computation rules and some are no longer entirely accurate. Read the following sections with this in mind: 1.665(a)–0A, 1.665(a)–1A(a), 1.665(b)–1A(a), 1.665(b)–1A(b) (except (b)(2)), 1.665(e)–1A(b), 1.666(a)–1A(a), 1.666(a)–1A(b), 1.666(a)–1A(d), 1.666(a)–1A(e), 1.666(b)–1A, 1.666(c)–1A, 1.666(c)–2A, 1.666(d)–1A, and 1.667(a)–1A.

The accumulation distribution and throwback rules of Subpart D of Subchapter J are necessitated by the fact that complex trusts may accumulate current income, for distribution in subsequent years. Designed to minimize the advantage to be gained by taxing accumulated income to a trust (rather than current distribution of that income, with current taxation thereof to its recipients), these rules have no application to trusts that have no "outside income" and have never accumulated income, nor to estates (which are ignored because they ostensibly pose slight risk of prolonged abusive administration for tax minimization purposes). Treasury Regulation section 1.665(a)–0A(d). Many professional personal representatives are fully aware of tax minimization opportunities available through post-mortem income tax planning in estates of decedents, but the fundamental assumption regarding estate administration is probably accurate in the vast majority of cases.

With the 1986 changes, which reduced to a very small amount the savings attributable to treating a trust as a separate taxpaying entity, it can be argued that Subpart D is no longer necessary. Congress has yet to be persuaded to repeal Subpart D, because there is still real value in making accumulations today in order to avoid increasing a beneficiary's brackets, even if taking advantage of the trust's run through the rate brackets is worth very little. That is, the savings generated by taxing accumulated income to the trust may be slight (due to the relatively compressed rate brackets that apply), but the value to a beneficiary of not receiving the trust's income may be great, in terms of avoiding application of the section 1(g) gradual adjustment or minimizing the amount of lost deductions due to the section 67 and 213 floors on certain itemized and medical expense deductions.

The rules of Subpart D of Subchapter J usually apply only if a section 665(b) "accumulation distribution" is made by a complex trust. (While a simple trust can be subject to throwback in very limited circumstances, as illustrated by Treasury Regulation section 1.665(e)–1A(b), these unusual situations are ignored for purposes herein.) An accumulation distribution is essentially a distribution in excess of the greater of DNI and fiduciary accounting income for the taxable year (see the last sentence of section 665(b)). Recall that the priority rules treat DNI as passing first to section 662(a)(1) Tier 1 distributees. Also recall that, by definition under 651(a) (last sentence: simple trusts lose that status in any year in which distributions exceed the amount of income for the year) and under 661(a)(1) (Tier 1 distributions being limited to income for the current year that was required to be distributed), Tier 1 distributions from a complex trust (and all distributions from a simple trust) cannot exceed the amount of fiduciary accounting income. Thus, only Tier 2 distributions from complex trusts may invoke application of the accumulation distribution and throwback rules. For this reason the technical definition of an accumulation distribution under section 665(b) (which makes reference to amounts specified in section 661(a)(2), which are Tier 2 distributions) is met only to the extent Tier 2 distributions exceed DNI remaining after all Tier 1 distributions. Moreover, by virtue of the last sentence of section 665(b), an accumulation distribution exists only if total Tier 1 and Tier 2 distributions exceed fiduciary accounting income for the current year, and then only to the extent prior years' UNI has not yet been distributed by prior accumulation distributions, as dictated under the second sentence of section 666(a) and Treasury Regulation section 1.666(a)–1A(e).

By way of example, if a trust has $20,000 of current fiduciary accounting income, $19,000 of DNI (due to $1,000 of expenses that were deducted but charged to and paid from corpus for fiduciary accounting purposes), $10,000 of UNI and makes aggregate Tier 1 and Tier 2 distributions of no more than $20,000 (the amount of fiduciary accounting income), there would be no accumulation distribution, even though the amount distributed exceeded DNI. However, if as little as one more dollar (for a total of $20,001) were distributed, an accumulation distribution would exist, now because Tier 1 and Tier 2 distributions exceed the greater of DNI and fiduciary accounting income. Moreover, by virtue of a flaw in the statute, the amount of this accumulation distribution could be anywhere from $1 to $1001, as illustrated as follows:

(a) If Tier 1 distributions were $20,000 (distributions that were required and that did not exceed fiduciary accounting income for the year), the Tier 2 distribution would be $1. Only to the extent the Tier 2 distribution ($1) exceeds DNI ($19,000), as reduced (but not below zero) by Tier 1 distributions ($20,000), would there be an accumulation distribution. Here that excess would be only $1.

(b) If Tier 1 distributions were $19,000, the Tier 2 distribution would be $1001. Again to the extent this Tier 2 distribution exceeded DNI ($19,000) reduced by Tier 1 distributions ($19,000), there would be an accumulation distribution. Here that amount would be $1001.

(c) If Tier 1 distributions were anything less than $19,000, the accumulation distribution could not exceed $1001. For example, if the Tier 1 distribution were $0, the Tier 2 distributions would be $20,001 and would exceed DNI ($19,000), reduced by Tier 1 distributions ($0), by only $1001.

This disparity should not exist, but it does because the last sentence of section 665(b) reads "*if* the amounts properly paid * * * do not exceed the income * * *." The disparity described here would be removed if this provision were to read instead "*to the extent* amounts properly paid, credited, or required to be distributed by the trust for the taxable year do not exceed the income of the trust for such year, there shall be no accumulation distribution for such year." In the foregoing examples, amounts distributed exceeded fiduciary accounting income by only $1 in each case and only to that extent would they be regarded as an accumulation distribution by the suggested change.

Subject to an exception for distributions of income that was accumulated before the recipient reached the age of 21 years (the "minority exception" granted by the penultimate sentence of section 665(b)), accumulation distributions are subject to taxation in the beneficiary's hands under the "throwback" rules. Originally envisioned as a precise determination of the tax the beneficiary would have paid if the income had been distributed rather than accumulated in the year it was received by the trust, the Tax Reform Act of 1976 eliminated the old exact and short-cut methods of determining the tax on accumulation distributions. This change was due to a recognition that the pre–1976 short-cut method, although intended to simplify calculations, had the opposite effect because taxpayers were compelled to compute the tax under both it and the exact method in order to determine which produced the least tax. The present computation has evolved into only a rough approximation of the tax the beneficiary would have paid had the trust been a simple trust in the year of accumulation, and the current "modified short-cut" method of computation may be performed in seven fundamental steps:

(1) *Allocation to "preceding taxable years":* under section 667(b)(1)(A), it is necessary to know the number of years during which distributed UNI was accumulated. Applying a first-in, first-out rule, accumulation distributions are attributed to the earli-

est year of the trust (beginning after 1968)[1] during which UNI was accumulated and has not yet been deemed distributed by a prior section 666(a) accumulation distribution. Thus, for example, if an accumulation distribution were $20,000 in year four of a trust's existence and UNI had been $15,000 in each of the first three years of the trust's existence, the number of preceding taxable years to which the accumulation distribution would be allocated would be two, carrying out all the UNI from year one ($15,000) and one-third of the UNI from year two ($5000). If, in year five, an added $10,000 accumulation distribution were made, it would carry out the balance of the year two UNI and the maximum number of preceding taxable years would be reduced to only one for future computation purposes.

(2) *"Gross up" rule applied:* having determined the preceding taxable years to which the accumulation distribution is attributable, taxes paid by the trust, attributable under sections 661(b) and 661(c) to the accumulation distribution, are added to the accumulation distribution. Both the allocation of taxes paid by the trust on UNI for years as to which the entire accumulation is deemed distributed, and the pro ration for years as to which only a portion is deemed distributed, are computed on a "pro rata," rather than an "incremental," basis. Thus, if the trust would pay $1000 tax on capital gains allocated to principal and an *added* $1200 tax on an equal amount of accumulated income (under the progressive rates, the accumulation being taxed in a higher bracket), the credit allowed would not be for the $1200 increase; instead, it would be $1100 (half the aggregate tax imposed on the trust). Treasury Regulation section 1.665(d)–1A(b). Thus, while an accumulation increases the tax incrementally under a progressive rate schedule, the taxes deemed allocable thereto are not similarly determined.

This allocation method is not appropriate, in light of the rationale underlying the gross up rule, which is simply that, had the accumulated income been distributed in the year of receipt, the beneficiary would have been taxed on the full amount of the income in the trust, not just on UNI remaining after the trust paid the incremental tax on the accumulated income. Recall that, under section 665(a), UNI is defined as DNI remaining after current distributions and after payment of tax on the remaining DNI. While UNI could be defined differently and this issue avoided entirely, exclusion of taxes

1. Section 665(e)(1)(B) provides that taxable years beginning prior to 1969 are disregarded for purposes of allocating the accumulation distribution. This appears to mean that pre–1969 UNI is entirely disregarded for allocation purposes, not that allocation is made to such years and then either the UNI for that year or the year itself is disregarded for computation purposes. See Treasury Regulation sections 1.665(a)–0A(a)(3), 1.665(e)–1A(a)(1)(ii), 1.666(a)–1A(b)(1), and Schedule J to Form 1041.

paid by the trust in determining UNI, followed by the gross up rule addition of taxes paid in determining the accumulation distribution, permits exclusion of taxes paid on taxable capital gains that are not subject to throwback and also permits partial allocation of taxes for partial distributions of accumulated UNI. The present rule assists in making all these allocations administratively workable.

In order to perform the gross up function, as well as the earlier allocation to preceding taxable years, the trustee is required by Treasury Regulation section 1.666(d)–1A(a) to retain all tax returns and information pertaining thereto, (and section 666(d) provides a simple rule for allocation of income and gross up of taxes if adequate records do not exist). This gross up step is waived in a section 667(c)(1) so-called "third trust", as discussed below.

(3) *Average accumulation determined:* having determined the amount of the accumulation distribution, as grossed up by taxes attributable to that distributed UNI, and having established the number of preceding taxable years to which the distribution is attributable, an average accumulation is computed under section 667(b)(1)(C) by dividing the former (the grossed up accumulation distribution) by the latter (the number of preceding taxable years).

(4) *"De minimis" exclusion:* because the average accumulation determined in step (3) is fundamental to the throwback tax ultimately payable (a smaller average will ultimately result in a lower tax), and because that average is reduced if the number of preceding taxable years is increased, there is an incentive to increase the number of preceding years by intentionally distributing only a small amount of income attributable to a prior year. This can be accomplished by accumulating a small amount in every year of the trust. It can also be accomplished by carefully planning accumulation distributions to carry out a small amount of income from prior years that had large accumulations.

For example, if all accumulated income allocable to year 1 were carried out by a prior distribution, the next accumulation would be deemed to begin with UNI allocable to year 2. Abuse would exist if the prior distribution were limited so as to carry out all but a small amount of year 1 UNI, so the next distribution could carry out that small residue and cause year 1 to be counted in the number of allocation years. Similarly, abuse is possible by making the distribution carry a de minimis amount of income from the last year to which allocable, also causing an increase in the number of years involved in a computation (for example, if the accumulation distribution that carried out all the year 1 UNI had been a bit larger, in order to carry out a tiny amount of the year 2 accumulation as well). To prevent such planning from distorting the throwback computation, any year for which allocated distributed UNI (prior to being grossed up under section 666(b) or (c)) is less than 25 percent of the average determined in step (3) is disregarded under the de minimis rule of section 667(b)(3). Step (1) is not affected thereby, but step (3) is reperformed using the reduced number and a new, higher average accumulation is determined.[2]

(5) *Average tax computed:* using the average accumulation determined in step (3), as recomputed in step (4) (if necessary), an average increase in the beneficiary's tax is computed under section 667(b)(1). To determine the average increase, the average accumulation is first added to the mid-three of the beneficiary's five previous years' taxable income,[3] excluding for these purposes the years of the highest and lowest taxable income[4] and treating any loss year as having zero income.[5] The increase in the beneficiary's tax that would have resulted from this addition is computed for each of the three years, using those years' rates, and those increases are simply averaged under section 667(b)(1)(D).

In making this computation, no provision appears to preserve the special character of any accumulated income other than tax exempt income (to which the parenthetical in section

2. Reapplication of this step (4) could cause exclusion of additional years falling below 25 percent of the new average, which would necessitate further recomputations, which could again cause further exclusions. For example, if the grossed up accumulation were $36,000 and the number of preceding taxable years were four, consisting of accumulations of $850, $2900, $4400, $20,000 and the balance in grossed up taxes paid by the trust, the initial average accumulation would be $9000 ($36,000 ÷ 4) and the de minimis exclusion would apply to the $850 accumulation. By recomputing the average to be $12,000 ($36,000 ÷ 3) and again applying the de minimis exclusion, the $2900 accumulation would fall below the new 25 percent amount ($3000). If again the average accumulation were determined, this time as $18,000 ($36,000 ÷ 2), the $4400 accumulation would be excluded, leaving only one preceding taxable year for computation purposes. While the Code gives no indication whether the de minimis exclusion is to be applied more than once, and the Regulations are similarly silent on the issue, only the initial determination and any necessary one time only redetermination should be required.

3. Section 666(b)(1)(C). Addition to taxable income prevents the need to recompute the beneficiary's gross and adjusted gross incomes and any computations based thereon. In making these computations, taxable income is treated as including previous accumulation distributions that were allocated to the same tax years, under section 667(b)(4). Moreover, distributions from multiple trusts (subject to computation in the same year of distribution) are considered in any order the beneficiary selects, under section 667(b)(5).

4. Section 667(b)(1)(B). By using the five previous years instead of the actual preceding taxable years to which the accumulation distribution is allocable, the beneficiary need not retain tax records for a significant period. Exclusion of the high and low years is intended to minimize distortions that might arise due to aberrational years.

5. Section 667(b)(2) (for purposes of treating an individual's taxable income as zero prior to repeal in 1986 of the Zero Bracket Amount, the Code treated income as equal to the taxpayer's zero bracket amount for that year).

667(a) is directed).[6] No provision identifies other special classes of income (such as passive activity income) included in DNI and consequently included in UNI, subsequently distributed subject to throwback.

(6) *Partial tax computed:* using the average increase in tax as determined in step (5), a partial tax is computed by multiplying this average increase by the number of preceding taxable years as determined in step (1) and adjusted in step (4).[7] The result is the amount of tax attributable to the accumulation distribution.

(7) *Tax payable:* the tax attributable to the accumulation distribution, as computed in step (6), may be reduced by either of two credits available to the beneficiary.

(a) One credit is granted under section 667(b)(6) if any estate or generation-skipping tax was imposed on the accumulated income while held in the trust. The theory behind this credit is that, if no accumulation had been made, the beneficiary would have paid an income tax on the accumulated income and the income tax dollars paid would not have been subjected to the estate or generation-skipping tax. The credit effects a rough justice without recomputing the wealth transfer tax after the income tax is paid. Thus, an *income* tax (rather than a wealth transfer tax) credit is given for the estate or generation-skipping tax that is attributable to the income tax on those accumulations that were subject to estate or generation-skipping tax. Computation of the credit may be performed under sections 667(b)(6)(A) and 667(b)(6)(C) according to a formula:

credit = section 667(b) partial tax, multiplied by:

$$\frac{\text{accumulation subject to estate or generation-skipping tax}}{\text{total accumulation}} \times \frac{\text{estate or generation-skipping tax attributable to accumulation}}{\text{accumulation subject to estate or generation-skipping tax}}$$

This cumbersome formula nets out to a more manageable formula:

$$\text{credit} = \text{partial tax multiplied by } \frac{\text{estate or generation-skipping tax attributable to accumulation}}{\text{total accumulation}}$$

(b) The other credit is granted by the last clause of the last sentence of section 667(b)(1) (to all but any section 667(c)(1) third trusts) for any income taxes already paid by the trust on the accumulation, thus avoiding double taxation in most cases. For example, assume a trust has income of $16,000 in year 1. It distributes $10,000 and accumulates the balance, paying $1,000 of tax thereon in year 1 (so UNI = $5,000). In year 2

6. For example, see Treasury Regulation section 1.665(f)–1A (applicable prior to the revision in 1976 repealing the throwback rule with respect to capital gains).

7. Section 667(b)(1), last sentence.

the trust distributes the full year 2 current DNI, plus an added $5000; that $5000 is treated as 100% of the year 1's accumulation. If the trust paid tax of $1000 thereon in year 1 and the beneficiary's throwback tax is $1200 (computed under the throwback rule as if that income had been distributed in year 1), the beneficiary will receive a credit for the $1000 already paid by the trust. The beneficiary would, therefore, pay for year 2 only the $200 of throwback tax in excess of this $1000. If the trust paid more tax on the accumulation than is owed by the beneficiary under throwback on the distribution, the beneficiary's tax would be reduced to zero, but section 666(e) denies a refund for any excess tax paid by the trust, meaning that some double taxation may occur.

If there is a risk of any excess credit being wasted in a year in which more than one trust is making accumulation distributions, the beneficiary may choose the order in which the various distributions will be taxed under section 667(b)(5). Because section 667(b)(4) adds previously taxed distributions to the beneficiary's taxable income for subsequent computation purposes, higher taxes will result under the progressive rate tables on subsequent distributions. Thus, the beneficiary might elect to tax last any trust for which the excess credit will be lost, on the assumption that it would be best to make that trust's distribution the one taxed at the highest rates because the available credit will cover those taxes in any event, the least excess credit will be left, and the loss will be minimized. In those multiple trusts in which the credit is denied in toto (by section 667(c), as discussed below), double tax is the unremitted consequence, and this same provision allows the beneficiary to choose which will be the so-called third trust as to which this result will apply. In any case, the trustee must be careful to avoid inadvertent accumulation of income if more tax will be paid by the trust than would be paid on distribution to the beneficiary, either currently or as an accumulation distribution.

As an example of the foregoing computation procedure, assume a trust has the following accumulations, and that the total accumulation is distributed at one time.

Year	Excess DNI	Taxes [8]	UNI
1	$ 20,000	$ 6,070	$ 13,930
2	21,000	6,550	14,450
3	22,050	7,055	14,995
4	23,153	7,606	15,547
5	24,310	8,184	16,126
6	25,526	8,793	16,733
7	26,802	9,455	17,347
8	28,142	10,165	17,977
TOTAL	$190,983	$63,878	$127,105

8. All attributable to income.

Actual accumulation	=	$127,105		
Plus taxes paid	=	63,878		
TOTAL		$190,983	÷ 8 accumulation years =	$23,873

Beneficiary's last five years:	Income	Taxes
	$29,549	$6,506
	31,027	7,038
	32,578	7,637
	34,207	8,273
	35,917	8,961

Average accumulation added to beneficiary's mid-three of	$ 31,027	$ 32,578	$ 34,207
	23,873	23,873	23,873
five prior years = TOTAL	$ 54,900	$ 56,451	$ 58,080
Tax on Total (Assume)	$ 17,910	$ 18,722	$ 19,586
Less tax paid by beneficiary	(7,038)	(7,637)	(8,273)
Tax Attributable to Accumulation	$ 10,872	$ 11,085	$ 11,313

Total tax on accumulations	$ 33,270
Average tax on accumulations	11,090
Times eight years of accumulation	88,720
Less taxes paid by trust on accumulations	(63,878)
TAX DUE ON ACCUMULATION DISTRIBUTION	$ 24,842

The foregoing example and the description of the computation steps ought to illustrate that the tax imposed is only an approximation of what those taxes would have been if the trust had been simple in each prior year and no accumulation had been made. The rules go a long way toward imposition of the same tax as if there had been no accumulation and the reduced benefit of taxing some income to the trust as a separate tax paying entity means that accumulation trusts are no longer as desirable for tax minimization purposes as they once were. However, the minority exception (discussed below) provides one continued benefit. This is, in part, a reflection of the fact that accumulation is desirable for many family planning objectives, and may be advisable even if no tax savings result therefrom. Moreover, even if throwback results in a higher tax ultimately being payable by the beneficiary, the complex trust rules do nothing to diminish the benefits that may be gained by avoiding the section 1(g) gradual adjustment or the section 67 and 213 limits on certain deductions, or by deferring the added tax until the year of actual distribution. In the simple example at pages 65–66 above of the beneficiary who would have paid tax of $1200 had there been no accumulation, even though an added $200 in tax was imposed under the throwback rules, the beneficiary had the use of that money between the time the trustee paid its tax and the imposition of the throwback tax. In the more complex example immediately above, a more attractive deferral of almost $25,000 was gained, without payment of interest. In both cases the beneficiary is effectively using the government's money and no interest or penalty is imposed thereon. In many larger situations this alone may justify the added administrative inconvenience of making all the complex trust calculations, and is a benefit that is available with no other taxable entity.

Question

Assume DNI is $45,000, that required current distributions total $15,000 and that discretionary distributions total $60,000. Prior years' accumulations were:

Year	UNI
7	$ 3,000
6	250
5	9,750
4	19,000
3	1,500
2	8,500
1	4,000
current	0

Assume for gross up purposes that taxes of $10,000 would be allocated to the accumulation distribution here. Perform only steps 1 through 4 of a throwback computation.

MINORITY EXCEPTION AND THIRD TRUST RULES

Read Code sections 665(b) and 667(c)

An exception to the accumulation distribution and throwback rules exists under the penultimate sentence of section 665(b) for accumulations made while the ultimate recipient thereof was under the age of 21 (which prima facie includes accumulations before the ultimate recipient's birth as well). If subsequently distributed to that beneficiary, at any time (including after (s)he has reached 21), the "minority exception" will prevent application of the throwback rules to the distribution and no throwback tax will be due thereon. To qualify for the exception, however, it is not enough to accumulate income while some beneficiary is under the age of 21. If distribution is to some *other* beneficiary who was over 21 when the income was accumulated, the exception does not apply. Distribution must be to a beneficiary who was under 21 in the year of the accumulation.

As with the balance of the throwback rules, for purposes of determining when an accumulation was made, the allocation rules of section 666(a) apply, meaning the first-in, first-out rule is applicable to any minority exception accumulation distribution. Finally, even though a trust may make an accumulation distribution to another trust that is less than 21 years old, Treasury Regulation section 1.665(b)–1A(b)(1) makes it clear that the minority exception will not apply.

As discussed below, the minority exception is lost with respect to distributions made from certain multiple trusts. In addition, if a distribution to a beneficiary is deemed to discharge some other person's legal obligation of support, Treasury Regulation section 1.665(b)–1A(b)(3) provides that the obligated person will be regarded as the beneficiary, with the result that the exception may be inapplicable. This is because, for purposes of taxing the "beneficiary" of a distribution, Treasury Regulation section 1.643(c)–1(a) specifies that a person obliged to support the actual recipient will be regarded as the beneficiary to the extent the obligated person's support obligation is discharged or satisfied by distribution. This regulation, along with Treasury Regulation section 1.662(a)–4, which establishes the "discharge of obligation" concept for purposes of Subchapter J, appears never to have been applied or challenged and is probably unsupportable under the law of most jurisdictions.[9]

Section 667(c) "third trusts" receive special disfavorable treatment for purposes of each of (1) the section 665(b) (see the parenthetical clause in the penultimate sentence) minority exception to the accumulation distribution rules, (2) the gross up rule of sections 666(b) and 666(c), and (3) the section 667(b)(1) (last clause of last sentence) credit for income taxes paid by the trust.

While the "third trust" rule is intended to minimize use of multiple trusts for the same beneficiary, each accumulating income for subsequent distribution after taxation at the trusts' lower rates, the rule is unlike section 643(f) because it does not look to whether each trust was created by the same grantor with substantially the same beneficiary and a tax avoidance intent. Rather, required is only that more than two trusts make accumulation distributions to the same beneficiary, allocable to the same preceding taxable year under section 666(a). Consequently, administration of trusts created independently by various individuals (for example, by parents, grandparents, or by a spouse) may raise the spectre of this third trust rule unless accumulations and subsequent distributions from each are well coordinated.

For administrative ease, accumulation distributions allocable to any year in which aggregate accumulation distributions were less than $1000 (before gross up) are excepted from application of the rule by section 667(c)(2). The exception is an all or nothing proposition. Exceeding the $1000 amount by any sum causes loss of the entire exception, not just the amount in excess of $1000. However, if UNI in any trust for any year is no greater than $999, the trustee need not worry about the timing of subsequent distributions and their coordination with other trusts' accumulation distributions to the same beneficiary.

The third trust rule is of great significance in throwback computations because, while the gross up rule is made inapplicable under section 667(c)(1), the beneficiary loses the credit for taxes already paid by the trust, resulting in double taxation. This severity is lessened in two respects. First, only those trusts in excess of two (the so-called "third trusts," regardless of how many in excess of two there are) making accumulation distributions allocable to the same preceding taxable year are subject to the rule. Second, because each accumula-

9. See Pennell, "Custodians, Incompetents, Trustees and Others: Taxable Powers of Appointment?," 15 U.Miami Inst.Est. Plan. ¶ 1602.3B (1981).

tion distribution throwback computation is performed separately, and seriatim, the beneficiary may, under section 667(b)(5), choose the order in which several distributions will be taxed and may choose which of several trusts will be treated as the first two trusts. As a result, the beneficiary may order the distributions for tax purposes so that the smallest distributions are taxed last, resulting in the smallest exposure to double taxation.

Chapter Five

DISTRIBUTIONS AND TERMINATION

DISTRIBUTIONS IN-KIND

Read Code sections 643(e), 661, 662, 663 and 691.

As we discovered in Chapter Three, distributions from a trust or an estate carry out income (first DNI, then UNI, to the extent either is available in the year of distribution), regardless of whether the distribution constitutes fiduciary accounting income or corpus and regardless of whether the fiduciary distributes cash or property in-kind. Section 643(e) was adopted in 1984 to (1) limit the amount of income deemed distributed by a complex trust or an estate on a Tier 2 in-kind transfer of property and (2) establish the basis of such distributed property. Notice, however, that section 643(e) establishes these special rules for distributions and basis only for purposes of sections 661(a)(2) and 662(a)(2) (Tier 2 distributions) and has no application to simple trusts that are governed by sections 651 and 652, nor to Tier 1 distributions that are governed by sections 661(a)(1) and 662(a)(1). Thus, prior law will apply with respect to all but Tier 2 in-kind distributions.

If section 643(e) does not apply, income equal to the fair market value of a distributed asset is carried out by distribution of an asset in-kind (to the extent there is sufficient DNI and, after distribution of all DNI, to the extent of UNI as well), unless distribution qualifies as a specific bequest under section 663(a). To the extent applicable, section 643(e)(2) limits the income carryout on such a distribution to the lesser of (1) the asset's fair market value or (2) the adjusted basis of the asset (plus or minus any gain or loss realized on the distribution), with an election granted to the fiduciary under section 643(e)(3) to intentionally incur gain or loss on the distribution. Further, adjusted basis to the distributee is a carryover of the distributing entity's basis (again, as adjusted for gain or loss realized on the distribution).

To illustrate the effect of this provision, if an asset has a fair market value of $100 and an adjusted basis of $40, distribution as a

Tier 2 in-kind transfer prior to adoption of section 643(e) (governed by Treasury Regulation section 1.661(a)–2(f)(3) under prior law) would have carried out $100 of income (assuming there was, in the aggregate, that much DNI and UNI available for distribution) and basis of the asset to the distributee would become its fair market value ($100) by virtue of the described distribution, that being the amount of income carried out. Congress was persuaded that this increase in basis to fair market value, accomplished without realization of the $60 of appreciation by either the distributing entity or the recipient, was a problem that needed correction. Thus, under the provisions of section 643(e), with a basis less than fair market value, the amount of income carried out by the described distribution would be $40, and basis to the distributee would be $40, being a carryover of the distributing entity's basis (with no adjustment for gain or loss because none was incurred on distribution). The effect of section 643(e) is thus two-fold. First, unless the election is made to incur gain or loss, or the distribution is itself a realization event (for example, because distribution is in satisfaction of an obligation of the fiduciary, as discussed more fully below), less income is now carried out by a Tier 2 distribution of an appreciated asset in-kind. Second, the prior tax free step-up in basis for such a distribution is eliminated.

Queer about the change made by section 643(e) was that the sole intent of Congress was to override the rule of Treasury Regulation section 1.661(a)–2(f)(3), that a Tier 2 distribution of an appreciated asset in-kind received a new basis equal to its fair market value to the extent the distribution carried out income to the recipient. Had Congress wanted to address only that problem, it would have been easy to dictate only that basis of such an asset distributed in-kind would be a carryover of the entity's basis (adjusted for gain or loss incurred on the distribution), regardless of the amount of income carried out by distribution and without changing, in any respect, the income carry out rules. For example, if a trustee wanted to distribute $70 to a beneficiary, it could do so by distributing (1) an asset with fair market value of $70 and a basis of any amount, (2) cash of $70, or (3) any combination of the two. Were the rule otherwise than that adopted by Congress, each distribution would effect the same income carryout without altering the basis of distributed assets in the process.

As adopted, however, a Tier 2 distribution of cash will carry out $70 of income but a Tier 2 distribution in-kind will carry out no more income than the basis of the distributed asset. The justification for this limited carry out of income is a feeling that it is inequitable to saddle a distributee with income equal to fair market value *plus* any unrealized appreciation (or ordinary income in the case of IRD) represented by a basis that is lower than fair market value.

Questions

1. If section 643(e) limits the amount of income carried out on a Tier 2 distribution of property in-kind, does the distribution carry out UNI to the

extent fair market value exceeds the amount of DNI deemed to be carried out?

2. Why does section 643(e) apply only to sections 661(a)(2) and 662(a)(2) and is inapplicable in all respects to Tier 1 distributions governed by sections 661(a)(1) and 662(a)(1) and to distributions from simple trusts governed by sections 651 and 652?

3. Assume DNI equals $18,000, there is no UNI, and Tier 2 distributions for the year are (1) $13,000 of cash and (2) an asset with a fair market value of $13,000 and an adjusted basis of $9000. What are the tax consequences of the distribution of these items? Would it matter if distributions were made to several beneficiaries rather than just to one? Consider the penultimate sentence of Treasury Regulation section 1.661(a)–2(f)(3).

4. If several assets are distributed in a given year, the available income (whether DNI, UNI or both) must be pro rated among them. What are the income tax consequences of the following Tier 2 distributions if there is no UNI, DNI is $100x, and no gain or loss is realized on any distribution?

Asset	Fair Market Value	Adjusted Basis	Recipient
Blackacre	$75x	$50x	A
A Corp. Stock	$60x	$10x	A
Cash	$15x	—	A
Greenacre	$50x	$50x	B
B Corp. Stock	$45x	$30x	B
C Corp. Bonds	$15x	$ 5x	B
Cash	$40x	—	B

An especially intriguing issue is created by the interrelation of Income In Respect of a Decedent (IRD) and the carryover of basis rule of section 643(e). In reading the following cases, consider the effect of that interplay. What was the taxpayer hoping to accomplish by distributing IRD, and what is the effect of section 643(e)?

ROLLERT RESIDUARY TRUST v. COMMISSIONER

United States Tax Court, 1983
80 T.C. 619, aff'd, 752 F.2d 1128 (6th Cir.1985).

WHITAKER, JUDGE: * * * This case was submitted fully stipulated. * * * The primary issue for decision [is] * * * whether rights to income in respect of a decedent [in the form of rights to receive future installment payments of bonus awards earned by the decedent during life,] which were distributed by the decedent's estate to petitioner in prior years acquired a basis in the hands of petitioner equal to their fair market value on the date of distribution. With respect to this * * * issue, we must specifically decide whether the rights to income in respect of a decedent were amounts "properly paid or credited" for purposes of sections 661(a)(2) and 662(a)(2). * * *

Each of the distributions of the rights to future bonus installments was treated by the estate and petitioner in essentially the following manner. With respect to each right that was distributed, the present value of the right was determined as of the date of distribution. The estate claimed a distribution deduction for this amount on its U.S. Fiduciary Income Tax Return, Form 1041. Petitioner reported on its U.S. Fiduciary Income Tax Return, Form 1041, for the year of distribution the same value as gross income received from the estate. In each of the years in which rights to bonus installments were distributed, the estate had distributable net income, as defined in section 643, consisting primarily of bonus installments actually received by the estate in that year. For each year, the amount of distributable net income exceeded the total of the correct date-of-distribution value of rights to future bonus installments plus the amount of cash distributions which were made in each of these years to the marital trust.

In the subsequent years, when the bonus installments were due, General Motors paid them directly to petitioner. Petitioner reported on its income tax return as ordinary income only the amount, if any, by which the bonus installment paid to it by General Motors exceeded the corrected value of the right to the bonus installment as of the date the right was distributed to it. Due to fluctuations in stock prices, two of the bonus installments had values lower than the bases previously assigned to the rights to these installments. Petitioner claimed no losses in these instances. The estate did not include in income any portion of the bonus installments that were paid directly to petitioner.

The following description of the treatment by the estate and petitioner of the stock portion of the distribution on December 30, 1970, illustrates how the distributions of the rights were treated. On December 30, 1970, the executor distributed to petitioner the right to receive future payment and delivery of the bonus installment of 1,446 shares of General Motors common stock which was payable and deliverable by General Motors to the estate on January 10, 1973. Both the estate and petitioner used $92,941 as the value as of December 30, 1970, of this bonus right. The estate claimed a distribution deduction of $92,941 on its income tax return, and petitioner reported $92,941 on its income tax return. The trustee subsequently made an adjustment on the books of petitioner to increase the reported present value of the right distributed to it as of December 30, 1970, from $92,941 to $108,242, which was the correct present value of the right as of December 30, 1970. On January 10, 1973, General Motors paid the installment due on that date by delivery of the 1,446 shares of common stock to petitioner. As of this date, the total fair market value of the 1,446 shares was $119,476. Petitioner reported on its 1973 income tax return $11,234 as a receipt of ordinary income. This amount represented the difference between the fair market value of the stock on January 10, 1973 ($119,476), and the corrected December 30, 1970, present value of the right to receive the stock ($108,242). The estate reported no gain or income with respect to this payment either in 1973, when the installment of the bonus award was paid to petitioner, or in any other year.

* * *

We must determine * * * whether the estate's distribution to petitioner of the rights to receive bonus installments in subsequent years gave petitioner a basis in these rights equal to their fair market values when distributed, and whether such basis could be used by petitioner to reduce the income it received when the bonus installments were actually paid to it. This is a question of first impression.

* * *

In resolving this case, we must analyze the relationship between the rules of section 691 for the taxation of income in respect of a decedent and those of subchapter J, part I, governing the income taxation of estates. In general, the provisions of subchapter J, part I, are designed to allocate between the estate and its beneficiaries taxable income received by the estate, so that income will be taxed at only one level. For an estate that may accumulate income, such as Mr. Rollert's estate, this general allocation scheme is accomplished through the distribution rules of sections 661 through 663. Section 691 serves a totally different purpose. It is designed to deal with the problem of how to tax income that has been earned but not received by an individual as of the date of his or her death. Under section 691, income that has accrued to a decedent prior to death but has not yet been received is not included in the decedent's final income tax return, even though the right to such income may be included on the estate's estate tax return. Instead, the income is reported when received by the person who actually receives the income.

Here, petitioner used the distribution rules of section 662 in an attempt to reduce the income taxed to it under section 691. In effect, what petitioner did here was to report part of the payments of income in respect of a decedent as income under section 662, even before the payments were made by General Motors. When the payments were actually made in subsequent years, petitioner excluded the previously reported amounts from its section 691 income. Because the treatment of payments of income in respect of a decedent in this manner would completely undermine the mandate of section 691 that the recipient of such income report it for the year when received, we agree with respondent that petitioner had no right to reduce its income in respect of a decedent in the year it received the bonus payments by the amounts it had previously reported as income under section 662.

Section 691(a)(1) provides that the amount of all items of income in respect of a decedent shall be included in gross income, for the taxable year when received. This rule applies to income in respect of a decedent received by (A) the decedent's estate if it has acquired from the decedent the right to receive such income; (B) a person who has acquired, by reason of the decedent's death, the right to receive such income if the right to receive such income was not acquired by the decedent's estate from decedent; and (C) a person who has acquired the right to receive the amount by bequest, devise, or inheritance from the decedent, after a distribution by the decedent's estate of such right. See also sec. 1.691(a)–2(a), Income Tax Regs. In this case, subparagraph (A) required Mr. Rollert's estate to include in income amounts received with respect to those rights to bonus installments that it did not distribute to petitioner, and subparagraph (C) required petitioner to include those bonus installments that it received with respect to rights the estate had distributed to it.

Under section 661(a), an estate deducts in computing its taxable income (1) any amount of income required to be distributed currently and (2) "any other amounts properly paid or credited or required to be distributed for such taxable year." However, the total amount of these deductions may not exceed the estate's distributable net income. Under section 662, the beneficiary to whom these distributions are made must include in gross income a corresponding amount. Sections 661(b) and 662(b) are designed to assure that the character of the amounts deducted by the estate and taken into income by the beneficiary is proportionate to the character of items entering into the computation of distributable net income.

Petitioner and the estate applied the distribution rules of sections 661 and 662 to the distribution of the rights to receive subsequent bonus installments. With respect to each bonus right it distributed, the estate deducted the entire fair market value of the right as a distribution of its distributable net income. Petitioner took this same amount into income and used it as its basis in the right to the bonus installment. The character of petitioner's income was determined under sections 661(b) and 662(b) by reference to the character of the estate's distributable net income rather than by reference to the character of the bonus, itself.

Petitioner treated section 691 as coming into play only when the actual payments of the bonus installments were made. It treated each bonus payment as income when received but only to the extent, if any, that the amount paid to it exceeded the basis it had previously assigned the bonus right.

Petitioner claims that the distribution to it of the rights to the bonus installments falls squarely within the literal language of sections 661(a)(2) and 662(a)(2) as "amounts properly paid or credited." Since the rights were irrevocably transferred to petitioner and had an acknowledged value to it at the time of distribution, which was taken into income as a distribution from the estate, the distribution appears on its face to fall within the ambit of these provisions. However, the terms "amounts properly paid or credited" would be excessively broad if read literally. Thus, these words must be interpreted in the light of the statutory framework and overall legislative objectives of subchapter J.

In characterizing the distribution of the rights to the bonus installments as amounts properly paid or credited, petitioner placed particular reliance upon section 1.661(a)–2(c) and (f). Section 1.661(a)–2(c) specifies that the term "any other amounts properly paid or credited or required to be distributed" includes a distribution of property in kind, which petitioner believes includes the distribution here of the rights to the bonus installments. Section 1.661(a)–2(f)(2) states that, in determining the amount deductible by the estate and includable in gross income of the beneficiary, the property distributed in kind is taken into account at its fair market value at the time it was distributed, credited, or required to be distributed. There is no dispute in this case as to the fair market values of the rights on the dates of distribution. Section 1.661(a)–2(f)(3) provides that to the extent the fair market value of the property is included in a beneficiary's gross income, the beneficiary takes such amount as its basis for the property.

Respondent points out that the assigning of tax basis to the rights to income in respect of a decedent has enabled petitioner to escape income taxation on much of the income payable under those rights. In each year in which the rights to the bonus installments were distributed, the estate had distributable net income consisting primarily of bonus payments actually received by it in that year. The estate retained part of this income, but offset this action by distributing to petitioner rights to bonus installments that had not yet been paid to the estate. Because it treated the transfers of the rights as distributions of distributable net income, the estate's deduction for distributions of distributable net income included the date-of-distribution values of the bonus rights. The estate thereby reduced its taxable income by carrying its distributable net income out to petitioner, even though it retained much of the income it had received. Petitioner increased its income in the years of distribution by taking into income the date-of-distribution values of the bonus rights, in other words, the discounted value of the future installments of income. However, by assigning basis under section 1.661(a)–2(f)(3) to these rights, its income was reduced by the same amounts in the later years when the bonus installments were actually paid. * * * Thus, the net effect of the treatment of the bonus rights by petitioner and the estate was to reduce the aggregate taxable income of the estate and petitioner by the fair market values of the bonus rights as of the dates of distribution.[16] * * *

16. The following examples illustrate the escape from taxation caused by petitioner's treating the distribution of a right to income in respect of a decedent (IRD) as a distribution of distributable net income (DNI).

EXAMPLE A (right to IRD not distributed):

Fact *Year 1:* Estate has DNI of $50,000. No DNI distributed.
Year 2: Estate has no DNI except for IRD of $30,000. After receiving the $30,000, estate distributed it to legatee.

Tax treatment
Year 1: $50,000 income to estate; no income to legatee
Year 2: $30,000 income to legatee; no income to estate

We therefore agree with respondent that the approach taken by petitioner and the estate allowed substantial sums of income to escape taxation.[17] Section 691 and its legislative history evince a clear purpose to tax income in respect of a decedent in the same manner as if it had been received by the decedent. Allowing the escape from taxation suggested by petitioner would undermine this purpose. * * *

Petitioner would have us accept its taking into income under section 662(a) the value of the bonus rights when distributed as satisfying the objective of section 691 to tax all income in respect of a decedent to the actual *recipient* of the income. Petitioner is correct that the overall amount of income reported by it under either section 662(a) or section 691 was similar to the amount it would have reported had it not treated the receipt of the rights to future bonus installments as distributions of the estate's distributable net income. However, as we have explained above, the aggregate amount of income reported by the estate and petitioner was substantially reduced by petitioner's approach since the distributions of the rights to future bonus installments were treated as carrying out to petitioner the estate's distributable net income. The estate thereby reduced its reported income and was able to accumulate funds which could subsequently be paid out, tax-free, to petitioner, the residuary legatee.

EXAMPLE B (right to IRD distributed in year 1 and treated as DNI distribution):

Fact	*Year 1:*	Estate has DNI of $50,000. No DNI distributed except that right to IRD payable in year 2 is distributed to legatee. Present value of this right to IRD is $28,000.
	Year 2:	Estate has no DNI. The $30,000 of IRD is paid directly to legatee.
Tax treatment		
	Year 1:	$22,000 income to estate; $28,000 income to legatee.
	Year 2:	No income to estate; $2,000 income to legatee (i.e., $30,000 IRD minus basis of $28,000).

COMPARISON:

	Income to estate	Income to legatee	Aggregate income to estate and legatee
Example A	$50,000	$30,000	$80,000
Example B	22,000	30,000 *	52,000
			28,000 (Amount escaping taxation)

[* $28,000 in year 1 = DNI on distribution
$ 2,000 in year 2 = IRD in excess of basis in right to receive payment. Ed.]

17. Commentators who have examined the tax consequences of an estate's distribution of rights to income in respect of a decedent have generally recognized that application of the distribution rules of secs. 661 and 662 would allow substantial sums to escape taxation. But they also recognize that a literal reading of secs. 661 and 662 and the regulations thereunder would allow this result. Some of the commentators believe these provisions of the Code and regulations must be interpreted as inapplicable to the distribution of rights to income in respect of a decedent. See 2 A. Casner, Estate Planning 804–805 (1980); M. Ferguson, J. Freeland & R. Stephens, Federal Income Taxation of Estates and Beneficiaries 533–534 (1970); Rammel, "'Income in Respect of Decedent' Provisions Lend Themselves to Postmortem Estate Planning," 7 Tax'n for Acct. 358, 361 (1971). Others have concluded, however, that the distribution of the rights to income in respect of a decedent should be

For this reason, we do not believe that petitioner's reporting income under section 662 when it received the rights to subsequent bonus installments should be treated as satisfying the requirement that the *recipient* report all income in respect of a decedent. Furthermore, even if we were to assume that petitioner's treatment of the bonus rights and installments satisfied the requirement of section 691 that income in respect of a decedent be taxed to the recipient of such income, we see no way that it could also satisfy the timing and characterization rules of that section.

Section 691(a)(1) requires income in respect of a decedent to be included in income "for the taxable year when received." It is designed to defer taxation of these amounts until actual receipt. Were we to accept petitioner's view that its reporting income when the rights to bonus installments were distributed satisfied the objective that it be taxed on the income in respect of a decedent, it would be apparent that the timing rule had been violated. Under petitioner's approach, the only income deferred until actual receipt would be the excess of the amount received over the amount reported in the year the right was distributed.

Section 691(a)(3) requires the character of income in respect of a decedent to be the same as it would have been in the hands of the decedent if the decedent had lived and received such income. Here, however, only that income actually reported in the year of receipt as income in respect of a decedent took its character under section 691(a)(3). The character of the rights to income in respect of a decedent that were distributed was determined under section 662(b) by reference to the character of the estate's distributable net income. Thus, it is apparent that petitioner's approach would also cripple the characterization rule for income in respect of a decedent.

It is a well-accepted principle of law that a specific statute controls over a general one, even if the latter might otherwise appear to govern. *Bulova Watch Co. v. United States,* 365 U.S. 753, 758 (1961). As we have explained, there is an apparent conflict between section 691 and the distribution rules of sections 661 and 662. In view of the nature of section 691 as a specific statutory scheme for the taxation of income in respect of a decedent, which would be largely defeated were rights to income in respect of a decedent allowed to acquire basis under the distribution rules, we believe section 691 must take precedence, here.

Although the legislative history of section 691 and the regulations under that section do not specifically address the issue presented in this case, they do tend to support our conclusion that sections 661 and 662

accepted as "amounts distributed" for purposes of secs. 661 and 662. See Quigley, "The IRS's Position on Income in Respect of a Decedent," 121 Tr. & Est. 15 (1982); Wilf, "Planning for Distributions of Property-in-Kind After the Tax Reform Act," 12 Inst. on Est. Plan., sec. 1612 (1978); "Income in Respect of a Decedent," 5 Real Prop.Prob. & Tr.J. 307, 309 (1970).

should not be applied to an estate's distribution of rights to income in respect of a decedent. Example 1 of section 1.691(a)–2(b) which illustrates the application of the general principle of taxing income in respect of decedent, when received, involves a fact situation quite similar to that now before us. A decedent was entitled to salary payments in five annual installments after his death. The estate collected the first two payments and then distributed to the residuary legatee the right to the remaining three installments. The example states that the estate must include the first two installments in its gross income and the legatee must include the subsequent three installments in his gross income. This example does not even refer to the possibility of the right to the final three installments being treated as a distribution governed by sections 661 and 662. If the distribution rules were meant to apply to distributions of rights to income in respect of a decedent, the absence of any reference to this effect in the regulation is incomprehensible.

The current rules in section 691 for the taxation of income in respect of a decedent are derived primarily from section 126, I.R.C. 1939, which was added by section 134 of the Revenue Act of 1942, 56 Stat. 831. The legislative history of that provision clearly states Congress' intent that amounts of income in respect of a decedent—

> be treated, in the hands of the persons receiving them, as income of the same nature and to the same extent as such amounts would be income if the decedent remained alive and received such amounts. [S.Rept. 1631, 77th Cong., 2d Sess. (1942), 1942–2 C.B. 504, 580.]

At several points, the Senate report indicates the provision was designed to place the recipient of the income in respect of a decedent in the *same position* as the decedent with respect to both the amount and character of income. Nothing in the legislative history of the Internal Revenue Code of 1954, which introduced the distribution rules of sections 661 and 662, indicates any congressional desire to change the requirement that income in respect of a decedent be taxed in the same manner as it would have been treated if it had been received by the decedent, himself. The decedent would normally report for tax purposes each installment as received, with the full installment being included as income. The provisions of the legislative history cited by petitioner do not indicate otherwise. All that these provisions are concerned with is the general rule of sections 661 and 662 that all distributions are deductible by the estate and includable by the beneficiary when distributed. They do not deal, however, with the question before us now of whether a distribution of rights to income in respect of a decedent is a distribution subject to sections 661 and 662.

Contrary to petitioner's contention, the changes made when the Internal Revenue Code of 1954 was enacted actually support respondent. Congress extended section 691(a)(1) so that it applies to rights to income in respect of a prior decedent that are acquired by a beneficiary from a second decedent. As an example of how this provision works, the committee reports mention a widow who was entitled to receive insurance renewal commissions but who died before receiving such commission income. Under the pre–1954 law, the fair market value of the right to receive the commissions had to be included in the widow's final income tax return, even though she left to her son the right to receive the commissions. Congress explained that section 691 was being expanded so that no income would be realized on the transfer to the widow's estate of the right to income from the prior decedent. The commissions earned by the prior decedent should be taxed to the recipient upon receipt and their character determined by reference to the prior decedent. These results outlined in the reports under the post–1954 law could not be obtained if petitioner's theory were accepted, since petitioner would treat the distribution from the estate of the prior decedent to the widow as a distribution of a right to income in respect of a decedent, which would require the widow to recognize income and would create a basis in the right to receive future commissions. The rights to the commission income had necessarily been distributed from the estate of the prior decedent to the widow, and under petitioner's theory, the widow would have reported the fair market value of such rights when they were distributed to her and taken such value as her basis in the rights. Nowhere do the committee reports even intimate that this might be the proper treatment.

We address finally petitioner's contention that its treatment of the bonus rights did not defeat the overall scheme of section 691, since section 1.661(a)–2(f) forgives any income tax on the appreciation in value of property in kind distributed by an estate or trust. It is apparent that this regulation does cause the nonrecognition of some unrealized appreciation. However, there are several key distinctions between the nonrecognition sanctioned by this regulation and the situation before us now. First of all, petitioner has assumed that the difference between the value of a right to income in respect of a decedent and its basis can properly be labeled as appreciation. However, the right to income in respect of a decedent is the right to compensation income, which was already earned by the decedent and became nonforfeitable upon his death. This is simply income that has been earned but not yet reported, and thus cannot be seen as constituting appreciation in the value of property. Any increase in the value of bonus rights resulted from the fact that they were initially discounted because of the delay that had to be borne until the recipient could actually enjoy receipt of the income.

More importantly, petitioner's analogy to appreciated property is misplaced because it fails to consider that section 1014(a) generally allows a step-up in basis to the date-of-death valuation for property acquired from a decedent, while section 1014(c) denies a basis step-up for rights to income in respect of a decedent. Petitioner's approach would allow an escape from income taxation for all income in respect of a decedent represented by the value of the right to such income when distributed. This would have the effect of allowing a step-up in basis for increases in value of rights to income in respect of a decedent occurring before the decedent's death, as well as those occurring between the date of death and the date of distribution. Thus, petitioner's interpretation of section 1.661(a)–2(f) sees respondent as having allowed by regulation what was specifically denied by statute under section 1014(c), i.e., a step-up basis to the date-of-death value for rights to income in respect of a decedent.

We hold as a general principle that section 691 overrides sections 661 and 662 and precludes the assignment of a basis to a right to income in respect of a decedent when that right is transferred by an estate to a legatee. Therefore, we find in this case that petitioner improperly offset against its income in respect of a decedent, basis previously assigned to the rights to the bonus installments. * * *

ESTATE OF DEAN v. COMMISSIONER

United States Tax Court, 1983.

1983 T.C.M. 276, 46 T.C.M. (CCH) 184, 52 T.C. Memo (P–H) 1133.

FAY, JUDGE: * * *

After concessions, the only issue is whether an estate is entitled to a deduction under section 661(a)(2) when it makes a distribution to its beneficiaries of a promissory note representing a right to receive income in respect of a decedent under section 691.

* * *

Jack Dean (decedent) died on July 26, 1972. Prior to his death, he sold cattle to Paul C. Dean (Buyer). Buyer executed a $221,252.69 promissory note (the Note) payable in 8 equal annual installments with interest of 7 percent on the unpaid balance. Decedent elected to report gain on the sale on the installment basis under section 453.

* * *

The parties agree the Note is income in respect of a decedent under section 691. At issue is whether an estate is entitled to a section 661(a)(2) deduction when it distributes a note representing a right to receive income in respect of a decedent. The Estate claims it is entitled to the deduction since such distribution comes within the literal language of section 661(a)(2) as "amounts properly paid." Respondent acknowledges a literal reading of that section might include a distribution of a right to receive income. Respondent contends, however, that section 691 overrides section 661(a)(2) and, therefore, governs the tax treatment of both the Estate and its beneficiaries upon distribution of the Note.

This very issue was decided in respondent's favor in a recent opinion of this Court wherein we held section 691 must take precedence over section 661. *Rollert Residuary Trust v. Commissioner,* 80 T.C. 619 (1983). Briefly, the basis of our decision is as follows.

* * *

When the right to receive income in respect of a decedent is distributed by an estate, the distribution rules of sections 661 and 662 conflict with the provisions of section 691.

Although most property acquired from a decedent receives a stepped-up basis equal to its date of death value, section 691 property receives no such step-up in basis. Sec. 1014(c). By allowing the estate a deduction for a distribution of the section 691 property (in the same manner as a distribution of any other property) the estate and its beneficiaries escape income taxation by the amount of such deduction.[4] This effectively subverts sections 691 and 1014(c) which contemplate that the entire amount of income in respect of a decedent be subject to income tax.

Moreover, the timing and characterization rules of sections 661 and 662, and section 691, are inconsistent. Sections 661 and 662 require income to be included at the time of distribution whereas section 691 requires income to be reported at the time of its actual receipt. Additionally, section 691(a)(3) requires the character of section 691 property to be the same as it would have been in the hands of the decedent had he lived to receive such income. Under the distribution rules, the character of the income is determined by reference to the character of the estate's distributable net income.

Given these inconsistencies, and given the well-settled principle that a specific statute controls over a general one, we held that section 691 overrides sections 661 and 662. *Rollert Residuary Trust v. Commissioner,* 80 T.C. 619 (1983). Property representing a right to receive income in respect of a decedent is subject to its own statutory provisions. Thus, the transfer by an estate of section 691 property is treated as a neutral event, and is not subject to the distribution rules of sections 661 and 662. Accordingly, we hold for respondent on this issue.

In a typical situation, IRD has little or no basis. Assume, for example, that fair market value of a right to receive IRD is $40 but that

4. The following example taken from respondent's brief illustrates this point. An estate has distributable net income (DNI) of $100,000 in 1974 representing interest paid on a certificate of deposit held by the estate. The estate also holds sec. 691 property in the form of a note with a value of $120,000 and with zero basis. In 1974 the estate distributes the sec. 691 property and retains the interest income. In 1974, soon after the distribution, the beneficiary received the $120,000 payment on the note.

Applying sec. 661(a)(2), the estate receives a $100,000 deduction in 1974 based on its distribution of the note. The deduction carries out all distributable net income totally eliminating any tax liability of the estate. Under sec. 662, the beneficiary is required to include $100,000 in his gross income at the date of distribution. He also takes a $100,000 basis in the note. Sec. 1.661(a)–2(f)(3). Because of this increased basis, the beneficiary need only include $20,000 in his gross income when he receives actual payments of $120,000 on the note. Thus, although $220,000 in income has been realized, only $120,000 has been taxed. Moreover, no income will result upon the later distribution by the estate of the $100,000 of interest income. Therefore, $100,000, the amount of the distribution deduction, escapes income taxation altogether.

its basis is $0 under section 1014(c). Also assume that the right to this IRD could be distributed from a simple trust or as a Tier 1 distribution from a complex trust, in either case in satisfaction of a right to receive $40. In either case, distribution of the right to receive the IRD would work an acceleration of the income represented under section 691(a)(2) and an increase in basis to $40. The right to receive this IRD could also be distributed from a complex trust as a Tier 2 distribution pursuant to an exercise of the trustee's discretion, in which case there would be no acceleration and basis would remain at $0. An unresolved question with respect to either distribution is how *Rollert* and *Dean* will apply to either the accelerating or the discretionary distribution of the right to receive IRD.

In the Tier 2 discretionary distribution, if the right to IRD has a basis of $0 and there is no acceleration under section 691(a)(2) to step up the basis, section 643(e) would dictate that the amount of DNI carried out to the recipient is zero because that is the lesser of basis and fair market value. This is consistent with *Rollert* and *Dean.*

Questions

1. In the accelerating distribution, because income is recognized and basis is stepped up to fair market value, will income equal to fair market value be carried out to the recipient, or will *Dean* be deemed to apply to specify that no income is carried out in both an accelerating distribution as well as a nonaccelerating distribution?

2. If *Dean* is not applicable, may the distributing entity make the section 643(e)(3) election in the otherwise nonaccelerating situation in order to intentionally accelerate the income represented by the right to receive IRD, thereby stepping basis up to fair market value and allowing income to be carried out to that extent?

REALIZATION EVENTS

The carryover of basis and income carry out limitation of section 643(e) is affected by distributions that otherwise generate a new basis. Gain or loss may be realized under Treasury Regulation section 1.661(a)–2(f)(1) by distribution of an asset in-kind, with a concomitant adjustment to basis (to fair market value) if (1) the distribution is in satisfaction of the distributee's right to receive some other asset (for example, if Blackacre were distributed instead of a specific bequest of stock), or (2) the distribution is in satisfaction of the distributee's right to receive cash (for example, if Blackacre were distributed to satisfy a debt owed to a creditor or to satisfy a beneficiary's right to receive a specific legacy). In either case, the income tax treatment is as if the proper asset or cash were distributed and then used to purchase the actual asset distributed, with gain or loss generated on that sale if the asset had unrealized appreciation or depreciation (and nonrecognition under the Code did not otherwise apply). As illustrated by Revenue Ruling 69–486, which is reproduced below, gain or loss may also be realized by the beneficiaries of a distribution if a non-pro-rata division of property occurs in a situation requiring a fractional division of the property. These principles are illustrated by the following materials.

REVENUE RULING 74–178

1974–1 Cumulative Bulletin 196.

* * *

At the time of his death * * *, the decedent owned 150 shares of common stock in a domestic corporation. These shares were acquired from the decedent by his estate and valued for Federal estate tax purposes at $70 per share, which was the fair market value of a share at the date of his death. On the Federal estate tax return filed on behalf of the decedent's estate, the executor did not elect the alternate valuation date prescribed by section 2032 of the Internal Revenue Code of [1986]. An unrelated creditor of the decedent subsequently filed a claim against the estate for $8,000. The claim was based upon an indebtedness of $8,000 that the decedent owed the creditor at the date of his death. In an arm's-length transaction the executor of the estate transferred 100 shares of the stock to the creditor in satisfaction of the claim. The fair market value of a share at the time of the transfer was $80.

Section 1001(a) of the Code provides, in part, that the gain from the disposition of property shall be the excess of the amount realized therefrom over the adjusted basis provided in section 1011 for determining gain.

* * *

Section 1014(a) of the Code provides, generally, that the basis of property in the hands of a person acquiring the property from a decedent shall be the fair market value of the property at the date of the decedent's death or, where there is an appropriate election, at the alternate valuation dates as provided in section 2032.

* * *

Rev.Rul. 66–207, 1966–2 C.B. 243, holds, in part, that where an executor distributes appreciated property in partial satisfaction of a pecuniary legacy, the estate realizes gain to the extent of the difference between the amount of the bequest satisfied and the estate's basis in the property. That Revenue Ruling states that the effect of the distribution will be the same as if the executor sold the assets of the estate and distributed the proceeds.

In the instant case the fair market value of the shares of stock at the time such stock was transferred to the creditor is equal to the amount of the claim satisfied ($8,000). However, since the executor did not elect the alternate valuation date, the estate's basis in the shares transferred is the fair market value of the shares at the date of the decedent's death ($7,000). Accordingly, it is held that upon such transfer the estate realized a gain of $1,000, which is the excess of the amount of the claim satisfied by the transfer over the estate's basis in the shares. Had the estate's basis in the shares of stock transferred exceeded the amount of the claim satisfied, the estate would have sustained a loss deductible to the extent allowed in sections 1211 and 1212 of the Code.

SUISMAN v. EATON

United States District Court, District of Connecticut, 1935.
15 F.Supp. 113, aff'd, 83 F.2d 1019 (2d Cir.1936), cert. denied, 299 U.S. 573, 57 S.Ct. 37, 81 L.Ed. 422 (1936).

* * *

1. The testator's daughter, Minerva, under the will upon the testator's death acquired an equitable right to receive the sum of $50,000 in cash from the general assets of the trust corpus, upon attaining the age of 25 years. This legacy was general rather than specific; it was equitable rather than legal; if I considered it material, I should hold it contingent rather than absolute or vested.

2. Under the will the said Minerva acquired no title, legal or equitable, to any specific assets of the estate.

3. Under the will, the legacy was a general charge upon the trust corpus. The trustee was in equity under obligation to pay to the said Minerva when she became 25 the sum of $50,000 in cash out of the assets of the trust estate, and had full power to convert the assets into cash at least in so far as necessary to satisfy said obligation.

4. When the said Minerva received stock of the value of $50,000 in full satisfaction of her legacy, her right, against the trustee and trust corpus, and the correlative liabilities were wholly satisfied and extinguished; a conclusion which is required even if Minerva's equitable right under the will vested upon the testator's death.

5. The transfer of said securities by the trustee to the said Minerva was a "sale or other disposition" of said securities. * * *

6. The property which the trust estate received from the "sale or other disposition" of said stocks was the discharge of the corpus from Minerva's equitable right to receive $50,000 therefrom; the amount realized, i.e., the "fair market value of the property (other than money) received," * * * was $50,000; and the excess of the amount realized over the basis was properly computed by the Commissioner, legally assessed as part of the taxable income of the trust estate, and the tax thereon was legally collected.

* * *

KENAN v. COMMISSIONER

United States Court of Appeals, Second Circuit, 1940.
114 F.2d 217.

AUGUSTUS N. HAND, CIRCUIT JUDGE.

The testatrix, Mrs. Bingham, died * * * leaving a will under which she placed her residuary estate in trust and provided in item

"Seventh" that her trustees should pay a certain amount annually to her niece, Louise Clisby Wise, until the latter reached the age of forty, "at which time or as soon thereafter as compatible with the interests of my estate they shall pay to her the sum of Five Million ($5,000,000.00) Dollars." The will provided in item "Eleventh" that the trustees, in the case of certain payments including that of the $5,000,000 under item "Seventh", should have the right "to substitute for the payment in money, payment in marketable securities of a value equal to the sum to be paid, the selection of the securities to be substituted in any instance, and the valuation of such securities to be done by the Trustees and their selection and valuation to be final."

Louise Clisby Wise became forty years of age * * *. The trustees decided to pay her the $5,000,000 partly in cash and partly in securities. The greater part of the securities had been owned by the testator and transferred as part of her estate to the trustees; others had been purchased by the trustees. All had appreciated in value during the period for which they were held by the trustees, and the Commissioner determined that the distribution of the securities to the niece resulted in capital gains which were taxable to the trustees * * * as taxable income on the "sale or exchange" of capital assets.

* * *

In support of their petition the taxpayers contend that the delivery of the securities of the trust estate to the legatee was a donative disposition of property pursuant to the terms of the will, and that no gain was thereby realized. They argue that when they determined that the legacy should be one of securities, it became for all purposes a bequest of property, just as if the cash alternative had not been provided, and not taxable for the reason that no gain is realized on the transfer by a testamentary trustee of specific securities or other property bequeathed by will to a legatee.

We do not think that the situation here is the same as that of a legacy of specific property. The legatee was never in the position occupied by the recipient of specific securities under a will. She had a claim against the estate for $5,000,000, payable either in cash or securities of that value, but had no title or right to the securities, legal or equitable, until they were delivered to her by the trustees after the exercise of their option. She took none of the chances of a legatee of specific securities or of a share of a residue that the securities might appreciate or decline in value between the time of the death of the testator and the transfer to her by the trustees, but instead had at all times a claim for an unvarying amount in money or its equivalent.

If there had merely been a bequest to the legatee of $5,000,000 and she had agreed with the trustees to take securities of that value, the transaction would have been a "sale or other disposition" of the securities under Suisman v. Eaton, 15 F.Supp. 113. * * *

In the present case, the legatee had a claim which was a charge against the trust estate for $5,000,000 in cash or securities and the trustees had the power to determine whether the claim should be satisfied in one form or the other. The claim, though enforceable only in the alternative, was, like the claim in Suisman v. Eaton, supra, a charge against the entire trust estate. If it were satisfied by a cash payment securities might have to be sold on which (if those actually delivered in specie were selected) a taxable gain would necessarily have been realized. Instead of making such a sale the trustees delivered the securities and exchanged them pro tanto for the general claim of the legatee, which was thereby satisfied.

It is said that this transaction was not such a "sale or other disposition" as * * * in Suisman v. Eaton, because it was effectuated only by the will of the trustees and not, as in Suisman v. Eaton, through a mutual agreement between trustee and legatee. The Board made no such distinction, and we are not inclined to limit thus the meaning of the words "other disposition" * * * or of "exchange". * * * The word "exchange" does not necessarily have the connotation of a bilateral agreement which may be said to attach to the word "sale." Thus, should a person set up a trust and reserve to himself the power to substitute for the securities placed in trust other securities of equal value, there would seem no doubt that the exercise of this reserved power would be an "exchange" within the common meaning of the word, even though the settlor consulted no will other than his own, although, of course, we do not here advert to the problems of taxability in such a situation.

The Board alluded to the fact that both here and in Suisman v. Eaton the bequest was fixed at a definite amount in money, that in both cases there was no bequest of specific securities (nor of a share in the residue which might vary in value), that the rights of the legatee, like those in the Suisman case, were a charge upon the corpus of the trust, and that the trustees had to part either with $5,000,000 in cash or with securities worth that amount at the time of the transfer. It added that the increase in value of the securities was realized by the trust and benefited it to the full extent, since, except for the increase, it would have had to part with other property, and it cited in further support of its position United States v. Kirby Lumber Co., 284 U.S. 1, 52 S.Ct. 4, 76 L.Ed. 131. Under circumstances like those here, where the legatee did not take securities designated by the will or an interest in the corpus which might be more or less at the time of the transfer than at the time of decedent's death, it seems to us that the trustees realized a gain by using these securities to settle a claim worth $5,000,000, just as the trustee in Suisman v. Eaton realized one.

It seems reasonably clear that the property was not "transmitted at death" or "acquired by bequest * * * from the decedent." It follows that the fears of the taxpayers that double taxation of this appreciation will result because the legatee will take the basis of the decedent under Brewster v. Gage, 280 U.S. 327, 50 S.Ct. 115, 74 L.Ed. 457, are groundless. It is true that the basis for property "acquired by bequest, devise, or inheritance" is "the fair market value of such property at the time of such acquisition" and that under Brewster v. Gage, supra, the date of acquisition has been defined as the date of death of the testator [with no tax free step-up in basis. Ed.] But the holding of the present case is necessarily a determination that the property here acquired is acquired in an exchange and not "by bequest, devise or inheritance," * * *. The legatee's basis would seem to be the value of the claim surrendered in exchange for the securities; and the Board of Tax Appeals has so held. Sherman Ewing v. Commissioner of Internal Revenue, 40 B.T.A. 911.

* * *

REVENUE RULING 82–4

1982–1 Cumulative Bulletin 99.

* * *

In 1980 *A* gratuitously transferred to *B*, *A* 's adult child, 100,000 shares of *X* company stock. *A* died in 1981. *A* 's will provides that after the payment of debts, expenses, taxes, and the satisfaction of certain specific bequests, the residue of the estate is to be divided equally between the decedent's adult children, *B* and *C*. However, the will further provides that the executor, in determining the allocation of the residue to *B* and *C*, is to take into account the date of death value of the 100,000 shares of stock transferred to *B*. This provision was intended to equalize, to the extent possible, the value of the property transferred to *B* and *C*, taking into consideration the lifetime transfer to *B*. The will also provides that any assets distributed in kind are to be valued at the date of distribution.

At the time of final distribution, the residuary estate consisted solely of 60,000 shares of *X* company stock with a value of $3 per share. The value of the stock at the date of death was $2 per share. Because the value of the residue at the date of distribution ($180,000) was less than the value at the date of death of the stock previously transferred by the decedent to *B* ($200,000), the executor, in accordance with the terms of the decedent's will, distributed the entire residuary estate to *C*.

* * *

Section 1.661(a)–2(f)(1) of the Income Tax Regulations provides that an estate does not realize a gain or loss from the distribution of property in kind unless the distribution is in satisfaction of a right to receive a distribution in a specific dollar amount. Under this provision of the regulations, whenever an estate distributes property other than money to any beneficiary in satisfaction of a specific dollar amount, the estate realizes gain or loss measured by the difference between the amount of the bequest satisfied and the basis to the estate of the distributed property.

Section 663(a) of the Code excludes from amounts falling within section 661(a) any amount that, under the terms of the governing instrument, is properly paid or credited as a gift or bequest of a specific sum of money or of specific property.

Section 1.663(a)–1(b)(1) of the regulations provides that in order to qualify as a gift or bequest of a specific sum of money or of specific property under section 663(a) of the Code, the amount of money or the identity of the specific property must be ascertainable under the terms of a decedent's will as of the date of the decedent's death.

In Rev.Rul. 66–207, 1966–2 C.B. 243, the decedent's will created a trust and provided for a bequest of a specific sum of money, 250*x* dollars, to the trust. After payment of all debts, costs of administration, claims, and specific bequests, other than the 250*x* dollars, the estate consisted of assets (including 10*x* dollars in cash) having a fair market value of 200*x* dollars and an aggregate basis to the estate of 150*x* dollars. Rev.Rul. 66–207 holds that the bequest of 250*x* dollars is a "bequest of a specific sum of money" as that term is defined in section 1.663(a)–1(b)(1) of the regulations. The fact that the fair market value of the property remaining in the estate is not equal to the bequest of the specific sum of money does not transform that bequest into a bequest of the residue of the estate. Rather, the bequest of a specific sum has been abated by 50*x* dollars and thereby reduced from 250*x* dollars to 200*x* dollars. Because the distribution is in satisfaction of a bequest of a specific sum of money, as defined by section 1.663(a)–1(b)(1), no amount is deductible by the estate under section 661 of the Code or includible in gross income of the trust under section 662.

Rev.Rul. 66–207 further holds that upon distribution of the property remaining in the estate to the trust, the estate will realize a gain of 50*x* dollars under section 1.661(a)–2(f) of the regulations equal to the difference between the amount of the bequest satisfied by distribution of property other than cash (200*x* dollars less 10*x* dollars cash, or 190*x* dollars) and the basis (150*x* dollars less 10*x* dollars cash or 140*x* dollars) to the estate of the property other than cash so distributed. The effect of the distribution is the same as if the executor of the estate sold the remaining assets of the estate and distributed the proceeds to the trustee.

In the present situation, the decedent's will provides that the residue of the estate is to be divided equally between *B* and *C*. However, in order to equalize to the extent possible the respective shares of *B* and *C*, the executor must take into account the value at the date of death of the stock previously transferred to *B*.

In this case, as in Rev.Rul. 66–207, the residue equal to the value of 100,000 shares of *X* company stock as of date of death bequeathed to *C* is a "bequest of a specific sum of money," as that term is defined in section 1.663(a)–1(b)(1) of the regulations, because the amount is ascertainable under the terms of *A* 's will as of the date of A's death. Thus, no amount is deductible by the estate under section 661 of the Code or includible in the gross income of *B* under section 662. Also, under section 1.661(a)–2(f)(1), the estate realizes a gain on the distribution in kind of appreciated property in satisfaction of *C*'s right to receive a distribution in a specific dollar amount.

The estate realizes gain of $60,000 (date of distribution value ($180,000) less the basis of the property in the estate ($120,000)) for federal income tax purposes when the executor distributes the entire residuary estate to *C* to equalize to the extent possible the respective shares of total transfers received from the decedent.

If in this case the value of the residuary estate had been, for example, $250,000, the property remaining after satisfaction of the $200,000 bequest to *C* ($50,000) would pass to *B* and *C* in equal shares. The estate would realize no gain or loss under section 1.661(a)–2(f)(1) of the regulations upon distribution of this portion of the $50,000 residue because the distribution would not be in satisfaction of the right to receive a distribution in a specific dollar amount.

REVENUE RULING 56–270

1956–1 Cumulative Bulletin 325.

The decedent bequeathed in trust for the benefit of his wife an amount sufficient to utilize the marital deduction to the maximum extent authorized by section 2056 of the Internal Revenue Code of [1986] after taking into consideration any other property with respect to which such deduction is allowable. The income from the trust is given to the surviving spouse for life with a power exercisable by her alone at death to appoint the entire interest to any other person or persons, or to her estate. *Held,* the marital trust fund was provided for in a fixed and definite "dollar amount." Accordingly, capital gains were realized by the estate to the extent that the fair market value of the property on the date of distribution to the trustee exceeds the fair market value thereof on the date of the decedent's death (or, in the event alternate valuation is elected, the fair market value thereof on the alternate valuation date). Consistent with the foregoing conclusion, it is further held that losses measured by the difference between the basis of the property in the hands of the executor and the value thereof at the date of distribution to the marital trust may be offset against the gains realized.

REVENUE RULING 60–87

1960–1 Cumulative Bulletin 286.

* * *

The decedent was a resident of a community property state. The estate consisted almost entirely of community property. The decedent's will provided that, after certain distributions of his personal property, a part of the residue and remainder of the estate be placed in trust for the benefit of his wife. The trust was to include the wife's share of certain community property, plus an amount of the decedent's separate property which, when added to the value of certain other property included in the decedent's gross estate, would equal one-half of his adjusted gross estate as finally determined for Federal estate tax purposes. * * *

After the final determination of the value of the decedent's adjusted gross estate for Federal estate tax purposes, the executor of the estate transferred to the testamentary marital deduction trust securities sufficient in value, together with the other items to be included therein, to bring the value of the trust to the required one-half of the adjusted gross estate. In determining the value of the property to be transferred to the trust, the executor of the estate used the fair market value of the property at the date of the distribution. However, since the fair market value of the property transferred, at the date of the transfer to the trust, was greater than the value used for Federal estate tax purposes, the specific question arises whether gain is realized by the estate because of such transfer. A corollary question is whether such marital deduction trust may be considered as being provided for in a fixed and definite "dollar amount."

Revenue Ruling 56–270, C.B. 1956–1, 325, stands for the proposition that, if a marital deduction trust comprises a fraction or percentage of the "adjusted gross estate" of a decedent, the marital trust fund is considered to have been provided for in a fixed and definite "dollar amount." Therefore, capital gain or loss is recognized upon the distribution of property to a trust.

Insofar as is here pertinent, section 663(a) of the Internal Revenue Code of [1986] provides, in general, that a gift or bequest of a specific sum of money shall neither be allowed as a deduction to an estate or trust under section 661 of the Code nor included in the gross income of the beneficiary under section 662(a) of the Code. To qualify for this exclusion, the amount of money bequeathed must be ascertainable as of the date of death. The effect of the regulations is that a bequest under a marital deduction trust formula clause does not qualify for exclusion since the amount of the trust fund is not ascertainable at the date of the decedent's death.

Section 1.663(a)–1(b)(1) of the Income Tax Regulations provides as follows:

> In order to qualify as a gift or bequest of a specific sum of money or of specific property under section 663(a), the amount of money or the identity of the specific property must be ascertainable under the terms of the testator's will as of the date of his death, or under the terms of an inter vivos trust instrument as of the date of the inception of the trust. For example, bequests to a decedent's son of the decedent's interest in a partnership and to his daughter of a sum of money equal to the value of the partnership interest are bequests of specific property and of a specific sum of money, respectively. On the other hand, a bequest to the decedent's spouse of money or property, to be selected by the decedent's executor, equal in value to a fraction of the decedent's "adjusted gross estate" is neither a bequest of a specific sum of money or of specific property. The identity of the property and the amount of

money specified in the preceding sentence are dependent both on the exercise of the executor's discretion and on the payment of administration expenses and other charges, neither of which are facts existing on the date of the decedent's death. It is immaterial that the value of the bequest is determinable after the decedent's death before the bequest is satisfied (so that gain or loss may be realized by the estate in the transfer of property in satisfaction of it).

Unlike section 1.663(a)–1(b)(1) of the regulations, Revenue Ruling 56–270, supra, is not concerned with the ascertainability of a specific amount at the date of death but rather whether the marital trust fund is provided for in a fixed and definite amount at the time of the distribution. Thus, to qualify for the exclusion provided for in section 663(a) of the Code, the above-quoted regulation prescribes an entirely different test from that prescribed in Revenue Ruling 56–270, which has application only for capital gain purposes. Further, the last sentence of the above-quoted regulations recognizes the fact that a different rule applies for capital gain purposes and clearly implies that the regulations are not to be considered inconsistent with that rule.

In the instant case, the marital deduction trust comprises a portion of the residue of the decedent's estate. However, instead of using a residuary formula clause, which leaves a percentage or fraction of the value of the residuary estate to the surviving spouse or trust, the will uses a pecuniary formula clause, as [in] Revenue Ruling 56–270, supra, which leaves a percentage of the "adjusted gross estate" to the surviving spouse or trust. There is a significant distinction between a marital deduction trust of the pecuniary formula type and one of the residuary formula type.

The rationale of Revenue Ruling 56–270, supra, is that a marital deduction trust of the pecuniary formula type provides for a trust fund in a fixed and definite amount, once the value of the adjusted gross estate is finally determined, which amount is unaffected by any appreciation or depreciation in value of the assets comprising the estate.

The difference is that under a pecuniary formula clause the trust will receive assets of a fixed and definite amount at the time of distribution, whereas under the residuary formula clause the percentage or fraction will be applied for the purpose of making distribution of the residuary estate as constituted at the time of distribution. Therefore, under a residuary formula clause, the trust will share in appreciation and depreciation of the value of the estate, which is not the case under a pecuniary formula clause. Thus, Revenue Ruling 56–270, supra, is not inconsistent with section 1.663(a)–1(b)(1) of the regulations.

The facts in the instant case show that the marital deduction trust comprising a portion of the residue of the estate is measured by a percentage of the value of the adjusted gross estate. Under such circumstances, the marital trust fund is considered as being provided for in a fixed and definite "dollar amount." Accordingly, gain or loss is realized by the estate measured by the difference between the fair market value of the property at the date of distribution and the value of the property determined for Federal estate tax purposes.

REVENUE RULING 69–486

1969–2 Cumulative Bulletin 159.

* * *

Under terms of the trust instrument, the trustee is required to distribute currently all trust income to *B* for her life and upon her death distribute one-half of the trust corpus to *C*, an individual, and one-half to *X*, a charitable organization exempt from tax under section 501(c)(3) of the Internal Revenue Code of [1986].

* * *

At the time of *B* 's death, the trust corpus to be distributed to *C* and *X* consisted in part of notes that had been purchased by the trust and that had a total adjusted basis of 300*x* dollars and a total fair market value of an equal amount. The balance of the trust corpus consisted of common stock acquired by purchase with a total adjusted basis of 100*x* dollars and a total fair market value of 300*x* dollars.

The trust instrument as well as local law was silent as to the authority of the trustee to make a non-pro rata distribution of property in kind.

By mutual agreement, the two beneficiaries requested that the trustee distribute all of the notes to *C* and all of the common stock to *X*.

* * *

Since the trustee was not authorized to make a non-pro rata distribution of property in kind but did so as a result of the mutual agreement between *C* and *X*, the non-pro rata distribution by the trustee to *C* and *X* is equivalent to a distribution to *C* and *X* of the notes and common stock pro rata by the trustee, followed by an exchange between *C* and *X* of *C* 's pro rata share of common stock for *X* 's pro rata share of notes.

* * *

The basis of the pro rata shares of notes and common stock in the hands of *C* and *X* is the same as the adjusted basis in the hands of the trust. See section 1.1015–2(b) of the regulations.

Furthermore, *C* in substance exchanged his pro rata share of common stock with *X* for *X* 's pro rata share of notes. The amount of recognized gain to *C* is determined under sections 1001 and 1002 of the Code. Since *X* is a charitable organization exempt from tax under section 501(c)(3) of the Code, it has no tax consequence as a result of the exchange.

LETTER RULING 8145026

National Office Technical Advice Memorandum
July 31, 1981.

* * *

The decedent * * * established a marital trust for the benefit of his spouse and bequeathed to that trust:

> a part of my estate, selected by my Executor, having a value determined as follows: (1) determine the value of my entire estate passing under this Will, (2) add thereto the value of any and all insurance and other property passing outside of this Will but includable in my estate for federal estate tax purposes, (3) deduct therefrom all debts and expenses of administration allowed as a deduction for federal estate tax purposes but not any estate or inheritance tax, (4) ascertain one-half of the remainder, (5) deduct from such one-half the value of any and all insurance and other property passing to my said wife either outside this Will or under any other Item of this Will in such manner as to qualify as a part of the marital deduction under the federal estate tax law, and (6) the remainder of such one-half shall be the value of the part of my estate bequeathed in this Item.
>
> The determination of this bequest and the division of my estate shall be on the basis of values existing on the date of division in the case of property then divided, or on the date of distribution in the case of any property previously distributed, or on such estate tax value as finally determined in the case of any property passing outside of this Will, and this bequest shall carry with it its proportionate part of [the] income of my estate from the date of my death.

Clause 12(f) of A's will states:

> In the distribution of my estate and the division into separate trusts and shares, the Executor and Trustee shall be authorized to make the division in money or in kind or in both, and the division made and the values established by my Executor or Trustee shall be binding and conclusive on all persons taking hereunder. My Executor or Trustee may in making such division allot undivided interests in the same property to several trusts or shares.

At the close of administration, the value of the bequest due the marital trust was calculated to be $2,980,392.54 with $2,961,621.42 due to be paid at termination. In satisfaction of this bequest, the estate distributed cash in the amount of $158.92 and property having an aggregate fair market value of $2,961,462.50 and an aggregate basis of $990,908.85. At distribution the marital trust received specific assets instead of fractional interests in each asset of the estate.

One of the adjustments proposed by the examining agent during examination of the estate's final Form 1041 is the recognition of long-term capital gain of $1,970,553.65 due to the satisfaction of the bequest to the marital trust with assets that appreciated between the date of A's death and final distribution.

This office issued a technical advice memorandum on October 23, 1980, concerning the subject transaction and concluded that the bequest in question was a specific dollar amount bequest within the meaning of section 1.661(a)–2(f)(1) and that the estate realized a capital gain when it distributed assets which had appreciated in value between the date of A's death and the time of distribution of the assets to the trust.

The district director's office that requested the technical advice has requested that this office reconsider the technical advice of October 23, 1980.

Section 1.661(a)–2(f)(1) of the regulations provides that if property is paid, credited, or required to be distributed in kind, no gain or loss is realized by the trust or estate (or the other beneficiaries) by reason of the distribution, unless the distribution is in satisfaction of a right to receive a distribution in a specific dollar amount or in specific property other than that distributed.

Where an estate satisfies a pecuniary bequest with appreciated property, the estate recognizes gain to the extent the amount of the bequest exceeds the basis of the property used to satisfy the bequest in the hands of the estate. For example, in *Kenan v. Commissioner,* 114 F.2d 217 (2d Cir.1940), the testatrix provided in her will that her niece be paid the sum of five million dollars when the niece became forty years of age. The trustees satisfied the bequest partly in cash and partly in appreciated securities.

The court stated that the beneficiary had a claim against the estate for five million dollars, payable either in cash or securities of that value, but had no title or right to the securities, legal or equitable, until they were delivered to her by the trustees. The trustees had the power to determined whether the claim should be satisfied in cash or in kind. If the trustees had satisfied the bequest in cash, they would have had to sell assets and recognized gain. By using appreciated assets, the trustees satisfied a claim against the estate and the estate received the benefit of the appreciation of those assets.

The court made a distinction between the situation and one in which the beneficiary takes property specifically designated in the will or where the beneficiary has an interest in the corpus which might be more or less at the time of the transfer than at the time of decedent's death. The court thus distinguishes a situation where the beneficiary's interest fluctuates in value with the corpus of the estate.

Rev.Rul. 56–270, 1956–1 C.B. 325, holds that a bequest which provides that a trust for the benefit of decedent's wife be paid an amount sufficient to utilize the marital deduction to the maximum extent is a bequest of a fixed and definite dollar amount. The formula is a fraction or percentage of the adjusted gross estate. Accordingly, the estate recognizes a capital gain to the extent appreciated assets are used to satisfy the bequest.

Rev.Rul. 56–270 was clarified by Rev.Rul. 60–87, 1960–1 C.B. 286. Rev.Rul. 60–87 holds that gain or loss is realized by an estate upon the distribution of property by the executor to a marital deduction trust where the amount of property distributed is a portion of the residue of the estate which is measured by a percentage of the adjusted gross estate. * * *

The executor transferred to the marital deduction trust securities sufficient in value, together with the other items to be included therein, to bring the value of the trust to the required one-half of the adjusted gross estate. The executor used date of distribution fair market values in order to determine the value of the property to be transferred to the trust. The fair market value of the property transferred exceeded the value of the property used for federal estate tax purposes (thus exceeded the basis in the hands of the estate).

Rev.Rul. 60–87 concludes that where the marital deduction trust is to receive a portion of the residue of the estate measured by a percentage of the value of the adjusted gross estate, the trust is considered as being provided for in a fixed and definite dollar amount. Rev.Rul. 60–87 characterizes the bequest as a pecuniary formula clause because the trust will receive a percentage of the "adjusted gross estate."

The revenue ruling contrasts the pecuniary formula clause with a residuary formula clause by stating that the residuary formula clause leaves a percentage or fraction of the value of the residuary estate to the surviving spouse or trust. The difference between the two is noted as being that in the residuary formula clause, the trust (the beneficiary) will share in appreciation and depreciation of the value of the estate, which is not the case under a pecuniary formula clause.

In this situation the value of the claim of the marital deduction trust fluctuates with the value of the assets of the estate. Furthermore, the claim is not a claim for cash against the estate, but is a claim of a percentage of the value of the residuary estate as in Rev.Rul. 60–87 to be satisfied with money or in kind or both at the discretion of the executor.

Because the bequest to the marital deduction trust gives the trust a claim which fluctuates in value up until the date of distribution and is not a claim for cash and the executor has the unrestricted discretion to satisfy the bequest with money or in kind or both, the claim is not for a specific dollar amount within the meaning of section 1.661(a)–2(f)(1) of the regulations.

Accordingly, the estate does not recognize gain upon satisfaction of the marital deduction trust bequest. * * *

REVENUE RULING 67–74

1967–1 Cumulative Bulletin 194.

Under the terms of the instrument which created a trust, the trustee is required to distribute currently to the beneficiary all of the income of the trust for each year. For the taxable year under consideration, the trustee had sufficient cash on hand to enable him to distribute in cash all of the trust income for that year which he was required to distribute to the beneficiary. However, in accordance with an agreement with the beneficiary, the trustee distributed, in lieu of cash, stock which was a part of the trust corpus and which had a fair market value equal to the amount of trust income for that year required to be distributed to the beneficiary. The value of the stock so distributed exceeded the basis of the stock in the hands of the trust.

Held, for Federal income tax purposes, the transaction is treated as though the trustee had actually distributed to the beneficiary cash in an amount equal to the trust income required to be distributed currently, and the beneficiary had purchased the stock from the trustee with cash. The trust is allowed a deduction under section 651(a) limited by the distributable net income of the trust, for the amount of income required to be distributed currently, and the beneficiary must report a like amount in gross income under section 652(a). The instant transfer, involving stock having a fair market value equal to the trust income for the year in question which the trustee was required to distribute to the beneficiary, resulted in a capital gain to the trust equal to the difference between the basis of the stock in the hands of the trustee and the amount of the obligation satisfied by the transfer. Further, the basis of the stock in the hands of the beneficiary is his cost, that is, the price he is deemed to have paid for it.

LETTER RULING 8447003

National Office Technical Advice Memorandum
June 8, 1984.

* * *

In 1957, Grantor created Trust for the benefit of Beneficiary, the grandchild of Grantor. Article First paragraph (1) of the trust agreement for Trust provides that during the minority of Beneficiary, the trustees of Trust must accumulate all of the net income of Trust. When Beneficiary reaches the age of 21, the trustees must pay to Beneficiary all of the accumulated income. Thereafter, the trustees must pay to Beneficiary, at least quarter-annually, all of the net income of Trust.

Article First, paragraph (2) of the trust agreement provides that when Beneficiary reaches the age of 25, the trustees must distribute to Beneficiary an amount equal to one-fourth of the principal of Trust, valued as then constituted.

Under Article Second, paragraph (4) of the trust agreement, the trustees have the power to make any distribution in cash or in other property or partly in cash and partly in property. The property distributed may be real or personal, and the trustees may distribute undivided interests in property.

In 1980, the trustees distributed stock in satisfaction of Beneficiary's right to receive net income of Trust. The trustees also distributed cash and stock in satisfaction of Beneficiary's right to receive an amount equal to one-fourth of the principal of Trust. Each share of stock had appreciated in value from the time it was transferred by Grantor to Trust until the date it was distributed to Beneficiary. * * *

This office issued a technical advice memorandum on October 17, 1983, on this same transaction and concluded that no gain was realized by Trust in 1980 when the trustees distributed appreciated stock under either the direction to pay net income or the direction to pay an amount equal to one-fourth of the principal. The district director's office that originally requested the technical advice issued on October 17, 1983 has now requested that this office reconsider it.

Section 1.661(a)–2(f)(1) of the Income Tax Regulations provides that if property is paid, credited, or required to be distributed in kind, no gain or loss is realized by the trust by reason of the distribution, unless the distribution is in satisfaction of a right to receive a distribution in a specific dollar amount or specific property other than that distributed.

In *Kenan v. Commissioner,* 114 F.2d 217 (2d Cir.1940), the beneficiary had a right to receive a distribution in the amount of $5,000,000 upon reaching age 40. The trust instrument authorized the trustee "to substitute for the payment in money, payment in marketable securities of a value equal to the sum to be paid, the selection of the securities to be substituted in any instance, and the valuation of such securities to be done by the Trustees and their selection and valuation to be final." The trustees conveyed appreciated securities to the beneficiary in partial satisfaction of the required $5,000,000 distribution. The court held that, notwithstanding the lack of a bilateral agreement between the parties, the distribution was a sale or other disposition of the securities, and the trust realized gain.

In Rev.Rul. 67–74, 1967–1 C.B. 194, a trust agreement required the trustee to distribute currently to the beneficiary all of the income of the trust for each year. For the taxable year under consideration, the trustee had sufficient cash to make the required distribution of income entirely in cash. However, under an agreement with the beneficiary, the trustee did not distribute the cash but instead distributed appreciated stock that had a fair market value equal to the amount of income that was to be distributed. Rev.Rul. 67–74 held that the distribution caused the trust to realize gain. The transaction was treated as though the trustee had distributed cash to the beneficiary and then the beneficiary had purchased the stock from the trustee.

In Rev.Rul. 55–117, 1955–1 C.B. 233, a trust was formed under the will of a decedent. The will directed the trustees to pay the net income of the trust to the beneficiary until she reached a specified age. At that time, the trustees were to pay her one-fourth of the principal of the trust, valued on the date of distribution. The balance of the principal was to be retained by the trust for five years, and the net income distributed to the beneficiary. The will further provided that distributions could be made in kind or in money or partly in each. When the beneficiary reached the specified age, the trustees distributed stock that had appreciated between the date of death and the date of distribution. The distribution of stock satisfied the requirement under the will to distribute one-fourth of the trust principal. Rev.Rul. 55–117 held that there was no sale or exchange when the stock was distributed. The distribution was not in satisfaction of an obligation of the trust to distribute a definite amount of cash or equivalent value in securities, but instead was in the nature of a partial distribution of a share of the trust principal.

Rev.Rul. 60–87, 1960–1 C.B. 286, held that gain was realized by an estate upon the distribution of appreciated property to a marital trust when the bequest was of a portion of the residue of the estate that was measured by a percentage of the adjusted gross estate. The bequest was made under a pecuniary formula clause, rather than a residuary formula clause, and thus was in a fixed and definite dollar amount.

1. Income Distribution

The trust instrument for Trust required at least a quarter-annual distribution of the net income of Trust. Through this provision, Beneficiary acquired the right to receive a specific dollar amount, within the meaning of section 1.661(a)–2(f)(1) of the regulations. Beneficiary had a right to all of the net income, the specific amount of which was fixed at the time of each distribution. There is no requirement in the regulation that the specific dollar amount must be determined prior to the date of distribution. Accordingly, Trust realizes gain on the transfer [of] appreciated property in satisfaction of its obligation to distribute net income for 1980.

Rev.Rul. 67–74 is consistent with this result. It does not cite section 1.661(a)–(2)(f)(1) of the regulations. Rather, in reconstructing the transaction as a distribution of cash to the beneficiary followed by a purchase of the stock by the beneficiary from the trustee with the cash, the ruling relies on the agreement by the beneficiary to accept the stock instead of a cash distribution. In the present case, there was no such agreement; the trustee did not need Beneficiary's consent because the trust agreement specifically allows distributions to be made in property other than cash, at the trustee's discretion. This difference in facts, however, does not call for a different result. Section 1.661(a)–(2)(f)(1) makes no distinction pertaining to the source of a trustee's authority to make a non-cash distribution. It literally applies whenever property is conveyed in satisfaction of a right to receive a distribution in a specific dollar amount. The distribution by

Trust is clearly covered by the regulation. In *Kenan v. Commissioner,* the court considered an in-kind distribution based not on the beneficiary's consent but on the authority granted in the trust instrument. Holding that a sale or other disposition of securities had occurred, the court specifically rejected the distinction that there was no bilateral agreement between the parties.

2. PRINCIPAL DISTRIBUTION

The present case is nearly identical to Rev.Rul. 55–117. Although Article First, paragraph (2) of the trust agreement provides that the trustees must distribute an *amount* equal to one-fourth of the principal of Trust, this direction does not substantively differ from a direction to pay one-fourth of the trust principal. Therefore, this provision is similar to a residuary formula clause in a will rather than a pecuniary formula clause. As illustrated in Rev.Rul. 60–87, appreciation and depreciation of the assets of a trust or estate will cause the economic right of a beneficiary to fluctuate under a residuary formula. The economic right under a pecuniary formula will remain unaffected. Because the right of Beneficiary fluctuated from the date Trust was created until the date of distribution, Beneficiary had a right under a residuary clause, that was not a right to receive a fixed amount. As in Rev.Rul. 55–117, the distribution of an amount equal to one-fourth of the value of the principal was in the nature of a partial distribution of a share of the trust principal rather than a satisfaction of a right to receive a fixed dollar amount. Thus, there is a longstanding position that a distribution of a portion of principal or residue, whether pro-rata or non-pro-rata, valued at the time of distribution is not a taxable event. Accordingly, Trust did not realize gain on the distribution.

ELECTION TO REALIZE GAIN OR LOSS

Read Code section 643(e)(3).

By section 643(e)(3), the fiduciary of an estate or trust that is making a distribution may voluntarily elect to incur gain or loss, even though distribution otherwise would not constitute a realization event. By virtue of the election, gain or loss is realized by the trust or estate as if the distributed asset were sold to the distributee for its fair market value, causing basis in the asset to be adjusted to reflect the gain or loss realized. In the case of an appreciated asset, the election causes basis to be stepped-up to fair market value, thereby allowing a greater income carry out, a larger distribution deduction to the trust or estate making the distribution and, once available DNI has been exhausted, permitting an accumulation distribution subject to throwback to the extent fair market exceeds DNI and there is available UNI to be carried out.

Under section 643(e)(3)(B), the election must be made for the tax year of the distribution, by the fiduciary required to file the tax return for the estate or trust making the distribution, by reporting on Schedule D of Form 1041 for the year of the distribution (timely filed, including any extensions granted), showing the gain or loss realized on the deemed sale and reporting the name and taxpayer identification number of the distributee, all as dictated by Temporary Treasury Regulation section 5h.4(h) (promulgated by T.D. 7976). By allowing the election on the tax return for the year of distribution, the fiduciary is permitted to evaluate all the facts involving both its and the distributee's taxable situation before deciding whether to cause the additional consequences of the election, all while having already given the distributee the benefit of the asset distributed. Hardly a more accommodating procedure could be granted, but with this flexibility attends a high responsibility to elect in a reasonable and prudent fashion.

Questions

1. By a Technical Correction enacted as part of the Tax Reform Act of 1986, Congress clarified section 643(e)(3) by specifying that the election must be made on an "all-or-nothing" basis, thereby precluding asset-by-asset elections. Why might Congress have chosen this less flexible alternative as the procedure for making a proper election, and is the correction a proper interpretation of the original statute?

2. Assume the trustee of a discretionary trust is authorized to make Tier 2 distributions as it deems appropriate, but is required to treat beneficiaries A and B equally. Thus, if the trustee determines that A needs funds, a distribution to A must be matched by an equal distribution to B. The trustee has decided to distribute Blackacre to beneficiary A and will make an equal distribution to beneficiary B of stock with a fair market value equal to the fair market value of Blackacre. What issue must the trustee consider in making these equal distributions and how, if at all, may the trustee deal with the problem(s) you foresee?

Three immediate results flow from making the section 643(e)(3) election. First, if basis carries over from the entity making the distribution, the holding period of the asset tacks under section 1223(1). The election to incur gain or loss should prevent this, based on the vision that election is as if a sale had occurred. While basis to the distributee under section 643(e)(1) is a carryover of the entity's stepped-up basis, tacking is not proper under the analogy of a deemed sale. This will seldom be significant, however, because gain or loss up to the time of distribution will have been realized by the entity.

A second immediate result of an election to incur gain (but not loss) is that realization by a trust (but not an estate) could constitute a recapture event under section 1239. As a result, gain may be converted to ordinary income. Because section 643(a)(3) (gain excluded from the computation of DNI) is applicable only with respect to *gains* from the sale of capital assets, the effect of recapture may be to cause this ordinary income to become part of DNI in a situation in which the gain realized would not be includible in DNI. If included in DNI, the result of recapture would include both a potentially higher tax bite (due to conversion of the character of the item), plus a larger potential carry out of income by virtue of a higher basis in the asset distributed and the increase in DNI caused by recapture.

A third immediate consequence of the election flows from section 643(e)(3)(A)(ii), by which realized gain or loss is deemed to be incurred on a sale between the entity and the distributee. As a consequence, distribution may be a section 469 passive asset disposition and, for both sections 469 and 267, if a trust (but not an estate) [1] makes the election, any loss would be deferred. See sections 267(b)(6) and 469(g)(1)(B). While election in such a situation would cause adjusted basis to be reduced to fair market value of the asset, this would not result in a lower carry out of income than if the loss had not been realized, because the carry out is limited under section 643(e) in all events to the lesser of adjusted basis or fair market value. While it is true that, by virtue of section 267(d), the loss is not lost if the asset is ultimately sold by the distributee at a gain (in which case the distributee may use the previously disallowed loss to offset gain on the subsequent sale), this preservation is relevant only if the asset is sold, at a gain. Section 469(g)(1)(B) will prevent the trust from claiming the passive activity loss until the year the related distributee sells the asset.

The issue that a trustee must confront is who should take advantage of the loss in such situations. If the trust can make the best use of the loss, the trustee should sell the asset and incur the loss for the benefit of the trust. If, however, it is appropriate to preserve the asset from sale outside the group consisting of the trust and the beneficiaries, or if the distributee can make best use of the loss, it is possible to preserve the loss for use by the distributee by simply distributing the asset in-kind and not making the section 643(e)(3) election. In either event, the result is better than under prior law because the loss is not lost under section 643(e) by virtue of distribution of the asset in-kind. Under prior law, Treasury Regulation section 1.661(a)–2(f)(3) would have wiped out the loss by virtue of its new basis rule, to the extent distribution carried out income equal to fair market value. Moreover, because the amount of income carried out will be the same regardless of the election made, this distribution alternative should be without tax consequence to the distributee. The ultimate conclusion based on this third consequence of the election is that, while estates may want in all events to make the election to recognize losses, trusts may never want

1. The related party transaction rules of section 267 are not applicable to estates, and this treatment would flow over to section 469 as well. Thus, an estate may elect to realize loss without adverse consequence. Indeed, some planners have suggested that section 643(e)(3) creates a new obligation on personal representatives to revalue all assets that may have declined in value during estate administration, in order to make the section 643(e)(3) election upon final distribution, thus benefiting from the loss even if the asset will be retained by the distributee. In some cases, it may prove to be more favorable to follow this approach than to elect alternate valuation under section 2032 in the case of estate assets that decline in value.

to make the election, preferring instead to actually sell and incur the loss or, alternatively, allow the distributee to sell and incur the loss, in each case preserving the loss from disallowance under section 267.

With respect to assets that have appreciated, planning relating to the section 643(e)(3) election must consider whether the entity or the distributee is best suited to incur any gain on sale of the asset. If the beneficiary is in a lower income tax bracket than the entity, or has losses that may be used to offset any gain, it may be preferable for the fiduciary to distribute the asset in-kind, not make the section 643(e)(3) election, and permit the beneficiary to incur the gain. Were the transfer of the appreciated asset moving in the other direction (into the entity), section 644 would prevent this shifting of gain to a lower tax bracket taxpayer unless sale were delayed at least two years (as discussed in Chapter Eight). There is, however, (yet) no provision of the Code that will prevent this "reverse–644" gaming when the entity distributes an appreciated asset to a beneficiary for the same gain shifting purpose.

Perhaps the biggest question surrounding the section 643(e)(3) election is whether gain incurred on a deemed sale by the entity will be included in DNI and thereby increase the amount of income that may be carried out on any distribution. The carry out would be increased in two ways. The first is because the asset would have a higher basis (reflecting realization of the gain). The second would be due to any increase in the amount of DNI available for distribution, to the extent gain is includible therein. Consider the effect of the following ruling on this issue.

REVENUE RULING 68–392

1968–2 Cumulative Bulletin 284

* * *

Under the will of *A*, assets with a fair market value of 268*x* dollars were transferred to a trust for the benefit of his daughter, *B*. The testator directed that 24*x* dollars be paid annually to *B* for her lifetime, first out of income of the trust and if necessary, out of corpus.

For its first taxable year, the trust had income of 10*x* dollars, all of which was distributed by the trustee to *B*. In satisfaction of her right to receive an additional 14*x* dollars, *B* agreed to accept securities that were part of trust corpus. The securities had a fair market value of 14*x* dollars at the time of distribution and a basis of 12*x* dollars in the hands of the trust.

The governing instrument is silent on the treatment of capital gains. However, in the absence of a provision in the trust instrument, local law requires that such gains be allocated to corpus.

The transaction whereby the trustee distributed securities to *B* in partial satisfaction of the annuity payments, to the extent of their fair market value, is treated as though the trustee sold the securities to *B* for cash, and immediately thereafter the trustee distributed the entire proceeds from the sale to her. Since the securities distributed had a fair market value in excess of their basis at the time of distribution, this excess must be included in the gross income of the trust as capital gain.

* * *

Section 643(a)(3) of the Code provides, in part, that gains from the sale or exchange of capital assets shall be excluded from distributable net income to the extent that such gains are allocated to corpus and are not (A) paid, credited, or required to be distributed to any beneficiary during the taxable year, or (B) paid, permanently set aside, or to be used for the purposes specified in section 642(c) of the Code.

Section 1.643(a)–3(a) of the regulations provides that gains from sale or exchange of capital assets are ordinarily excluded from distributable net income, and are not ordinarily considered as paid, credited, or required to be distributed to any beneficiary unless they are:

(1) Allocated to income under the terms of the governing instrument or local law by the fiduciary on its books or by notice to the beneficiary,

(2) Allocated to corpus and actually distributed to beneficiaries during the taxable year, or

(3) Utilized (pursuant to the terms of the governing instrument or the practice followed by the fiduciary) in determining the amount which is distributed or required to be distributed.

The first instance under the regulations for inclusion in distributable net income requires that capital gains be allocated to income under the terms of the governing instrument or local law by the fiduciary on its books or by notice to the beneficiary. This requisite is not met in the instant case since the governing instrument is silent as to allocation of capital gains and, in the absence of a provision therein, local law requires that capital gains be allocated to corpus.

The second instance under the regulations for inclusion in distributable net income requires that capital gains be allocated to corpus and actually distributed to beneficiaries during the taxable year. As illustrated by Examples (3), (4) and (5) of section 1.643(a)–3(d) of the regulations, this provision regarding the inclusion of capital gains in distributable net income applies only where there is a distribution required by the terms of the governing instrument upon the happening of a specified event. In the instant case, such a condition for inclusion of capital gains in distributable net income is not present.

The third instance under the regulations for inclusion in distributable net income requires that capital gains be utilized (pursuant to the terms of the governing instrument or the practice followed by the fiduciary) in determining the amount that is distributed or required to be distributed. In the instant case, capital gains are not being utilized pursuant to the terms of the governing instrument in determining the amount that is distributed or required to be distributed. Furthermore, since this is the first taxable year of the trust, capital gains are not utilized pursuant to the practice followed by the fiduciary in determining the amount that is distributed or required to be distributed.

Accordingly, under the facts set forth above, where income of the trust for its first taxable year is insufficient to make the annuity payment to *B* and in accordance with the agreement with her, the trustee distributes securities to her in partial satisfaction of the annuity payment, capital gain * * * resulting from the transaction is includible in gross income of the trust but is excludable from its distributable net income.

B is required to include 10*x* dollars (the trust's distributable net income as determined under section 643 of the Code) in gross income as ordinary income. Also *B* is treated as having received 14*x* dollars (such amount being in excess of the trust's distributable net income) as a distribution of corpus.

The basis of the securities in the hands of *B* is 14*x* dollars representing fair market value on the date of transfer.

Consistent with repeal of the capital gain throwback rule as part of the Tax Reform Act of 1976, section 643(a)(3) specifies that capital gain is not includible in DNI unless the gain is paid, credited or required to be distributed during the current year, (or it is set aside or distributed to or for the benefit of a charity). Treasury Regulation section 1.643(a)–3(a) lists three general circumstances (excluding for these purposes the effect of gains allocated to charity) in which gains will be includible in DNI.

First, gain is includible in DNI to the extent the gain is allocated to income under either local law or the governing instrument. Under the Principal and Income Act in most states, this is not the dictate of local law *except* to the extent allocation of a share of any gain is required pursuant to an unproductive or underproductive property provision, which was the case in Letter Ruling 8431004. Most un(der)productive property statutes require that a portion of the proceeds of a sale be allocated to income to compensate for delayed sale of an investment that did not generate a reasonable rate of income. With the exception of these provisions, few garden variety trusts and virtually no estates will encounter a dictate that capital gains be allocated to income. Nevertheless, it would be permissible (and may prove attractive) to alter the local law allocation of capital gain to corpus, and this usually would cause no significant problems unless a gift tax computation is involved and depends upon valuation methods that assume gains will be allocated to corpus.

Second, gain is includible in DNI to the extent the gain is allocated to corpus but actually distributed to beneficiaries during the current tax year. This would be the case if the trust or estate terminated in the year the gain was incurred. The interesting question is whether this is the case in the event of a "partial" termination, either by virtue of a directed distribution of a portion of the trust occurring on a stated event or by virtue of an asset being distributed in the trustee's discretion. While there is very little authority on the entire question of the proper interpretation of section 643(a)(3), what little there is indicates that normal distributions will not qualify under this second provision to cause gain to be added to DNI. For example, Letter Ruling 8429005 generally defines the concept of "termination" for purposes of section 643(a)(3), stating that an entity is "considered terminated if all the assets have been distributed, except for amounts retained to meet unascertained or contingent liabilities and expenses," which is not the situation presented on a discretionary distribution or even on a partial termination dictated by the terms of the document. In addition, a number of rulings indicate that capital gains incurred upon a partial termination or incident to distribution of an asset in kind are the *last* items in corpus to be distributed, not the first nor even a proportionate amount.[2]

Finally, gain is includible in DNI to the extent the gain is utilized to determine the amount (required to be) distributed. As interpreted by several provisions in the regulations, this third condition is met in either of two circumstances. First, it occurs upon an event specified in the document that requires distribution. See Treasury Regulation section 1.643(a)–3(d) Examples (3) and (4). Second, it occurs if there is a practice customarily followed by the fiduciary of distributing capital gains, such as customary distribution of the exact net proceeds of a sale of trust or estate properties. See Treasury Regulation section 1.643(a)–3(d) Example (1). It is not likely that the former circumstance will exist with respect to capital gains incurred by virtue of the section 643(e)(3) election. This is because, if distribution were required, it is usually going to be the case that gain will be incurred in satisfaction of the requisite distribution (and not due to the section 643(e)(3) election), or the distribution will qualify as a section 663(a) specific bequest and, therefore, will qualify as an exception to section 643(e) under subsection (4) thereof. It is difficult to conjure a situation in which a required distribution, measured in whole or in part by the amount of gain, does not fit either of these two scenarios.

However, there is an argument that the second condition (customary distribution of the exact proceeds) is routinely met if it is distribution of the appreciated asset that generates the gain, because it is in

2. See Letter Ruling 8506005 (gain not deemed distributed unless distribution was required under trust terms upon the occurrence of a specified event) and Letter Ruling 8429005 (distribution deemed to carry out a limited amount of gain, but only because the amount remaining in trust after the distribution was less than the total amount of capital gains allocated to corpus). And see Letter Ruling 6404234660A (specifying that "the coincidence of a capital gain which is allocated to principal and a discretionary distribution of that amount of principal does not make the gain includible in distributable net income," this ruling being responsive to the suggestion that distribution and realization at the same time is sufficient to regard the gain as distributed and, therefore, includible in DNI).

such a case that it most appears that the proceeds of the sale are in fact being distributed. Existing authority, slim as it is, probably rejects this latter argument as well. In a sense, Revenue Ruling 68–392 and Letter Ruling 8324002 both illustrate this proposition. Each ruling concludes that gain is not includible in DNI when realized in the first year of an estate's administration, followed immediately by distribution of an amount equal to the net capital gain, because there could be no established fiduciary practice to distribute gain in the first year of estate administration. An unstated conclusion in each appears to be that the coincidence of distribution of the exact amount of the gain is not itself sufficient to satisfy the condition of customary distribution according to fiduciary practice; something more is required.

Letter Ruling 8105028 is perhaps the closest authority to the type of situation presented under section 643(e)(3). In this ruling the executor of an estate sold several securities at a gain. Later in the same year the executor distributed assets in-kind, together having a fair market value in excess of the amount of gain recognized on the previous sales, and argued that the gain was includible in DNI under the authority of Treasury Regulation section 1.643(a)–3(a). In rejecting this contention, the Service determined that the executor had not established a practice of taking capital gain into account in determining the amount of the distribution, citing Revenue Ruling 68–392 and making reference to the short duration of the estate. In addition, the Service stated that the gains were not themselves actually distributed, because the assets distributed in-kind "could have been distributed * * * regardless of any gain recognized by the estate." This last notation seems particularly relevant in the case of a section 643(e)(3) election to incur gain because distribution is made during the year with the election to incur gain not being made until *after* year end, when filing the tax return for that year. In this sense it could be argued that the gain is not taken into account in determining the amount of the distribution.

To the suggestion that the fiduciary *knows* the amount of the gain at the time of distribution, and may make distribution in anticipation of that gain, the Service is likely to respond that the timing is wrong for gain to be included in determining the amount of any distribution. Thus, the Service could draw an analogy to cases such as Kenan v. Commissioner, 114 F.2d 217 (2d Cir.1940), that would regard the realization of gain as if the fiduciary had distributed cash, followed by the distributee's purchase of the asset from the fiduciary using that cash, causing the gain, in which case the gain would not be deemed considered by the fiduciary in determining the amount of the distribution. While Revenue Ruling 68–392 treats the distribution as if the fiduciary sold the asset first and then distributed the proceeds, which the distributee subsequently used to purchase the asset, the conclusion reached there was that the gain was not includible in DNI, presumably meaning that the coincidence of gain and distribution will not result in inclusion in DNI.

Because none of this is clear, perhaps the only certain conclusion regarding the question whether DNI includes gain incurred on an election under section 643(e)(3) is that it will require regulations or a specific ruling on point before fiduciaries and tax planners are sure. The treatment of losses incurred under section 643(e)(3) is more definite, however, because losses are includible in DNI only to the extent applied against gains that are also included in DNI. The effect is that losses are partially "enjoyed" by those beneficiaries who receive DNI for the year, to the extent (if any) the losses are applied to offset gains that are actually included in DNI. Otherwise, however, losses are not regularly reflected in DNI.

Question

Given the effects of making the section 643(e)(3) election and the overall operation of section 643(e), what factors might a fiduciary want to consider in dealing with distributions under the new rules?

TERMINATING DISTRIBUTIONS

Read Code section 642(h).

Read Regulation section 1.642(h).

Additional aspects of trust and estate distributions relate to termination of the entity and allocation of deductions available to the trust or estate. Ordinarily, deductions allowable to a trust or an estate only indirectly benefit income recipients by reducing taxable income and, thus, DNI. Deductions exceeding taxable income, however, do not pass out to the beneficiaries and are wasted unless constituting a section 172(a) net operating loss or a section 1212(b)(1) capital loss carryover to the entity's next tax year. As illustrated in the following materials, however, deductions (such as a termination fee) that exceed income, along with any net operating loss or capital loss carryover not utilized by the entity, pass through to the beneficiaries under section 642(h) in the year of the entity's termination, in most respects as if the entity had not existed for the year. In addition, passive activity losses ought to carry out with the underlying passive activity investment if distribution is not regarded as a section 469(g) disposition. Note, however, that not all deductions will carry over. For example, by virtue of the parenthetical clause in section 642(h)(2), the section 642(b) deduction in lieu of the personal exemption and the section 642(c) charitable deduction do not carry over. See Treasury Regulation section 1.642(h)–2(a).

REVENUE RULING 58–191

1958–1 Cumulative Bulletin 149.

Advice has been requested (1) whether income received by a beneficiary from a trust engaged in farming may be used by the beneficiary in computing his allowable deduction for soil or water conservation expenses for his own form, and (2) whether, upon termination of the trust, the beneficiary may claim a deduction for such expenses of the trust which exceed the gross income of the trust for its year of termination.

Section 175 of the Internal Revenue Code of [1986] provides generally that a taxpayer engaged in the business of farming may treat expenditures which are paid or incurred by him during the taxable year for the purpose of soil or water conservation in respect of land used in farming as expenses which are not chargeable to capital account. Under the Code, any expenditure properly so treated is allowed as a deduction, but the deduction thus allowed is limited to an amount which does not exceed 25 per cent of the gross income derived by the taxpayer from farming in the taxable year. However, the excess of such expenditures over 25 per cent of the gross income derived from farming in the taxable year is deductible in succeeding taxable years to the extent that, when combined with like deductions in a succeeding taxable year, the total does not exceed 25 percent of the gross income from farming for such succeeding year.

* * *

* * * [S]ection 1.642(h) of the Income Tax Regulations provides separate treatment for unused loss carryovers to the beneficiaries on termination of a trust or an estate, and for deduction by the beneficiaries of the excess of deductions over gross income of the trust or estate in its last taxable year. Section 1.642(h)–1 of the regulations provides, in part, that if, on the final termination of an estate or trust, a net operating loss carryover or a capital loss carryover would be allowable to the estate or trust in a taxable year subsequent to the taxable year of termination but for the termination, the carryovers are allowed under section 642(h)(1) of the Code to the beneficiaries succeeding to the property of the estate or trust.

Section 1.642(h)–2 of the regulations provides, in part, that if, on the termination of an estate or trust, the estate or trust has for its last taxable year, deductions (other than for personal exemption or relating to charitable contributions) in excess of gross income, the excess is allowed under section 642(h)(2) of the Code as a deduction to the beneficiaries succeeding to the property of the estate or trust; and that the deduction is allowable only in the taxable year of the beneficiary in which or with which the estate or trust terminates.

Accordingly, it is held that:

(1) In the absence of any specific provisions in the Code (other than section 642(h)) for a carryover of a deduction from the trust to the beneficiary, the excess of the soil or water conservation expenditures of the trust over 25 per cent of its gross income from farming does not follow the income to the beneficiary, whether or not such beneficiary has farm income separate from that of the trust.

(2) Where the trust has had soil or water conservation expenditures and such expenditures (to the extent deductible under section 175 of the Code) have entered into the computation of a net operating loss

carryover of the trust under section 172 of the Code, upon termination of the trust the beneficiary succeeding to its property would be entitled under section 642(h)(1) of the Code to the net operating loss carryover as thus computed subject to the limitations imposed by section 1.642(h)–2(b) and (c) of the regulations.

(3) If, on termination, the trust has for its last taxable year, deductions (including expenditures for soil or water conservation to the extent deductible under section 175 of the Code) in excess of gross income for such year, then such excess (including the aforesaid soil or water conservation expenditures to the extent deductible by the trust) is allowable under section 642(h)(2) of the Code as a deduction to the beneficiary succeeding to the property of the trust subject to the limitations imposed by section 1.642(h)–2(b) and (c) of the regulations.

(4) Since the trust for its last taxable year (as in any other taxable year) is not entitled to deduct soil or water conservation expenditures in excess of 25 per cent of its gross income for such taxable year derived from farming, the excess amounts which, except for the termination of the trust, would, under section 175(b) of the Code, carry over as deductions to successive years of the trust are lost to the beneficiary, since a deduction allowable under section 642(h)(2) of the Code to a beneficiary succeeding to the property of the trust is limited to the excess of allowable deductions of the trust over gross income for its last taxable year.

REVENUE RULING 57–31

1957–1 Cumulative Bulletin 201.

Advice has been requested whether excess deductions allowable to a residuary testamentary trust on the termination of an estate, which trust distributes all of its current income, will be available to the income beneficiary of the trust should such deductions exceed the gross income of the trust for its taxable year.

Section 642(h)(2) of the Internal Revenue Code of [1986] provides that any deductions (other than deductions for personal exemption and charitable contributions) in excess of the gross income of an estate or trust for its year of termination may be allowed as a deduction to the beneficiaries succeeding to the property of the estate or trust. A testamentary trust may be a legatee or beneficiary of an estate for purposes of section 642(h). * * *

* * *

If a testamentary trust has deductions in excess of its gross income after the allowance of deductions from an estate made available to it through section 642(h)(2), the amount in excess of the gross income would not be deductible by the income beneficiary of the trust. However, if the trust also terminates during the taxable year in which it is allowed the section 642(h)(2) deductions, the deductions in excess of its gross income will be available under section 642(h)(2) to the remaindermen succeeding to the property.

* * *

In addition, character of the items is the same for the beneficiaries as it was to the trust or estate,[3] deductions that would be disallowed to the entity because allocable to tax exempt income are similarly disallowed to the beneficiary,[4] and the number of years for carryforward of carryovers is the same as if the trust or estate had not terminated.[5] Unanswered is the question whether a deduction that the entity could claim but that the beneficiary could not (such as fees for administration, fully deductible by the entity under section 212 but subject to the 2% floor if incurred by an individual) are made subject to the limitation or are lost entirely when they pass out of the entity. Section 67(c) would appear to indicate that these items do not lose their deductibility by virtue of passing out of a trust or estate, but section 642(h) can be read as if the entity's deductions were original to the beneficiaries, in which case it might be argued that they should be subject to the same limitations as if the entity had not existed and the beneficiary had generated the items in the first instance.

Excepted by section 642(h)(2) from the carryout of excess deductions is the section 642(b) deduction in lieu of the personal exemption and any section 642(c) charitable deduction. Consider the dispute with respect to this latter exception, illustrated by the following case.

O'BRYAN v. COMMISSIONER

United States Tax Court, 1980.
75 T.C. 304.

NIMS, JUDGE:

* * *

This is a case of first impression. At issue is the interpretation and construction of section 642(h)(2), which provides as follows:

If on the termination of an estate or trust, the estate or trust has—

* * *

(2) for the last taxable year of the estate or trust deductions (*other than the deductions allowed under subsections (b) or (c)*) in excess of gross income for such year,

then such carryover or such excess shall be allowed as a deduction, in accordance with regulations prescribed by the Secretary, or his delegate, to the beneficiaries succeeding to the property of the estate or trust.

[Emphasis added.]

3. See, e.g., Treasury Regulation sections 1.642(h)–1(b) and 1.642(h)–2, preserving even the tax preference nature of items for purposes of the minimum tax on those preference items.

4. See Whittemore v. United States, 383 F.2d 824 (8th Cir.1967), rev'g 257 F.Supp. 1008 (E.D.Mo.1966).

5. Dorfman v. Commissioner, 294 F.2d 651 (2d Cir.1968), rev'g 48 T.C. 478 (1967), holding Treasury Regulation section 1.642(h)–1(b) invalid to the extent it reduces the number of carryover years.

The focal point of the dispute before us is the application of the parenthetical clause "(other than the deductions allowed under subsections (b) or (c))." Section 642(b) permits a $600 personal exemption deduction and section 642(c) permits a deduction for amounts paid or permanently set aside for a charitable purpose.

Like many simple rules, the rule contained in section 642(h)(2), when applied to a concrete set of facts, creates an enigma. We are told that no part of the charitable deduction may be included in "excess deductions," but we are not told how to determine whether, on facts such as ours, the excess of deductions over income actually includes any charitable deduction.

Respondent contends that section 642(h)(2) invokes a simple one-step procedure in which all deductions are totaled, except for the personal exemption and charitable contribution, and that figure is given first priority in reducing gross income to determine whether there are any excess deductions.[3]

Petitioner reads the section 642(h)(2) parenthetical clause as excluding the section 642(c) deduction, not from total deductions calculated under section 642(h)(2), but only from the amount determined to be the excess. Arithmetically, this translates into a two-step calculation: the first step is to determine the amount by which total deductions exceeds gross income, and the second step is to determine what amount of this excess consists of deductions other than the section 642(b) and (c) deductions. In essence, says petitioner, the amount by which total estate deductions exceed gross income is an excess deduction under section 642(h)(2) to the extent that the estate has deductions other than a section 642(c) deduction.[4]

From the above it is apparent that, regardless of the arguments made to support the respective positions, each party is simply asking us to afford priority to a preferred type of deduction in reducing estate gross income. If, under petitioner's theory, gross income is first to be

3. Respondent's computation is as follows:

a.	Gross income of estate		$879,446.55
	Less deductions:		
b.	Interest, taxes, fees, and miscellaneous expenses	($165,349.96)	
c.	Sec. 642(c) charitable deductions	0	
d.	Total deductions		(165,349.96)
e.	Excess of deductions over gross income (0 if line a exceeds line d)		0

4. The following computation results from petitioner's approach:

a.	Gross income of estate		$879,446.55
	Less deductions:		
b.	Interest, taxes, fees, and miscellaneous expenses	($165,349.96)	
c.	Sec. 642(c) deduction	(776,500.00)	
d.	Total deductions		(941,849.96)
e.	Excess of deductions over income		(62,403.41)
f.	Amount attributable to deductions other than sec. 642(c) deductions		(165,349.96)
g.	Deduction allowable to beneficiary (lower of e or f)		(62,403.41)

reduced (but not below zero) by the charitable deduction, the excess deductions allowable to the trust, and ultimately in fact to petitioner, must perforce consist of allowable deductions. Under respondent's theory, the reverse would be true.

There can be little argument that respondent's construction follows more comfortably the literal dictates of the statute. Petitioner asks the Court to look beyond a literal construction of the statute and to read section 642(h) in the context of the entire statutory scheme of subchapter J. Petitioner argues that her interpretation preserves the integrity of the section 642(c) charitable deduction and also balances the goal of section 642(h) to ameliorate wastage of deductions with what she perceives as the purpose of the parenthetical in section 642(h)(2) to prevent any charitable deduction from being passed from an estate or trust to a noncharitable beneficiary.

* * *

Petitioner has drawn on two themes present in subchapter J in an attempt to show her construction of section 642(h)(2) best implements policy considerations underlying subchapter J. One is the familiar axiom that Congress seeks to encourage charitable contributions and foster charitable organizations and that this policy is manifested in section 642(c). The second is that unused deductions for expenses incurred in the year of termination should be passed on to beneficiaries.

While these themes are present in subchapter J, countervailing considerations surface in section 642(h)(2). Charitable deductions are allowed "without limitation" on the estate side only for purposes of calculating the *estate's* taxable income. On the beneficiary side, the section 662(a) tier system imposes a substantial limitation by barring first-tier beneficiaries from gaining any tax benefit from the presence of a section 642(c) charitable distribution deduction. The structure of section 662 reflects a distinct lack of concern on the part of Congress for "wastage" of charitable deductions insofar as determining the tax liability of income beneficiaries.

In the instant case all the deductions, other than the section 642(b) personal exemption and the section 642(c) charitable deduction, have already been taken into account in determining the pool of income potentially taxable to beneficiaries. The only deduction that has been wasted here, i.e., that does not operate to reduce the income beneficiary's tax liability, is the section 642(c) deduction for charitable distributions. Given the lack of concern evinced by Congress in section 662 for wasted charitable deductions, we are not troubled by a reading of section 642(h)(2) which allows these deductions to go unused. Mathematically, this result is accomplished by excluding altogether the section 642(c) charitable deduction from the section 642(h)(2) computation, which is the construction of the statute called for by respondent.

Under the circumstances, we reject petitioner's argument that the policy considerations underlying subchapter J are best implemented by her reading of section 642(h)(2). In summary, we hold that to determine whether there are excess deductions available to beneficiaries under section 642(h)(2), deductions exclusive of the personal exemption under section 642(b) and the charitable deduction under section 642(c) are to be totaled and matched against the gross income of the terminating estate or trust. If the deductions so computed in fact exceed such gross income, then, and only then, will there be excess deductions as contemplated by section 642(h)(2).

For purposes of the section 642(h) pass through, Treasury Regulation section 1.642(h)–3 provides that any beneficiary receiving assets of the trust or estate that generated the deduction or that would abate or suffer any loss attributable to the net operating or capital losses is the beneficiary entitled to the pass through. In a typical estate this would be the residuary beneficiaries and, if there is no residue, any beneficiary whose pre-residuary amounts would next abate due to any losses in the estate. Similar principles are applied to trusts, under Treasury Regulation section 1.642(h)–3(d). Consequently, the remainder beneficiaries, not the income beneficiaries, are entitled to these benefits,[6] and any carry through to a trust becomes the trust's deduction, not its beneficiaries'.[7]

Questions

1. Assume an estate is distributable $10,000 to A, the residue equally to B and C. There is, however, only $9000 available in the entire estate. To whom is any section 642(h) entitlement allocable, and in what amounts or portions?

2. In the year of its termination an estate borrowed funds for investment purposes and incurred an interest expense. Assume that, under section 67(e), the interest expense would not be subject to the 2% floor on miscellaneous itemized deductions on the estate's income tax return. Unfortunately, under section 163(d), the estate does not have sufficient investment income to permit full deduction of the interest in the year it is paid. Upon termination of the estate, however, this expense will constitute a section 642(h) excess deduction and will pass out to beneficiary A, who has plenty of investment income in excess of investment interest. To what extent will the interest expense be deductible by A?

TRAPPING DISTRIBUTIONS

With respect to all distributions from an entity, not just those upon termination, significant planning opportunities are made possible by the income carry out rules and proper timing of distributions, as illustrated by the following ruling.

6. Revenue Ruling 59–392, 1959–2 C.B. 163.

7. Revenue Ruling 57–31, 1957–1 C.B. 201.

LETTER RULING 7809057

National Office Technical Advice Memorandum
November 30, 1977.

* * *

The taxpayer is the wife of the decedent. * * * Paragraph 6B of the will of the decedent provided for the transfer of the assets in his residuary estate to a trust under which the trustees are to invest and reinvest the assets and pay the income derived therefrom at least quarter-annually to his wife during her lifetime.

In 1973 and 1974, the executors of his estate made partial distributions of principal to the residuary trust created under paragraph 6B of his will. Various other distributions, not here in question, were also made during this time. The decedent's estate claimed a deduction each year under section 661(a) of the Internal Revenue Code of [1986] for the amounts distributed to the residuary trust for that year to the extent of the allocable portion of distributable net income. Pursuant to section 662 of the Code, the residuary trust included in its gross income each year the corresponding amount deducted by the estate under section 661(a) of the Code.

You contend that the distributions to the residuary trust are includible in the taxpayer's gross income because of the decision in *United States v. Britten,* 161 F.2d 921 (3d Cir.1947). It is your position that under *Britten* a testamentary trust may not be recognized during the period of administration. Thus, the distributions pass through the trust and are includible in the taxpayer's gross income.

* * *

Section 1.643(c)–1 of the regulations provides that a trust created under a decedent's will is a beneficiary of the decedent's estate.

With respect to his estate, Paragraph 7(5) of the decedent's will grants his executors, in their absolute discretion and without the prior consent of any court, the power, which the decedent intended to be construed in the "broadest possible manner", to make distributions in cash or in specific property real or personal, or an undivided interest therein, or partly in cash and partly in such property.

Under New York law, the executors are permitted to make partial distributions to testamentary trusts during the period of administration.

In *Britten,* the testator, after providing for certain specific devises and bequests, directed that the residuary estate be held in trust for the benefit of his wife and two children in three separate trusts. During the years 1934 and 1935 the executors sold certain securities from which capital gains were realized. The issue in *Britten* was whether the capital gains realized on these sales were taxable to the plaintiffs as executors or were taxable to the three trusts of which the plaintiffs were trustees.

The taxpayers in *Britten* argued that the capital gains were includible in the trusts' gross incomes because the trusts were created by the will and took effect at the testator's death. The court, however, held that under New Jersey law a testamentary trust did not vest immediately upon the death of the testator but required the occurrence of further events, and, therefore, the capital gains were includible in the gross income of the estate.

We do not believe that the "further events" necessary for recognition of the trust in *Britten* required that the estate be settled before the testamentary trusts could be recognized. At page 926, the court in *Britten* stated: "As we see it, appellee's position really amounts to an asserted purpose on their part to sell the stock as trustees. Under local law such a sale by them as trustees is both conceivable and permissible."

Thus, the partial distributions made in this case were valid under local law, were made in accordance with the terms of the decedent's will and constituted amounts properly paid to a beneficiary (within the meaning of section 1.643(c)–1 of the regulations) for purposes of section 661(a) and 662(a) of the Code.

* * *

Section 643(b) of the Code provides, in part, that the term "income", when not preceded by the words "taxable", "distributable net", "undistributed net", or "gross", means the amount of income of the estate or trust for the taxable year determined under the terms of the governing instrument and applicable local law.

Under New York law the distributions from the estate to the trust in this case are to be considered as receipts of "principal" rather than "income".

Based on the foregoing, we conclude that to the extent the distributions in this case do not exceed the distributable net income of the estate, such amounts are allowable as a deduction in computing the estate's taxable income under section 661(a) of the Code, and are includible in the gross income of the residuary trust created under paragraph 6B of decedent's will under section 662(a) of the Code. Furthermore, because these distributions are not "income" to the trust within the meaning of section 643(b) of the Code, they are not required to be included in the taxpayer's gross income under section 652 of the Code.

Often utilized by estates that make pour-over distributions to following trusts, but also available in instances in which one trust makes distributions to another trust, "trapping" distributions may fragment income among various potential taxpayers. If properly done, the result overall is minimization of the aggregate tax payable by reducing the marginal tax bracket at which the aggregate income is assessed. To illustrate, assume that Decedent's estate is to be divided among two trusts, one requiring distribution of all income annually (a simple trust, such as the typical marital deduction trust), the other permitting accumulations of income (a complex trust, such as the typical "bypass" trust), with Decedent's surviving spouse as beneficiary of both. Under Treasury Regulation section 1.643(c)–1, partial funding, and the trusts created thereby, is recognized for income tax purposes. Thus, if the estate were to partially fund the two trusts during a year prior to termination of the estate, there are four potential taxpayers in whose pockets income originally received by the estate might be taxed. By distributing fiduciary accounting principal to each trust, income may be carried out to those trusts and, because the principal will be classified and remain as principal in the trusts, that income will be "trapped" and taxable to the trusts. Coincidentally, the estate could distribute fiduciary accounting income to either trust which, because it similarly would be classified and remain as income in the trusts, may be distributed and taxed to the surviving spouse. By retaining a portion of total income, the estate itself would pay tax on the balance of the year's income, making it the fourth taxpayer. With added income beneficiaries of either trust, extra pockets are available for further fragmentation of income and minimization through equalization of the tax brackets of each.

The difficult aspect of these distributions is estimating the other income of each potential taxpayer and, based thereon, determining the amount of income to distribute in an effort to best equalize brackets and reduce taxes. An ancillary difficulty arises from the potential for inequality if one taxpayer is in a lower tax bracket and thus is intentionally saddled with a greater than proportionate share of income. An equitable adjustment may be required in this event, which is a topic that we address shortly. Further, with reduced income tax rates, the advantages to be gained may not justify the added costs of administration that are involved in this form of planning.

Question

If a fully funded inter vivos trust takes the place of a decedent's estate at death, how should income be taxed from that revocable grantor trust following the death of the grantor but before implementation of a direction to divide the principal of the trust into two or more irrevocable continuing trusts or distributive shares, assuming that the governing instrument is silent on the question? See Fleming, "Taxation of Income of Grantor Trusts After Death of Grantor and Before Implementation of Successor Trusts or Shares," 63 Ill.B.J. 78 (1974).

POST–MORTEM PLANNING

The following materials investigate distribution related topics, including selection of fiscal year and the sometimes inequitable consequences of distributions that are properly made to save taxes.

INCOME TAX OPPORTUNITIES AND PITFALLS IN ESTATE DISTRIBUTIONS

13 Real Property, Probate and Trust Journal 854 (1978).

FISCAL YEAR SELECTION

One of the most important initial decisions facing the executor is the selection of the fiscal year for the estate. As a new taxpayer, the estate may adopt the calendar year or any fiscal year for income tax purposes that does not end more than twelve months after the decedent's death. The estate's taxable year is particularly significant because net income of an estate is taxed to it if not required to be distributed currently or if not in fact distributed within the taxable year in which the estate receives the income.

In reaching a decision as to the selection of a fiscal year, the executor must forecast the flow of income to the estate, the timing of deductible expenses incurred by the estate, the rate of tax applicable to the estate, the income tax brackets of the beneficiaries of the estate to whom distributions ultimately will be made, and the likely time at which such distributions either will or can be made. Nonrecurring items of income that might result in "bunching" of income shortly after death could include items of income in respect of the decedent such as final payments of current compensation and initial installments of deferred compensation paid to the estate, accrued interest from the sale of Series E Savings Bonds, etc., as well as gains realized by the estate on the sale of assets by the executor to raise cash and preserve the value of the estate. * * *

If it is anticipated that there will be unusually large amounts of taxable income received by the estate during the first few months after death, the initial fiscal year of the estate might be ended after three or four months. Following this short initial fiscal year, "normal" amounts of income received by the estate can be taxed over regular twelve-month periods. Also, if a distribution of tangible personal property which is not specifically bequeathed will be made shortly after death, a fiscal year can be chosen ending right after the distribution to prevent too much income from being taxed to the beneficiaries. On the other hand, if the estate incurs large deductible expenses shortly after the decedent's death, the selection of a long initial fiscal year might be preferable, in order to utilize all of these deduction for income tax purposes. * * *

While electing a calendar year, intentionally or by default, can increase income tax paid by an estate or its beneficiaries, use of a fiscal year also can cause problems. First, bunching of income taxable to the beneficiaries in the year of termination of the estate can occur through inaccurate forecasting of the time of closing, the flow of income in the final year or the misuse of deductions available to the estate. Also, the executor must be aware of the need to coordinate the taxable year of the estate with the fiscal year of a Subchapter S corporation of which the estate may be a shareholder. [The same would be true of a partnership of which the decedent was a partner. Ed.] * * * Furthermore, to the extent income producing assets are distributed, the estate will be lost as a separate taxpayer in the future because thereafter the income from the assets will be taxed directly to the beneficiaries.

Where the residuary beneficiaries' top income tax brackets are likely to be significantly higher than that of the estate during the period of administration, the personal representative should delay the distribution of income-producing assets to the beneficiaries as long as possible. On the other hand, if nonincome producing assets such as tangible personal property and principal or vacation homes have not been specifically bequeathed and early distribution of these items is desired for nontax reasons, the personal representative should consider distributing them soon after death during a short initial fiscal year in which little or no taxable income will be carried out to the high bracket beneficiaries.

Conversely, where the top income tax bracket of the estate is likely to be significantly higher than the residuary beneficiaries' top brackets during administration, equalization of the top brackets could be achieved in at least two ways: (1) by making a partial distribution of an appropriate amount of the estate income to the beneficiaries each year, or (2) by distributing some of the income-producing assets to the beneficiaries during the short initial fiscal year of the estate. * * *

The equalization of the top income tax brackets of the estate and the residuary beneficiaries is difficult when the top brackets of the beneficiaries vary significantly. If a distribution is made to just one of several residuary beneficiaries because he is in a lower top bracket than the estate, the income tax impact, to the extent of the estate's taxable income, falls entirely on that beneficiary. If equalizing distributions are made to the other beneficiaries in a subsequent year when there is not as much DNI, or in such a way that the estate's income is divided among more than one beneficiary, the result may be that the beneficiary who received the earlier distribution, received less after taxes than the other equally entitled beneficiaries. Since the personal representative represents the interests of all beneficiaries and must not favor one over another, it is conceivable that a further equalizing distribution might have to be made to adjust for the disproportionate tax impact caused by the non pro rata distribution.

Ordinarily, the executor should make distributions on a pro rata basis, so as not to cause more than a pro rata share of the estate's net income to be taxed to one beneficiary as opposed to the other beneficiaries, even though some beneficiaries may be in higher top brackets than others. The recordkeeping problems can be difficult where non pro rata distributions of income-producing assets are made. Furthermore, the fact that less overall income tax is paid as the result of a non pro rata distribution is small consolation to a low income beneficiary who nevertheless pays more income tax than he would have if the distribution had been pro rata.

Proper timing of a distribution can also result in the deferral of a beneficiary's obligation to pay the tax on the income when the estate and the beneficiary have different tax years. This deferral of tax is possible because of the basic rule that estate income distributed to a beneficiary is taxable to him for his tax year in which or with which the taxable year of the estate ends.

* * *

In the final year of distribution, it is possible that the beneficiaries may be taxed on more than twelve months of income of the estate. This could happen, for example, where the estate's last full fiscal year ends early in the calendar year and its final short fiscal year ends late in the calendar year. In such a case, a calendar-year beneficiary would have to include in his return for the year in which or with which the estate's final fiscal year ends, the income for the last two fiscal years of the estate. This bunching effect can be avoided or minimized by electing a calendar year for the estate, or electing a fiscal year ending late in a calendar year and making sure that the estate's final short fiscal year ends in the calendar year after the calendar year of the preceding full fiscal year. For example, if the estate's fiscal year ends on September 30, 1978, and if the estate's final short fiscal year ends on March 30, 1979, beneficiaries will be taxed in 1978 on estate income distributed to them for the estate's fiscal year ending September 30, 1978, and will be taxed in 1979 on estate income distributed to them in the estate's final year. In addition, careful timing of terminating distributions and of the payment of expenses which reduce DNI serve to defer and reduce the impact of bunching.

The executor should also consider timing the final distribution and the payment of fees and expenses so they fall in the estate's final year and can be utilized by the beneficiaries, along with any unused net operating or capital loss carryovers, in their individual returns. This is particularly important where the beneficiaries are in high maximum tax brackets relative to the estate. Where a trust is the residuary beneficiary of the estate, the loss carryovers and excess deductions are not allowable directly to the beneficiary of the trust, but to the extent they reduce the distributable net income of the trust, the trust beneficiary receives an indirect benefit.

Disproportionate Residuary Distributions

Inequitable allocation of income tax on estate income occurs whenever estate distributions to residuary beneficiaries during any taxable year are not in the same proportion as the respective interests of the beneficiaries in the residuary estate. The Code requires the allocation of estate DNI among the beneficiaries in direct proportion to the amounts actually distributed during the taxable year, whether or not the distributions in that period were in the proportions specified in the will. Further, the Code does not distinguish between distributions of principal or income, in the accounting sense, so that a distribution of principal carries with it a proportionate distribution of DNI.

Thus if, in a taxable year of an estate, each of two equal residuary beneficiaries receives a $5,000 income distribution and one of them also receives a $5,000 principal distribution, the amount of estate income includible in the gross income of the principal recipient may be twice the amount includible in the gross income of the beneficiary who received only income. This is the result of the section 662(a) fiction that principal distributions are deemed to be distributions of income for income tax purposes.

Unfair income tax apportionment also results when a beneficiary of estate principal who does not share in estate income is nevertheless required to include estate income in his gross income. Such is the predicament of outright residuary beneficiaries of bequests that are not "specific" within the meaning of section 663(a)(1), and of trusts that receive so-called "trapping" distributions.

Clearly, it is sometimes possible to eliminate or reduce inequitable tax apportionment by making only proportionate distributions, although minor adjustments may be required because of the inability to determine the exact proportions in which beneficiaries are entitled to share. Such adjustments are ordinarily necessary when a tentative determination of a marital deduction formula fraction is made before completion of tax proceedings. Other devices to reduce inequity include the satisfaction of non-residuary bequests by distributions during years when the estate has little distributable net income, e.g., a short initial fiscal year of the estate or a year during which deducted administration expense payments nearly equal gross income of the estate.

However, proportionate distribution and other devices for the reduction of inequity as between beneficiaries often conflict with the goals of post-mortem tax planning. Disproportionate distributions may be intended to reduce the total income tax on a family group by evening out tax brackets. Similarly, disproportionately large distributions to older beneficiaries may be employed to reduce the prospective estates of members of an older generation by having them bear the burden of income taxes on income that will ultimately be paid to their descendants.

What may be viewed as inequitable as between beneficiaries from one point of view may be seen from another as the achievement of family tax planning goals. The situation would appear to call for planning designed to strike a proper balance between conflicting considerations for a beneficiary group.

HARKNESS v. UNITED STATES

United States Claims Court, 1972.
469 F.2d 310.

PER CURIAM:

In her 1955 federal income tax return, plaintiff included in her gross income $413,379.04 as income received during that year from her husband's estate. In 1961, the District Director of Internal Revenue for the Manhattan District, New York, took the position that, instead of such sum, plaintiff should have included the amount of $630,740.04, *i.e.*, an additional $217,361. * * *

Plaintiff's husband * * * gave plaintiff one-half of his residuary estate. The remaining half was, after the deduction therefrom of any "legacy, succession, transfer, estate or inheritance taxes payable by [the] estate with respect to any property disposed of by [the] Will or payable by any recipient of any such property," given, in equal shares, to the trustees of four testamentary trusts for the children of plaintiff and the decedent (*i.e.*, the issue of their or prior marriages). The will provided that such taxes "shall be paid by [the] Executors out of [the] estate as part of the expenses of administration thereof," with the proviso that "no part of such taxes shall be deducted from or payable out of the one-half (½) of [the] residuary estate" which the decedent bequeathed to plaintiff.

During 1955, and prior to the ultimate distribution of the residuary estate, the executors made distributions to the five beneficiaries thereof in the total sum of $36,004,082.23. Of this amount plaintiff, by eleven payments, received $27,467,768.51. The four trusts, by ten payments to each, received the balance of $8,436,295.75 (in equal shares of approximately $2,134,000). All the distributions were in the form of cash, stocks and bonds. None of the distributions were required by the will to be made prior to the ultimate distribution of the residuary estate.

The federal fiduciary income tax return filed by the executors on behalf of the estate showed distributable net income for 1955 in the amount of $1,005,682.94. A deduction of $826,758.68 was shown on the return for distributions of such income to the five residuary estate beneficiaries, the difference of $178,924.26 between such two figures consisting of tax-exempt income (and expenses allocable thereto).

Section 662(a)(2)(B) of the Internal Revenue Code of [1986] (26 U.S.C. § 662(a)(2)(B) (1958)) provides that, where the amounts distributed to all beneficiaries of an estate accumulating income or distributing corpus exceed the distributable net income of the estate, each beneficiary shall include in his gross income an amount which bears the same ratio to distributable net income as the total amount distributed to him bears to the total of the amounts distributed to all the beneficiaries.

The amount of $27,467,768.51 which plaintiff received in 1955 from the residuary estate equaled 76.2907 percent of the total amount of

$36,004,082.23 distributed to all beneficiaries during such taxable year. Since such total amount distributed exceeded the distributable net income, the District Director concluded that the provisions of Section 662(a)(2)(B) were applicable and accordingly applied the same percentage to the taxable distributable net income of the estate, the resulting figure being regarded as the amount which plaintiff should have included in her gross income. Application of such 76.2907 percent to the taxable distributable net income figure of $826,758.68 produces the aforementioned figure of $630,740.04 as the amount the District Director concluded plaintiff was required by the statute to have included in her gross income. The inclusion of such amount in plaintiff's gross income produced the additional income tax which is the subject of this suit.

Plaintiff contends that, pursuant to accurate accounting by the executors in calculating the amount of the estate corpus and income which they distributed to the five beneficiaries in 1955, she in fact actually received during the year only the taxable amount of $413,379.34, which amount was but one-half of the taxable distributable net income, and not 76.2907 percent thereof, the figure that the statutory formula produces. Such accounting in the administration of the estate was, plaintiff says, in no way tax motivated, but was in accordance with common practices followed at that time by executors in New York in the administration of estates, and was permitted by the terms of the will and applicable local law. Furthermore, she points out, the accounts of the executors for the year 1955, which set forth the income distributions to plaintiff and the four trusts on a basis of one-half to plaintiff and the other half to the trusts, were judicially settled and allowed by the Surrogate Court of New York County, New York.

Although the approximately $27,500,000 paid to plaintiff during the year greatly exceeded the aggregate amount of approximately $8,500,000 paid to the four trusts, each of such total payments concededly consisting of both corpus and income, plaintiff says that such unequal amounts nevertheless included the equal amounts of $413,379.34 of taxable net income. For this result, plaintiff relies upon the manner in which the executors made their distributions of what they designated as "corpus." The executors, in accordance with a common New York practice, made simultaneous distributions of "principal" and "income" among all the residuary legatees on a basis proportionate to their respective interests in the residuary estate. Further, since here the will directed that all legacy, succession, transfer, estate, or inheritance taxes (sometimes collectively referred to as "death taxes") were to be paid as administration expenses of the estate, but with plaintiff's share of the residuary estate to be undiminished thereby, whenever the executors made any such tax payments (which were, according to their accounting, entirely out of corpus), they also made, again following a common New York practice where wills provided for payment of death taxes out of one or more shares of the residue but not out of one or more other shares, "corpus" distributions to the plaintiff simultaneously with and in the same amounts as such tax payments. Thus, these simultaneous distributions to plaintiff always served, says plaintiff, to keep the remaining corpus interests of the plaintiff and the four trusts in the residuary estate in equal balance, with such equal corpus shares therefore always generating equal amounts to income. The result of adopting these simultaneous distribution practices was the avoidance of complicated calculations of shares of income earned, over varying periods of time, by unequal shares of principal (or by undistributed income). (In this case the decedent's will specifically provided that the income should be distributed proportionately to the residuary legatees, and that if distribution of the residuary estate was not made simultaneously, "an adjustment of the income shall be made by my Executors.") To illustrate, when, on January 1, 1955, the executors distributed $1,125,000 to each of the trusts—amounts which the executors designated as coming entirely from corpus—they simultaneously paid plaintiff $4,500,000, also designated as a corpus distribution. And when, on February 8, 1955, they paid $4,310,000 on account of the New York estate tax, they distributed the identical amount (again designated as principal on their accounts) to plaintiff. Similarly, when on November 14, 1955, they paid $14,621,454.81 on account of the federal estate tax, plus an amount aggregating $3,524,558.49 to the four trusts, such sums totaling $18,146,013.29, they distributed the identical total sum to plaintiff (all amounts again being designated as coming entirely out of principal). In accordance with the will, the New York and federal estate tax payments were deducted from the trusts' aggregate one-half interest in the residuary estate. The several 1955 distributions to plaintiff and the four trusts which the executors designated as distributions of estate income were so calculated by the executors that the amount of such income distributed to plaintiff on any date equaled the aggregate amount distributed to the trusts on the same date.

It is on the above basis that plaintiff argues she actually received only one-half of the distributable net income of the estate in 1955, and not 76 percent.

In a situation such as the instant one, plaintiff contends, Section 662(a)(2)(B) was not intended to be applicable for the formula there prescribed would attribute to plaintiff income which she in fact did not receive. She should not, she argues, have attributed to her more than her actual share of estate income simply because the executors, in their authorized discretion, made principal distributions to her in order to balance the death tax payments and other principal distributions to the trusts. The purpose of the statutory provision here involved was, she contends, to prevent fiduciaries, where the estate had principal, current income, and accumulated income, from controlling tax consequences by manipulating distributions, as, for instance, making distributions designated as coming from "income" to beneficiaries in low income tax brackets, while distributions designated as coming from "principal" are made to beneficiaries in high brackets, and therefore not taxable at all.

There was no intent here on the part of the executors, she argues, to gain any kind of income tax advantage for plaintiff.

These contentions cannot be accepted as justifying recovery. There can be no doubt but that plaintiff's situation falls squarely within the literal provisions of Section 662(a)(2)(B), and plaintiff is not understood to contend otherwise. The nub of her contention is that the payments here involved should not be treated as being covered by the statute because the executors' actions were not tax motivated. Even so, the section applies. Clear statutory coverage of this kind, based upon a presumption that any distribution is deemed to be a distribution of the estate's income to the extent of its income for the year, does not and cannot be made to depend on such intangible factors as the subjective intent of executors.

Section 662(a)(2)(B) was specifically intended, for the purposes of that section, "to avoid the necessity for tracing of income." Such tracing was required by the 1939 Code, which provided that distributions by an estate or trust to its beneficiaries were taxed to the beneficiaries for the taxable year in which they received the distributions only if the distributions were made from the current income of the estate or trust. As shown, this lent itself to various kinds of manipulations by executors in the labeling of estate moneys as "income" or "principal." To eliminate such manipulations and tax consequences based upon such estate tax accounting designations of what was "principal" and "income" and from which source a distribution had been made, the "tracing" requirement was, for such distribution purposes, eliminated. Instead, "[t]he beneficiary's proportionate share of the distributable net income * * * is determined by taking the same fractional part of [the] distributable net income * * * as the * * * amounts * * * distributed to him * * * bear to the total of [the] amounts * * * distributed to all beneficiaries." [8] In short, Congress

8. 3 U.S.C.Cong. & Adm.News, *supra* n. 6, at pp. 4340, 4990. The portions of the House and Senate Reports here involved are identical. *Id.*, at pp. 4339–40, 4989–90. In pertinent part, they stated:

> Subsection (a) provides that the beneficiary of an estate or trust * * * must include in gross income any amounts paid, credited, or required to be distributed to him for the taxable year of the estate or trust; however, the amount so includible may not exceed the beneficiary's proportionate share of the distributable net income. The effect of limiting the taxation of a beneficiary to his proportionate share of the distributable net income is to preserve the conduit principle by providing that all distributions * * * from an estate or trust will be taxable but not to an extent in excess of the taxable income of the estate or trust * * *. It is thus possible largely to avoid the necessity for tracing of income which exists generally under existing law. Instead of determining whether a particular distribution represents amounts of current or accumulated trust income, this revision, broadly speaking, provides that any distribution is considered a distribution of the trust or estate's current income to the extent of its taxable income for the year. This principle is similar to the determination of whether a dividend has been distributed, i.e., that every distribution made by a corporation is deemed to be out of earnings and profits to the extent thereof and from the most recently accumulated earnings and profits.
>
> * * *
>
> If the estate or trust pays * * * to beneficiaries amounts other than income which is required to be distributed currently, paragraph (2) provides that these

wished to establish an easily useable formula, and to avoid both the necessity of "tracing" and an inquiry into the subjective intention of executors or trustees. As was pointed out in Manufacturers Hanover Trust Co. v. United States, 312 F.2d 785, 793, 160 Ct.Cl. 582, 596, cert. denied, 375 U.S. 880, 84 S.Ct. 150, 11 L.Ed.2d 111 (1963):

> * * * Around this concept of "distributable net income" the Code builds its provisions for (a) the deduction allowed the trust for its current distributions to the beneficiaries, and (b) the distributions which the beneficiaries must include in their own gross incomes. "Thus, distributable net income has been termed the measuring rod or yardstick to be employed in determining, on the one hand, the maximum deduction for distributions which may be allowed to the estate or trust and for gauging, on the other hand, the extent to which beneficiaries may be taxable on the distributions." 6 Mertens "Law of Federal Income Taxation" § 36.04.

We accept plaintiff's contention that there were no tax motivations on the part of the executors in making the distributions at the times and in the amounts they did, and that they made the "balancing" corpus distributions to plaintiff only to avoid complicated calculations of estate income due to the beneficiaries which would result from their having disproportionate interests in the residuary estate.[9] The fact nevertheless remains that, by making the discretionary "balancing" distributions as they did—required neither by the will nor state law—plaintiff received, under their estate accounting, less of the distributable net income than she probably otherwise would have. There is no showing that—either by not making distributions until the estate was wound up finally, or otherwise—the residuary estate could not have been so managed as to produce the same result as the statutory formula. Thus, in that sense (and not in the sense of tax avoidance), the distributions were "manipulated" so that plaintiff, who received over 75 percent of the 1955 payments, is nevertheless said to have received in that year only 50 percent of the taxable distributable net income. On its face and as its purpose is shown by its development and legislative history, the statute was designed to prevent such a result for tax purposes. Indeed, the statutory formula could be considered as providing the more natural and logical result—income earned during the administration of the residuary estate is allocated to the beneficiaries in the same ratio as their interest in the corpus of such estate. Generally, of course, various percentages of corpus will produce like

other amounts * * * are includible in the gross income of the recipient beneficiaries but only to the extent of each beneficiary's proportionate share of the distributable net income * * *. * * * The beneficiary's proportionate share of the distributable net income * * * is determined by taking the same fractional part of such distributable net income * * * as the other amounts paid * * * bear to the total of other amounts paid * * * to all beneficiaries. * * *

9. Such as would occur after the death taxes were paid and deducted from the shares of the trusts, thereby diminishing the interests of the trusts in the residuary estate from the dates of such payments, with proportionate diminutions in the income which would be produced after such dates from such diminished shares.

percentages of income. It is thus plain that plaintiff's situation is, by the unambiguous provisions thereof, covered by the statute and although recognizing, of course, the difficulties involved in envisaging every specific situation that could arise under general statutory language, it would nevertheless appear to constitute the type of situation that Congress intended should be covered.

Plaintiff further contends that, even if Section 662(a) is applicable, its formula was erroneously applied because the death taxes should be included in the "amounts properly paid, credited, or required to be distributed to * * * beneficiaries." Crediting the trusts with such taxes as if they constituted distributions to the trusts would result in plaintiff and the trusts receiving equal total amounts. Accordingly, they would, under the statutory formula, be considered as having received equal amounts of the taxable distributable net income.

Plaintiff's basis for treating the payment of the death taxes as distributions to the trusts is based upon the provisions of Regulations § 1.662(a)–4 (26 C.F.R.) that "[a]ny amount which, pursuant to the terms of a will * * * is used in full or partial discharge or satisfaction of a legal obligation of any person is included in the gross income of such person under section 662(a) * * * (2) * * * as though directly distributed to him as a beneficiary, * * *." Since the taxes were not deductible from or payable out of plaintiff's one-half of the residuary estate, they therefore were, argues plaintiff, a charge upon, or obligation of, the remaining one-half passing to the trusts. As such an obligation, they should, plaintiff says, be considered, under the Regulations, as expenditures made on behalf of the trusts.

This contention too cannot be sustained. The death tax moneys never constituted a part of, nor were they ever incorporated in, the trusts. The will bequeathed one-half of the residuary estate to the trusts "*after* the deduction therefrom of all of the [death] taxes * * *." (Emphasis supplied.) There is, therefore, no warrant for adding to the amounts paid to the trusts the amount of the death taxes, an amount which was never paid or payable to the trusts and which the trusts were, under the will, never to receive. Furthermore, these taxes were the legal obligations of the estate, and not of the trusts, the will specifically so recognizing and providing that such taxes, "payable by my estate * * * shall be paid * * * out of my estate as part of the expenses of administration thereof * * *." The taxes were a "charge" upon, or an "obligation" of, the trusts only in the loose sense that, in calculating the net amount of the residuary estate which the trusts were to receive, the amount of the taxes was to be deducted from the share left to the trusts. They were not a "legal obligation" of the trusts in the sense used by the regulation upon which plaintiff relies.

The trusts received $8,536,313.72 from the estate in 1955. It is such amount that is properly to be considered as the amount "properly paid, credited, or required to be distributed to" them under the statute. The $18,931,454.81 in death taxes paid during the year by the executors, described by the will as part of the administration expenses of the estate, were not "amounts properly paid, credited, or required to be distributed to * * * beneficiaries" within the meaning of the statute or the regulation.

* * *

EQUITABLE ADJUSTMENTS IN POSTMORTEM INCOME TAX PLANNING: AN UNREMITTING DIET OF *WARMS*

Dobris,* 65 Iowa Law Review 103 (1979).

> *"Very delicate, and often very intricate questions arise in the adjustment of the rights and duties of the different parties in the inheritance."*

Postmortem tax planning under the Internal Revenue Code of [1986] is a matter of substantial concern in estate administration because of the tax savings available with proper planning. Postmortem, or after death, tax planning is the grand label applied to the intricate process of maximizing for estates and beneficiaries the tax opportunities that lie in the counterworkings of state fiduciary power law, state fiduciary accounting law, and the complex Internal Revenue Code provisions that pertain to taxation of estate and trust income.[2]

In an effort to obtain maximum tax advantage it is easy to overlook the problem created when tax savings are achieved at a cost to a particular beneficiary. The problem can arise, for example, under section 642(g) of the Internal Revenue Code. Many estate expenses can be deducted as either estate tax deductions or income tax deductions. Section 642(g) forces an executor to elect to take deductible estate expenditures as either death tax deductions on the death tax return or as income tax deductions on the estate's annual fiduciary income tax returns. The expenditure will usually be allocated to, and paid from, the estate principal account. Therefore, executors often use the deduction on the death tax return because it is a principal return. However, the deduction will often save more taxes if it is taken on a fiduciary income tax return. Thus, the use of a deduction paid from the principal account on a fiduciary income tax return saves more money, but causes inequity in those situations where principal goes to one beneficiary and income goes to another—where the principal account makes the expenditure, but the deduction benefits the income account. This inequity is caused by the uncorrelated relationship of the law of

* Professor of Law, University of California, Davis. B.A. 1963, Yale College; LL.B. 1966, University of Minnesota. * * *

2. The tax planning process is similar for trusts. In this Article the expression "postmortem tax planning" is used interchangeably with the expression "fiduciary tax planning." * * *

fiduciary administration, the law of fiduciary accounting, and federal tax law. The numerous tax problems and opportunities that ensue form the basis of the arcane art of postmortem tax planning.

The 1955 case of *Estate of Warms* [10] presented the first opportunity for a court to deal with this problem. The fiduciaries in *Warms* took deductible expenditures on a fiduciary income tax return rather than on the death tax return. More taxes were saved, but the deductible expenditures came out of the principal account under standard fiduciary accounting rules, with the income account receiving the advantage. The court applied principles of equity and required the income account to transfer to the principal account the lost value of the deduction, but permitted the income account to keep the advantage of the deduction to the extent it exceeded the reimbursement. Later cases have adopted what has come to be known as the "*Warms* adjustment," and also have required adjustments of fiduciaries in other situations.

That the first equitable adjustment case did not appear until 1955 is not surprising. Postmortem planning is a phenomenon of mid-twentieth-century income and estate taxation and, presently, there exists only a thin body of law dealing with adjustments.[15] The enactment of Subchapter J of the Internal Revenue Code of [1986] as well as the widespread social respectability of sharp tax planning through the manipulation of deductions and the long-term postponement of taxes are factors that have contributed to today's world of postmortem tax planning.

The cases dealing with equitable adjustments come from states where there is a tradition of creating trusts and paying close attention to the niceties of fiduciary administration. It is quite common to find as counsel in equitable adjustment cases highly visible members of the trusts and estates specialty bar. These cases are usually lower court decisions that often are not reported in bound volumes. The impact of these cases on fiduciary action and on the advice given by estates lawyers is unknown, but is likely to be widespread. The jurisdictions where the cases are decided, and the fact that virtually all are lower court decisions, are not as important as they might seem, because the cases are read as a single body of law by lawyers, judges, and commentators. While certain equitable adjustments have gained acceptance, a clear rationale for making adjustments has yet to emerge.

* * *

II. Unfair Allocation of Tax Burden or Benefit When Rules Conflict

Standard postmortem planning techniques have emerged since the passage of the Internal Revenue Code of [1986]. Some of these tech-

10. 140 N.Y.S.2d 169 (Sur.Ct.1955).

15. There is an even thinner body of law dealing with surcharge for poor postmortem planning. *See generally* Taggart, *Fiduciary's Liability in Utilizing Post-Mortem Estate Planning Techniques,* in P. Asofsky, Post Mortem Estate Planning 1979, at 339; Comment, *Surcharging an Executor for Negligent Administration of Tax Responsibilities,* 45 Temp.L.Q. 42 (1971).

niques minimize taxes while imposing unfair results on beneficiaries. These tax savings techniques are based on the exercise of discretionary administrative powers that are subject to the duty of impartiality, and on the conflicting rules of fiduciary administration, fiduciary accounting, and fiduciary income taxation. The techniques often involve the appropriation of a tax benefit that fiduciary accounting rules would locate in one beneficial interest and the transfer of that benefit to another beneficial interest. Frequently, it is a deduction that is appropriated, and often it is transferred from principal to income. The particular problems that have led to equitable adjustments cluster around the following administrative decisions; the use of deductions, the timing and amounts of distributions of estate income and principal, and the sale of assets. The focus of this section will be on these administrative decisions, the inequities that often result, and the particular types of adjustments that have been required by the courts to remedy the inherent unfairness.

A. *Use of Deductions*

The expenses of estate administration—such as commissions, lawyers' fees, accountants' fees, and guardians' fees—can be deducted at the executor's election,[108] either as estate tax deductions or as income tax deductions. If the expenses are used as estate tax deductions, the estate tax is lower and the income tax is higher, but if the expenses are used as income tax deductions, the estate tax is higher and the income tax is lower. Simple calculations inform the executor which use of deductions saves more overall taxes for the estate, and, to oversimplify somewhat, the executor chooses the tax return with the higher marginal rate.

The savings can be dramatic. In *Estate of Bixby*[112] the executor used expenses as income tax deductions on a fiduciary income tax return and saved about $100,000 in taxes. If the expenses had been used as death tax deductions, the savings would have been approximately $60,000. The duty to save taxes required the executor to use the deductions on a fiduciary income tax return.

The problem is that estate administration expenses are allocated to the principal account under standard fiduciary accounting rules. When income and principal go to different beneficiaries—that is, when successive interests are created—the tax decision will affect the amount of money each beneficiary receives. The income beneficiary in *Bixby* would have received a $100,000 saving at a cost to the principal beneficiary of $60,000.

* * * There is no initially impartial method to obtain the savings generated by the transfer of a deduction. The transfer of the deduction to the higher bracket income tax return is incidentally unfair to the

108. *See* I.R.C. § 642(g).

112. 140 Cal.App.2d 326, 295 P.2d 68 (1956).

beneficiary whose account paid the expense that generates the deduction. The judicial response to the problem has been uniform: to make an equitable adjustment, to require the return of the value of the lost deduction—the extra estate taxes paid—from the income account to the principal account. * * *

The most important case is *Estate of Bixby.* That opinion clearly based the adjustment on the duty of impartiality. The court recognized the duty to "minimize the aggregate of taxes paid by the estate . . . [when] there is a wide disparity between [tax brackets]." The court stated that the duty to save taxes does not allow "the severe disruption and disarrangement of . . . the beneficial interests of the legatees" without an adjustment, which suggests that tax savings must be foregone if the inequity is too great and the equitable adjustment cannot be used. *Bixby* demonstrates that the goals of tax savings and impartiality may be reached if principal is returned to the status quo by receipt of a transfer from the income account of an amount equal to the death tax increase.[135]

To summarize, *Warms* requires that when an executor deducts an administrative expense paid out of the principal account on an estate income tax return to save overall taxes for the estate, the income account must make the principal account whole for the increased tax caused by the lost use of the deduction. This is accomplished by transferring from the income account to the principal account an amount equal to the increased death tax.

* * *

B. Timing and Amounts of Distributions of Estate Income and Principal

A fiduciary ultimately has a duty to distribute the principal held in trust and the income earned thereon. An executor must distribute after a reasonable period of administration and settlement, and a trustee must distribute under the terms of the trust. Since termination must always occur at some point in time, the powers to implement a termination distribution are in one sense mandatory. However, because of the substantial leeway involved in accomplishing a termination, especially in the case of an estate, distribution powers are also discretionary in nature. Inequities attributable to unfair allocations of tax benefits and burdens can arise when an executor exercises discretionary administrative powers to determine the timing and amounts of distributions of estate income and principal. Planning the distribu-

135. The court in *In re* Veith's Estate, 26 Fla.Supp. 145 (Dade County Ct.1965), adopted the *Warms* adjustment in view of three factors: the duty to minimize taxes; the testator's intent; and the duty of impartiality. *Id.* at 149–50. The court found all three factors vindicated under the facts by adopting the adjustment. *Id.* at 150. The intention of the testator carried out by the § 642(g) election and the adjustment is not specified, but presumably the intention was to save taxes and favor the income beneficiary (the surviving spouse) without encroaching on the principal of the trusts established for the charitable remainder beneficiaries of the nonmarital trust. *Cf.* Rev.Rule 78–445, 1978–2 C.B. 242 (computation of value of charitable remainder interest).

tions of estate income and principal is a function of several factors: (1) tax minimization; (2) the beneficiaries' current needs for income and principal; (3) the time needed to administer a particular estate; and (4) the fiduciary's desire to limit the risk of surcharge for investment error by distributing assets to legatees to enable them to assume investment responsibility. Distribution techniques designed to save taxes include: (1) spreading estate income among multiple taxpayers to even tax brackets—that is, using distributions to transfer estate income to related taxpayers with lower marginal brackets; and (2) delaying the payment of taxes in order to retain the tax money for short-term investments.[139]

1. *Trapping Distributions*

A standard distribution technique used to tax estate income to lower marginal brackets is the so-called "trapping distribution," which takes advantage of the counterworkings of the following: (1) the DNI income tax system, which treats all distributions out of an estate up to the DNI ceiling as taxable income without regard to whether the

139. * * * If the estate's income tax bracket is higher than that of the beneficiaries—typically if individual beneficiaries have low taxable incomes or if estate beneficiaries include trusts that have no income at their inception—it is good tax sense to distribute from the estate to equalize tax brackets. If the estate's income tax bracket is lower than that of the beneficiaries, from a tax viewpoint it will be beneficial to retain the income, taxing the estate. *See* 302 TAX MNGM'T, *supra* note 2, at A–17. A variety of techniques exist. For example, if a small estate is left to a high bracket income taxpayer who can afford to wait for distributions, an executor will keep the estate open as long as possible to earn income in low brackets, take all deductions possible as estate income tax deductions, bunch all of the deductions in the final year, and pass them out as excess deductions to the beneficiary. Here the estate income tax bracket is so much lower, by hypothesis, than that of the residuary legatee, that equalization distributions do not make sense. *See id.*

If the residuary estate goes to a trust for a person with a moderate taxable income, a year's income can be split three ways (to oversimplify); by distributing principal in an amount equal to one-third of the estate's income to principal (a "trapping distribution," that will trap that amount of income in the trust, with principal paying the tax bill); by distributing one-third of estate income directly to the trust income beneficiary on account of his or her trust income interest * * *; and, by retaining one-third of the estate's income in the estate. If the estate had $90,000 in income, and $30,000 of principal went to the trust and $30,000 of income went to the beneficiary, for income tax purposes the trust will be deemed to have received $30,000 of income and the remaining $30,000 will be seen as left in the estate to be taxed to it. A *Holloway* or "trapping" adjustment would have to be made.

If the trust income beneficiary is a high bracket taxpayer, it is possible to give income to the beneficiary at low tax cost—to avoid the beneficiary's high bracket—by making a substantial funding of the trust with principal far in excess of estate income and, at the same time, giving the beneficiary a meaningful, but much smaller, amount of income. The estate will be lost as a taxpayer because all of its income will have been taken out by distributions in excess of DNI. Since most of the distribution has gone to the trust, however, most of the year's income will be taxed to the trust, and if it is the first year of the trust's existence, and therefore it is in a relatively low tax bracket because it has no principal to produce income, the tax bill will not be much more than if the estate kept the income. The beneficiary will be deemed to have received only a very small amount of income and will have gotten a distribution at little or no tax cost. A *Holloway* or "trapping" adjustment would have to be made.

Postponement of taxes is accomplished primarily by manipulating the tax year of the estate. * * *

property distributed is income or principal; (2) the executor's discretionary power to make distributions of estate income and principal during administration; and (3) the fiduciary accounting rule that requires estate assets characterized as income or principal in the estate to retain that character when distributed to a trust.

The executor of an estate has a discretionary power to make partial distributions of estate principal to legatees before administration is completed and to structure the income tax consequences of the termination of the estate. For tax purposes, a distribution of principal to a trust will be treated as if it consisted of income rather than principal under the DNI rules, notwithstanding that the distribution is principal on the books of the estate and is to be allocated to principal on the books of the trust. For tax purposes, the receiving trust will be treated as if it had received income and will be liable for the income tax due. When the income items in the estate that actually generated the income tax are later distributed to the life tenant, there is little or no tax due because the tax has already been paid by the trust principal account as recipient of the principal that is treated as income. The DNI rules that cause income to be taxed to the first beneficiaries to receive distributions from the estate provide an opportunity to minimize taxes by the timing of distributions. A skillful executor, in order to save overall taxes, will use this opportunity to appropriate the trust's separate taxpayer status, its low income tax bracket in its first year, and its lower tax bracket in later years. * * *

A very simple example may prove helpful. Assume an estate of $1,000,000, with taxable income of $40,000. The income tax would be about $16,000. Assume $20,000 of principal is distributed to a previously unfunded testamentary trust created under the will. The estate then will have only $20,000 of income and the tax would be about $6000. The trust would be deemed to have $20,000 of income because of the $20,000 of principal distributed to it, and the income tax would also be about $6000. Thus, the tax saving because of the small funding of the trust would be about $4000.

When such a distribution is purposely made, it is called a "trapping distribution," because the taxable income attributed to the principal distribution remains in the trust and is said to be "trapped" there. Inequity exists because the burden of paying the income tax on estate income is allocated—by the combined effect of the DNI system, fiduciary accounting law, and the discretionary distribution decision—to the trust principal account.

There is a recognized fiduciary adjustment that requires the income account to compensate the principal account for the income tax paid. This adjustment might be called the *Holloway* or "trapping adjustment." The executors in *In re Estate of Holloway,*[148] a New York Surrogate's Court decision, funded four residuary trusts in the manner

148. *In re* Estate of Holloway, 67 Misc. 2d 132, 323 N.Y.S.2d 534 (Sur.Ct.1971), *modified,* 68 Misc.2d 361, 327 N.Y.S.2d 865 (Sur.Ct.1972).

described above, thus transferring income tax liability from the estate income account to the trust principal account. Presumably, the executors made the trapping distributions to principal in pursuit of tax savings, although they may have funded the trust without any post-mortem income tax savings plan. A guardian ad litem appointed for the principal beneficiaries proposed an adjustment in the amount of the income tax that had been paid by the principal account. * * * The approval of the equitable adjustment was based on the surrogate's acceptance of the bankers' statement that corporate fiduciaries routinely made the adjustment and on the expressed goal of an "equitable approach" based on an equitable apportionment of the tax burden.

* * *

The *Holloway* or trapping adjustment is a sensible extension of *Warms* and a sensible application of the doctrine of equitable apportionment. The inherent unfairness in requiring the trust principal account to pay income tax attributable to receipts that are allocable to the estate income account had to be adjusted under the duty of impartiality, just as the executors had to make trapping distributions to discharge the duty to save taxes. The exercise of discretionary administrative powers that contribute to the inequity formed the basis for the adjustment. Because the discretionary power that caused the unfair result is not found in the Internal Revenue Code, *Holloway* makes clear that the existence of a Code election is not a prerequisite to a court's making an equitable adjustment.

2. *Disproportionate Distributions*

Trapping distributions are not the only exercise of a fiduciary's discretionary powers of distribution that can cause unfair allocation of tax benefits and burdens. Disproportionate or non-prorated distributions can also cause inequity when tax benefits and burdens are allocated. A disproportionate or non-prorated distribution is one that does not mirror in its proportion the entitlement of the beneficiaries to principal under the instrument. For example, if *A* and *B* are to receive equal shares of a decedent's residuary estate of $100,000 and in the first year of administration *A* gets $20,000 of principal on account and *B* gets nothing, then a disproportionate distribution has been made.[163]

Inequity exists under the DNI system when there is a partial distribution of estate income or principal before completion of administration, and the distribution is disproportionate to the beneficiary's underlying entitlement to estate principal. The inequity exists when one beneficiary has to pay income taxes on income receipts allocable to another beneficiary. The inequity occurs for several reasons. All distributions out of an estate are deemed to carry out estate income for the tax year without regard to character as current income, income

163. Distinguish a heterogeneous distribution, a distribution that is different in kind. For example, if the residuary consists of two holdings of equal fair market value, 100 shares of X stock and 100 shares of Y stock, and if the executor gives all the X stock to *A* and all the Y stock to *B*, then a heterogeneous distribution has been made. They, too, may be unfair without adjustment. * * *

from a prior year, or principal, and without regard to ultimate entitlement to income and principal.[165] Estate income for fiduciary accounting purposes is distributed on a pro rata basis by reference to the beneficiaries' respective entitlement to estate principal. Using the previous example, if *A* and *B* have equal entitlement to a $100,000 estate that has $5000 of income in a given year, both are entitled to $2500 of income on account of their entitlement to estate principal. If *A* were entitled to four-fifths of the estate and *B* to one-fifth, *A* would be entitled to $4000 of income and *B* would be entitled to $1000. If a distribution is made to a residuary legatee and if that distribution in its relationship to all estate distributions made in that tax year exceeds the pro rata amount of trust accounting income allocable to the beneficiary, the beneficiary is paying more than his or her share of the income tax for that year. Again, assume *A* and *B* take a residuary net estate of $100,000 in equal shares and are therefore entitled to half of the income earned by the estate during administration. In the first year of the estate there is $5000 of estate income. *A* receives a partial distribution of $20,000 of principal on account of his or her $50,000 share of estate principal, and *B* receives no income or principal in that year. In effect, a disproportionate distribution has been made. For trust accounting purposes, the $5000 of income is still in the trust and will go to *A* and *B* in equal shares. For income tax purposes, the $5000 of income is taxed to *A* under conduit income taxation of estate principles because of the $20,000 distribution of principal to *A*. Without an adjustment, *A* will have paid the tax on all $5000 of income and *B* will receive his or her share of income tax-free in a later year.[172] That is, *A* will have paid *B*'s income tax.[173]

165. This is not true for distributions from trusts that are subject to the separate share rule of I.R.C. § 663.

172. That *A* pays *B*'s taxes was confirmed in Harkness v. United States, 469 F.2d 310, 319–21 (Ct.Cl.1972), *cert. denied,* 414 U.S. 820 (1973). In *Harkness* the surviving spouse received one-half of the decedent's residuary estate. In 1955, almost immediately after the enactment of the new rules for income taxation of trusts and estates, the executor sought to keep the flow of estate income balanced after the estate tax had been paid from the nonmarital share—thereby reducing that half of principal and therefore reducing entitlement to income during the remaining days of the estate. This was done by distributing an amount of principal equal to the tax money to the surviving spouse so the principal on hand would be equally payable to the two legatees. *Id.* at 312–13. Under the DNI system of the Code, this distribution caused the surviving spouse to be taxed on more than her fair share of estate income. The Court of Claims refused to allow a refund of the tax. *Id.* at 321. Obviously, no question of adjustment or surcharge arose in the tax proceeding. Given the newness and the complexity of the question in 1955, and the faithfulness of the fiduciary, a remedy beyond an adjustment would be most unlikely.

A different result obtains if a revocable trust is the instrument chosen to dispose of a decedent's property. The separate share rule of the Code then limits the amount of income that can be deemed distributed to a beneficiary to a percentage that is a fraction of his or her share of the principal, with any income beyond that principal share remaining taxable to the trust. *See* I.R.C. § 663(c). The separate share rule does not apply to estates. *See id.*

173. The transfer hypothesized can never make sense from a tax viewpoint because use of the estate as a separate taxpayer is forfeited. The greatest tax savings come from even taxable income in the hands of as many taxpayers as possible. If *A, B,* and the estate all have no other income, the best tax result, to slightly oversimplify, comes if the $5000 in in-

Disproportionate distributions can take place under a variety of circumstances and are often the result of poor postmortem tax planning. There are basically two ways, given the DNI system, that the inequity of having to pay another beneficiary's taxes can occur because of a disproportionate distribution. The first, like the example above, is when a disproportionate distribution of assets departs avoidably, and usually significantly, from the ratio of entitlement to estate principal. This inequity could be avoided through the use of balancing distributions. * * *

The second way inequity can occur is when a disproportionate distribution of assets departs unavoidably, and usually in a de minimus [sic] amount, from the ratio of entitlement to estate principal. This happens when it is impossible or extremely difficult to determine the beneficiaries' exact entitlement to estate principal within the tax year that the partial distribution is made.[175] Pro rata or balancing distributions can only minimize the impact of these distributions. * * *

To summarize, inequitable allocation of tax benefits and burdens often occurs when a fiduciary makes a disproportionate partial distribution of estate income or principal. A fiduciary equitable adjustment should be made. Available authority and experience suggest that an adjustment is not customarily made. This is, in part, because no standard postmortem planning technique is based on disproportionate distributions, and the number of occasions to make the adjustment is therefore limited.

C. Sales of Assets

* * *

When an asset is sold by a fiduciary, the sale typically generates deductible expenditures, such as commissions and state capital gains taxes, allocable under fiduciary accounting rules to principal. The allocation of the costs to principal is appropriate since the costs relate to management of principal and activity in the principal account. Moreover, it is only fair that the principal account—the account charged with the deductible expenditure—obtain the benefit of the deduction. The Internal Revenue Code, however, in order to avoid wasting deductions in years when there is no capital gain, automatically first allocates those deductions in *all* years to taxable income going to life tenants. The effect is to deprive principal, the source of the

come is split three ways, with $1666 going to each. This is done by passing no more than that amount of value, in the form of either income or principal, to *A* and *B*, which will have the effect of giving one-third of the taxable income to each of *A* and *B*, leaving $1666 of taxable income in the estate. Any distribution to *A* in excess of an amount designed to reduce taxes, which can never be higher than one-half of the estate's income for tax purposes, can never be justified as a tax savings distribution.

175. This uncertainty can arise when a will contains a formula legacy based on the decedent's adjusted gross estate, where the exact breakdown of estate ownership cannot be known until several years after the testator dies. Such legacies are used to obtain maximum marital deductions in decedents' estates without overfunding such legacies for tax purposes. Such uncertainty can also arise when taxes and expenses are not borne ratably, but are assessed against particular legacies.

deductible expenditure, in those years when it has taxable gain, of the use of the deduction. For example, assume a trust with ordinary income of $10,000 in a tax year and sales in the same year generating deductions of $2000. Those deductions will reduce the $10,000 of income, but not the capital gain, if any.

Thus, when a fiduciary makes a sale recognizing gain and generating deductible expenses allocable to the principal account, an unfair allocation is made by the DNI system—a tax burden is placed on the principal account by the transfer of deductions to the income account. There is a split of authority on whether an equitable adjustment must be made [200] from the income account to make the principal account whole for the transfer of the deduction.

* * *

III. The Abstract Form of the Adjustments

Courts will require a fiduciary to make a *Warms* adjustment to remedy the inequities created by the section 642(g) election and will require a *Holloway* adjustment to eliminate the unfairness inherent in a trapping distribution. Courts also may require fiduciaries to make a *Cooper* adjustment to eliminate inequities created by disproportionate or non-prorated distributions, and a *Rice* adjustment to eliminate inequities in a DNI transfer of deductions from principal to income.

But, when a court has decided to make an adjustment, what form is it to take? * * * The adjustment cases involve taking a tax benefit from the account of one beneficiary and transferring it to the account of another beneficiary. In *Warms,* because of the section 642(g) election, and in *Rice,* because of the DNI system, a deduction attributable to an expenditure from the principal account was transferred to the income account. In *Holloway* and *Cooper* separate taxpayer status was appropriated, thus saving taxes. When asked to remedy the inequitable effects of the transfer of a tax benefit, the courts had a choice between two remedies. The courts could have required an adjustment that returned the injured beneficiary to the status quo or could have required an adjustment that returned the tax benefit with some or all of its increase to the beneficiary.

For example, in *Bixby,* the California case that followed *Warms,* the deductible expenditures made out of the principal account were worth approximately $60,000 in tax savings on the death tax return and about $100,000 on the fiduciary income tax return. The court was asked to provide a remedy. The equitable adjustment was the transfer of approximately $60,000 from the income account to the principal account. This was a compensatory adjustment that restored to the principal account the value of the lost deduction. It was an adjustment

200. *Compare* Rice Estate, 8 Pa.D. & C.2d 379, 413, 6 Pa.Fiduc. 225, 242 (Orphans' Ct.1956) (allowing adjustment) *with In re* Estate of Dick, 29 Misc.2d 648, 651, 218 N.Y.S.2d 182, 185 (Sur.Ct.1961) *and* Estate of Adler, N.Y.L.J., June 21, 1974, at 15, col. 1 (Sur.Ct.1974) (denying adjustment).

in the nature of the damages remedy because it returned the accounts to the status quo and compensated for the harm.

The court did not transfer the $100,000 income tax savings to the principal account. Had the court transferred the entire $100,000, it would have been transferring the fruit of the taking of the deduction, and the court would have been providing an adjustment in the nature of a restitutionary remedy—restoring the deduction plus its incremental value. The court would have been treating the tax benefit as property and would have been restoring it to principal along with the "profit" earned by its use as an income tax deduction.

The basic pattern of the cases considered is to provide a compensatory adjustment in the nature of the damages remedy. The basis of the pattern lies in *Warms*. There the court implicitly rejected an adjustment that treated the deduction as property—in effect, a proprietary adjustment. That is, the court rejected a restitutionary remedy that would have led to a partial or total reallocation of the income tax savings to the principal account. The *Warms* court instead chose an adjustment focused on the injury to the principal account, not the enrichment of the income account.

The choice of a compensatory, rather than a restitutionary, adjustment can be rationalized. A compensatory adjustment is sensible because the compensatory remedy of damages is the standard remedy courts provide. An adjustment that mirrors the damages remedy and simply returns the lost value of the tax benefit is all that is required. All that a diminished beneficiary is entitled to is a return to the norm, to the status quo. There is no property right in the tax benefits involved in these cases, and it is the taking of property that requires a restitutionary remedy. For example, in the *Warms* situation, as a matter of property law, to give the principal account more than compensation for the lost tax benefit—for example, to give the principal account part or all of the tax increase from the transfer of a deduction—would be to recognize the benefit as a transferable item of property, which it is not. Restitution is a proprietary remedy—it assumes a property interest impinged on, and in these situations there is none. Thus, there should be no restitutionary adjustments. * * *

Moreover, restitution is often made in response to an unjust enrichment. While the income account has been enriched in the *Warms* situation and there has been an imposition on the principal account for which there must be compensation, the enrichment is not unjust. The adjustment was in response to a faithful nonobservance of the duty of impartiality by an executor responding to the fiduciary duty to minimize taxes. Thus, the conduct of the parties, which can form the basis for the conclusion that there is unjust enrichment, does not suggest the use of a restitutionary remedy. * * *

CONCLUSION

The system for taxing income of estates and trusts, the fundamental fiduciary accounting rules, the duty to save taxes, and the duty of impartiality do not always mesh. Fiduciaries have a clear duty to save taxes through the use of mixed mandatory and discretionary administrative powers. Fiduciaries must synthesize the terms of the instrument setting forth the settlor's intent, the duty to save taxes, and the duty of impartiality. Action taken to save taxes must be reasonable, which usually means, among other things, either initially fair under fiduciary accounting rules or fair through equitable apportionment. Equitable adjustment is a form of equitable apportionment, the doctrine that requires fiduciaries, in order to deal with beneficiaries fairly, to reallocate or reapportion benefits or burdens received in an initially unfair form under standard accounting rules.

Equitable allocation rules and equitable apportionment rules trace back to the duty of impartiality. Cases to date suggest that equitable adjustments in postmortem planning can be made because the exercise of a discretionary power has caused an inequitable allocation. That is a rational theory. Looking beyond, it seems correct to say that external impositions that do not ensue directly from the exercise of discretionary powers are also subject to adjustment under general doctrines of equitable apportionment.

The equitable adjustment cases decided to date constitute a gloss on fundamental and sound rules of fiduciary accounting that do not always work fairly in a modern tax context. When adjustments are made, they are structured to return the lost value of the tax benefit to the unfairly burdened beneficiary. This form can be explained by reference to general principles of equitable remedies, property law, and equitable apportionment. The courts have fashioned adjustments that return the lost value of a tax benefit to the burdened beneficiary account, but have refused to require adjustments that treat tax benefits as property, contenting themselves instead with returning matters to the point where they stood before the particular unjust imposition.

Equity requires equality. That is, equity requires harmony, classical forms, proportion. Equitable adjustments provide order in the baroque world of postmortem planning.

An article summarizing the equitable adjustment law in the 50 states is Carrico and Bondurant, "Equitable Adjustments: A Survey and Analysis of Precedents and Practice", 36 Tax Lawyer 545 (1983).

Questions

1. During the course of trust administration the trustee properly depreciated trust assets pursuant to section 168. Recapture upon a subsequent sale caused some of the gain on that disposition to be converted to ordinary income. If, under state law, that income was nevertheless taxable

to corpus (because the gain was allocable to principal notwithstanding its conversion to ordinary income status for income tax purposes), what form of equitable adjustment might be required? See Will of Pross, 90 Misc.2d 895, 396 N.Y.S.2d 309 (Surr.Ct.1977).

2. Consider the deduction granted to the recipient of income in respect of a decedent under section 691(c) (which we study in Chapter Six), in terms of the equitable adjustment issues it creates. The Treasury Department has indicated in the past that it would like for section 691(c) to provide a basis adjustment to the IRD, rather than a deduction to the recipient thereof. Would this solve the equitable adjustment problem?

3. Is the adjustment called for in *Warms* correct, or would a more equitable alternative be proper?

4. What are the proper income tax consequences of an equitable adjustment? See, e.g., Letter Rulings 8501011 and 8501084, and Boyle, "Tax Consequences of Equitable Adjustments", 37 South Carolina L.Rev. 583 (1986).

Chapter Six

INCOME AND DEDUCTIONS IN RESPECT OF A DECEDENT

Read Code sections 691(a) through 691(c) and 1014(c).

Read Regulation sections 1.691(a) through 1.691(c).

Neither income in respect of a decedent (IRD) nor deductions in respect of a decedent (DRD) is a concept unique to the income taxation or administration of trusts and estates or the taxation of beneficiaries. Nevertheless, because each applies to any taxpayer receiving income to which a decedent was entitled, or paying specified deductible expenses on the decedent's behalf, IRD and DRD are common to fiduciary administration and the income taxation of trusts, estates and beneficiaries. With respect to all taxpayers, the fundamental tax objective of both the IRD and DRD concepts is to maintain the same character of the income and deductions as if received or incurred by the decedent while alive and, for fiduciary tax purposes, any IRD received or DRD incurred by a trust or estate enters into the computation of its taxable income, and thus into the amount of DNI.

One disconcerting aspect of this concept is the initial difficulty in determining whether an item constitutes IRD. The Internal Revenue Code contains no definition of IRD, though Treasury Regulation section 1.691(a)–1(b) refers to "amounts to which a decedent was entitled as gross income" but that were not includible prior to death. Consider whether the following materials establish any tests that could be useful in identifying IRD.

ESTATE OF SIDLES v. COMMISSIONER

United States Tax Court, 1976.

65 T.C. 873, aff'd, 553 F.2d 102 (8th Cir.1977), acquiescence, 1976–2 C.B. 2.

DAWSON, CHIEF JUDGE: Respondent determined deficiencies of $160,203 and $2,197 in petitioners' Federal income taxes for the taxable years ended May 31, 1969, and May 31, 1970, respectively.

Some issues have been conceded by petitioners. The primary issue for our decision is whether a liquidating distribution received by the

Estate of Harry B. Sidles from Bi-State Distributing Corp. constituted "income in respect of a decedent" within the meaning of section 691(a)(1). If this distribution is determined to be "income in respect of a decedent," then we must decide whether the deduction provided by section 691(c) is to be offset only against section 691(a) income.

* * *

In his notice of deficiency * * * respondent determined that the gain realized from the liquidation of Bi-State constituted income in respect of a decedent. The gain ($673,129.81) was calculated by subtracting the decedent's adjusted basis in his Bi-State stock ($29,701.04) from the net fair market value of the assets received by the estate as a liquidating distribution ($702,830.85). * * *

Petitioners contend that the liquidating distribution received by the estate from Bi-State is not governed by section 691(a) and, even if it did constitute income in respect of a decedent, the deduction provided by section 691(c) should not be limited solely to section 691(a) income items.

The principal issue is whether the liquidating distribution received by the estate from Bi-State constituted "income in respect of a decedent" as that term is used in section 691, which provides, in relevant part, that:

The amount of all items of gross income in respect of a decedent which are not properly includible in respect of the taxable period in which falls the date of his death or a prior period (including the amount of all items of gross income in respect of a prior decedent, if the right to receive such amount was acquired by reason of the death of the prior decedent or by bequest, devise, or inheritance from the prior decedent) shall be included in the gross income, for the taxable year when received, of:

(A) the estate of the decedent, *if the right to receive* the amount is acquired by the decedent's estate from the decedent; [Emphasis added.]

Section 1.691(a)–1(b), Income Tax Regs., defines "income in respect of a decedent" as:

those amounts to which a decedent was *entitled* as gross income but which were not properly includible in computing his taxable income for the taxable year ending with the date of his death or for a previous taxable year under the method of accounting employed by the decedent. * * * [Emphasis added.]

Respondent determined that the liquidation proceeds were income in respect of the decedent because, as of the date of his death, the decedent was entitled to and possessed the right to receive the liquidating distribution from Bi-State.

Petitioners argue that the criterion for determining whether an item constitutes "income in respect of a decedent" within the meaning of the Code and regulations sections quoted above is that the decedent must be entitled to the item in the sense that he had a right to the income at the time of his death, which right had been earned during his lifetime. Petitioners further contend that neither the adoption of the plan of liquidation nor decedent's activities or economic efforts created the requisite right to income under section 691 and the regulations thereunder. They argue that the decedent had no right and was not entitled to the liquidation proceeds until the distribution had been authorized by Bi-State's board of directors.

Income in respect of a decedent is defined only in the regulations and not in the statute. An attempt to add such a definition to the Code in 1959 failed. H.R. 3041, 86th Cong., 1st Sess. (1959). However, some guidelines can be gleaned from an examination of congressional intent as reflected in the legislative history of section 691 and its antecedents.

Prior to 1934 an accrual basis taxpayer was required to pay income tax on those amounts accrued but not received as of the date of his death. However, neither a cash basis taxpayer nor his estate was required to pay a Federal income tax on such amounts because they were considered corpus rather than income. *Nichols v. United States,* 64 Ct.Cl. 241 (1927), cert. denied 277 U.S. 584 (1928). Furthermore, no income tax liability arose when capital assets were transferred after death since the estate's basis in such assets was fair market value at date of death and the amounts received generally did not exceed this amount.[3]

Congressional concern with this discrimination between taxpayers and loss of revenue led to the enactment of section 42 of the Revenue Act of 1934. This section required all income accrued to the date of death but not otherwise properly includable in income for that period or any prior period to be included in the decedent's income tax return for the period ending with his death regardless of his method of accounting. See S.Rept. No. 558, 73d Cong., 2d Sess. 28 (1934).

While this section achieved an equality between cash and accrual basis decedents, it resulted in bunching of income since amounts which would have been received over several years and taxed at lower rates were required to be reported in the year of death. This situation was aggravated by the imposition of war surtaxes and by the realization that taxpayers might be taxed on substantial sums which they had not yet received or might never receive. See S.Rept. No. 1631, 77th Cong., 2d Sess. 100–105 (1942), 1942–2 C.B. 504, 579–583. Furthermore, the decision of the Supreme Court in *Helvering v. Enright,* 312 U.S. 636 (1941), greatly expanded the meaning of "accrued" as used in section 42. In that case, the Supreme Court, after giving the reasons for the enactment of section 42, explained that it was endeavoring to effectuate the legislative objective of ensuring that income, which would have been taxable had decedent lived to receive it, should not escape income taxation by reason of his death.

3. Under present law, sec. 1014(c) provides that the general rule of sec. 1014(a) that the basis of property acquired from a decedent shall be the fair market value of the property on the date of the decedent's death, "shall not apply to property which constitutes a right to receive an item of income in respect of a decedent under section 691."

Accruals here are to be construed in furtherance of the intent of Congress to cover [sic] into income the assets of decedents, earned during their life and unreported as income, which on a cash return, would appear in the estate returns. Congress sought a fair reflection of income. [312 U.S. at 644–645.]

Section 134 of the Revenue Act of 1942 added section 126 of the 1939 Internal Revenue Code. This section, the predecessor of section 691 of the Internal Revenue Code of [1986], eliminated the undesirable pyramiding effects of the prior law through formulation of the concept of "income in respect of a decedent." Under this section income accruing to a decedent because of his death was not to be included in his final return, but was to be treated as income and reported as such by the person receiving such income. As noted in *Commissioner v. Linde,* 213 F.2d 1, 5–6 (9th Cir.1954), cert. denied 348 U.S. 871 (1954):

there is nothing in the legislative history or in the text of Sec. 126 to indicate that it was intended to be anything other than an improved device to accomplish the general purpose of the internal revenue code that all income should pay a tax and that death should not rob the United States of the revenue which otherwise it would have had. We think it clear that the intent of Congress continued to be as stated in the Enright case "to cover into income the assets of decedents, earned during their life and unreported as income". * * * [Fn. ref. omitted.]

* * *

it is our view that section 126 was but an improved method adopted by Congress in aid of its continuing effort to avoid the loss of tax upon income merely because of the death of the decedent who would have paid a tax upon the same economic returns had he lived to receive them.

Section 691 includes in gross income "all items of gross income in respect of a decedent which are not properly includible" in the taxable year ending with the date of his death or prior period. This reflects the same general congressional intent to tax all items which can constitutionally be considered income, but which are not exempted from taxation, as that underlying section 61 which defines gross income. However, for income to be considered "income in respect of a decedent," section 691 requires that the decedent possess a right to that income as of his date of death. This is a question of fact and each case depends upon its "subsisting facts." *Trust Co. of Georgia v. Ross,* 392 F.2d 694, 695 (5th Cir.1967), cert. denied 393 U.S. 830 (1968). One of the factors to be considered is whether the income received after death resulted from the decedent's activities and economic efforts during his lifetime. But this right must be distinguished from the activity which created it. No matter how great the activity or effort, there can be no income in respect of a decedent under section 691 unless the decedent possessed a right to receive such income on his date of death. *Trust Co. of Georgia v. Ross, supra* at 695. Our point of inquiry must be whether the transaction had sufficiently matured as of decedent's death so as to create in him a right to receive the income when it was subsequently realized.

The facts and circumstances of this case lead us to the conclusion that the amounts received by the decedent's estate on the liquidation of Bi-State constituted income in respect of a decedent within the meaning of section 691.

On February 28, 1968, the board of directors of Bi-State Distributing Corp., consisting of Harry B. Sidles, Janice P. Sidles, and Areta L. Kelly, passed a resolution calling for the complete liquidation and dissolution of the corporation. The sole stockholder of Bi-State, Harry B. Sidles, approved the resolution that same day.

The liquidating distribution had its source exclusively in decedent's actions. His affirmative vote for liquidation created a right to receive that distribution, which right existed at his death. Although decedent had the power to rescind the transaction creating such a right, he had not attempted to do so before his death. Had the decedent lived to receive the liquidating distribution, it would have constituted income to him, and consequently such amounts constitute income in respect of a decedent when received by the estate.

There can be no doubt that the estate acquired the right to receive the liquidation distribution from the decedent. The estate's right to such proceeds derived solely from decedent's death and not from its own efforts. Whatever actions the estate took were of no material significance here.

Furthermore, the actions of Bi-State's board of directors which remained to be done at the time of decedent's death do not derogate decedent's right to receive the liquidating distribution. The resolution of November 29, 1968, to distribute the assets in liquidation to decedent's estate, the declaration of the liquidating dividend and the filing of articles of dissolution were mere formalities; ministerial acts necessary to complete the liquidation under State law. On the date of his death the decedent had performed enough substantive acts within his control to perfect his right to receive the liquidating distribution for purposes of section 691.[6] Cf. *Hudspeth v. United States,* 471 F.2d 275 (8th Cir.1972); *Kinsey v. Commissioner,* 477 F.2d 1058 (2d Cir.1973), affg. 58 T.C. 259 (1972).

In *Keck v. Commissioner,* 415 F.2d 531 (6th Cir.1969), revg. 49 T.C. 313 (1968), the Commissioner determined a deficiency in the income tax of George W. Keck and Mary Ann Keck, and also asserted transferee liability against Mary Ann Keck, as transferee of the assets of the Estate of Arthur D. Shaw, deceased. The issue there was whether

6. Although the decedent's right to the liquidating distribution at his death was an absolute and unconditional one, it should be noted that sec. 1.691(a)–1(b)(3), Income Tax Regs., provides that income to which the decedent had a "contingent claim" at the time of his death is sufficient to create income in respect of a decedent. See also Rev.Rul. 60–227, 1960–1 C.B. 262, 263.

Further, it has been held that the requisite right need not be a legally enforceable one, *O'Daniel's Estate v. Commissioner,* 173 F.2d 966 (2d Cir.1949), but merely free from contingencies, *Estate of Nilssen v. United States,* 322 F.Supp. 260, 264–265 (D.Minn.1971).

certain amounts received in 1960 by Mary Ann Keck and by the estate, were taxable as income in respect of a decedent under section 691. The deceased, Arthur D. Shaw, owned stock in three affiliated corporations as of March 1, 1956. On that date an agreement was entered into prior to the sale of the assets of the corporation. The sale, however, was contingent upon approval of the Interstate Commerce Commission. The shares of stock were placed in escrow pending such approval.

Mr. Shaw died November 27, 1958. ICC approval was not obtained until May 5, 1960. On July 21, 1960, pursuant to authority granted by the ICC, the three companies were liquidated pursuant to the agreement earlier agreed upon, and the cash received from the sale was distributed in exchange for shares of the stock of the three companies. The executor of the Estate of Mr. Shaw paid over to Mrs. Keck $314,328.53 in exchange for 100 shares of one of the companies liquidated. The court there held that at the time of the decedent's death, his stock had not been converted into section 691 income in respect of a decedent. The Court of Appeals agreed with the dissenting opinion of Judge Featherston in *George W. Keck,* 49 T.C. 313 (1968), that the sale was subject to a number of contingencies which operated to prevent the cash from becoming income in respect of a decedent: (1) The sale was subject to approval of the ICC, which approval did not come until 18 months after decedent's death; (2) as of the time of decedent's death, neither decedent nor the other stockholders were contractually committed to the plan to liquidate the corporation; (3) the majority stockholder (who in this case was not decedent) might have decided not to liquidate the corporation; and (4) the decedent's own stock was not committed to vote for the plan until May 23, 1960, when the proxies were signed and delivered.

The *Keck* case is clearly distinguishable on its facts. Unlike *Keck,* the decedent, as Bi-State's sole shareholder, possessed the power to compel payment of the liquidating distribution, as well as the right to that payment, when he died. His right to the liquidation distribution was not subject to the many contingencies involved in *Keck.* The transaction was not subject to the approval of any Government agency; there was no other stockholder who could vote not to liquidate the corporation. The distribution made to the Estate of Harry B. Sidles, was clearly "income in respect of a decedent" within the meaning of section 691.

* * *

HALL, J., concurring in the result: I believe the liquidation gains did constitute income in respect of a decedent. However, some of the language in the Court's opinion could be construed as going farther than I would in stating the criteria for distinguishing income in respect of a decedent from mere unrealized appreciation in value of property. The issue, as properly framed by the Court's opinion, is whether at death decedent had a *right* to receive the Bi-State liquidation proceeds. Under Nebraska law, the filing of a statement of intent to dissolve without more obligates the corporation to cease doing business and distribute its assets to its shareholders. Nebraska Business Corporation Act, Neb.Rev.Stat. secs. 21–2085 and 21–2086 (1974). Should the corporate directors fail to make such a distribution, within a reasonable period the shareholders would apparently be able to sustain an action to compel such a distribution in the absence of shareholder action reversing the original dissolution resolution. At that point the shareholders are vested with a legal right to the proceeds, and the postdeath gains are income in respect of a decedent. The case is analogous to the execution of an enforceable executory contract of sale. *Trust Co. of Georgia v. Ross,* 392 F.2d 694 (5th Cir.1967), cert. denied 393 U.S. 830 (1968). However, I do not consider it significant that decedent, as Bi-State's sole shareholder, had the *power* to compel payment of the liquidating distribution when he died, for any sole shareholder, as a practical matter, has such power at all times. Reference to the sole shareholder's *power* proves too much. He has the effective power, for example, to cause an ordinary dividend to be declared. But when no formal directors' action declaring such a dividend has been taken, a postdeath declaration would not give rise to income in respect of a decedent, for the decedent had no *right* at death to such a distribution. What counts is whether the formal corporate actions have been taken which would give even a *minority* shareholder the legal right to compel a liquidating distribution. References to cases holding that a "right" need not be a "legal" right are also inapposite here in the context of realization of gains on appreciated property. Such cases involve compensation income. Indeed, it may well be that even in the compensation cases a *right* existed to compensation in quantum meruit, as evidenced by the very postdeath, nondonative payment which was held to be income in respect of a decedent. In any event, short of the existence of a fixed, predeath *legal* right to the proceeds of a sale or exchange, I would not consider realization of gains on the sale or exchange of property to be income in respect of a decedent.

WILBUR, J., agrees with this concurring opinion.

* * *

FEATHERSTON, J., dissenting: I respectfully disagree with the majority's conclusion on the first issue. Section 691(a), which prescribes the general rule for the taxation of "income in respect of a decedent," refers to the "right to receive" items of gross income. Generally speaking, the term "income in respect of a decedent" applies only to "those amounts to which a decedent was entitled as gross income" but which were not properly includable in his final return. Sec. 1.691(a)–1(b), Income Tax Regs. As stated in *Trust Co. of Georgia v. Ross,* 392 F.2d 694, 695 (5th Cir.1967), cert. denied 393 U.S. 830 (1968): "the right [to income] is to be distinguished from the activity which creates the right. Absent such a right, no matter how great the activities or efforts, there would be no taxable income under sec. 691." While the right to income need not be a legal right to *collect* a sum ascertainable on the date of death, see *Commissioner v. Linde,* 213 F.2d 1 (9th Cir.

1954), remanding 17 T.C. 584 (1951), cert. denied 348 U.S. 871 (1954); *O'Daniel's Estate v. Commissioner,* 173 F.2d 966 (2d Cir.1949), affg. 10 T.C. 631 (1948), the right to collect the income *when realized* must have arisen prior to or at the decedent's death. The problem in the instant case, therefore, is not to weigh and assess the probabilities at decedent's death that his estate or some other beneficiary would or would not ultimately receive the proceeds of the liquidation of Bi-State, but rather to determine the *rights* of the decedent or that beneficiary as of the date of decedent's death.

This imprecise test is not easily applied to cases involving the liquidation of corporations. In my opinion, in such cases "The crucial question should be whether the redemption or liquidation has proceeded to a point beyond the control of the decedent prior to his death." Ferguson, Freeland & Stevens, Federal Income Taxation of Estates and Beneficiaries 208 (1970). The issue of whether a contract for the disposition of property has created income in respect of a decedent, e.g., via sale, is analogous. In contract cases, the issue is whether, on the date of death, the transaction has proceeded to the point where the value of the property has been converted into an intangible right to receive the ultimate proceeds of the sale or other disposition. Sec. 1.691(a)–2(b), *Example 4,* Income Tax Regs. Such a conversion occurs only when the property is somehow put beyond the control of decedent prior to his death. See *Commissioner v. Linde, supra; Estate of Helen Davison,* 155 Ct.Cl. 290, 292 F.2d 937 (1961), cert. denied 368 U.S. 939 (1961); *Stephen H. Dorsey,* 49 T.C. 606, 633 (1968). In *Trust Co. of Georgia v. Ross, supra,* for example, the court, holding that the disposition of certain stock by decedent prior to his death created income in respect of a decedent, stated (392 F.2d at 696):

> [Decedent] entered into a binding contract prior to his death. That contract required the conveyance of the property from whence the income in litigation was derived. The contract created a right to these proceeds in [decedent] at the time the contract was executed. The contract inured to and was binding upon his executor. * * *

In contrast, in *Keck v. Commissioner,* 415 F.2d 531 (6th Cir.1969), revg. 49 T.C. 313 (1968), discussed at length in the majority opinion, where a contingent or informal agreement to liquidate a corporation did not constitute a binding contract, the Court of Appeals refused to find income in respect of a decedent.

I do not think the liquidation of Bi-State, at decedent's death, had proceeded to a point beyond his control so that his stock had been converted to a mere right to receive income. It bears reiterating that decedent was *sole* shareholder of Bi-State. To the extent possible under a scheme of State regulation his control of that corporation was absolute, and his rights were in no way diluted by the presence of minority shareholders. His estate succeeded to the same quantum of control.

At any time prior to his death, decedent, the sole shareholder, could have reversed the decision to liquidate Bi-State. Neb.Rev.Stat. secs. 21–2087, 21–2088 (1974). Similarly, at any time after his death and prior to the distributions on November 29 and 30, 1968, decedent's estate, as sole shareholder, could have rescinded the resolution to liquidate and sold the stock to a third party or could have decided to keep the corporation alive so that, for example, it could continue the operation of the gift shop or the ownership of the real and personal property located at 4827 Dodge Street in Omaha. Had the estate taken either one of those steps, clearly it would not have received income in respect of a decedent. The estate received the liquidation proceeds only because it, as sole shareholder, did not revoke the liquidation resolution.

Under the *Trust Co. of Georgia* reasoning, since there was no commitment by either the decedent or his executor to permit Bi-State to be liquidated, decedent's stock at his death had not been converted to income.

The importance of the power to rescind a decision to liquidate a corporation has been emphasized in cases dealing with the transfer of stock in a corporation after the adoption of a resolution to liquidate. In *Rushing v. Commissioner,* 441 F.2d 593 (5th Cir.1971), affg. 52 T.C. 888 (1969), the court held that the transfer of a controlling interest in the corporation relieved the transferor of tax on the liquidation proceeds of the transferred shares. An opposite result was reached in *Hudspeth v. United States,* 471 F.2d 275 (8th Cir.1972), where the taxpayer transferred shares to a charity but retained a controlling interest in the corporation. The *Hudspeth* court explained the dichotomy as follows (471 F.2d at 278):

> we read *Rushing* [*Rushing v. Commissioner,* 441 F.2d 593 (5th Cir.1971)] as evincing the proposition that if the donor or vendor transfers a *controlling interest* in a corporation, such that the transferee will have the legal capacity to suspend or rescind the liquidation and thereby have the power to supercede the donor's initial intent to provide the donee only with the otherwise imminent liquidation proceeds, then the gains are not taxable to the transferor. But, in the case where the taxpayer retains control of the corporation and the transferee will be unable to vitiate the taxpayer's intent to liquidate, the shareholders' vote remains sufficient to constitute the necessary severance of gain.

To the same effect, see *Kinsey v. Commissioner,* 477 F.2d 1058, 1062 (2d Cir.1973), affg. 58 T.C. 259 (1972); *Simmons v. United States,* 341 F.Supp. 947, 951 (M.D.Ga.1972); cf. *Jacobs v. United States,* 280 F.Supp. 437 (S.D.Ohio 1966), affd. 390 F.2d 877 (6th Cir.1968). While these cases involved the alleged constructive receipt or anticipatory assignment of income, I think their reasoning is apposite in resolving the present controversy. The right of the decedent or his estate to rescind the liquidation resolution shows that the liquidation had not proceeded to a point beyond the control of the decedent-shareholder. His unbridled right unilaterally to reverse the liquidation decision eviscerated any claim to a "right" to the liquidation proceeds under the Nebraska statute.

Deciding the first issue in this fashion would obviate the necessity for dealing with the second one.

FORRESTER and DRENNEN, JJ., agree with this dissent.

CLAIBORNE v. UNITED STATES

United States Court of Appeals, Sixth Circuit, 1981.
648 F.2d 448.

EDWARDS, CHIEF JUDGE.

* * *

The facts in the case were stipulated before the District Judge who decided in favor of the administratrix. Our question is whether or not the stipulated facts showed that at the time of Simcoe's death she was entitled to the income from the sale of a piece of property.

Decedent Simcoe in 1967 was an elderly widow living on her farm in Jefferson County, Kentucky. The preceding year the Ford Motor Company had decided to purchase real estate for the site of a Ford heavy duty truck assembly plant in the vicinity of Louisville, and for that purpose had signed a contract with the Louisville and Nashville Railroad (L & N). A wholly-owned subsidiary of L & N (Houston-McCord Realty Company) began negotiations with landowners, including Simcoe, and entered into an option contract with Simcoe for the purchase of her property at $4,000 per acre. With the signing of the option contract, Simcoe received $6,000, which was described in the contract as being the total of liquidated damages the purchaser would be subject to pay in the event the option was not picked up or the contract for sale was not consummated.

Four events happened thereafter: Simcoe appointed her son, Newton Simcoe, as her personal representative and gave him power of attorney to act on her behalf. Thereafter on August 12, 1967, Houston-McCord exercised its option rights on the Simcoe property. On August 15, Newton Simcoe entered into an agreement with Houston-McCord giving them immediate possession of the property at issue. In early September, Ford actually entered upon the Simcoe farm and began clearing and site preparation work for the construction of an access road.

Maude Simcoe died October 1, 1967, before the closing of the sale and before anything had been paid except the $6,000 previously referred to.

The applicable statute does not in its specific language appear to shed much light upon the issue which is currently before us.

* * *

The Treasury Regulation adopted to elucidate § 691 adds at least something to the construction of the statute in applicable part as follows:

> (b) *General definition.* In general, the term "income in respect of a decedent" refers to those amounts *to which a decedent was entitled as gross income* but which were not properly includible in computing his taxable income for the taxable year ending with the date of his death or for a previous taxable year under the method of accounting employed by the decedent. See the regulations under section 451. Thus, the term includes—
>
> (1) All accrued income of a decedent who reported his income by use of the cash receipts and disbursements method;
>
> (2) Income accrued solely by reason of the decedent's death in case of a decedent who reports his income by use of an accrual method of accounting; and
>
> (3) Income to which the decedent had a contingent claim at the time of his death.

Treas.Reg. § 1.691(a)–1(b) (1965).

The legal arguments which have followed the enactment of this statute and the regulation just quoted have divided approximately as follows: The taxpayers have contended that entitlement meant an immediate and legally enforceable right to payment as of the date of death. The IRS, on the contrary, has taken the point of view that where the income was produced by the activities of the decedent prior to death, it was income "in respect of a decedent" within the meaning of the statute, regardless of whether or not the decedent could on the date of death have enforced payment through legal process. The District Judge who heard this case reasoned as follows:

The terms of the contract concerning liquidated damages are plain and unambiguous. They are such that they can only reasonably be construed to be a limitation of the rights of the parties, and not security for the performance of the contract. The terms specifically refer to the consideration as liquidated damages. True it is that the Court must look at the entire agreement. If it is clear that the intention of the parties was to limit their rights, the Court must give that interpretation to the contract. The Court must also look at the surrounding circumstances.

Here, Houston-McCord was not negotiating for itself but for Ford. Had Ford, for whatever reason, changed its plans, Houston-McCord cannot be found to have intended to purchase the property for itself. Thus, the liquidated damages provision must be interpreted as just that. *See* 71 Am.Jur.2d, *Specific Performance,* Section 58.

Defendant further urges that Ford, by taking possession of Mrs. Simcoe's property in August, indicated that the contract would be performed by Houston-McCord and that both Ford and Houston-McCord treated the transaction as having been consummated except for the formal signing of the deed. Whether or not this position has merit, it is agreed that Ford entered the property pursuant to authority granted by Newton Simcoe under the power of attorney referred to above. The reading of that power of attorney raises serious doubt as to the validity of Newton Simcoe's acts. The Court finds no special significance in Houston-McCord's and Ford's activities.

In sum, the Court finds that, at the date of her death, Mrs. Simcoe was not entitled to the amounts yet unpaid by Houston-McCord and that, therefore, the amounts ultimately paid were not income in respect of a decedent as that term is used in Section 691. Since there was no right, there was no taxable income. *Keck v. Commissioner of Internal Revenue,* 415 F.2d 531 (6th Cir.1969).

We observe that our examination of the power of attorney Mrs. Simcoe gave her son does not raise in this court's mind such serious doubts as to the validity of Newton Simcoe's actions as the District Judge found therein. We recognize, of course, that the broad power granted in the first sentence was limited by Mrs. Simcoe by the phrase "under such terms or conditions as I may deem proper." Nothing in this record, however, suggests that Mrs. Simcoe disagreed with her son's grant of authority to the Ford Motor Company to enter upon her land and begin site preparation, and the second paragraph of the power of attorney seems to us to resolve any question of Newton Simcoe's authority.

At that point where the Ford Motor Company began the work of site preparation, Houston-McCord had already exercised its option to purchase this property. In addition, the purchasing parties (Ford, L & N and Houston-McCord) had had Mrs. Simcoe's property rezoned to industrial use and had secured a building permit for it.

Furthermore, Houston-McCord had agreed with Mrs. Simcoe to purchase a farm and some income-producing property which would be accepted by her as part of the purchase price. These negotiations were far advanced at the time of Mrs. Simcoe's death and were completed shortly thereafter. The closing of the purchase of Mrs. Simcoe's farm (with the exchange of properties referred to above and payment of $690,258.86 in cash) took place just 16 days after Mrs. Simcoe's death.

Assuming that the test for taxability of the current disputed income is the enforceability of Mrs. Simcoe's right to the full purchase price as of the date of her death, we find it impossible to agree that no such enforcement rights existed. While as a strict matter of law Mrs. Simcoe would not be "entitled" to the purchase price until after the closing, we believe that Ford's entry upon the land after Houston-McCord had exercised its option would have occasioned the success of a suit by Mrs. Simcoe for specific performance if at that advanced point in the transaction the Ford Motor Company had for some reason refused to complete the purchase. As we construe the term "entitlement," it includes both legal and equitable rights.

Kentucky, of course, recognizes an action for specific performance.
* * *

Under the factual posture of this case, at the moment of decedent's death, we believe that there was entitlement in Mrs. Simcoe to the specific performance of the purchase agreement on tender of a deed.

We also believe where, by agreement, Ford Motor Company had taken possession of Mrs. Simcoe's land and had begun reshaping it, Ford's agent would be regarded by the Kentucky courts as having so exercised its contract rights as to be liable for full payment of the contract price.

* * *

The leading case in this Circuit upon interpretation of § 691 of the Revenue Act of 1954 is *Keck v. Commissioner,* 415 F.2d 531 (6th Cir. 1969). *Keck* relied in part on *Trust Co. of Georgia v. Ross,* 392 F.2d 694 (5th Cir.1967), *cert. denied,* 393 U.S. 830, 89 S.Ct. 97, 21 L.Ed.2d 101 (1968). In *Keck* we said:

> We agree with the United States Court of Appeals for the Fifth Circuit in holding that the right to income, under the provision of the statute here pertinent, is to be distinguished from the economic activities that create that right and that, absent such a right, no matter how great the activities, there is no taxable income under Section 691.
>
> It is our conclusion that, at the date of his death, decedent Arthur D. Shaw possessed neither the right nor the power to require the corporations to liquidate and did not, prior to his death, possess the right to receive any proceeds from the contemplated liquidation. It follows that the amounts herein involved are not taxable under Section 691.

Keck v. Commissioner, supra at 534–35.

In *Keck* the transaction involved required the approval of the Interstate Commerce Commission before there could be any consummation of the sales of the shares concerned. Such approval was not received until a year and a half after the death of the owner of the shares concerned. Neither in law nor in equity could the owner of the shares have enforced the purchase agreement there involved.

We recognize that the United States in this appeal argues for an "economic activities" test which would exclude any consideration of enforceability as an aspect of entitlement. To this degree the government appears to be asking for an overruling of the *Keck* opinion. Since we believe that for the reasons outlined above the factual situation in this case is sufficiently distinguishable from the facts in *Keck* to warrant a different result, we decline the suggestion which we believe is strongly implied in the government's brief that we now overrule the legal conclusion in *Keck.*

For the reasons set forth above, we hold that decedent was entitled to the completion of this transaction and the payment of the funds as of the time of her death. The basic thrust of the Congressional purpose appears to us to be to include in income accounted for under § 691 all income where economic activities had progressed to the point of either legal or equitable entitlement.

The judgment of the District Court is therefore vacated and this case is remanded to the District Court for further proceedings in accordance with this opinion.

ESTATE OF PETERSON v. COMMISSIONER

United States Tax Court, 1980.
74 T.C. 630, aff'd, 667 F.2d 675 (8th Cir.1981).

HALL, JUDGE:

* * *

The sole issue for decision is whether the proceeds from the sale of 2,398 calves received by the Estate of Charley W. Peterson constituted "income in respect of a decedent" as that term is used in section 691.

* * *

Respondent contends that the sale proceeds in issue were income in respect of Charley W. Peterson (hereinafter referred to as the decedent) because, as of the date of his death, the decedent was entitled to receive those proceeds. Respondent claims that the decedent's entitlement arose from a combination of two factors, the livestock sales contract executed on July 11, 1972, between the decedent and the Max Rosenstock Co. (hereinafter referred to as the Rosenstock contract) and the activities performed by the decedent pursuant to the contract. As a result of his determination, respondent asserts that the estate should report as income the difference between the sale proceeds and the decedent's adjusted basis in the calves. See sec. 1014(c).[5]

On the other hand, petitioners contend that the criterion for determining whether an item constitutes income in respect of a decedent is whether the decedent "performed under the contract to the extent that a fixed, legal right at death exists, which will ultimately result in payment without any conditions precedent or contingencies with respect to the decedent's performance." Petitioners argue that when the decedent died on November 9, 1972, he did not possess such an unconditional right to the sale proceeds. Rather, petitioners assert that it was the postdeath activities of the estate that consummated the sale and gave rise to the accompanying entitlement to the proceeds. Accordingly, petitioners claim that the sale proceeds were not income in respect of the decedent and that the estate must recognize as income only the difference between the sale proceeds and the fair market value of the calves as of November 9, 1972. See sec. 1014(a). For the reasons stated below, we agree with petitioners.

5. Sec. 1014(a) generally provides that the basis of property in the hands of a person acquiring the property from a decedent shall be the fair market value of the property at the date of the decedent's death. However, sec. 1014(c) provides that the above statutory provision "shall not apply to property which constitutes a right to receive an item of income in respect of a decedent under section 691."

* * *

Although the present statute describes how income in respect of a decedent is to be reported, nowhere does it define what it is. The only definition appears in section 1.691(a)–1(b), Income Tax Regs., but a reading of that definition readily demonstrates its imprecision. As a result, the courts have been called upon to establish the dimensions of the term.

Certain general propositions have evolved from prior cases. For income to be considered "income in respect of a decedent," section 691 requires that the decedent possess a *right* to that income as of the date of death. See *Estate of Sidles v. Commissioner,* 65 T.C. 873, 880 (1976), affd. without opinion 553 F.2d 102 (8th Cir.1977). This right to the income is not limited to those items which, on the date of decedent's death, would satisfy the requirements of the "all events" test of accrual tax accounting. Rather the expansive view of "accrual" established in *Helvering v. Enright* has been subsumed by section 691. See *Commissioner v. Linde,* 213 F.2d 1, 6 (1954); *Estate of Davison v. United States,* 155 Ct.Cl. 290, 292 F.2d 937, 940–941 (1961). Whether a decedent possesses a right to certain income on the date of his death must be determined on a case-by-case basis upon "the subsisting facts." *Trust Co. of Georgia v. Ross,* 392 F.2d 694, 695 (5th Cir.1967), cert. denied 393 U.S. 830 (1968). One of the facts to be considered is whether the income received after death resulted from the decedent's activities during his lifetime. But this right must be distinguished from the activity which created it, for no matter how great that activity was, there can be no income in respect of a decedent under section 691 unless the decedent possessed a right to receive such income on his death. *Trust Co. of Georgia v. Ross, supra* at 695. The problem in the instant case is to apply these abstract and general propositions to the facts before us. As succinctly stated elsewhere:

> At times, it may be difficult to determine whether the decedent's steps prior to his death had proceeded sufficiently to treat sales proceeds received after death as income in respect of a decedent. The test here is not quite whether the decedent "closed" the sale or transferred title and possession of an asset before death. Rather, it is whether his successor acquired a right to receive proceeds from an asset's disposition on the one hand, or acquired the asset itself on the other. Depending upon the subject and terms of a sale, death may interrupt the transaction at a number of stages which do not fall clearly on either side of this rather murky distinction. The result has been frequent litigation and critical commentary on its results. Despite its importance, the test still defies easy application in a given case. [M. Ferguson, J. Freeland & R. Stephens, Federal Income Taxation of Estates and Beneficiaries 178–179 (1970).]

Our examination of the prior cases involving postdeath sales proceeds and the applicable portions of the regulations under section 691 has distilled at least four requirements which have been applied to test whether a decedent possessed the requisite right to sales proceeds at the time of his death.[9]

The first requirement is that the decedent must have entered into a legally significant arrangement, e.g., a contract, regarding the disposition of the subject matter of the sale. This arrangement may take a variety of forms: an express executory contract of sale (see *Trust Co. of Georgia v. Ross, supra;* Rev.Rul. 78–32, 1978–1 C.B. 198); an implied contract of sale (e.g., if X, a decedent, delivered unsolicited apples to Y, who accepted the apples but had not paid for them prior to X's death); or a contractual arrangement with a cooperative marketing association (see *Commissioner v. Linde, supra*). The significance of these arrangements is to elevate the decedent's right beyond the level of a mere expectancy.[10] Cf. *Estate of Burnett v. Commissioner,* 2 T.C. 897 (1943), cited in Rev.Rul. 58–436, 1958–2 C.B. 366, modified on other grounds in Rev.Rul. 64–289, 1964–2 C.B. 173. (The "mere ownership" of livestock or harvested crops which were marketable on the date of decedent's death does not constitute income in respect of a decedent.)

The second requirement is that the decedent has performed the substantive (nonministerial) acts required of him as preconditions to the sale, i.e., the subject matter of the sale was in a deliverable state on the date of the decedent's death. The nature and scope of the decedent's activities will depend on the subject matter of the sale. For instance, the decedent's activities associated with a sale of corporate stock will be substantially less than the activities associated with the building and sale of a house or the raising and sale of crops. Whereas the acts required of a decedent to make stock deliverable are generally ministerial in nature (see *Estate of Sidles v. Commissioner,* 65 T.C. 873, 881 (1976), affd. without opinion 553 F.2d 102 (8th Cir.1977)), the same is not true for the house or crops which require the sweat of the decedent's brow. The decedent's right will not sufficiently ripen for purposes of section 691 if the decedent has not performed the substantive acts required of him as a precondition to the sale.[11] In other words, the estate's right to sale proceeds must derive from the decedent's death and not from its own efforts. See *Estate of Sidles v. Commissioner, supra* at 881.

9. The list of requirements is not meant to be an ironclad formulation of the hurdles which an item of income must clear before it will be categorized as income in respect of a decedent. The innumerable types of sales transactions and the different stages at which the seller's death may intervene, make any formulation of a list of criteria susceptible to change. Yet this list represents the present status of the law and is a reasonable line of demarcation considering the potentially broad scope of the statute.

10. Whether an arrangement that is legally significant for purposes of determining the existence of income in respect of decedent must also be legally enforceable is not decided here. Cf. *O'Daniel's Estate v. Commissioner,* 173 F.2d 966 (2d Cir.1949) (involving a postdeath bonus). See *Estate of Sidles v. Commissioner,* 65 T.C. 873, 888 (1976) (Judge Hall's concurring opinion).

11. For example, if X, the decedent, enters into an executory contract to sell the crops to be grown next season on X's farm and X dies prior to the plowing and seeding of his fields, no one would argue that the proceeds from the crop sale were income in respect of a decedent.

One indicium of whether a decedent has performed the applicable substantive acts is whether he has delivered, or somehow placed, the subject matter of the sale beyond his control prior to his death. Thus a predeath delivery to the purchaser (see sec. 1.691(a)–2(b) *Example 5(1),* Income Tax Regs.), to an escrow agent (see *Trust Co. of Georgia v. Ross,* 262 F.Supp. 900 (N.D.Ga.1966), affd. 392 F.2d 694 (5th Cir.1967)), or to a cooperative marketing association (see *Commissioner v. Linde, supra*) indicates that the decedent has performed the necessary substantive acts. However, the absence of delivery or otherwise placing the subject matter beyond the decedent's control does not preclude a finding that the sale proceeds are income in respect of a decedent.[12]

The third requirement is that there existed, at the time of the decedent's death, no economically material contingencies which might have disrupted the sale. For example, if a sale is contingent on a nonroutine or nonperfunctory approval by the Interstate Commerce Commission and such approval has not been given prior to the decedent's death, the sale proceeds are not income in respect of a decedent. See *Keck v. Commissioner,* 415 F.2d 531, 534 (6th Cir.1969), revg. 49 T.C. 313 (1968) ("the sale of the stock was subject to a number of contingencies; that it was, at that time, subject to the approval of the Interstate Commerce Commission, a condition precedent which was not met until eighteen months after decedent's death, and that such approval was neither routine or perfunctory"); *Estate of Sidles v. Commissioner,* 65 T.C. 873, 889–890 (1976) (Judge Tannenwald concurring in part and dissenting in part). In this respect, the test departs from the "all events" test of accrual accounting, which is normally not met even if a remaining contingency which would preclude receipt is sufficiently remote as not to have economic materiality.

The fourth requirement is that the decedent, himself, would have eventually received (actually or constructively) the sale proceeds if he had lived. This situation may be best exemplified by a typical date-of-death buy-sell agreement between a decedent and his corporation; since, by its terms, the sale is only effective upon the decedent's death, the decedent could not have received the sale proceeds if he had lived. Therefore, the proceeds from such a sale are not income in respect of a decedent. See sec. 1.691(a)–2(b) *Example 4.*

The facts and circumstances of this case lead us to the conclusion that the proceeds received by the decedent's estate on the sale of the 2,398 calves did not constitute income in respect of a decedent within the meaning of section 691. In reaching this conclusion, we have considered the four requirements delineated above.

Initially, the facts indicate that the decedent entered into an executory sales contract, i.e., a legally significant arrangement, with the Max Rosenstock Co. for the sale of calves. This characterization is

12. For example, the result in *Trust Co. of Georgia* would not be any different if the decedent in that case had held his stock until death rather than placing it with an escrow agent.

contrary to petitioners' assertion that the Rosenstock contract did not represent a valid executory sales contract. Rather, petitioners view the Rosenstock contract as creating "illusory" obligations on the contracting parties much in the nature of an option to buy or sell. Petitioners' position appears to stem from a combination of three factors—the decedent's relative freedom to select delivery dates, the buyer's ability to reject any calves which he considered too young, too old, or unmerchantable, and the imprecise number of calves to be sold.

There is no dispute between the parties that the Nebraska version of the Uniform Commercial Code (UCC) is applicable to the Rosenstock contract. Using the UCC as our guidepost, we have no doubt that the Rosenstock contract was a valid executory sales contract. The UCC takes a very liberal view of contract formation. * * *

None of the provisions of the Rosenstock contract cited by petitioners supports their position that performance by either party to the contract was optional. Although the delivery dates were not specifically spelled out in the contract, the decedent was obligated to deliver prior to December 15, 1972. Furthermore, even though the buyer possessed the right to reject calves, this right was not unbridled. Rather, the buyer could only reject calves which were too young, too old, or unmerchantable and, even then, these rejection rights were tempered by a "good faith" obligation. See Neb.Rev.Stat. secs. 1–203, 2–103(1)(b) (1971 reissue). Moreover, although the contract only approximated the number of calves to be delivered, the use of an estimate did not mean that either party was free to disavow his obligation under the contract. See 67 Am.Jur.2d 282–283 (1973). The decedent had a good-faith obligation to deliver approximately 3,300 calves, and the buyer had a good-faith obligation to accept those calves, assuming they met his requirements. See Neb.Rev.Stat. sec. 1–203 (1971 reissue).

In sum, petitioners have failed to convince us that the title of the agreement "Livestock Sales Contract" is a misnomer. Rather, the terms of the agreement and the prior dealings between the parties for almost 50 years support our finding that the parties created a valid executory sales contract.

Second, at the time of the decedent's death there existed no economically material contingencies which could potentially disrupt the sale. While it is true that the calves could have been destroyed by disease, etc., prior to delivery, so that the "all events" test would not have been met, petitioners failed to prove that this was anything but a remote possibility. Therefore, potential destruction of the subject matter of the sale did not pose a "real" or "significant" obstacle to the completion of the sale.

Third, the decedent would have received the proceeds of the sale had he lived since the terms of the sale did not make it effective only upon the decedent's death.

Although three of the four requirements tend to support a conclusion opposite to the one reached, all four elements are necessary to support a finding that the decedent possessed a right to the sale proceeds as of his date of death. Accordingly, the absence of one of these requirements precludes the applicability of section 691.

The missing link in this case is the decedent's failure to perform the substantive acts required under the Rosenstock contract. As a precondition to the sale of the calves and consequently, to the receipt of the sale proceeds, it was necessary for the decedent to raise and feed the calves so that they would satisfy the terms of the Rosenstock contract. One such term was that the calves be between 3 months and 11 months old at the time of delivery.

We have found as a fact that of the 2,398 calves eventually delivered by the decedent's estate under the Rosenstock contract only two-thirds were deliverable as of November 9, 1972, the date of the decedent's death. The remainder were too young for delivery. Viewed in its entirety [18] and as impliedly modified by the parties,[19] the contract was not deliverable on November 9, 1972.

The premature status of such a significant number of calves required the decedent's estate to continue the raising and feeding of the calves. Each delivered calf gained approximately one-half to 3 pounds per day between the date of decedent's death (November 9) and the delivery date in December. Had the estate not daily fed, watered, and cared for the calves from the date of decedent's death until the delivery date, these calves would have perished. The activities performed by the estate were not perfunctory or ministerial but substantial and essential acts not performed by the decedent prior to his death. In sum, the estate's right to the sale proceeds derived from its own efforts as well as those of the decedent. This contribution by the estate is sufficient to remove the sale proceeds from the reach of section 691. Cf. *Trust Co. of Georgia v. Ross, supra* at 696. ("It is true that some aspects of the transaction which the contract contemplated had to be performed by [the decedent's] executor but these were not of such scope as would negate the right which was [the decedent's] under the contract.")

Respondent does not deny the estate's role in the sale of the calves. Rather, respondent argues that we should focus on the substantial activities undertaken by the decedent to fulfill the Rosenstock contract and the status of those efforts at the time of his death. At the time of the decedent's death, two-thirds of the 2,398 calves were deliverable under the contract and the remaining one-third were in existence.[21]

18. Neither party contends that the Rosenstock contract was divisible.

19. The written contract required decedent to deliver the Brown County calves on or before Nov. 1, 1972. The calves were not in fact delivered until December at which time Brickley accepted them. Brickley's waiver of the Nov. 1 delivery date resulted in an implied modification of the contract. See Neb.Rev.Stat. sec. 2–206 (1971 reissue).

21. In support of his position, respondent cites the language of regulations section 1.691(a)–1(b), which states that income in respect of a decedent includes "Income to which the decedent had a contingent claim at the time of his death." In his brief, respondent states:

We do not doubt that the decedent's efforts contributed far more to the completion of the contract than those of the estate, but a weighing of the relative efforts is not the test envisioned by section 691. See *Trust Co. of Georgia v. Ross, supra* at 695. Under respondent's formulation, any work-in-progress which was the subject of a predeath contract of sale could constitute income in respect of a decedent if the major part of the work had been completed prior to the decedent's death. The statute, however, does not reach so broadly. As noted in *Commissioner v. Linde, supra* at 5 (9th Cir.1954): "We think it clear that the intent of Congress [in section 691] continued to be as stated in the *Enright* case 'to cover into income the assets of decedents, *earned* during their life and unreported as income.'" (Emphasis supplied.) See also *Estate of Sidles v. Commissioner, supra* at 879. Although the legislative history of section 691 indicates that it is not necessary for an item to have been *earned* by the decedent in any tax reporting sense or in any technical accounting sense, we believe the use of the term "earned" is appropriate insofar as it connotes the practical completion of a transaction. While there is some imprecision in this commonsense approach, it is more precise than respondent's formulation which we find to be "open-ended and somewhat inadequate as a precedent when considered in the scope of the statute." *Trust Co. of Georgia v. Ross, supra* at 695.

SIMPSON, J., concurring: I accept the result reached by the majority since the Commissioner never sought to allocate the proceeds from the sale of the calves between those calves which were deliverable at the date of the decedent's death and those not so deliverable.[1] However, I disagree with the majority's opinion. Such opinion appears to indicate that, as a matter of law, none of the proceeds from the sale of the calves is income in respect of a decedent since some of such proceeds do not constitute such income. Such opinion overlooks the basic proposition

"Respondent's regulation is a reasonable interpretation of the statute. It looks not only to that [to] which the decedent was entitled but also to that [to] which he had a contingent claim. In so doing, it reflects the intent of Congress to go beyond the test of receipt for cash basis taxpayers or the all events test for accrual basis taxpayers. The regulation reflects Congress' intent that a decedent's income be fairly reflected."

We agree that the phrase "contingent claim" as used in respondent's regulation is reflective of congressional intent to go beyond the "all events" test, but this does not mean there is no limit to the scope of that phrase or that the facts of this case are not beyond that limit. Clearly, not all "contingent" claims held by a decedent at the time of his death are within the purview of sec. 691. See *Keck v. Commissioner*, 415 F.2d 531 (6th Cir.1969), revg. 49 T.C. 313 (1968). On the other hand, that phrase does properly include such "contingent" claims as renewal insurance commissions. See *Latendresse v. Commissioner*, 26 T.C. 318 (1956), affd. 243 F.2d 577 (7th Cir. 1957). On balance, respondent's regulation is no more enlightening than the legislative history previously outlined and, accordingly, we are left to chart our own course in the murky waters of sec. 691.

1. Had this case been presented to me, I would have given serious consideration to requesting the parties to consider an allocation of the proceeds and offering them a further trial if necessary to present additional evidence relating to a proper allocation of the proceeds. It might have been preferable to pursue such a course rather than to proceed to announce and apply an unsound construction of sec. 691. However, the question of whether to decide the case as presented or to request further development of it is a matter of judicial discretion, and I accept Judge Hall's decision on this matter.

that under section 691, income earned by a decedent is to be subject to the income tax and not exempt from such tax by giving it a stepped-up basis under section 1014(a). The Court finds that two-thirds of the calves were deliverable on the date of the decedent's death, and as to those calves, virtually all of the income from their sale was earned during the lifetime of the decedent. I agree that the income attributable to the sale of the other one-third is not income in respect of a decedent, but that fact should not have the effect of exempting all the proceeds from the sale of the calves from income tax.

* * *

The issues in this case can be more easily understood if we simplify the facts: Suppose the seller had agreed to sell two calves, one deliverable on November 1, and the other on December 15, and payment was not to be made until both calves had been delivered. If a calf had in fact been delivered on November 1, it is clear that the proceeds from the sale of that calf would be income in respect of a decedent. *Trust Co. of Georgia v. Ross,* 392 F.2d 694 (5th Cir.1967), cert. denied 393 U.S. 830 (1968); *Commissioner v. Linde,* 213 F.2d 1 (9th Cir.1954); *Estate of Sidles v. Commissioner,* 65 T.C. 873 (1976), affd. without opinion 553 F.2d 102 (8th Cir.1977). Similarly, even if the one calf had not been delivered on November 1, but if it was deliverable at the date of the decedent's death, it is clear that substantially all of the conditions of the sale would have been performed before the date of the decedent's death and that the proceeds from the sale of the calf should be treated as income in respect of a decedent. *Trust Co. of Georgia v. Ross, supra; Estate of Sidles v. Commissioner, supra.* Although there were many more calves involved in this case, the applicable principles are the same, and the proceeds attributable to the calves which were deliverable at the time of the decedent's death should be treated as income in respect of a decedent.

As to the two-thirds of the calves which were deliverable at the date of the decedent's death, his efforts had earned a right to the income from their sale. Such right was "the fruits of the man's * * * activity during his lifetime" (*Riegelman's Estate v. Commissioner,* 253 F.2d at 319) and "stemmed solely from * * * [the decedent's] efforts" (*United States v. Ellis,* 264 F.2d at 327). As to those calves, actual delivery of the calves to the purchaser was all that was required to complete the sale. We do not know why none of the calves was delivered before the death of the decedent, but whether those calves were delivered was wholly within the control of the decedent and those managing his affairs. It was their decision not to deliver the calves before his death, and their decision not to perform that ministerial act of delivery should not result in the income from the sale of such calves being exempt from income tax.[2] The opinion of the majority may lead

2. Here, we are not dealing with the sale of an indivisible product, such as a house or a building, which was partially completed before the death of the decedent; nor are we dealing with a situation in which none of the product was to be delivered before the death of the decedent. I

some persons to conclude that in similar situations it is advisable to postpone the completion of a sale in order to avoid the income tax.

The effect of the opinion of the majority is to exempt from income tax the proceeds of the sale of all the calves simply because some of them were not deliverable at the time of the decedent's death. In other words, because one-third of the calves were not yet ready for delivery, none of the income earned during the lifetime of the decedent is to be subject to the income tax. In my judgment, such a result clearly frustrates the purpose of section 691. *Davison's Estate v. United States,* 292 F.2d at 941.

The conclusion of the majority cannot be justified by any administrative difficulties involved in allocating the proceeds of the sale. It is true that we may not be able to identify the actual calves which were deliverable at the time of the decedent's death and that, therefore, we do not know the prices brought by them. It is also true that such calves gained some additional weight after the death of the decedent. As a result of these circumstances, it may be impossible to ascertain the exact amount of income earned during the life of the decedent; yet, these difficulties should not result in exempting all of such income from taxation.

In construing the predecessor of section 691, the Supreme Court held in *Helvering v. Enright,* 312 U.S. 636 (1941), that the fact that the exact amount earned by the decedent cannot be determined should not frustrate the provision; the Court said at page 645:

> The completion of the work in progress was necessary to fix the amount due but the right to payment for work ordinarily arises on partial performance. Accrued income under § 42 for uncompleted operations includes the value of the services rendered by the decedent, capable of approximate valuation whether based on the agreed compensation or on quantum meruit. * * *

Similarly, when a court is convinced that a taxpayer is entitled to a deduction, it is generally not denied him merely because he cannot establish the precise amount thereof. *Cohan v. Commissioner,* 39 F.2d 540 (2d Cir.1930); *Merians v. Commissioner,* 60 T.C. 187 (1973). A similar approach should have been adopted in this case.

DRENNEN, DAWSON, TANNENWALD, and CHABOT, JJ., agree with this concurring opinion.

REVENUE RULING 64–289

1964–2 Cumulative Bulletin 173.

Reconsideration has been given to Revenue Ruling 58–436, C.B. 1958–2, 366, in light of the decision of the United States Court of Claims in the case of *Estate of Helen Davison v. United States,* 292 Fed. (2d) 937 (1961), certiorari denied, 368 U.S. 939 (1961).

express no opinion concerning the applicability of sec. 691 in such situations.

In Revenue Ruling 58–436 a decedent owned livestock and farm crops in various stages of growth at the time of his death. The ruling holds, in pertinent part, that livestock and farm crops (harvested or unharvested, raised by a decedent prior to his death or received from tenants as rent for farm lands, held for sale or for feeding purposes) which a decedent, who had reported his income on the cash method of accounting, owned at the time of his death, constitute items of property or inventory and not rights to, or items of, income in respect of a decedent.

Section 1.61–4 of the Income Tax Regulations, relating to the gross income of farmers, provides, in part, that crop shares (whether or not considered rent under State law) shall be included in gross income as of the year in which the crop shares are reduced to money or the equivalent of money.

In the *Davison* case, the decedent, who had employed the cash receipts and disbursements method of accounting, died on December 24, 1952, owning two parcels of real property. One parcel had been leased by the decedent for the period January 1, 1952, to January 1, 1953, under terms providing that she was to be paid as rent one-fourth of all crops grown on the land. The second parcel of land had been leased by the decedent for the period February 1952, to January 1, 1953, under terms providing that she was to be paid as rent one-half of the net proceeds of all crops grown on the land. In 1953 and 1954 the decedent's estate received payments in respect of the two leases in the form of (1) proceeds from the sale of crops, and (2) crops, which were then sold for the account of the estate. The court held that the rental payments received by the decedent's estate in 1953 and 1954 were taxable to the estate, under section 126 of the Internal Revenue Code of 1939 and section 691 of the Internal Revenue Code of 1954, as income in respect of a decedent.

In the *Davison* case, the court stated, in part, as follows:

> * * * Crops received as rent exist in the hands of the lessor as a unique kind of property which can be described, like a right to receive future income, as a potential income asset. * * *
>
> Now if a landlord died while in possession of certain crops which he had received as rent we believe that under present law the essential income nature of these crops would follow the crops into the landlord's estate. The crops would remain *crop-rents* in the hands of the estate and would represent a form of income in respect of a decedent. Furthermore, under section 126 [of the 1939 Code] these crop-rents would be considered in the hands of the estate to have the same character which they had in the hands of the decedent—the potential of producing taxable income through sale. Only when the estate finally sold the crops would income be recognized. But at that point the money derived from the sale would be taxable, and taxable as income in respect of a decedent.

Upon reconsideration, in light of the *Davison* decision, it is held that crop shares or livestock received as rent by a decedent, who had employed the cash method of accounting, prior to his death, and owned by him at the time of his death, as well as crop shares or livestock which he had a right to receive as rent at the time of his death for economic activities occurring before his death, constitute income in respect of a decedent which is required to be included in gross income, for Federal income tax purposes, in the year in which the crop shares or livestock are sold, or otherwise disposed of.

Where the decedent dies during a rent period, only the net proceeds attributable to the portion of the rent period ending with his death are income in respect of a decedent. The proceeds attributable to the portion of the rent period which runs from the day after death to the end of the rent period are ordinary income to the estate.

Where crop shares or livestock received as rent are reduced to cash and received by the lessor prior to his death, or received by the lessor in kind and sold by him before his death, the proceeds thus received are includible in gross income and reportable in the final return of the decedent. No proration is required even though the rental period does not terminate until after his death. Likewise, cash rent received by the lessor prior to his death should be reported on his final return.

Where crop shares or livestock rentals are received in kind and held by the lessor at the time of his death, and are sold later by the executor or by a beneficiary who acquires the property in kind by inheritance, the proceeds from the sale of such crop shares or livestock should be allocated between income in respect of a decedent and income under section 61 of the Code.

The amount to be allocated to income in respect of a decedent is determined by multiplying the proceeds by a fraction of which the numerator is the number of days in the part of the rental period which ends with the date of death of the lessor and the denominator is the total number of days in the rental period.

The amount to be allocated to income under section 61 of the Code is determined by multiplying the proceeds by a fraction of which the numerator is the number of days in the rental period after the date of the lessor's death and the denominator is the number of days in the total rental period.

The allocation of the proceeds from crop shares or livestock rentals, where the decedent dies during a rent period, may be illustrated by the following examples:

Example 1.—A farm owner, who used the cash receipts and disbursements method of accounting, leased land to a tenant for one-third of the crop, payable in cash when the crop share is sold at the direction of the lessor. The rental period was for 1 year beginning March 1, 1963. The lessor died June 30, 1963. He was alive 122 days of the rental period. The rental was paid in cash to the decedent's estate on October 31, 1963. $^{122}/_{365}$ of the amount received by the estate is income in respect of a decedent. The remainder is income under section 61 of the Code.

Example 2.—On January 1, 1962, a farm owner, who employed the cash receipts and disbursements method of accounting, leased land to a tenant for 1 year for one-third of the crop (wheat and corn). The lessor died August 28, 1962. He was alive 240 days of the rental period. The lessor's share of the wheat crop was delivered to him on July 31, 1962, and was sold by him on August 5, 1962, for 12*x* dollars. No part of the 12*x* dollars is income in respect of a decedent since it should be reported on the lessor's final return. The deceased lessor's share of the corn crop was delivered on December 6, 1962, to his estate. The executor of his estate sold one-half of the corn on December 20, 1962, and sold the balance of the corn on February 10, 1963. 240/365 of the proceeds of each sale by the executor will constitute income in respect of a decedent and 125/365 of the proceeds of each sale will constitute income to the estate under section 61 of the Code.

The foregoing holding is applicable only to crop shares or livestock received as rent. It is not applicable to items received in a sharing arrangement in which the landowner, as well as the tenant, participates materially in the farming operation.

Revenue Ruling 58–436, C.B. 1958–2, 366, is hereby modified to remove therefrom the holding that livestock and farm crops received as rent by the decedent prior to his death, and owned by him at the time of his death, do not constitute items of income in respect of a decedent.

REVENUE RULING 64–308

1964–2 Cumulative Bulletin 176.

Advice has been requested whether a proportionate part of the income of *X* company, an electing small business corporation, which was included in the gross income of *A* 's estate, is income in respect of a decedent under section 691 of the Internal Revenue Code of 1954 with respect to which a deduction is allowable under subsection (c) of section 691 of the Code.

* * *

Section 691 of the Code does not apply to dividends declared on stock owned by a taxpayer but unpaid at his death if he dies before the record date. See *Estate of Henry W. Putnam v. Commissioner,* 324 U.S. 393 (1945), C.B.1945, 345. The decedent must be identified as the owner of the right to the income at his death.

Since only persons who are shareholders of an electing small business corporation on the last day of the taxable year of the corporation are required to include in their gross income the amounts specified in section 1373 of the Code, it cannot be said that any part of the corporation's undistributed taxable income for its taxable year in which *A* died was includible in his gross income. Furthermore, since the corporation had declared no dividend payable to stockholders of record on a date prior to the death of *A*, at the time of his death *A* had no right to receive as gross income any amount of the undistributed taxable income of *X* company for its fiscal year ended June 30, 1959.

The amount includible in the gross income of *A* 's estate for its first taxable year is the amount it would have received as a dividend if, on the last day of *X* company's taxable year, there had been distributed to *A* 's estate one-half of *X* company's undistributed taxable income for its fiscal year ended June 30, 1959. The amount so includible is treated as a dividend distributed on June 30, 1959, subsequent to the death of *A*.

Accordingly, it is held that no part of the undistributed taxable income of *X* company included in the gross income of *A* 's estate is "income in respect of a decedent" under section 691 of the Code. Therefore, no deduction is allowable under subsection (c) of section 691 of the Code.

Helpful guidelines for identifying IRD refer to income that would have been taxable to decedent had death not occurred prior to receipt.[1] *Peterson* refers to there being a legally significant arrangement that elevated the income above a mere expectancy and there were no outstanding economically material contingencies at decedent's death. To establish that decedent would have received and included the income had death not intervened, it is necessary to establish that decedent, not the ultimate recipient, performed the substantive acts that spawned the entitlement. Thus, according to *Claiborne*, the recipient's acquisition must be "passive," not due to efforts made to generate the right (as opposed to enforcing it) after decedent's death.

Questions

Using these guidelines, which of the following items would constitute IRD? [2]

1. Decedent was employed at an hourly wage, payable bimonthly two weeks after the close of each pay period involved. At death, decedent had yet to receive the paycheck for the pay period prior to the one in which death occurred, and had accumulated hours for the pay period in which death occurred. Will the paychecks for those periods constitute IRD?

2. Decedent was a medical doctor whose office staff had neither billed nor collected for services rendered prior to death. Will the fees subsequently collected by decedent's staff be IRD?

3. Decedent was an insurance agent entitled to substantial renewal commissions payable for many years after death on policies sold during decedent's life. To be entitled to those commissions, however, the owners of the policies must renew them annually. Will those continuing commis-

1. See Ferguson, Freeland & Stephens, Federal Income Taxation of Estates and Beneficiaries 146–48 (1970).

2. For exhaustive studies of what constitutes IRD, see Ferguson, Freeland & Stephens, Federal Income Taxation of Estates and Beneficiaries 162–271 (1970), and Annot., 13 ALR Fed. 613 (1972).

sion payments constitute IRD? Would it affect your answer if decedent's insurance agency performs acts intended to encourage existing owners to continue to renew their policies, whether originally purchased from decedent or other members of the agency?

4. Although not obliged to do so, decedent's employer paid decedent's surviving spouse a year end bonus for the year in which decedent died. Is the bonus IRD? Would it matter whether the employer deducted the bonus as a salary expense under section 162, and are the estate tax consequences of the payment relevant to the income taxation thereof? Should decedent's surviving spouse care whether the bonus is IRD?

5. Decedent's estate received a cash liquidation of accrued vacation and sick leave credited to decedent's account. Is this payment IRD?

6. Is the noncontributory portion of decedent's qualified employee benefit plan IRD? The contributory portion? Would it matter if the plan were not a qualified plan under section 401?

7. Decedent's estate received a cash payment under a death benefit only (DBO) plan maintained as an employee benefit by decedent's employer. Is the payment IRD, and should it matter whether the plan was qualified under section 401?

8. Decedent was a partner in a law firm. After death the partnership made a liquidating distribution of decedent's interest in the partnership, and continued to make periodic payments representing decedent's share of contingent fees received in cases in various stages of litigation at the time of decedent's death and either completed or settled by the firm thereafter. Are any of these payments IRD?

9. Decedent owned EE bonds that accrued interest during decedent's life. Under the regulations dealing with these savings bonds, decedent had elected to defer reporting that interest during life. Does any portion of the bond represent IRD?

10. Decedent owned commercial rental property for which rentals were paid in advance. Is any portion of the payment made for the period during which decedent died excludible from decedent's gross income on decedent's final return, and is any portion IRD?

11. Decedent was income beneficiary of a trust that paid income quarterly. Following death in the middle of the present quarter, how much, if any, of the next income payment will constitute IRD? Would it matter whether that payment were made to decedent's estate as opposed to the next income beneficiary?

12. With respect to stocks that pay dividends, which of the declaration date, record date or payment date must occur before decedent's death in order for dividends to constitute IRD?

13. Is the unrealized gain in property held by decedent at death IRD when ultimately realized? Would it matter if the property were an asset, such as artwork, that decedent created during life?

14. Decedent owned Greenacre on which a partially mature crop was growing at the time of death. If the crop is harvested and marketed after decedent's death, is any portion of the proceeds therefrom IRD and, if so,

how would that portion be determined? Would it matter if the crop were being grown by a tenant farmer and constituted rent for use of decedent's land?

15. In *Claiborne,* if decedent's son died prior to collecting on the contract for sale, and his entire estate were inherited by his surviving spouse, would amounts collected by her constitute IRD?

16. Decedent sold Homeacre to a child on installments with notes payable over 30 years. The notes were self cancelling on decedent's death. What are the estate tax and IRD consequences of the self cancellation provision?

17. Grantor established a section 677 trust during life. If that trust sold appreciated property on installments prior to grantor's death, and some of the installments are collected after grantor's death, does any part of the gain represented in those installments constitute IRD to grantor's successors or to the next income beneficiaries of the trust?

18. Under an enforceable buy-sell agreement, decedent's estate was obliged to sell stock in decedent's closely held business after death. Is any of the gain on that sale IRD?

19. In Revenue Ruling 64–308, why did the taxpayer *want* the item to constitute IRD?

TAX CONSEQUENCES OF IRD

There are essentially four tax consequences of an item being regarded as IRD, not all of which being disadvantageous, depending on the circumstances. First, even if the decedent was not a cash basis taxpayer, income represented by the right to receive IRD is taxable in the year it is received. There is no tax consequence attributable to that income in the recipient's tax year in which the *right* to the IRD was acquired. Be prepared to explain the difference apparent in the last sentence of Treasury Regulation section 1.691(a)–2(a) between the concept of receipt of the right to IRD as opposed to receipt of the income represented by that right.

Second, under section 691(a)(3), the character of the income is the same as if received by the decedent.

Third, rather than a new basis at death, the item has a section 1014(c) basis equal to what decedent's basis would have been if living. Do you understand why this treatment is necessary?

Finally, if the right to IRD is transferred prior to collection, such as in paying an obligation (for example, in funding a marital deduction bequest or in satisfaction of other obligations imposed on an estate), realization of the income represented by that right is accelerated under section 691(a)(2). According to Treasury Regulation section 1.691(a)–4(a), the amount includible in the year of transfer is the greater of fair market value of the IRD item or the amount of any consideration received on the transfer, less any basis in the item. As a consequence of acceleration, the recipient receives the item with a new basis equal to its fair market value, thus protecting against subsequent income taxation of the IRD a second time. Acceleration, and any DNI carryout on distribution of a right to IRD, is avoided entirely under Treasury Regulation sections 1.691(a)–4(b)(2) and 1.691(a)–4(b)(3) if distribution is in satisfaction of a specific bequest of the right to receive the IRD or, under Treasury Regulation sections 1.691(a)–4(b)(1) and 1.691(a)–4(b)(3), if distribution occurs on the death of the person (or termination of the estate or trust) entitled thereto. In such a case, income is not realized on transfer of the right to receive the IRD. Instead, income is deferred until receipt by the beneficiary of the income represented by that right. While this says nothing about the distribution deduction and inclusion rules of sections 651, 652, 661 and 662, sections 663(a) and 643(e) ought to provide these answers, as we saw in Chapter Five.

Question

If acceleration is avoidable by deferring distribution until termination of an estate or trust, why would a fiduciary make an accelerating distribution, especially from an estate?

DEDUCTIONS IN RESPECT OF A DECEDENT

As a counterpart to the rules governing income in respect of a decedent, a taxpayer who makes certain payments that would have been deductible if paid by a decedent is entitled to a section 691(b) deduction in respect of the decedent. Those expenditures are specificially limited to section 162 business expenses, section 212 expenses of producing income or managing or safeguarding income producing property, section 163 interest, and section 164 deductible taxes (or the section 33 credit for foreign taxes). In addition, the recipient of depletable property is entitled to any section 611 percentage depletion attributable to income received therefrom, under Treasury Regulation section 1.691(b)–1(b). In each case, the deduction is available to the recipient of property to which the expenditure is attributable, and without limitation by the otherwise applicable section 642(g) rule denying double duty for deductions that may be taken on either the estate or income tax return.

Questions

1. Why are deductions in respect of a decedent specifically excepted from the operation of section 642(g)?

2. During life, Decedent borrowed against the cash surrender value of insurance on Decedent's life, never repaying the principal of the loans and, as authorized under the policy, allowing interest to go unpaid so long as annual increases in cash surrender value equalled or exceeded the interest accrued in the prior year. At death, also pursuant to terms of the policy, the proceeds payable to Decedent's designated beneficiary were reduced by the amount of the loans and accrued interest. The beneficiary deducted the interest element of the offset amount as a deduction in respect of the

Decedent, which the IRS disallowed. What grounds would you put forward in defense of the Service's disallowance, and should the deduction be allowed? See Hooks v. Commissioner, 22 T.C. 502 (1954), acquiescence, 1955–1 C.B. 5.

DEDUCTION FOR TAXES ATTRIBUTABLE TO IRD

In addition to deductions in respect of a decedent, an income tax deduction is also allowed under section 691(c) for estate or generation-skipping taxes attributable to IRD. This deduction is based on a theory that, had the income been received by the decedent during life, any income tax incurred thereon would have been paid prior to imposition of the estate or generation-skipping tax, resulting in a smaller estate subject to those taxes and, thus, less of those taxes being payable. In order to approximate that result without recomputing the estate or generation-skipping tax after the income tax on the IRD has been computed, Congress substituted an income tax deduction for the estate or generation-skipping taxes attributable to the IRD. While the result is not necessarily the same, the general objective is to obtain a result that is administratively easier than recomputation of the wealth transfer tax and that gives some rough approximation of what would have happened if the IRD had been received during the decedent's life.

The deduction is equal to the incremental amount of tax attributable to inclusion of the section 691(c)(2)(B) net amount of IRD. Net IRD means total IRD less total DRD, with this offset required by Treasury Regulation section 1.691(c)–1(a)(1) even if the recipient of the IRD (to whom the deduction for taxes incurred is allowed) is not the taxpayer who is entitled to claim the DRD (by virtue of having paid the deductible expenditures). Similarly, the deduction for taxes paid is an entitlement of the recipients of the IRD, even if other taxpayers bore the burden of the taxes that generate that deduction. Quaere whether this disparity warrants an equitable adjustment in favor of the payor of the estate or generation-skipping tax.

Determination of the incremental taxes attributable to inclusion of the net IRD requires a calculation of the amount these taxes would have been had the net IRD not been included. For example, if the decedent's estate were $1,000,000 and net IRD were $50,000, the tax on an estate of $950,000 would be determined and the difference between that tax and the tax paid on the $1,000,000 estate would be the incremental amount that would be deductible under section 691(c). This computation becomes more complex if a marital or charitable deduction is involved, as illustrated by the following case.

ESTATE OF KINCAID v. COMMISSIONER

United States Tax Court, 1985.
85 T.C. 25.

CLAPP, JUDGE: Respondent determined a deficiency in Nelle W. Kincaid's income tax for 1976 of $98,864.18 and a deficiency in her income tax for 1977 of $223,080.75. Because of concessions by both parties, the only issue for our determination is the proper method of computing the deduction under section 691(c) for estate tax attributable to income in respect of a decedent where there is a formula maximum marital deduction bequest.

* * *

Mrs. Kincaid was the widow of Garvice Kincaid, who died on November 21, 1975. Mrs. Kincaid died during the pendency of these proceedings, and her estate was substituted as party petitioner. Mr. Kincaid's employment contract with Kentucky Finance Co. (KFC) provided that his annual bonus payments were to continue after his death and were to be paid to Mrs. Kincaid. The value of the right to the KFC payments was includable in Mr. Kincaid's gross estate and was eligible for the marital deduction provided by section 2056(a).

Most of Mr. Kincaid's other property was bequeathed to a trust. After payment of taxes, debts, and the expenses of administering his estate, the trust property was divided into a "marital part" and a "nonmarital part." The "marital part" consisted of property equal in value to the maximum deduction allowable to his estate less the value of non-trust property includable in his gross estate which passed to Mrs. Kincaid and qualified for the marital deduction. The KFC payments were such non-trust property. Thus, the value of the right to the KFC payments was subtracted from the maximum marital deduction in determining the "marital part." The "marital part" passed to Mrs. Kincaid and was eligible for the marital deduction. The "nonmarital part" consisted of the remainder of the trust property. From the notice of deficiency in the estate tax for Mr. Kincaid's estate and from his estate tax return, there can be no dispute that there were other assets in his estate which would have qualified to fund "the marital part" which were not income in respect of a decedent.

* * *

The section 691(c)(1)(A) deduction is computed by creating a fraction in which the numerator is the IRD received by Mrs. Kincaid during the year and included in her income and in which the denominator is the value of all IRD included in Mr. Kincaid's gross estate. That fraction is multiplied by the estate tax attributable to all IRD included in his gross estate. The result is the section 691(c)(1)(A) deduction.

The focus of the controversy here is how to calculate the estate tax attributable to the KFC payments pursuant to section 691(c)(2)(C). This section defines the amount of estate tax attributable to the KFC payments to be the difference between the actual estate tax and the estate tax computed without including the KFC payments in the gross estate (recomputed tax). Thus, one must recompute the estate tax by excluding from the value of the gross estate the value of the KFC payments. The heart of the dispute is the effect the exclusion of the KFC payments has on the recomputed marital deduction.

Respondent, relying on Rev.Rul. 67–242, 1967–2 C.B. 227, which in turn relies on section 1.691(c)–1(a)(2), and section 1.691(d)–1(e), *Example 2,* Income Tax Regs., contends that the proper method of recomputation is to subtract from both the gross estate and the marital deduction the KFC payments. This method produces a marital deduction less than the maximum allowed by the 50 percent of the adjusted gross estate limitation. It also produces no change in the taxable estate, because the reduction in the gross estate is equaled by the reduction in the marital deduction and, therefore, the estate tax remains the same. Petitioner contends that the full maximum marital deduction subject only to the 50 percent of adjusted gross estate limitation should be allowed in recomputing the estate tax. Petitioner relies on the testamentary documents which call for a maximum marital deduction bequest based on a formula and on the fact that there are sufficient non-IRD assets in the estate to fully fund this formula marital deduction.

As the following table shows, these approaches produce substantially different results:

	Actual computation	Petitioner's recomputation	Respondent's recomputation
Gross estate	$1,000,000	$900,000	$900,000
Adjusted gross estate	1,000,000	900,000	900,000
Marital deduction	(500,000)	(450,000)	400,000
Exemption	(60,000)	(60,000)	(60,000)
Taxable estate	440,000	390,000	440,000
Estate tax	126,500	100,500	126,500
Sec. 691(c)(1)(A) deduction	—	16,000	0

* * * Although there is no guidance in the statute or the legislative history on the specific point at issue here, we conclude that petitioner's method is consistent with the purpose of the statute. The formula bequest here required that Mrs. Kincaid receive property equal in value to the maximum marital deduction out of the assets of the estate available for distribution. In the recomputation there is no IRD available in the recomputed gross estate to satisfy the marital bequest. The bequest, therefore, by its own terms, must be funded to its full extent by non-IRD property.

This method fits more logically into the scheme of the statute. The value of KFC payments was included in Mr. Kincaid's estate and taxed there. Even though the payments went to the marital share, there were other assets which could have funded the marital share to fully fund the formula maximum marital deduction bequest. The other assets which were allocated to the nonmarital share were subject to tax. The important fact is that the existence of the IRD produced additional estate tax on Mr. Kincaid's estate. The allocation of assets as between marital and nonmarital shares should be irrelevant to the discussion. Therefore, logically, it must be concluded that the surviving spouse is entitled to some deduction for the excess estate tax paid because of the inclusion of the IRD in the estate. This conclusion should not be nullified by the happenstance that the IRD passed to the marital share rather than the nonmarital share.

Respondent relies on Rev.Rul. 67–242, 1967–2 C.B. 227, which in turn relies on section 1.691(c)–1(a)(2), Income Tax Regs. Initially, we note that revenue rulings represent only the conclusions of respondent and do not have the force and effect of a Treasury regulation. *Helvering v. New York Trust Co.,* 292 U.S. 455 (1934). Moreover, the revenue ruling involves a specific marital bequest rather than a formula bequest. Respondent also relies on section 1.691(d)–1(e), *Example 2,* in the regulations which assumes that the only qualifying gift to the spouse is an annuity, a portion of which constitutes the IRD. The example does not specifically address the issue of the recomputed marital deduction but rather is used to illustrate the application of section 691(d) involving a joint and survivor annuity contract. Neither the revenue ruling nor the example in the regulations should control the result of this case which involves a formula maximum marital deduction bequest. Our holding is entirely consistent with section 1.691(c)–1(a)(2), Income Tax Regs., which provides:

In computing the estate tax without including the [income in respect of a decedent] in the gross estate, any estate tax deduction (such as the marital deduction) which may be based upon the gross estate shall be recomputed so as to take into account the exclusion of the [income in respect of a decedent] from the gross estate.

Under our method, the marital deduction does not include IRD and is also limited to 50 percent of the recomputed gross estate, as required by section 2056.

Respondent also relies on dicta in *Chastain v. Commissioner, supra.* That case involved the recomputation of the tax on an estate which was distributed as follows: first, $1 million, which was paid in part out of IRD to the decedent's son; second, several other specific bequests; and third, the residue to a charitable foundation. The Court found that the correct recomputation under section 691(c)(2)(C) required the elimination of the IRD from the gross estate without otherwise changing the amount of the residuary bequest that was actually paid to the foundation. In that case, respondent relied on Rev.Rul. 67–242 and section 1.691(c)–1(a)(2) and *Example 2* in section 1.691(d)–1(e), Income Tax Regs., to support his argument that the residuary bequest should be recast to account for the exclusion of the IRD which passed to the son. The Court in rejecting the relevancy of the ruling and the regulations to the case at hand stated that "[the] recomputation * * * assumes as fact only the elimination of the section 691 items; there is no assumption of any modification of any gift to the surviving spouse (except to the extent that a 691 item may have been part of the bequest to that spouse)," and all statutory rules "governing the determination of the amount of the marital deduction" apply in the recomputation of the tax. 59 T.C. at 467–468. Respondent relies on this language to support his argument. However, neither the revenue ruling nor the regulations address the problem of a formula maximum marital deduction bequest. The facts in *Chastain* did not involve such a bequest, and the Court recognized that the marital deduction situation is different from the case presented before it:

It is * * * fallacious to treat the residuary charitable bequest as comparable to the marital deduction. The marital deduction involves merely a *computation* based upon certain assumed facts. The charitable deduction, on the other hand, depends upon the amount actually bequeathed to the charitable beneficiary * * *. [59 T.C. at 468; emphasis in original.]

Therefore, we do not believe our holding is inconsistent with the holding in *Chastain.*

* * *

Questions

1. Assume Decedent's estate is valued at $1,000,000 for Federal estate tax purposes and includes a right to receive $50,000 of net IRD. If Decedent's surviving spouse is entitled to receive that amount necessary to reduce estate taxes to zero (a so-called "optimum" marital bequest), what would be the incremental difference in taxes and the allowable section 691(c) deduction? A so-called "optimum" marital bequest is that amount needed to reduce taxes payable to zero, after application of the Decedent's unified credit (which, if not otherwise consumed, will shelter $600,000 from estate tax payment). In answering this question, don't necessarily assume that Treasury Regulation section 1.691(c)–1(a)(2) is not applicable.

2. If, instead of an optimum marital bequest, the bequest were a specified fraction of the estate, how would the section 691(c) computation work? Assume an estate of $2,000,000 with $50,000 of net IRD and a bequest of half the estate to the surviving spouse.

3. Consider the section 642(g) election for deductions not in respect of a decedent. In light of section 691(c), if an estate has expenses that may be deducted on either the estate tax Form 706 or the income tax Form 1041 for the estate, which would be preferable?

4. Under section 691(c)(1)(A), if there is more than one recipient of IRD, the allowable deduction is pro rated among them on the basis of the pro rata amount of net IRD receivable by each. If beneficiaries A and B were each entitled to receive half of an $80,000 net IRD item includible in an estate, compute the pro ration of the allowable deduction assuming A collects a full $40,000 but B collects only $35,000. See Treasury Regulation section 1.691(c)–1(d) *Example 1.* If A were to actually collect $45,000, how would that affect the allocation? No authority appears to support this regulatory position, though it also appears never to have been challenged.

If IRD is capital gain, its character will, by virtue of section 691(a)(3), remain the same as if the decedent were alive. The *Quick* case reproduced below arose at a time when section 1202 allowed a 50% deduction of net long term capital gain. In response to the decision, Congress amended section 691(c)(4)[3] to require the taxpayer to first apply the section 691(c) deduction against the long term capital gain IRD. In 1986, Congress repealed section 1202 and correspondingly amended section 691(c)(4). Consider, in light of *Quick,* what the effect will be if Congress ever allows the rate of tax for capital gains to differ from that for ordinary income in a year in which the taxpayer has long term capital gain IRD.

QUICK v. UNITED STATES

United States Court of Appeals, Tenth Circuit, 1974.
503 F.2d 100.

MOORE, CIRCUIT JUDGE:

* * *

Prior to his death, plaintiff's husband, Edmund T. Quick (the decedent) had contracted to sell 640 acres of land for $1,100,000 on an installment basis. * * * The balance remaining to be paid on the date of decedent's death was $1,060,000, an amount which was included in his estate.

During each of the years in question, 1968, 1969 and 1970, plaintiff received * * * income in respect of a decedent * * * pursuant to the sales contract which * * * she reported as a net long-term capital gain. * * * Plaintiff then, pursuant to Section 1202 of the Internal Revenue Code of 1954, took advantage of the 50% capital gains deduction provided for therein, thus reducing capital gains. * * * In addition, she deducted the estate tax deduction allowed by Section 691(c) of the Code * * * and reported the balance * * * as a net taxable gain for each of the tax years in question.

Upon audit the government accepting the same figures rearranged them slightly by deducting the [section 691(c)] estate tax allowance * * * from the entire net capital gain * * * before applying the [section 1202] 50% deduction thereto.

* * *

In the District Court, the parties stipulated the issue as follows:

> Whether the deduction of estate tax provided by Section 691(c) of the Internal Revenue Code of [1986] should be taken as an offset against the long-term capital gain representing income in respect of a decedent before deducting fifty percent (50%) of the long-term capital gain (as provided by Section 1202 of the Internal Revenue Code of [1986]) or whether the Section 691(c) estate tax deduction should be taken against the sum of the net of long-term capital

3. Section 691(c)(4) was added by section 702(b)(1) of the Revenue Act of 1978, Pub.L. No. 95–600, 92 Stat. 2925, at a time prior to repeal of the section 1202 deduction by the Tax Reform Act of 1986.

gain (after the fifty percent (50%) Section 1202 deduction) and ordinary income. * * *

As the District Court pointed out, although the statute reads that the estate tax deduction "shall be allowed," it does not specifically state "from what." However, the very omission of a "from what" specification is a sufficient basis for the courts to fill in a purpose * * * by holding that the method most advantageous to the taxpayer [is] proper. Here the estate tax deduction was roughly $20,000. * * * The law (section 1202) cut the capital gains in half before taxes. It did not cut the deduction in half. Yet if the deduction had to be taken before the cut, the net effect would have been to reduce the allowance from $20,000 to $10,000. Therefore, if any meaning is to be given to the "most advantageous" principle, it should be applied here. The income against which it is being applied is the statutory income, i.e., 50%.

Questions

1. Assume taxpayer has long term capital gain IRD of $100,000 and a section 691(c) deduction of $20,000 attributable to that long term capital gain IRD. If the taxpayer's effective tax rate for ordinary income were 40% but the section 1(j) maximum rate for long term capital gain were 28%, determine how section 691(c)(4) will operate in this case.

2. Explain how the Treasury Department's proposal to make section 691(c) a basis adjustment instead of an income tax deduction would solve the 691(c)(4) problem involved in *Quick*.

Chapter Seven

CHARITABLE TRUSTS AND DISTRIBUTIONS

Read Code section 642(c)(1) and skim Code section 664.

Read Treasury Regulation sections 1.663(a)–2, 1.642(c)–1(a), 1.642(c)–1(b)(1), 1.642(c)–3(b), 1.664–1(a)(1)(i) and 1.664–1(d)(1)(i).

There are four federal income tax regimes that may apply to trusts that benefit charity.

1. Wholly charitable trusts may qualify under section 501, in which case they are totally exempt from federal income taxation.

2. Qualified charitable remainder trusts are also exempt from federal income tax; unless tainted with unrelated business taxable income, section 664(c) provides a total exemption for qualified charitable remainder annuity trusts and qualified charitable remainder unitrusts. However, distributions made from these trusts to noncharitable beneficiaries may carry income out to the recipient, under section 664(b), which contains special character rules that specify how distributions will be treated in the hands of the beneficiary, even in years in which the trust has lost its exemption due to the existence of any unrelated business taxable income. These character rules override the normal pro rata allocation rules of the balance of Subchapter J and provide that, up to the full amount thereof, a distribution is first regarded as ordinary income of the trust from the "pool" of current year or undistributed prior years' net ordinary income, then as net short term capital gain (on a cumulative basis) from the pool of current year or undistributed prior years' net short term capital gain, followed by net long term capital gain (on a cumulative basis) from the pool of current year or undistributed prior years' net long term capital gain, followed by "other" (such as tax exempt or previously taxed) income of the current and prior years and, finally, as a tax free distribution of corpus, with each pool being depleted seriatim by distributions until entirely exhausted before any part of the distribution is deemed to carry out any part of the next pool. Under Treasury Regulation section 1.664–1(d), losses and deductions within a given category are

netted against income or gains in that category in determining the net amount available in the pool, with a carryover from prior years of items that are not carried out from the prior year.

3. Nonqualified trusts (including so-called charitable "lead" trusts, which are functional opposites of the charitable remainder annuity trust or charitable remainder unitrust but are not subject to the special rules of section 664 for income tax purposes) that make distributions to charity may qualify for the section 642(c) deduction.

4. Finally, nonqualified trusts *might* (as we will see shortly, there is quite a debate on this question) qualify for the section 661(a)(2) distribution deduction if [to the extent?] section 642(c) is not applicable.

Because exempt organizations, private foundations and section 664 could make up an entirely separate course of study, the primary focus of this chapter is section 642(c) because it provides the primary rules for the income tax deduction of amounts distributed from nonqualified (taxable) trusts to qualified charities, supplanting the section 170 charitable deduction rules otherwise applicable to individuals.

Relevant (by virtue of the first parenthetical of section 642(c)) only with respect to estates and complex trusts (by definition, a trust cannot be a simple trust if it provides for charity), section 642(c)(1) permits an unlimited deduction for amounts of gross income that are applied to a section 170(c) qualified charitable purpose during the taxable year,[1] as authorized or permitted by the terms of the governing instrument. If the document is silent as to whether distribution is to be from income or principal, the local governing law and the apparent intent of the grantor will be scrutinized to determine whether section 642(c) is met. Rev.Rul. 71–285, 71–2 C.B. 248.

Similarly, section 642(c)(2) permits a deduction for estates and older trusts that permanently set aside amounts of gross income for a qualified charitable purpose.[2] Also established by section 642(c) are rules applicable to pooled income funds and private foundations which, because of their relatively limited and specialized use, are not the subject of study in these materials.

Income taxation is no concern for qualified wholly charitable trusts because the trust is (except in years in which the trust has unrelated business taxable income) exempt from federal income tax. In contrast, if section 642(c) is the source of the deduction for a nonqualified charitable trust, only amounts currently paid or, in proper but limited circumstances, set aside for charity are currently deductible, and then they are deductible only to the extent those distributions are from gross income of the trust or estate. Thus, under Treasury Regulation section 1.642(c)–3(b), tax exempt items of income distributed to charity do not

1. Subject to the election available in the penultimate sentence of section 642(c)(1).

2. Section 642(c)(2) was replaced with respect to trusts by section 664 and, because enactment was in 1969, generally it is only pre-October 9, 1969 trusts that are still eligible for the section 642(c)(2) set aside deduction.

generate a section 642(c) deduction, nor can distributions of corpus be deducted under section 642(c).

If a trust or estate distributes fiduciary accounting corpus to a qualified charity in any year in which there is DNI in the entity, is the normal section 661(a)(2) distribution deduction available to generate a "pseudo-charitable" deduction? Read Treasury Regulation section 1.663(a)–2 and the following materials with an eye to the policy and abuse issues involved. Does it matter whether section 642(c) or 661(a) is the source of the deduction?

MOTT v. UNITED STATES

United States Claims Court, 1972.
462 F.2d 512.

COWEN, CHIEF JUDGE:

This tax case, apparently one of first impression, comes before the court on the parties' cross-motions for summary judgment. The issue is whether an estate is entitled to a deduction from its gross income, pursuant to Section 661(a)(2) of the Internal Revenue Code of [1986], when it makes a distribution of corpus of an estate to a qualified charitable beneficiary pursuant to a general pecuniary bequest. We have concluded that the claimed deduction is not available.

The pertinent facts, which have been stipulated, are as follows: Walter C. Teagle died on January 9, 1962, leaving a gross estate in excess of $36,000,000. Under the terms of his will, two-thirds of the estate, after payment of debts, expenses, and specific bequests, was left to the Teagle Foundation, a tax-exempt charitable corporation. The residue of the estate, including all income earned during its administration, was left in trust for the benefit of Jane W. Teagle, an alternate life beneficiary, with specified remainders over.

The years involved in this suit are the estate's taxable years ending July 31, 1963, 1964, and 1965. During this period, the executors of the estate made the following payments out of the corpus of the estate in partial satisfaction of the bequest to the Teagle Foundation:

1963	$13,165,575.75
1964	405,379.02
1965	375,000.00

The executors also made several distributions of income to Jane during the administration period before the trust came into operation, including during the years involved here, a $100,000 payment in 1963.

In computing Mr. Teagle's taxable estate, the executors were allowed an estate tax deduction of $14,107,420.90 for the charitable bequest to the Teagle Foundation. They now assert that they are also entitled to a deduction, in computing the estate's taxable income for the years involved here, for the payments described above which they made in satisfaction of the charitable bequest. Briefly stated, they contend that such a deduction is permitted by the plain terms of Section 661(a)(2), which provides in pertinent part that:

> In any taxable year there shall be allowed as a deduction in computing the taxable income of an estate * * * any * * * amounts properly paid * * * for such taxable year * * *.

The Government, while conceding that a literal reading of Section 661(a)(2) would permit plaintiffs to prevail, maintains that that section cannot properly be interpreted without reference to its purpose, and that when the provision is read in the context of the entire statutory scheme of Subchapter J of Chapter 1 of the Code, it is clear that the distribution to the charitable organization in this case cannot qualify for the deduction permitted by Section 661(a)(2).

* * *

Both parties agree that the amount of the payments, although made to a charitable organization, are not deductible under Section 642(c) in computing the estate's taxable income. Mr. Teagle's will did not provide, as Section 642(c) requires, that the payments be made out of the estate's gross income. In fact, the payments here were made out of the corpus of the estate.

In addition, the parties seem to agree that none of the provisions of Section 663(a) expressly excludes the payments here from the operation of Section 661. The exception of Section 663(a)(1), for gifts or bequests of a specific sum or of specific property which is paid or credited all at once or in not more than three installments, is not applicable here because the bequest has not been satisfied in three installments or less. Moreover, it is not a bequest of a specific sum of money since its amount, expressed as a percentage of the estate after payment of administrative expenses and other charges, was not ascertainable at the time of Mr. Teagle's death. *See* Treas.Reg. § 1.663(a)–1(b)(1) (1956). Section 663(a)(2), which provides that an estate may not deduct under Section 661 any amount paid, permanently set aside, or otherwise qualifying for the charitable deduction permitted by Section 642(c), would also seem to be inapplicable because the amounts here, as noted above, do not qualify under Section 642(c) for the charitable deduction.

Plaintiffs contend that since none of the express exceptions to Section 661 applies here, the amounts paid to the Teagle Foundation are properly deductible under that section because they constitute "amounts properly paid * * * for such taxable year * * *." The Government contends that "amounts" cannot be read literally and that Section 661(a)(2) does not apply to these charitable distributions. It relies principally on Section 1.663(a)–2 of the Regulations which provides in pertinent part:

> Any amount paid, permanently set aside, or to be used for the charitable, etc., purposes specified in section 642(c) and which is allowable as a deduction under that section is not allowed as a deduction to an estate or trust under section 661 or treated as an amount distributed for purposes of determining the amounts in-

cludible in gross income of beneficiaries under section 662. *Amounts paid, permanently set aside, or to be used for charitable, etc., purposes are deductible by estates or trusts only as provided in section 642(c).* * * *

From our reading of this regulation, two things seem clear. First, the italicized language is dispositive of the issue in this case, since it prevents an estate from claiming as a deduction under Section 661(a)(2) any amounts distributed to a charitable beneficiary except as permitted by Section 642(c). Second, however, there is nothing in Section 663(a)(2), the statutory provision under which this regulation was promulgated, which expressly supports the rule announced in the regulation. Section 663(a)(2) provides only that an estate or trust may not deduct under Section 661 any amounts which are also deductible under Section 642(c); it does not specifically cover situations like the one here, where amounts paid to a charitable organization do not qualify for the charitable deduction.

The validity of this regulation must be sustained unless it is "unreasonable and plainly inconsistent with the revenue statutes * * *." Commissioner of Internal Revenue v. South Texas Lumber Co., 333 U.S. 496, 501, 68 S.Ct. 695, 698, 92 L.Ed. 831 (1948). *See also, e.g.,* Estate of Bahen v. United States, 305 F.2d 827, 829, 158 Ct.Cl. 141, 145 (1962), and cases cited therein. After carefully considering the parties' contentions in this case, as well as the entire distribution scheme of Subchapter J, we think that the regulation is valid and also that any other rule would be an unreasonable interpretation of the statute.

We do not adopt plaintiff's argument that Section 661(a)(2) must be read according to its literal terms. If an estate were entitled to a distribution deduction for "*any* other amounts properly paid," as that section provides, then all payments made by an estate, whether or not to a beneficiary, would be deductible. For example, contrary to Thomas Lonergan Trust, 6 T.C. 715 (1946), an estate would be allowed a distribution deduction when it makes payments to a creditor in satisfaction of a judgment against the estate. * * *

Obviously, the phrase "any other amounts paid" should not be read as broadly as its literal terms suggest. It must be interpreted in its own particular context, with reference to its relationship with the other provisions of Subchapter J, and in accordance with the consequences which Congress sought to achieve when it enacted Section 661 in 1954.

The most logical reference point in attempting to delineate the scope of Section 661 is the corollary provision of Section 662. That the two sections should be read together is not only implicit from the fact that they are similarly structured and in some instances identically worded, but also explicit from Section 662's express reference to Section 661. Thus, Section 662(a), in imposing its tax on distributees, states that "there shall be included in the gross income of a beneficiary to whom an amount specified in section 661(a) is paid, credited, or required to be distributed * * * the sum of the following amounts * * *." By this reference, we think it is proper to confine Section 661 to distributions to *beneficiaries* of the estate, even though Section 661(a) does not specifically so provide.[16] Such a construction, implied in Section 662(a), prevents the absurd results mentioned above which would occur if the phrase "any other amounts properly paid" in Section 661(a)(2) were applied literally.

Of course, an interpretation which limits Section 661 to distributions to beneficiaries does not put an end to the matter here, since the Teagle Foundation is a beneficiary of the estate. Therefore, the Government also asks us to interpret Section 661(a) as permitting a deduction only for distributions to *taxable* beneficiaries, based upon its argument that Section 661 must be read as interdependent with Section 662. That is, as we understand the Government's argument, the incidence of the tax on the income of an estate must be allocated between estate and beneficiary, and to the extent that the beneficiary is exempt from the tax imposed by Section 662, any distributions to that beneficiary would not be deductible by the estate under Section 661.

The Government's position seems to be correct in the context of this case, but we do not hold that it is a general rule which may be applied in every conceivable situation that may arise under the provisions of the Code here considered. We think it is sufficient to say that, under the facts of this case, the Government's position accords with the general intent of Congress in enacting the distribution rules[17] and, as we discuss below, is in accord with what we believe to be an implied Congressional intent to prevent all charitable distributions, whether or not deductible under Section 642(c), from entering into the operation of the distribution rules.

As we noted above, when Congress enacted the present distribution rules its primary purpose was to eliminate the necessity for tracing the source of distributions. Under prior law, in general, beneficiaries were taxed only on amounts of current income distributed by an estate or trust. Such a simple rule led to manipulation, and in 1942 Congress attempted to tighten up the statute by enacting the 65–day rules of Section 162(d) of the 1939 Code. The end result was that the distribution rules became so difficult to apply, and so entrenched in the tracing

16. This construction is confirmed by the legislative history of Section 661. *See* H.R.Rep. No. 1337, 83d Cong., 2d Sess. A198 (1954); S.Rep. No. 1622, 83d Cong., 2d Sess. 347 (1954); U.S.Code Cong. & Admin.News, p. 4988:

"§ *661. Deduction for estates and trusts accumulating income or distributing corpus.*

* * *

"This section (subject to the limitations discussed below) allows an additional deduction to estates or trusts for amounts paid, credited, or required to be distributed *to beneficiaries.* * * * [Emphasis added]"

17. *See* H.R.Rep. No. 1337, 83d Cong., 2d Sess. 60 (1954); S.Rep. No. 1622, 83d Cong. 2d Sess. 82 (1954), U.S.Code Cong. & Admin.News, p. 4714:

"The bill adopts the general principle that to the extent of the trust's current income all distributions are deductible by the estate or trust and taxable to the beneficiaries."

requirements, that Congress abandoned the old system in favor of the present scheme. Tracing was eliminated by providing in Section 662 that all amounts distributed to beneficiaries would be considered to be distributions of income, subject to the modifications of Section 663 and the quantitative limitation of D.N.I. Consistent with the conduit principle, an estate or trust making such distributions would be entitled to a deduction under Section 661.

As we read Sections 661(a) and 662(a), Congress intended to do nothing more than combine the conduit principle with a conclusive presumption that distributions subject to the operation of those sections are distributions of income. Such a presumption is, we think, inapplicable to charitable distributions. As Section 642(c) provides, a charitable deduction is available only if the source of the distribution is gross income. Tracing of charitable distributions is still required under Section 642(c), and to the extent that a charitable distribution is not paid out of gross income in accordance with the requirements of Section 642(c), then we think that Congress intended that no deduction is allowable.

Without the distinction between charitable and noncharitable distributions, Congress' general intent in enacting the present provisions—to prevent manipulative distributions—would be seriously thwarted. The facts of this case are a good illustration. Both the Teagle Foundation and Jane, the sole income distributee, would be second-tier beneficiaries. If the estate could deduct under Section 661(a)(2) the payments made out of the corpus of the estate in satisfaction of the charitable bequest, then the following will result: the estate will pay no tax on the income which it accumulates, because that income will be offset by deductions for its distributions of corpus to the Teagle Foundation. Later on, the estate can distribute the accumulated income to Jane tax-free. With regard to current payments to Jane, concededly out of estate income, her tax would be greatly reduced. Thus, in 1963, she received $100,000 while the Teagle Foundation received approximately $13,200,000. If both amounts were considered distributions to beneficiaries within the meaning of Section 662, then Jane would be taxable on only 1/133 of the estate's D.N.I. for 1963, up to the amount of her distribution.

Based upon our reading of the distribution sections of Subchapter J and their legislative history, we conclude that Section 1.663(a)–2 of the Regulations, which provides that amounts distributed by an estate or trust to a charitable organization are deductible only under Section 642(c), is consistent with the statutory scheme and a reasonable interpretation thereof. It necessarily follows that plaintiffs are not entitled to a deduction pursuant to Section 661(a)(2) for the amounts of corpus distributed in satisfaction of the charitable bequest. * * *

ESTATE OF O'CONNOR v. COMMISSIONER

United States Tax Court, 1977.
69 T.C. 165.

STERRETT, J., dissenting: I respectfully dissent from the majority's conclusion that "a literal interpretation of section 661(a)(2), which would permit (subject to the distributable net income ceiling) the deductibility of all amounts distributed and not otherwise expressly disallowed (see *Mott v. United States,* 462 F.2d 512, 517 (Ct.Cl.1972)) would be inconsistent with the statutory framework and overall legislative objectives of subchapter J and that, as applied to the circumstances herein, respondent's regulations should be sustained." In my view, analysis of the applicable statutes and legislative history amply supports the opposite result.

Although the majority's view that the marital trust should not be recognized for Federal income tax purposes seems questionable, in any event, resolution of the alleged conflict between sections 642(c) and 661(a)(2) must be determined. This is so because even if the marital trust is recognized for Federal tax purposes, section 661 permits the estate a deduction for all amounts distributed by it (subject to the D.N.I. ceiling), and then upon distribution by the trust to the foundation, the sections 642(c) and 661(a)(2) issue must be scrutinized.

The legislative history under subchapter J, part I, provides us with three general principles relating to distributions by estates and trusts, to wit: (1) While estates and trusts are to be treated as separate taxable entities, they are treated substantially as conduits through which income passes to the beneficiary; (2) all distributions are deductible by the estate or trust and are taxable to the beneficiaries to the extent of the estate's or trust's current income; and (3) under the concept of distributable net income, the tracing of such distributions is not required. S.Rept. 1622, 83d Cong., 2d Sess. (1954), U.S.Code Cong. & Adm.News 4715–4717; see also H.Rept. 1337, 83d Cong., 2d Sess. (1954), U.S.Code Cong. & Adm.News 4086–4087.

Implementation of these principles, for the estate and trusts herein, is accomplished by sections 661 and 662. Section 661(a) allows a deduction by an estate or trust, not exceeding D.N.I., for any amount of income "required to be distributed currently" (sec. 661(a)(1)) and "any other amounts properly paid or credited or required to be distributed" (sec. 661(a)(2)). Then, with some limitations, section 662(a) includes in "the gross income of a beneficiary" amounts "paid, credited or required to be distributed" as specified in section 661(a).

In addition to the distribution deduction, Congress has provided in section 642(c) that an estate or trust shall be allowed a deduction, in computing its taxable income (in lieu of a section 170(a) deduction), for any amounts of gross income paid, permanently set aside, or otherwise used exclusively for charitable purposes. Therefore, "a trust or estate is allowed an unlimited deduction for charitable contributions and is not subject to the limitation imposed on the charitable contributions of individuals." H.Rept. 1337, *supra,* U.S.Code Cong. & Adm.News at 4332. See also S.Rept. 1622, *supra,* U.S.Code Cong. & Adm.News at 4982. In view of this broad deduction Congress enacted section 663(a)(2) as follows:

(a) EXCLUSIONS.—There shall not be included as amounts falling within section 661(a) or 662(a)—

* * *

(2) CHARITABLE, ETC., DISTRIBUTIONS.—Any amount paid or permanently set aside or otherwise qualifying for the deduction provided in section 642(c) * * *

Therefore, upon a reading of sections 642(c) and 663(a)(2), there is no doubt that if an amount qualifies for deduction under section 642(c) it cannot also be deducted under section 661(a). This was the result intended by Congress and it is supported by the legislative record as follows:

Subsection (a)(2) corresponds to subsection (b)(3) of the House bill. It provides that any amount paid, permanently set aside, or to be used for the purposes specified in section 642(c) (relating to charitable, etc., deductions) is excluded from the provisions of sections 661 and 662. For this purpose the deduction provided in section 642(c) is computed without regard to section 681. Since the estate or trust is allowed a deduction under section 642(c) for amounts paid, permanently set aside, or otherwise qualifying for the deduction provided in that section, such amounts are not allowed as an additional deduction for distributions, nor are they treated as amounts distributed for purposes of section 662 in determining the amounts includible in gross income of the beneficiaries. [S.Rept. 1622, *supra,* U.S.Code Cong. & Adm.News at 4995. See also H.Rept. 1337, *supra,* U.S.Code Cong. & Adm.News at 4344.]

Furthermore, the Court of Appeals for the Second Circuit, to which an appeal in this case lies, has stated that section 642(c) was enacted "apparently because Congress did not wish charitable gifts by trusts to be subject to the percentage limitations imposed on individuals in section 170(b). Having authorized this broad deduction in section 642(c), Congress enacted section 663(a)(2) to prevent the trust from having a double deduction and a beneficiary from claiming a charitable deduction already taken by the trustee." *Statler Trust v. Commissioner,* 361 F.2d 128, 132 (2d Cir.1966).

Therefore, neither the legislative history nor the statute requires a conclusion that an amount distributed by an estate or trust to a charity, which does not meet the requirements of section 642(c), cannot under any circumstances qualify for a deduction under section 661(a). Under a literal interpretation of the statute a finding that section 642(c) is inapplicable (the majority did so at page 173) in fact automatically makes section 663(a)(2) inapplicable.

In my opinion section 1.663(a)–2, Income Tax Regs., is inapplicable to the facts before us; the regulation is consistent with the aforenoted statute and legislative history. Congress having authorized an exceptionally broad deduction for charitable gifts under section 642(c) understandably wanted to prevent a double deduction under section 661. To deny the deduction under section 642(c) because of its inapplicability and then to further deny a distribution deduction under section 661 would be the killing of two birds with one stone. In my view the second sentence of section 1.663(a)–2, Income Tax Regs., must be read with the first sentence to preclude a deduction under section 661 when both sections 642(c) and 661 are applicable. However, where section 642(c) is inapplicable one must then test the deductibility of the distribution to the foundation under section 661.

It cannot be gainsaid that distributions to the foundation were amounts "properly paid" within the meaning of section 661(a)(2). It becomes necessary, however, to determine whether the foundation qualifies as a "beneficiary" of decedent's estate so as to permit the deduction of distributions to it under section 661(a). Implicit in this is that section 661 deductions are confined to distributions properly paid to beneficiaries.

Section 643(c) provides that "the term 'beneficiary' includes heir, legatee, and devisee." For purposes of the provisions here in issue "includes" is not deemed to exclude "other things otherwise within the meaning of the term defined." Sec. 7701(b). In construing section 643(c) there is no legislative history to aid us and judicial authorities are almost nonexistent.[6]

In *duPont Testamentary Trust v. Commissioner,* 66 T.C. 761, 767 (1976), we held that to be deductible under section 661, "a distribution must be made to a beneficiary in his status as a beneficiary, not as a creditor or in some other capacity." In the present case the source of the foundation's interest is the gratuitous assignment by Mrs. O'Connor of her right to income and corpus of the marital trust.

The validity of an assignment is determined under local law, *Blair v. Commissioner,* 300 U.S. 5 (1937), and under New York law Mrs. O'Connor's assignment was valid. See New York Est., Powers & Trusts Law, Sec. 7–1.5 (McKinney 1967). Thus, the question narrows to whether the foundation, as an assignee-donee, is a "beneficiary" under section 643(c). Absent judicial construction or legislative history we must look to the plain meaning of the term "beneficiary."

The beneficiary of an estate or trust is simply the person for whose benefit the trust property is held by the trustee. See G. Bogert, The Law of Trusts and Trustees, sec. 1, p. 4 (2d ed. 1965). Although the majority opinion correctly notes that *Blair v. Commissioner, supra,* specifically involved the issue of whether an assignor of an income

6. Except for *duPont Testamentary Trust v. Commissioner,* 66 T.C. 761 (1976), the cases cited by the majority (at p. 179 of its opinion) pertain to the definition of beneficiary under sec. 642(h). In my opinion these cases are inapposite to the inquiry herein involved because the term "beneficiary" under sec. 642(h) has a narrower purpose than in sec. 643(c) in that it is intended as a relief provision to the beneficiary. See *Sletland v. Commissioner,* 43 T.C. 602, 610 (1965).

interest continued to be liable for the tax upon the income or whether the assignees were so liable, in my opinion, the case is helpful in defining the term "beneficiary" herein. The Court stated at 300 U.S. 12:

> The Government points to the provisions of the revenue acts imposing upon the beneficiary of a trust the liability for the tax upon the income distributable to the beneficiary. But the term is merely descriptive of the one entitled to the beneficial interest. These provisions cannot be taken to preclude valid assignments of the beneficial interest, or to affect the duty of the trustee to distribute income to the owner of the beneficial interest, whether he was such initially or becomes such by valid assignment. The one who is to receive the income as the owner of the beneficial interest is to pay the tax. *If under the law governing the trust the beneficial interest is assignable, and if it has been assigned without reservation, the assignee thus becomes the beneficiary and is entitled to rights and remedies accordingly.* We find nothing in the revenue acts which denies him that status.

Thus an assignee steps into the shoes of its assignor, here the transferring beneficiary. "It does not matter how the benefits are to come to the beneficiary. The important trust concept is that he has a right to obtain them." G. Bogert, The Law of Trusts and Trustees, *supra,* sec. 188 at 289 (2d ed. 1965). It is an elementary principle of trust law that the trustee holds the trust property for the benefit of the beneficiary. After the assignment the foundation was entitled to and did receive the benefits of the trust. Clearly, it was entitled to enforce the duty of the trustee. Thus, in my opinion, the foundation received the benefits of the trust in its capacity as a "beneficiary."

Having decided that the foundation qualifies as a "beneficiary" one final point remains. That is, whether deductions should be denied for amounts distributed to the foundation because section 661(a) permits deductions only for distributions to *taxable* beneficiaries. In my opinion the answer is no.

As previously stated sections 661 and 662 together apply the "conduit principle" to the basic pattern of taxability of complex trusts. Without these provisions a trust would compute its taxable income and pay the tax thereon according to rules substantially similar to those applicable to individuals. See secs. 641–643. Sections 661 and 662 in general require, however, that the beneficiary and not the trust be taxed (to the extent of the trust's distributable net income) on any amounts which are paid, credited, or required to be distributed to that beneficiary. Section 661 permits the trust a deduction for the amounts so distributed whereas section 662 requires their inclusion in the gross income of the beneficiary. See *duPont Testamentary Trust v. Commissioner, supra* at 765–766.

In my opinion, even if the beneficiary is exempt from tax on distributions required to be included in gross income under section 662, distributions to that beneficiary would still be deductible by the trust under section 661. Congress' intent in enacting the distribution rules cannot be read in a vacuum. Thus Congress' statement that "The bill adopts the general principle that to the extent of the trust's current income all distributions are deductible by the estate or trust and taxable to the beneficiaries," must be read in conjunction with other statutory provisions specifically exempting income. In *Helvering v. Butterworth,* 290 U.S. 365 (1933), which antedated the enactment of subchapter J, the Court, in discussing the statute then in effect, stated at 290 U.S. 369, that the evident general purpose of the statute was "to tax in some way the whole income of all trust estates." However, the Court observed at 290 U.S. 369, that "Certainly, Congress did not intend any income from a trust should escape taxation *unless definitely exempted.*" (Emphasis supplied.) It follows that, since the income to the foundation is "definitely exempted" under section 501, effect must be given to such provision.

Similarly in Rev.Rul. 74–299, 1974–1 C.B. 154, a nonexempt employees' trust was permitted a deduction under section 661 despite the fact that the specific provisions of section 402(b), rather than section 662(a), applied to the employee as beneficiary of the trust. Additionally, in *Estate of Tait v. Commissioner,* 11 T.C. 731 (1948), remanded by stipulation in compromise (4th Cir. 7/20/49), the parties agreed that the trust would be permitted a deduction for payments made to four foreign domiciliaries who were exempt from U.S. tax under a treaty between the United States and Canada.

I respectfully submit that the trust or estate, as one may have it, should be allowed a section 661(a) deduction for amounts distributed to the foundation and, accordingly, the foundation will then pick up its allocable share of D.N.I. under section 662.

DRENNEN and WILES, JJ., agree with this dissenting opinion.

In the most recent case involving the issue of a charitable distribution qualifying for a deduction under section 661(a)(2) when it could not qualify under section 642(c), an added wrinkle complicated the issue. In United States Trust Co. v. I.R.S., 803 F.2d 1363 (5th Cir.1986), the decedent's estate distributed income earned during administration of the estate in satisfaction of a pecuniary formula bequest to charity. The value of the bequest had been deducted under section 2055 for Federal estate tax purposes, but did not qualify for the section 642(c) income tax deduction because the estate was not directed to make the distribution from income. Thus, the issue presented to the court was whether the estate should be allowed a section 661(a)(2) Tier 2 distribution deduction for the amount of its current income that was distributed to the qualified charitable beneficiary.

In holding that it did not qualify for the section 661(a)(2) distribution deduction, the Court of Appeals for the Fifth Circuit reversed the District Court (617 F.Supp. 575), stating

> As the plain language of sections 2055(a)(2) and 642(c) demonstrates, Congress intended that the benefit for a charitable bequest be conferred only once—either as an offset against the gross value of the estate or as an offset against income. This intent is accomplished by limiting section 2055(a)(2) deductions to the value of the property that is included in the gross estate at the time of decedent's death. Thus, no estate tax deduction is available for amounts that are paid to a charitable organization at the direction of the governing instrument from estate income. The tax benefit for income distributions is then bestowed by section 642(c) which allows deductions for amounts payable out of gross income. 803 F.2d at 1367.

Lest the facts escape us, the estate did in fact claim, and was allowed, a section 2055 estate tax charitable deduction for its distribution of estate income in satisfaction of the pecuniary bequest under decedent's Will. Thus, the court must have been thinking that the source of payment would not be relevant for estate tax purposes if the bequest was not specifically a bequest of income earned after the date of decedent's death.

On the fundamental issue whether both an income and an estate tax charitable deduction could be claimed for the same distribution, the District Court had earlier stated:

> The statute itself is explicit and unambiguous and indicates that Congress intended only to prevent an estate from taking two *income tax* deductions for the same distribution: one under § 642(c) and one under § 661. [emphasis in original]

Then, having reviewed the legislative history, the District Court held that:

> There is no statute, cited to or found by this Court, which prohibits a double deduction such as that sought in the instant case. The Estate having taken an estate tax deduction under § 2055 now seeks an income tax deduction under § 661. The government argues that the Estate should not be allowed to claim an estate tax deduction and an income tax deduction for the same distribution. The Court is of the opinion that the estate tax provisions in the Internal Revenue Code are separate and distinct from the income tax provisions and are not mutually exclusive.
>
> * * *
>
> Congress has specifically addressed the disallowance of double deductions and has not disallowed the one sought by the Estate. In § 642(g) Congress provided as follows:
>
> > Disallowance of Double Deductions.—Amounts allowable under Section 2053 [estate tax deduction for expenses, indebtedness or taxes] or 2054 [estate tax deduction for losses] as a deduction in computing the taxable estate of a decedent shall not be allowed as a deduction. . . .

> If Congress had intended to disallow a deduction under § 2055 it could have and would have included that section in § 642(g). In the face of clear Congressional intent not to disallow double deductions under Section 2055 and the income provisions of the Code, the Court will not infer one.
>
> * * *

The statute quite clearly and simply creates a loophole by which income accumulated by the Estate and distributed to a charity is never taxed, when the same distribution qualifies for an estate tax deduction. Treas.Reg. § 1.663(a)–2 is an attempt by the IRS to close this loophole. It is up to Congress, however, and not the IRS or this Court to close this loophole. 617 F.Supp. at 583.

Questions

1. What is the "loophole" that was perceived by the District Court in *U.S. Trust,* should section 661(a)(2) apply in those situations in which section 642(c) does not, and how does section 2055 affect the situation?

2. Consider the interplay of sections 642(c), 661(a)(2) and 664(b) in the situation in which an estate is directed to fund a qualified charitable remainder annuity trust. For example, assume that the estate realizes $20,000 of fiduciary accounting income for the current year, of which $15,000 is taxable dividends and $5,000 is tax exempt interest. During the current year the personal representative of the estate distributes $40,000 in cash to the charitable trust, charging the distribution to fiduciary accounting principal, and distributes $10,000 directly to A, the noncharitable beneficiary of the trust, in satisfaction of income that A is entitled to receive under the terms of the trust. What are the income tax consequences to the estate, to A and to the trust?

Chapter Eight

GRANTOR TRUSTS

INTRODUCTION

Read Code section 671.

Read Regulation sections 1.671–1, 1.671–2 and 1.671–4.

Subchapter J establishes three categories into which trusts may fall. Two we studied in Chapter Three, being simple and complex trusts. As you may recall, unlike estates, which are always taxed as a complex trust, trusts may be either simple or complex for income tax purposes, and some trusts fluctuate between simple and complex from year to year. Now we come to the third category and again estates are treated differently: by virtue of section 671, estates cannot be subject to the following rules. However, any trust (whether simple or complex) may be subject in whole or in part to this third category of rules, being Subpart E (sections 671 through 679) of Subchapter J. Trusts subject to these rules are called "grantor trusts" and may be subject to Subpart E in some years but not in others. To the extent these rules apply, Subpart E overrides the balance of Subchapter J.

Fundamental to application of the grantor trust rules is possession of prohibited enjoyment or control of trust income or principal by a grantor or, under section 678, someone treated as the grantor. By the last sentence of section 671, normal principles for imputing ownership of income for Federal income tax purposes, such as principles that look to dominion and control, are supplanted by the grantor trust rules (though assignment of income and discharge of obligation theories continue to apply under Treasury Regulation section 1.671–1(c)). In place of these general principles, Subpart E defines reasonably limited circumstances in which a specified portion of a trust will be ignored for income tax purposes. To the extent this happens, income, losses, deductions and credits allocable to that portion of the trust are attributed to the actual or deemed grantor, rather than to the trust or its beneficiaries, and retain their character in the grantor's hands, in most respects, as if no trust had been created. Thus, for example, a trust loss would be the grantor's deduction, a distribution to charity would be treated as the grantor's contribution, and capital gains in the trust would be aggregated with the grantor's capital gains and losses.

The key to application of the grantor trust rules is whether the grantor enjoys trust benefits, has retained so much control, or has left so many "strings" attached to the trust that the grantor should be regarded as the true owner of the trust property for income tax purposes. Accordingly, the grantor trust provisions read like a laundry list of prohibited powers and interests in the trust, any one of which being sufficient to invoke grantor trust treatment. Prior to enactment of the Tax Reform Act of 1986, each was tied to an arbitrary policy that, if the interest or power could not affect the enjoyment of trust benefits within ten years after the final transfer of property into the trust, it would not be considered as a prohibited power or interest until the greater than ten year deferral period had run. Thus, to avoid grantor trust treatment under prior law, control over trust property was not necessarily relinquished forever; relinquishment for over ten years would suffice. As a result, trusts drafted for the purpose of diverting income to low bracket taxpayers were usually recognizable by virtue of their slightly longer than ten years duration, and are collectively referred to as "Clifford" trusts in recognition of the following case. By an amendment to section 673, and indirectly to other provisions of Subpart E, the former 10 year rule has been repealed, effective for transfers in trust after March 1, 1986 ("post-TRA '86 trusts").

HELVERING v. CLIFFORD

Supreme Court of the United States, 1940.
309 U.S. 331, 60 S.Ct. 554, 84 L.Ed. 788.

MR. JUSTICE DOUGLAS delivered the opinion of the Court.

In 1934 respondent declared himself trustee of certain securities which he owned. All net income from the trust was to be held for the "exclusive benefit" of respondent's wife. The trust was for a term of five years, except that it would terminate earlier on the death of either respondent or his wife. On termination of the trust the entire corpus was to go to respondent, while all "accrued or undistributed net income" and "any proceeds from the investment of such net income" was to be treated as property owned absolutely by the wife. During the continuance of the trust respondent was to pay over to his wife the whole or such part of the net income as he in his "absolute discretion" might determine. And during that period he had full power (a) to exercise all voting powers incident to the trusteed shares of stock; (b) to "sell, exchange, mortgage, or pledge" any of the securities under the declaration of trust "whether as part of the corpus or principal thereof or as investments or proceeds and any income therefrom, upon such terms and for such consideration" as respondent in his "absolute discretion may deem fitting"; (c) to invest "any cash or money in the trust estate or any income therefrom" by loans, secured or unsecured, by deposits in banks, or by purchase of securities or other personal property "without restriction" because of their "speculative character" or "rate of return" or any "laws pertaining to the investment of trust funds"; (d) to collect all income; (e) to compromise, etc., any claims held by him as trustee; (f) to hold any property in the trust estate in the names of "other persons or in my own name as an individual" except as otherwise provided. Extraordinary cash dividends, stock dividends, proceeds from the sale of unexercised subscription rights, or any enhancement, realized or not, in the value of the securities were to be treated as principal, not income. An exculpatory clause purported to protect him from all losses except those occasioned by his "own wilful and deliberate" breach of duties as trustee. And finally it was provided that neither the principal nor any future or accrued income should be liable for the debts of the wife; and that the wife could not transfer, encumber, or anticipate any interest in the trust or any income therefrom prior to actual payment thereof to her.

It was stipulated that while the "tax effects" of this trust were considered by respondent they were not the "sole consideration" involved in his decision to set it up, as by this and other gifts he intended to give "security and economic independence" to his wife and children. It was also stipulated that respondent's wife had substantial income of her own from other sources; that there was no restriction on her use of the trust income, all of which income was placed in her personal checking account, intermingled with her other funds, and expended by her on herself, her children and relatives; that the trust was not designed to relieve respondent from liability for family or household expenses and that after execution of the trust he paid large sums from his personal funds for such purposes.

Respondent paid a federal gift tax on this transfer. During the year 1934 all income from the trust was distributed to the wife who included it in her individual return for that year. The Commissioner, however, determined a deficiency in respondent's return for that year on the theory that income from the trust was taxable to him. The Board of Tax Appeals sustained that redetermination. The Circuit Court of Appeals reversed. We granted certiorari because of the importance to the revenue of the use of such short term trusts in the reduction of surtaxes.

Sec. [61] includes among "gross income" all "gains, profits, and income derived * * * from professions, vocations, trades, businesses, commerce, or sales, or dealings in property, whether real or personal, growing out of the ownership or use of or interest in such property; also from interest, rent, dividends, securities, or the transaction of any business carried on for gain or profit, or gains or profits and income derived from any source whatever." The broad sweep of this language indicates the purpose of Congress to use the full measure of its taxing power within those definable categories. Cf. Helvering v. Midland Mutual Life Insurance Co., 300 U.S. 216, 57 S.Ct. 423, 81 L.Ed. 612, 108 A.L.R. 436. Hence our construction of the statute should be consonant with that purpose. Technical considerations, niceties of the law of trusts or conveyances, or the legal paraphernalia which inventive genius may construct as a refuge from surtaxes should not obscure the basic issue. That issue is whether the grantor after the trust has been established may still be treated, under this statutory scheme as the owner of the corpus. See Blair v. Commissioner, 300 U.S. 5, 12, 57 S.Ct. 330, 333, 81 L.Ed. 465. In absence of more precise standards or guides supplied by statute or appropriate regulations, the answer to that question must depend on an analysis of the terms of the trust and all the circumstances attendant on its creation and operation. And where the grantor is the trustee and the beneficiaries are members of his family group, special scrutiny of the arrangement is necessary lest what is in reality but one economic unit be multiplied into two or more by devices which, though valid under state law, are not conclusive so far as § [61] is concerned.

In this case we cannot conclude as a matter of law that respondent ceased to be the owner of the corpus after the trust was created. Rather, the short duration of the trust, the fact that the wife was the beneficiary, and the retention of control over the corpus by respondent all lead irresistibly to the conclusion that respondent continued to be the owner for purposes of § [61].

So far as his dominion and control were concerned it seems clear that the trust did not effect any substantial change. In substance his control over the corpus was in all essential respects the same after the trust was created, as before. The wide powers which he retained included for all practical purposes most of the control which he as an individual would have. There were, we may assume, exceptions, such as his disability to make a gift of the corpus to others during the term of the trust and to make loans to himself. But this dilution in his control would seem to be insignificant and immaterial, since control over investment remained. If it be said that such control is the type of dominion exercised by any trustee, the answer is simple. We have at best a temporary reallocation of income within an intimate family group. Since the income remains in the family and since the husband retains control over the investment, he has rather complete assurance that the trust will not effect any substantial change in his economic position. It is hard to imagine that respondent felt himself the poorer after this trust had been executed or, if he did, that it had any rational foundation in fact. For as a result of the terms of the trust and the intimacy of the familial relationship respondent retained the substance of full enjoyment of all the rights which previously he had in the property. That might not be true if only strictly legal rights were considered. But when the benefits flowing to him indirectly through the wife are added to the legal rights he retained, the aggregate may be said to be a fair equivalent of what he previously had. To exclude from the aggregate those indirect benefits would be to deprive § [61] of considerable vitality and to treat as immaterial what may be highly relevant considerations in the creation of such family trusts. For where the head of the household has income in excess of normal needs, it may well make but little difference to him (except income-tax-wise) where portions of that income are routed—so long as it stays in the family group. In those circumstances the all-important factor might be retention by him of control over the principal. With that control in his hands he would keep direct command over all that he needed to remain in substantially the same financial situation as before. Our point here is that no one fact is normally decisive but that all considerations and circumstances of the kind we have mentioned are relevant to the question of ownership and are appropriate foundations for findings on that issue. Thus, where, as in this case, the benefits directly or indirectly retained blend so imperceptibly with the normal concepts of full ownership, we cannot say that the triers of fact committed reversible error when they found that the husband was the owner of the corpus for the purposes of § [61]. To hold otherwise would be to treat the wife as a complete stranger; to let mere formalism obscure the normal consequences of family solidarity; and to force concepts of ownership to be fashioned out of legal niceties which may have little or no significance in such household arrangements.

* * *

The judgment of the Circuit Court of Appeals is reversed and that of the Board of Tax Appeals is affirmed.

Reversed.

You may recall from your individual income tax course that tax liability cannot be shifted by "anticipatory arrangements and contracts * * * skillfully devised" to attribute earned income to another taxpayer for income tax purposes. *Clifford* is consistent with the long line of income tax cases that began with Lucas v. Earl, 281 U.S. 111, 50 S.Ct. 241, 74 L.Ed. 731 (1930), prohibiting such gratuitous assignments of earned income. You may also have studied Helvering v. Horst, 311 U.S. 112, 61 S.Ct. 144, 85 L.Ed. 75 (1940), which essentially held that an assignment of income from property (as opposed to an assignment of income from services) was equally improper if the assignor retained ownership of the income producing property. This subsequently raised questions of what constitutes a relinquishment of both the income from property and ownership of the underlying property itself, sufficient to generate an effective income shift.

With cases like Blair v. Commissioner, 300 U.S. 5, 57 S.Ct. 330, 81 L.Ed. 465 (1937), courts began to realize that trusts create their own special income shifting problems and opportunities in the income shifting arena. In *Blair,* the taxpayer was the income beneficiary of a trust who gratuitously assigned that income interest. In keeping with earlier principles established outside the trust context, the Court found the assignment to be valid for income tax purposes, essentially on a theory that all the taxpayer owned was a right to receive income, which had been relinquished in its entirety. Notable about the case was that the assignor never owned the trust corpus and had not created the trust; it was not analogous to the taxpayer in *Clifford* who sought to take his own income producing properties and place them in a trust, followed by an assignment of the right to receive trust income. And it was decidedly unlike the spate of "Constitutional" or "family" trusts that generated significant amounts of litigation in the early to mid 1980's, by which a taxpayer would attempt to assign the right to income from personal services to a trust and make other family members the trust income beneficiaries.

Clifford may be seen as standing for a simple proposition that, if a taxpayer relinquishes sufficient control over income producing property, the assignment of income game will work. The difficult question is what constitutes a sufficient relinquishment that will suffice for these purposes? Most of the following material deals directly or indirectly with that question. Before embarking on that study, however, we pause for a moment to inspect one situation in which an otherwise sufficient relinquishment of income producing property will not effectively shift income to the intended assignee.

Adopted in 1986 (though advocated in a rudimentary form as early as 1947, in Hearings Before the Committee on Ways & Means, 80th Cong. 1st Sess., on Proposed Revisions of the Internal Revenue Code (Miscellaneous Recommendations) at 3837 (1947)), the so-called "Kiddie Tax" of section 1(i) was added to the Code by the Tax Reform Act of 1986 in an effort to curtail a form of perceived widespread abuse of the income tax system. Originally proposed to tax only the unearned (that is, not compensation from personal services) income of a young child derived from property that was transferred to the child by a parent, the provision finally adopted applies to all unearned income of such a minor child, thus avoiding difficult tracing and step or sham transaction problems. As finally enacted, the Kiddie Tax simply requires a child who is under the age of 14 at the end of the tax year to compute the child's tax liability on more than a de minimis amount (usually $1,000, though it could be larger) of unearned income, as if that income had belonged to the child's parents. Special provisions dictate which parent's tax rates to apply in determining the tax liability on unearned income if the parents are divorced or legally separated or if the child lives with foster parents, and special provisions apply if the parents' tax liability would be less than the child's. But in normal circumstances, the child is made to pay the income tax on unearned income at the parents' marginal income tax rate, effectively preventing any donor (not just the parents themselves) from transferring income producing property to a young taxpayer in an effort to cause the income therefrom to be taxed at the youngster's (hopefully lower) marginal rates.

The tax is arbitrary (for example, why focus only on the unearned income of prepubescent children instead of requiring all members of a single household or nuclear family to file a joint return?) and it will be avoided by those who are well advised (for example, by investing in tax exempts until the child turns 14), but it may have curtailed a certain amount of activity designed solely to reduce the tax liability on income produced by assets that are otherwise enjoyed by members of the young taxpayer's family. The Kiddie Tax will certainly affect certain forms of planning popular prior to 1987. But consider whether it (or *Clifford* itself) will affect the type of planning illustrated by the following case.

LERNER v. COMMISSIONER

United States Tax Court, 1978.
71 T.C. 290, acquiescence, 1984–1 C.B. 1.

DRENNEN, JUDGE:

* * *

The basic facts in this case are relatively simple and undisputed. In 1970, Dr. Lerner, who until that time had been a self-employed ophthalmologist, incorporated his practice into a professional service corporation, Hobart A. Lerner, M.D., P.C., which was formed for the purpose of engaging in the practice of ophthalmology. Dr. Lerner acquired all of the issued stock of the corporation for $500 cash; he did not transfer the furnishings and equipment he used in his practice to the corporation. Instead, Dr. Lerner established a trust, with his attorney as trustee, to which he transferred his medical furnishings and equipment. The net income of the trust was to be distributed to his children at least annually. The trust was to terminate in 10 years and approximately 1 month, at which time the corpus and any accumulated income of the trust was to revert to Dr. Lerner. The trustee, in turn, leased the medical furnishings and equipment to the corporation at a fair and reasonable rental for a period coextensive with the life of the trust. The corporation paid the rent to the trustee, who either distributed it to the children or invested some portion thereof in additional medical equipment which was included in the lease for additional and reasonable rental. Dr. Lerner became an employee of the corporation and the corporation charged and received the usual fees for his services and those of certain other employees.

Respondent, in a rather scattergun approach, disallowed the rental as a deduction to the corporation and taxed such rental, which had been paid to the trust, as income to Dr. Lerner, presumably as dividends from the corporation. It is not entirely clear whether respondent determined that the rent was taxable to Dr. Lerner as a dividend received directly from the corporation or as the owner for tax purposes of the trust and taxable on the income thereof. One thing is clear—respondent recognized the corporation as a separate taxable entity, taxing to it the income from the practice of ophthalmology, but disallowing the rental deductions, thus resulting in the deficiency determined to be due from the corporation.

We turn first to the deductibility of the rent, and we find no valid reason to deny it to the corporation. The equipment and furnishings covered by the lease were used by the corporation in its business and were required for the production of the income on which it is being taxed. Respondent does not question the reasonableness of the rent and indeed the evidence would not support him if he did. Therefore, the rental was an ordinary and necessary expense of the corporation's business.

* * *

We conclude that the corporate petitioner is entitled to deduct the rent it paid for use of the medical equipment and furnishings.

The second issue is whether the rental paid by the corporation to the trust is taxable income to the beneficiaries of the trust or to the Lerners. The rationale for taxing the income to the Lerners set forth in the notice of deficiency and in respondent's opening statement assumes that the gift and lease are invalid for Federal income tax purposes.

* * *

By enacting section 671 of the [1986] Code, Congress certainly recognized that usually a grantor of a family trust will not be treated as the owner of the trust for tax purposes solely on the grounds of his dominion and control of the trust unless he is treated as owner for one of the reasons specified in sections 673–677. Respondent does not point to any of those reasons for treating Dr. Lerner as owner of the trust and seems to recognize the trust as a "Clifford Trust." However, it is clear from S.Rept. 1622, 83d Cong., 2d Sess. 365 (1954), that the provision of section 671 relative to dominion and control does not affect the principles governing the taxability of income to a grantor of a trust other than by reason of his dominion and control over the trust, i.e., a transfer of future earnings of the grantor, etc. It is also clear that subpart E (secs. 671–679) has no application in determining the right of a grantor to deductions for payments to a trust under a transfer and leaseback arrangement. See also sec. 1.671–1(c). Thus, while this is not a typical sale and leaseback arrangement, and we are more concerned at this point with the taxability of the income produced by, rather than the deductibility of, the rent, we believe we should examine the arrangement in the light of case law to determine whether there is any reason, other than dominion and control, to tax the income of the trust to the Lerners rather than the beneficiaries of the trust.

* * *

In *Van Zandt v. Commissioner,* 40 T.C. 824 (1963), affd. 341 F.2d 440, 443 (5th Cir.1965), cert. denied 382 U.S. 814 (1965), this Court held that a physician who transferred a building and equipment he used in his medical practice to trusts created for the benefit of his children, naming himself as trustee, and immediately leased the building and equipment back from the trust for use in his medical practice could not deduct the rent paid by the physician to the trusts because it would not have been necessary for him to pay the rent had he not transferred the property to the trusts. There the taxpayer, as trustee, retained complete control of the property and continued to use it in his business. The Court of Appeals for the Fifth Circuit affirmed our decision emphasizing, however, that while taxpayers have every right to avail themselves of all provisions of the law to minimize their taxes, the obligation of the taxpayer to pay rent arose not out of business necessity nor for any business purpose but solely for the purpose of permitting a division of taxpayer's income tax. The appellate court recognized "that from the standpoint of taxability of income of the trust, not deductions which a payor of that 'income' may take, this was a perfectly valid trust. It met not only the minimum but all the statutory tests so that its income will be taxed to it, not the settlors."

In *Mathews v. Commissioner,* under somewhat similar circumstances, we held the rents paid were deductible by the settlors. We distinguished *Van Zandt* for the reasons that there the grantor was himself the trustee and thus failed to relinquish effective control of the property while in *Mathews,* as here, there was an independent trustee. In our opinion, we also listed certain requirements that have to be met to permit the grantor to deduct rent paid to the trustee in the typical two-party gift-leaseback transaction. Those requirements were:

(1) The grantor must not retain substantially the same control over the property that he had before he made the gift.

(2) The leaseback should normally be in writing and must require payment of a reasonable rental.

(3) The leaseback (as distinguished from the gift) must have a bona fide business purpose.

(4) The grantor must not possess a disqualifying "equity" in the property within the meaning of section 162(a)(3).

We do not believe that an arrangement that is bona fide and arm's length in all respects but which results in splitting family income must be disregarded for tax purposes for the latter reason alone. The so-called Clifford provisions in the Code recognize that valid trusts can be created which result in splitting the family income and minimizing taxes if the grantor does not retain control of the property for his own benefit. The Fifth Circuit recognized this in its opinion in *Van Zandt v. Commissioner.* There need be no business purpose for a father to transfer income-producing property to a trust for his children and have them taxed on the income produced. There is a difference, of course, if the father attempts to assign to the trust his future earnings and have the trust pay tax thereon. But in the case before us Dr. Lerner, having decided to incorporate his medical practice, could either have transferred his medical furnishings and equipment to the corporation, he could have retained ownership of it and rented it to the corporation himself, or he could do as he did—transfer the furnishings and equipment to a trust created for the benefit of his children and have the trust lease it to the corporation. The fact that the latter course of action would result in less taxes does not justify taxing the income of the trust to Dr. Lerner as long as he does not use that income for his own purposes or violate any of the restrictions contained in sections 673–677 of the Code. We believe respondent erred in not recognizing the trust as the true recipient and owner of the rental income and attempting to tax that income to the Lerners.

Question

With the 1986 changes to section 673, consider what kind of trust Dr. Lerner would need to create today to work his income shifting intent. Would it matter how old the Lerner children were? Consider section 1(i). In light of *Lerner,* is it fair to say that income shifting is, or ever was, precluded either as a matter of proper policy or in practical application?

Among the powers and interests that will, under Subpart E, queer an effort to divert income, the most common include:

(a) a reversion to the grantor or grantor's spouse, if the value of the reversion exceeds 5% of the trust or portion to which the reversion relates. A reversion on the death before age 21 of a minor beneficiary who holds all the present interests in a trust (such as a section 2503(c) qualified minors' trust) or a portion of a trust is *not* a prohibited interest if the beneficiary is a lineal descendant of the grantor;

(b) power in the grantor or grantor's spouse to control beneficial enjoyment without consent of an adverse party (subject to numerous exceptions, such as powers limited by a proper standard and testamentary powers of appointment);

(c) administrative powers permitting the grantor or grantor's spouse to deal at less than arms' length with the trust property;

(d) power in the grantor or grantor's spouse to amend or revoke the trust; and

(e) an interest in income that may be used "for the benefit of the grantor," including income that may be paid to the grantor or to the grantor's spouse, and income that is actually distributed to a person either the grantor or grantor's spouse is obliged to support or maintain (for example, a child).

In addition, a final section of Subpart E has the effect of taxing someone other than the grantor as if (s)he were the grantor, usually if that other person is given a withdrawal right over the trust. In recognition of a leading case in this area, such a trust is often referred to as a "Mallinckrodt" trust.

One final tax provision fleshes out another historical source of tax minimization through the use of trusts. At a time when the applicable income tax rates of trusts were likely to be lower than those applicable to the grantor thereof, a grantor who owned assets with a substantial amount of appreciation and wished to dispose thereof might find the income tax imposed on such a disposition to be prohibitive if taxed to the grantor at the grantor's marginal income tax rates but acceptable if the grantor were to transfer those assets to a valid trust, to be disposed of by the trust with the income therefrom taxed at the trust's lower marginal bracket. To curb this abuse, section 644 was added to the Code in 1976 to provide that, if disposed of by the trust within two years of transfer by the grantor, the tax on that income will be imposed at the same rate as if the grantor had disposed thereof. The two year period is an arbitrary term selected as a sufficient period to indicate that transfer and subsequent disposition were not part of a tax avoidance scheme. As with many of the other rules involving the income taxation of trusts, the trustee must be aware of the timing of any disposition, and has increased administrative (and perhaps liability) problems on a disposition inadvertently invoking this rule. But quaere whether the effect of bracket compression in 1986 may be to encourage the exact converse of the gaming to which section 644 was directed, and whether there is any reason for planners and their clients to avoid such "reverse–644" planning.

DEFINITIONS

Read Code sections 643(b) and 672.

Read Regulation sections 1.671–2(b) (second sentence) and 1.672.

Subpart E contains several concepts, terms and unique definitions that should be assimilated before studying specific sections and rules. Perhaps the most unfortunate unique definition is of the term "income," which is defined by section 643(b) to mean "fiduciary accounting income" for the balance of Subchapter J. By the penultimate sentence of Treasury Regulation section 1.671–2(b), applicable for purposes of the regulations under Subpart E (but not specifically for purposes of the Code itself), income means "taxable income," reflecting gross income, deductions, losses, credits and other items that enter into the determination of taxable income for income tax purposes. Further complicating the terminology, "ordinary income" is used in the last sentence of the same regulation, but not in a traditional tax sense; instead, it refers (again, in the Subpart E regulations) to "fiduciary accounting income."

A second frequently used term in Subpart E is found in provisions that refer to powers exercisable by the actual or any deemed grantor, or by a "nonadverse" party, in either case without the consent of an "adverse" party. See, for example, sections 674(a), 675(1), 675(2), 676 and 677. Indeed, in all of Subpart E except sections 673, 675(3), 675(4), and perhaps 676 (compare the Code with Treasury Regulation section 1.676(a)–1, for which there is no statutory authority), the requirement of consent of an adverse party will insulate powers held by, or act as a buffer against tax exposure to, the actual or any deemed grantor. As defined in section 672(a), an adverse party is one with a substantial beneficial interest that would be adversely affected by exercise or nonexercise of the power. Under section 672(b), a nonadverse party is anyone else. According to Treasury Regulation section 1.672(a)–1(b), in addition to direct beneficiaries of the trust, a person may have an indirect "beneficial interest" in a trust or, under the penultimate sentence of Treasury Regulation section 1.672(a)–1(a), be a beneficiary because (s)he possesses a general power of appointment. And "substantial" (as defined in the last sentence of Treasury Regulation section 1.672(a)–1(a) but without much guidance) means "not insignificant" in relation to total property subject to the power.

In relying on these exceptions, it is essential to remember several important caveats. First, under Treasury Regulation sections 1.672(a)–1(b), 1.672(a)–1(c) and 1.672(a)–1(d), a beneficiary is adverse with respect to only that portion of a trust in which (s)he is beneficially interested. Thus, for example, an income beneficiary of a portion of trust income may not be adverse with respect to powers over corpus, income allocable to corpus, or income from the balance of the trust. Second, in referring to a "general" power, there is no guidance in the statute, regulations or case law to determine whether a power is general as defined at common law (exercisable in favor of the donee or his or her estate) or for transfer tax purposes (exercisable in favor of the donee, his or her estate, or creditors of either), nor is there a compelling or logical reason to suggest that a nongeneral power (that could permit appointment to any one or more of every person in the world except the donee, the donee's estate, or creditors of either) is *not* a sufficient beneficial interest to constitute the donee as an adverse party. Third, "not insignificant," though lacking in clarity, is also not defined. For example, the last sentence of Treasury Regulation section 1.672(a)–1(c) suggests that a contingent income beneficiary may be an adverse party, without discussing the nature or remoteness of the contingency nor whether it can be regarded as significant, and there is virtually no other guidance. Thus, it can be questionable whether a person is adverse with respect to a particular power or portion of a trust, or sufficiently adverse to act as an appropriate buffer. Due to a relative dearth of litigation to enlarge upon these concepts, it may prove unwise to rely on adversity in planning for administration of trusts free from application of the grantor trust rules.

A third useful but less often utilized concept in Subpart E is that of the "related or subordinate" party. This term is integral to the definition of an "independent trustee" under section 674(c), which provides that, if not more than half the trustees of a trust are related or subordinate, the trustee will be deemed independent and, therefore, the trustee's powers will not cause section 674(a) grantor trust exposure. There is a similar "related or subordinate trustee" concept in the last sentence of section 675(3), relating to powers to borrow trust funds. For both, a "related or subordinate" party under section 672(c) must be (1) nonadverse, (2) subservient to the grantor (subservience is presumed by the last sentence of section 672(c) unless disproven by a preponderance of available evidence, such as proof that the trustee acts contrary to the grantor's wishes), and (3) any of grantor's spouse (if living with the grantor), parent, sibling, descendent, or employee of the grantor or of any corporation in which the grantor is a superior executive or significant stockholder (in terms of aggregate voting control of the grantor and of the trust). Neither "executive" nor "significant" voting control is defined. Because both the nonadverse and the subservient aspects of the definition are also uncertain, the only certain escape from the related or subordinate definition is by falling outside the defined class of related parties.

A final introductory concept relates to efforts to obfuscate the true grantor of a trust or portion thereof. One facet of the effort to identify the "grantor" is application of the "reciprocal trust doctrine" that may be utilized to ascertain whether an individual is only an ostensible, but not a recognizable, grantor, as illustrated by the following case.

KRAUSE v. COMMISSIONER

United States Tax Court, 1972.
57 T.C. 890, aff'd, 497 F.2d 1109 (6th Cir.1974).

STERRETT, JUDGE:

* * *

Adolph * * * and Janet S. Krause, * * * husband and wife, * * * executed a partnership agreement pursuant to the Michigan Limited Partnership Statutes, wherein they created a limited partnership.

* * *

Contemporaneous with the execution of this partnership agreement, petitioners * * * created six trusts for the benefit of their children and grandchildren. Adolph entered into a trust agreement between himself and Old Kent Bank & Trust Co. and Sidney A. Veltman as cotrustees, creating three trusts: The Janice K. Ziegler Trust for the benefit of Janice K. Ziegler; the Shirley K. Brackett Trust for the benefit of Shirley K. Brackett; and the Jack A. Krause Trust for the benefit of Jack A. Krause (hereinafter referred to as the children's trusts). The trusts were each funded with $100 in cash and 50 shares of Wolverine Shoe & Tanning Corp. (hereinafter sometimes referred to as Wolverine).

Janet also executed a trust agreement creating three trusts: The Janice K. Ziegler's Children's Trust for the benefit of the children of Janice K. Ziegler; the Shirley K. Brackett's Children's Trust for the benefit of the children of Shirley K. Brackett; and the Jack A. Krause's Children's Trust for the benefit of the children of Jack A. Krause (hereinafter referred to as the grandchildren's trust). Jack A. Krause had no children at the time of the creation of the above-noted trust. Janet named the same trustees as had been selected by her husband. The trusts were each funded with $100 in cash and 25 shares of Wolverine.

The express provisions of each trust executed by the respective petitioners provided in pertinent part, as follows:

3. BENEFICIARIES OF THE TRUSTS

(a) * * *

The Trustees shall hold, invest and reinvest the principal of each such Trust and may accumulate the income therefrom, add the same to principal, or retain it as undistributed income, or may pay the same or any part thereof, at such times and in such manner * * * and in such shares * * * as the Trustees shall determine, in their sole and absolute discretion * * * to or for the benefit of each such first life beneficiary of each respective Trust, or to such first life beneficiary's spouse * * * or to the issue of such first life beneficiary or to any other issue of the Grantor.

(e) The Grantor hereby expressly disclaims and waives any and all interest in and control over the Trusts, or the property thereof, for himself and for his estate.

* * *

5. POWERS OF TRUSTEES

(n) To terminate in whole or in part, any or all of such Trusts, at any time after the expiration of a period of twelve (12) years, commencing on the date the Trusts herein are created, and upon such termination, to pay the principal accumulations and unpaid income thereof to the then life beneficiary, if living; or if such first life beneficiary be dead, to the then living issue of such first life beneficiary; or if there be no such issue then living, in equal shares to the first life beneficiaries of the other Trusts, or if either of such first life beneficiaries be dead, to such deceased first life beneficiary's issue then living; or if there be no such issue then living, to the surviving first life beneficiary, or if such life beneficiary also be dead, to his or her issue then living; if all of such first life beneficiaries and their respective issue be dead, to those who would take the Grantor's personal property under the laws of Michigan then in force had the Grantor died intestate.

* * *

Notwithstanding the foregoing, my Trustees shall also have the power in their sole and absolute discretion to make any such payment of principal and accumulated income upon termination hereunder to the * * * [spouse] of the Grantor if she [or he] be then living * * *.

7. POWERS OF INVASION OF PRINCIPAL

[O]r, if in the judgment of my Trustees, the principal of such Trust is needed for the care, comfort, and necessities of the Grantor's * * * [spouse], or for sickness or for emergencies of any nature whatsoever occurring to the Grantor's * * * [spouse], the beneficiaries of the Trusts, or their families, it shall become the duty of the Trustees to devote so much of the income, and if necessary, the principal of such Trust funds as may be required for the use of such person or persons and for such purpose or purposes, in the discretion of the Trustees. * * *

* * *

13. No Power of Revocation

The Trusts herein created shall be irrevocable. The Grantor intends by this instrument to divest himself of all rights, title and interest in the property herein given to the Trustees.

* * *

15. Resignation, Removal and Appointment of Trustees

(b) My * * * [spouse] * * * shall have the power to remove any Trustee * * *.

* * *

Respondent contends that the reciprocal-trust doctrine is applicable to the instant case and therefore each petitioner is considered to be the grantor of the trust created by his or her spouse. Petitioners on the one hand assert that the reciprocal-trust doctrine is inapplicable to the present set of facts, but even if determined to be applicable, it does not cause petitioners to be taxed on the trust income as the grantor trust provisions have not been violated.

We agree with respondent. The Supreme Court in *United States v. Estate of Grace,* 395 U.S. 316 (1969), in affirming the validity of the reciprocal-trust doctrine in the estate tax area, specifically section 2036(a)(1), stated:

> we hold that application of the reciprocal trust doctrine is not dependent upon a finding that each trust was created as a *quid pro quo* for the other. Such a "consideration" requirement necessarily involves a difficult inquiry into the subjective intent of the settlors. Nor do we think it necessary to prove the existence of a tax-avoidance motive. As we have said above, standards of this sort, which rely on subjective factors, are rarely workable under the federal estate tax laws. Rather, we hold that application of the reciprocal trust doctrine requires only that the trusts be interrelated, and that the arrangement, to the extent of mutual value, leaves the settlors in approximately the same economic position as they would have been in had they created trusts naming themselves as life beneficiaries. [395 U.S. at 324. Footnote omitted.]

Further, this doctrine has been held to apply to the income tax as well as the estate tax area. See *Estate of Newberry,* 17 T.C. 597 (1951), revd. 201 F.2d 874 (C.A.3, 1953), on the facts but not on the above-noted principle of law; *Margaret Batts Tobin,* 11 T.C. 928 (1948), reversed in part 183 F.2d 919 (C.A.5, 1950), on the facts but not on the principle of law; *Henry F. Haldeman,* 6 T.C. 345 (1946); *Werner A. Wieboldt,* 5 T.C. 946 (1945); *Purdon Smith Whiteley,* 42 B.T.A. 316 (1940).

The trusts in the instant case were interrelated; all were created on the same day, named the same trustees and contained identical provisions. The primary beneficiaries were the natural objects of the grantors' bounty. However, each trust contained provisions permitting the trustees to pay the accumulated income and corpus to the grantor's spouse. It is therefore apparent that, though petitioners mutually desired to make provision for their children and grandchildren, they did not wish such provision to separate them irrevocably from financial security. Hence the "crossed" power to aid each other. As a result they maintained the same economic position throughout the entire transaction. As the Second Circuit stated in *Lehman v. Commissioner,* 109 F.2d 99, 100 (C.A.2, 1940), affirming 39 B.T.A. 17 (1939), the case which initiated the reciprocal-trust doctrine:

The fact that the trusts were reciprocated or "crossed" is a trifle, quite lacking in practical or legal significance.

Petitioners however contend that section 671 which states in part:

No items of a trust shall be included in computing the taxable income and credits of the grantor or of any other person solely on the grounds of his dominion and control over the trust under section 61 (relating to definition of gross income) or any other provision of this title, except as specified in this subpart.

precludes the applicability of the reciprocal-trust doctrine to the grantor trust provisions. Further, they argue that section 677(a) which provides:

SEC. 677. Income for Benefit of Grantor.

(a) GENERAL RULE.—The grantor shall be treated as the owner of any portion of a trust * * * whose income * * * may be—

(1) distributed to the grantor or the *grantor's spouse;*

(2) held or accumulated for future distribution to the grantor or the *grantor's spouse;* or

(3) applied to the payment of premiums on policies of insurance on the life of the grantor or the *grantor's spouse* * * *. [Emphasis supplied.]

closes the "loophole" present in the instant case. Petitioners point out however that such language was added with the enactment of the "69 Tax Reform Act," after the taxable years in question.

We cannot agree with either argument. First, section 671 merely precludes the applicability of any other section in taxing the grantor on the income of the trust. It does not prevent the use of the reciprocal-trust doctrine. As will be seen *infra,* the reciprocal-trust doctrine is applied only so that this Court can determine whether in fact petitioners are taxable under the grantor trust provisions. Secondly, Congress in amending section 677 to include grantor "or the grantor's spouse" clearly was not attempting to deal with a reciprocal trust. Rather, as we noted above, the courts first disposed of this issue in *Lehman v. Commissioner, supra,* a decision promulgated in 1940. The addition of the term "spouse" merely contemplated a situation wherein "*a* trust [is] created by *a* taxpayer for the benefit of his spouse." (Emphasis supplied. H.Rept. No. 91–413 (Part 1), 91st Cong., 1st Sess., p. 97 (1969), 1969–3 C.B. 261)

* * *

Having determined that petitioners, through the application of the reciprocal-trust doctrine and grantor trusts provisions, are taxed on the income of the trusts, we must now decide to what extent they must be taxed. The Supreme Court in *United States v. Estate of Grace, supra,* held that the petitioner would be required to include in the deceased's estate, the value of the trust created by his spouse, "to the extent of mutual value," 395 U.S. at 324. * * *

In the instant case the three trusts created by Adolph were funded with $100 and 50 shares of Wolverine, while Janet's trusts contained $100 and only 25 shares of Wolverine. Therefore, following the rationale of *Grace,* petitioners are taxed to the extent of the income produced by 25 shares of Wolverine held by each of the six trusts.

* * *

If the trusts in *Krause* had been post–TRA'86 trusts, the reciprocal trust doctrine would have been unnecessary because the Service could regard each grantor as taxable by virtue of the interests and powers granted to the grantor's spouse, pursuant to section 672(e). However, the reciprocal trust doctrine could apply in numerous situations in which section 672(e) will not apply. For example, consider the creation of two mirror image trusts, one established by sibling A with sibling B as trustee and the other established by B with A as trustee. To the extent the trusts are found to be "interrelated," they may be regarded as trusts created by A with A as trustee and by B with B as trustee, after which the trustee powers held by the deemed grantors would have the potential for grantor trust exposure.

For these purposes, "interrelation" is not a function of any intent on the part of A and B but, rather, is deemed to exist under mechanical tests that look to (1) whether the trusts were created at approximately the same time, (2) whether they have substantially identical terms, and (3) whether each of A and B are in approximately the same economic position as if the trusts had been created as viewed—as opposed to as actually structured. United States v. Estate of Grace, 395 U.S. 316, 89 S.Ct. 1730, 23 L.Ed.2d 332 (1969), rev'g 393 F.2d 939 (Ct.Cl.1968) (establishing these tests in an estate tax application of the reciprocal trust doctrine, uncrossing trusts created by husband and wife for each other). For purposes of the approximately same economic position aspect of the interrelation test, the doctrine looks to mutual value so that, if one trust were $100x at creation and the other were $60x, all of the smaller trust and 60 percent of the larger would be treated as reciprocal. The remaining 40 percent of the larger trust would remain unchanged by application of the doctrine. See Revenue Ruling 74–533, 74–2 C.B. 293.

In a similar vein, if two identical trusts were created by X, one with A as trustee for B and the other with B as trustee for A, the reciprocal trust doctrine may serve to uncross these trusts to regard A as beneficiary of the trust as to which A is trustee and B as beneficiary of the trust as to which B is trustee, with the potential for grantor trust exposure under the deemed grantor provision in section 678. Thus, for example, in Letter Ruling 8029001, the reciprocal trust doctrine was so applied in a gift tax setting, entirely unrelated to the tax consequences flowing from any powers held as trustee. Historically, "uncrossing" has occurred only at the "settlor" level, not at the trustee or beneficiary level (for example, A>——>B as trustee for C would be deemed to be B>——>B as trustee for C). This ruling appears to be the first use of the doctrine to uncross at the trustee level (for example, F>——>A as trustee for B would be deemed to be F>——>B as trustee for B). Flato v. Commissioner, 195 F.2d 580 (5th Cir.1952) is a similar case with a similar result, but not based on the reciprocal trust doctrine.

Other efforts to disguise the true grantor or nature of a trust will be ignored, as would be likely if A transferred property to B with the understanding that B would use the property to create a trust thereof for the benefit of A, or granting A powers that would otherwise cause grantor trust exposure were A the grantor. In such a case, A would be regarded as grantor of the trust for purposes of Subchapter J.[1] Finally, it is necessary to recognize that any trust may have multiple grantors, as would equally be true if A and B originally created a trust or if B added assets to a trust originally created by A. Thus, Treasury Regulation section 1.671–3(a)(3) establishes rules for allocation among several individuals as grantors of a single trust. One common but often overlooked source of multiple grantor treatment is lapse of a withdrawal power with the property subject to the power remaining in trust and the donee thereafter being regarded as grantor of that property, as if it had been withdrawn and recontributed to the trust. For example, Letter Ruling 8517052 and Revenue Ruling 67–241, 67–2 C.B. 225, both involved "five or five" withdrawal rights, the lapse of which not being taxable under section 2514(e), but still being regarded as a contribution as to which the powerholder is the grantor for future income tax purposes.

REVERSIONARY INTERESTS

Read Code section 673.

Section 673, as the first grantor trust rule, was a keystone provision in Subpart E prior to its amendment in 1986. For example, each of sections 674(b)(2), 676(b) and 677(a) incorporated the same 10 year term of pre–TRA'86 section 673 by simple reference to the period that would not cause exposure under section 673.

Under prior law (which still applies generally with respect to trusts that were irrevocable before March 2, 1986, and as to which no tainting addition or other transfer was made after March 1, 1986), a reversion would cause grantor trust exposure only if it would, or might reasonably be expected to, take effect within 10 years of transfer of that portion

1. *See, e.g.,* Whiteley v. Commissioner, 120 F.2d 782 (3d Cir.1941), cert. denied, 314 U.S. 657, 62 S.Ct. 110, 86 L.Ed. 527 (1941), aff'g, 42 B.T.A. 402 (1940) (husband treated as grantor of trust created by wife to hold stock previously transferred by husband to wife).

to the trust. Required, under Treasury Regulation section 1.673(a)–1(c), for application of section 673 was only a reasonable expectation that the reversion would occur within 10 years. Specifically excepted from the need to make an actuarial determination was a reversion that would occur only on the death of the income beneficiary. Under section 673(c) and Treasury Regulation section 1.671(a)–1(b), such a reversion did not cause grantor trust treatment under pre–TRA'86 law, regardless of the beneficiary's life expectancy.

Also provided under prior law was the opportunity to purify a trust that contained an otherwise taxable reversion. For example, assume that Grantor executed a trust on December 31, 1983, to run until January 1, 1994. During early January of 1984, Grantor made the requisite transfers to fund the trust, so that all assets were in place and the trust was prepared to receive all income generated after 1983. In this case, notwithstanding creation of the trust more than 10 years prior to termination and reversion to Grantor, the relevant time for testing section 673 was funding of the trust, which occurred within 10 years of termination, making this a grantor trust. See Bibby v. Commissioner, 44 T.C. 638 (1965) (10 year and a day Clifford trust with assets transferred approximately 11 months after execution). Now assume that Grantor is informed of this failure to draft and fund the trust in such a manner to avoid application of section 673. In the second year of the trust, Grantor extends the term of the trust to 13 years total, with the income tax consequence of purifying the originally defective term and, not inconsequentially, also making the additional three year term a qualified transfer that itself also avoids application of section 673.

This last matter is not insignificant. For example, assume that Grantor had created an effective 11 year trust that avoided grantor trust exposure and that, with two years left to run, Grantor extended the term to 15 years by postponing the reversion an added four years. In this case the original term would be unaffected by the extension but, under section 673(d) and Treasury Regulation section 1.673(d)–1, the new term of four years would be subject to grantor trust treatment when it became the present interest because, with respect to it, Grantor made a transfer that would revert within six years (the transfer having been made by the extension in year nine). Under similar authority, any extension of a term after March 1, 1986, should be regarded as a new transfer into trust, as to which the new section 673 rules will apply.

Today, while section 673 has waned in importance, it remains one of the easiest and most straightforward provisions in Subpart E. Disregarded by virtue of section 673 is any portion of a trust as to which the grantor has a reversion of either income or corpus that exceeds five percent in value of the portion that may revert. An exception exists if the grantor may acquire by reversion either the income or corpus of a trust created for a lineal descendant who possesses all the present interests in the trust and who dies prior to reaching the age of 21 years. An example of such a trust is contained in the Committee Reports, which mention a section 2503(c) qualified minor's trust.

The consequence of a reversion that is not excepted from application of section 673 is that the subject portion of the trust is ignored. Thus, under section 671, all tax items allocable thereto or flowing therefrom (including the character, timing and other tax attributes of those items) are regarded as those of the grantor, as if no trust had been created.[2]

Most events triggering a reversion are subject to actuarial determination under established rules. For example, the most common event triggering a reversion is death of another person, usually a beneficiary of the trust. The appropriate actuarial tables (now found in Treasury Regulation section 20.2031–7(f)) may be used to determine life expectancy of such an individual and the value of the reversion will presumably be determined in the same manner as under section 2037, which incorporates the same five percent valuation standard. Events that are not subject to actuarial determination would be dangerous to use if avoidance of section 673 is desired,[3] though there are tables of probability of some events (such as likelihood of remarriage or divorce) upon which an actuary may estimate the probability of some reversion events. For all these purposes, it is important to consider that Revenue Ruling 80–80, 1980–1 C.B. 194, holds that the actuarial tables in Treasury Regulation section 20.2031–7(f) must be used if valuation of an individual's life interest is required for purposes of the federal estate or gift taxes, unless the individual whose life expectancy is the measuring event is known to be afflicted with an incurable physical condition that is in such an advanced stage that death is clearly imminent. While Revenue Ruling 80–80 is not specifically directed at valuation for purposes of section 673, most commentators assume that the same principles will apply.

Questions

1. A common source of confusion regarding the reversion rule of section 673 relates to items of taxable income (and losses) that are allocated to principal, either as accumulations made in the trustee's discretion or because allocable thereto under local law (for example, capital gains and losses that are allocated to corpus under RUPIA section 3(b)(8)). Even if the trust avoids section 673 notwithstanding an otherwise permissible reversion retained by the grantor, the last paragraph of Treasury Regulation section 1.673(a)–1(a) establishes that those items that are allocated to

2. See Schmolka, "Selected Aspects of the Grantor Trust Rules", 9 U.Miami Inst. Est.Plan. ¶ 1400, 1403 (1975), dealing with definition of the "portion" of the trust of which the grantor is treated as owner. With respect to timing, see Scheft v. Commissioner, 59 T.C. 428 (1972), reproduced at page 262.

3. See Treasury Regulation section 1.673(a)–1(d) ("[i]t is immaterial that a reversionary interest in corpus or income is subject to a contingency if the reversionary interest may, taking the contingency into consideration, reasonably be expected to take effect in possession or enjoyment . . .").

principal and that will ultimately return to the grantor are taxable to the grantor under section 677(a)(2), pertaining to income accumulated for future distribution to the grantor. Thus, even though the trust is drafted properly to prevent application of section 673 to the grantor, this is not a total protection against grantor trust exposure. With this in mind, why might Congress have thought that section 673 needs to apply to a reversion of income?

2. In a post–TRA'86 section 2503(c) trust, Grantor directed that income and principal may be paid to a minor grandchild of the grantor as beneficiary until termination of the trust at the grandchild's age 21. If the grandchild dies before reaching 21, the trust is distributable to Grantor's spouse, with what income tax consequences?

POWER TO REVOKE

Read Code section 676.

Read Regulation section 1.676.

Section 676 is a second straightforward provision that puts grantors who retain a power of revocation (allowing reacquisition of trust property in the grantor's discretion) on an even footing with those who retain a section 673 automatic reversion. To maintain a concept of equality between a power to revoke and a reversion, section 676(b), as it applied prior to TRA'86, contained an exception that incorporated by reference the 10 year period of section 673 as it existed prior to 1986. That exception is applicable to any pre–TRA'86 trust with a power of revocation that is exercisable only with respect to income and that affects enjoyment only after "the expiration of a period such that the grantor would not be treated as the owner under section 673 if the power were a reversionary interest . . ." (that is, a 10 year period, or the earlier death of the income beneficiary). Such a power will not cause grantor trust exposure prior to expiration of the 10 year (or earlier death) period and, by Treasury Regulation section 1.676(b)–1, this exception is applicable even if the power is presently vested or exercisable, if the effect of exercise is properly postponed.

With respect to post–TRA'86 trusts, section 676(b) now refers to the new section 673 exception for a reversion on the death of a minor lineal descendant who is the sole present interest beneficiary of a trust, presumably meaning that a power to revoke that is triggered on such a death will not cause section 676 exposure until such death occurs.

If section 676(b) is not applicable, then section 676(a) will attribute to the grantor those items of income, deductions, and credits of any portion of the trust that is subject to a power to revoke, if the power is exercisable (even if not actually exercised) by the grantor or any nonadverse party, without the consent of an adverse party (Treasury Regulation section 1.676(a)–1 provides an adverse party exception though there is no direct authority therefor in the statute). Powers that will trigger section 676(a) include (1) a direct power to terminate (either expressly retained or existing under state law due to a failure to make the trust irrevocable), as well as powers (2) to purchase trust assets for less than a full and adequate consideration, or (3) to invade, withdraw, alter, amend or appoint, in each case if exercisable by, in favor of, or for the benefit of the grantor (or, under section 672(e), the grantor's spouse in a post–TRA'86 trust).

Questions

1. Grantor created a pre–TRA'86 trust, reserving a power to revoke if the trust's ten year old income beneficiary dies before distribution at the beneficiary's age 40. Is section 676 applicable? See Rovensky v. Commissioner, 37 B.T.A. 702 (1938).

2. What portion of trust income will be taxable to a grantor if the only power retained in a pre–TRA'86 trust is a protected section 676(b) power of revocation, not exercisable before expiration of ten years after funding the trust? See Duffy v. United States, 487 F.2d 282 (6th Cir.1973).

3. Client assists an elderly relative with the fixed monthly costs of a nursing home. At present, Client uses after tax income earned on certain investments, but would like to find a method to reduce the cost of this assistance and thereby increase the amount that Client can afford to contribute. The relative is in a lower tax bracket and Client considered giving some of these income producing assets to the relative, but was turned away from that idea by the gift tax cost of the initial transfer and the fact that Client might lose control of the assets if the relative fails to bequeath them back at death (to say nothing of potential estate tax costs to reacquire the assets). What might you recommend to Client to reduce the tax cost of the assistance without losing ultimate control of the assets?

4. What are the grantor trust consequences of making a demand loan to a trust?

INCOME FOR GRANTOR'S BENEFIT

Read Code section 677.

Read Regulation section 1.677.

Many inter vivos trusts are not created for the purpose of shifting income from the grantor to another taxpayer. For these trusts, income tax liability to the grantor is not unexpected because it flows from intentional retention of enjoyment of trust income. A grantor is treated under section 677(a) as owner of any portion of a trust as to which the income, without the consent of an adverse party, either (1) must be paid or (2) in the discretion of the grantor or any nonadverse party, either may be paid currently or may be accumulated for future payment to the grantor (or, as we will see, in most modern trusts, for the grantor's spouse as well). In each case, the income must be available for the direct or indirect benefit of the grantor.

Benefit to the grantor is a broad concept, obviously encompassing direct payments to the grantor. Unexpected income tax liability does arise in some cases, however, because benefit to the grantor extends to a wide range of indirect or constructive distributions. For example, in trusts created after 1969, distributions to or for the benefit of the grantor's spouse are treated under section 677(a) and Treasury Regulation section 1.677(a)–1(b)(2) essentially as if the grantor were the beneficiary. This is true even if the spouse is not living with the grantor: compare sections 672(c), 672(e), and 674(d), which all require the spouse to be living with the grantor; no such requirement appears in section 677(a). However, if the grantor is separated from the spouse, either of sections 71 or 682 may apply to distributions to the spouse. Generally, section 71 applies to trusts created for the purpose of making alimony payments to the spouse (pursuant to a divorce decree or separation agreement), and section 682 applies to payments from trusts that antedated a divorce or legal separation and that discharge grantor's subsequently incurred obligations. In either case, pre–TRA'86 trust income payable to the spouse (not as child support) is taxed to the spouse, not to the grantor, under the last sentence of Treasury Regulation section 1.682(a)–1(a)(2). See Zaritsky, "Special Trusts and Unique Problems: Grantor Trusts After the Grantor's Death, Alimony Trusts, and Foreign Trusts Versus Domestic Trusts", 37 N.Y.U. Inst.Fed.Tax § 42.03[2] (1979). However, section 672(e) apparently applies to post–TRA'86 trusts that make payments to a spouse who was living with the grantor as of creation of the trust, meaning that the grantor would be taxed on trust income, though this result may not have been the intent of Congress in drafting the effective date of section 1401(b) of TRA'86. Compare TRA'86 § 1402(c)(2).

In addition, payment of premiums for insurance on the life of the grantor (or, in post–1969 trusts, on the life of grantor's spouse as well) will cause section 677(a)(3) to apply. While the apparent theory behind this rule is that the grantor or grantor's spouse benefits from such insurance being carried, the policies need not be owned by the grantor or spouse nor must they designate either as beneficiary. Payment of premiums for insurance owned by the grantor or grantor's spouse on the life of someone other than the grantor or grantor's spouse is not covered under section 677(a)(3) but would probably be covered under either section 677(a)(1) or (a)(2) as an indirect distribution to the grantor or grantor's spouse or an indirect accumulation of income (through any increase in the cash surrender or other value of the policy). Finally, payments that discharge a legal or contractual obligation of the grantor or grantor's spouse are regarded as indirectly beneficial to the grantor under Treasury Regulation section 1.677(a)–1(c), which deals with distributions at the direction of the grantor or grantor's spouse and 1.677(a)–1(d), which deals with distributions to discharge legal obligations.

Questions

1. For purposes of section 677, the penultimate clause of Treasury Regulation section 1.677(a)–1(b)(2) provides that the grantor's spouse cannot

be an adverse party in any trust created after 1969, on the theory that the spouse's adverse interest would constitute an indirect benefit to the grantor and thus would not be adverse at all. See Amabile v. Commissioner, 1986 T.C.M. 180, 51 T.C.M. (CCH) 963, 55 T.C. Memo (P–H) 772 (1986). In a post-TRA'86 trust, the section 672(e) equivalence of the grantor and grantor's spouse will make these issues irrelevant in most cases. In a pre–TRA'86 trust, however, is it possible for the spouse's interest to be adverse to that of the grantor, even though it is deemed to be an indirect benefit to the grantor? For example, assume that, in a pre–TRA'86 trust, grantor's spouse is entitled to all principal and accrued income at the death of the grantor, and has a power during the grantor's life to veto any proposed distributions of income to the grantor. Is the spouse an adverse party with respect to the grantor's income interest?

2. If the trustee of a trust is not precluded from making distributions to pay premiums for insurance on the grantor's life, but is also not authorized to do so and the trust owns no insurance, will section 677(a)(3) apply because income could, in the trustee's discretion, be so used in the future? See Corning v. Commissioner, 104 F.2d 329 (6th Cir.1939); Weil v. Commissioner, 3 T.C. 579 (1944), acquiescence, 1944 C.B. 29; and Moore v. Commissioner, 39 B.T.A. 808 (1939), acquiescence, 1979–2 C.B. 25.

3. Assume Grantor is a party to a buy-sell agreement relating to closely held business stock owned by Grantor and several of Grantor's siblings. To provide the liquidity to permit each sibling to purchase the stock of a deceased party to the agreement, each sibling establishes a trust, the income from which being used to pay premiums for insurance that the other siblings own on the grantor's life. Thus, Grantor's trust pays the premiums for insurance that each sibling owns on Grantor's life. When Grantor dies, that insurance will pay to the siblings the necessary cash with which to purchase Grantor's stock. For whose benefit is this insurance held? Does section 677(a)(3) apply with respect to the income from Grantor's trust? Should it?

4. Why might a grantor want section 677(a)(3) to apply to a trust created to own insurance on the grantor's life?

Consider the concept of a grantor's indirect beneficial enjoyment, as illustrated by the following case.

KRAUSE v. COMMISSIONER

United States Tax Court, 1971.
56 T.C. 1242.

FEATHERSTON, JUDGE: Respondent determined a deficiency in petitioners' Federal income tax for 1964 in the amount of $91,249.05. The issue for decision is whether funds derived by trusts from dividends and loans and used, pursuant to the trust instruments, to pay the gift taxes resulting from the creation of the trusts are income taxable to petitioners.

* * *

[P]etitioner created three trusts: One for the benefit of the children of his son, Gordon C. Krause (hereinafter the Gordon trust), and one for the benefit of the children of each of his daughters, Elizabeth K. Sherwood and Ruth K. Sherwood (hereinafter the Elizabeth and Ruth trusts, respectively). * * *

The Gordon trust agreement provides:

2. The Trustees shall promptly pay all Federal Gift Taxes and all other taxes which shall arise out of or be attributable to the transfer by this Trust Agreement of the above mentioned shares of corporate stock, and said corporate stock is transferred hereby subject to the duty and obligation of the Trustees to promptly pay all such taxes. In order to provide funds with which to pay said taxes the Trustees in their sole and absolute discretion may sell and convert to cash such portions of said corporate stock as they may deem necessary for that purpose or they may borrow sufficient funds for that purpose from such sources, including themselves or either of them, as they may deem proper, and pledge any part of the principal and income of this Trust as security for such loan, or they may obtain funds for the payment of all such taxes partly by sale of assets of said Trust and partly by loan secured by all or any part of the principal and income of this Trust, all in accordance with their sole and absolute discretion.

3. All income and earnings of this Trust shall be used and applied by the Trustees in such amounts and at such times as they in their sole and absolute discretion from time to time shall determine for the following purposes, namely:

First—for the payment of all taxes and assessments and other governmental charges which may be lawfully imposed upon the principal and/or income of this Trust.

Second—for the payment of all proper charges and expenses incurred by the Trustees and their agents and attorneys in and about the faithful administration of this Trust.

The Elizabeth and Ruth trust agreements contain basically similar provisions, differing only in that each further provides that the trustees—

may obtain funds for the payment of all such [gift] taxes partly by sale of assets of the principal of said trust, partly from income thereof, and partly by loan secured by all or any part of the principal and/or income of this trust * * *

In April of 1964, the trustees of the three trusts pledged the stock which they had received from petitioner to Old Kent Bank & Trust Co., one of the trustees, as security for loans in the total amount of $134,500. With these funds, the trustees, on April 14, 1964, paid the joint and several gift tax liabilities of petitioner and his wife, both of whom had consented pursuant to section 2513 to having the gifts treated as made one-half by each of them. The total amount of taxes so paid was $134,331.65.

During their fiscal years ending August 31, 1964, the trusts received the following amounts of dividend income:

	Sept. to Apr. 14	Apr. 15 to Aug. 31	Total
Gordon	$3,600	$4,050	$7,650
Elizabeth	2,400	2,700	5,100
Ruth	2,400	2,700	5,100
Total	8,400	9,450	17,850

Beginning in September of 1964 and continuing through August of 1970, the trusts made periodic payments to Old Kent Bank & Trust Co. to discharge the loans and the interest thereon. These payments were made with dividend income received by the trusts from the stock.

The Code provides generally that the gift tax "shall be paid by the donor." Sec. 2502. When a husband and wife have consented to have a gift made by one of them treated as if made one-half by each of them, they are jointly and severally liable for the full amount of the tax liability arising from the transfer. Sec. 2513(d). The donee, under section 6324(b), is personally liable for the tax only if it is not paid when due. *Fletcher Trust Co. v. Commissioner,* 141 F.2d 36, 39 (C.A. 7, 1944), affirming 1 T.C. 798 (1943), certiorari denied 323 U.S. 711 (1944). Thus, notwithstanding his agreements with the trustees and his wife, petitioner was liable under the Code for the payment of all the gift taxes arising from the transfers to the trusts.

Relying upon these Code provisions, respondent determined that petitioner transferred "stock in trust for several donees, reserving an income interest in the transfer for the payment of * * * [his] gift tax liability in the amount of $134,331.65; and that * * * [his] reservation of the income interest subjects * * * [him] to the provisions of section 677 of the Internal Revenue Code * * *. Accordingly, the net income of the trusts in 1964 is taxable to * * * [him] in the amount of $14,091.62." Respondent further determined that petitioner's "income interest in the trusts terminated in 1964 when the trusts paid * * * [his] gift tax liability in full; and that such payment, from funds other than trust income, constitutes a purchase in liquidation of * * * [his] income interest and results in ordinary income" in the additional amount of $120,240.03.

Section 677(a) provides in pertinent part:

The grantor shall be treated as the owner of any portion of a trust * * * whose income without the approval or consent of any adverse party is, or, in the discretion of the grantor or a nonadverse party, or both, may be—

(1) distributed to the grantor;

Amplifying this provision, section 1.677(a)–1(d) provides:

(d) Under section 677 a grantor is, in general, treated as owner of a portion of a trust whose income is, or in the discretion of the grantor or a nonadverse party, or both, may be applied in discharge of a legal obligation of the grantor. * * *

* * *

To the extent of the amount of the income realized by the trusts prior to the payment of the gift taxes ($8,400), respondent's position is quite clearly correct. Where a person transfers property to a trust and, as a condition to the transfer, the trustee agrees to pay the resulting gift tax liability, the donor is taxable on any trust income which the trustee may use for that purpose. Within the meaning of section 677, he is treated as an owner of a portion of the trust because its income, in the discretion of the trustee, may be used to discharge his legal obligation. Under section 671, the donor is taxable on the income attributable to such portion of the trust—i.e., the income which may be used to discharge his legal obligation to pay the gift tax. *Estate of Craig R. Sheaffer,* 37 T.C. 99 (1961), affd. 313 F.2d 738 (C.A. 8, 1963), certiorari denied 375 U.S. 818 (1963); *Estate of A.E. Staley, Sr.,* 47 B.T.A. 260 (1942), affd. 136 F.2d 368 (C.A. 5, 1943), certiorari denied 320 U.S. 786 (1943). It is of no avail to petitioner in the instant case that the proceeds of the loans rather than the trust income were used for this purpose. The controlling consideration under section 677 is the described "discretion," not the way in which that discretion is actually exercised.

* * *

Paragraph 2 of the Gordon trust agreement, quoted above, is permissive; it allows the trustee to sell part of the corpus or to borrow on the corpus to pay the gift taxes, but it does not prohibit the use of trust income for this purpose. Indeed, paragraph 3, dealing with trust income, gives the trustee wide discretion to use the trust income "for the payment of *all* taxes and assessments * * * which may be lawfully imposed upon the principal and/or income" (emphasis added) of the trust and "for the payment of all proper charges and expenses incurred by the Trustees and their agents and attorneys." Since the trust agreements required the trustees to pay the gift tax liabilities arising from the transfers in trust, such liabilities became proper charges against the principal and income of the trusts. The trustees, therefore, had the discretionary power to use the trust income to meet this charge without violating the trust agreement. In these circumstances, sections 671 and 677 require all such income received prior to the payment of the taxes to be included in petitioner's taxable income.

The income received by the trusts after April 14, 1964, when the gift taxes were paid, however, is not taxable to petitioner. As a result of the payment of the taxes, all of his obligations with respect thereto were satisfied, and, within the meaning of section 1.677(a)–1(d), *supra,* he had no further obligations to which the trust income could be applied. Thus, the payment of the gift taxes denuded petitioner of every interest in the trusts, and section 1.677(a)–1(c) provides: "If the grantor strips himself permanently and definitively of every interest

* * * he is not treated as an owner under section 677 after that divesting."[5]

Since petitioner, after April 14, 1964, no longer had any interest in the trusts within the meaning of section 677, none of the trust income received after that date is taxable to him. * * *

Question

Grantor transferred Blackacre to an irrevocable trust. What are the income tax consequences if the trustee pays mortgage installments relating to Blackacre as they come due during the term of the trust?

An often misunderstood section 677 exception is found in the last sentence of section 677(a) and Treasury Regulation section 1.677(a)–1(e), applicable to the extent enjoyment of benefits is deferred in a pre-TRA'86 trust for a 10 year period (or until the earlier death of an income beneficiary other than the grantor or grantor's spouse), or in a post-TRA'86 trust until the occurrence of a section 673 event (death of a present interest minor lineal descendant beneficiary). Clearly excepted from current grantor trust treatment under this exception is a power that permits enjoyment of (1) income earned by a pre-TRA'86 trust no sooner than 10 years after the transfer of trust property to the trust, or (2) income earned by a post-TRA'86 trust after the death of a minor lineal descendant beneficiary. Until enjoyment actually begins, such a provision will not invoke grantor trust liability (though grantor trust liability begins under Treasury Regulation section 1.677(a)–1(e) when current enjoyment becomes possible under the terms of the deferral provision). *Not* protected, however, as illustrated by Treasury Regulation section 1.677(a)–1(f), is a power to accumulate *current* income, even though distribution is postponed for the same 10 year period or until the death of a minor lineal descendant beneficiary.

Thus, for example, if items of trust taxable income are added to principal, either as accumulations made in the trustee's discretion or because allocable thereto under local law (for example, capital gains),

5. The language of sec. 39.167–1(b)(5), Regs. 118, is even more explicit in stating that a grantor whose interest in a trust has been extinguished does not thereafter realize taxable income from the trust as follows:

> 5. If the grantor strips himself permanently and definitely of every * * * interest retained by him—[which would cause the trust income to be taxed to him under sec. 167, I.R.C.1939], the income of the trust realized after such divesting takes effect is not taxable to the grantor. * * *

The differences in the language of this regulation and the current regulation sec. 1.677(a)–1(c), quoted in the text, are only differences in form. Sec. 677 treats the grantor as the owner of a portion of the trust if income may be distributed or applied for his benefit; sec. 167, I.R.C.1939, on the other hand, requires the portion of the trust income which may be used for the grantor's benefit to be included in his gross income. Both sections, however, were designed to aid in achieving the same objective—i.e., "to determine when a trust's income is to be taxed to the grantor because of the grantor's substantial dominion and control of the trust property or income." S.Rept. No. 1622, to accompany H.R. 8300 (Pub.L. No. 591), 83d Cong., 2d Sess., pp. 86, 371 (1954).

and if there is (a) a reversion to the grantor or grantor's spouse at any time or upon the occurrence of any event, (b) discretion in the trustee to distribute accumulations to the grantor or grantor's spouse at any time, present or future, or (c) any power in the grantor or grantor's spouse to reach those accumulations at any time, present or future, grantor trust exposure will *currently* exist, as illustrated in the following case.

DUFFY v. UNITED STATES

United States Court of Appeals, Sixth Circuit, 1973.
487 F.2d 282.

McCREE, CIRCUIT JUDGE.

* * *

The taxpayers, F. Paul Duffy, a physician, and his wife, Virginia H. Duffy, purchased improved real estate in Cincinnati, Ohio on July 31, 1962, for use by Dr. Duffy in his medical practice. Shortly thereafter, on February 26, 1963, the Duffys executed a trust agreement pursuant to which they conveyed this property to the Provident Bank as trustee. On the same day, the Duffys and the bank executed a five year lease-back agreement, renewable for an additional five years, in which Dr. Duffy agreed to pay an annual rent of $8,650, an amount stipulated as reasonable.

The trust agreement created four trusts, one for the benefit of each of their children. * * * These trusts were made irrevocable for 10 years and 30 days and amendable and revocable thereafter. The trust instrument provides that a beneficiary, while a minor, may receive, if necessary in the sole discretion of the trustee, his share of the trust principal or the income generated by it for his education, maintenance or welfare. Income not distributed for these purposes is to be accumulated by the trustee. When each child reaches his majority, his share of the accumulated and unexpended trust income is to be made part of the trust corpus. However, his share of the trust income accruing thereafter must be distributed to him. Moreover, unless the trust is revoked or amended as it may be after 10 years and 30 days, the principal and the income accumulated during the minority of each child will be distributed among the beneficiaries when the youngest becomes 25. No beneficiary has ever received any income during his minority. * * *

During the tax years 1963 through 1966, taxpayers did not include in their income the taxable income received by the trust from the rental of the property to Dr. Duffy. Moreover, during the same period of time, taxpayers deducted as an ordinary and necessary business expense the rent paid by Dr. Duffy to the trust.

Pursuant to an audit of taxpayers' joint returns for the tax years 1963, 1964, 1965, and 1966, the Internal Revenue Service (IRS) concluded that either the taxable income of the trust should have been included in taxpayers' income for these years or alternatively, that the rent paid by Dr. Duffy, less the depreciation allowance for the building was not an ordinary and necessary business expense. Deficiencies of tax and interest were therefore assessed.

After paying the assessed deficiencies, taxpayers filed a claim for refund for each year involved. * * *

Taxpayers * * * filed a suit in United States District Court. The district court found that the taxable trust income for the years in question was not includible in taxpayers' income and that the rent paid by Dr. Duffy was an ordinary and necessary business expense. The court, therefore, granted the taxpayers recovery of assessed income taxes and interest. * * * Duffy v. United States, 343 F.Supp. 4 (S.D. Ohio 1972).

In this appeal the government argues that * * * the Duffys should have included in their income the taxable trust income under section 677(a)(2) of the Internal Revenue Code, * * * or that the district court erred in holding that the Duffys were entitled to deduct the rent paid for Dr. Duffy's office as an ordinary and necessary business expense under section 162 of the Code. * * *

We hold that the taxable income of the trust should have been included in the taxpayers' income under section 677(a)(2) of the Internal Revenue Code. * * *

Section 677(a)(2) of the Internal Revenue Code, Income for benefit of grantor, provides in relevant part:

> (a) General rule. The grantor shall be treated as the owner of any portion of a trust * * * whose income without the approval or consent of any adverse party is, or, in the discretion of the grantor or a nonadverse party, or both, may be * * *.
>
> (2) held or accumulated for future distribution to the grantor * * *.

This provision is followed immediately by an "excepting" clause which provides that

> [t]his subsection shall not apply to a power the exercise of which can only affect the beneficial enjoyment of the income for a period commencing after the expiration of a period such that the grantor would not be treated as the owner under section 673 if the power were a reversionary interest; but the grantor may be treated as the owner after the expiration of the period unless the power is relinquished.

This section is dispositive of the issues in this case: first, whether the taxpayers are exempt from the application of the general rule of the section by virtue of the excepting clause, and second, if the taxpayers do not come within the excepting clause, whether the institutional trustee is an "adverse party" within the meaning of the general rule. We hold that the taxpayers cannot avail themselves of the excepting clause and that the Provident Bank is not an adverse party.

To come within the excepting clause, taxpayers argue, they need only show that they had no power during the initial ten years of the trusts to control the beneficial enjoyment of the trust income. If during this period they could not control the disposition of trust income, they argue that the taxable trust income should be taxed to the trust, not to them. Taxpayers attempt to bolster this argument by referring to section 673 of the Code, Reversionary interests, which provides in relevant part:

> (a) *General Rule.*—The grantor shall be treated as the owner of any portion of a trust in which he has a reversionary interest in either the corpus or the income therefrom if, as of the inception of that portion of the trust, the interest will or may reasonably be expected to take effect in possession or enjoyment within 10 years commencing with the date of the transfer of that portion of the trust.

We, however, interpret the reference to section 673 in the excepting clause to section 677 as referring not merely to the ten year period of time during which the grantor of a trust may not have an existing exercisable power to affect the distribution of trust income but also to the income received by the trust during that ten year period. Thus, we do not agree with taxpayers that a grantor of a trust is entitled to the benefits of the excepting clause of section 677 as long as he may not during the initial ten year period of the trust affect the disposition of the trust income even though after ten years and a day the grantor may cause the accumulated trust income to be distributed to himself.

Nor does the last part of the excepting clause, "but the grantor may be treated as the owner after the expiration of the [ten year] period unless the power is relinquished," compel a contrary interpretation. That part of the excepting clause provides only that subsection 677(a) does not apply to powers the exercise of which can affect the beneficial enjoyment of trust income received only after ten years. This provision was intended to insure that a power over trust income received after the initial ten year period would not itself taint the trust income received during the ten year period. It was not intended to exempt a grantor from taxation on trust income received during the ten year period if after the expiration of that period the grantor has the power to dispose of that very income. S.Rep. No. 1622, 83d Cong., 2d Sess. 371; 3 United States Code Cong. & Admin.News, pp. 4621, 5012 (1954).

Our interpretation of the excepting clause of section 677 is supported by the considered interpretation of the agencies charged with administering the tax laws. Thus, Treas.Reg. § 1.677(a)–1(e), (f) (1965) explains the excepting clause as follows:

> (e) The last sentence of section 677(a) provides an exception to the general rule when a discretionary right can only affect the beneficial enjoyment of the income of a trust received after a period of time which is such that a grantor would not be treated as

an owner under section 673 if the power were a reversionary interest. See §§ 1.673(a)–1 and 1.673(b)–1. For example, if the ordinary income of a trust is payable to B for 10 years and then in the grantor's discretion income or corpus may be paid to B or to the grantor, the grantor is not treated as an owner with respect to ordinary income under section 677 during the first 10 years. He will be treated as an owner under section 677 after the expiration of the 10–year period unless the power is relinquished.

(f) However, if income is accumulated in any taxable year for future distribution to the grantor, section 677(a)(2) treats the grantor as an owner for that taxable year. *The exception set forth in the last sentence of section 677(a) does not apply merely because the grantor must await the expiration of a period of time before he can receive or exercise discretion over previously accumulated income of the trust, even though the period is such that the grantor would not be treated as an owner under section 673 if a reversionary interest were involved.* Thus, if income (including capital gains) of a trust is to be accumulated for 10 years and then will be, or at the discretion of the grantor may be, distributed to the grantor, the grantor is treated as the owner of the trust from its inception. (emphasis added.) [3]

Moreover, in 1957, the Internal Revenue Service issued a ruling in which it adopted the same interpretation of the excepting clause of section 677 under the following circumstances. The grantor created a trust, irrevocable for 12 years, in which an independent trustee was empowered to expend any and all of the trust principal and income for the education, maintenance and welfare of the beneficiary, the grantor's child. Any income not expended or distributed could be accumulated or invested by the trustee at his discretion. At the expiration of the trust, the trustee was required to return to the grantor any principal not expended or distributed and to the grantor or the beneficiary any accumulations of income. In that case the grantor-taxpayer also argued that the trust provisions fell within the excepting clause of section 677. However, the IRS found that because the trustee's power over current income, that is, income accruing to the trust during its 12 year life, might in fact result in the accumulation of income not for the

3. The Treasury Regulation also provides the following example to illustrate the application of Section 677(a):

* * *

Example (2). G creates a trust whose ordinary income is payable to his adult son. Ten years from the date of transfer or on the death of his son, whichever is earlier, corpus is to revert to G. * * * Under the terms of the trust instrument and applicable local law capital gains must be applied to corpus. During the taxable year 1955 the trust had the following items of income and deductions:

Dividends	$10,000
Capital gain	2,000
Expenses allocable to income	400
Expenses allocable to corpus	200

Since the capital gain is held or accumulated for future distributions to G, he is treated under section 677(a)(2) as an owner of a portion of the trust to which the gain is attributable. Therefore, he must include the capital gain in the computation of his taxable income. (Had the trust sustained a capital loss in any amount, G would likewise include that loss in the computation of his taxable income.) * * *

benefit of the beneficiary but for the benefit of the grantor, the grantor was taxable for trust income received during the 12 year period. The IRS expressed its opinion in the following rule: "where the trustee has a power to withhold distribution of trust income from the beneficiary and accumulate the amount so withheld for ultimate distribution to the grantor or to his estate, the grantor will be treated as the owner of the trust under the provisions of section 677(a)(2) of the Internal Revenue Code of [1986], and the income therefrom will be taxable to him." Rev. Rul. 363, 1957–2 Cum.Bull. 326, 329.

This Revenue Ruling was relied upon by the court in Humphrey v. United States, 245 F.Supp. 49 (D.Kan.1965), where the court reached the result we reach here in considering the taxability of the grantor of a trust having provisions similar to the trust in this case. There, the grantor-taxpayer created a trust for the benefit of his children, irrevocable for 15 years, in which the trust corpus consisted of the grantor's one-third interest in a partnership. The trustee, the grantor, his brother and his father, were authorized to invest or accumulate the earnings of the trust. The trust instrument provided that after the expiration of the trust, all trust property remaining and unexpended would at the option of the grantor revert to him. The court found that because the trustees were empowered to accumulate trust income which might, after 15 years, be distributed to the grantor, the grantor should be treated as the owner of the trust from its inception.

We believe that the Code, the regulations and rulings promulgated thereunder, and the court's decision in *Humphrey, supra,* require that when a trustee has the power to accumulate trust income during the initial ten years of the trust and this income may thereafter be received by the grantor, the grantor may not avail himself of the excepting clause of section 677.

* * *

Probably the most commonly overlooked aspect of section 677(a)(2) liability is with respect to capital gains allocable to principal in trusts with a reversion that is protected by section 673. Even if no other power or interest would cause grantor trust exposure, gains and losses allocable to principal that will ultimately revert to the grantor are currently attributable to the grantor because they constitute income accumulated for future distribution to the grantor.[4] This tax exposure is particularly unsettling to many grantors because, in most cases, the grantor receives no distributions from the trust with which to pay the tax generated by inclusion of those gains. Prior to TRA'86, there were a number of alternatives to minimize or avoid this exposure, but each had drawbacks and frequently nothing was done to circumvent this treatment. With respect to post-TRA'86 trusts, however, the problem

4. Treasury Regulation section 1.677(a)–1(g) *Example 2*; Rev.Rul. 75–267, 1975–2 C.B. 254. See Berall, "How to deal with the capital gains problem of the settlor of a short term trust," 7 Estate Planning J. 56 (1980).

is likely to apply only if the grantor has created a minor's trust and retained a protected section 673 reversion. Here one simple solution would be to alter the principal and income allocations dictated by local law by providing in the trust instrument that all items of taxable income be allocated to the income account and paid currently to the minor beneficiary. The problem with this approach is that, considering the needs of the minor beneficiary, such allocations may cause too much income to be distributable, especially if sales of highly appreciated assets are contemplated. The trust could prohibit sale of assets at a gain, either absolutely or unless the grantor consents to the sale but, in the case of a veto provision, section 675(4)(B) must be avoided if assets in the trust include stock in a business in which the grantor and the trust's ownership is significant. More important, perhaps, is that this suggestion is likely to be acceptable investment policy only in unusual circumstances.

It is true that, to deal with the problem of gains being taxable to a grantor who has inadequate assets to pay the tax thereon, the trust might authorize withdrawal of sufficient amounts of income or principal to pay those taxes or might direct the trustee to distribute a sufficient amount of income or principal for that purpose. The problem here is that (1) section 676 (withdrawal) or 677 (distribution power) exposure would attach to the grantor, (2) even if grantor trust exposure did not exist, distributions would likely be taxable income to the grantor, meaning that a withdrawal or distribution amount deemed sufficient to pay the tax on gains generated by the trust would also be taxable to the grantor, presumably requiring an additional distribution to pay the tax thereon, and (3) if income were subject to the withdrawal or distribution provision, the trust would fail to meet the requirements of section 2503(c), meaning that the annual exclusion could be unavailable on creation of the trust, if that section were being relied upon for this benefit.

Question

Of the options noted to deal with the capital gains problem, which would you recommend to a client? Be prepared to explain why any would be preferable.

A second major exception to section 677(a) liability applies if the trustee has discretion to distribute income for the support or maintenance of someone the grantor is obliged to support or maintain. Despite the fact that this discretion is regarded as essentially a power to indirectly benefit the grantor, trust income is taxable to the grantor under section 677(b) as a result of the power only to the extent income is actually distributed for the support or maintenance of such a dependent. Again, however, misunderstanding is rife with respect to the scope and application of the exception.

For example, by virtue of Treasury Regulation section 1.677(b)–1(f), the exception does not apply to distributions that are mandatory instead of discretionary and it does not apply to distributions of principal because all of section 677 is restricted to distributions of income. Fortunately (perhaps), a special rule under Treasury Regulation section 1.677(b)–1(c) regards distributions from a trust to be made from income for the year to the fullest extent possible and distributions not out of current trust income may be regarded, under the last sentence of section 677(b) and Treasury Regulation section 1.677(b)–1(b), as accumulation distributions that are subject to the throwback rules and thereby invoke application of section 677(b).

Finally, the parenthetical provision in section 677(b) prevents application of the exception to distributions to the grantor's spouse (even if for support or maintenance of the spouse, notwithstanding the spouse being grantor's dependent), nor does the statute appear to apply the exception to distributions for the support or maintenance of someone grantor's spouse, but not the grantor, must support or maintain. In this respect, compare section 677(a) with section 677(b) (the former makes repeated reference to grantor's spouse for trusts created after 1969 while the latter does not). Also compare the last clause of the first sentence of Treasury Regulation section 1.677(b)–1(a), which makes reference to a child "whom the grantor *or his spouse* is legally obligated to support" (emphasis added), and the last clause of Treasury Regulation section 1.677(a)–1(d), with Treasury Regulation section 1.677(b)–1(d), which provides that "[t]he exception provided in section 677(b) relates *solely* to the satisfaction of the *grantor's* legal obligation to support or maintain a beneficiary." (Emphasis added).

If the exception is not applicable to distributions for the support or maintenance of someone grantor's spouse, but not the grantor, is obliged to support or maintain, then the discretion to make such distributions will generate grantor trust liability even if not exercised, constituting a power to make distributions indirectly to grantor's spouse that would fall within section 677(a)(1). Unfortunately, this result is not directly addressed by section 672(e), which dictates that powers and interests of a grantor's spouse shall be deemed to be those of the grantor. Nevertheless, if the theory of this obligation provision is that distributions to dependents are an indirect benefit to the grantor, it ought to hold true that distributions to the spouse's dependents constitute the spouse as having an interest that should be treated as a section 672(e) interest of the grantor, causing the protection of section 677(b) to spread across both situations. Such a result would certainly be consistent with Congress' intent in 1969 when it amended section 677(a) and again in 1986 when it added section 672(e).

A final curiosity under section 677(b) is that its protection applies only to legal, as opposed to contractual, obligations, as illustrated by Treasury Regulation section 1.677(b)–1(d). Thus, distributions for such nonlegally obligated items as private schooling, music and dance lessons, special camps and other nonessentials may constitute section 677(a)(1) distributions for a grantor's indirect benefit if the grantor is deemed to have a contractual obligation to the provider of those items, which is being discharged by distributions. See, for example, Morrill v. United States, 228 F.Supp. 734 (D.Me.1964), and Braun v. Commissioner, 1984 T.C.M. 285, 48 T.C.M. (CCH) 210, 53 T.C. Memo (P–H) 1116 (finding private secondary and post-secondary education to be a parent's legal obligation in New Jersey, based on the grantor's station in life).

Perhaps most importantly, section 677(b) does not require that distributions be made that *satisfy* the grantor's legal obligation of support or maintenance. Section 677(b) is very carefully worded to apply to distributions for the support or maintenance of someone the grantor is obligated to support or maintain, not to distributions that *discharge* that obligation. Treasury Regulation section 1.662(a)–4 even recognizes that such distributions probably cannot, under most states' laws, have the effect of discharging such obligations. But see the first sentence of Treasury Regulation section 1.677(b)–1(d), which refers to "satisfaction of grantor's legal obligation to support or maintain a beneficiary", and Treasury Regulation section 1.677(a)–1(d), which also refers to the discharge of grantor's obligation of support.

Question

To prevent grantor trust exposure under section 677(b) for any distributions made, how should a trust for minor children of the grantor be drafted? See Upjohn v. United States, 72–2 U.S. Tax Cas. (CCH) ¶ 12,888, 30 A.F.T.R.2d (P–H) ¶ 147,708 (W.D.Mich.1972) (clause prohibiting distributions that discharge grantor's obligations did not constitute a "substantial restriction" for purposes of section 2503(c)).

POWERS OVER BENEFICIAL ENJOYMENT

Read Code section 674.

Read Regulation section 1.674.

Probably the most cumbersome provision in Subpart E is section 674. It imposes grantor trust liability with respect to any portion of a trust as to which either the grantor, grantor's spouse (with respect to post–TRA'86 trusts) or a nonadverse party (in each case acting without the consent of an adverse party) has a power to affect beneficial enjoyment of income or principal. Consider whether the following description of the rationale for section 674 adequately explains why grantor trust exposure is imposed in situations in which neither the grantor nor the grantor's spouse is the trustee or a beneficiary of the trust.

COMMISSIONER v. BUCK

United States Court of Appeals, Second Circuit, 1941.
120 F.2d 775.

FRANK, CIRCUIT JUDGE.

* * *

We can best approach the instant case by enumerating the significant factors to be considered: That the donees are members of the donor's family, of which he is the head; that he has "income in excess of normal needs"; that, during his life, he is unrestricted as to the disposition of any part of the corpus or income, excepting that he may not divert any portion for his personal use; that, while he lives, he has entire control of the management of the corpus, and, at his pleasure, may remove the trustee and appoint another.

Respondent argues, in effect, that the income is non-taxable to him because he has deprived himself of certain of his prior "bundle of rights", i.e. the rights to have the income paid directly to him, to use any of the income or principal for his personal consumption expenditures, and to make a testamentary disposition of the income or corpus. As we read the recent decisions of the Supreme Court, such a diminution of the congeries of rights and privileges called "ownership" is not sufficient to immunize the grantor of a trust from a tax on the income, in a case where, as here (to revert to our enumeration of significant factors), the beneficiaries are members of the donor's family and he has "income in excess of normal needs". In such a case, at any rate, a potent factor which melts off the grantor's insulation from income taxation is the donor's power to dispose of the income, for that power "is the equivalent of ownership of it." Helvering v. Horst, (1940) 311 U.S. 112, 118, 61 S.Ct. 144, 147, 85 L.Ed. —, 131 A.L.R. 655; * * * taxable income, said the court, is to be measured by the "satisfactions which are of economic worth" (311 U.S. 112, 117, 61 S.Ct. 144, 147, 85 L.Ed. —, 131 A.L.R. 655), and chief among them, it held, is the power to make gifts. We understand the Supreme Court to say that, certainly where the family-entente element is present, the elimination of the donor's power to expend the income for satisfactions flowing from his personal consumption does not afford him shelter from the tax.

The outstanding fact, which distinguishes this case from Helvering v. Palmer, 2 Cir., 115 F.2d 368 and Blair v. Commissioner, 1937, 300 U.S. 5, 57 S.Ct. 330, 81 L.Ed. 465, is that respondent has reserved to himself during his life, the power, at any time, and from time to time, to "alter or amend in any respect whatsoever," the provisions of the indenture relating to "the disposition of the income and principal of the trust estate or the separate shares into which the same may be divided, and to change any beneficial interest" thereunder. True, he cannot do so in such a way as to "revest in himself title" or "so as to direct that any part of the income * * * be distributed to him or be held or accumulated for future distribution to him." But he has unlimited power, at any moment to reduce or obliterate the share of principal or interest originally allotted to his wife or any child, if for any reason, or for no reason, he decides, in the exercise of his uncontrolled discretion, that any of the beneficiaries is receiving more than seems desirable. Consequently, he has deprived himself merely of (1) the power to dispose by will and (2) the power to use the income or principal for personal consumption purposes. During his life, he has entire control of the sale and investment of the corpus, in whole or in part, and the voting power of any stock now or later constituting that corpus. When to such control there is coupled the power, until his death, freely to sprinkle the income about among any beneficiaries he may select (as if he were playing a hose), it is impossible to conclude, in the light of the recent decisions of the Supreme Court, that the income is not taxable to him. For here we have the central fact which the Supreme Court emphasized in Helvering v. Clifford, supra: the beneficiaries named in the trust instrument are members of respondent's "intimate family group", there is a "reallocation of income" within that group so that (unless respondent otherwise decides) the "income remains in the family"; and it "is hard to imagine that respondent felt himself the poorer after this trust had been executed or, if he did, that it had any rational foundation in fact." In the Clifford case, the court said that "where the head of the household has income in excess of normal needs, it may well make but little difference to him (except income-tax-wise) where portions of that income are routed—so long as it stays in the family group". Here, in addition, this respondent can, during his life, determine precisely where, at any moment, the income is to be routed. In apportioning the family budget—and in thus reducing the amounts he may contribute to specific members of his family out of his non-trusteed income—he may take into account what he has decided to be the current destination of the trusteed income. And, while Clifford was under a "disability to make a gift of the corpus to others" than the originally named donee, respondent Buck is under no such constraint; indeed, he may route it outside the family.

The retained "satisfactions which are of economic worth" are so numerous, that Buck, like Clifford, "has rather complete assurance that the trust will not effect any substantial change in his economic position"; while he lives, he has as much to say about the management of the corpus as before he made the trust; neither he nor his acquaintances will observe any important practical difference [2]. His household will run on substantially as before, since the incomes of the members of his family will still be subject to his whims; should any of his family

2. We note, in passing, that Buck had expressly in mind the importance of retaining voting power in a considerable block of stock in conjunction with a small group of persons who, together with him, were the dominant stockholders of the Wrigley company. It has often been observed (in economic treatises, government reports, based upon extensive investigations, and judicial decisions), that control of such a block yields corporate control from which in turn may flow numerous pecuniary emoluments of substance, to say nothing of more indirect "satisfactions * * * of economic worth" of the sort to which the court referred in the Horst case.

expend what he received in a manner displeasing to Buck, or offend Buck in any way, a few words written by Buck can cut off that beneficiary's portion of the income and, later, a few more can restore it. The direct satisfactions of pater familias are thus virtually undiminished, as are those indirect satisfactions (stemming from the vicarious pleasure of consumption of the income by his wife and children) which the Supreme Court regards as noteworthy indicia of taxability.

The one feature of this case which calls for special mention is the fact that the trust is of long duration. But the decisions of the Supreme Court disclose that the dominant fact, in the family group cases, is the extent of the donor's actual control. We conclude that, the control factor is sufficiently present when the trust is of short duration, as in the Clifford case (because the grantor will soon reacquire complete dominion), even if there are no express reservations of control; while, if the trust is of long duration, then the donor is to be regarded as the "owner", if he expressly reserved, as here, a very substantial measure of control of the disposition of the income.

* * *

By Treasury Regulation section 1.674(a)–1(a), section 674(a) can apply whether the power is held in a fiduciary capacity as a direct power over disposition, is a beneficial interest in the form of a power of appointment, or is held in any other manner. Because of the breadth of section 674(a), were there no exceptions to it few trusts would escape grantor trust treatment during the grantor's life. Fortunately, there are numerous exceptions to the general rule, most being subject to three overriding cautions. First, under Treasury Regulation section 1.674(d)–2(a), a person (whether the grantor or anyone else) will be considered to possess powers held by a trustee (and therefore an exception may fail to apply) if the person has a power to remove, substitute or add trustees and is not prohibited from naming the powerholder as a successor trustee. However, under the parenthetical provision of Treasury Regulation section 1.674(d)–2(a), attribution of trustee powers will not occur in any year in which no vacancy exists and the powerholder cannot create one, nor will attribution occur if the powerholder must replace a removed trustee with a comparable trustee (other than the powerholder). See the last sentence of Treasury Regulation section 1.674(d)–2(a). An example of a "comparable" trustee would be a corporate replacement to a corporate trustee. This provision is directly contrary to that taken in Revenue Ruling 79–353, 1979–2 C.B. 325, which was modified by Revenue Ruling 81–51, 1981–1 C.B. 458 (limiting Revenue Ruling 79–353 to prospective application after 28 October 1979), for estate and gift tax purposes, by which the Service opined that a "revolving door" power to remove and replace trustees at will, even if the powerholder cannot become successor trustee and must name a comparable successor, will suffice to regard the powerholder as holding all powers of the trustee.

The second overriding caution is relevant with respect to sections 674(b)(5), 674(b)(6), 674(b)(7), 674(c) and 674(d). As explained by Treasury Regulation section 1.674(d)–2(b), the exceptions provided by these sections are expressly lost if any person may add beneficiaries to the trust, except by exercise of a power of appointment or by birth or adoption. The third caution raised under the penultimate sentence of Treasury Regulation section 1.674(b)–1(b)(5)(i), which establishes that the exceptions relating to the exercise of fiduciary discretion under section 674(b)(5)(A) (and, indirectly, under section 674(d) due to the parenthetical provision in Treasury Regulation section 1.674(d)–1), will not apply if the trustee's powers are conclusive or exempt from judicial supervision, as may occur inadvertently under a broadly drawn exoneration or exculpatory provision. Though there is no direct authority for the extension of this caution, it would be reasonable for the same reservation to apply for purposes of discretionary actions under sections 674(b)(8) and 674(c) as well.

Before studying the section 674(b), 674(c) and 674(d) exceptions below, consider the message of the following case in terms of the degree of restriction imposed by the need to avoid various classes of individuals in selecting trustees.

ESTATE OF GOODWYN v. COMMISSIONER

United States Tax Court, 1976.
1976 T.C.M. 238, 35 T.C.M. (CCH) 1026, 45 T.C. Memo (P–H) 1012.

QUEALY, JUDGE:

* * *

Under the terms of the deeds creating these trusts, the trustees were granted broad discretionary powers with respect to both the distribution of income to the beneficiaries and the investment and management of the corpus of the trusts. Notwithstanding the designation of Richards and Russell as trustees, it further appears that at all times from the establishment of the trusts until his last illness, with the acquiescence of the trustees, the decedent made all decisions with respect to the purchase and sale of trust assets and the investment of any proceeds and determined the amounts, if any, to be distributed to the respective beneficiaries.

There is no question that Goodwyn created legally valid trusts under state law. The provisions of these trust instruments, including those regarding the rights, duties and obligations of the trustees demonstrate the grantor's intent to relinquish the ownership of the involved assets. Although many of the beneficiaries were unaware of the existence of these trusts, such notice is not a requirement for a valid trust.

Regarding the effect of the Federal income tax laws on these trusts, it is not contended here that the decedent reserved any right or power in any of the trusts whereby the income of these trusts could be attributed to the grantor. Additionally, it is clear that during the years in issue the trustees were not related or subordinate parties within the definition of 672(c) whose discretionary power to distribute or accumulate income to beneficiaries would attribute the income to the grantor. Rather, these trustees were independent trustees within the meaning of section 674(c), who may have such a discretionary power over income.

While the record indicates that the legal formalities have been complied with, it also indicates that the designated "independent" trustees, whether by agreement or otherwise, entrusted the management of the trusts' assets and the distribution of income therefrom to the sole discretion of the decedent. The decedent kept all the records, made all of the investments and decided the amount to be distributed to beneficiaries. The trustees merely acquiesced in these actions.

On the basis of these facts, the judicial decisions following the Supreme Court's decision in *Helvering v. Clifford* 309 U.S. 331 (1940), and the later so-called *Clifford* regulations might well warrant the attribution of the income from these trusts to the decedent. However, to the extent these previous principles are not embodied in the present statutory provisions of the Code, they must be considered no longer applicable. Section 671 provides that subpart E represents the sole criterion of dominion and control under section 61 (relating to the definition of gross income) and thereby also under the *Clifford* doctrine.

The Report of the Committee on Ways and Means on the Internal Revenue Code of 1954 explains clearly that this exclusivity was the intent of Congress:

> It is also provided in this section [671] that no items of a trust shall be included in computing the income or credits of the grantor (or another person) solely on the grounds of his dominion and control over the trust under the provisions of section 61 (corresponding to sec. 22(a) of existing law). The effect of this provision is to insure that taxability of *Clifford* type trusts shall be governed solely by this subpart. However, this provision does not affect the principles governing the taxability of income to a grantor or assignor other than by reason of his dominion and control over the trust. Thus, this subpart has no application in situations involving assignments of future income to the assignor, as in *Lucas v. Earl* (281 U.S. 111), *Harrison v. Schaffner* (312 U.S. 579), and *Helvering v. Horst* (311 U.S. 112), whether or not the assignment is to a trust; nor are the rules as to family partnerships affected by this subpart.

Consequently, in order for a grantor to be held taxable pursuant to subpart E on the income of a trust which he has established, he must have one of the powers or retained interests proscribed by subpart E.

The grantor's power to control beneficial enjoyment of either the principal or the income, within the limits defined in section 674, would result in attribution of the income to the grantor. Section 674 provides as a general rule:

(a) General Rule.—The grantor shall be treated as the owner of any portion of a trust in respect of which the beneficial enjoyment of the corpus or the income therefrom is subject to a power of disposition, exercisable by the grantor or a nonadverse party, or both, without the approval or consent of any adverse party.

* * *

Although the trustees here would not be adverse parties, section 674(c) excepts the application of the general rule in certain circumstances which are applicable here.

Respondent would concede that none of the provisions of the trusts in issue would give the decedent the power proscribed by this section. It is respondent's argument, however, that although grantor does not specifically have such a power, his relationship to the trust res through its management and to the administration of these trusts generally is such that he should be deemed to be a trustee, in fact, during his life. Being considered a trustee, the trustee's power under the trust agreement to distribute or accumulate the income from these trusts would then make such income attributable to him under subpart E.

Respondent's contention in this respect is similar to that respondent raised in the *Estate of Hilton W. Goodwyn, supra.* As relevant here, respondent argued in that case that the decedent should be treated as trustee, in fact, possessing such rights and powers as to cause the inclusion of the assets thereof in his gross estate under section 2036(a)(2). That section required the inclusion in decedent's gross estate any property for which the decedent has retained the right, either alone or in conjunction with any person, to designate the persons who shall possess or enjoy the property or the income therefrom.

We found in that case there was no basis for such inclusion. The Supreme Court has held in *United States v. Byrum,* 408 U.S. 125, 136–7 (1972), that the right, upon which the inclusion under section 2036(a)(2) is predicated, is "an ascertainable and legally enforceable power," reserved in the trust instrument or by some other means. See also *Estate of Charles Gilman,* 65 T.C. 296, 316 (1975), on appeal (2d Cir., February 6, 1976). We found that Goodwyn had not retained such a right in the case of the Richards and Russell Trusts of which he was grantor.

In this case, while a different test is applicable, the tests are similar in character. Where section 2036(a) uses the term "right," section 674 uses the term "power." The House Ways and Means Committee Report, cited supra, in its explanation of this section uses the term power in the legal sense of having an enforceable authority or right to perform some action. The use of this term in this legal sense suggests that the power of a grantor upon which he will be taxed is a power reserved by instrument or contract creating an ascertainable and legally enforceable right, not merely the persuasive control which he might exercise over an independent trustee who is receptive to his wishes. Such interpretation is also, we believe, indicated by the holding in the *Byrum* case.

In this case, the trustees in question accepted the rights, duties and obligations granted them in the trust instruments. Regardless of the fact they had entrusted to the decedent the complete management and control of these trusts, this informal delegation did not discharge them from the legal responsibility they had as the trustees. As a matter of law, the trustees were liable and answerable for the decedent's acts on their behalf. See 2 Scott, Trusts 1388, 1391 (3rd ed., 1967); 3 Scott, Trusts 1794 (3rd ed., 1967).

There is nothing in the record to show that the trustees could not have undertaken exclusive control of the trust res if they had elected to do so. Whatever power Goodwyn exercised over the trust assets, administration or distribution, he did so on the trustee's behalf and not in his own right.

Because of Goodwyn's failure to have a legally enforceable right, we have already held, following *Byrum,* that the assets of these trusts were not includable in the decedent's estate under 2036(a)(2). Since a similar legal right or power is a prerequisite under section 674(a), consistency appears to require the same decision with respect to the applicability of this section. We see no other possible decision.

Section 671 precludes attributing the income to Goodwyn on any other theory of dominion and control under the definition of gross income, including the *Clifford* doctrine. We interpret this limitation to mean that if Goodwyn cannot be considered as a trustee, in fact, under the statutory provisions of subpart E, he cannot be considered as such by virtue of the judicial doctrines arising from the *Clifford* case which Congress intended to limit through the enactment of subpart E.

* * *

The section 674(b), 674(c), and 674(d) exceptions to the general rule of section 674(a) may be grouped first according to who may hold a particular power, without causing grantor trust liability, and second by the portions of a trust (for example, income or principal) over which the power may apply. Progressing from the most restrictive class of powerholder to the most expansive, the exceptions to grantor trust exposure for powers over the trust are:

(a) Under section 674(c) *independent trustees* may have powers to accumulate income or to distribute either income or corpus to anyone, without restraint by any limitation or standard. "Independent" trustee means (1) not the grantor and (2) not more than half of the trustees are related or subordinate parties who are subservient to the grantor. Remember that, within post-TRA'86 trusts, section 672(e) regards grantor's spouse as if (s)he were the grantor, which presumably means that neither the grantor nor grantor's spouse may act as trustee and comply with the definition of an independent trustee.

(b) Under section 674(d), *anyone except the grantor or grantor's spouse (if living with the grantor), acting as trustee* may have power to distribute income to any beneficiary, if the power is limited by a "reasonably definite external standard." Though the requisite standard is not defined for purposes of section 674(d), Treasury Regulation section 1.674(d)–1 specifies that the standard is the same as a "reasonably definite standard" as defined at Treasury Regulation section 1.674(b)–1(b)(5)(i), despite the one word ("external") difference in their titles. Thus, such a standard could include the terms "education," "support," "maintenance," "health," "to maintain his accustomed standard of living," "reasonable support and comfort" and "to meet an emergency."

(c) *Anyone acting as trustee* (including the grantor or grantor's spouse) may have the following powers.

Over both income and principal:

(1) Under section 674(a), unlimited powers if exercisable only with the consent of an adverse party.

(2) Under section 674(b)(4), power to allocate without limitation among charities.

(3) Under section 674(b)(8), power to determine proper allocation of receipts and distributions between income and principal, notwithstanding any incidental effect on the rights of beneficiaries.

Over principal only:

(1) Under section 674(b)(5)(B), power to make distributions to income beneficiaries without limitation by any standards, provided the distribution is charged against the share of the trust producing that beneficiary's income interest, but it is not necessary that the income beneficiary be a remainder beneficiary and, as a consequence, the charging requirement does not refer to future distribution of any anticipated share of principal that the beneficiary might otherwise ultimately receive.

(2) Under section 674(b)(5)(A), power to make distributions (without charging shares) if limited by a "reasonably definite standard."

Over income only:

(1) Under section 674(b)(2), a power to affect enjoyment of income received (a) in a post–TRA'86 trust after the death of the present interest minor lineal descendant beneficiary, or (b) in a pre–TRA'86 trust after expiration of a greater than 10 year period (or the earlier death of the income beneficiary) is harmless, but only until it actually

becomes exercisable. This provision incorporates the section 673 period, including the principles thereunder dealing with contingent powers and postponement of the deferral period, as established by the last sentence of Treasury Regulation section 1.674(b)–1(b)(2).

(2) Under section 674(b)(1), a power to distribute income for the support or maintenance of a beneficiary the grantor is obliged to support or maintain is harmless under section 674, because section 677(b) will apply to such a power to the extent exercised, meaning that this section is merely adopting a hands off approach so that section 677(b) may be the exclusive authority.

(3) Section 674(b)(7) exempts a power to accumulate income while the beneficiary is under the age of 21 years or is suffering from a legal disability.

(4) Powers to accumulate income are protected under certain limitations. This accumulation power is harmless under section 674(b)(6)(A) only to the extent accumulated income is ultimately payable:

  (a) to the beneficiary from whom withheld;

  (b) to that beneficiary's estate;

  (c) as that beneficiary appoints pursuant to a statutory power of appointment. The statutory power of appointment *must* (not may) be exercisable in favor of anyone except the beneficiary, the beneficiary's estate or creditors of either, and is the broadest power available without causing section 2041 estate tax or section 2514 gift tax consequences on exercise, release or lapse. By the parenthetical provision in section 674(b)(6)(A), the document may designate default beneficiaries to take the accumulation to the extent it is not effectively appointed; or

  (d) the accumulation is harmless under section 674(b)(6)(B) if it is payable in previously specified shares to all current income beneficiaries on termination of the trust.

  (e) There is also a proviso under the penultimate sentence of section 674(b)(6) that, if termination and distribution of the trust may reasonably be expected to occur within the beneficiary's lifetime but the beneficiary in fact dies prior to termination, distribution on termination may be made to the beneficiary's appointees or to designated alternative takers (other than the grantor, grantor's estate or, presumably, grantor's spouse or the spouse's estate in post–TRA'86 trusts) and, again, the document may designate default takers.

(d) Anyone acting in any capacity may have a testamentary power under section 674(b)(3) to appoint either income or principal; however, by Treasury Regulation section 1.674(b)–1(b)(3), this exception does not apply to a power in the grantor or, for post-TRA'86 trusts, in grantor's spouse to appoint income that was (or that could have been) specifically accumulated without the consent of an adverse party for purposes of testamentary appointment.

Questions

1. Given these limitations, a grantor's testamentary power of appointment will likely inadvertently cause current taxation of what kinds of income in most trusts? How should the power be drafted to avoid this exposure?

2. Prepare a list of interests or powers that a grantor may retain or create in the grantor's spouse without running afoul of the grantor trust limitations studied to this point.

3. If a grantor were to create an inter vivos trust for family members, such as a children's educational fund, would it be possible for the grantor or grantor's spouse to be trustee? Be prepared to explain the extent of any powers that would be permissible and the limits that would be necessary to prevent grantor trust exposure.

ADMINISTRATIVE POWERS

Read Code section 675.

Read Regulation section 1.675.

Probably the most infrequently applied source of grantor trust exposure relates to administrative powers that permit the grantor (or, for post-TRA'86 trusts, grantor's spouse) to deal with closely held stock or to engage in what amounts in many cases to self-dealing with the trust. While no authority exists in the Code to support the penultimate sentence of Treasury Regulation section 1.675–1(a), it specifies that, if the grantor or the grantor's spouse has a power to amend the trust, even if that power would not otherwise suffice to cause section 676 grantor trust exposure, the trust will be treated as if such an amendment had already been made if it would permit the grantor or the spouse to establish any of the following powers.

Under section 675(1), a grantor is treated as owner of any portion of a trust as to which the grantor, the grantor's spouse, or a nonadverse party (acting without the consent of an adverse party) may deal with, dispose of or exchange either income or principal for less than full and adequate consideration, regardless of whether the grantor may personally benefit from exercise of the power.

Sections 675(2) and (3) deal with loans to the grantor or grantor's spouse from the trust. The former treats the grantor as owner of any portion of a trust as to which the grantor or the spouse has the power to borrow, or a nonadverse party has been given a power to make loans to the grantor or the spouse, in either case on less than adequate interest or security. It does not apply, however, to any trustee other than the grantor or the spouse who is generally authorized by the document to make loans to any person, including the grantor or grantor's spouse, without regard to interest or security.

Section 675(3) treats the grantor as owner of any portion of the trust that the grantor or grantor's spouse has actually borrowed and has not completely repaid before the tax year began (which necessarily includes amounts borrowed during the current tax year). It does not apply, however, if (1) the loan was made for an adequate interest and security, (2) by a trustee other than the grantor or a related or subordinate party.

Section 675(4) applies only to the extent a nonadverse party (including the grantor or grantor's spouse) has any power to act in a nonfiduciary capacity, without the consent of a fiduciary, either (1) under section 675(4)(A) or 675(4)(B), to vote, invest or direct either, with respect to securities in any corporation in which the aggregate holdings of the grantor or grantor's spouse and the trust are significant, or (2) under section 675(4)(C), to reacquire principal by swapping it for property of equivalent value.

Among other troublesome aspects of section 675, the nonadverse party requirement appears to arise only from Treasury Regulation section 1.675–1(b)(4), with no statutory support and, under the same regulation, the "nonfiduciary capacity" issue in section 675(4) presumably means action that is not in the interests of the beneficiaries nor subject to judicial supervision. For purposes of sections 675(4)(A) and 675(4)(B), "significant" holdings is nowhere defined and, most disconcerting of all, the need for some of these rules in the first instance is not at all apparent, as illustrated by the following questions.

Questions

1. What is the effect to the grantor under section 675(3) if there are no items of taxable income in a trust to be taxed to the grantor, by virtue of the grantor having borrowed the full corpus on an interest free basis? What if the grantor were to borrow only half the corpus? How would the tax consequences differ if the grantor paid interest, at a less than market rate, or paid adequate interest but invoked application of section 675(3) by virtue of borrowing with inadequate security or because the trustee was related or subordinate? The *Benson* case that follows and the Revenue Ruling after it may be helpful in dealing with this problem.

2. How does the type of power subject to section 675(1) differ from a section 676 power to revoke, and does that difference make any sense?

BENSON v. COMMISSIONER

United States Tax Court, 1981.
76 T.C. 1040.

FAY, JUDGE: * * * The only issue for decision is what part of a trust created by petitioner-husband is to be treated as being owned by him during 1974 and 1975 under section 675(3).

* * *

On March 31, 1972, petitioners, by quitclaim deeds, transferred the "property" to the "L. William Benson Short Term Irrevocable Trust," a trust created by petitioner Larry Benson on the same date. Petitioner June Benson was named trustee of the trust. The trust is to terminate 10 years and 10 days after the last contribution to it is made. All net trust income is to be paid annually to petitioners' four children or for their benefit with all capital gains and losses being allocated to principal. When the trust terminates, all accrued but undistributed net income will be distributed to the children or to the children's appointees, while the trust principal will revert to petitioner Larry Benson.

Petitioner June Benson, as trustee, has the power to invest, sell, or exchange trust property and the power to borrow money pledging trust property as security. Additionally she may as trustee, "loan trust property to any person with provision for reasonable interest and security."

Evidently the only asset ever transferred to the trust was the "property" which housed the home appliance center. Therefore, the rents paid by Benson's Maytag, Inc., were the trust's only source of income. * * *

Petitioner June Benson, as trustee, made several loans to petitioner Larry Benson. Each of those loans was unsecured, bore interest of 8 percent, and was represented by a promissory demand note. The loans were as follows:

Date of loan	Amount
May 1, 1973	$17,215
Sept. 1, 1974	5,000
Sept. 1, 1974	1,500
Nov. 1, 1974	24,000

No payments on the loans were made before January 1, 1976. The loans, including accrued interest, were paid in full on December 30, 1977. The total principal and interest amounts outstanding at the beginning of the taxable years involved herein were as follows:

	Principal	Interest	Total
Jan. 1, 1974	$17,215	916.87	$18,131.87
Jan. 1, 1975	47,715	2,782.06	50,497.06

The trust reported the following income and deductions on its returns for 1973, 1974, and 1975:

	Income	Taxes	Depreciation	Distributions
1973	$22,150	($5,097)	($3,016)	$14,037
1974	20,400	(3,619)	—	16,781
1975	20,400	(3,724)	—	16,676

Thus, the trust reported zero taxable income for each of those 3 years.

Although distribution deductions were taken, the beneficiary children received no money or property from the trust. All net trust receipts until November 1, 1974, were loaned to petitioner Larry Benson.

In his statutory notice of deficiency, respondent determined that petitioner Larry Benson should be treated as owning the entire trust during 1974 and 1975. Thus, per section 671, respondent increased petitioners' gross income by the amount of the trust's income * * * in each of those years and allowed petitioners those deductions otherwise allowable to the trust.

The only issue for decision is what part of a trust created by petitioner-husband is to be treated as being owned by him during 1974 and 1975 as a result of loans made by the trust to him. Petitioner-husband, a trust grantor, borrowed trust funds without security and did not repay the loans before the beginning of 1974 or before the beginning of 1975, the taxable years involved herein. Thus, under section 675(3), the "portion of [the] trust in respect of which" petitioner-husband borrowed is treated as being owned by petitioner-husband. The parties disagree as to what "portion" means.

Petitioners contend that "portion" refers to the part of the trust borrowed in comparison to the entire trust. Accordingly, they maintain that the part of the trust income taxable to them is an amount which bears the same ratio to the trust's entire income as the amount of loans, including interest, outstanding at the beginning of the taxable year bears to the fair market value of the trust at the beginning of the taxable year. Respondent argues that "portion" means the entire trust whenever a grantor has the power to borrow all corpus or income and any trust property is borrowed. Alternatively, respondent contends that "portion" is a fraction arrived at by dividing the amount borrowed, including interest, by the trust's income for the year calculated without the sections 651 and 661 distribution deductions. We do not adopt respondent's analysis but sustain his determination in this case for the reasons below.

Section 675 is one of a series of Internal Revenue Code sections collectively known as the grantor trust rules. See secs. 671 through 679. Sections 673 through 677 enumerate the instances in which a trust grantor is treated as owning all or part of a trust. For tax purposes, a grantor is credited with the trust income, deductions, and credits allocable to the trust "portion" he is treated as owning. Sec. 671. The purpose of those grantor trust rules is to tax a trust grantor on trust items over which he has retained substantial dominion and control, see section 1.671–2(b), and it is with that purpose in mind that we interpret section 675(3) and "portion."

At the outset, we note that while "portion" is used throughout the Code sections comprising the grantor trust rules, its meaning varies from section to section and from case to case. Sec. 1.671–3.[12] "Portion's" flexible meaning is necessary to fulfill the purpose of the grantor trust rules—taxation of a grantor only on trust items over which he has retained substantial dominion and control. See sec. 1.671–2(b). Given a myriad of dispositive variables, "portion" must have an adaptable meaning. For example, under section 676, a trust grantor is treated as owning any trust "portion" which he can revoke. If the grantor can revoke the entire trust, then "portion" means the entire trust. However, if the grantor can revoke only the remainder interest and has no power to alter the income interest, "portion" means only the remainder interest, since the grantor has no power over the income interest and should not be taxed on it. See sec. 1.671–3(b)(2).

In determining what "portion" of a trust should be treated as being owned by its grantor, most of the grantor trust rules focus on powers set forth in the trust instrument which evidence a grantor's dominion and control over trust property without regard to whether or not those powers are ever exercised. In most cases, it is fairly simple to tell over what part of a trust a power extends; therefore, the meaning of "portion" is easily decided. For example, if a grantor has the power to distribute the entire trust to his spouse, the entire trust is treated as his even if only part of the trust is actually so distributed. See sec. 677(a)(1). On the other hand, if a grantor has the power to distribute only current income to his spouse, he is treated as owning only the current income interest in the trust. In the latter case, "portion" means only the current income interest, because that is the only trust segment over which the grantor has any power.

Section 675(3) differs from the other provisions which provide rules for determining grantor ownership of a trust, because it requires an affirmative act, borrowing, rather than a mere power, before it applies. Nevertheless, the same theme underlies section 675(3) as underlies the other Code sections which treat a grantor as owning the trust. In both cases, the justification for taxation of the grantor is evidence of substantial grantor dominion and control. Thus, our proper inquiry is not what the grantor has borrowed but what the grantor's borrowing represents in terms of the grantor's dominion and control over the trust.

12. The regulations recognize six possible meanings of "portion": the entire trust; the trust accounting income; the trust corpus; a fraction or dollar amount of trust accounting income; a fraction or dollar amount of corpus; or specific trust property. See sec. 1.671–3(a) to (c), Income Tax Regs. See also, Schmolka, "Selected Aspects of the Grantor Trust Rules," U. Miami 9th Inst. on Estate Planning par. 1400 (1975).

In order fully to understand the implications of grantor borrowing, section 675(3) must be read in conjunction with section 675(2). Section 675(2) treats a grantor as the owner of the trust anytime the grantor, a nonadverse party, or both have the power to loan income or corpus to the grantor without adequate security or without adequate interest, unless a nongrantor trustee may make such loans to any and all persons. Thus, the mere power to loan trust property to the grantor on favorable terms, vested in the grantor or a nonadverse party, evidences enough grantor dominion and control over the trust to justify taxing all the trust income to the grantor. However, if a nongrantor trustee can make unsecured or no-interest loans to anyone, the grantor is seemingly on equal footing with the rest of the world, and the evidence of grantor dominion and control is less.

Section 675(2) can be avoided easily. A trust grantor can install a "friendly" trustee and give that trustee a general power to make unsecured or no-interest loans to anyone. In all probability, the "friendly" trustee would not make such loans to anyone except the grantor; but, nevertheless, section 675(2) would not apply. However, a grantor cannot rely on such an escape from section 675(2) if he contemplates actually borrowing from the trust. When actual borrowing occurs, section 675(3) must be considered.

As previously noted, section 675(3) treats a trust grantor as owning any "portion of a trust in respect of which" he borrows, if the loans are either unsecured or bear no interest or are made by a "friendly" trustee, unless the grantor repays the loans before the beginning of the taxable year. It might seem that section 675(3) serves to tax the grantor only on the part of the trust he actually borrows. But, such an interpretation would read 675(3) as treating the grantor as owning the "portion" he borrowed rather than owning the "portion of [the] trust in respect of which" he borrowed, which is what the statute mandates. Moreover, such a reading would produce an unacceptable result. The power to make unsecured or no-interest loans to a trust grantor causes the grantor to be treated as owner of the entire trust under section 675(2). It would be incongruous if unsecured or no-interest loans actually made to the grantor caused only the part of the trust actually borrowed to be treated as the grantor's under section 675(3). That result would make avoidance of section 675(2) not only easy, but relatively harmless from the grantor's viewpoint—he could still obtain trust property in the form of favorable loans but without having to worry about being treated as owning any substantial part of the trust. Therefore, we refuse to read "portion of [the] trust in respect of which" to mean merely "portion."

Likewise, we reject petitioners' contention that "portion" refers to the amount borrowed in comparison to the entire trust. Petitioner would have us calculate a fraction arrived at by dividing the amount borrowed by the trust corpus, and treat that fraction as the trust "portion" owned by the grantor. If such were the case, a trust grantor could borrow the entire trust income derived from the entire trust corpus but only be treated as owning a fraction of the trust, even though his borrowing evidences dominion and control over the entire trust. We find such a result patently unreasonable and unsupported by the statutory language or any other authority.

On the other hand, we need not address respondent's contention that "portion" means the entire trust whenever a grantor has the power to borrow all corpus or income and any trust property is borrowed. See *Mau v. United States,* 355 F.Supp. 909 (D.Hawaii 1973). In this case, petitioner-husband borrowed all the trust income and that income was derived from the entire trust corpus. Thus, it is clear that petitioner-husband should be treated as owner of the entire trust. It does not matter in this case whether we reach that result via respondent's automatic entire trust rule or via calling petitioner-husband owner of the entire trust simply because he actually borrowed "in respect of" the entire trust. The same result is reached either way. It is best to wait for a case clearly presenting the problem to analyze fully respondent's "entire trust" contention.

Petitioners in this case have made no showing that less than all the trust should be treated as being owned by petitioner-husband. As previously noted, he borrowed all the trust income which was in respect of all the trust corpus. His borrowings undoubtedly indicate significant dominion and control over the entire trust. Accordingly, we conclude that petitioner-husband is treated as owning the entire trust during 1974 and 1975.

REVENUE RULING 86-82

1986-1 Cumulative Bulletin 253

On May 11, 1985, *A* created an irrevocable trust for the benefit of *A*'s children. The trust instrument names *A* trustee and gives *A* power to borrow trust corpus or income at the market rate of interest with adequate security. On June 11, 1985, *A* borrowed 100*x* dollars from the trust in compliance with these requirements. The borrowed funds comprised the entire trust corpus. On November 3, 1985, *A* repaid the loan plus interest. Both *A* and the trust are calendar year taxpayers.

Section 671 of the Code provides that if any section of subpart E of subchapter J treats the grantor as the owner of any portion of the trust, then the grantor must include in computing taxable income those items of income, deductions, and credits which are attributable to that portion of the trust.

Section 675(3) of the Code provides that, generally, the grantor of a trust will be treated as the owner of any portion of a trust in respect to which the grantor has borrowed the corpus or income and has not completely repaid the loan, including any interest, before the beginning of the taxable year.

In *Mau v. United States,* 355 F.Supp. 909 (D.Hawaii 1973), the taxpayer established five separate trusts, with the taxpayer designated trustee of each. In 1965, the taxpayer borrowed money from each of the trusts. These amounts were not repaid until 1969. The taxpayer argued that section 675(3) of the Code did not cause the taxpayer-grantor to be liable for federal income tax on the trusts' 1965 income because the loans were not outstanding at the beginning of the year. The court rejected this interpretation of the statute, reasoning that section 675(3) was enacted to prevent the shifting of taxable income in situations where a grantor retained control and use of trust properties through borrowing. Therefore, the court held that the borrowing of trust corpus or income by a grantor at any time during a taxable year would result in the grantor being taxed on trust income for that entire year under section 675(3). The court concluded that the taxpayer was taxable on income of the trusts in 1965, the year the borrowing occurred, even though the loans were made after the beginning of the year. If section 675(3) otherwise applies for a given year, its effect is not avoided by making repayment before the year closes. *Mau* therefore stands for the principle that section 675(3) applies for any year during any part of which a loan by a trust to the grantor-trustee is outstanding.

In the present case, *A* borrowed the entire trust corpus during calendar 1985. Accordingly, *A* is treated as the owner of the entire trust under section 675(3) of the Code in spite of the fact that *A* made full payment of principal and interest before the close of 1985. *See* section 1.671–3(b)(3) of the regulations. Hence, under section 671, *A* must include in gross income all income earned by the trust in 1985.

Do you agree with the characterization of the transaction under section 675(3) in the following case? Consider the favorable income tax planning opportunities that it may present.

ROTHSTEIN v. UNITED STATES

United States Court of Appeals, Second Circuit, 1984.
735 F.2d 704.

FRIENDLY, CIRCUIT JUDGE:

* * *

The district court found the facts to be as follows: In 1951 decedent Alexander Rothstein ("taxpayer") and Abraham Savin formed a real estate holding company known as Industrial Developers, Inc. ("IDI"). * * *

On February 18, 1957, taxpayer contributed his 300 shares of IDI to an irrevocable trust he established for the benefit of his three children. * * *

In October 1964, taxpayer bought Savin's 300 shares of IDI for $500,000, agreeing to pay the purchase price at a later date. On November 13, 1964, he purchased from his wife as trustee the trust's 300 shares for $320,000. Payment was made by an unsecured promissory note bearing an interest rate of 5% per annum, payable semi-annually beginning May 13, 1965. These payments were duly made * * * until the full sum of $320,000 had been paid.

In January 1965, taxpayer, having become owner of all of IDI's stock as a result of the transactions with Savin and the trust, dissolved IDI and had all its assets transferred to himself. * * *

In their joint federal income tax return for 1965 taxpayer and his wife claimed deductions for (1) $16,000 in interest paid to the trust on the promissory note, and (2) a short-term capital loss of $33,171 on the liquidation of IDI. * * * The Commissioner, however, asserted a deficiency of $56,664 based on his disallowance of the interest deduction and his determination that taxpayer had in fact realized a substantial gain on the liquidation of IDI. As now presented by the Government, the Commissioner's theory was that, under IRC § 675(3), the taxpayer was to be treated as the "owner" of the trust assets and that this crucially affected the tax consequences of the events described above. On this view, transactions involving trust assets were to be re-analyzed after substituting the taxpayer (as the "owner" of those assets) for the trust. Thus, the Commissioner disallowed the $16,000 interest deduction, since the taxpayer was not entitled to a deduction for amounts paid to himself as "owner" of the promissory note held by the trust. Similarly, in computing taxpayer's gain on the liquidation of IDI, the Commissioner reduced taxpayer's basis in the shares acquired from the trust from $320,000 to $30,000. His rationale, apparently, was that the taxpayer could not claim a full "cost" basis in stock acquired in a sale that involved nothing more than a transfer of the property from the taxpayer (as "owner" of the stock) to himself.

* * *

Taxpayer's principal argument on the merits is that his purchase, on credit, of the 300 shares of IDI did not involve a "borrowing" from the trust and therefore did not come within IRC § 675(3), which applies only when the grantor "has directly or indirectly borrowed the corpus or income and has not completely repaid the loan, including any interest, before the beginning of the taxable year". The image most immediately conveyed by the statutory language is that of a grantor who has obtained an asset from the trust, whether money or otherwise, in exchange for a promise to return the same asset at some future time. Taxpayer is correct in noting that a transaction like that here in question—a sale of a trust asset on credit—involves no borrowing of the asset sold. However, the Commissioner's argument is that what was "directly or indirectly borrowed" was not the IDI stock but money in the amount of the purchase price. On the Commissioner's view, the trust's extension of credit was a "loan" within the meaning of § 675(3), notwithstanding that the loan "proceeds" were immediately used to pay for the shares.

Whether an extension of credit in a sale should be deemed a "loan" for purposes of § 675(3) is not easily answered on the basis of the language of the statute alone. On the one hand, Black's Law Dictionary 844 (5th ed. 1979) defines "loan" quite narrowly as the "[d]elivery by one party to and receipt by another party of [a] sum of money upon agreement, express or implied, to repay it with or without interest". This definition suggests that an extension of credit is not a loan unless there is actual delivery of loan proceeds to the obligor. A similar distinction appears to underlie the numerous decisions holding that, for purposes of a usury statute, a sale on credit is not a loan. *See, e.g., Bartholomew v. Northampton Nat'l Bank,* 584 F.2d 1288, 1295 (3 Cir. 1978) (Pennsylvania law). On the other hand, it is common enough to conceive of a credit sale as involving a loan, as witness the many statutes referred to as "truth-in-lending" laws, *see, e.g.,* Consumer Credit Protection Act, 15 U.S.C. § 1601 *et seq.* ("Truth in Lending Act"), although one hardly says that the purchaser has borrowed the property purchased.[3]

More important in deciding whether § 675(3) should apply in the instant case is the object which the statute was intended to serve. As is well known, the purpose of IRC §§ 671–79 and the regulations that preceded them was to bring order out of the chaos that has been created by the decision in *Helvering v. Clifford,* 309 U.S. 331, 60 S.Ct. 554, 84 L.Ed. 788 (1940), that a grantor's continued domination of a trust might render trust income taxable to him. This led to over a hundred decisions in the courts of appeals, some holding *Clifford* to be applicable and others holding the contrary, with little difference in the facts, see 1 Surrey & Warren, Federal Income Taxation 1340 (1972 ed.). The purpose of the regulations, originally issued in 1945, amended in 1947, and codified in 1954, was "to establish a definite line separating 'Clifford trusts' where income is taxable to the grantor from trusts falling under the general trust sections [where income is taxable to the trust or its distributees]." *Id.* at 1341. The statute directs that the grantor shall be treated as "owner" of a portion of a trust * * * in many * * * instances where * * * the grantor's powers or acts were thought by the Commissioner and later by Congress to indicate that he remained in effective control.

Section 675, entitled "Administrative powers", is a subset of the many provisions dealing with the retention of substantial interests in and powers over a trust. Broadly speaking, it requires that the grantor be treated as "owner" of a trust when he could engage or has engaged in certain transactions with the trust without providing adequate consideration. In particular, § 675(3) addresses those situations in which the grantor has exercised "dominion and control" over a trust by

3. It could be further contended on behalf of the taxpayer that Congress dealt with the subject of purchases from a trust in § 675(1) (regarding certain powers "to purchase, exchange, or otherwise deal with or dispose of the corpus or the income therefrom for less than an adequate consideration"), thus arguing for a narrower interpretation of § 675(3). Against this is the fact that § 675(1) applies only to powers permitting purchases for inadequate consideration, whereas § 675(3) applies, irrespective of a previously existing power, where the loan is either inadequately secured or made by "a related or subordinate trustee subservient to the grantor."

borrowing from it at less than an adequate rate of interest or without giving adequate security for his promise to repay the loan. Indeed, § 675(3)'s determination to prevent a grantor's treating a trust as his private bank without paying the tax consequences is so strong that the grantor is to be treated as "owner" even if the rate of interest and the security *are* adequate, unless the loan is made by a trustee other than the grantor or "a related or subordinate trustee subservient to the grantor".

There can be no doubt that the extension of credit in the present case, made without adequate security by a subservient trustee, would fall within the scope of the statute should we deem it a "borrowing" or "loan" under § 675(3). We think it is consistent with the overall purpose of Congress to do so. *First,* in view of the fact that the statute is to apply to any grantor who has "borrowed" from the trust, whether "directly *or indirectly*" (emphasis supplied), we cannot attach much weight to the distinction, mentioned above, between (1) an extension of credit in which the proceeds are actually delivered to and received by the obligor, and (2) one in which they are immediately applied to the purchase of an asset from the obligee. *Second,* we must consider the consequences of a decision that an extension of credit like this is *not* within the scope § 675(3). A grantor wishing to obtain a loan from a trust while steering clear of the statute could always do so by arranging for the trust to purchase, for example, marketable securities with a value equal to the amount of the contemplated loan, which the grantor would then purchase from the trust in exchange for his note. The grantor could then sell the securities on the market, leaving him with cash and the trust with his note—just as if it had made him a conventional loan. The only difference would be that § 675(3) would not apply, since the extension of credit in the sale did not involve actual delivery of loan proceeds to the grantor. Accepting taxpayer's argument would in effect largely annul § 675(3). We therefore adopt the district court's conclusion that the extension of credit here was, at least "indirectly", a "borrowing" within the meaning of the statute.

FEINBERG, CHIEF JUDGE (concurring and dissenting):

I feel compelled to write a separate opinion because my view of the transaction in question is entirely different from that of my colleagues. In my judgment, the crucial issue is whether IRC § 675(3) applies at all to the trust's installment sale of stock to Rothstein. This issue turns on whether that transaction is a "borrowing" within the meaning of § 675(3) or a sale. Although they disagree on the consequences flowing therefrom, both Judges Friendly and Oakes agree that § 675(3) applies because they apparently view the installment sale as either a "borrowing" of the purchase price of the stock or an extension of credit equal to the purchase price. I disagree.

The transaction was not a sham sale. There was a mutual exchange of consideration that made both parties better off and that had genuine economic substance. For over seven years prior to the sale, the trust's asset was stock in a closely held corporation, which had paid no dividends to stockholders and for which there was apparently no market. After the sale, the trust held an asset, Rothstein's promissory note, that paid interest and that conceivably could be discounted for cash. It is significant that the advisory jury and the district judge found that the $320,000 installment note was adequate consideration for the stock. For his part, Rothstein received full title to the stock to do with whatever he pleased (which, incidently, is the reason no one is arguing the stock was borrowed). This, and the coordinate purchase of Savin's stock, enabled Rothstein to liquidate the company, reorganize and refinance it and continue the enterprise, another factor suggesting economic substance to the transaction rather than an attempt to evade the Clifford regulations. The government makes much of the fact that Rothstein did not give security for the promissory note until after the end of the taxable year. Yet Savin gave full title to his stock to Rothstein in October 1964, but was not paid until after Rothstein liquidated the company and took out a mortgage on its former assets in January 1965. Surely, that was not a loan of Savin's stock, nor do I view it as a loan of the purchase price, but simply a deferred payment date. Whatever risk Savin incurred by accepting a deferred payment date without interim security was apparently offset in his view by the economic gain to him from the deal. The same is true for the trust.

In this case, the Commissioner seeks to recharacterize the transaction because he apparently does not like the favorable tax consequences for Rothstein. In a case analogous to this one and also involving the Clifford Regulations, the Ninth Circuit was presented with a sale of stock and other property to a grantor trust in return for a lifetime annuity. It refused to recharacterize the transaction as a reservation of a life estate, which would have caused the trust income to be taxable to the grantor under IRC §§ 677(a) and 671. *Lafargue v. C.I.R.*, 689 F.2d 845 (9th Cir.1982). The court found that the sale had genuine substance and was not a disguised conduit for distribution of the trust income. The annuity was fixed and was not an attempt to approximate the income production of the trust assets. The taxpayer-annuitant bore the risk of early death or appreciation of the trust assets; the trust bore the risk of late demise or depreciation of the trust assets. The court concluded that "[i]n these circumstances, Taxpayer's formal characterization of the transaction as a sale in exchange for an annuity should not be disregarded for tax purposes." Id. at 850. Similarly, because of the economic substance behind the transaction at bar, I do not believe it should be recharacterized as a "borrowing" within § 675(3).

The sham sale analysis that I would apply in determining the applicability of § 675(3) does not produce the undesirable consequences suggested by Judge Friendly's hypothetical case in which "[a] grantor wishing to obtain a loan from a trust while steering clear of the statute could always do so by arranging for the trust to purchase, for example, marketable securities with a value equal to the amount of the contemplated loan, which the grantor would then purchase from the trust in exchange for his note." * * * The hypothesized transaction would be patently a sham. There would be no reason for the trust to engage in such a transaction. Why would the trust give up freely marketable securities it had just purchased for a promissory note? Alternatively, if a promissory note was attractive to the trust for some reason, why wouldn't it simply give cash for the promissory note? Because of the lack of economic substance, the government would be permitted to recharacterize the two steps of the hypothetical transaction as a loan of money with which the taxpayer happened to purchase marketable securities.

The real objection that the Commissioner and Judge Oakes appear to have is to the use of the installment sale device between a grantor and a trust to produce favorable tax consequences in addition to accomplishing whatever other economic objectives the parties may have. However, as long as the transaction is not a sham, the choice is one Congress has made. The taxpayer is free to structure his transactions, and specifically may choose to employ the installment sale device, to minimize his tax consequences.

* * *

DEMAND TRUSTS

Read Code section 678.

Read Regulation section 1.678.

Section 678 is a provision that is not technically a "grantor trust" provision because it applies only to someone other than the grantor who has (or, under proper circumstances, who has released or modified) certain powers. It is included in Subpart E of Subchapter J and it is appropriate to consider it as part of the grantor trust rules, however, because it has the effect of treating that person as if (s)he were the owner of that portion of the trust as to which the power applies, just as if the person were a grantor who transferred property into the trust and retained certain powers or interests.

MALLINCKRODT v. NUNAN

United States Court of Appeals, Eighth Circuit, 1945.
146 F.2d 1, cert. denied, 324 U.S. 871, 65 S.Ct. 1017, 89 L.Ed. 1426 (1945).

SANBORN, CIRCUIT JUDGE.

The Tax Court of the United States determined deficiencies in the income taxes due from petitioner for the calendar years 1934 to 1937, inclusive. 2 T.C. 1128. The deficiencies resulted from including in the petitioner's income for each of the years the undistributed income of an irrevocable trust created by his father in 1918. By the terms of the instrument creating the trust, this undistributed income was payable to petitioner annually upon his request, but, if not paid to him at his request, it was to be added to the corpus of the trust estate at the end of each year.

The question presented is whether the undistributed income of the trust in the years in question was taxable to petitioner or taxable to the trust.

* * *

The factual situation out of which this controversy arises is, in substance, as follows: Edward Mallinckrodt, Sr. (who died in 1928), on April 17, 1918, executed a trust instrument, by which he transferred to St. Louis Union Trust Company and the petitioner, as trustees, property and securities under the terms and conditions stated in the instrument. * * * The grantor's intention in creating the trust was primarily to provide for petitioner's children and grandchildren. Petitioner had already received a large amount of property from his father. By the terms of the trust instrument, the net income of the trust was to be devoted first to paying certain debts, obligations, and burdens growing out of a building enterprise, and, after those obligations had been paid and satisfied in full, the trustees were directed: to pay to petitioner's wife out of the annual net income of the trust $10,000 each year during her life and that of petitioner; to pay the residue of such annual trust income to petitioner during his life, upon his request; to accumulate the undistributed annual net income and, at the end of each year, to add it to the principal of the trust estate.

* * *

The petitioner did not request that any of the income of the trust be paid to him in 1934 and 1935. In 1936 the trustees distributed, upon petitioner's request, out of the trust income, $15,000, which was disbursed to certain educational and charitable organizations, and $4,075.82, which was transferred to a trust which petitioner had created for the benefit of his wife. Petitioner reported in his income tax return for 1936 so much of the $15,000 distribution as was taxable. He did not report in his return the taxable portion of the $4,075.82 distribution. In 1937, the trustees distributed out of trust income, upon petitioner's request, $3,109.14 by transferring that amount to the trust which he had created for his wife's benefit. The taxable portion of this distribution was not included in petitioner's income tax return for 1937. During each of the taxable years, petitioner's wife reported and paid the tax upon the $10,000 of trust income which was distributable to her and which she received from the trustees. All of the undistributed net annual income of the trust for each of the years in question was reported by the trustees as income taxable to the trust, and they paid the tax due upon it. At the end of each of the years, the trustees, as directed by the trust instrument, added the undistributed net income for that year to the corpus of the trust.

The respondent determined that the undistributed trust income for each of the years was taxable to petitioner. Petitioner had a very large taxable income. The Tax Court sustained the respondent's determination.

It seems apparent from the grantor's purpose in creating the trust, from the elaborate provisions of the trust instrument relative to the continuance of the trust beyond the lifetime of the petitioner for the benefit of others, and from other circumstances, that the powers conferred upon the petitioner and upon the trustees over the disposition of the income and corpus of the trust were not granted with the thought that they would be exercised for the sole use or benefit of petitioner. The grantor evidently conferred the powers in the belief that the petitioner and the trustees, during petitioner's lifetime, should have discretion to alter the provisions of the trust instrument relative to the disposition of the trust estate or to terminate the trust if deemed necessary or wise in the interests of the beneficiaries of the trust. It is apparent that the grantor intended that the wife and descendants of petitioner were to have a real and subsisting interest in the income and the corpus of the trust estate. It is a fair assumption that the grantor contemplated that petitioner would not, during his lifetime, seek to withdraw either income or principal from the trust estate unless he needed it or unless he believed that it could be used advantageously by him for the benefit of the family.

A majority of the judges of the Tax Court were of the opinion that, because of the powers granted to petitioner by the trust instrument, the undistributed income of the trust in each of the years in question was his income, for purposes of taxation, by virtue of the provisions of section [61]. The basis for their opinion is indicated by the following excerpt (at pages 1136–1137 of 2 T.C.):

"Certainly with such powers and rights in and to the trust corpus, and particularly to the income produced, there can be no question that if petitioner were the grantor he would be taxable on the income under section 22(a), Helvering v. Clifford, supra [309 U.S. 331, 60 S.Ct. 554, 84 L.Ed. 788], and petitioner makes no claim to the contrary. The fact that the powers and rights are not the retained powers and rights of a grantor but were received by petitioner as beneficiary of the trust and by grant from his father makes them no less substantial. As in the Clifford case, the rights and powers of the petitioner in and to the trust corpus and the income therefrom did not include all of the incidents of ownership, but we think it may definitely be said that the benefits held by and belonging to petitioner, directly or indirectly, were such as to require the conclusion that he was the owner of the income here in question, within the meaning of section 22(a), supra. In Corliss v. Bowers, 281 U.S. 376 [50 S.Ct. 336, 74 L.Ed. 916], the Supreme Court said:

" 'But taxation is not so much concerned with the refinements of title as it is with actual command over the property taxed—the actual benefit for which the tax is paid. * * * Still speaking with reference to taxation, if a man disposes of a fund in such a way that another is allowed to enjoy the income which it is in the power of the first to appropriate it does not matter whether the permission is given *by* *assent or by failure to express dissent.* The income that is subject to a man's unfettered command and that he is free to enjoy at his own option may be taxed to him as his income, whether he sees fit to enjoy it or not. * * * (Italics supplied.)' "

* * *

Two of the judges who concurred were of the opinion that it was unnecessary to consider the effect of section [61]. They thought that the undistributed trust income was taxable to petitioner as income "to be distributed currently" by the fiduciaries to the petitioner as beneficiary, within the meaning of section [652(a)].

Five of the judges of the Tax Court dissented. The conclusion of four of the dissenting judges is concisely stated as follows (at pages 1151, 1152 of 2 T.C.):

"Trust No. 3660 here involved was no mere tax saving device. It was unquestionably a real trust set up for legitimate purposes and one which, it seems to me, Congress intended to tax according to the provisions of sections 161 and 162. Under section 161 it was the duty of the trust to include in its income tax return all taxable gross income and from this gross income it was entitled to take all the ordinary deductions granted to an individual by the statute. In addition to these deductions the trust was entitled to take the deductions granted by subparagraph (b) of section 162, * * *.

"The trust was directed to pay annually out of the net income of the trust $10,000 to Elizabeth E. Mallinckrodt, wife of petitioner. This was income which was clearly 'to be distributed currently' to her within the meaning of (b) of section 162 and under the terms of that subparagraph was deductible by the trust and taxable to the beneficiary, Elizabeth E. Mallinckrodt. Concerning this $10,000 there is no issue in this case.

"The remainder of the net income of the trust was not currently distributable to petitioner, Edward Mallinckrodt, Jr., but only such part of the remainder of the net income of the trust, after the $10,000 distribution to Elizabeth, was distributable to him as he might request. The settlor of the trust directed that such part of the net income of the trust as might not be requested by petitioner should be accumulated and should at the end of the year become a part of the principal of the trust estate, subject to such further disposition as was in the trust indenture provided for the principal of the trust estate. Under these provisions only that part of the net income requested by petitioner was currently distributable to him and taxable to him under the provisions of section 162(b). The balance of the net income not so requested was 'income accumulated or held for future distribution under the terms of the will or trust' within the meaning of section 161(a)(1) and was taxable to the trust. The findings of fact show that 'the trustees filed income tax returns with respect to the undistributed taxable income of the trust and paid the tax shown on the returns.' In my opinion the law does not require more."

The conflicting contentions of the parties as to the applicable law are clearly reflected in the opinions of the judges of the Tax Court. 2 T.C. 1133–1138, 1150–1155. No useful purpose would be served by a further discussion.

We shall briefly state our conclusions and our reasons for them. We think that the undistributed income of the trust in suit was not income "to be distributed currently" by the fiduciaries to petitioner as beneficiary, within the meaning of section [652(a)]. This, for the reason that, by the terms of the trust instrument, the trustees could not distribute trust income to petitioner except upon his request, and were obliged to accumulate and to add to trust corpus all undistributed net income at the end of each year. The trustees were bound to abide by the exact terms and conditions of the trust instrument. By its terms, trust income was not distributable to petitioner unless he elected to withdraw it by requesting that it be paid to him.

* * *

We agree with the majority of the Tax Court that implications which fairly may be drawn from the opinions of the Supreme Court in Corliss v. Bowers, 281 U.S. 376, 378, 50 S.Ct. 336, 74 L.Ed. 916, Helvering v. Clifford, 309 U.S. 331, 60 S.Ct. 554, 84 L.Ed. 788, and other cases relative to the taxability of trust income to one having command over it, justify, if they do not compel, the conclusion that the undistributed net income of the trust in suit, during the years in question, was taxable to petitioner under section [61]. This, because the power of petitioner to receive this trust income each year, upon request, can be regarded as the equivalent of ownership of the income for purposes of taxation. In Harrison v. Schaffner, 312 U.S. 579, 580, 61 S.Ct. 759, 760, 85 L.Ed. 1055, the Supreme Court approved "the principle that the power to dispose of income is the equivalent of ownership of it and that the exercise of the power to procure its payment to another, whether to pay a debt or to make a gift, is within the reach of the statute taxing income 'derived from any source whatever.' " It seems to us, as it did to the majority of the Tax Court, that it is the possession of power over the disposition of trust income which is of significance in determining whether, under section [61], the income is taxable to the possessor of such power, and that logically it makes no difference whether the possessor is a grantor who retained the power or a beneficiary who acquired it from another. See Jergens v. Commissioner, supra, at page 498 of 136 F.2d. Since the trust income in suit was available to petitioner upon request in each of the years involved, he had in each of those years the "realizable" economic gain necessary to make the income taxable to him. See Helvering v. Stuart, 317 U.S. 154, 168, 169, 63 S.Ct. 140, 87 L.Ed. 154; Helvering v. Clifford, supra, at pages 336, 337 of 309 U.S., 60 S.Ct. 554, 84 L.Ed. 788; Helvering v. Gordon, 8 Cir., 87 F.2d 663, 667.

The decision of the Tax Court is affirmed.

Applicable in two parts, it is the first portion of section 678(a) that treats a person as owner of that portion of a trust as to which the person has a power to demand or withdraw either income or principal. Under the penultimate sentence of Treasury Regulation section 1.678(a)–1(b), powers held in conjunction with another, even if a nonadverse party, will not cause the powerholder to be treated as owner. Thus, to apply, section 678 requires that the power be exercisable solely by the powerholder. Classic forms of exposure under section 678(a)(1) stem from five or five and Crummey withdrawal rights, granted to avoid taxable lapses under section 2514(e) while qualifying for the annual exclusion of section 2503(b), along with general inter vivos powers of appointment, most often found in section 2056(b)(5) marital deduction trusts, as illustrated by the following rulings.

REVENUE RULING 67–241

1967–2 Cumulative Bulletin 225.

A decedent in his will gave his widow a power, exercisable solely by her, to require the trustees of the residuary trust created under his will to pay to her at her request from corpus during any calendar year an amount equal to the greater of five percent of the value of the trust corpus or $5,000. The widow's right to exercise such power was not cumulative, so that upon her failure to exercise it before the end of any calendar year, her right as to that year lapsed. The trust income was payable in equal amounts to the decedent's two sons.

Section 678(a)(1) of the Internal Revenue Code of [1986] provides a general rule that a person other than the grantor shall be treated as the owner of any portion of a trust with respect to which such person has a power exercisable solely by himself to vest the corpus or the income therefrom in himself.

* * *

Since the widow has a power exercisable solely by herself to vest a portion of the trust corpus in herself, she is treated as the owner of that portion of the trust under section 678 of the Code.

As the owner of a portion of the trust corpus, there are included in computing her tax liability those items of income, deduction, and credit against tax attributable to or included in that portion. Pursuant to the provisions of section 1.671–4 of the regulations, these items should not be reported by the trust on Form 1041, U.S. Fiduciary Income Tax Return (for estates, and trusts), but should be shown on a separate statement to be attached to that form.

The portions of trust corpus considered owned by the widow are not subject to the provisions of sections 661(a)(2) and 662(a)(2) of the Code when distributed to her.

REVENUE RULING 81-6

1981-1 Cumulative Bulletin 385.

* * *

C is a minor who is a beneficiary of an irrevocable inter vivos trust created by *C*'s parent, *P*, in 1979. Under the terms of the trust agreement, an independent trustee is authorized to accumulate the net income of the trust unless, in the judgment of the trustee, all or part of the current or accumulated net income should be distributed to, or for the benefit of, *C* for *C*'s support, maintenance in reasonable comfort, health, and education until *C* reaches 25 years of age. Also, the trustee may distribute principal to *C* subject to the above standard.

The trust also provides that *C* has the noncumulative power in any calendar year to withdraw from principal the lesser of (1) all amounts added to the trust during such year by the grantor; or (2) the sum of $3,000. *C* also has the power to withdraw the entire income of the trust until *C* reaches age 25.

Unless sooner exhausted by withdrawal or distributions, the trust is to terminate upon the death of *C* or at such time as *C* reaches age 25, and any remaining amount of trust principal and income is to be distributed to *C* or *C*'s estate.

The instrument provides that trust income may be used to discharge *P*'s obligation to support *C* only if *P* is unable to personally discharge that obligation.

Under applicable state law, *C*, as a minor, is legally incapable of exercising the above powers in the absence of an appointed guardian. Although no legal guardian has been appointed for *C*, there is no impediment under the trust agreement or local law to the appointment of a guardian.

* * *

In *Trust No. 3 v. Commissioner*, 285 F.2d 102 (7th Cir.1960), beneficiaries who were minors were granted a power to terminate a trust and to take possession of the trust property. The court held that the fact that no guardians had been duly appointed for the beneficiaries was immaterial in determining whether the beneficiaries became vested with a present right to use all or any part of the property of the trust upon making due demand. The court noted that the taking of such routine steps as appointing a guardian would have no bearing upon the fundamental question of the legal right of the beneficiaries to terminate the trust.

In the present case, as in *Trust No. 3*, no guardian has been appointed for the minor beneficiary of a trust with respect to which the beneficiary has a power exercisable solely by the beneficiary to vest the corpus or the income therefrom in the beneficiary. Here, *C*, in the absence of an appointed guardian, is legally incapable of exercising the power; however, *C*'s inability to exercise the power because *C* is a minor does not affect the existence of the power. For purposes of section 678 of the Code it is the existence of a power rather than the capacity to exercise such a power that determines whether a person other than the grantor shall be treated as the owner of any part of a trust.

* * *

Questions

1. Consistent with Revenue Ruling 67–241, beneficiaries who may exercise a five or five power to withdraw annually an amount not to exceed the greater of $5000 or five percent of the trust corpus are treated as owners of a portion of the trust under section 678. A corresponding portion of all income and deductions and of all realized capital gains and losses in the trust must be taxed annually to the holder of the power, even if the power is not exercised in a given year and the beneficiary has no cash distributions from the trust with which to pay the resulting income tax. Moreover, the trustee must maintain accurate records so as to properly inform the powerholder of those tax consequences and avoid having the trust or some other beneficiary pay the tax thereon. For these reasons, some planners limit withdrawal rights to $5000 annually. Can you ascertain why?

2. Taxpayer is income beneficiary of one-third of a trust and may withdraw $5000 annually from corpus. What are the income tax consequences of lapse of that withdrawal right?

Under the first sentence of Treasury Regulation section 1.678(a)–1(b), section 678(a)(1) also reaches any power to directly or indirectly apply either income or principal to the person's individual benefit. In most respects, taxation under this first part of the rule is very similar to traditional grantor trust exposure flowing from a grantor's retention of enjoyment or powers, and it is fitting that two exceptions from other grantor trust rules find application here as well.

The first, while based on three very old cases, appears to provide that restrictions on the person's powers, in the form of a limitation such as a "reasonably definite (external) standard," will serve to treat the power as if nonexistent.[5] The second is analogous to the section 677(b) exception for a grantor's indirect enjoyment flowing from distributions for the support or maintenance of grantor's dependents: if the person has a power, as trustee, to apply income to the support or maintenance of a dependent, grantor trust exposure is limited under section 678(c) to the amount of actual distributions made. Notable about this limitation is that it applies only with respect to the person's

5. United States v. DeBonchamps, 278 F.2d 127 (9th Cir.1960) (power to consume principal limited by "needs, maintenance and comfort;" capital gains in trust not taxed to powerholder); Funk v. Commissioner, 185 F.2d 127 (3d Cir.1950) ("needs" deemed a sufficient limitation); and Smither v. United States, 108 F.Supp. 772 (S.D. Tex.1952), aff'd, 205 F.2d 518 (5th Cir.1953) (power limited by "support, maintenance, comfort and enjoyment").

power as a fiduciary and only with respect to income distributions. By Treasury Regulation section 1.678(c)–1(a), other aspects of the section 677(b) related limitation, such as that regarding certain distributions as being accumulation distributions to the person that are subject to throwback, are also applicable here.

One interesting question exists, raised by the last clause of Treasury Regulation section 1.678(c)–1(c), for which no answer appears to exist. The question is whether a power to distribute income for a dependent's support or maintenance that falls under the protection of the *DeBonchamps* exception for powers limited by a reasonably definite standard is a power described in section 678(a). If it is not (because of the limitation), then according to the regulation, section 678(c) cannot apply with respect thereto. It would seem that the better reasoned result is to regard the power as one described in section 678(a) but as to which no tax consequences attach due to the protection afforded by a properly confined standard. Any other result would be perverse, in effect saying that an excepted power under section 678(a) cannot enjoy the protection afforded to more extensive powers under section 678(c).

The second part of the *Mallinckrodt* trust rule is applicable under section 678(a)(2) only if the person previously released or modified a power over the trust in such a fashion that any of the grantor trust rules would apply were the release or modification a transfer by a grantor. For example, assume the person has a power to withdraw income from the trust each year, and allows that power to lapse so that income that could have been withdrawn is instead added to principal. In the next year the same power to withdraw income will apply to income generated by the prior year's accumulation. If the prior year's income had been property transferred to the trust by a grantor, this continuing withdrawal right would cause grantor trust liability under section 677(a)(1) with respect to that portion of the trust represented by the accumulation. Consequently, the continuing withdrawal right will cause the person to be treated as the owner of that same portion of the trust, and multiple lapses over several years can cause the beneficiary to be regarded as owner of an increasing portion of the trust each year. See, e.g., Mallinckrodt v. Nunan, 146 F.2d 1 (8th Cir.1945), aff'g 2 T.C. 1128 (1943), acquiescence, 1944 C.B. 18.

Given this pseudo-grantor trust treatment, the position taken in Treasury Regulation section 1.665(b)–1A(d) Example (4), that any distribution from the trust in the future may be an accumulation distribution to the person with the withdrawal right, is improper. Being treated as owner of that portion of the trust, and having paid tax thereon under section 678 in the year the income was earned, the accumulation distribution rules should not apply at a future date because their purpose is to impose the tax that would have been imposed had the trust never made the accumulation. Because the grantor trust rules will have imposed just such a tax, no further computation or imputation of tax is necessary. Moreover, because the trust never paid a tax on that accumulation (because of the grantor trust treatment), there is no provision in the accumulation distribution rules to give the deemed grantor a credit for the taxes already paid by the deemed grantor, meaning that the technical result of application of the accumulation distribution rules could be double taxation, which is thoroughly improper.

Two overriding exceptions apply to both parts of section 678(a). One is the disclaimer rule of section 678(d), applicable if renunciation of a power is made within a reasonable time of learning thereof. "Reasonable time" is not defined, though it probably would be construed similarly to the same language found in the gift tax disclaimer rule applicable prior to adoption of section 2518. The other is section 678(b), which simply provides that, with respect to powers over income only, if the grantor is also regarded as owner of the same portion of the trust, grantor trust liability will preempt liability under section 678, thereby avoiding taxation of the same items of taxable income to two different taxpayers.

Questions

1. A beneficiary is given a power to distribute income among a class consisting of the beneficiary and the beneficiary's siblings, in the beneficiary's uncontrolled discretion. What are the beneficiary's income tax consequences attributable to the power?

2. What would be the income tax consequences in question 1 if the beneficiary were to release so much of the power as permits distributions to the beneficiary?

3. How would your answer to question 1 differ if the beneficiary's power were exercisable only by Will?

4. How would your answer to question 1 differ if the beneficiary's power were exercisable only in conjunction with another sibling?

5. How would your answer to question 2 differ if the beneficiary released the entire power within several months after creation of the trust? Within several years? What if a prior interest came before the beneficiary's interest and the release occurred within several months after termination of that prior interest?

6. How would your answer to questions 1 and 2 differ if the beneficiary's power were limited to distributions of corpus (not income) for the support and maintenance of the permissible recipients?

PORTION RULES

Read Regulation section 1.671–3.

Grantor trust treatment may not apply with respect to an entire trust. Thus, the Code provides that the grantor (or a section 678 third party who is treated like a grantor) shall be treated as the owner of any "portion" of the trust as to which the requisite power or interest exists.

This raises two issues: (1) what is that portion, and (2) what income, deductions and credits are allocable thereto?

Treasury Regulation section 1.671–3 identifies several different "portions" that may be subject to the grantor trust rules, each causing items allocable to that portion to be attributed to the grantor. The following examples illustrate those portions in the context of interests or powers that generate grantor trust exposure with respect to that particular portion.

(1) *Entire Trust.* A grantor with a section 673 reversion or a section 676 power to revoke the trust in its entirety would be treated as owner of every item of income, deduction and credit in the trust. Similarly, if the grantor or any nonadverse party were trustee with no restrictions on powers over income and principal, section 674(a) exposure could apply to the entire trust. In addition, if the grantor were income beneficiary with section 677(a)(1) exposure and the remainder passed to the grantor's spouse, generating section 677(a)(2) liability as well, the two together (but neither alone, as noted below) would cause grantor trust exposure with respect to the entire trust.

(2) *Ordinary Income.* Meaning fiduciary accounting income, this portion is to be distinguished from ownership of corpus, which would pick up items of taxable income that are allocable to principal. Under Treasury Regulation section 1.671–3(b)(1), the ordinary income portion is those items allocable to the income account and would be the proper portion if the grantor retained a section 674(a) power to distribute only ordinary income among beneficiaries with no applicable section 674(b) or 674(d) exception, or if the grantor possessed only a section 677(a)(1) income interest. Under section 677(a)(1), it may be possible to argue that a standard limiting distributions to amounts necessary for the grantor's support or maintenance would limit the portion to that amount of income needed for those purposes. See Rev.Rul. 56–484, 1956–2 C.B. 23. If section 677(b) were applicable, the portion would be limited to the amount used for the beneficiaries' support and maintenance (or, more technically, the grantor would be deemed to own that portion—along with its income, credits and deductions—needed to produce the amount of net income distributed to the beneficiaries).

In computing the ordinary income portion, an interesting issue is raised by Treasury Regulation section 1.671–3(c), which treats the grantor as if (s)he were the current income beneficiary of the portion. By way of example, if taxable income allocable to income were $5,000, taxable income allocable to corpus were $2,000 and deductible expenses were $6,000, the current income beneficiary would be taxed on zero income and the excess deduction of $1,000 would reduce income allocable to corpus; that excess deduction would not pass through to the income beneficiary. It is thus assumed here that the same result would apply for grantor trust purposes and that the grantor would not be entitled to deductions in excess of ordinary income in this situation. This, however, is not the same treatment as if no trust had been created, which is the frequent assumption about the application of the grantor trust rules.[6]

(3) *Corpus.* This portion is all items not reflected in the ordinary income portion, meaning income and deductions allocable to corpus (and all income earned thereon after accumulation as a part of corpus).[7] In the prior example, the income allocable to corpus that would be taxable to the owner of this portion would be $1,000, being the $2,000 of gain allocable to corpus reduced by the $1,000 of excess deductions. Treasury Regulation section 1.671–3(b)(2) contains a classic example of the applicability of this portion, being a trust in which the grantor has a reversion that escapes section 673 but not section 677(a)(2). In a far less common example, the court held in Greenough v. Commissioner, 74 F.2d 25 (1st Cir.1934), that the grantor should be treated as owner of gains allocable to corpus by virtue of a section 677(a)(1) right to all income, because the grantor also had power to allocate receipts between income and principal. However, under Treasury Regulation section 1.671–3(b)(3), a section 674 power over corpus alone could result in the grantor being treated as owner of all income, not just income allocable to corpus, if the power over corpus could affect enjoyment of current income as well. For example, a power to distribute corpus currently (as opposed to a power to distribute corpus only after the occurrence of a section 673 event or, in a pre–TRA'86 trust, after expiration of a section 673 period) would affect enjoyment of current income because income would flow with corpus to any appointee.

(4) *Fractional Amount of Ordinary Income* or *Fractional Amount of Corpus.* Both these portions reflect rights that would cause grantor trust exposure above, limited to less than all of the trust (for example, a section 677(a)(1) right to receive half the income from a trust, or a section 673 reversion of half the corpus). Under the antepenultimate sentence of Treasury Regulation section 1.671–3(a)(3), an interest or power stated in terms of a specific dollar amount of corpus must be converted into a fraction, using the dollar amount as the numerator and the value of the trust as the denominator, valued as of the later to occur of the beginning of the tax year in question or existence of the interest or power. If the interest or power is computed in reference to a stated dollar amount of income, the last two sentences of Treasury Regulation section 1.671–3(c) require an added step in determining the numerator, being to identify the portion of trust corpus needed to produce that amount of income, then using this amount of corpus as the numerator. For example, if the grantor retained a section 677(a)(1) right to receive $5,000 of income each year, the current actuarial tables would specify that it requires $50,000 of corpus to produce that income, so the numerator would seem to be $50,000, not the $5,000 of income

6. See Edgar v. Commissioner, 56 T.C. 717 (1971); and see Schmolka, "Selected Aspects of the Grantor Trust Rules," 9 U. Miami Inst. Est. Plan. ¶ 1400 at ¶ 1403.2 Example (4) (1975).

7. Revenue Ruling 66–161, 1966–1 C.B. 164.

specified. Nevertheless, Treasury Regulation section 1.677(a)–1(g) Example (2) uses *actual* income to determine the fraction rather than income presumed to be generated using the applicable interest assumptions.

(5) *Specific Asset(s).* In the unusual circumstance covered in Treasury Regulation section 1.671–3(a)(2) of a taxable power over a particular asset, such as a section 675(4)(A) power to vote closely held stock transferred to a trust, the grantor will report the income, deductions and credits attributable to that asset as if the grantor were its owner, along with a pro rata share of any deductions not specifically identifiable with respect to the asset but properly spread among all trust assets (such as an otherwise unallocated trustee's fee).

Questions

1. If a trust had the following items of income and deduction for the current year, what would be the ordinary income and the corpus portions?

Dividend income	$20,000
Tax exempt income	5,000
Capital gains	16,000
Capital losses	(4,000)
Trustee fees, paid half from income and half from corpus	(3,000)

2. For the following interests and powers, identify the relevant grantor trust Code section(s) and select the appropriate portion that the grantor will be deemed to own from among the following five possibilities: (1) ordinary income only, (2) corpus only, (3) all income and corpus (that is, the entire trust), (4) a fractional portion of one of the above, or (5) specific asset(s).

a. Power to revoke the trust immediately.

b. Power in a nonadverse, non-independent, trustee (other than the grantor or grantor's spouse) to distribute corpus among A, B and C for their happiness and best interests, from a pot trust with no "advancements" provision.

c. In a pre-TRA'86 trust, power to revoke the trust in year 11.

d. The power in b. above, limited to current income, with a provision for accumulation of income not paid pursuant thereto.

e. Testamentary power to appoint the corpus (and all accrued or accumulated income added or allocated thereto).

f. Right to the current income, payable annually.

g. Power to sprinkle income among A, B and C.

h. Right to half the current income, payable annually.

i. In a pre-TRA'86 trust, reversion 132 months after creation of the trust. An additional contribution was made to corpus 24 months into the trust's existence.

j. A five or five withdrawal right, applicable with respect to corpus of the trust. Would your answer differ if it allowed withdrawal of income in an amount not to exceed $5,000 or five percent of the value of the trust?

k. Power to vote closely held stock in the trust.

3. What is the portion if the trust provides the grantor with power to withdraw gains annually but, to the extent not withdrawn, they are accumulated and added to principal, with the entire trust corpus returning to the grantor pursuant to a protected section 673 reversion?

RETURN REQUIREMENTS

Read Regulation section 1.671–4.

Notwithstanding the portion rules, which do not completely result in a trust being "ignored" for income tax purposes when a given grantor trust provision is triggered, the following materials illustrate how pervasive the grantor trust rules can be in "ignoring" the existence of a subject trust.

SCHEFT v. COMMISSIONER

United States Tax Court, 1972.
59 T.C. 428.

FEATHERSTON, JUDGE: Respondent determined a deficiency in petitioners' income tax for 1968 in the amount of $103,184. The only issue is whether sections 451(a) and 671 require the capital gains realized on the sales of property which had been placed in trust by petitioner William Scheft to be included in his income for the taxable year (1968) in which the property was sold or in the following year (1969) during which the fiscal year of the trusts ended.

* * *

Petitioner reports his income using a calendar year. Each of the six trusts reports its income using a fiscal year ending March 31. During the calendar year 1968, but within the trusts' fiscal year ending March 31, 1969, the trustees of the six trusts sold stocks and debentures in transactions which produced net long-term capital gains in the total amount of $383,943. Petitioner has agreed that he is taxable under section 677(a)(2) on the capital gains realized on these sales. This concession and a stipulation that the amount of the total capital gain shown in the statutory notice is not in dispute narrow the controversy to the issue, stated above, whether the trusts' gains are taxable to petitioner in 1968 or 1969.

We hold the gains are taxable in 1968 when the property was sold. We think this conclusion is required by the language of sections 451(a) 671, and 677(a)(2) and the accompanying interpretative regulations, particularly when read in the light of related provisions prescribing the general scheme for the taxation of trust income.

* * *

Where the taxable year of a "beneficiary" is different from that of the trust, section 662(c) provides that the amount to be included in the gross income of the beneficiary shall be based upon (1) the distributable net income of the trust, and (2) the amounts properly paid, credited, or required to be distributed during the taxable year of the trust ending within the beneficiary's taxable year. See also sec. 652(c). Thus, if the capital gains here in dispute were regarded as income taxable to a "beneficiary" under subparts A through D, they would be taxable in 1969 as contended by petitioner.

However, section 677(a)(2), the provision which both parties agree causes the capital gains to be taxed to petitioner, is not part of subparts A through D but is one of the so-called grantor trust provisions in subpart E, part I, of subchapter J. This subpart enunciates the rules to be applied where, in described circumstances, a grantor has transferred property to a trust but has not parted with complete dominion and control over the property or the income which it produces. S.Rept. No. 1622, to accompany H.R. 8300 (Pub.L. No. 591), 83d Cong., 2d Sess., p. 86 (1954). In such circumstances, prior to the grantor's transfer to a trust of his own creation, he owns the property, is entitled to its income, and is liable for taxes on that income. Where the grantor makes a formal but incomplete transfer of that property in trust, retaining the enjoyment of the fruits of ownership through the power to control or receive the income or reacquire the corpus, subpart E provides, in substance, that the transfer of legal title is to be disregarded insofar as such enjoyment has been retained. See *Kent v. United States,* 60 F.Supp. 203, 210 (Ct.Cl.1945). The obvious purpose is to prevent the use of a temporary or incomplete transfer in trust as a means of tax avoidance. *Crane v. Commissioner,* 368 F.2d 800, 802 (C.A. 1, 1966), affirming 45 T.C. 397 (1966); *Kent v. Rothensies,* 120 F.2d 476, 478 (C.A. 3, 1941).

Thus, sections 673 through 677 of that subpart each provides that where a grantor retains rights or powers over a portion of a trust in the manner therein described, he shall be "treated as the owner" of that "portion" of the trust. This includes the situations covered by section 677(a)(2), as in the instant case, where the capital gains or other income may be accumulated for the grantor's benefit. See *Archbishop Samuel Trust,* 36 T.C. 641, 650–651 (1961), affd. 306 F.2d 682 (C.A. 1, 1962); *Ralph L. Humphrey,* 39 T.C. 199, 202–203 (1962). When the grantor is so treated, section 671 provides that in computing the grantor's taxable income there shall be included the "items of income, deductions, and credits against tax of the trust which are attributable to that portion of the trust." And section 1.671–2(c), Income Tax Regs., further provides that: "An item of income, deduction, or credit included in computing the taxable income and credits of a grantor * * * under section 671 *is treated as if it had been received or paid directly by the grantor.*" (Emphasis added.)

Significantly, the inclusion in the grantor's taxable income under section 671 is not keyed to the trust's gross, net, or distributable income. Rather, the inclusion is in terms of the "items" of income and the "items" of deductions attributable to the portion of the trust of which the grantor is treated as the owner. And those items are to be taken into account to the same extent they would be "in computing taxable income * * * of an individual." This means that the trust is to be ignored in computing the taxable income from the grantor's portion of the trust, and the section expressly provides that: "Any remaining portion of the trust shall be subject to subparts A through D."

* * *

Accordingly, in the case of a trust falling within both subparts A through D *and* subpart E, the gross income and deductions are segregated into two categories: (1) Items which are taken into account in computing the grantor's taxable income by reason of his being treated as owner of all or a portion of the trust under subpart E, and (2) the income taxed to the fiduciary or the beneficiary under subparts A through D. This segregation is carried forward to the trust's income tax return pursuant to section 1.671–4, which provides that any items of income, deduction, and credit attributable to the grantor should not be reported in the trust's fiduciary return but should be shown on a separate statement attached to the return.

The absence from subpart E of a provision comparable with section 662(c), discussed above, specifying when income is to be reported by the grantor in case his taxable year and that of the trust do not coincide, is consistent with the scheme of treating the grantor as the "owner" of a portion of the trust. Since the trust is disregarded to the extent possible and the grantor is taxed on the income as if he received it directly, the general rule of section 451(a) governs the year of the inclusion in the grantor's taxable income. In pertinent part, that section provides that: "The amount of any item of gross income shall be included in the gross income for the taxable year in which received by the taxpayer." This means that the gains here in dispute are taxable to petitioner in 1968, when they were realized from the sales of property, rather than in 1969, when the trusts' fiscal year ended.

While the direct issue here presented has not been decided previously, we think our conclusion is compelled not only by the statutory language and the regulations but also by the underlying rationale of the above-cited cases applying various sections, or their predecessors, of subpart E.

* * *

In summary, because of petitioner's retained right to receive ultimately the capital gains realized on the sales of the property in trust, section 677(a)(2) requires petitioner to be "treated as the owner" of that portion of each of the trusts. In computing his taxable income, he is required by section 671 to include the items of capital gains which are attributable to that portion. And each such item, according to section 1.671–2(c), "is treated as if it had been received * * * directly by the grantor." We hold that these provisions can be given their intended meaning and effect in the instant case only if the trust entity is disregarded in determining the year in which the capital gains are taxable and such gains are taxed to petitioner in 1968, the year in which they were realized.

In the *Rothstein* case studied at page 244, the Service successfully argued that a purchase of assets from a trust, in exchange for a promissory note from the grantor, constituted a section 675(3) indirect borrowing, resulting in grantor trust treatment. In that case, however, the government argued but lost a second issue, whether the trust would be recognized as a separate taxpaying entity for purposes of entering into the sale transaction with the grantor and thereby creating a new basis in the assets purportedly purchased from the trust. In *Rothstein,* the Court of Appeals for the Second Circuit disagreed with the Service's assertion that the grantor could not claim a new basis by virtue of the purported sale. In Revenue Ruling 85–13, 1985–1 C.B. 184, the Service issued its nonacquiescence to this aspect of *Rothstein,* stating:

In *Rothstein v. United States,* 735 F.2d 704 (2d Cir.1984), the court considered a transaction that is in substance identical to the facts described in this ruling. The court held that the grantor was the owner of a trust under section 675(3) of the Code because by exchanging an unsecured note for the entire trust corpus, the grantor had indirectly borrowed the trust corpus. The court held further, however, that although the grantor must be treated as the owner of the trust, this means only that the grantor must include items of income, deduction, and credit attributable to the trust in computing the grantor's taxable income and credits, and that the trust must continue to be viewed as a separate taxpayer. The court held, therefore, that the transfer of trust corpus to the grantor in exchange for an unsecured promissory note was a sale and that the taxpayer acquired a cost basis in the assets.

In *Rothstein,* as in this case, section 671 of the Code requires that the grantor include in computing the grantor's tax liability all items of income, deduction, and credit of the trust as though the trust were not in existence during the period the grantor is treated as the owner. Section 1.671–3(a)(1) of the regulations. It is anomalous to suggest that Congress, in enacting the grantor trust provisions of the Code, intended that the existence of a trust would be ignored for purposes of attribution of income, deduction, and credit, and yet, retain its vitality as a separate entity capable of entering into a sales transaction with the grantor. The reason for attributing items of income, deduction, and credit to the grantor under section 671 is that, by exercising dominion and control over a trust, either by retaining a power over or an interest in the trust, or, as in this case, by dealing with the trust property for the grantor's benefit, the grantor has treated the trust property as though it were the grantor's property. The Service position of treating the owner of an entire trust as the owner of the trust's assets is, therefore, consistent with and supported by the rationale for attributing items of income, deduction, and credit to the grantor.

The court's decision in *Rothstein,* insofar as it holds that a trust owned by a grantor must be regarded as a separate taxpayer capable of engaging in sales transactions with the grantor, is not in accord with the views of the Service. Accordingly, the Service will not follow *Rothstein.*

The Service's position in *Rothstein* and Revenue Ruling 85–13 is consistent with its treatment of grantor trusts in other circumstances. For example, in Revenue Ruling 84–14, 1984–1 C.B. 147, Settlor created a 121 month Clifford trust into which Settlor transferred proven oil and gas properties. As directed by the terms of the trust instrument, the trustee allocated income of the trust to a depletion reserve in the full amount of the percentage depletion deduction allowable for Federal income tax purposes under section 613A. Because of Settlor's reversion, which applied with respect to both principal and accumulated income, Settlor was treated under section 677(a)(2) as owner of that portion of the trust that represented income accumulated for future distribution, in this case being the depletion reserve. Letter Ruling 8307022 involved similar facts. Pursuant to section 611(b)(3) and regulation section 1.611–1(c)(4), the allowable depletion deduction in that case was allocable to the trust in the amount of the depletion reserve created. As a consequence of section 677(a)(2) grantor trust treatment with respect to that portion of the trust, the full amount of the depletion deduction allocable to the depletion reserve was attributable to the grantor under section 677(a)(2). In both situations, the ultimate consideration was section 613A(c)(9), which specifies that a transfer of proven oil and gas producing properties after 1974 will result in a disqualification for the percentage depletion deduction. The issue presented in both rulings was whether the grantor's transfer of those proven producing properties into trust caused such a loss of the deduction. By virtue of the full deduction being attributable to the grantor under section 677(a)(2), the Service determined that no transfer had been made for purposes of section 613(c)(9)(A) and, as a consequence thereof, that the grantor would not become ineligible for percentage depletion by virtue of the transfer into trust. In addition, the Service similarly held that no disqualifying transfer would occur upon termination of the trust and reversion of the trust accumulated income and corpus to the grantor. As a result, no portion of the depletion deduction was lost in either the creation or subsequent termination of those grantor trusts.

In the easier situation of Revenue Ruling 85–45, 1985–1 C.B. 183, a principal personal residence was held in a marital deduction trust that created section 678 pseudo-grantor trust exposure to the surviving spouse as beneficiary thereof. The question in that situation was the availability of the section 121 exclusion of gain on the trust's sale of the residence. The Service applied consistent reasoning and treated the trust as if it did not exist, allowing application of section 121 as if the spouse were the outright owner of the residence. And in Revenue Ruling 66–159, 1966–1 C.B. 162, the same essential treatment was given for purposes of section 1034 because of grantor trust treatment under section 676.

Finally, in Revenue Ruling 85–158, 1985–2 C.B. 175, the grantor was a clearinghouse that created a trust to satisfy its financial obligations to customers, with section 677(a) grantor trust treatment flowing from this trust's discharge of the grantor's legal obligations. The issue raised was the deductibility of transfers made by the grantor to fund the trust. The Service, again applying consistent reasoning, denied a deduction on the initial transfer into trust because the trust, as a grantor trust, was ignored for all income tax purposes. Instead, if payments were made by the trust to customers, those payments would be treated as if the grantor made direct deductible distributions at that time.

Significant about these rulings is the Service's continuing recognition that treatment as a grantor trust is tantamount for most purposes to there being no trust entity at all. In some of these situations grantor trust treatment worked to the settlor's advantage; in *Rothstein* and Revenue Ruling 85–158 the effect to the taxpayer was not advantageous but the treatment was consistent. Consider the effect of grantor trust treatment in the following case, involving a situation of such common application that the decision represents a highly significant holding.

MADORIN v. COMMISSIONER

United States Tax Court, 1985.
84 T.C. 667.

DAWSON, CHIEF JUDGE:

* * *

Bernard Madorin (petitioner), as grantor, established four separate irrevocable trusts: the Miles Trust; the Mark Trust; the Melanie Trust; and the Bernard Descendant's Trust. A provision in the trust agreement gave the trustee the power to add one or more section 501(c)(3) charitable organizations as beneficiaries to any of the trusts. As a result of this provision, petitioner, the grantor, was treated as the owner of the four trusts pursuant to the provisions of section 674(a).

On petitioners' 1975 through 1977 Federal income tax returns they reported the following losses and income from the four trusts:

1975	Loss	($50,709.60)
1976	Loss	(20,753.92
1977	Income	1,544.28

On January 1, 1978, Coen, the trustee of the four trusts, irrevocably renounced his power to add beneficiaries to each trust. As a result, the trusts ceased to be grantor trusts and petitioner, the grantor, was no longer considered the owner of the trusts under section 674(a). Petitioners reported no gain or loss from the trusts on their 1978 return.

In August 1981, respondent sent petitioners a notice of deficiency. Relying on section 1.1001–2(c), example (5) (hereinafter referred to as example (5) or the regulation), respondent determined that the grantor was the owner of the partnership interests, and when the trusts ceased to be grantor trusts, there was a disposition of the trusts' assets by the grantor to the four trusts.

I. Validity of the Regulation

Petitioners contend that *Example 5* is invalid as an unreasonable interpretation of sections 671, 674, and 1001. Petitioners argue that the grantor of a trust should be "treated as the owner" only for the limited purpose of attributing to him items of income, deductions, and credits. This contention embodies petitioners' argument that (1) the trust should be treated as the partner and owner of the partnership interest, and (2) the trust maintains a separate transactional identity. According to petitioners, the interpretation of "owner" in example (*5*) to mean owner of the trust's assets is inconsistent with section 671. Respondent contends, however, that *Example 5* is a valid interpretation of the applicable statutory provisions. We agree with respondent.

* * *

The Supreme Court has ruled that statutory terms should be given their "usual, ordinary and everyday meaning." *Old Colony Railroad Co. v. Commissioner,* 284 U.S. 552, 561 (1932). We agree with respondent's contention that defining "owner * * * of a trust" under section 674 (and section 671) to mean owner of the trust's assets is consistent with the usual, ordinary, and everyday meaning of the word. Application of the grantor trust provisions generally results in nonrecognition of the trust (or a portion thereof) as an entity separate from the grantor. See *Estate of O'Connor v. Commissioner,* 69 T.C. 165, 174 (1977).

Petitioners set forth several arguments toward establishing that "owner" as defined in *Example 5* is inconsistent with the intended meaning of section 671. First, they appeal to the language of section 671. Section 671 states in part:

> Where it is specified in this subpart that the grantor or another person shall be treated as the owner of any portion of a trust, there shall then be included in computing the taxable income and credits of the grantor or the other person those items of income, deductions, and credits against tax of the trust which are attributable to that portion of the trust to the extent that such items would be taken into account under this chapter in computing taxable income or credits against the tax of an individual. * * *

Petitioners assert that the plain language of section 671 limits the attributes of ownership to the imputation of income, deductions, and credits only. We disagree. There is nothing on the face of the statute which tells us that that is the exclusive attribute of ownership. Section 671 specifies one result of being an "owner," but it does not specifically limit the meaning to that result.

Second, petitioners point to the legislative history of section 671. Petitioners assert that the Senate and House committee reports indicate that Congress intended to limit the attributes of ownership to the reporting of income, deductions, and credits. Petitioners argue that the stated purpose for enacting sections 671 through 679 was to bring together "the rules for determining taxability of trusts falling within the purview of section 22(a) as well as those covered by sections 166 and 167 [of the Internal Revenue Code of 1939]." As such "These provisions generally adopt the approach of the [Clifford] regulations (and the two provisions of existing law)." Petitioners state that prior to 1954, the existing grantor trust rules attributed only income to the grantor. They assert that congressional intent in using the word "owner" was to remedy the preexisting condition by also allowing deductions, losses, and credits attributable to the trust to flow through to the grantor's individual tax return along with the items of income.

We find petitioners' argument to be unpersuasive. The authorities cited in support of petitioners' argument do not specifically state that "owner" was used solely as a device to include items of deductions, losses, and other allowances. Absent a clear and unambiguous legislative directive in this matter, limiting the usage of the word "owner," we will apply the usual, ordinary, and everyday meaning of the word.

Third, petitioners argue that a grantor trust maintains its existence as a transactional entity separate and distinct from its grantor for Federal income tax purposes. In support of their contention, petitioners direct us to several cases. Petitioners' reliance upon these cases is misplaced.

Petitioners rely heavily upon *W & W Fertilizer Corp. v. United States,* 208 Ct.Cl. 443, 527 F.2d 621 (1975), in which the Court of Claims addressed the issue of whether a corporation's subchapter S status was automatically terminated when a shareholder transferred his stock into a grantor trust of which he was the grantor. The Commissioner contended that when the shareholder transferred his stock to the trust, the subchapter S election terminated because having a trust as a shareholder disqualified the corporation as a "small business corporation." The taxpayer, however, argued that a separate trust entity did not exist because the grantor was considered the "owner" of the trust corpus. After examining the language of sections 671 and 1371(a) and their legislative history, the court held that "ownership" extended only to the attribution of income, deductions, and credits from the trust.

In *W & W Fertilizer Corp.,* the court rendered its decision on the basis of the congressional policy inherent in restricting the ownership of subchapter S corporations to individuals and estates. The intent was to provide a narrow benefit to certain classes of taxpayers. A specific requirement of form was established. Hence, when the grantor trust was examined, its specific form rather than the substance was accepted. The court wrote:

The "grantor trust rules" treat the grantor as if he were the owner in cases where he has reserved to himself some of the powers normally attendant to outright ownership. Thus, their design is to expand the coverage of the taxing statute. On the other hand, Subchapter S was enacted as a remedial measure to relieve qualifying small business corporations of a tax otherwise payable. Section 1371(a)(2) limits the benefits of the Act to corporations whose stock is owned solely by individuals or estates. Where such a deliberately specific qualification is imposed, we must strictly apply it lest the narrow benefit intended by Congress be unduly broadened. Hence, the "grantor trust rules," with the very purpose of expansion, and the qualification requirements of section 1371(a), with their restrictive purpose, are not analogous, and their comparison is not supportive of the taxpayer in this case. [208 Ct.Cl. at 455; 527 F.2d at 627–628.]

We, therefore, think that *W & W Fertilizer Corp.* has limited applicability. It is an exceptional example where form of ownership controls in order that congressional intent be carried out. We are not concerned in the instant case with a statute that requires that a specific form be satisfied. Moreover, the effect of the decision in *W & W Fertilizer Corp.* is not that the grantor is not considered the owner of the trust corpus for other tax purposes but that there is a disqualification from a benefit that was not intended to be bestowed upon a particular form of ownership.

Petitioners also cite *Swanson v. Commissioner,* 518 F.2d 59 (8th Cir. 1975), affg. T.C. Memo. 1974–61, and *Estate of O'Connor v. Commissioner,* 69 T.C. 165 (1977). We agree with respondent, however, that these cases more aptly support respondent's position than that of petitioners.

In *Swanson v. Commissioner, supra,* life insurance policies on the grantor's life were transferred to grantor trusts for valuable consideration. The Commissioner contended that pursuant to section 101(a)(2) each of the trusts was required to recognize as gross income a proportionate amount of the proceeds of the policies that matured upon the grantor's death. The taxpayer claimed that the transfer was to the grantor/insured, and therefore, an exception to section 101(a)(2) had been met. At issue in *Swanson* was whether the trusts and the grantor/insured were the same entity per the definition of "owner" under section 671. While this Court did not directly address this issue, the Eighth Circuit, in its affirmance of our opinion held that "owner" under section 671 meant "owner" in the legal sense of the word, and held that the policies had in fact been transferred to the grantor/insured. The Eighth Circuit declared:

We cannot accept the government's contention that in this case Swanson, the grantor of the grantor-trusts, is not deemed the owner of the trusts for any purpose other than that of taxing trust income to him, and trusts, therefore, retain their identity as a separate tax entity under Section 101(a)(2)(B). [518 F.2d at 63.]

Estate of O'Connor v. Commissioner, supra, involved a testamentary marital trust in which the decedent's wife held certain rights which made the trust a grantor trust. Subsequent to the establishment of the trust, the decedent's wife assigned all of her interest in the trust to a section 501(c)(3) charitable foundation. One issue in *Estate of O'Connor* was whether the estate was entitled to a distribution deduction under section 661(a) for amounts passed through the marital trust to the foundation. The resolution of that issue turned upon whether the foundation/grantor should be treated as the "owner." If the foundation were treated as the "owner," then the trust entity would be ignored, and the estate would be deemed to have made its distributions directly to the foundation and not through the trust. This Court held that the trust was not a recognizable tax entity, and disallowed the estate's deduction. In so holding we stated:

> When a grantor or other person has certain powers in respect of trust property that are tantamount to dominion and control over such property, the Code "looks through" the trust form and deems such grantor or other person to be the owner of the trust property and attributes the trust income to such person. See secs. 671, et seq. By attributing such income directly to a grantor or other person, the Code, in effect, disregards the trust entity. [69 T.C. at 174.]

Petitioners also rely upon *Rothstein v. United States,* 735 F.2d 704 (2d Cir.1984), wherein the issues were whether the grantor of irrevocable trusts was (1) entitled to a new cost basis when he purchased shares of corporate stock from the trusts, which he originally contributed to the trusts, and (2) entitled to a deduction for interest paid to the trustee on the promissory note used to purchase the stock. The Commissioner contended that the step-up in basis and the interest deduction should be disallowed because the grantor/owner had in effect purchased the stock from himself and had paid interest to himself. The District Court held for the Commissioner, but the Second Circuit reversed. In reversing the District Court, the Second Circuit wrote:

> Section 671 makes it plain that it was not Congress's intention that the taxation of grantor/"owners" be governed by what might otherwise seem the sensible general principle that a taxpayer may not have meaningful dealings with himself. Rather, the statute envisions (1) that the income and deductions of the grantor and the trust will be computed in the normal fashion, the trust being treated as a fully independent tax-paying entity, and (2) that the relevant "items of income, deductions, and credits against tax" that would ordinarily appear on the trust's return will instead "be included in computing the taxable income and credits of the grantor." * * * Consistently with the objective of *Clifford* to prevent high-bracket taxpayers from shifting income to low-bracket trusts over which they retain or exercise excessive controls, § 671 dictates that, when the grantor is regarded as "owner," the trust's income shall be attributed to him—this and nothing more. [735 F.2d at 709; fn. ref. omitted.]

We need not comment on the result reached by the Second Circuit in *Rothstein,* nor on the rationale applied by the court in reaching such result. In that case, the court was concerned with a trust while it was still in effect, and the court had to decide whether the tax consequences for the taxpayer-grantor were governed by the specific provisions of sections 671 et seq. or whether to apply the general doctrine that he was to be treated as the owner. The court concluded that those consequences were governed by the specific statutory provisions. Since the transaction at issue in that case was different from that at issue in this case, the court was not concerned with the validity of any regulations. However, the case before us involves a significantly different issue. Here, we must decide what are the tax consequences when a grantor trust is terminated as such. There are no specific statutory provisions relating to such a transaction, and we do have a Treasury regulation dealing specifically with the transaction. Under such circumstances, it is not at all clear that the Second Circuit would apply its rationale to those facts, and we believe that our case is entirely distinguishable.

In the instant case, there is an interplay between section 671 and the partnership provisions of subchapter K, along with the recognition of gain or loss provisions of section 1001. These sections require the recognition of gain upon the sale or disposition of a partnership interest where the amount realized exceeds the adjusted basis of the partnership interest. The basis of a partnership interest includes the partner's share of partnership liabilities. Secs. 722 and 752. As the adjusted basis of the partnership interest is often reduced by partnership losses resulting from depreciation and other writeoffs, the goal is to force a recapture upon disposition. This is accomplished by including, as amounts realized, liabilities previously included in basis. *Crane v. Commissioner,* 331 U.S. 1 (1947).

This scheme of taxation is frustrated here if petitioners are allowed to escape recapture through a formalistic, piecemeal application of the law. The trusts were created with a built-in defect, causing them to be grantor trusts. The trusts then invested in a limited partnership interest that produced significant paper losses for the grantor. At the "cross-over" point, when the partnership began to generate income, the defect in the trusts was cured, and the tax burden was placed on the lower bracket beneficiaries. A formalistic approach, as suggested by petitioners, would result in a finding that ownership never changed hands—since the trusts have technically been the owners of the partnership interests—which would then allow petitioners to escape recapture.

Although *Edgar v. Commissioner,* 56 T.C. 717 (1971), was not cited by either party, we think it necessary to comment upon that opinion in light of the instant case. In *Edgar,* we held that a grantor who was also the income beneficiary of a grantor trust could not be treated as the owner of the corpus portion of the trust. Accordingly, we held that the loss generated by a partnership interest owned by the trust was not deductible on the grantor's individual tax return, because the loss belonged to the corpus portion of the trust, while the grantor was owner only of the income portion. The key issue in *Edgar* was the definition of "portion" in section 677. In *Edgar,* [it] was determined that under section 677 a grantor who was also an income beneficiary could only "own" the income portion of the trust. We did not imply in *Edgar* that it was not possible to own the entire trust, i.e., income and corpus. Our previous cases presuppose this. See, e.g., *Estate of O'Connor v. Commissioner,* 69 T.C. 165 (1977); *Swanson v. Commissioner,* T.C.Memo. 1974–61, affd. 518 F.2d 59 (8th Cir.1975). See also sec. 1.671–3(a)(1). In the instant case, the trust became a grantor trust by virtue of section 674(a):

> The grantor shall be treated as the owner of any portion of a trust in respect of which the beneficial enjoyment of the corpus or the income therefrom is subject to a power of disposition, exercisable by the grantor or a nonadverse party, or both, without the approval or consent of any adverse party.

Because the trustee, the nonadverse party, has a power of disposition over all of the corpus and income, the grantor must be considered owner of the whole trust, both income and corpus. *Edgar,* therefore, is distinguishable from the instant case.

Petitioners also contend that even if the grantor is the owner of the trust assets, a mere change in the trust's status is not a disposition triggering the recognition of gain. On brief, petitioners argue that a sale or other disposition did not occur, noting that no transfer documents were ever executed, nor was there any other method of conveyance at the time of trust perfection. While this is true in form, a different event took place in substance.

The situation at hand is analogous to cases dealing with part-sale, part-gift transactions. Under section 1.1001–1(e), if a transfer of property is in part a sale and in part a gift, the transferor must recognize gain to the extent his amount realized exceeds his adjusted basis in the property. This doctrine has been applied by the courts to situations where the transferred gift property is subject to a debt. To the extent the debt assumed by the transferee exceeds the transferor's adjusted basis in the property, a disposition is deemed to occur, and a corresponding gain must be recognized by the transferor. *Estate of Levine v. Commissioner,* 634 F.2d 12 (2d Cir.1980), affg. 72 T.C. 780 (1979); *Johnson v. Commissioner,* 495 F.2d 1079 (6th Cir.1974), affg. 59 T.C. 791 (1973). See *Diedrich v. Commissioner,* 457 U.S. 191 (1982). Here, the grantor's proportionate share of the partnership's nonrecourse liability exceeded his adjusted basis in the partnership interest. Therefore, a disposition is deemed to have occurred, and gain must be recognized.

Petitioners finally contend that, applying section 704(e) and section 1.704–1(e)(2) to the facts of the instant case, the trustee of the four trusts is the "partner" for purposes of subchapter K. Petitioners argue that since the grantor is not the partner for purposes of subchapter K, section 741, which governs the recognition of gain or loss by the "transferor partner" in the case of a sale or exchange of the transferor's interest in a partnership, is not applicable in the instant case. Respondent contends that an examination of the ownership tests contained in section 1.704–1(e)(2) is unnecessary and inappropriate in a grantor trust situation. Rather, respondent argues that section 671 et seq. (the grantor trust provisions) and the principle of substance over form result in the grantor's being the owner of the partnership interest.

We do not agree with respondent's contention that an examination of the ownership test of the family partnership rules is inappropriate in a grantor trust situation. Section 1.671–1(c) provides, in part, as follows:

> Except as provided in such subpart E, income of a trust is not included in computing the taxable income and credits of a grantor or another person solely on the grounds of his dominion and control over the trust. However, the provisions of subpart E do not apply in situations involving an assignment of future income, whether or not the assignment is to a trust. * * * *Nor are the rules as to family partnerships affected by the provisions of subpart E even though a partnership interest is held in trust.* * * * [Emphasis added.]

In addition, this Court has noted that the language of section 704(e) is sufficiently broad to cover nonfamily partnership situations even though section 704(e) is primarily directed towards "family partnerships." *Carriage Square, Inc. v. Commissioner,* 69 T.C. 119, 126 n. 4 (1977), citing *Evans v. Commissioner,* 54 T.C. 40, 51 (1970), affd. 447 F.2d 547 (7th Cir.1971).

We do agree, however, with respondent that the grantor trust provisions result in the grantor's being treated as the owner of the partnership interest. We do not accept petitioners' contention that the application of section 704(e) and the regulations thereunder overrides the grantor trust provisions and necessitates the opposite conclusion.

We do not think that a detailed analysis of the interrelationship of the grantor trust provisions and section 704(e) nor a reconciliation of the various tax principles involved would be helpful in resolving the issues in this case. In general, we think that where there exists a complex arrangement of tiered partnership interests placed in a grantor trust, both subchapter K and subpart E of subchapter J are applicable. In computing income, deductions, and credits of the various taxpayers involved, subchapter K is applied to the partnerships and subpart E operates to tax the grantor on the income, deductions, and credits. Thus in general, the grantor is treated as the owner of the partnership interest for tax purposes. Application of section 704(e) and the regulations thereunder to conclude that the trustee rather than the grantor is the owner of the partnership interest under section 704(e) is ineffective to change this scheme of taxation, because section 704(e) does not operate to override subchapter E.

SALE OF APPRECIATED "TWO YEAR" PROPERTY

Read Code section 644.

Under section 644, "quasi-grantor trust" treatment is imposed on any gain incurred with respect to appreciated assets sold by a trust within two years after any transferor's addition thereof to the trust. The rule was originally designed to compensate for the repeal in 1976 of the capital gains throwback rule and to prevent abuse whereby a transferor would contribute appreciated assets to a trust that would immediately sell the assets to incur gain at the trust's lower income tax rate for the year. Thus, under section 644(a)(1)(B), the rule is applicable only to assets in which fair market value exceeds adjusted basis immediately after the transfer. Because an asset purchased by the trust for full and adequate consideration would have a basis equal to fair market value, only assets transferred for less than full and adequate consideration (for example, by gift or by part-sale, part-gift) or assets with a substituted basis from such assets are subject to this rule, in this latter case by virtue of section 644(d)(2). Special rules under sections 644(d)(1) and 644(f) prevent avoidance of the two year period through installment sales, short sales or the use of puts and calls.

With the changes made in 1986 to the rate brackets that apply to trusts and estates, it is probable that, in most cases, section 644 addresses a game that will not be played very often. Indeed, if minimization of the tax rate is the only consideration, it is likely that the transferor's rate will be lower than the entity's. Nevertheless, there is no provision that prevents "reverse-644" gaming.

If section 644 does apply, it essentially imposes a tax under section 644(a)(2) on any recognized gain at the transferor's incremental tax rates, as if the transferor had sold the asset, with the character of the gain determined under section 644(c) as if sold by the transferor. Moreover, any gain subject to this special rule is limited under section 644(b) to the lesser of all the gain recognized by the trust or the built in appreciation as of the transfer into trust. Thus, the section 644 gain is limited to the excess of fair market value over adjusted basis immediately after the transfer (as adjusted for gift taxes incurred, as provided by section 1015(b)(6)). Any excess gain is taxed at the trust's rates.

The tax result under section 644 is not exactly the same as if no transfer into the trust had occurred and the transferor had sold the asset individually, because the trust actually pays any tax due. Because the trust pays the tax, section 641(c) excludes the gain so taxed from the trust's taxable income for purposes of computing the trust's other income taxes, thereby avoiding double taxation. The time for reporting gain on the sale also may be slightly different under section 644(a)(3) than if the transferor had sold the asset. For example, if the trust sold an asset in its year ending sometime during the transferor's tax year, with taxes being due from the trust before the transferor's year ended, the computation of taxes the transferor would have incurred would be impossible. Consequently, the gain is taxed to the trust in its year that *begins* in the transferor's year during which sale occurred. For example, if the transferor is on a June 30 fiscal year but the trust is on a calendar year, a sale after June 30 of year one would be taxed to the trust for the year beginning January 1 of year two and ending December 31 of year two. Because of the delay in paying the tax necessitated thereby, interest is imposed under section 644(a)(2)(B) at the statutory rate specified by section 6621. In most cases both the trust and the transferor will be on a calendar year and this problem will not arise. Finally, for obvious reasons, under sections 644(e)(1) and 644(e)(4), the rule has no application if the transferor is deceased at the time of the sale.

S CORPORATION SHAREHOLDERS

Read Code section 1361.

Though not a part of Subchapter J, the income tax consequences under Subchapter S of the use of trusts or estates as a section 1361(a) S Corporation shareholder is of concern in fiduciary administration. A qualified S Corporation for Federal income tax purposes may have an estate as a shareholder, but only four types of trust may qualify under section 1361(c)(2) as permissible S Corporation shareholders.

For example, any voting trust is a permissible S Corporation shareholder under section 1361(c)(2)(A)(iv), with each beneficiary of the trust being regarded as a shareholder of the corporation under section 1361(c)(2)(B)(iv) for purposes of complying with the qualified S Corporation shareholder limitation under section 1361(b)(1)(A). Second, under section 1361(c)(2)(A)(iii), any trust is a qualifying shareholder for up to 60 days with respect to any stock received pursuant to the terms of a Will, with section 1361(c)(2)(B)(iii) treating the distributing estate as the qualifying shareholder during the 60 day period. Permitted is retention for 60 days after "transfer" of stock pursuant to the terms of a Will, but no provision specifies whether "transfer" is effective upon actual conveyance and receipt by the trust or only upon later reflection on the corporation's books. Because the administrative acts of the corporation or its transfer agent should not affect the qualification of an S Corporation, actual transfer and receipt is presumably the intended measuring event. It might also be questioned whether stock would qualify if transferred to one trust by the terms of another trust operating as a decedent's primary estate planning document, rather than by the terms of an actual "Will." While this situation may in many cases be covered under section 1361(c)(2)(A)(ii), it is quite possible to fail to meet the technical requirements of that provision but still be in the analogous situation to an estate making the transfer. Because the apparent intent of both subparagraphs (A)(ii) and (A)(iii) is to grant a transition period following the death or termination of a qualified shareholder, it should be held that a previously qualifying trust that makes distribution to a following trust shall be regarded the same as an estate making distribution pursuant to a "Will" for purposes of section 1361(c)(2)(A)(iii).

Third, under section 1361(c)(2)(A)(i), many grantor trusts will qualify as permissible S Corporation shareholders if entirely subject to the grantor trust provisions of Subpart E of Subchapter J. Because foreign trusts cannot qualify as S Corporation shareholders due to their exclusion under the last sentence of section 1361(c)(2)(A), only trusts subject to sections 673 to 678 are relevant (excluding for these purposes section 679, which is a part of Subpart E), and only if all of the trust "is treated . . . as owned by an individual who is a citizen or resident of the United States." By use of the singular, "an individual," it also seems likely that a multiple grantor trust cannot qualify, even if all of the trust is taxed as a grantor trust, unless the trust may be regarded as several separate trusts under the last sentence of section 1361(d)(3)(B). Lending support to a theory that only a single grantor trust will qualify is use of the singular "owner" and "shareholder" therein.

If the trust does qualify then, under section 1361(c)(2)(B)(i), the deemed owner of the trust for income tax purposes is regarded as the shareholder for S Corporation qualification purposes. In addition, if such a trust continues in existence after the death of the individual taxed as its owner under Subpart E, it will continue to qualify as an S Corporation shareholder for at least 60 days (and potentially for two years) thereafter, pursuant to section 1361(c)(2)(A)(ii), with the two year period being applicable if the entire corpus is includible in the deemed owner's gross estate for Federal estate tax purposes. In determining whether the trust continues in existence after the individual's death, administrative actions such as division into several separate following shares or trusts should be disregarded under Treasury Regulation section 1.641(b)–3(b) until the original trust is regarded as having terminated under state law. Under section 1361(c)(2)(B)(ii), the qualifying estate is regarded as the shareholder for S Corporation purposes.

Finally, upon filing a requisite election,[8] a "Qualified Subchapter S Trust" becomes a permissible S Corporation shareholder under section 1361(d)(1), with the election being retroactive under section 1361(d)(2)(D) for up to two months and 15 days at the electing trust's option. To qualify under section 1361(d)(3), (1) the trust must have only one current beneficiary of either income or principal,[9] (2) all fiduciary accounting income must be required to be or actually distributed

8. Code section 1361(d)(2)(B) requires a separate election for each S Corporation represented by shares held in the trust, but requires only one election per trust, regardless of any change of beneficiaries. Once made, an election is made revocable under section 1361(d)(2)(C) only with the consent of the Commissioner or upon the affirmative act of a new beneficiary within 60 days of becoming the beneficiary. See section 1361(d)(2)(B)(ii) and Temporary Treasury Regulation section 18.1361–1(b). Formal requirements of the election itself may be found in Temporary Treasury Regulation section 18.1361–1(a) and Proposed Treasury Regulation section 1.1361–1A.

9. In Letter Ruling 8514017 the Service conditioned its determination that a trust was a Qualified Subchapter S Trust on distributions of trust income not making the trustee a pseudo-grantor under section 678(c), by virtue of the discharge of obligation theory discussed at page 256.

currently to the beneficiary, (3) the beneficiary must be a citizen or resident of the United States and, (4) if the trust terminates during the beneficiary's life, all trust assets must be distributed to the beneficiary. For purposes of satisfying the first requirement, the separate share rule of section 663(c) is applicable and the 65 day rule of section 663(b) should be applicable for purposes of the second requirement. The effect of an election is to cause the trust to be regarded as a grantor trust for purposes of qualification under section 1361(d)(1)(A) (which causes the trust to be regarded as a section 1361(c)(2)(A)(i) grantor trust) and to cause taxation to the beneficiary of trust income and deductions attributable to the S Corporation under section 1361(d)(1)(B) (which specifies that the beneficiary is to be regarded as the owner under section 678 of that portion of the trust that consists of S Corporation stock as to which the requisite election has been made).

Chapter Nine

FOREIGN TRUSTS AND ESTATES

Read Code sections 668 & 679.

United States citizen or resident grantors and beneficiaries of foreign trusts and estates suffer special disadvantageous tax consequences by virtue of approximately half a dozen rules unique to the income taxation of foreign trusts and estates. Because nonresident aliens are not United States income taxable as grantors or beneficiaries of foreign trusts and estates, of concern here are only grantors and beneficiaries who are "United States persons" as defined in section 7701(a)(30), meaning citizens or residents of the United States. Section 7701(a)(31) defines a "foreign trust" or "foreign estate" as one the income of which is not includible in gross income and section 871 supplies a rule that only nondomestic income of a nonresident alien is not includible in gross income. See Treasury Regulation section 1.871-1(a). Thus, a trust or estate is "foreign" only if (1) it is a nonresident alien and (2) its income is not includible in gross income because it is from sources outside the United States that are not connected with the conduct of a trade or business within the United States.

To determine whether a trust or estate is a nonresident alien requires a balancing of factors such as the situs of the trust or estate, the place of its creation and administration, and the nationality and residence of the trustee, personal representative, grantor and beneficiaries. An exhaustive exegesis of the various elements contained in the definition of a foreign trust or estate may be found in Zaritsky, 427 Tax Mgmt. (BNA) Foreign Trusts, Estates and Beneficiaries A-6 to A-9 (1981) [herein cited as Zaritsky].

GRANTOR TRUST CONSEQUENCES

Most important among the deviations from the familiar rules applicable to domestic trusts and estates is section 679, a special grantor trust provision treating the transferor of property to a foreign trust as the owner of the income of that foreign trust if the trust has at least one United States citizen or resident beneficiary. Effectively overriding any other provision for the taxation of trust income, section 679 is triggered by the actual or deemed existence of a proper beneficiary. By the expansive rule of section 679(c)(1), a trust is deemed to have a United States beneficiary if any part of the income or principal may be accumulated for or paid to or for the benefit of a United States citizen or resident, including upon termination of the trust during the taxable year or pursuant to exercise of any power of appointment. See Staff of the Joint Committee on Taxation, 94th Cong., 2d Sess., General Explanation of the Tax Reform Act of 1976 at 222 (Comm.Print 1976) [the "Bluebook"]. In addition, under section 679(c)(2), attribution rules may treat a foreign corporation, partnership, trust or estate as a United States beneficiary if United States beneficiaries own sufficient stock in the corporation, are partners of the partnership or are beneficiaries of the trust or estate. In addition, if a foreign trust acquires a United States beneficiary some time after its creation (for example, by marriage, birth or immigration of a trust beneficiary), section 679 will be triggered for future income and, under section 679(b), the grantor will be taxed in that year upon all previously undistributed net income in the transferred portion of the trust.

If applicable, section 679 applies to any portion of a trust transferred directly or indirectly [1] by a United States citizen or resident prior to death. Section 679(a)(2)(A) excepts transfers made by reason of a transferor's death, and the special rule has no application after a transferor's death. See Bluebook at 222. An exception applies under section 679(a)(2)(B) if the transfer was a sale or exchange for fair market value, causing immediate realization and either immediate or installment recognition of the full gain or loss in transferred assets. In the absence of incurring such gain, the grantor will be liable for a 35 percent excise tax imposed under section 1491 on the gain element of property transferred to a foreign trust. Alternatively, a grantor may elect under section 1057 to treat the transfer as a sale or exchange for purposes of realizing any gain in the transferred assets.

SPECIAL RULES FOR NONGRANTOR TRUSTS AND ESTATES

With respect to any portion of a foreign estate, or a foreign trust as to which the grantor is not taxable as owner (for example, because of death, or because transfer to the trust qualified under section 679(a)(2)(B)), several additional special rules affect the tax consequences of the trust or estate to its beneficiaries. First, distributable net income of the trust or estate is computed differently than in a domestic trust or estate. Minor deviations from the normal computation of DNI are itemized in section 643(a)(6) and include (1) a provision directing inclusion of net foreign source income (as reduced by deductions allocable

1. The Bluebook at 222 makes reference to both direct transfers and such indirect transfers as having a foreign trust borrow funds upon a loan, the repayment of which is guaranteed by a United States person.

thereto), (2) an exception to application of the foreign treaty exempt income rules of section 894, and (3) special rules relating to capital gains.

The most important deviation, however, is inclusion in DNI of all net capital gains of the trust or estate (without benefit of any deduction for long term capital gains),[2] even if those gains are allocated to principal. This treatment differs from the treatment of domestic trusts and estates under section 643(a)(3), which excludes from DNI any capital gains that are allocable to principal. The effect of this deviation is felt with respect to the accumulation distribution and throwback rules and their application to foreign trusts (but not foreign estates, which are not subject to Subpart D) because the inclusion of gain increases DNI, which increases UNI under section 665(a) for future accumulation distribution computation purposes (if those gains are allocated to principal rather than currently paid out, which would normally be the case). While capital gains distributed currently by either a foreign or a domestic trust retain their character as capital gain under sections 652(b) and 662(b), capital gain allocated to principal may lose its special character if subsequently carried out to a beneficiary by an accumulation distribution.

In the case of an accumulation distribution to a nonresident alien, section 667(e) preserves the special character of the gain, but all other distributions are subject to the parenthetical provision in the first sentence of section 667(a), which has the effect of denying a character pass through on any accumulation distribution except of tax exempt income. This is completely contrary to the consequence in a domestic trust, in which capital gain allocated to principal is not thereafter carried back out to beneficiaries by accumulation distributions because the gain is not includible in DNI or, thus, in UNI. By virtue of the exclusion from DNI of capital gain in a domestic trust, this means the gain is taxed as gain to the trust. In a foreign trust, however, because the gain loses its character if subsequently carried out to the beneficiary, inclusion of the gain in DNI means that it can be carried out to the beneficiary by a subsequent accumulation distribution and taxed without capital gain treatment. See the Bluebook at 225. Consequently, foreign trusts with United States beneficiaries pose disfavorable capital gain consequences.

To exacerbate this treatment of foreign trusts (but, again, not foreign estates), two added deviations deny both the minority exception of the penultimate sentence of section 665(b) and the section 665(e)(1) pre–1969 exception to the accumulation distribution and throwback rules.

Further negatively affecting the beneficiaries of a foreign trust is the section 667(a)(3) special (and, by section 668(c)(1), nondeductible) six

2. The deduction permitted before repeal of section 1202 was specifically denied, except in the case of accumulation distributions of pre–1976 taxable year undistributed net income, as to which the deduction is still permitted under section 643(a)(6)(D).

percent annual simple interest[3] excise assessed on the throwback tax computed on accumulation distributions. The interest charge is determined on the basis of an average number of years to which the accumulation distribution is attributable. As an example, if income deemed distributed in 1985 was accumulated in years 1977, 1978 and 1979, a fraction would be produced with the aggregate number of years accumulation was deferred as the numerator and the number of accumulation years as the denominator, in this case being $7 + 6 + 5 \div 3 = 18 \div 3 = 6$. For computation purposes, determining the number of years each accumulation was deferred involves counting the full year in which the income was accumulated but not the year of distribution. For example, under section 668(a)(1), 1977 to 1984 is seven years, even if the accumulation was late in 1977 and the distribution was early in 1984. Moreover, under section 668(c)(2), pre–1977 accumulations are deemed to have been made in the first taxable year of the trust beginning after 1976.

Some modest relief may be available, however, by virtue of the introduction to the de minimis rule of section 667(b)(3) (reading "for purposes of paragraph (1)"), by which it appears that the computation of the average under section 668(a) includes de minimis years. If this is correct, a trustee could intentionally make a minor accumulation in a year just prior to the year of an expected accumulation distribution so as to increase both the numerator and denominator by one, which would have the effect of reducing the average number of accumulation years determined under the computation. For example, in the computation example above, the numerator would be 19, the denominator 4, and the average reduced to less than the 6 previously determined, thereby reducing the total excise imposed.

In assessing interest, partial years count as full years. Thus, if an accumulation were made late in year one and distribution were made early in year two, the accumulation would be assessed a full year's interest. Bluebook at 224. By section 668(b), the added interest charge is limited only to an amount that, when added to taxes otherwise generated on the accumulation distribution, may be no greater than the beneficiary's actual receipts from the trust in the year of distribution. Moreover, in computing the throwback tax to be imposed on the recipient of an accumulation distribution, foreign taxes determined under section 665(d)(2) imposed on the trust in the year of, and attributable to, the accumulation are applied differently than are other similar taxes. Unlike the normal application of taxes paid against the final amount of throwback tax computed under section 667, the credit for foreign taxes is instead applied under section 667(d)(1)(A) against the increase in taxes prior to determination of the average increase in those taxes. Moreover, section 667(d)(1)(B) grants the beneficiary an option to apply the taxes as a deduction in lieu of the credit in

3. Interest is not compounded. Bluebook at 224.

computing the beneficiary's taxable income. For a detailed explanation of the operation of section 667(d), see Zaritsky at A–53 to A–56. Finally, special returns and reporting requirements are imposed with respect to foreign trusts.[4]

4. See Zaritsky at A–57 to A–59. Included among the special returns required are Forms 926, 3520 and 3520A (relating to settlors of and transferors to foreign trusts), Form 1040NR (nonresident alien income tax return) and the reports required by the Foreign Investment in Real Property Tax Act of 1980 under section 6039C.

Appendix A

UNIFORM PRINCIPAL AND INCOME ACT

REVISED 1962 ACT

Sec.

§ 1. [Definitions]

As used in this Act:

(1) "income beneficiary" means the person to whom income is presently payable or for whom it is accumulated for distribution as income;

(2) "inventory value" means the cost of property purchased by the trustee and the market value of other property at the time it became subject to the trust, but in the case of a testamentary trust the trustee may use any value finally determined for the purposes of an estate or inheritance tax;

(3) "remainderman" means the person entitled to principal, including income which has been accumulated and added to principal;

(4) "trustee" means an original trustee and any successor or added trustee.

§ 2. [Duty of Trustee as to Receipts and Expenditure]

(a) A trust shall be administered with due regard to the respective interests of income beneficiaries and remaindermen. A trust is so administered with respect to the allocation of receipts and expenditures if a receipt is credited or an expenditure is charged to income or principal or partly to each—

(1) in accordance with the terms of the trust instrument, notwithstanding contrary provisions of this Act;

(2) in the absence of any contrary terms of the trust instrument, in accordance with the provisions of this Act; or

(3) if neither of the preceding rules of administration is applicable, in accordance with what is reasonable and equitable in view of the interests of those entitled to income as well as of those entitled to principal, and in view of the manner in which men of ordinary prudence, discretion and judgment would act in the management of their own affairs.

(b) If the trust instrument gives the trustee discretion in crediting a receipt or charging an expenditure to income or principal or partly to each, no inference of imprudence or partiality arises from the fact that the trustee has made an allocation contrary to a provision of this Act.

§ 3. [Income; Principal; Charges]

(a) Income is the return in money or property derived from the use of principal, including return received as

(1) rent of real or personal property, including sums received for cancellation or renewal of a lease;

(2) interest on money lent, including sums received as consideration for the privilege of prepayment of principal except as provided in section 7 on bond premium and bond discount;

(3) income earned during administration of a decedent's estate as provided in section 5;

(4) corporate distributions as provided in section 6;

(5) accrued increment on bonds or other obligations issued at discount as provided in section 7;

(6) receipts from business and farming operations as provided in section 8;

(7) receipts from disposition of natural resources as provided in sections 9 and 10;

(8) receipts from other principal subject to depletion as provided in section 11;

(9) receipts from disposition of underproductive property as provided in section 12.

(b) Principal is the property which has been set aside by the owner or the person legally empowered so that it is held in trust eventually to be delivered to a remainderman while the return or use of the principal is in the meantime taken or received by or held for accumulation for an income beneficiary. Principal includes

(1) consideration received by the trustee on the sale or other transfer of principal or on repayment of a loan or as a refund or replacement or change in the form of principal;

(2) proceeds of property taken on eminent domain proceedings;

(3) proceeds of insurance upon property forming part of the principal except proceeds of insurance upon a separate interest of an income beneficiary;

(4) stock dividends, receipts on liquidation of a corporation, and other corporate distributions as provided in section 6;

(5) receipts from the disposition of corporate securities as provided in section 7;

(6) royalties and other receipts from disposition of natural resources as provided in sections 9 and 10;

(7) receipts from other principal subject to depletion as provided in section 11;

(8) any profit resulting from any change in the form of principal except as provided in section 12 on underproductive property;

(9) receipts from disposition of underproductive property as provided in section 12;

(10) any allowances for depreciation established under sections 8 and 13(a)(2).

(c) After determining income and principal in accordance with the terms of the trust instrument or of this Act, the trustee shall charge to income or principal expenses and other charges as provided in section 13.

§ 4. [When Right to Income Arises; Apportionment of Income]

(a) An income beneficiary is entitled to income from the date specified in the trust instrument, or, if none is specified, from the date an asset becomes subject to the trust. In the case of an asset becoming subject to a trust by reason of a will, it becomes subject to the trust as of the date of the death of the testator even though there is an intervening period of administration of the testator's estate.

(b) In the administration of a decedent's estate or an asset becoming subject to a trust by reason of a will

(1) receipts due but not paid at the date of death of the testator are principal;

(2) receipts in the form of periodic payments (other than corporate distributions to stockholders), including rent, interest, or annu-

ities, not due at the date of the death of the testator shall be treated as accruing from day to day. That portion of the receipt accruing before the date of death is principal, and the balance is income.

(c) In all other cases, any receipt from an income producing asset is income even though the receipt was earned or accrued in whole or in part before the date when the asset became subject to the trust.

(d) On termination of an income interest, the income beneficiary whose interest is terminated, or his estate, is entitled to

(1) income undistributed on the date of termination;

(2) income due but not paid to the trustee on the date of termination;

(3) income in the form of periodic payments (other than corporate distributions to stockholders), including rent, interest, or annuities, not due on the date of termination, accrued from day to day.

(e) Corporate distributions to stockholders shall be treated as due on the day fixed by the corporation for determination of stockholders of record entitled to distribution or, if no date is fixed, on the date of declaration of the distribution by the corporation.

§ 5. [Income Earned During Administration of a Decedent's Estate]

(a) Unless the will otherwise provides and subject to subsection (b), all expenses incurred in connection with the settlement of a decedent's estate, including debts, funeral expenses, estate taxes, interest and penalties concerning taxes, family allowances, fees of attorneys and personal representatives, and court costs shall be charged against the principal of the estate.

(b) Unless the will otherwise provides, income from the assets of a decedent's estate after the death of the testator and before distribution, including income from property used to discharge liabilities, shall be determined in accordance with the rules applicable to a trustee under this Act and distributed as follows:

(1) to specific legatees and devisees, the income from the property bequeathed or devised to them respectively, less taxes, ordinary repairs, and other expenses of management and operation of the property, and an appropriate portion of interest accrued since the death of the testator and of taxes imposed on income (excluding taxes on capital gains) which accrue during the period of administration;

(2) to all other legatees and devisees, except legatees of pecuniary bequests not in trust, the balance of the income, less the balance of taxes, ordinary repairs, and other expenses of management and operation of all property from which the estate is entitled to income, interest accrued since the death of the testator, and taxes imposed on income (excluding taxes on capital gains) which

accrue during the period of administration, in proportion to their respective interests in the undistributed assets of the estate computed at times of distribution on the basis of inventory value.

(c) Income received by a trustee under subsection (b) shall be treated as income of the trust.

§ 6. [Corporate Distributions]

(a) Corporate distributions of shares of the distributing corporation, including distributions in the form of a stock split or stock dividend, are principal. A right to subscribe to shares or other securities issued by the distributing corporation accruing to stockholders on account of their stock ownership and the proceeds of any sale of the right are principal.

(b) Except to the extent that the corporation indicates that some part of a corporate distribution is a settlement of preferred or guaranteed dividends accrued since the trustee became a stockholder or is in lieu of an ordinary cash dividend, a corporate distribution is principal if the distribution is pursuant to

(1) a call of shares;

(2) a merger, consolidation, reorganization, or other plan by which assets of the corporation are required by another corporation; or

(3) a total or partial liquidation of the corporation, including any distribution which the corporation indicates is a distribution in total or partial liquidation or any distribution of assets, other than cash, pursuant to a court decree or final administrative order by a government agency ordering distribution of the particular assets.

(c) Distributions made from ordinary income by a regulated investment company or by a trust qualifying and electing to be taxed under federal law as a real estate investment trust are income. All other distributions made by the company or trust, including distributions from capital gains, depreciation, or depletion, whether in the form of cash or an option to take new stock or cash or an option to purchase additional shares, are principal.

(d) Except as provided in subsections (a), (b), and (c), all corporate distributions are income, including cash dividends, distributions of or rights to subscribe to shares or securities or obligations of corporations other than the distributing corporation, and the proceeds of the rights or property distributions. Except as provided in subsections (b) and (c), if the distributing corporation gives a stockholder an option to receive a distribution either in cash or in its own shares, the distribution chosen is income.

(e) The trustee may rely upon any statement of the distributing corporation as to any fact relevant under any provision of this Act concerning the source or character of dividends or distributions of corporate assets.

§ 7. [Bond Premium and Discount]

(a) Bonds or other obligations for the payment of money are principal at their inventory value, except as provided in subsection (b) for discount bonds. No provision shall be made for amortization of bond premiums or for accumulation for discount. The proceeds of sale, redemption, or other disposition of the bonds or obligations are principal.

(b) The increment in value of a bond or other obligation for the payment of money payable at a future time in accordance with a fixed schedule of appreciation in excess of the price at which it was issued is distributable as income. The increment in value is distributable to the beneficiary who was the income beneficiary at the time of increment from the first principal cash available or, if none is available, when realized by sale, redemption, or other disposition. Whenever unrealized increment is distributed as income but out of principal, the principal shall be reimbursed for the increment when realized.

§ 8. [Business and Farming Operations]

(a) If a trustee uses any part of the principal in the continuance of a business of which the settlor was a sole proprietor or a partner, the net profits of the business, computed in accordance with generally accepted accounting principles for a comparable business, are income. If a loss results in any fiscal or calendar year, the loss falls on principal and shall not be carried into any other fiscal or calendar year for purposes of calculating net income.

(b) Generally accepted accounting principles shall be used to determine income from an agricultural or farming operation, including the raising of animals or the operation of a nursery.

§ 9. [Disposition of Natural Resources]

(a) If any part of the principal consists of a right to receive royalties, overriding or limited royalties, working interests, production payments, net profit interests, or other interests in minerals or other natural resources in, on or under land, the receipts from taking the natural resources from the land shall be allocated as follows:

(1) If received as rent on a lease or extension payments on a lease, the receipts are income.

(2) If received from a production payment, the receipts are income to the extent of any factor for interest or its equivalent provided in the governing instrument. There shall be allocated to principal the fraction of the balance of the receipts which the unrecovered cost of the production payment bears to the balance owed on the production payment, exclusive of any factor for interest or its equivalent. The receipts not allocated to principal are income.

(3) If received as a royalty, overriding or limited royalty, or bonus, or from a working, net profit, or any other interest in minerals or other natural resources, receipts not provided for in the preceding paragraphs of this section shall be apportioned on a yearly basis in accordance with this paragraph whether or not any natural resource was being taken from the land at the time the trust was established. Twenty-seven and one-half per cent of the gross receipts (but not to exceed 50% of the net receipts remaining after payment of all expenses, direct and indirect, computed without allowance for depletion) shall be added to principal as an allowance for depletion. The balance of the gross receipts, after payment therefrom of all expenses, direct and indirect, is income.

(b) If a trustee, on the effective date of this Act, held an item of depletable property of a type specified in this section he shall allocate receipts from the property in the manner used before the effective date of this Act, but as to all depletable property acquired after the effective date of this Act by an existing or new trust, the method of allocation provided herein shall be used.

(c) This section does not apply to timber, water, soil, sod, dirt, turf, or mosses.

§ 10. [Timber]

If any part of the principal consists of land from which merchantable timber may be removed, the receipts from taking the timber from the land shall be allocated in accordance with section 2(a)(3).

§ 11. [Other Property Subject to Depletion]

Except as provided in sections 9 and 10, if the principal consists of property subject to depletion, including leaseholds, patents, copyrights, royalty rights, and rights to receive payments on a contract for deferred compensation, receipts from the property, not in excess of 5% per year of its inventory value, are income, and the balance is principal.

§ 12. [Underproductive Property]

(a) Except as otherwise provided in this section, a portion of the net proceeds of sale of any part of principal which has not produced an average net income of at least 1% per year of its inventory value for more than a year (including as income the value of any beneficial use of the property by the income beneficiary) shall be treated as delayed income to which the income beneficiary is entitled as provided in this section. The net proceeds of sale are the gross proceeds received, including the value of any property received in substitution for the property disposed of, less the expenses, including capital gains tax, if any, incurred in disposition and less any carrying charges paid while the property was underproductive.

(b) The sum allocated as delayed income is the difference between the net proceeds and the amount which, had it been invested at simple interest at [4%] per year while the property was underproductive, would have produced the net proceeds. This sum, plus any carrying charges and expenses previously charged against income while the property was underproductive, less any income received by the income beneficiary from the property and less the value of any beneficial use of the property by the income beneficiary, is income, and the balance is principal.

(c) An income beneficiary or his estate is entitled to delayed income under this section as if it accrued from day to day during the time he was a beneficiary.

(d) If principal subject to this section is disposed of by conversion into property which cannot be apportioned easily, including land or mortgages (for example, realty acquired by or in lieu of foreclosure), the income beneficiary is entitled to the net income from any property or obligation into which the original principal is converted while the substituted property or obligation is held. If within 5 years after the conversion the substituted property has not been further converted into easily apportionable property, no allocation as provided in this section shall be made.

§ 13. [Charges Against Income and Principal]

(a) The following charges shall be made against income:

(1) ordinary expenses incurred in connection with the administration, management, or preservation of the trust property, including regularly recurring taxes assessed against any portion of the principal, water rates, premiums on insurance taken upon the interests of the income beneficiary, remainderman, or trustee, interest paid by the trustee, and ordinary repairs;

(2) a reasonable allowance for depreciation on property subject to depreciation under generally accepted accounting principles, but no allowance shall be made for depreciation of that portion of any real property used by a beneficiary as a residence or for depreciation of any property held by the trustee on the effective date of this Act for which the trustee is not then making an allowance for depreciation;

(3) one-half of court costs, attorney's fees, and other fees on periodic judicial accounting, unless the court directs otherwise;

(4) court costs, attorney's fees, and other fees on other accountings or judicial proceedings if the matter primarily concerns the income interest, unless the court directs otherwise;

(5) one-half of the trustee's regular compensation, whether based on a percentage of principal or income, and all expenses reasonably incurred for current management of principal and application of income;

(6) any tax levied upon receipts defined as income under this Act or the trust instrument and payable by the trustee.

(b) If charges against income are of unusual amount, the trustee may by means of reserves or other reasonable means charge them over a reasonable period of time and withhold from distribution sufficient sums to regularize distributions.

(c) The following charges shall be made against principal:

(1) trustee's compensation not chargeable to income under subsections (a)(4) and (a)(5), special compensation of trustees, expenses reasonably incurred in connection with principal, court costs and attorney's fees primarily concerning matters of principal, and trustee's compensation computed on principal as an acceptance, distribution, or termination fee;

(2) charges not provided for in subsection (a), including the cost of investing and reinvesting principal, the payments on principal of an indebtedness (including a mortgage amortized by periodic payments of principal), expenses for preparation of property for rental or sale, and, unless the court directs otherwise, expenses incurred in maintaining or defending any action to construe the trust or protect it or the property or assure the title of any trust property;

(3) extraordinary repairs or expenses incurred in making a capital improvement to principal, including special assessments, but, a trustee may establish an allowance for depreciation out of income to the extent permitted by subsection (a)(2) and by section 8;

(4) any tax levied upon profit, gain, or other receipts allocated to principal notwithstanding denomination of the tax as an income tax by the taxing authority;

(5) if an estate or inheritance tax is levied in respect of a trust in which both an income beneficiary and a remainderman have an interest, any amount apportioned to the trust, including interest and penalties, even though the income beneficiary also has rights in the principal.

(d) Regularly recurring charges payable from income shall be apportioned to the same extent and in the same manner that income is apportioned under section 4.

§ 14. [Application of Act]

Except as specifically provided in the trust instrument or the will or in this Act, this Act shall apply to any receipt or expense received or incurred after the effective date of this Act by any trust or decedent's estate whether established before or after the effective date of this Act and whether the asset involved was acquired by the trustee before or after the effective date of this Act.

§ 15. [Uniformity of Interpretation]

This Act shall be so construed as to effectuate its general purpose to make uniform the law of those states which enact it.

§ 16. [Short Title]

This Act may be cited as the Revised Uniform Principal and Income Act.

§ 17. [Severability]

If any provision of this Act or the application thereof to any person or circumstance is held invalid, the invalidity does not affect other provisions or applications of the Act which can be given effect without the invalid provision or application and to this end the provisions of this Act are severable.

Appendix B

SUBCHAPTER J CODE AND REGULATIONS

SUBCHAPTER J—ESTATES, TRUSTS, BENEFICIARIES, AND DECEDENTS

Part

I. Estates, trusts, and beneficiaries.
II. Income in respect of decedents.

PART I—ESTATES, TRUSTS, AND BENEFICIARIES

Subpart

A. General rules for taxation of estates and trusts.
B. Trusts which distribute current income only.
C. Estates and trusts which may accumulate income or which distribute corpus.
D. Treatment of excess distributions by trusts.
E. Grantors and others treated as substantial owners.
F. Miscellaneous.

Subpart A—General Rules for Taxation of Estates and Trusts

§ 641. Imposition of tax

(a) Application of tax.—The tax imposed by section 1(e) shall apply to the taxable income of estates or of any kind of property held in trust, including—

(1) income accumulated in trust for the benefit of unborn or unascertained persons or persons with contingent interests, and income accumulated or held for future distribution under the terms of the will or trust;

(2) income which is to be distributed currently by the fiduciary to the beneficiaries, and income collected by a guardian of an infant which is to be held or distributed as the court may direct;

(3) income received by estates of deceased persons during the period of administration or settlement of the estate; and

(4) income which, in the discretion of the fiduciary, may be either distributed to the beneficiaries or accumulated.

(b) Computation and payment.—The taxable income of an estate or trust shall be computed in the same manner as in the case of an individual, except as otherwise provided in this part. The tax shall be computed on such taxable income and shall be paid by the fiduciary.

(c) Exclusion of includible gain from taxable income.—

(1) General rule.—For purposes of this part, the taxable income of a trust does not include the amount of any includible gain as defined in section 644(b) reduced by any deductions properly allocable thereto.

(2) Cross reference.—

For the taxation of any includible gain, see section 644.

§ 642. Special rules for credits and deductions

(a) Foreign tax credit allowed.—An estate or trust shall be allowed the credit against tax for taxes imposed by foreign countries and possessions of the United States, to the extent allowed by section 901, only in respect of so much of the taxes described in such section as is not properly allocable under such section to the beneficiaries.

(b) Deduction for personal exemption.—An estate shall be allowed a deduction of $600. A trust which, under its governing instrument, is required to distribute all of its income currently shall be allowed a deduction of $300. All other trusts shall be allowed a deduction of $100. The deductions allowed by this subsection shall be in lieu of the deductions allowed under section 151 (relating to deduction for personal exemption).

(c) Deduction for amounts paid or permanently set aside for a charitable purpose.—

(1) General rule.—In the case of an estate or trust (other than a trust meeting the specifications of subpart B), there shall be allowed as a deduction in computing its taxable income (in lieu of the deduction allowed by section 170(a), relating to deduction for charitable, etc., contributions and gifts) any amount of the gross income, without limitation, which pursuant to the terms of the governing instrument is, during the taxable year, paid for a purpose specified in section 170(c) (determined without regard to section 170(c) (2) (A)). If a charitable contribution is paid after the close of such taxable year and on or before the last day of the year following the close of such taxable year, then the trustee or administrator may elect to treat such contribution as paid during such taxable year. The election shall be made at such time and in such manner as the Secretary prescribes by regulations.

(2) Amounts permanently set aside.—In the case of an estate, and in the case of a trust (other than a trust meeting the specifications of subpart B) required by the terms of its governing instrument to set aside amounts which was—

(A) created on or before October 9, 1969, if—

(i) an irrevocable remainder interest is transferred to or for the use of an organization described in section 170(c), or

(ii) the grantor is at all times after October 9, 1969, under a mental disability to change the terms of the trust; or

(B) established by a will executed on or before October 9, 1969, if—

(i) the testator dies before October 9, 1972, without having republished the will after October 9, 1969, by codicil or otherwise,

(ii) the testator at no time after October 9, 1969, had the right to change the portions of the will which pertain to the trust, or

(iii) the will is not republished by codicil or otherwise before October 9, 1972, and the testator is on such date and at all times thereafter under a mental disability to republish the will by codicil or otherwise,

there shall also be allowed as a deduction in computing its taxable income any amount of the gross income, without limitation, which pursuant to the terms of the governing instrument is, during the taxable year, permanently set aside for a purpose specified in section 170(c), or is to be used exclusively for religious, charitable, scientific, literary, or educational purposes, or for the prevention of cruelty to children or animals, or for the establishment, acquisition, maintenance, or operation of a public cemetery not operated for profit. In the case of a trust, the preceding sentence shall apply only to gross income earned with respect to amounts transferred to the trust before October 9, 1969, or transferred under a will to which subparagraph (B) applies.

(3) Pooled income funds.—In the case of a pooled income fund (as defined in paragraph (5)), there shall also be allowed as a deduction in computing its taxable income any amount of the gross income attributable to gain from the sale of a capital asset held for more than 6 months, without limitation, which pursuant to the terms of the governing instrument is, during the taxable year, permanently set aside for a purpose specified in section 170(c).

(4) Coordination with section 681.—In the case of a trust, the deduction allowed by this subsection shall be subject to section 681 (relating to unrelated business income).

(5) Definition of pooled income fund.—For purposes of paragraph (3), a pooled income fund is a trust—

(A) to which each donor transfers property, contributing an irrevocable remainder interest in such property to or for the use of an organization described in section 170(b) (1) (A) (other than in clauses (vii) or (viii)), and retaining an income interest for the life of one or more beneficiaries (living at the time of such transfer),

(B) in which the property transferred by each donor is commingled with property transferred by other donors who have made or make similar transfers,

(C) which cannot have investments in securities which are exempt from the taxes imposed by this subtitle,

(D) which includes only amounts received from transfers which meet the requirements of this paragraph,

(E) which is maintained by the organization to which the remainder interest is contributed and of which no donor or beneficiary of an income interest is a trustee, and

(F) from which each beneficiary of an income interest receives income, for each year for which he is entitled to receive the income interest referred to in subparagraph (A), determined by the rate of return earned by the trust for such year.

For purposes of determining the amount of any charitable contribution allowable by reason of a transfer of property to a pooled fund, the value of the income interest shall be determined on the basis of the highest rate of return earned by the fund for any of the 3 taxable years immediately preceding the taxable year of the fund in which the transfer is made. In the case of funds in existence less than 3 taxable years preceding the taxable year of the fund in which a transfer is made, the rate of return shall be deemed to be 6 percent per annum, except that the Secretary may prescribe a different rate of return.

(6) Taxable private foundations.—In the case of a private foundation which is not exempt from taxation under section 501(a) for the taxable year, the provisions of this subsection shall not apply and the provisions of section 170 shall apply.

(d) Net operating loss deduction.—The benefit of the deduction for net operating losses provided by section 172 shall be allowed to estates and trusts under regulations prescribed by the Secretary.

(e) Deduction for depreciation and depletion.—An estate or trust shall be allowed the deduction for depreciation and depletion only to the extent not allowable to beneficiaries under sections 167(h) and 611(b).

(f) Amortization deductions.—The benefit of the deductions for amortization provided by sections 169, 184, 187, and 188 shall be allowed to estates and trusts in the same manner as in the case of an individual. The allowable deduction shall be apportioned between the income beneficiaries and the fiduciary under regulations prescribed by the Secretary.

(g) Disallowance of double deductions.—Amounts allowable under section 2053 or 2054 as a deduction in computing the taxable estate of a decedent shall not be allowed as a deduction (or as an offset against the sales price of property in determining gain or loss) in computing the taxable income of the estate or of any other person, unless there is filed, within the time and in the manner and form prescribed by the Secretary, a statement that the amounts have not been allowed as deductions under section 2053 or 2054 and a waiver of the right to have such amounts allowed at any time as deductions under section 2053 or 2054. This subsection shall not apply with respect to deductions allowed under part II (relating to income in respect of decedents).

(h) Unused loss carryovers and excess deductions on termination available to beneficiaries.—If on the termination of an estate or trust, the estate or trust has—

(1) a net operating loss carryover under section 172 or a capital loss carryover under section 1212, or

(2) for the last taxable year of the estate or trust deductions (other than the deductions allowed under subsections (b) or (c)) in excess of gross income for such year,

then such carryover or such excess shall be allowed as a deduction, in accordance with regulations prescribed by the Secretary, to the beneficiaries succeeding to the property of the estate or trust.

* * *

§ 643. Definitions applicable to subparts A, B, C, and D

(a) **Distributable net income.**—For purposes of this part, the term "distributable net income" means, with respect to any taxable year, the taxable income of the estate or trust computed with the following modifications—

(1) **Deduction for distributions.**—No deduction shall be taken under sections 651 and 661 (relating to additional deductions).

(2) **Deduction for personal exemption.**—No deduction shall be taken under section 642(b) (relating to deduction for personal exemptions).

(3) **Capital gains and losses.**—Gains from the sale or exchange of capital assets shall be excluded to the extent that such gains are allocated to corpus and are not (A) paid, credited, or required to be distributed to any beneficiary during the taxable year, or (B) paid, permanently set aside, or to be used for the purposes specified in section 642(c). Losses from the sale or exchange of capital assets shall be excluded, except to the extent such losses are taken into account in determining the amount of gains from the sale or exchange of capital assets which are paid, credited, or required to be distributed to any beneficiary during the taxable year.

(4) **Extraordinary dividends and taxable stock dividends.**—For purposes only of subpart B (relating to trusts which distribute current income only), there shall be excluded those items of gross income constituting extraordinary dividends or taxable stock dividends which the fiduciary, acting in good faith, does not pay or credit to any beneficiary by reason of his determination that such dividends are allocable to corpus under the terms of the governing instrument and applicable local law.

(5) **Tax-exempt interest.**—There shall be included any tax-exempt interest to which section 103 applies, reduced by any amounts which would be deductible in respect of disbursements allocable to such interest but for the provisions of section 265 (relating to disallowance of certain deductions).

(6) **Income of foreign trust.**—In the case of a foreign trust—

(A) There shall be included the amounts of gross income from sources without the United States, reduced by any amounts which would be deductible in respect of disbursements allocable to such income but for the provisions of section 265(1) (relating to disallowance of certain deductions).

(B) Gross income from sources within the United States shall be determined without regard to section 894 (relating to income exempt under treaty).

(C) Paragraph (3) shall not apply to a foreign trust. In the case of such a trust, (i) there shall be included gains from the sale or exchange of capital assets, reduced by losses from such sales or exchanges to the extent such losses do not exceed gains from such sales or exchanges, and (ii) the deduction under section 1202 (relating to deduction for excess of capital gains over capital losses) shall not be taken into account.

(D) Effective for distributions made in taxable years beginning after December 31, 1975, the undistributed net income of each foreign trust for each taxable year beginning on or before December 31, 1975, remaining undistributed at the close of the last taxable year beginning on or before December 31, 1975, shall be redetermined by taking into account the deduction allowed by section 1202.

(b) Income.—For purposes of this subpart and subparts B, C, and D, the term "income", when not preceded by the words "taxable", "distributable net", "undistributed net", or "gross", means the amount of income of the estate or trust for the taxable year determined under the terms of the governing instrument and applicable local law. Items of gross income constituting extraordinary dividends or taxable stock dividends which the fiduciary, acting in good faith, determines to be allocable to corpus under the terms of the governing instrument and applicable local law shall not be considered income.

(c) Beneficiary.—For purposes of this part, the term "beneficiary" includes heir, legatee, devisee.

* * *

(e) Treatment of property distributed in kind.—

(1) Basis of beneficiary.—The basis of any property received by a beneficiary in a distribution from an estate or trust shall be—

(A) the adjusted basis of such property in the hands of the estate or trust immediately before the distribution, adjusted for

(B) any gain or loss recognized to the estate or trust on the distribution.

(2) Amount of distribution.—In the case of any distribution of property (other than cash), the amount taken into account under sections 661(a)(2) and 662(a)(2) shall be the lesser of—

(A) the basis of such property in the hands of the beneficiary (as determined under paragraph (1)), or

(B) the fair market value of such property.

(3) Election to recognize gain.—

(A) In general.—In the case of any distribution of property (other than cash) to which an election under this paragraph applies—

(i) paragraph (2) shall not apply,

(ii) gain or loss shall be recognized by the estate or trust in the same manner as if such property had been sold to the distributee at its fair market value, and

(iii) the amount taken into account under sections 661(a)(2) and 662(a)(2) shall be the fair market value of such property.

(B) Election.—Any election under this paragraph shall apply to all distributions made by the estate or trust during a taxable year and shall be made on the return of such estate or trust for such taxable year.

Any such election, once made, may be revoked only with the consent of the Secretary.

(4) Exception for distributions described in section 663(a).—This subsection shall not apply to any distribution described in section 663(a).

(f) Treatment of multiple trusts.—For purposes of this subchapter, under regulations prescribed by the Secretary, 2 or more trusts shall be treated as 1 trust if—

(1) such trusts have substantially the same grantor or grantors and substantially the same primary beneficiary or beneficiaries, and

(2) a principal purpose of such trusts is the avoidance of the tax imposed by this chapter.

For purposes of the preceding sentence, a husband and wife shall be treated as 1 person.

(g) Certain payments of estimated tax treated as paid by beneficiary.—

(1) In general.—In the case of a trust—

(A) the trustee may elect to treat any portion of a payment of estimated tax made by such trust for any taxable year of the trust as a payment made by a beneficiary of such trust,

(B) any amount so treated shall be treated as paid or credited to the beneficiary on the last day of such taxable year, and

(C) for purposes of subtitle F, the amount so treated—

(i) shall not be treated as a payment of estimated tax made by the trust, but

(ii) shall be treated as a payment of estimated tax made by such beneficiary on January 15 following the taxable year.

The preceding sentence shall apply only to the extent the payments of estimated tax made by the trust for the taxable year exceed the tax imposed by this chapter shown on its return for the taxable year.

(2) Time for making election.—An election under paragraph (1) may be made—

(A) only on the trust's return of the tax imposed by this chapter for the taxable year, and

(B) only if such return is filed on or before the 65th day after the close of the taxable year.

§ 644. Special rule for gain on property transferred to trust at less than fair market value

(a) Imposition of tax.—

(1) In general.—If—

(A) a trust (or another trust to which the property is distributed) sells or exchanges property at a gain not more than 2 years after the date of the initial transfer of the property in trust by the transferor, and

(B) the fair market value of such property at the time of the initial transfer in trust by the transferor exceeds the adjusted basis of such property immediately after such transfer,

there is hereby imposed a tax determined in accordance with paragraph (2) on the includible gain recognized on such sale or exchange.

(2) Amount of tax.—The amount of the tax imposed by paragraph (1) on any includible gain recognized on the sale or exchange of any property shall be equal to the sum of—

(A) the excess of—

(i) the tax which would have been imposed under this chapter for the taxable year of the transferor in which the sale or exchange of such property occurs had the amount of the includible gain recognized on such sale or exchange, reduced by any deductions properly allocable to such gain, been included in the gross income of the transferor for such taxable year, over

(ii) the tax actually imposed under this chapter for such taxable year on the transferor, plus

(B) if such sale or exchange occurs in a taxable year of the transferor which begins after the beginning of the taxable year of the trust in which such sale or exchange occurs, an amount equal to the amount determined under subparagraph (A) multiplied by the underpayment rate established under section 6621.

The determination of tax under clause (i) of subparagraph (A) shall be made by not taking into account any carryback, and by not taking into account any loss or deduction to the extent that such loss or deduction may be carried by the transferor to any other taxable year.

(3) Taxable year for which tax imposed.—The tax imposed by paragraph (1) shall be imposed for the taxable year of the trust which begins with or within the taxable year of the transferor in which the sale or exchange occurs.

(4) Tax to be in addition to other taxes.—The tax imposed by this subsection for any taxable year of the trust shall be in addition to any other tax imposed by this chapter for such taxable year.

(b) Definition of includible gain.—For purposes of this section, the term "includible gain" means the lesser of—

(1) the gain recognized by the trust on the sale or exchange of any property, or

(2) the excess of the fair market value of such property at the time of the initial transfer in trust by the transferor over the adjusted basis of such property immediately after such transfer.

(c) Character of includible gain.—For purposes of subsection (a)—

(1) The character of the includible gain shall be determined as if the property had actually been sold or exchanged by the transferor, and any activities of the trust with respect to the sale or exchange of the property shall be deemed to be activities of the transferor, and

(2) the portion of the includible gain subject to the provisions of section 1245 and section 1250 shall be determined in accordance with regulations prescribed by the Secretary.

(d) Special rules.—

(1) Short sales.—If the trust sells the property referred to in subsection (a) in a short sale within the 2-year period referred to in such subsection, such 2-year period shall be extended to the date of the closing of such short sale.

(2) Substituted basis property.—For purposes of this section, in the case of any property held by the trust which has a basis determined in whole or in part by reference to the basis of any other property which was transferred to the trust—

(A) the initial transfer of such property in trust by the transferor shall be treated as having occurred on the date of the initial transfer in trust of such other property,

(B) subsections (a) (1) (B) and (b) (2) shall be applied by taking into account the fair market value and the adjusted basis of such other property, and

(C) the amount determined under subsection (b) (2) with respect to such other property shall be allocated (under regulations prescribed by the Secretary) among such other property and all properties held by the trust which have a basis determined in whole or in part by reference to the basis of such other property.

(e) Exceptions.—Subsection (a) shall not apply to property—

(1) acquired by the trust from a decedent or which passed to a trust from a decedent (within the meaning of section 1014), or

(2) acquired by a pooled income fund (as defined in section 642(c) (5)), or

(3) acquired by a charitable remainder annuity trust (as defined in section 664(d) (1)) or a charitable remainder unitrust (as defined in sections 664(d) (2) and (3)), or

(4) if the sale or exchange of the property occurred after the death of the transferor.

(f) Special rule for installment sales.—If the trust reports income under section 453 on any sale or exchange to which subsection (a) applies, under regulations prescribed by the Secretary—

(1) subsection (a) (other than the 2-year requirement of paragraph (1) (A) thereof) shall be applied as if each installment were a separate sale or exchange of property to which such subsection applies, and

(2) the term "includible gain" shall not include any portion of an installment received by the trust after the death of the transferor.

§ 645. Taxable year of trusts

(a) In general.—For purposes of this subtitle, the taxable year of any trust shall be the calendar year.

(b) Exception for trusts exempt from tax and charitable trusts.—Subsection (a) shall not apply to a trust exempt from taxation under section 501(a) or to a trust described in section 4947(a)(1).

Subpart B—Trusts Which Distribute Current Income Only

§ 651. Deduction for trusts distributing current income only

(a) Deduction.—In the case of any trust the terms of which—

(1) provide that all of its income is required to be distributed currently, and

(2) do not provide that any amounts are to be paid, permanently set aside, or used for the purposes specified in section 642(c) (relating to deduction for charitable, etc., purposes),

there shall be allowed as a deduction in computing the taxable income of the trust the amount of the income for the taxable year which is required to be distributed currently. This section shall not apply in any taxable year in which the trust distributes amounts other than amounts of income described in paragraph (1).

(b) Limitation on deduction.—If the amount of income required to be distributed currently exceeds the distributable net income of the trust for the taxable year, the deduction shall be limited to the amount of the distributable net income. For this purpose, the computation of distributable net income shall not include items of income which are not included in the gross income of the trust and the deductions allocable thereto.

§ 652. Inclusion of amounts in gross income of beneficiaries of trusts distributing current income only

(a) Inclusion.—Subject to subsection (b), the amount of income for the taxable year required to be distributed currently by a trust described in section 651 shall be included in the gross income of the beneficiaries to whom the income is required to be distributed, whether distributed or not. If such amount exceeds the distributable net income, there shall be included in the gross income of each beneficiary an amount which bears the same ratio to distributable net income as the amount of income required to be distributed to such beneficiary bears to the amount of income required to be distributed to all beneficiaries.

(b) Character of amounts.—The amounts specified in subsection (a) shall have the same character in the hands of the beneficiary as in the hands of the trust. For this purpose, the amounts shall be treated as consisting of the same proportion of each class of items entering into the computation of distributable net income of the trust as the total of each class bears to the total distributable net income of the trust, unless the terms of the trust specifically allocate different classes of income to different beneficiaries. In the application of the preceding sentence, the items of deduction entering into the computation of distributable net income shall be allocated among the items of distributable net income in accordance with regulations prescribed by the Secretary.

(c) Different taxable years.—If the taxable year of a beneficiary is different from that of the trust, the amount which the beneficiary is required to include in gross income in accordance with the provisions of this section shall be based upon the amount of income of the trust for any taxable year or years of the trust ending within or with his taxable year.

Subpart C—Estates and Trusts Which May Acccumulate Income or Which Distribute Corpus

§ 661. Deduction for estates and trusts accumulating income or distributing corpus

(a) Deduction.—In any taxable year there shall be allowed as a deduction in computing the taxable income of an estate or trust (other than a trust to which subpart B applies), the sum of—

(1) any amount of income for such taxable year required to be distributed currently (including any amount required to be distributed which may be paid out of income or corpus to the extent such amount is paid out of income for such taxable year); and

(2) any other amounts properly paid or credited or required to be distributed for such taxable year;

but such deduction shall not exceed the distributable net income of the estate or trust.

(b) Character of amounts distributed.—The amount determined under subsection (a) shall be treated as consisting of the same proportion of each class of items entering into the computation of distributable net income of the estate or trust as the total of each class bears to the total distributable net income of the estate or trust in the absence of the allocation of different classes of income under the specific terms of the governing instrument. In the application of the preceding sentence, the items of deduction entering into the computation of distributable net income (including the deduction allowed under section 642(c)) shall be allocated among the items of distributable net income in accordance with regulations prescribed by the Secretary.

(c) Limitation on deduction.—No deduction shall be allowed under subsection (a) in respect of any portion of the amount allowed as a deduction under that subsection (without regard to this subsection) which is treated under subsection (b) as consisting of any item of distributable net income which is not included in the gross income of the estate or trust.

§ 662. Inclusion of amounts in gross income of beneficiaries of estates and trusts accumulating income or distributing corpus

(a) Inclusion.—Subject to subsection (b), there shall be included in the gross income of a beneficiary to whom an amount specified in section 661(a) is paid, credited, or required to be distributed (by an estate or trust described in section 661), the sum of the following amounts:

(1) Amounts required to be distributed currently.—The amount of income for the taxable year required to be distributed currently to such beneficiary, whether distributed or not. If the amount of income required to be distributed currently to all beneficiaries exceeds the distributable net income (computed without the deduction allowed by section 642(c), relating to deduction for charitable, etc., purposes) of the estate or trust, then, in lieu of the amount provided in the preceding sentence, there shall be included in the gross income of the beneficiary an amount which bears the same ratio to distributable net income (as so computed) as the amount of income required to be distributed currently to such beneficiary bears to the amount required to be distributed currently to all beneficiaries. For purposes of this section, the phrase "the amount of income for the taxable year required to be distributed currently" includes any amount required to be paid out of income or corpus to the extent such amount is paid out of income for such taxable year.

(2) Other amounts distributed.—All other amounts properly paid, credited, or required to be distributed to such beneficiary for the taxable year. If the sum of—

(A) the amount of income for the taxable year required to be distributed currently to all beneficiaries, and

(B) all other amounts properly paid, credited, or required to be distributed to all beneficiaries

exceeds the distributable net income of the estate or trust, then, in lieu of the amount provided in the preceding sentence, there shall be included in the gross income of the beneficiary an amount which bears the same ratio to distributable net income (reduced by the amounts specified in (A)) as the other amounts properly paid, credited or required to be distributed to the beneficiary bear to the other amounts properly paid, credited, or required to be distributed to all beneficiaries.

(b) Character of amounts.—The amounts determined under subsection (a) shall have the same character in the hands of the beneficiary as in the hands of the estate or trust. For this purpose, the amounts shall be treated as consisting of the same proportion of each class of items entering into the computation of distributable net income as the total of each class bears to the total distributable net income of the estate or trust unless the terms of the governing instrument specifically allocate different classes of income to different beneficiaries. In the application of the preceding sentence, the items of deduction entering into the computation of distributable net income (including the deduction allowed under section 642(c)) shall be allocated among the items of distributable net income in accordance with regulations prescribed by the Secretary. In the application of this subsection to the amount determined under paragraph (1) of subsection (a), distributable net income shall be computed without regard to any portion of the deduction under section 642(c) which is not attributable to income of the taxable year.

(c) Different taxable years.—If the taxable year of a beneficiary is different from that of the estate or trust, the amount to be included in the gross income of the beneficiary shall be based on the distributable net income of the estate or trust and the amounts properly paid, credited, or required to be distributed to the beneficiary during any taxable year or years of the estate or trust ending within or with his taxable year.

§ 663. Special rules applicable to sections 661 and 662

(a) Exclusions.—There shall not be included as amounts falling within section 661(a) or 662(a)—

(1) Gifts, bequests, etc.—Any amount which, under the terms of the governing instrument, is properly paid or credited as a gift or bequest of a specific sum of money or of specific property and which is paid or credited all at once or in not more than 3 installments. For this purpose an amount which can be paid or credited only from the income of the estate or trust shall not be considered as a gift or bequest of a specific sum of money.

(2) Charitable, etc., distributions.—Any amount paid or permanently set aside or otherwise qualifying for the deduction provided in section 642(c) (computed without regard to sections 508(d), 681, and 4948(c) (4)).

(3) Denial of double deduction.—Any amount paid, credited, or distributed in the taxable year, if section 651 or section 661 applied to such amount for a preceding taxable year of an estate or trust because credited or required to be distributed in such preceding taxable year.

(b) Distributions in first sixty-five days of taxable year.—

(1) General rule.—If within the first 65 days of any taxable year of a trust, an amount is properly paid or credited, such amount shall be considered paid or credited on the last day of the preceding taxable year.

(2) Limitation.—Paragraph (1) shall apply with respect to any taxable year of a trust only if the fiduciary of such trust elects, in such manner and at such time as the Secretary prescribes by regulations, to have paragraph (1) apply for such taxable year.

(c) Separate shares treated as separate trusts.—For the sole purpose of determining the amount of distributable net income in the application of sections 661 and 662, in the case of a single trust having more than one beneficiary, substantially separate and independent shares of different beneficiaries in the trust shall be treated as separate trusts. The existence of such substantially separate and independent shares and the manner of treatment as separate trusts, including the application of subpart D, shall be determined in accordance with regulations prescribed by the Secretary.

§ 664. Charitable remainder trusts

(a) General rule.—Notwithstanding any other provision of this subchapter, the provisions of this section shall, in accordance with regulations prescribed by the Secretary, apply in the case of a charitable remainder annuity trust and a charitable remainder unitrust.

(b) Character of distributions.—Amounts distributed by a charitable remainder annuity trust or by a charitable remainder unitrust shall be considered as having the following characteristics in the hands of a beneficiary to whom is paid the annuity described in subsection (d) (1) (A) or the payment described in subsection (d) (2) (A):

(1) First, as amounts of income (other than gains, and amounts treated as gains, from the sale or other disposition of capital assets) includible in gross income to the extent of such income of the trust for the year and such undistributed income of the trust for prior years;

(2) Second, as a capital gain to the extent of the capital gain of the trust for the year and the undistributed capital gain of the trust for prior years;

(3) Third, as other income to the extent of such income of the trust for the year and such undistributed income of the trust for prior years; and

(4) Fourth, as a distribution of trust corpus.

For purposes of this section, the trust shall determine the amount of its undistributed capital gain on a cumulative net basis.

(c) Exemption from income taxes.—A charitable remainder annuity trust and a charitable remainder unitrust shall, for any taxable year, not be subject to any tax imposed by this subtitle, unless such trust, for such year, has unrelated business taxable income (within the meaning of section 512, determined as if part III of subchapter F applied to such trust).

(d) Definitions.—

(1) Charitable remainder annuity trust.—For purposes of this section, a charitable remainder annuity trust is a trust—

(A) from which a sum certain (which is not less than 5 percent of the initial net fair market value of all property placed in trust) is to be paid, not less often than annually, to one or more persons (at least one of which is not an organization described in section 170(c) and, in the case of individuals, only to an individual who is living at the time of the creation of the trust) for a term of years (not in excess of 20 years) or for the life or lives of such individual or individuals,

(B) from which no amount other than the payments described in subparagraph (A) may be paid to or for the use of any person other than an organization described in section 170(c), and

(C) following the termination of the payments described in subparagraph (A), the remainder interest in the trust is to be transferred to, or for the use of, an organization described in section 170(c) or is to be retained by the trust for such a use.

(2) Charitable remainder unitrust.—For purposes of this section, a charitable remainder unitrust is a trust—

(A) from which a fixed percentage (which is not less than 5 percent) of the net fair market value of its assets, valued annually, is to be paid, not less often than annually, to one or more persons (at least one of which is not an organization described in section 170(c) and, in the case of individuals, only to an individual who is living at the time of the creation of the trust) for a term of years (not in excess of 20 years) or for the life or lives of such individual or individuals,

(B) from which no amount other than the payments described in subparagraph (A) may be paid to or for the use of any person other than an organization described in section 170(c), and

(C) following the termination of the payments described in subparagraph (A), the remainder interest in the trust is to be transferred to, or for the use of, an organization described in section 170(c) or is to be retained by the trust for such a use.

(3) Exception.—Notwithstanding the provisions of paragraphs (2) (A) and (B), the trust instrument may provide that the trustee shall pay the income beneficiary for any year—

(A) the amount of the trust income, if such amount is less than the amount required to be distributed under paragraph (2) (A), and

(B) any amount of the trust income which is in excess of the amount required to be distributed under paragraph (2) (A), to the extent that (by reason of subparagraph (A)) the aggregate of the amounts paid in prior years was less than the aggregate of such required amounts.

(e) Valuation for purposes of charitable contribution.—For purposes of determining the amount of any charitable contribution, the remainder interest of a charitable remainder annuity trust or charitable remainder unitrust shall be computed on the basis that an amount equal to 5 percent of the net fair market value of its assets (or a greater amount, if required under the terms of the trust instrument) is to be distributed each year.

(f) Certain contingencies permitted.—

(1) General rule.—If a trust would, but for a qualified contingency, meet the requirements of paragraph (1)(A) or (2)(A) of subsection (d), such trust shall be treated as meeting such requirements.

(2) Value determined without regard to qualified contingency.—For purposes of determining the amount of any charitable contribution (or the actuarial value of any interest), a qualified contingency shall not be taken into account.

(3) Qualified contingency.—For purposes of this subsection, the term "qualified contingency" means any provision of a trust which provides that, upon the happening of a contingency, the payments described in paragraph (1)(A) or (2)(A) of subsection (d) (as the case may be) will terminate not later than such payments would otherwise terminate under the trust.

Subpart D—Treatment of Excess Distributions by Trusts

§ 665. Definitions applicable to subpart D

(a) Undistributed net income.—For purposes of this subpart, the term "undistributed net income" for any taxable year means the amount by which the distributable net income of the trust for such taxable year exceeds the sum of—

(1) the amounts for such taxable year specified in paragraphs (1) and (2) of section 661(a), and

(2) the amount of taxes imposed on the trust attributable to such distributable net income.

(b) Accumulation distribution.—For purposes of this subpart, the term "accumulation distribution" means, for any taxable year of the trust, the amount by which—

(1) the amounts specified in paragraph (2) of section 661(a) for such taxable year, exceed

(2) distributable net income for such year reduced (but not below zero) by the amounts specified in paragraph (1) of section 661(a).

For purposes of section 667 (other than subsection (c) thereof, relating to multiple trusts), the amounts specified in paragraph (2) of section 661(a) shall not include amounts properly paid, credited, or required to be distributed to a beneficiary from a trust (other than a foreign trust) as income accumulated before the birth of such beneficiary or before such beneficiary attains the age of 21. If the amounts properly paid, credited, or required to be distributed by the trust for the taxable year do not exceed the income of the trust for such year, there shall be no accumulation distribution for such year.

* * *

(d) Taxes imposed on the trust.—For purposes of this subpart—

(1) In general.—The term "taxes imposed on the trust" means the amount of the taxes which are imposed for any taxable year of the trust under this chapter (without regard to this subpart or part IV of subchapter A) and which, under regulations prescribed by the Secretary, are properly allocable to the undistributed portions of distributable net income and gains in excess of losses from sales or exchanges of capital assets. The amount determined in the preceding sentence shall be reduced by any amount of such taxes deemed distributed under section 666(b) and (c) or 669(d) and (e) to any beneficiary.

(2) Foreign trusts.—In the case of any foreign trust, the term "taxes imposed on the trust" includes the amount, reduced as provided in the last sentence of paragraph (1), of any income, war profits, and excess profits taxes imposed by any foreign country or possession of the United States on such foreign trust which, as determined under paragraph (1), are so properly allocable.

(e) Preceding taxable year.—For purposes of this subpart—

(1) in the case of a trust (other than a foreign trust created by a United States person), the term "preceding taxable year" does not include any taxable year of the trust—

(A) which precedes by more than 5 years the taxable year of the trust in which an accumulation distribution is made, if it is made in a taxable year beginning before January 1, 1974, or

(B) which begins before January 1, 1969, in the case of an accumulation distribution made during a taxable year beginning after December 31, 1973; and

(2) in the case of a foreign trust created by a United States person, such term does not include any taxable year of the trust to which this part does not apply.

In the case of a preceding taxable year with respect to which a trust qualifies (without regard to this subpart) under the provisions of subpart B, for purposes of the application of this subpart to such trust for such taxable year, such trust shall, in accordance with regulations prescribed by the Secretary, be treated as a trust to which subpart C applies.

§ 666. Accumulation distribution allocated to preceding years

(a) **Amount allocated.**—In the case of a trust which is subject to subpart C, the amount of the accumulation distribution of such trust for a taxable year shall be deemed to be an amount within the meaning of paragraph (2) of section 661(a) distributed on the last day of each of the preceding taxable years, commencing with the earliest of such years, to the extent that such amount exceeds the total of any undistributed net income for all earlier preceding taxable years. The amount deemed to be distributed in any such preceding taxable year under the preceding sentence shall not exceed the undistributed net income for such preceding taxable year. For purposes of this subsection, undistributed net income for each of such preceding taxable years shall be computed without regard to such accumulation distribution and without regard to any accumulation distribution determined for any succeeding taxable year.

(b) **Total taxes deemed distributed.**—If any portion of an accumulation distribution for any taxable year is deemed under subsection (a) to be an amount within the meaning of paragraph (2) of section 661(a) distributed on the last day of any preceding taxable year, and such portion of such distribution is not less than the undistributed net income for such preceding taxable year, the trust shall be deemed to have distributed on the last day of such preceding taxable year an additional amount within the meaning of paragraph (2) of section 661(a). Such additional amount shall be equal to the taxes (other than the tax imposed by section 55) imposed on the trust for such preceding taxable year attributable to the undistributed net income. For purposes of this subsection, the undistributed net income and the taxes imposed on the trust for such preceding taxable year attributable to such undistributed net income shall be computed without regard to such accumulation distribution and without regard to any accumulation distribution determined for any succeeding taxable year.

(c) **Pro rata portion of taxes deemed distributed.**—If any portion of an accumulation distribution for any taxable year is deemed under subsection (a) to be an amount within the meaning of paragraph (2) of section 661(a) distributed on the last day of any preceding taxable year and such portion of the accumulation distribution is less than the undistributed net income for such preceding taxable year, the trust shall be deemed to have distributed on the last day of such preceding taxable year an additional amount within the meaning of paragraph (2) of section 661(a). Such additional amount shall be equal to the taxes (other than the tax imposed by section 55) imposed on the trust for such taxable year attributable to the undistributed net income multiplied by the ratio of the portion of the accumulation distribution to the undistributed net income of the trust for such year. For purposes of this subsection, the undistributed net income and the taxes imposed on the trust for such preceding taxable year attributable to such undistributed net income shall be computed without regard to the accumulation distribution and without regard to any accumulation distribution determined for any succeeding taxable year.

(d) Rule when information is not available.—If adequate records are not available to determine the proper application of this subpart to an amount distributed by a trust, such amount shall be deemed to be an accumulation distribution consisting of undistributed net income earned during the earliest preceding taxable year of the trust in which it can be established that the trust was in existence.

(e) Denial of refund to trusts and beneficiaries.—No refund or credit shall be allowed to a trust or a beneficiary of such trust for any preceding taxable year by reason of a distribution deemed to have been made by such trust in such year under this section.

§ 667. Treatment of amounts deemed distributed by trust in preceding years

(a) General rule.—The total of the amounts which are treated under section 666 as having been distributed by a trust in a preceding taxable year shall be included in the income of a beneficiary of the trust when paid, credited, or required to be distributed to the extent that such total would have been included in the income of such beneficiary under section 662(a) (2) (and, with respect to any tax-exempt interest to which section 103 applies, under section 662(b)) if such total had been paid to such beneficiary on the last day of such preceding taxable year. The tax imposed by this subtitle on a beneficiary for a taxable year in which any such amount is included in his income shall be determined only as provided in this section and shall consist of the sum of—

(1) a partial tax computed on the taxable income reduced by an amount equal to the total of such amounts, at the rate and in the manner as if this section had not been enacted,

(2) a partial tax determined as provided in subsection (b) of this section, and

(3) in the case of a foreign trust, the interest charge determined as provided in section 668.

(b) Tax on distribution.—

(1) In general.—The partial tax imposed by subsection (a) (2) shall be determined—

(A) by determining the number of preceding taxable years of the trust on the last day of which an amount is deemed under section 666(a) to have been distributed,

(B) by taking from the 5 taxable years immediately preceding the year of the accumulation distribution the 1 taxable year for which the beneficiary's taxable income was the highest and the 1 taxable year for which his taxable income was the lowest,

(C) by adding to the beneficiary's taxable income for each of the 3 taxable years remaining after the application of subparagraph (B) an amount determined by dividing the amount deemed distributed under section 666 and required to be included in income under subsection (a) by the number of preceding taxable years determined under subparagraph (A), and

(D) by determining the average increase in tax for the 3 taxable years referred to in subparagraph (C) resulting from the application of such subparagraph.

The partial tax imposed by subsection (a) (2) shall be the excess (if any) of the average increase in tax determined under subparagraph (D), multiplied by the number of preceding taxable years determined under subparagraph (A), over the amount of taxes (other than the amount of taxes described in section 665(d) (2)) deemed distributed to the beneficiary under sections 666(b) and (c).

(2) Treatment of loss years.—For purposes of paragraph (1), the taxable income of the beneficiary for any taxable year shall be deemed to be not less than zero.

(3) Certain preceding taxable years not taken into account.—For purposes of paragraph (1), if the amount of the undistributed net income deemed distributed in any preceding taxable year of the trust is less than 25 percent of the amount of the accumulation distribution divided by the number of preceding taxable years to which the accumulation distribution is allocated under section 666(a), the number of preceding taxable years of the trust with respect to which an amount is deemed distributed to a beneficiary under section 666(a) shall be determined without regard to such year.

(4) Effect of other accumulation distributions.—In computing the partial tax under paragraph (1) for any beneficiary, the income of such beneficiary for each of his prior taxable years shall include amounts previously deemed distributed to such beneficiary in such year under section 666 as a result of prior accumulation distributions (whether from the same or another trust).

(5) Multiple distributions in the same taxable year.—In the case of accumulation distributions made from more than one trust which are includible in the income of a beneficiary in the same taxable year, the distributions shall be deemed to have been made consecutively in whichever order the beneficiary shall determine.

(6) Adjustment in partial tax for estate and generation-skipping transfer taxes attributable to partial tax.—

(A) In general.—The partial tax shall be reduced by an amount which is equal to the pre-death portion of the partial tax multiplied by a fraction—

(i) the numerator of which is that portion of the tax imposed by chapter 11 or 13, as the case may be, which is attributable (on a proportionate basis) to amounts included in the accumulation distribution, and

(ii) the denominator of which is the amount of the accumulation distribution which is subject to the tax imposed by chapter 11 or 13, as the case may be.

(B) Partial tax determined without regard to this paragraph.—For purposes of this paragraph, the term "partial tax" means the partial tax imposed by subsection (a) (2) determined under this subsection without regard to this paragraph.

(C) Pre-death portion.—For purposes of this paragraph, the pre-death portion of the partial tax shall be an amount which bears the same ratio to the partial tax as the portion of the accumulation distribution which is attributable to the period before the date of the death of the decedent or the date of the generation-skipping transfer bears to the total accumulation distribution.

(c) Special rule for multiple trusts.—

(1) In general.—If, in the same prior taxable year of the beneficiary in which any part of the accumulation distribution from a trust (hereinafter in this paragraph referred to as "third trust") is deemed under section 666(a) to have been distributed to such beneficiary, some part of prior distributions by each of 2 or more other trusts is deemed under section 666(a) to have been distributed to such beneficiary, then subsections (b) and (c) of section 666 shall not apply with respect to such part of the accumulation distribution from such third trust.

(2) Accumulation distributions from trust not taken into account unless they equal or exceed $1,000.—For purposes of paragraph (1), an accumulation distribution from a trust to a beneficiary shall be taken into account only if such distribution, when added to any prior accumulation distributions from such trust which are deemed under section 666(a) to have been distributed to such beneficiary for the same prior taxable year of the beneficiary, equals or exceeds $1,000.

(d) Special rules for foreign trust.—

(1) Foreign tax deemed paid by beneficiary.—

(A) In general.—In determining the increase in tax under subsection (b) (1) (D) for any computation year, the taxes described in section 665(d) (2) which are deemed distributed under section 666(b) or (c) and added under subsection (b) (1) (C) to the taxable income of the beneficiary for any computation year shall, except as provided in subparagraphs (B) and (C), be treated as a credit against the increase in tax for such computation year under subsection (b) (1) (D).

(B) Deduction in lieu of credit.—If the beneficiary did not choose the benefits of subpart A of part III of subchapter N with respect to the computation year, the beneficiary may in lieu of treating the amounts described in subparagraph (A) (without regard to subparagraph (C)) as a credit may treat such amounts as a deduction in computing the beneficiary's taxable income under subsection (b) (1) (C) for the computation year.

(C) Limitation on credit; retention of character.—

(i) Limitation on credit.—For purposes of determining under subparagraph (A) the amount treated as a credit for any computation year, the limitations under subpart A of part III of subchapter N shall be applied separately with respect to amounts added under subsection (b) (1) (C) to the taxable income of the beneficiary for such computation year. For purposes of computing the increase in tax under subsection (b) (1) (D) for any computation year for which the beneficiary did not choose the benefits of subpart A of part III of subchapter N, the beneficiary shall be treated as having chosen such benefits for such computation year.

(ii) Retention of character.—The items of income, deduction, and credit of the Trust shall retain their character (subject to the application of section 904(f) (5)) to the extent necessary to apply this paragraph.

(D) Computation year.—For purposes of this paragraph, the term "computation year" means any of the three taxable years remaining after application of subsection (b) (1) (B).

(e) Retention of character of amounts distributed from accumulation trust to nonresident aliens and foreign corporations.—In the case of a distribution from a trust to a nonresident alien individual or to a foreign corporation, the first sentence of subsection (a) shall be applied as if the reference to the determination of character under section 662(b) applied to all amounts instead of just to tax-exempt interest.

§ 668. Interest charge on accumulation distributions from foreign trusts

(a) General rule.—For purposes of the tax determined under section 667(a), the interest charge is an amount equal to 6 percent of the partial tax computed under section 667(b) multiplied by a fraction—

(1) the numerator of which is the sum of the number of taxable years between each taxable year to which the distribution is allocated under section 666(a) and the taxable year of the distribution (counting in each case the taxable year to which the distribution is allocated but not counting the taxable year of the distribution), and

(2) the denominator of which is the number of taxable years to which the distribution is allocated under section 666(a).

(b) Limitation.—The total amount of the interest charge shall not, when added to the total partial tax computed under section 667(b), exceed the amount of the accumulation distribution (other than the amount of tax deemed distributed by section 666(b) or (c)) in respect of which such partial tax was determined.

(c) Special rules.—

(1) Interest charge not deductible.—The interest charge determined under this section shall not be allowed as a deduction for purposes of any tax imposed by this title.

(2) Transitional rule.—For purposes of this section, undistributed net income existing in a trust as of January 1, 1977, shall be treated as allocated under section 666(a) to the first taxable year beginning after December 31, 1976.

Subpart E—Grantors and Others Treated as Substantial Owners

§ 671. Trust income, deductions, and credits attributable to grantors and others as substantial owners

Where it is specified in this subpart that the grantor or another person shall be treated as the owner of any portion of a trust, there shall then be included in computing the taxable income and credits of the grantor or the other person those items of income, deductions, and credits against tax of the trust which are attributable to that portion of the trust to the extent that such items would be taken into account under this chapter in computing taxable income or credits against the tax of an individual. Any remaining portion of the trust shall be subject to subparts A through D. No items of a trust shall be included in computing the taxable income and credits of the grantor or of any other person solely on the grounds of his dominion and control over the trust under section 61 (relating to definition of gross income) or any other provision of this title, except as specified in this subpart.

§ 672. Definitions and rules

(a) Adverse party.—For purposes of this subpart, the term "adverse party" means any person having a substantial beneficial interest in the trust which would be adversely affected by the exercise or nonexercise of the power which he possesses respecting the trust. A person having a general power of appointment over the trust property shall be deemed to have a beneficial interest in the trust.

(b) Nonadverse party.—For purposes of this subpart, the term "nonadverse party" means any person who is not an adverse party.

(c) Related or subordinate party.—For purposes of this subpart, the term "related or subordinate party" means any nonadverse party who is—

(1) the grantor's spouse if living with the grantor;

(2) any one of the following: The grantor's father, mother, issue, brother or sister; an employee of the grantor; a corporation or any employee of a corporation in which the stock holdings of the grantor and the trust are significant from the viewpoint of voting control; a subordinate employee of a corporation in which the grantor is an executive.

For purposes of sections 674 and 675, a related or subordinate party shall be presumed to be subservient to the grantor in respect of the exercise or nonexercise of the powers conferred on him unless such party is shown not to be subservient by a preponderance of the evidence.

(d) Rule where power is subject to condition precedent.—A person shall be considered to have a power described in this subpart even though the exercise of the power is subject to a precedent giving of notice or takes effect only on the expiration of a certain period after the exercise of the power.

(e) Grantor treated as holding any power or interest of grantor's spouse.—For purposes of this subpart, if a grantor's spouse is living with the grantor at the time of the creation of any power or interest held by such spouse, the grantor shall be treated as holding such power or interest.

§ 673. Reversionary interests

(a) General rule.—The grantor shall be treated as the owner of any portion of a trust in which he has a reversionary interest in either the corpus or the income therefrom, if, as of the inception of that portion of the trust, the value of such interest exceeds 5 percent of the value of such portion.

(b) Reversionary interest taking effect at death of minor lineal descendant beneficiary.—In the case of any beneficiary who—

(1) is a lineal descendant of the grantor, and

(2) holds all of the present interests in any portion of a trust,

the grantor shall not be treated under subsection (a) as the owner of such portion solely by reason of a reversionary interest in such portion which takes effect upon the death of such beneficiary before such beneficiary attains age 21.

§ 674. Power to control beneficial enjoyment

(a) General rule.—The grantor shall be treated as the owner of any portion of a trust in respect of which the beneficial enjoyment of the corpus or the income therefrom is subject to a power of disposition, exercisable by the grantor or a nonadverse party, or both, without the approval or consent of any adverse party.

(b) Exceptions for certain powers.—Subsection (a) shall not apply to the following powers regardless of by whom held:

(1) Power to apply income to support of a dependent.—A power described in section 677(b) to the extent that the grantor would not be subject to tax under that section.

(2) Power affecting beneficial enjoyment only after occurrence of events.—A power, the exercise of which can only affect the beneficial enjoyment of the income for a period commencing after the occurrence of an event such that a grantor would not be treated as the owner under section 673 if the power were a reversionary interest; but the grantor may be treated as the owner after the occurrence of the event unless the power is relinquished.

(3) Power exercisable only by will.—A power exercisable only by will, other than a power in the grantor to appoint by will the income of the trust where the income is accumulated for such disposition by the grantor or may be so accumulated in the discretion of the grantor or a nonadverse party, or both, without the approval or consent of any adverse party.

(4) Power to allocate among charitable beneficiaries.—A power to determine the beneficial enjoyment of the corpus or the income therefrom if the corpus or income is irrevocably payable for a purpose specified in section 170(c) (relating to definition of charitable contributions).

(5) Power to distribute corpus.—A power to distribute corpus either—

(A) to or for a beneficiary or beneficiaries or to or for a class of beneficiaries (whether or not income beneficiaries) provided that the power is limited by a reasonably definite standard which is set forth in the trust instrument; or

(B) to or for any current income beneficiary, provided that the distribution of corpus must be chargeable against the proportionate share of corpus held in trust for the payment of income to the beneficiary as if the corpus constituted a separate trust.

A power does not fall within the powers described in this paragraph if any person has a power to add to the beneficiary or beneficiaries or to a class of beneficiaries designated to receive the income or corpus, except where such action is to provide for after-born or after-adopted children.

(6) Power to withhold income temporarily.—A power to distribute or apply income to or for any current income beneficiary or to accumulate the income for him, provided that any accumulated income must ultimately be payable—

(A) to the beneficiary from whom distribution or application is withheld, to his estate, or to his appointees (or persons named as alternate takers in default of appointment) provided that such beneficiary possesses a power of appointment which does not exclude from the class of possible appointees any person other than the beneficiary, his estate, his creditors, or the creditors of his estate, or

(B) on termination of the trust, or in conjunction with a distribution of corpus which is augmented by such accumulated income, to the current income beneficiaries in shares which have been irrevocably specified in the trust instrument.

Accumulated income shall be considered so payable although it is provided that if any beneficiary does not survive a date of distribution which could reasonably have been expected to occur within the beneficiary's lifetime, the share of the deceased beneficiary is to be paid to his appointees or to one or more designated alternate takers (other than the grantor or the grantor's estate) whose shares have been irrevocably specified. A power does not fall within the powers described in this paragraph if any person has a power to add to the beneficiary or beneficiaries or to a class of beneficiaries designated to receive the income or corpus except where such action is to provide for after-born or after-adopted children.

(7) Power to withhold income during disability of a beneficiary.—A power exercisable only during—

(A) the existence of a legal disability of any current income beneficiary, or

(B) the period during which any income beneficiary shall be under the age of 21 years,

to distribute or apply income to or for such beneficiary or to accumulate and add the income to corpus. A power does not fall within the powers described in this paragraph if any person has a power to add to the beneficiary or beneficiaries or to a class of beneficiaries designated to receive the income or corpus, except where such action is to provide for after-born or after-adopted children.

(8) Power to allocate between corpus and income.—A power to allocate receipts and disbursements as between corpus and income, even though expressed in broad language.

(c) Exception for certain powers of independent trustees.—Subsection (a) shall not apply to a power solely exercisable (without the approval or consent of any other person) by a trustee or trustees, none of whom is the grantor, and no more than half of whom are related or subordinate parties who are subservient to the wishes of the grantor—

(1) to distribute, apportion, or accumulate income to or for a beneficiary or beneficiaries, or to, for, or within a class of beneficiaries; or

(2) to pay out corpus to or for a beneficiary or beneficiaries or to or for a class of beneficiaries (whether or not income beneficiaries).

A power does not fall within the powers described in this subsection if any person has a power to add to the beneficiary or beneficiaries or to a class of beneficiaries designated to receive the income or corpus, except where such action is to provide for after-born or after-adopted children.

(d) Power to allocate income if limited by a standard.—Subsection (a) shall not apply to a power solely exercisable (without the approval or consent of any other person) by a trustee or trustees, none of whom is the grantor or spouse living with the grantor, to distribute, apportion, or accumulate income to or for a beneficiary or beneficiaries, or to, for, or within a class of beneficiaries, whether or not the conditions of paragraph (6) or (7) of subsection (b) are satisfied, if such power is limited by a reasonably definite external standard which is set forth in the trust instrument. A power does not fall within the powers described in this subsection if any person has a power to add to the beneficiary or beneficiaries or to a class of beneficiaries designated to receive the income or corpus except where such action is to provide for after-born or after-adopted children.

§ 675. Administrative powers

The grantor shall be treated as the owner of any portion of a trust in respect of which—

(1) **Power to deal for less than adequate and full consideration.**—A power exercisable by the grantor or a nonadverse party, or both, without the approval or consent of any adverse party enables the grantor or any person to purchase, exchange, or otherwise deal with or dispose of the corpus or the income therefrom for less than an adequate consideration in money or money's worth.

(2) **Power to borrow without adequate interest or security.**—A power exercisable by the grantor or a nonadverse party, or both, enables the grantor to borrow the corpus or income, directly or indirectly, without adequate interest or without adequate security except where a trustee (other than the grantor) is authorized under a general lending power to make loans to any person without regard to interest or security.

(3) **Borrowing of the trust funds.**—The grantor has directly or indirectly borrowed the corpus or income and has not completely repaid the loan, including any interest, before the beginning of the taxable year. The preceding sentence shall not apply to a loan which provides for adequate interest and adequate security, if such loan is made by a trustee other than the grantor and other than a related or subordinate trustee subservient to the grantor.

(4) **General powers of administration.**—A power of administration is exercisable in a nonfiduciary capacity by any person without the approval or consent of any person in a fiduciary capacity. For purposes of this paragraph, the term "power of administration" means any one or more of the following powers: (A) a power to vote or direct the voting of stock or other securities of a corporation in which the holdings of the grantor and the trust are significant from the viewpoint of voting control; (B) a power to control the investment of the trust funds either by directing investments or reinvestments, or by vetoing proposed investments or reinvestments, to the extent that the trust funds consist of stocks or securities of corporations in which the holdings of the grantor and the trust are significant from the viewpoint of voting control; or (C) a power to reacquire the trust corpus by substituting other property of an equivalent value.

§ 676. Power to revoke

(a) **General rule.**—The grantor shall be treated as the owner of any portion of a trust, whether or not he is treated as such owner under any other provision of this part, where at any time the power to revest in the grantor title to such portion is exercisable by the grantor or a non-adverse party, or both.

(b) **Power affecting beneficial enjoyment only after occurrence of event.**—Subsection (a) shall not apply to a power the exercise of which can only affect the beneficial enjoyment of the income for a period commencing after the occurrence of an event such that a grantor would not be treated as the owner under section 673 if the power were a reversionary interest. But the grantor may be treated as the owner after the occurrence of such event unless the power is relinquished.

§ 677. Income for benefit of grantor

(a) General rule.—The grantor shall be treated as the owner of any portion of a trust, whether or not he is treated as such owner under section 674, whose income without the approval or consent of any adverse party is, or, in the discretion of the grantor or a nonadverse party, or both, may be—

(1) distributed to the grantor or the grantor's spouse;

(2) held or accumulated for future distribution to the grantor or the grantor's spouse; or

(3) applied to the payment of premiums on policies of insurance on the life of the grantor or the grantor's spouse (except policies of insurance irrevocably payable for a purpose specified in section 170(c) (relating to definition of charitable contributions)).

This subsection shall not apply to a power the exercise of which can only affect the beneficial enjoyment of the income for a period commencing after the occurrence of an event such that the grantor would not be treated as the owner under section 673 if the power were a reversionary interest; but the grantor may be treated as the owner after the occurrence of the event unless the power is relinquished.

(b) Obligations of support.—Income of a trust shall not be considered taxable to the grantor under subsection (a) or any other provision of this chapter merely because such income in the discretion of another person, the trustee, or the grantor acting as trustee or co-trustee, may be applied or distributed for the support or maintenance of a beneficiary (other than the grantor's spouse) whom the grantor is legally obligated to support or maintain, except to the extent that such income is so applied or distributed. In cases where the amounts so applied or distributed are paid out of corpus or out of other than income for the taxable year, such amounts shall be considered to be an amount paid or credited within the meaning of paragraph (2) of section 661(a) and shall be taxed to the grantor under section 662.

§ 678. Person other than grantor treated as substantial owner

(a) General rule.—A person other than the grantor shall be treated as the owner of any portion of a trust with respect to which:

(1) such person has a power exercisable solely by himself to vest the corpus or the income therefrom in himself, or

(2) such person has previously partially released or otherwise modified such a power and after the release or modification retains such control as would, within the principles of sections 671 to 677, inclusive, subject a grantor of a trust to treatment as the owner thereof.

(b) Exception where grantor is taxable.—Subsection (a) shall not apply with respect to a power over income, as originally granted or thereafter modified, if the grantor of the trust or a transferor (to whom section 679 applies) is otherwise treated as the owner under the provisions of this subpart other than this section.

(c) Obligations of support.—Subsection (a) shall not apply to a power which enables such person, in the capacity of trustee or co-trustee, merely to apply the income of the trust to the support or maintenance of a person whom the holder of the power is obligated to support or maintain except to the extent that such income is so applied. In cases where the amounts so applied or distributed are paid out of corpus or out of other than income of the taxable year, such amounts shall be considered to be an amount paid or credited within the meaning of paragraph (2) of section 661(a) and shall be taxed to the holder of the power under section 662.

(d) Effect of renunciation or disclaimer.—Subsection (a) shall not apply with respect to a power which has been renounced or disclaimed within a reasonable time after the holder of the power first became aware of its existence.

(e) Cross Reference.—

For provision under which beneficiary of trust is treated as owner of the portion of the trust which consists of stock in an electing small business corporation, see section 1361(d).

§ 679. Foreign trusts having one or more United States beneficiaries

(a) Transferor treated as owner.—

(1) In general.—A United States person who directly or indirectly transfers property to a foreign trust (other than a trust described in section 404(a)(4) or 404A(a)(4)) shall be treated as the owner for his taxable year of the portion of such trust attributable to such property if for such year there is a United States beneficiary of any portion of such trust.

(2) Exceptions.—Paragraph (1) shall not apply—

(A) Transfers by reason of death.—To any transfer by reason of the death of the transferor.

(B) Transfers where gain is recognized to transferor.—To any sale or exchange of the property at its fair market value in a transaction in which all of the gain to the transferor is realized at the time of the transfer and is recognized either at such time or is returned as provided in section 453.

(b) Trusts acquiring United States beneficiaries.—If—

(1) subsection (a) applies to a trust for the transferor's taxable year, and

(2) subsection (a) would have applied to the trust for his immediately preceding taxable year but for the fact that for such preceding taxable year there was no United States beneficiary for any portion of the trust,

then, for purposes of this subtitle, the transferor shall be treated as having income for the taxable year (in addition to his other income for such year) equal to the undistributed net income (at the close of such immediately preceding taxable year) attributable to the portion of the trust referred to in subsection (a).

(c) Trusts treated as having a United States beneficiary.—

(1) In General.—For purposes of this section, a trust shall be treated as having a United States beneficiary for the taxable year unless—

(A) under the terms of the trust, no part of the income or corpus of the trust may be paid or accumulated during the taxable year to or for the benefit of a United States person, and

(B) if the trust were teminated at any time during the taxable year, no part of the income or corpus of such trust could be paid to or for the benefit of a United States person.

(2) Attribution of ownership.—For purposes of paragraph (1), an amount shall be treated as paid or accumulated to or for the benefit of a United States person if such amount is paid to or accumulated for a foreign corporation, foreign partnership, or foreign trust or estate, and—

(A) in the case of a foreign corporation, more than 50 percent of the total combined voting power of all classes of stock entitled to vote of such corporation is owned (within the meaning of section 958(a)) or is considered to be owned (within the meaning of section 958(b)) by United States shareholders (as defined in section 951(b)),

(B) in the case of a foreign partnership, a United States person is a partner of such partnership, or

(C) in the case of a foreign trust or estate, such trust or estate has a United States beneficiary (within the meaning of paragraph (1)).

Subpart 7—Miscellaneous

§ 681. Limitation on charitable deduction

(a) Trade or business income.—In computing the deduction allowable under section 642(c) to a trust, no amount otherwise allowable under section 642(c) as a deduction shall be allowed as a deduction with respect to income of a taxable year which is allocable to its unrelated business income for such year. For purposes of the preceding sentence, the term "unrelated business income" means an amount equal to the amount which, if such trust were exempt from tax under section 501(a) by reason of section 501(c) (3), would be computed as its unrelated business taxable income under section 512 (relating to income derived from certain business activities and from certain property acquired with borrowed funds).

* * *

§ 682. Income of an estate or trust in case of divorce, etc.

(a) Inclusion in gross income of wife.—There shall be included in the gross income of a wife who is divorced or legally separated under a decree of divorce or of separate maintenance (or who is separated from her husband under a written separation agreement) the amount of the income of any trust which such wife is entitled to receive and which, except for this section, would be includible in the gross income of her husband, and such amount shall not, despite any other provision of this subtitle, be includible in the gross income of such husband. This subsection shall not apply to that part of any such income of the trust which the terms of the decree, written separation agreement, or trust instrument fix, in terms of an amount of money or a portion of such income, as a sum which is payable for the support of minor children of such husband. In case such income is less than the amount specified in the decree, agreement, or instrument, for the purpose of applying the preceding sentence, such income, to the extent of such sum payable for such support, shall be considered a payment for such support.

(b) Wife considered a beneficiary.—For purposes of computing the taxable income of the estate or trust and the taxable income of a wife to whom subsection (a) applies, such wife shall be considered as the beneficiary specified in this part.

(c) **Cross reference.—**

For definitions of "husband" and "wife", as used in this section, see section 7701(a) (17).

* * *

PART II—INCOME IN RESPECT OF DECEDENTS

§ 691. Recipients of income in respect of decedents

(a) Inclusion in gross income.—

(1) **General rule.**—The amount of all items of gross income in respect of a decedent which are not properly includible in respect of the taxable period in which falls the date of his death or a prior period (including the amount of all items of gross income in respect of a prior decedent, if the right to receive such amount was acquired by reason of the death of the prior decedent or by bequest, devise, or inheritance from the prior decedent) shall be included in the gross income, for the taxable year when received, of:

(A) the estate of the decedent, if the right to receive the amount is acquired by the decedent's estate from the decedent;

(B) the person who, by reason of the death of the decedent, acquires the right to receive the amount, if the right to receive the amount is not acquired by the decedent's estate from the decedent; or

(C) the person who acquires from the decedent the right to receive the amount by bequest, devise, or inheritance, if the amount is received after a distribution by the decedent's estate of such right.

(2) **Income in case of sale, etc.**—If a right, described in paragraph (1), to receive an amount is transferred by the estate of the decedent or a person who received such right by reason of the death of the decedent or by bequest, devise, or inheritance from the decedent, there shall be included in the gross income of the estate or such person, as the case may be, for the taxable period in which the transfer occurs, the fair market value of such right at the time of such transfer plus the amount by which any consideration for the transfer exceeds such fair market value. For purposes of this paragraph, the term "transfer" includes sale, exchange, or other disposition, or the satisfaction of an installment obligation at other than face value, but does not include transmission at death to the estate of the decedent or a transfer to a person pursuant to the right of such person to receive such amount by reason of the death of the decedent or by bequest, devise, or inheritance from the decedent.

(3) **Character of income determined by reference to decedent.**—The right, described in paragraph (1), to receive an amount shall be treated, in the hands of the estate of the decedent or any person who acquired such right by reason of the death of the decedent, or by bequest, devise, or inheritance from the decedent, as if it had been acquired by the estate or such person in the transaction in which the right to receive the income was originally derived and the amount includible in gross income under paragraph (1) or (2) shall be considered in the hands of the estate or such person to have the character which it would have had in the hands of the decedent if the decedent had lived and received such amount.

(4) **Installment obligations acquired from decedent.**—In the case of an installment obligation reportable by the decedent on the installment

method under section 453 or 453A, if such obligation is acquired by the decedent's estate from the decedent or by any person by reason of the death of the decedent or by bequest, devise, or inheritance from the decedent—

(A) an amount equal to the excess of the face amount of such obligation over the basis of the obligation in the hands of the decedent (determined under section 453B) shall, for the purpose of paragraph (1), be considered as an item of gross income in respect of the decedent; and

(B) such obligation shall, for purposes of paragraphs (2) and (3), be considered a right to receive an item of gross income in respect of the decedent, but the amount includible in gross income under paragraph (2) shall be reduced by an amount equal to the basis of the obligation in the hands of the decedent (determined under section 453B).

(5) Other rules relating to installment obligations.—

(A) In general.—In the case of an installment obligation reportable by the decedent on the installment method under section 453 or 453A, for purposes of paragraph (2)—

(i) the second sentence of paragraph (2) shall be applied by inserting "(other than the obligor)" after "or a transfer to a person",

(ii) any cancellation of such an obligation shall be treated as a transfer, and

(iii) any cancellation of such an obligation occurring at the death of the decedent shall be treated as a transfer by the estate of the decedent (or, if held by a person other than the decedent before the death of the decedent, by such person).

(B) Face amount treated as fair market value in certain cases.—In any case to which the first sentence of paragraph (2) applies by reason of subparagraph (A), if the decedent and the obligor were related persons (within the meaning of section 453(f)(1)), the fair market value of the installment obligation shall be treated as not less than its face amount.

(C) Cancellation includes becoming unenforceable.—For purposes of subparagraph (A), an installment obligation which becomes unenforceable shall be treated as if it were canceled.

(b) Allowance of deductions and credit.—The amount of any deduction specified in section 162, 163, 164, 212, or 611 (relating to deductions for expenses, interest, taxes, and depletion) or credit specified in section 27 (relating to foreign tax credit), in respect of a decedent which is not properly allowable to the decedent in respect of the taxable period in which falls the date of his death, or a prior period, shall be allowed:

(1) Expenses, interest, and taxes.—In the case of a deduction specified in section 162, 163, 164, or 212 and a credit specified in section 27, in the taxable year when paid—

(A) to the estate of the decedent; except that

(B) if the estate of the decedent is not liable to discharge the obligation to which the deduction or credit relates, to the person who, by reason of the death of the decedent or by bequest, devise, or inheritance acquires, subject to such obligation, from the decedent an interest in property of the decedent.

(2) **Depletion.**—In the case of the deduction specified in section 611, to the person described in subsection (a) (1) (A), (B), or (C) who, in the manner described therein, receives the income to which the deduction relates, in the taxable year when such income is received.

(c) **Deduction for estate tax.**—

(1) **Allowance of deduction.**—

(A) **General rule.**—A person who includes an amount in gross income under subsection (a) shall be allowed, for the same taxable year, as a deduction an amount which bears the same ratio to the estate tax attributable to the net value for estate tax purposes of all the items described in subsection (a) (1) as the value for estate tax purposes of the items of gross income or portions thereof in respect of which such person included the amount in gross income (or the amount included in gross income, whichever is lower) bears to the value for estate tax purposes of all the items described in subsection (a) (1).

(B) **Estates and trusts.**—In the case of an estate or trust, the amount allowed as a deduction under subparagraph (A) shall be computed by excluding from the gross income of the estate or trust the portion (if any) of the items described in subsection (a) (1) which is properly paid, credited, or to be distributed to the beneficiaries during the taxable year.

(2) **Method of computing deduction.**—For purposes of paragraph (1)—

(A) The term "estate tax" means the tax imposed on the estate of the decedent or any prior decedent under section 2001 or 2101, reduced by the credits against such tax.

(B) The net value for estate tax purposes of all the items described in subsection (a) (1) shall be the excess of the value for estate tax purposes of all the items described in subsection (a) (1) over the deductions from the gross estate in respect of claims which represent the deductions and credit described in subsection (b). Such net value shall be determined with respect to the provisions of section 421(c) (2), relating to the deduction for estate tax with respect to stock options to which part II of subchapter D applies.

(C) The estate tax attributable to such net value shall be an amount equal to the excess of the estate tax over the estate tax computed without including in the gross estate such net value.

(3) **Special rule for generation-skipping transfers.**—In the case of any tax imposed by chapter 13 on a taxable termination or a direct skip occurring as a result of the death of the transferor, there shall be allowed a deduction (under principles similar to the principles of this subsection) for the portion of such tax attributable to items of gross income of the trust which were not properly includible in the gross income of the trust for periods before the date of such termination.

(4) **Coordination with capital gain provisions**—For purposes of sections 1(j), 1201, and 1211, the amount of any gain taken into account with respect to any item described in subsection (a)(1) shall be reduced (but

not below zero) by the amount of the deduction allowable under paragraph (1) of this subsection with respect to such item.

(5) Coordination with section 402(e).—For purposes of section 402(e) (other than paragraph (1) (D) thereof), the total taxable amount of any lump sum distribution shall be reduced by the amount of the deduction allowable under paragraph (1) of this subsection which is attributable to the total taxable amount (determined without regard to this paragraph).

(d) Amounts received by surviving annuitant under joint and survivor annuity contract.—

(1) Deduction for estate tax.—For purposes of computing the deduction under subsection (c) (1) (A), amounts received by a surviving annuitant—

(A) as an annuity under a joint and survivor annuity contract where the decedent annuitant died after December 31, 1953, and after the annuity starting date (as defined in section 72(c) (4)), and

(B) during the surviving annuitant's life expectancy period,

shall, to the extent included in gross income under section 72, be considered as amounts included in gross income under subsection (a).

(2) Net value for estate tax purposes.—In determining the net value for estate tax purposes under subsection (c) (2) (B) for purposes of this subsection, the value for estate tax purposes of the items described in paragraph (1) of this subsection shall be computed—

(A) by determining the excess of the value of the annuity at the date of the death of the deceased annuitant over the total amount excludable from the gross income of the surviving annuitant under section 72 during the surviving annuitant's life expectancy period, and

(B) by multiplying the figure so obtained by the ratio which the value of the annuity for estate tax purposes bears to the value of the annuity at the date of the death of the deceased.

(3) Definitions.—For purposes of this subsection—

(A) The term "life expectancy period" means the period beginning with the first day of the first period for which an amount is received by the surviving annuitant under the contract and ending with the close of the taxable year with or in which falls the termination of the life expectancy of the surviving annuitant. For purposes of this subparagraph, the life expectancy of the surviving annuitant shall be determined, as of the date of the death of the deceased annuitant, with reference to actuarial tables prescribed by the Secretary.

(B) The surviving annuitant's expected return under the contract shall be computed, as of the death of the deceased annuitant, with reference to actuarial tables prescribed by the Secretary.

(e) Cross reference.—

For application of this section to income in respect of a deceased partner, see section 753.

ESTATES, TRUSTS, BENEFICIARIES, AND DECEDENTS

Estates, Trusts, and Beneficiaries

General Rule for Taxation of Estates and Trusts

§ 1.641(a)–0 Scope of Subchapter J.

(a) In general. Subchapter J (sections 641 and following), Chapter 1 of the Code, deals with the taxation of income of estates and trusts and their beneficiaries, and of income in respect of decedents. Part I of Subchapter J contains general rules for taxation of estates and trusts (Subpart A), specific rules relating to trusts which distribute current income only (Subpart B), estates and trusts which may accumulate income or which distribute corpus (Subpart C), treatment of excess distributions by trusts (Subpart D), grantors and other persons treated as substantial owners (Subpart E), and miscellaneous provisions relating to limitations on charitable deductions, income of an estate or trust in case of divorce, and taxable years to which the provisions of Subchapter J are applicable (Subpart F). Part I has no application to any organization which is not to be classified for tax purposes as a trust under the classification rules of §§ 301.7701–2, 301.7701–3, and 301.7701–4 of this chapter (Regulations on Procedure and Administration). Part II of Subchapter J relates to the treatment of income in respect of decedents. However, the provisions of Subchapter J do not apply to employee trusts subject to Subchapters D and F, Chapter 1 of the Code, and common trust funds subject to Subchapter H, Chapter 1 of the Code.

(b) Scope of subparts A, B, C, and D. Subparts A, B, C, and D (section 641 and following), part I, subchapter J, chapter 1 of the Code, relate to the taxation of estates and trusts and their beneficiaries. These subparts have no application to any portion of the corpus or income of a trust which is to be regarded, within the meaning of the Code, as that of the grantor or others treated as its substantial owners. See subpart E (section 671 and following), part I, subchapter J, chapter 1 of the Code, and the regulations thereunder for rules for the treatment of any portion of a trust where the grantor (or another person) is treated as the substantial owner. So-called alimony trusts are treated under subparts A, B, C, and D, except to the extent otherwise provided in section 71 or section 682. These subparts have no application to beneficiaries of nonexempt employees' trusts. See section 402(b) and the regulations thereunder.

(c) Multiple trusts. Multiple trusts that have—

(1) No substantially independent purposes (such as independent dispositive purposes),

(2) The same grantor and substantially the same beneficiary, and

(3) The avoidance or mitigation of (a) the progressive rates of tax (including mitigation as a result of deferral of tax) or (b) the minimum tax for tax preferences imposed by section 56 as their principal purpose,

shall be consolidated and treated as one trust for the purposes of subchapter J.

[T.D. 6217, Dec. 19, 1956, as amended by T.D. 6989, Jan. 16, 1969; T.D. 7204, Aug. 24, 1972]

§ 1.641(a)–1 Imposition of tax; application of tax.

For taxable years beginning after December 31, 1970, section 641 prescribes that the taxes imposed by section 1(d), as amended by the Tax Reform Act of 1969, shall apply to the income of estates or of any kind of property held in trust. For taxable years ending before January 1, 1971, section 641 prescribes that the taxes imposed upon individuals by chapter 1 of the Code apply to the income of estates or of any kind of property held in trust. The rates of tax, the statutory provisions respecting gross income, and, with certain exceptions, the deductions and credits allowed to individuals apply also to estates and trust.

[T.D. 6217, Dec. 19, 1956, as amended by T.D. 7117, May 24, 1971]

§ 1.641(a)–2 Gross income of estates and trusts.

The gross income of an estate or trust is determined in the same manner as that of an individual. Thus, the gross income of an estate or trust consists of all items of gross income received during the taxable year, including:

(a) Income accumulated in trust for the benefit of unborn or unascertained persons or persons with contingent interests;

(b) Income accumulated or held for future distribution under the terms of the will or trust;

(c) Income which is to be distributed currently by the fiduciary to the beneficiaries, and income collected by a guardian of an infant which is to be held or distributed as the court may direct;

(d) Income received by estates of deceased persons during the period of administration or settlement of the estate; and

(e) Income which, in the discretion of the fiduciary, may be either distributed to the beneficiaries or accumulated.

The several classes of income enumerated in this section do not exclude others which also may come within the general purposes of section 641.

[T.D. 6217, Dec. 19, 1956]

§ 1.641(b)–1 Computation and payment of tax; deductions and credits of estates and trusts.

Generally, the deductions and credits allowed to individuals are also allowed to estates and trusts. However, there are special rules for the computation of certain deductions and for the allocation between the estate or trust and the beneficiaries of certain credits and deductions. See section 642 and the regulations thereunder. In addition, an estate or trust is allowed to deduct, in computing its taxable income, the deductions provided by sections 651 and 661 and regulations thereunder, relating to distributions to beneficiaries.

[T.D. 6217, Dec. 19, 1956]

§ 1.641(b)–2 Filing of returns and payment of the tax.

(a) The fiduciary is required to make and file the return and pay the tax on the taxable income of an estate or of a trust. Liability for the payment of the tax on the taxable income of an estate attaches to the person of the executor or administrator up to and after his discharge if, prior to distribution and discharge, he had notice of his tax obligations or failed to exercise due diligence in ascertaining whether or not such obligations existed. For the extent of such liability, see section 3467 of the Revised Statutes, as amended by section 518 of the Revenue Act of 1934 (31 U.S.C. 192). Liability for the tax also follows the assets of the estate distributed to heirs, devisees, legatees, and distributees, who may be required to discharge the amount of the tax due and unpaid to the extent of the distributive shares received by them. See section 6901. The same considerations apply to trusts.

(b) The estate of an infant, incompetent, or other person under a disability, or, in general, of an individual or corporation in receivership or a corporation in bankruptcy is not a taxable entity separate from the person for whom the fiduciary is acting, in that respect differing from the estate of a deceased person or of a trust. See section 6012(b)(2) and (3) for provisions relating to the obligation of the fiduciary with respect to returns of such persons.

[T.D. 6217, Dec. 19, 1956, as amended by T.D. 6580, Dec. 4, 1961]

§ 1.641(b)–3 Termination of estates and trusts.

(a) The income of an estate of a deceased person is that which is received by the estate during the period of administration or settlement. The period of administration or settlement is the period actually required by the administrator or executor to perform the ordinary duties of administration, such as the collection of assets and the payment of debts, taxes, legacies, and bequests, whether the period required is longer or shorter than the period specified under the applicable local law for the settlement of estates. For example, where an executor who is also named as trustee under a will fails to obtain his discharge as executor, the period of administration continues only until the duties of administration are complete and he actually assumes his duties as trustee, whether or not pursuant to a court order. However, the period of administration of an estate cannot be unduly prolonged. If the administration of an estate is unreasonably prolonged, the estate is considered terminated for Federal income tax purposes after the expiration of a reasonable period for the performance by the executor of all the duties of administration. Further, an estate will be considered as terminated when all the assets have been distributed except for a reasonable amount which is set aside in good faith for the payment of unascertained or contingent liabilities and expenses (not including a claim by a beneficiary in the capacity of beneficiary).

(b) Generally, the determination of whether a trust has terminated depends upon whether the property held in trust has been distributed to the persons entitled to succeed to the property upon termination of the trust rather than upon the technicality of whether or not the trustee has rendered his final accounting. A trust does not automatically terminate upon the happening of the event by which the duration of the trust is measured. A reasonable time is permitted after such event for the trustee to perform the duties necessary to complete the administration of the trust. Thus, if under the terms of the governing instrument, the trust is to terminate upon the death of the life beneficiary and the corpus is to be distributed to the remainderman, the trust continues after the death of the life beneficiary for a period reasonably necessary to a proper winding up of the affairs of the trust. However, the winding up of a trust cannot be unduly postponed and if the distribution of the trust corpus is unreasonably delayed, the trust is considered terminated for Federal income tax purposes after the expiration of a reasonable period for the trustee to complete the administration of the trust. Further, a trust will be considered as terminated when all the assets have been distributed except for a reasonable amount which is set aside in good faith for the payment of unascertained or contingent liabilities and expenses (not including a claim by a beneficiary in the capacity of beneficiary).

(c)(1) Except as provided in subparagraph (2) of this paragraph, during the period between the occurrence of an event which causes a trust to terminate and the time when the trust is considered as terminated under this section, whether or not the income and the excess of capital gains over capital losses of the trust are to be considered as amounts required to be distributed currently to the ultimate distributee for the year in which they are received depends upon the principles stated in § 1.651(a)-2. See § 1.663-1 et seq. for application of the separate share rule.

(2)(i) Except in cases to which the last sentence of this subdivision applies, for taxable years of a trust ending before September 1, 1957, subparagraph (1) of this paragraph shall not apply and the rule of subdivision (ii) of this subparagraph shall apply unless the trustee elects to have subparagraph (1) of this paragraph apply. Such election shall be made by the trustee in a statement filed on or before April 15, 1959, with the district director with whom such trust's return for any such taxable year was filed. The election provided by this subdivision shall not be available if the treatment given the income and the excess of capital gains over capital losses for taxable years for which returns have been filed was consistent with the provisions of subparagraph (1) of this paragraph.

(ii) The rule referred to in subdivision (i) of this subparagraph is as follows: During the period between the occurrence of an event which causes a trust to terminate and the time when a trust is considered as terminated under this section, the income and the excess of capital gains over capital losses of the trust are in general considered as amounts required to be distributed for the year in which they are received. For example, a trust instrument provides for the payment of income to A during her life, and upon her death for the payment of the corpus to B. The trust reports on the basis of the calendar year. A dies on November 1, 1955, but no distribution is made to B until January 15, 1956. The income of the trust and the excess of capital gains over capital losses for the entire year 1955, to the extent not paid, credited, or required to be distributed to A or A's estate, are treated under sections 661 and 662 as amounts required to be distributed to B for the year 1955.

(d) If a trust or the administration or settlement of an estate is considered terminated under this section for Federal income tax purposes (as for instance, because administration has been unduly prolonged), the gross income, deductions, and credits of the estate or trust are, subsequent to the termination, considered the gross income, deductions, and credits of the person or persons succeeding to the property of the estate or trust.

[T.D. 6217, Dec. 19, 1956, as amended by T.D. 6353, Jan. 13, 1959; T.D. 6462, May 5, 1960]

§ 1.642(b)-1 Deduction for personal exemption.

In lieu of the deduction for personal exemptions provided by section 151:

(a) An estate is allowed a deduction of $600.

(b) A trust which, under its governing instrument, is required to distribute currently all of its income for the taxable year is allowed a deduction of $300, and

(c) All other trusts are allowed a deduction of $100.

A trust which, under its governing instrument, is required to distribute all of its income currently is allowed a deduction of $300, even though it also distributes amounts other than income in the taxable year and even though it may be required to make distributions which would qualify for the charitable contributions deduction under section 642(c) (and therefore does not qualify as a "simple trust" under sections 651–652). A trust for the payment of an annuity is allowed a deduction of $300 in a taxable year in which the amount of the annuity required to be paid equals or exceeds all the income of the trust for the taxable year. For the meaning of the term "income required to be distributed currently", see § 1.651(a)–2.

[T.D. 6217, Dec. 19, 1956]

§ 1.642(c)–1 Unlimited deduction for amounts paid for a charitable purpose.

(a) In general. (1) Any part of the gross income of an estate, or trust which, pursuant to the terms of the governing instrument is paid (or treated under paragraph (b) of this section as paid) during the taxable year for a purpose specified in section 170(c) shall be allowed as a deduction to such estate or trust in lieu of the limited charitable contributions deduction authorized by section 170(a). In applying this paragraph without reference to paragraph (b) of this section, a deduction shall be allowed for an amount paid during the taxable year in respect of gross income received in a previous taxable year, but only if no deduction was allowed for any previous taxable year for the amount so paid.

(2) In determining whether an amount is paid for a purpose specified in section 170(c)(2) the provisions of section 170(c)(2)(A) shall not be taken into account. Thus, an amount paid to a corporation, trust, or community chest, fund, or foundation otherwise described in section 170(c)(2) shall be considered paid for a purpose specified in section 170(c) even though the corporation, trust, or community chest, fund, or foundation is not created or organized in the United States, any State, the District of Columbia, or any possession of the United States.

(3) See section 642(c)(6) and § 1.642(c)–4 for disallowance of a deduction under this section to a trust which is, or is treated under section 4947(a)(1) as though it were a private foundation (as defined in section 509(a) and the regulations thereunder) and not exempt from taxation under section 501(a).

(b) Election to treat contributions as paid in preceding taxable year—(1) In general. For purposes of determining the deduction allowed under paragraph (a) of this section, the fiduciary (as defined in section 7701(a)(6)) of an estate or trust may elect under section 642(c)(1) to treat as paid during the taxable year (whether or not such year begins before January 1, 1970) any amount of gross income received during such taxable year or any preceding taxable year which is otherwise deductible under such paragraph and which is paid after the close of such taxable year but on or before the last day of the next succeeding taxable year of the estate or trust. The preceding sentence applies only in the case of payments actually made in a taxable year which is a taxable year beginning after December 31, 1969. No election shall be made, however, in respect of any amount which was deducted for any previous taxable year or which is deducted for the taxable year in which such amount is paid.

(2) **Time for making election.** The election under subparagraph (1) of this paragraph shall be made not later than the time, including extensions thereof, prescribed by law for filing the income tax return for the succeeding taxable year. Such election shall, except as provided in subparagraph (4) of this paragraph, become irrevocable after the last day prescribed for making it. Having made the election for any taxable year, the fiduciary may, within the time prescribed for making it, revoke the election without the consent of the Commissioner.

(3) **Manner of making the election.** The election shall be made by filing with the income tax return (or an amended return) for the taxable year in which the contribution is treated as paid a statement which—

(i) States the name and address of the fiduciary,

(ii) Identifies the estate or trust for which the fiduciary is acting,

(iii) Indicates that the fiduciary is making an election under section 642(c)(1) in respect of contributions treated as paid during such taxable year,

(iv) Gives the name and address of each organization to which any such contribution is paid, and

(v) States the amount of each contribution and date of actual payment or, if applicable, the total amount of contributions paid to each organization during the succeeding taxable year, to be treated as paid in the preceding taxable year.

(4) **Revocation of certain elections with consent.** An application to revoke with the consent of the Commissioner any election made on or before June 8, 1970, must be in writing and must be filed not later than September 2, 1975.

No consent will be granted to revoke an election for any taxable year for which the assessment of a deficiency is prevented by the operation of any law or rule of law. If consent to revoke the election is granted, the fiduciary must attach a copy of the consent to the return (or amended return) for each taxable year affected by the revocation. The application must be addressed to the Commissioner of Internal Revenue, Washington, D.C. 20224, and must indicate—

(i) The name and address of the fiduciary and the estate or trust for which he was acting,

(ii) The taxable year for which the election was made,

(iii) The office of the district director, or the service center, where the return (or amended return) for the year of election was filed, and

(iv) The reason for revoking the election.

[T.D. 6217, Dec. 19, 1956, as amended by T.D. 7357, May 30, 1975]

§ 1.642(c)-2 Unlimited deduction for amounts permanently set aside for a charitable purpose.

(a) **Estates.** Any part of the gross income of an estate which pursuant to the terms of the will—

(1) Is permanently set aside during the taxable year for a purpose specified in section 170(c), or

(2) Is to be used (within or without the United States or any of its possessions) exclusively for religious, charitable, scientific, literary, or educational purposes, or for the prevention of cruelty to children or animals, or for the establishment, acquisition, maintenance, or operation of a public cemetery not operated for profit,

shall be allowed as a deduction to the estate in lieu of the limited charitable contributions deduction authorized by section 170(a).

(b) **Certain trusts—(1) In general.** Any part of the gross income of a trust to which either subparagraph (3) or (4) of this paragraph applies, that by the terms of the governing instrument—

(i) Is permanently set aside during the taxable year for a purpose specified in section 170(c), or

(ii) Is to be used (within or without the United States or any of its possessions) exclusively for religious, charitable, scientific, literary, or educational purposes, or for the prevention of cruelty to children or animals, or for the establishment, acquisition, maintenance, or operation of a public cemetery not operated for profit,

shall be allowed, subject to the limitation provided in subparagraph (2) of this paragraph, as a deduction to the trust in lieu of the limited charitable contributions deduction authorized by section 170(a). The preceding sentence applied only to a trust which is required by the terms of its governing instrument to set amounts aside. See section 642(c)(6) and § 1.642(c)-4 for disallowance of a deduction under this section to a trust which is, or is treated under section 4947(a)(1) as though it were, a private foundation (as defined in section 509(a) and the regulations thereunder) that is not exempt from taxation under section 501(a).

(2) **Limitation of deduction.** Subparagraph (1) of this paragraph applies only to the gross income earned by a trust with respect to amounts transferred to the trust under a will executed on or before October 9, 1969, and satisfying the requirements of subparagraph (4) of this paragraph or transferred to the trust on or before October 9, 1969. For such purposes, any income, gains, or losses, which are derived at any time from the amounts so transferred to the trust shall also be taken into account in applying subparagraph (1) of this paragraph. If any such amount so transferred to the trust is invested or reinvested at any time, any asset received by the trust upon such investment or reinvestment shall also be treated as an amount which was so transferred to the trust. In the case of a trust to which this paragraph applies which contains (i) amounts transferred pursuant to transfers described in the first sentence of this subparagraph and (ii) amounts transferred pursuant to transfers not so described, subparagraph (1) of this paragraph shall apply only if the amounts described in subdivision (i) of this subparagraph, together with all income, gains, and losses derived therefrom, are separately accounted for from the amounts described in subdivision (ii) of this subparagraph, together with all income, gains, and losses derived therefrom. Such separate accounting shall be carried out consistently with the principles of paragraph (c)(4) of § 53.4947-1 of this chapter (Foundation Excise Tax Regulations), relating to accounting for segregated amounts of split-interest trusts.

(3) **Trusts created on or before October 9, 1969.** A trust to which this subparagraph applies is a trust, testamentary or otherwise, which was created on or before October 9, 1969, and which qualifies under either subdivision (i) or (ii) of this subparagraph.

(i) **Transfer of irrevocable remainder interest to charity.** To qualify under this subdivision the trust must have been created under the terms of an instrument granting an irrevocable remainder interest in such trust to or for the use of an organization described in section 170(c). If the instrument granted a revocable remainder interest but the power to revoke such interest terminated on or before October 9, 1969, without the remainder interest having been revoked, the remainder interest will be treated as irrevocable for purposes of the preceding sentence.

(ii) **Grantor under a mental disability to change terms of trust.** (A) To qualify under this subdivision (ii) the trust must have been created by a grantor who was at all times after October 9, 1969, under a mental disability to change the terms of the trust. The term "mental disability" for this purpose means mental incompetence to change the terms of the trust, whether or not there has been an adjudication of mental incompetence and whether or not there has been an appointment of a committee, guardian, fiduciary, or other person charged with the care of the person or property of the grantor.

(B) If the grantor has not been adjudged mentally incompetent, the trustee must obtain from a qualified physician a certificate stating that the grantor of the trust has been mentally incompetent at all times after October 9, 1969, and that there is no reasonable probability that the grantor's mental capacity will ever improve to the extent that he will be mentally competent to change the terms of the trust. A copy of this certification must be filed with the first return on which a deduction is claimed by reason of this subdivision (ii) and subparagraph (1) of this paragraph. Thereafter, a statement referring to such medical opinion must be attached to any return for a taxable year for which such a deduction is claimed and during which the grantor's mental incompetence continues. The original certificate must be retained by the trustee of the trust.

(C) If the grantor has been adjudged mentally incompetent, a copy of the judgment or decree, and any modification thereof, must be filed with the first return on which a deduction is claimed by reason of this subdivision (ii) and subparagraph (1) of this paragraph. Thereafter, a statement referring to such judgment or decree must be attached to any return for a taxable year for which such a deduction is claimed and during which the grantor's mental incompetence continues. A copy of such judgment or decree must also be retained by the trustee of the trust.

(D) This subdivision (ii) applies even though a person charged with the care of the person or property of the grantor has the power to change the terms of the trust.

* * *

(c) **Pooled income funds.** Any part of the gross income of a pooled income fund to which § 1.642(c)–5 applies for the taxable year that is attributable to net long-term capital gain (as defined in section 1222(7)) which, pursuant to the terms of the governing instrument, is permanently set aside during the taxable year for a purpose specified in section 170(c) shall be allowed as a deduction to the fund in lieu of the limited charitable contributions deduction authorized by section 170(a). No deduction shall be allowed under this paragraph for any portion of the gross income of such fund which is (1) attributable to income other than net long-term capital gain (2) earned with respect to amounts transferred to such fund before August 1, 1969. However, see paragraph (b) of this section for a deduction (subject to the limitations of such paragraph) for amounts permanently set aside by a pooled income fund which meets the requirements of that paragraph. The principles of paragraph (b)(2) of this section with respect to investment, reinvestment, and separate accounting shall apply under this paragraph in the case of amounts transferred to the fund after July 31, 1969.

(d) Disallowance of deduction for certain amounts not deemed to be permanently set aside for charitable purposes. No amount will be considered to be permanently set aside, or to be used, for a purpose described in paragraph (a) or (b)(1) of this section unless under the terms of the governing instrument and the circumstances of the particular case the possibility that the amount set aside, or to be used, will not be devoted to such purpose or use is so remote as to be negligible. Thus, for example, where there is possibility of the invasion of the corpus of a charitable remainder trust, as defined in § 1.664-1(a)(1)(ii), in order to make payment of the annuity amount or unitrust amount, no deduction will be allowed under paragraph (a) of this section in respect of any amount set aside by an estate for distribution to such a charitable remainder trust.

For treatment of distributions by an estate to a charitable remainder trust, see paragraph (a)(5)(iii) of § 1.664-1.

[T.D. 6217, Dec. 19, 1956, as amended by T.D. 7357, May 30, 1975]

§ 1.642(c)-3 Adjustments and other special rules for determining unlimited charitable contributions deduction.

(a) Income in respect of a decedent. For purposes of §§ 1.642(c)-1 and 1.642(c)-2, an amount received by an estate or trust which is includible in its gross income under section 691(a)(1) as income in respect of a decedent shall be included in the gross income of the estate or trust.

(b) Reduction of charitable contributions deduction by amounts not included in gross income. **(1)** If an estate, pooled income fund, or other trust pays, permanently sets aside, or uses any amount of its income for a purpose specified in section 642(c)(1), (2) or (3) and that amount includes any items of estate or trust income not entering into the gross income of the estate or trust, the deduction allowable under § 1.642(c)-1 or § 1.642(c)-2 is limited to the gross income so paid, permanently set aside, or used. In the case of a pooled income fund for which a deduction is allowable under paragraph (c) of § 1.642(c)-2 for amounts permanently set aside, only the gross income of the fund which is attributable to net long-term capital gain (as defined in section 1222(7)) shall be taken into account.

(2) In determining whether the amounts of income so paid, permanently set aside, or used for a purpose specified in section 642(c)(1), (2), or (3) include particular items of income of an estate or trust not included in gross income, the specific provision controls if the governing instrument specifically provides as to the source out of which amounts are to be paid, permanently set aside, or used for such a purpose.

In the absence of specific provisions in the governing instrument, an amount to which section 642(c)(1), (2) or (3) applies is deemed to consist of the same proportion of each class of the items of income of the estate or trust as the total of each class bears to the total of all classes. See paragraph (b) of

§ 1.643(a)-5 for the method of determining the allocable portion of exempt income and foreign income.

(3) For examples showing the determination of the character of an amount deductible under § 1.642(c)-1 or § 1.642(c)-2, see examples (1) and (2) in § 1.662(b)-2 and paragraph (e) of the example in § 1.662(c)-4.

(4) For the purpose of this paragraph, the provisions of section 116 are not to be taken into account.

(c) **Capital gains included in charitable contribution.** Where any amount of the income paid, permanently set aside, or used for a purpose specified in section 642(c)(1), (2), or (3), is attributable to net long-term capital gain (as defined in section 1222(7)), the amount of the deduction otherwise allowable under § 1.642(c)-1 or § 1.642(c)-2, must be adjusted for any deduction provided in section 1202 of 50 percent of the excess, if any, of the net long-term capital gain over the net short-term capital loss. For determination of the extent to which the contribution to which § 1.642(c)-1 or § 1.642(c)-2 applies is deemed to consist of net long-term capital gains, see paragraph (b) of this section. The application of this paragraph may be illustrated by the following examples:

Example (1). Under the terms of the trust instrument, the income of a trust described in § 1.642(c)-2(b)(3)(i) is currently distributable to A during his life and capital gains are allocable to corpus. No provision is made in the trust instrument for the invasion of corpus for the benefit of A. Upon A's death the corpus of the trust is to be distributed to M University, an organization described in section 501(c)(3) which is exempt from taxation under section 501(a). During the taxable year ending December 31, 1970, the trust has long-term capital gains of $100,000 from property transferred to it on or before October 9, 1969, which are permanently set aside for charitable purposes. The trust includes $100,000 in gross income but is allowed a deduction of $50,000 under section 1202 for the long-term capital gains and a charitable contributions deduction of $50,000 under section 642(c)(2) ($100,000 permanently set aside for charitable purposes less $50,000 allowed as a deduction under section 1202 with respect to such $100,000).

Example (2). Under the terms of the will, $200,000 of the income (including $100,000 capital gains) for the taxable year 1972 of an estate is distributed, one-quarter to each of two individual beneficiaries and one-half to N University, an organization described in section 501(c)(3) which is exempt from taxation under section 501(a). During 1972 the estate has ordinary income of $200,000, long-term capital gains of $100,000, and no capital losses. It is assumed that for 1972 the estate has no other items of income or any deductions other than those discussed herein. The entire capital gains of $100,000 are included in the gross income of the estate for 1972, and N University receives $100,000 from the estate in such year. However, the amount allowable to the estate under section 642(c)(1) is subject to appropriate adjustment for the deduction allowable under section 1202. In view of the distributions of $25,000 of capital gains to each of the individual beneficiaries, the deduction allowable to the estate under section 1202 is limited by such section to $25,000 [($100,000 capital gains less $50,000 capital gains includible in income of individual beneficiaries under section 662) × 50%]. Since the whole of this $25,000 deduction under section 1202 is attributable to the distribution of $50,000 of capital gains to N University, the deduction allowable to the estate in 1972 under section 642(c)(1) is $75,000 [$100,000 (distributed to N) less $25,000 (proper adjustment for section 1202 deduction)].

Example (3). Under the terms of the trust instrument, 30 percent of the gross income (exclusive of capital gains) of a trust described in § 1.642(c)–2(b)(3)(i) is currently distributed to B, the sole income beneficiary. Net capital gains (capital gain net income for taxable years beginning after December 31, 1976) and undistributed ordinary income are allocable to corpus. No provision is made in the trust instrument for the invasion of corpus for the benefit of B. Upon B's death the remainder of the trust is to be distributed to M Church. During the taxable year 1972, the trust has ordinary income of $100,000, long-term capital gains of $15,000, short-term capital gains of $1,000, long-term capital losses of $5,000, and short-term capital losses of $2,500. It is assumed that the trust has no other items of income or any deductions other than those discussed herein. All the ordinary income and capital gains and losses are attributable to amounts transferred to the trust before October 9, 1969. The trust includes in gross income for 1972 the total amount of $116,000 [$100,000 (ordinary income)+$16,000 (total capital gains determined without regard to capital losses)]. Pursuant to the terms of the governing instrument the trust distributes to B in 1972 the amount of $30,000 ($100,000×30%). The balance of $78,500 [($116,000 less $7,500 capital losses)–$30,000 distribution] is available for the set-aside for charitable purposes. In determining taxable income for 1972 the capital losses of $7,500 ($5,000+$2,500) are allowable in full under section 1211(b)(1). The net capital gain (capital gain net income for taxable years beginning after December 31, 1976) of $8,500 ($16,000 less $7,500) is the excess of the net long-term capital gain of $10,000 ($15,000 less $5,000) over the net short-term capital loss of $1,500 ($2,500 less $1,000). The deduction under section 1202 is $4,250 ($8,500×50%), all of which is attributable to the set-aside for charitable purposes. Accordingly, for 1972 the deduction allowable to the trust under section 642(c)(2) is $74,250 [$78,500 (set-aside for M) less $4,250 (proper adjustment for section 1202 deduction)].

Example (4). During the taxable year a pooled income fund, as defined in § 1.642(c)–5, has in addition to ordinary income long-term capital gains of $150,000, short-term capital gains of $15,000, long-term capital losses of $100,000, and short-term capital losses of $10,000. Under the Declaration of Trust and pursuant to State law net long-term capital gain is allocable to corpus and net short-term capital gain is to be distributed to the income beneficiaries of the fund. All the capital gains and losses are attributable to amounts transferred to the fund after July 31, 1969. In view of the distribution of the net short-term capital gain of $5,000 ($15,000 less $10,000) to the income beneficiaries, the deduction allowed to the fund under section 1202 is limited by such section to $25,000 [($150,000 (long-term capital gains) less $100,000 (long-term capital losses) ×50%]. Since the whole of this deduction under section 1202 is attributable to the set-aside for charitable purposes, the deduction of $50,000 ($150,000 less $100,000) otherwise allowable under section 642(c)(3) is subject to appropriate adjustment under section 642(c)(4) for the deduction allowable under section 1202. Accordingly, the amount of the set-aside deduction is $25,000 [$50,000 (set-aside for public charity) less $25,000 (proper adjustment for section 1202 deduction)].

Example (5). The facts are the same as in example (4) except that under the Declaration of Trust and pursuant to State law all the net capital gain (capital gain net income for taxable years beginning after December 31, 1976) for the taxable year is allocable to corpus of the fund. The fund would thus include in gross income total capital gains of $165,000 ($150,000+$15,000). In determining taxable income for the taxable year the capital losses of $110,000 ($100,000+$10,000) are allowable in full under section 1211(b)(1). The net capital gain of $55,000 ($165,000 less $110,000) is available for the set-aside for charitable purposes under section 642(c)(3) only in the amount of the net long-term capital gain of $50,000 ($150,000 long-term gains less $100,000 long-term losses). The deduction under section 1202 is $25,000 ($50,000×50%), all of which is attributable to the set-aside for charitable purposes. Accordingly, the deduction allowable to the fund under section 642(c)(3) is $25,000 [$50,000 (set-aside for public charity) less $25,000 (proper adjustment for section 1202 deduction)]. The $5,000 balance of net capital gain (capital gain net income for taxable years beginning after December 31, 1976) is taken into account in determining taxable income of the pooled income fund for the taxable year.

* * *

[T.D. 6217, Dec. 19, 1956, as amended by T.D. 7357, May 30, 1975; T.D. 7728, Oct. 31, 1980]

§ 1.642(d)-1 Net operating loss deduction.

The net operating loss deduction allowed by section 172 is available to estates and trusts generally, with the following exceptions and limitations:

(a) In computing gross income and deductions for the purposes of section 172, a trust shall exclude that portion of the income and deductions attributable to the grantor or another person under sections 671 through 678 (relating to grantors and others treated as substantial owners).

(b) An estate or trust shall not, for the purposes of section 172, avail itself of the deductions allowed by section 642(c) (relating to charitable contributions deductions) and sections 651 and 661 (relating to deductions for distributions).

[T.D. 6217, Dec. 19, 1956]

§ 1.642(e)-1 Depreciation and depletion.

An estate or trust is allowed the deductions for depreciation and depletion, but only to the extent the deductions are not apportioned to beneficiaries under sections 167(h) and 611(b). For purposes of sections 167(h) and 611(b), the term "beneficiaries" includes charitable beneficiaries. See the regulations under those sections.

[T.D. 6217, Dec. 19, 1956, as amended by T.D. 6712, March 23, 1964]

§ 1.642(g)-1 Disallowance of double deductions; in general.

Amounts allowable under section 2053(a)(2) (relating to administration expenses) or under section 2054 (relating to losses during administration) as deductions in computing the taxable estate of a decedent are not allowed as deductions in computing the taxable income of the estate unless there is filed a statement, in duplicate, to the effect that the items have not been allowed as deductions from the gross estate of the decedent under section 2053 or 2054 and that all rights to have such items allowed at any time as deductions under section 2053 or 2054 are waived. The statement should be filed with the return for the year for which the items are claimed as deductions or with the district director for the internal revenue district in which the return was filed, for association with the return. The statement may be filed at any time before the expiration of the statutory period of limitation applicable to the taxable year for which the deduction is sought. Allowance of a deduction in computing an estate's taxable income is not precluded by claiming a deduction in the estate tax return, so long as the estate tax deduction is not finally allowed and the statement is filed. However, after a statement is filed under section 642(g) with respect to a particular item or portion of an item, the item cannot thereafter be allowed as a deduction for estate tax purposes since the waiver operates as a relinquishment of the right to have the deduction allowed at any time under section 2053 or 2054.

[T.D. 6217, Dec. 19, 1956]

§ 1.642(g)-2 Deductions included.

It is not required that the total deductions, or the total amount of any deduction, to which section 642(g) is applicable be treated in the same way. One deduction or portion of a deduction may be allowed for income tax purposes if the appropriate statement is filed, while another deduction or portion is allowed for estate tax purposes. Section 642(g) has no application to deductions for taxes, interest, business expenses, and other items accrued at the date of a decedent's death so that they are allowable as a deduction under section 2053(a)(3) for estate tax purposes as claims against the estate, and are also allowable under section 691(b) as deductions in respect of a decedent for income tax purposes. However, section 642(g) is applicable to deductions for interest, business expenses, and other items not accrued at the date of the decedent's death so that they are allowable as deductions for estate tax purposes only as administration expenses under section 2053(a)(2). Although deductible under section 2053(a)(3) in determining the value of the taxable estate of a decedent, medical, dental, etc., expenses of a decedent which are paid by the estate of the decedent are not deductible in computing the taxable income of the estate. See section 213(d) and the regulations thereunder for rules relating to the deductibility of such expenses in computing the taxable income of the decedent.

[T.D. 6217, Dec. 19, 1956]

§ 1.642(h)-1 Unused loss carryovers on termination of an estate or trust.

(a) If, on the final termination of an estate or trust, a net operating loss carryover under section 172 or a capital loss carryover under section 1212 would be allowable to the estate or trust in a taxable year subsequent to the taxable year of termination but for the termination, the carryover or carryovers are allowed under section 642(h)(1) to the beneficiaries succeeding to the property of the estate or trust. See § 1.641(b)-3 for the determination of when an estate or trust terminates.

(b) The net operating loss carryover and the capital loss carryover are the same in the hands of a beneficiary as in the estate or trust, except that the capital loss carryover in the hands of a beneficiary which is a corporation is a short-term loss irrespective of whether it would have been a long-term or short-term capital loss in the hands of the estate or trust. The net operating loss carryover and the capital loss carryover are taken into account in computing taxable income, adjusted gross income, and the tax imposed by section 56 (relating to the minimum tax for tax preferences). The first taxable year of the beneficiary to which the loss shall be carried over is the taxable year of the beneficiary in which or with which the estate or trust terminates. However, for purposes of determining the number of years to which a net operating loss, or a capital loss under paragraph (a) of § 1.1212–1, may be carried over by a beneficiary, the last taxable year of the estate or trust (whether or not a short taxable year) and the first taxable year of the beneficiary to which a loss is carried over each constitute a taxable year, and, in the case of a beneficiary of an estate or trust that is a corporation, capital losses carried over by the estate or trust to any taxable year of the estate or trust beginning after December 31, 1963, shall be treated as if they were incurred in the last taxable year of the estate or trust (whether or not a short taxable year). For the treatment of the net operating loss carryover when the last taxable year of the estate or trust is the last taxable year to which such loss can be carried over, see § 1.642(h)–2.

(c) The application of this section may be illustrated by the following examples:

Example (1). A trust distributes all of its assets to A, the sole remainderman, and terminates on December 31, 1954, when it has a capital loss carryover of $10,000 attributable to transactions during the taxable year 1952. A, who reports on the calendar year basis, otherwise has ordinary income of $10,000 and capital gains of $4,000 for the taxable year 1954. A would offset his capital gains of $4,000 against the capital loss of the trust and, in addition, deduct under section 1211(b) $1,000 on his return for the taxable year 1954. The balance of the capital loss carryover of $5,000 may be carried over only to the years 1955 and 1956, in accordance with paragraph (a) of § 1.1212–1 and the rules of this section.

Example (2). A trust distributes all of its assets, one-half to A, an individual, and one-half to X, a corporation, who are the sole remaindermen, and terminates on December 31, 1966, when it has a short-term capital loss carryover of $20,000 attributable to short-term transactions during the taxable years 1964, 1965, and 1966, and a long-term capital loss carryover of $12,000 attributable to long-term transactions during such years. A, who reports on the calendar year basis, otherwise has ordinary income of $15,000, short-term capital gains of $4,000 and long-term capital gains of $6,000, for the taxable year 1966. A would offset his short-term capital gains of $4,000 against his share of the short-term capital loss carryover of the trust, $10,000 (one-half of $20,000), and, in addition deduct under section 1211(b) $1,000 (treated as a short-term gain for purposes of computing capital loss carryovers) on his return for the taxable year 1966. A would also offset his long-term capital gains of $6,000 against his share of the long-term capital loss carryover of the trust, $6,000 (one-half of $12,000). The balance of A's share of the short-term capital loss carryover, $5,000, may be carried over as a short-term capital loss carryover to the succeeding taxable year and treated as a short-term capital loss incurred in such succeeding taxable year in accordance with paragraph (b) of § 1.1212–1. X, which also reports on the calendar year basis, otherwise has capital gains of $4,000 for the taxable year 1966. X would offset its capital gains of $4,000 against its share of the capital loss carryovers of the trust, $16,000 (the sum of one-half of each the short-term carryover and the long-term carryover of the trust), on its return for the taxable year 1966. The balance of X's share, $12,000, may be carried over as a short-term capital loss only to the years 1967, 1968, 1969, and 1970, in accordance with paragraph (a) of § 1.1212–1 and the rules of this section.

[T.D. 6217, Dec. 19, 1956, as amended by T.D. 6828, June 16, 1965; T.D. 7564, Sept. 11, 1978]

§ 1.642(h)-2 Excess deductions on termination of an estate or trust.

(a) If, on the termination of an estate or trust, the estate or trust has for its last taxable year deductions (other than the deductions allowed under section 642(b) (relating to personal exemption) or section 642(c) (relating to charitable contributions)) in excess of gross income, the excess is allowed under section 642(h)(2) as a deduction to the beneficiaries succeeding to the property of the estate or trust. The deduction is allowed only in computing taxable income and must be taken into account in computing the items of tax preference of the beneficiary; it is not allowed in computing adjusted gross income. The deduction is allowable only in the taxable year of the beneficiary in which or with which the estate or trust terminates, whether the year of termination of the estate or trust is of normal duration or is a short taxable year. For example: Assume that a trust distributes all of its assets to B and terminates on December 31, 1954. As of that date it has excess deductions, for example, because of corpus commissions on termination, of $18,000. B, who reported on the calendar year basis, could claim the $18,000 as a deduction for the taxable year 1954. However, if the deduction (when added to his other deductions) exceeds his gross income, the excess may not be carried over to the year 1955 or subsequent years.

(b) A deduction based upon a net operating loss carryover will never be allowed to beneficiaries under both paragraphs (1) and (2) of section 642(h). Accordingly, a net operating loss deduction which is allowable to beneficiaries succeeding to the property of the estate or trust under the provisions of paragraph (1) of section 642(h) cannot also be considered a deduction for purposes of paragraph (2) of section 642(h) and paragraph (a) of this section. However, if the last taxable year of the estate or trust is the last year in which a deduction on account of a net operating loss may be taken, the deduction, to the extent not absorbed in that taxable year by the estate or trust, is considered an "excess deduction" under section 642(h)(2) and paragraph (a) of this section.

(c) Any item of income or deduction, or any part thereof, which is taken into account in determining the net operating loss or capital loss carryover of the estate or trust for its last taxable year shall not be taken into account again in determining excess deductions on termination of the trust or estate within the meaning of section 642(h)(2) and paragraph (a) of this section (see example in § 1.642(h)-5).

[T.D. 6217, Dec. 19, 1956, as amended by T.D. 7564, Sept. 11, 1978]

§ 1.642(h)-3 Meaning of "beneficiaries succeeding to the property of the estate or trust".

(a) The phrase "beneficiaries succeeding to the property of the estate or trust" means those beneficiaries upon termination of the estate or trust who bear the burden of any loss for which a carryover is allowed, or of any excess of deductions over gross income for which a deduction is allowed, under section 642(h).

(b) With reference to an intestate estate, the phrase means the heirs and next of kin to whom the estate is distributed, or if the estate is insolvent, to whom it would have been distributed if it had not been insolvent. If a decedent's spouse is entitled to a specified dollar amount of property before any distribution to other heirs and next of kin, and if the estate is less than that amount, the spouse is the beneficiary succeeding to the property of the estate or trust to the extent of the deficiency in amount.

(c) In the case of a testate estate, the phrase normally means the residuary beneficiaries (including a residuary trust), and not specific legatees or devisees, pecuniary legatees, or other nonresiduary beneficiaries. However, the phrase does not include the recipient of a specific sum of money even though it is payable out of the residue, except to the extent that it is not payable in full. On the other hand, the phrase includes a beneficiary (including a trust) who is not strictly a residuary beneficiary but whose devise or bequest is determined by the value of the decedent's estate as reduced by the loss or deductions in question. Thus the phrase includes:

(1) A beneficiary of a fraction of a decedent's net estate after payment of debts, expenses, etc.;

(2) A nonresiduary legatee or devisee, to the extent of any deficiency in his legacy or devise resulting from the insufficiency of the estate to satisfy it in full;

(3) A surviving spouse receiving a fractional share of an estate in fee under a statutory right of election, to the extent that the loss or deductions are taken into account in determining the share. However, the phrase does not include a recipient of dower or curtesy, or any income beneficiary of the estate or trust from which the loss or excess deduction is carried over.

(d) The principles discussed in paragraph (c) of this section are equally applicable to trust beneficiaries. A remainderman who receives all or a fractional share of the property of a trust as a result of the final termination of the trust is a beneficiary succeeding to the property of the trust. For example, if property is transferred to pay the income to A for life and then to pay $10,000 to B and distribute the balance of the trust corpus to C, C and not B is considered to be the succeeding beneficiary except to the extent that the trust corpus is insufficient to pay B $10,000.

[T.D. 6217, Dec. 19, 1956]

§ 1.642(h)–4 Allocation.

The carryovers and excess deductions to which section 642(h) applies are allocated among the beneficiaries succeeding to the property of an estate or trust (see § 1.642(h)–3) proportionately according to the share of each in the burden of the loss or deductions. A person who qualified as a beneficiary succeeding to the property of an estate or trust with respect to one amount and does not qualify with respect to another amount is a beneficiary succeeding to the property of the estate or trust as to the amount with respect to which he qualifies. The application of this section may be illustrated by the following example:

Example. A decedent's will leaves $100,000 to A, and the residue of his estate equally to B and C. His estate is sufficient to pay only $90,000 to A, and nothing to B and C. There is an excess of deductions over gross income for the last taxable year of the estate or trust of $5,000, and a capital loss carryover of $15,000, to both of which section 642(h) applies. A is a beneficiary succeeding to the property of the estate to the extent of $10,000, and since the total of the excess of deductions and the loss carryover is $20,000, A is entitled to the benefit of one half of each item, and the remaining half is divided equally between B and C.

[T.D. 6217, Dec. 19, 1956]

§ 1.642(h)-5 Example.

The application of section 642(h) may be illustrated by the following example:

Example. (a) A decedent dies January 31, 1954, leaving a will which provides for distributing all her estate equally to A and an existing trust for B. The period of administration of the estate terminates on December 31, 1954, at which time all the property of the estate is distributed to A and the trust. A reports his income for tax purposes on a calendar year basis, and the trust reports its income on the basis of a fiscal year ending August 31. During the period of the administration, the estate has the following items of income and deductions:

Taxable interest	$ 2,500
Business income	3,000
Total	5,500
Business expenses (including administrative expense allocable to business income)	5,000
Administrative expenses and corpus commissions not allocable to business income	9,800
Total deductions	14,800

It also has a capital loss of $5,000.

(b) Under section 642(h)(1), an unused net operating loss carryover of the estate on termination of $2,000 will be allowable to: A to the extent of $1,000 for his taxable year 1954 and the next four taxable years in accordance with section 172; and to the trust to the extent of $1,000 for its taxable year ending August 31, 1955, and its next four taxable years. The amount of the net operating loss carryover is computed as follows:

Deductions of estate for 1954	$14,800
Less adjustment under section 172(d)(4) (deductions not attributable to a trade or business ($9,800) allowable only to extent of gross income not derived from such trade or business ($2,500))	7,300
Deductions as adjusted	$ 7,500
Gross income of estate for 1954	5,500
Net operating loss of estate for 1954	$ 2,000
(No deduction for capital loss of $5,000 under section 172(d)(2)).	

Neither A nor the trust will be allowed to carry back any part of the net operating loss made available to them under section 642(h)(1).

(c) Under section 642(h)(2), excess deductions of the estate of $7,300 will be allowed as a deduction to A to the extent of $3,650 for the calendar year 1954 and to the trust to the extent of $3,650 for the taxable year ending August 31, 1955. The deduction of $7,300 for administrative expenses and corpus commissions is the only amount which was not taken into account in determining the net operating loss of the estate ($9,800 of such expenses less $2,500 taken into account).

(d) Under section 642(h)(1), there will be allowable to A a capital loss carryover of $2,500 for his taxable year 1954 and for his next four taxable years in accordance with paragraph (a) of § 1.1212-1. There will be allowable to the trust a similar capital loss carryover of $2,500 for its taxable year ending August 31, 1955, and its next four taxable years (but see paragraph (b) of § 1.643(a)-3). (For taxable years beginning after December 31, 1963, net capital losses may be carried over indefinitely by beneficiaries other than corporations, in accordance with § 1.642(h)-1 and paragraph (b) of § 1.1212-1.)

(e) The carryovers and excess deductions are not allowable directly to B, the trust beneficiary, but to the extent the distributable net income of the trust is reduced by the carryovers and excess deductions B may receive indirect benefit.

[T.D. 6217, Dec. 19, 1956. Amended by T.D. 6828, June 16, 1965]

§ 1.643(a)-0 Distributable net income; deduction for distributions; in general.

The term "distributable net income" has no application except in the taxation of estates and trusts and their beneficiaries. It limits the deductions allowable to estates and trusts for amounts paid, credited, or required to be distributed to beneficiaries and is used to determine how much of an amount paid, credited, or required to be distributed to a beneficiary will be includible in his gross income. It is also used to determine the character of distributions to the beneficiaries. Distributable net income means for any taxable year, the taxable income (as defined in section 63) of the estate or trust, computed with the modifications set forth in §§ 1.643(a)-1 through 1.643(a)-7.

[T.D. 6217, Dec. 19, 1956]

§ 1.643(a)-1 Deduction for distributions.

The deduction allowable to a trust under section 651 and to an estate or trust under section 661 for amounts paid, credited, or required to be distributed to beneficiaries is not allowed in the computation of distributable net income.

[T.D. 6217, Dec. 19, 1956]

§ 1.643(a)-2 Deduction for personal exemption.

The deduction for personal exemption under section 642(b) is not allowed in the computation of distributable net income.

[T.D. 6217, Dec. 19, 1956]

§ 1.643(a)-3 Capital gains and losses.

(a) Except as provided in § 1.643(a)-6, gains from the sale or exchange of capital assets are ordinarily excluded from distributable net income, and are not ordinarily considered as paid, credited, or required to be distributed to any beneficiary unless they are:

(1) Allocated to income under the terms of the governing instrument or local law by the fiduciary on its books or by notice to the beneficiary,

(2) Allocated to corpus and actually distributed to beneficiaries during the taxable year, or

(3) Utilized (pursuant to the terms of the governing instrument or the practice followed by the fiduciary) in determining the amount which is distributed or required to be distributed.

However, if capital gains are paid, permanently set aside, or to be used for the purposes specified in section 642(c), so that a charitable deduction is allowed under that section in respect of the gains, they must be included in the computation of distributable net income.

(b) Losses from the sale or exchange of capital assets are excluded in computing distributable net income except to the extent that they enter into the determination of any capital gains that are paid, credited, or required to be distributed to any beneficiary during the taxable year (but see § 1.642(h)–1 with respect to capital loss carryovers in the year of final termination of an estate or trust).

* * *

(d) The application of this section may be illustrated by the following examples:

Example (1). A trust is created to pay the income to A for life, with a discretionary power in the trustee to invade principal for A's benefit. In the taxable year, $10,000 is realized from the sale of securities at a profit, and $10,000 in excess of income is distributed to A. The capital gain is not allocated to A by the trustee. During the taxable year the trustee received and paid out $5,000 of dividends. No other cash was received or on hand during the taxable year. The capital gain will not ordinarily be included in distributable net income. However, if the trustee follows a regular practice of distributing the exact net proceeds of the sale of trust property, capital gains will be included in distributable net income.

Example (2). The result in example (1) would have been the same if the trustee had been directed to pay an annuity of $15,000 a year to A (instead of being directed to pay the income to A with a discretionary power to distribute principal).

Example (3). The trustee of a trust containing Blackacre and other property is directed to hold Blackacre for ten years, and then sell it and distribute its proceeds to A. Any capital gain realized from the sale of Blackacre will be included in distributable net income.

Example (4). A trust instrument directs that the income shall be paid to A, and that the principal shall be distributed to A when he reaches age 35. All capital gains realized in the year of termination will be included in distributable net income. (See § 1.641(b)–3 for the determination of the year of final termination and the taxability of capital gains realized after the terminating event and before final distribution.)

Example (5). If in example (4) the trustee had been directed to distribute half of the principal to A when he reached 35, the capital gain would be included in distributable net income (and in the distribution to A) to the extent the capital gain is allocable to A under the governing instrument and local law. Thus, if the trust assets consisted entirely of 100 shares of corporation M stock and the trustee sold half the shares and distributed the proceeds to A, the entire capital gain would normally be considered as allocated to A. On the other hand, if the trustee sold all the shares and distributed half the proceeds to A, half the capital gain would be considered as allocable to A.

Example (6). If in example (4) the trustee had been directed to pay $10,000 to B before making distribution to A, no portion of the capital gains would be allocable to B since the distribution to B is a gift of a specific sum of money within the meaning of section 663(a)(1).

[T.D. 6217, Dec. 19, 1956, as amended by T.D. 6989, Jan. 16, 1969; T.D. 7357, May 30, 1975]

§ 1.643(a)–4 Extraordinary dividends and taxable stock dividends.

In the case solely of a trust which qualifies under subpart B (section 651 and following) as a "simple trust", there are excluded from distributable net income extraordinary dividends (whether paid in cash or in kind) or taxable stock dividends which are not distributed or credited to a beneficiary because the fiduciary in good faith determines that under the terms of the governing instrument and applicable local law such dividends are allocable to corpus. See section 665(e), paragraph (b) of § 1.665(e)–1 and paragraph (b) of § 1.665(e)–1A for the treatment of such dividends upon subsequent distribution.

[T.D. 6217, Dec. 19, 1956, as amended by T.D. 6989, Jan. 16, 1969; T.D. 7204, Aug. 24, 1972]

§ 1.643(a)–5 Tax-exempt interest.

(a) There is included in distributable net income any tax-exempt interest excluded from gross income under section 103, reduced by disbursements allocable to such interest which would have been deductible under section 212 but for the provisions of section 265 (relating to disallowance of deductions allocable to tax-exempt income).

(b) If the estate or trust is allowed a charitable contributions deduction under section 642(c), the amounts specified in paragraph (a) of this section and § 1.643(a)–6 are reduced by the portion deemed to be included in income paid, permanently set aside, or to be used for the purposes specified in section 642(c). If the governing instrument specifically provides as to the source out of which amounts are paid, permanently set aside, or to be used for such charitable purposes, the specific provisions control. In the absence of specific provisions in the governing instrument, an amount to which section 642(c) applies is deemed to consist of the same proportion of each class of the items of income of the estate or trust as the total of each class bears to the total of all classes. * * *

* * *

[T.D. 6217, Dec. 19, 1956]

§ 1.643(b)–1 Definition of "income".

For purposes of subparts A through D, part I, subchapter J, chapter 1 of the Code, the term "income" when not preceded by the words "taxable", "distributable net", "undistributed net", or "gross", means the amount of income of an estate or trust for the taxable year determined under the terms of its governing instrument and applicable local law. Trust provisions which depart fundamentally from concepts of local law in the determination of what constitutes income are not recognized for this purpose. For example, if a trust instrument directs that all the trust income shall be paid to A, but defines ordinary dividends and interest as corpus, the trust will not be considered one which under its governing instrument is required to distribute all its income currently for purposes of section 642(b) (relating to the personal exemption) and section 651 (relating to "simple" trusts).

[T.D. 6217, Dec. 19, 1956]

§ 1.643(b)–2 Dividends allocated to corpus.

Extraordinary dividends or taxable stock dividends which the fiduciary, acting in good faith, determines to be allocable to corpus under the terms of the governing instrument and applicable local law are not considered "income" for purposes of Subpart A, B, C, or D, Part I, Subchapter J, Chapter 1 of the Code.

* * *

[T.D. 6217, Dec. 19, 1956, as amended by T.D. 6989, Jan. 16, 1969; T.D. 7204, Aug. 24, 1972]

§ 1.643(c)–1 Definition of "beneficiary".

An heir, legatee, or devisee (including an estate or trust) is a beneficiary. A trust created under a decedent's will is a beneficiary of the decedent's estate. The following persons are treated as beneficiaries:

(a) Any person with respect to an amount used to discharge or satisfy that person's legal obligation as that term is used in § 1.662(a)–4.

(b) The grantor of a trust with respect to an amount applied or distributed for the support of a dependent under the circumstances specified in section 677(b) out of corpus or out of other than income for the taxable year of the trust.

(c) The trustee or cotrustee of a trust with respect to an amount applied or distributed for the support of a dependent under the circumstances specified in section 678(c) out of corpus or out of other than income for the taxable year of the trust.

[T.D. 6217, Dec. 19, 1956]

§ 1.643(d)–2 Illustration of the provisions of section 643.

(a) The provisions of section 643 may be illustrated by the following example:

Example. (1) Under the terms of the trust instrument, the income of a trust is required to be currently distributed to W during her life. Capital gains are allocable to corpus and all expenses are charges against corpus. During the taxable year the trust has the following items of income and expenses:

Dividends from domestic corporations	$30,000
Extraordinary dividends allocated to corpus by the trust in good faith	20,000
Taxable interest	10,000
Tax-exempt interest	10,000
Long-term capital gains	10,000
Trustee's commissions and miscellaneous expenses allocable to corpus	5,000

(2) The "income" of the trust determined under section 643(b) which is currently distributable to W is $50,000, consisting of dividends of $30,000, taxable interest of $10,000, and tax-exempt interest of $10,000. The trustee's commissions and miscellaneous expenses allocable to tax-exempt interest amount to $1,000 (10,000/50,000 × $5,000).

(3) The "distributable net income" determined under section 643(a) amounts to $45,000, computed as follows:

Dividends from domestic corporations		$30,000
Taxable interest		10,000
Nontaxable interest	$10,000	
Less: Expenses allocable thereto	1,000	
		9,000
Total		49,000

Less: Expenses ($5,000 less $1,000 allocable to tax-exempt interest)	$ 4,000
Distributable net income	45,000

In determining the distributable net income of $45,000, the taxable income of the trust is computed with the following modifications: No deductions are allowed for distributions to W and for personal exemption of the trust (section 643(a)(1) and (2)); capital gains allocable to corpus are excluded and the deduction allowable under section 1202 is not taken into account (section 643(a)(3)): the extraordinary dividends allocated to corpus by the trustee in good faith are excluded (sections 643(a)(4)); and the tax-exempt interest (as adjusted for expenses) and the dividend exclusion of $50 are included (section 643(a)(5) and (7)).

(b) See paragraph (c) of the example in § 1.661(c)–2 for the computation of distributable net income where there is a charitable contributions deduction.

[T.D. 6217, Dec. 19, 1956. Redesignated by T.D. 6989, Jan. 16, 1969]

Trusts Which Distribute Current Income Only

§ 1.651(a)–1 Simple trusts; deduction for distributions; in general.

Section 651 is applicable only to a trust the governing instruments of which:

(a) Requires that the trust distribute all of its income currently for the taxable year, and

(b) Does not provide that any amounts may be paid, permanently set aside, or used in the taxable year for the charitable, etc., purposes specified in section 642(c),

and does not make any distribution other than of current income. A trust to which section 651 applies is referred to in this part as a "simple" trust. Trusts subject to section 661 are referred to as "complex" trusts. A trust may be a simple trust for one year and a complex trust for another year. It should be noted that under section 651 a trust qualifies as a simple trust in a taxable year in which it is required to distribute all its income currently and makes no other distributions, whether or not distributions of current income are in fact made. On the other hand a trust is not a complex trust by reason of distributions of amounts other than income unless such distributions are in fact made during the taxable year, whether or not they are required in that year.

[T.D. 6217, Dec. 19, 1956]

§ 1.651(a)–2 Income required to be distributed currently.

(a) The determination of whether trust income is required to be distributed currently depends upon the terms of the trust instrument and the applicable local law. For this purpose, if the trust instrument provides that the trustee in determining the distributable income shall first retain a reserve for depreciation or otherwise make due allowance for keeping the trust corpus intact by retaining a reasonable amount of the current income for that purpose, the retention of current income for that purpose will not disqualify the trust from being a "simple" trust. The fiduciary must be under a duty to distribute the income currently even if, as a matter of practical necessity, the income is not distributed until after the close of the trust's taxable year. For example: Under the terms of the trust instrument, all of the income is currently distributable to A. The trust reports on the calendar year basis and as a matter of practical necessity makes distribution to A of each quarter's income on the fifteenth day of the month following the close of the quarter. The distribution made by the trust on January 15, 1955, of the income for the fourth quarter of 1954 does not disqualify the trust from treatment in 1955 under section 651, since the income is required to be distributed currently. However, if the terms of a trust require that none of the income be distributed until after the year of its receipt by the trust, the income of the trust is not required to be distributed currently and the trust is not a simple trust. For definition of the term "income" see section 643(b) and § 1.643(b)-1.

(b) It is immaterial, for purposes of determining whether all the income is required to be distributed currently, that the amount of income allocated to a particular beneficiary is not specified in the instrument. For example, if the fiduciary is required to distribute all the income currently, but has discretion to "sprinkle" the income among a class of beneficiaries, or among named beneficiaries, in such amount as he may see fit, all the income is required to be distributed currently, even though the amount distributable to a particular beneficiary is unknown until the fiduciary has exercised his discretion.

(c) If in one taxable year of a trust its income for that year is required or permitted to be accumulated, and in another taxable year its income for the year is required to be distributed currently (and no other amounts are distributed), the trust is a simple trust for the latter year. For example, a trust under which income may be accumulated until a beneficiary is 21 years old, and thereafter must be distributed currently, is a simple trust for taxable years beginning after the beneficiary reaches the age of 21 years in which no other amounts are distributed.

[T.D. 6217, Dec. 19, 1956]

§ 1.651(a)-3 Distribution of amounts other than income.

(a) A trust does not qualify for treatment under section 651 for any taxable year in which it actually distributes corpus. For example, a trust which is required to distribute all of its income currently would not qualify as a simple trust under section 651 in the year of its termination since in that year actual distributions of corpus would be made.

(b) A trust, otherwise qualifying under section 651, which may make a distribution of corpus in the discretion of the trustee, or which is required under the terms of its governing instrument to make a distribution of corpus upon the happening of a specified event, will be disqualified for treatment under section 651 only for the taxable year in which an actual distribution of corpus is made. For example: Under the terms of a trust, which is required to distribute all of its income currently, half of the corpus is to be distributed to beneficiary A when he becomes 30 years of age. The trust reports on the calendar year basis. On December 28, 1954, A becomes 30 years of age and the trustee distributes half of the corpus of the trust to him on January 3, 1955. The trust will be disqualified for treatment under section 651 only for the taxable year 1955, the year in which an actual distribution of corpus is made.

(c) See section 661 and the regulations thereunder for the treatment of trusts which distribute corpus or claim the charitable contributions deduction provided by section 642(c).

[T.D. 6217, Dec. 19, 1956]

§ 1.651(a)–4 Charitable purposes.

A trust is not considered to be a trust which may pay, permanently set aside, or use any amount for charitable, etc., purposes for any taxable year for which it is not allowed a charitable, etc., deduction under section 642(c). Therefore, a trust with a remainder to a charitable organization is not disqualified for treatment as a simple trust if either (a) the remainder is subject to a contingency, so that no deduction would be allowed for capital gains or other amounts added to corpus as amounts permanently set aside for a charitable, etc., purpose under section 642 (c), or (b) the trust receives no capital gains or other income added to corpus for the taxable year for which such a deduction would be allowed.

[T.D. 6217, Dec. 19, 1956]

§ 1.651(b)–1 Deduction for distributions to beneficiaries.

In computing its taxable income, a simple trust is allowed a deduction for the amount of income which is required under the terms of the trust instrument to be distributed currently to beneficiaries. If the amount of income required to be distributed currently exceeds the distributable net income, the deduction allowable to the trust is limited to the amount of the distributable net income. For this purpose the amount of income required to be distributed currently, or distributable net income, whichever is applicable, does not include items of trust income (adjusted for deductions allocable thereto) which are not included in the gross income of the trust. For determination of the character of the income required to be distributed currently, see § 1.652(b)–2. Accordingly, for the purposes of determining the deduction allowable to the trust under section 651, distributable net income is computed without the modifications specified in paragraphs (5), (6), and (7) of section 643(a), relating to tax-exempt interest, foreign income, and excluded dividends. For example: Assume that the distributable net income of a trust as computed under section 643(a) amounts to $99,000 but includes nontaxable income of $9,000. Then distributable net income for the purpose of determining the deduction allowable under section 651 is $90,000 ($99,000 less $9,000 nontaxable income).

[T.D. 6217, Dec. 19, 1956]

§ 1.652(a)–1 Simple trusts; inclusion of amounts in income of beneficiaries.

Subject to the rules in §§ 1.652(a)–2 and 1.652(b)–1, a beneficiary of a simple trust includes in his gross income for the taxable year the amounts of income required to be distributed to him for such year, whether or not distributed. Thus, the income of a simple trust is includible in the beneficiary's gross income for the taxable year in which the income is required to be distributed currently even though, as a matter of practical necessity, the income is not distributed until after the close of the taxable year of the trust. See § 1.642(a)(3)–2 with respect to time of receipt of dividends. See § 1.652(c)–1 for treatment of amounts required to be distributed where a beneficiary and the trust have different taxable years. The term "income required to be distributed currently" includes income required to be distributed currently which is in fact used to discharge or satisfy any person's legal obligation as that term is used in § 1.662(a)–4.

[T.D. 6217, Dec. 19, 1956]

§ 1.652(a)-2 Distributions in excess of distributable net income.

If the amount of income required to be distributed currently to beneficiaries exceeds the distributable net income of the trust (as defined in section 643(a)), each beneficiary includes in his gross income an amount equivalent to his proportionate share of such distributable net income. Thus, if beneficiary A is to receive two-thirds of the trust income and B is to receive one-third, and the income required to be distributed currently is $99,000, A will receive $66,000 and B, $33,000. However, if the distributable net income, as determined under section 643(a) is only $90,000, A will include two-thirds ($60,000) of that sum in his gross income, and B will include one-third ($30,000) in his gross income. See §§ 1.652(b)-1 and 1.652(b)-2, however, for amounts which are not includible in the gross income of a beneficiary because of their tax-exempt character.

[T.D. 6217, Dec. 19, 1956]

§ 1.652(b)-1 Character of amounts.

In determining the gross income of a beneficiary, the amounts includible under § 1.652(a)-1 have the same character in the hands of the beneficiary as in the hands of the trust. For example, to the extent that the amounts specified in § 1.652(a)-1 consist of income exempt from tax under section 103, such amounts are not included in the beneficiary's gross income. Similarly, dividends distributed to a beneficiary retain their original character in the beneficiary's hands for purposes of determining the availability to the beneficiary of the dividends received credit under section 34 (for dividends received on or before December 31, 1964) and the dividend exclusion under section 116. Also, to the extent that the amounts specified in § 1.652(a)-1 consist of "earned income" in the hands of the trust under the provisions of section 1348 such amount shall be treated under section 1348 as "earned income" in the hands of the beneficiary. Similarly, to the extent such amounts consist of an amount received as a part of a lump sum distribution from a qualified plan and to which the provisions of section 72(n) would apply in the hands of the trust, such amount shall be treated as subject to such section in the hands of the beneficiary except where such amount is deemed under section 666(a) to have been distributed in a preceding taxable year of the trust and the partial tax described in section 668(a)(2) is determined under section 668(b)(1)(B). The tax treatment of amounts determined under § 1.652(a)-1 depends upon the beneficiary's status with respect to them, not upon the status of the trust. Thus, if a beneficiary is deemed to have received foreign income of a foreign trust, the includibility of such income in his gross income depends upon his taxable status with respect to that income.

[T.D. 6217, Dec. 19, 1956, as amended by T.D. 6777, Dec. 15, 1964; T.D. 7204, Aug. 24, 1972]

§ 1.652(b)-2 Allocation of income items.

(a) The amounts specified in § 1.652(a)-1 which are required to be included in the gross income of a beneficiary are treated as consisting of the same proportion of each class of items entering into distributable net income of the trust (as defined in section 643(a)) as the total of each class bears to such distributable net income, unless the terms of the trust specifically allocate different classes of income to different beneficiaries, or unless local law requires such an allocation. For example: Assume that under the terms of the governing instrument, beneficiary A is to receive currently one-half of the trust income and beneficiaries B and C are each to receive currently one-quarter, and the distributable net income of the trust (after allocation of expenses) consists of dividends of $10,000, taxable interest of $10,000, and tax-exempt interest of $4,000. A will be deemed to have received $5,000 of dividends, $5,000 of taxable interest, and $2,000 of tax-exempt interest; B and C will each be deemed to have received $2,500 of dividends, $2,500 of taxable interest, and $1,000 of tax-exempt interest. However, if the terms of the trust specifically allocate different classes of income to different beneficiaries, entirely or in part, or if local law requires such an allocation, each beneficiary will be deemed to have received those items of income specifically allocated to him.

(b) The terms of the trust are considered specifically to allocate different classes of income to different beneficiaries only to the extent that the allocation is required in the trust instrument, and only to the extent that it has an economic effect independent of the income tax consequences of the allocation. For example:

(1) Allocation pursuant to a provision in a trust instrument granting the trustee discretion to allocate different classes of income to different beneficiaries is not a specific allocation by the terms of the trust.

(2) Allocation pursuant to a provision directing the trustee to pay all of one income to A, or $10,000 out of the income to A, and the balance of the income to B, but directing the trustee first to allocate a specific class of income to A's share (to the extent there is income of that class and to the extent it does not exceed A's share) is not a specific allocation by the terms of the trust.

(3) Allocation pursuant to a provision directing the trustee to pay half the class of income (whatever it may be) to A, and the balance of the income to B, is a specific allocation by the terms of the trust.

[T.D. 6217, Dec. 19, 1956]

§ 1.652(b)–3 Allocation of deductions.

Items of deduction of a trust that enter into the computation of distributable net income are to be allocated among the items of income in accordance with the following principles:

(a) All deductible items directly attributable to one class of income (except dividends excluded under section 116) are allocated thereto. For example, repairs to, taxes on, and other expenses directly attributable to the maintenance of rental property or the collection of rental income are allocated to rental income. See § 1.642(e)–1 for treatment of depreciation of rental property. Similarly, all expenditures directly attributable to a business carried on by a trust are allocated to the income from such business. If the deductions directly attributable to a particular class of income exceed that income, the excess is applied against other classes of income in the manner provided in paragraph (d) of this section.

(b) The deductions which are not directly attributable to a specific class of income may be allocated to any item of income (including capital gains) included in computing distributable net income, but a portion must be allocated to nontaxable income (except dividends excluded under section 116) pursuant to section 265 and the regulations thereunder. For example, if the income of a trust is $30,000 (after direct expenses), consisting equally of $10,000 of dividends, tax-exempt interest, and rents, and income commissions amount to

$3,000, one-third ($1,000) of such commissions should be allocated to tax-exempt interest, but the balance of $2,000 may be allocated to the rents or dividends in such proportions as the trustee may elect. The fact that the governing instrument or applicable local law treats certain items of deduction as attributable to corpus or to income not included in distributable net income does not affect allocation under this paragraph. For instance, if in the example set forth in this paragraph the trust also had capital gains which are allocable to corpus under the terms of the trust instrument, no part of the deductions would be allocable thereto since the capital gains are excluded from the computation of distributable net income under section 643(a)(3).

(c) Examples of expenses which are considered as not directly attributable to a specific class of income are trustee's commissions, the rental of safe deposit boxes, and State income and personal property taxes.

(d) To the extent that any items of deduction which are directly attributable to a class of income exceed that class of income, they may be allocated to any other class of income (including capital gains) included in distributable net income in the manner provided in paragraph (b) of this section, except that any excess deductions attributable to tax-exempt income (other than dividends excluded under section 116) may not be offset against any other class of income. See section 265 and the regulations thereunder. Thus, if the trust has rents, taxable interest, dividends, and tax-exempt interest, and the deductions directly attributable to the rents exceed the rental income, the excess may be allocated to the taxable interest or dividends in such proportions as the fiduciary may elect. However, if the excess deductions are attributable to the tax-exempt interest, they may not be allocated to either the rents, taxable interest, or dividends.

[T.D. 6217, Dec. 19, 1956]

§ 1.652(c)–1 Different taxable years.

If a beneficiary has a different taxable year (as defined in section 441 or 442) from the taxable year of the trust, the amount he is required to include in gross income in accordance with section 652(a) and (b) is based on the income of the trust for any taxable year or years ending with or within his taxable year. This rule applies to taxable years of normal duration as well as to so-called short taxable years. Income of the trust for its taxable year or years is determined in accordance with its method of accounting and without regard to that of the beneficiary.

[T.D. 6217, Dec. 19, 1956]

§ 1.652(c)–2 Death of individual beneficiaries.

If income is required to be distributed currently to a beneficiary, by a trust for a taxable year which does not end with or within the last taxable year of a beneficiary (because of the beneficiary's death), the extent to which the income is included in the gross income of the beneficiary for his last taxable year or in the gross income of his estate is determined by the computations under section 652 for the taxable year of the trust in which his last taxable year ends. Thus, the distributable net income of the taxable year of the trust determines the extent to which the income required to be distributed currently to the beneficiary is included in his gross income for his last taxable year or in the gross income of his estate. (Section 652(c) does not apply to such amounts.) The gross income for the last taxable year of a beneficiary on the cash basis includes only income actually distributed to the beneficiary before his death. Income required to be distributed, but in fact distributed to his estate, is included in the gross income of the estate as income in respect of a decedent under section 691. See paragraph (e) of § 1.663(c)–3 with respect to separate share treatment for the periods before and after the decedent's death. If the trust does not qualify as a simple trust for the taxable year of the trust in which the last taxable year of the beneficiary ends, see section 662(c) and § 1.662(c)–2.

[T.D. 6217, Dec. 19, 1956]

§ 1.652(c)–3 Termination of existence of other beneficiaries.

If the existence of a beneficiary which is not an individual terminates, the amount to be included under section 652(a) in its gross income for its last taxable year is computed with reference to §§ 1.652(c)–1 and 1.652(c)–2 as if the beneficiary were a deceased individual, except that income required to be distributed prior to the termination but actually distributed to the beneficiary's successor in interest is included in the beneficiary's income for its last taxable year.

[T.D. 6217, Dec. 19, 1956]

§ 1.652(c)–4 Illustration of the provisions of sections 651 and 652.

The rules applicable to a trust required to distribute all of its income currently to its beneficiaries may be illustrated by the following example:

Example. (a) Under the terms of a simple trust all of the income is to be distributed equally to beneficiaries A and B and capital gains are to be allocated to corpus. The trust and both beneficiaries file returns on the calendar year basis. No provision is made in the governing instrument with respect to depreciation. During the taxable year 1955, the trust had the following items of income and expense:

Rents	$25,000
Dividends of domestic corporation	50,000
Tax-exempt interest on municipal bonds	25,000
Long-term capital gains	15,000
Taxes and expenses directly attributable to rents	5,000
Trustee's commissions allocable to income account	2,600
Trustee's commissions allocable to principal account	1,300
Depreciation	5,000

(b) The income of the trust for fiduciary accounting purposes is $92,400, computed as follows:

Rents		$25,000
Dividends of domestic corporation		50,000
Tax-exempt interest		25,000
Total		100,000
Deductions:		
Expenses directly attributable to rental income	$5,000	
Trustee's commissions allocable to income account	2,600	
		7,600
Income computed under section 643(b)		92,400

One-half ($46,200) of the income of $92,400 is currently distributable to each beneficiary.

(c) The distributable net income of the trust computed under section 643(a) is $91,100, determined as follows (cents are disregarded in the computation):

Rents		$25,000
Dividends		50,000
Tax-exempt interest	$25,000	
Less: Expenses allocable there-to (25,000/100,000 × $3,900)	975	
		24,025
Total		99,025
Deductions:		
Expenses directly attributable to rental income	$ 5,000	
Trustee's commissions allocable to tax-exempt interest	2,925	
		7,925
Distributable net income		91,100

In computing the distributable net income of $91,100, the taxable income of the trust was computed with the following modifications: No deductions were allowed for distributions to the beneficiaries and for personal exemption of the trust (section 643(a)(1) and (2)); capital gains were excluded and no deduction under section 1202 (relating to the 50-percent deduction for long-term capital gains) was taken into account (section 643(a)(3)); the tax-exempt interest (as adjusted for expenses) and the dividend exclusion of $50 were included (section 643(a)(5) and (7)). Since all of the income of the trust is required to be currently distributed, no deduction is allowable for depreciation in the absence of specific provisions in the governing instrument providing for the keeping of the trust corpus intact. See section 167(h) and the regulations thereunder.

(d) The deduction allowable to the trust under section 651(a) for distributions to the beneficiaries is $67,025, computed as follows:

Distributable net income computed under section 643(a) (see paragraph (c))		$91,100
Less:		
Tax-exempt interest as adjusted	$24,025	
Dividend exclusion	50	
		24,075
Distributable net income as determined under section 651(b)		67,025

Since the amount of the income ($92,400) required to be distributed currently by the trust exceeds the distributable net income ($67,025) as computed under section 651(b), the deduction allowable under section 651(a) is limited to the distributable net income of $67,025.

(e) The taxable income of the trust is $7,200 computed as follows:

Rents		$25,000
Dividends ($50,000 less $50 exclusion)		49,950
Long-term capital gains		15,000
Gross income		89,950
Deductions:		
Rental expenses	$ 5,000	
Trustee's commissions	2,925	
Capital gain deduction	7,500	
Distributions to beneficiaries	67,025	
Personal exemption	300	
		82,750
Taxable income		7,200

The trust is not allowed a deduction for the portion ($975) of the trustee's commissions allocable to tax-exempt interest in computing its taxable income.

(f) In determining the character of the amounts includible in the gross income of A and B, it is assumed that the trustee elects to allocate to rents the expenses not directly attributable to a specific item of income other than the portion ($975) of such expenses allocated to tax-exempt interest. The allocation of expenses among the items of income is shown below:

	Rents	Dividends	Tax-exempt interest	Total
Income for trust accounting purposes	$25,000	$50,000	$25,000	$100,000
Less:				
Rental expenses	5,000			5,000
Trustee's commissions	2,925		975	3,900
Total deductions	7,925	0	975	8,900
Character of amounts in the hands of the beneficiaries	17,075	50,000	24,025	[1] 91,100

[1] Distributable net income.

Inasmuch as the income of the trust is to be distributed equally to A and B, each is deemed to have received one-half of each item of income; that is, rents of $8,537.50, dividends of $25,000, and tax-exempt interest of $12,012.50. The dividends of $25,000 allocated to each beneficiary are to be aggregated with his other dividends (if any) for purposes of the dividend exclusion provided by section 116 and the dividend received credit allowed under section 34. Also, each beneficiary is allowed a deduction of $2,500 for depreciation of rental property attributable to the portion (one-half) of the income of the trust distributed to him.

[T.D. 6217, Dec. 19, 1956, as amended by T.D. 6712, March 23, 1964]

Estates and Trusts Which May Accumulate Income or Which Distribute Corpus

§ 1.661(a)–1 Estates and trusts accumulating income or distributing corpus; general.

Subpart C, part I, subchapter J, chapter 1 of the Code, is applicable to all decedents' estates and their beneficiaries, and to trusts and their beneficiaries other than trusts subject to the provisions of subpart B of such part I (relating to trusts which distribute current income only, or "simple" trusts). A trust which is required to distribute amounts other than income during the taxable year may be subject to subpart B, and not subpart C, in the absence of an actual distribution of amounts other than income during the taxable year. See §§ 1.651(a)–1 and 1.651(a)–3. A trust to which subpart C is applicable is referred to as a "complex" trust in this part. Section 661 has no application to amounts excluded under section 663(a).

[T.D. 6217, Dec. 19, 1956]

§ 1.661(a)–2 Deduction for distributions to beneficiaries.

(a) In computing the taxable income of an estate or trust there is allowed under section 661(a) as a deduction for distributions to beneficiaries the sum of:

(1) The amount of income for the taxable year which is required to be distributed currently, and

(2) Any other amounts properly paid or credited or required to be distributed for such taxable year.

However, the total amount deductible under section 661(a) cannot exceed the distributable net income as computed under section 643(a) and as modified by section 661(c). See § 1.661(c)-1.

(b) The term "income required to be distributed currently" includes any amount required to be distributed which may be paid out of income or corpus (such as an annuity), to the extent it is paid out of income for the taxable year. See § 1.651(a)-2 which sets forth additional rules which are applicable in determining whether income of an estate or trust is required to be distributed currently.

(c) The term "any other amounts properly paid, credited, or required to be distributed" includes all amounts properly paid, credited, or required to be distributed by an estate or trust during the taxable year other than income required to be distributed currently. Thus, the term includes the payment of an annuity to the extent it is not paid out of income for the taxable year, and a distribution of property in kind (see paragraph (f) of this section). However, see section 663(a) and regulations thereunder for distributions which are not included. Where the income of an estate or trust may be accumulated or distributed in the discretion of the fiduciary, or where the fiduciary has a power to distribute corpus to a beneficiary, any such discretionary distribution would qualify under section 661(a)(2). The term also includes an amount applied or distributed for the support of a dependent of a grantor or of a trustee or cotrustee under the circumstances described in section 677(b) or section 678(c) out of corpus or out of other than income for the taxable year.

(d) The terms "income required to be distributed currently" and "any other amounts properly paid or credited or required to be distributed" also include any amount used to discharge or satisfy any person's legal obligation as that term is used in § 1.662(a)-4.

(e) The terms "income required to be distributed currently" and "any other amounts properly paid or credited or required to be distributed" include amounts paid, or required to be paid, during the taxable year pursuant to a court order or decree or under local law, by a decedent's estate as an allowance or award for the support of the decedent's widow or other dependent for a limited period during the administration of the estate. The term "any other amounts properly paid or credited or required to be distributed" does not include the value of any interest in real estate owned by a decedent, title to which under local law passes directly from the decedent to his heirs or devisees.

(f) If property is paid, credited, or required to be distributed in kind:

(1) No gain or loss is realized by the trust or estate (or the other beneficiaries) by reason of the distribution, unless the distribution is in satisfaction of a right to receive a distribution in a specific dollar amount or in specific property other than that distributed.

(2) In determining the amount deductible by the trust or estate and includible in the gross income of the beneficiary the property distributed in kind is taken into account at its fair market value at the time it was distributed, credited, or required to be distributed.

(3) The basis of the property in the hands of the beneficiary is its fair market value at the time it was paid, credited, or required to be distributed, to the extent such value is included in the gross income of the beneficiary. To the

extent that the value of property distributed in kind is not included in the gross income of the beneficiary, its basis in the hands of the beneficiary is governed by the rules in sections 1014 and 1015 and the regulations thereunder. For this purpose, if the total value of cash and property distributed, credited, or required to be distributed in kind to a beneficiary in any taxable year exceeds the amount includible in his gross income for that year, the value of the property other than cash is normally considered as includible in his gross income only to the extent that the amount includible exceeds the cash paid, credited, or required to be distributed to the beneficiary in that year. Further, to the extent that the value of different items of property other than cash is includible in the gross income of a beneficiary in accordance with the preceding sentence, a pro rata portion of the total value of each item of property distributed, credited, or required to be distributed is normally considered as includible in the beneficiary's gross income.

[T.D. 6217, Dec. 19, 1956, as amended by T.D. 7287, Sept. 26, 1973]

§ 1.661(b)-1 Character of amounts distributed; in general.

In the absence of specific provisions in the governing instrument for the allocation of different classes of income, or unless local law requires such an allocation, the amount deductible for distributions to beneficiaries under section 661(a) is treated as consisting of the same proportion of each class of items entering into the computation of distributable net income as the total of each class bears to the total distributable net income. For example, if a trust has distributable net income of $20,000, consisting of $10,000 each of taxable interest and royalties and distributes $10,000 to beneficiary A, the deduction of $10,000 allowable under section 661(a) is deemed to consist of $5,000 each of taxable interest and royalties, unless the trust instrument specifically provides for the distribution or accumulation of different classes of income or unless local law requires such an allocation. See also § 1.661(c)-1.

[T.D. 6217, Dec. 19, 1956]

§ 1.661(b)-2 Character of amounts distributed when charitable contributions are made.

In the application of the rule stated in § 1.661(b)-1, the items of deduction which enter into the computation of distributable net income are allocated among the items of income which enter into the computation of distributable net income in accordance with the rules set forth in § 1.652(b)-3, except that, in the absence of specific provisions in the governing instrument, or unless local law requires a different apportionment, amounts paid, permanently set aside, or to be used for the charitable, etc., purposes specified in section 642(c) are first ratably apportioned among each class of items of income entering into the computation of the distributable net income of the estate or trust, in accordance with the rules set out in paragraph (b) of § 1.643(a)-5.

[T.D. 6217, Dec. 19, 1956]

§ 1.661(c)-1 Limitation on deduction.

An estate or trust is not allowed a deduction under section 661(a) for any amount which is treated under section 661(b) as consisting of any item of distributable net income which is not included in the gross income of the estate or trust. For example, if in 1962, a trust, which reports on the calendar year basis, has distributable net income of $20,000, which is deemed to consist of $10,000 of dividends and $10,000 of tax-exempt interest, and distributes $10,000 to beneficiary A, the deduction allowable under section 661(a) (computed without regard to section 661(c)) would amount to $10,000 consisting of $5,000 of dividends and $5,000 of tax-exempt interest. The deduction actually allowable under section 661(a) as limited by section 661(c) is $4,975, since no deduction is allowable for the $5,000 of tax-exempt interest and the $25 deemed distributed out of the $50 of dividends excluded under section 116, items of distributable net income which are not included in the gross income of the estate or trust.

[T.D. 6217, Dec. 19, 1956, as amended by T.D. 6777, Dec. 15, 1964]

§ 1.661(c)–2 Illustration of the provisions of section 661.

The provisions of section 661 may be illustrated by the following example:

Example. (a) Under the terms of a trust, which reports on the calendar year basis, $10,000 a year is required to be paid out of income to a designated charity. The balance of the income may, in the trustee's discretion, be accumulated or distributed to beneficiary A. Expenses are allocable against income and the trust instrument requires a reserve for depreciation. During the taxable year 1955 the trustee contributes $10,000 to charity and in his discretion distributes $15,000 of income to A. The trust has the following items of income and expense for the taxable year 1955:

Dividends	$10,000
Partially tax-exempt interest	10,000
Fully tax-exempt interest	10,000
Rents	20,000
Rental expenses	2,000
Depreciation of rental property	3,000
Trustee's commissions	5,000

(b) The income of the trust for fiduciary accounting purposes is $40,000, computed as follows:

Dividends		$10,000
Partially tax-exempt interest		10,000
Fully tax-exempt interest		10,000
Rents		20,000
Total		50,000
Less:		
Rental expenses	$ 2,000	
Depreciation	3,000	
Trustee's commissions	5,000	
		10,000
Income as computed under section 643(b)		40,000

(c) The distributable net income of the trust as computed under section 643(a) is $30,000, determined as follows:

Rents			$20,000
Dividends			10,000
Partially tax-exempt interest			10,000
Fully tax-exempt interest		$10,000	
Less:			
Expenses allocable thereto (10,000/50,000 × $5,000)	$1,000		
Charitable contributions allocable thereto (10,000/50,000 × $10,000)	2,000		
		3,000	
			7,000
Total			47,000

Deductions:

Rental expenses	$ 2,000	
Depreciation of rental property	3,000	
Trustee's commissions ($5,000 less $1,000 allocated to tax-exempt interest)	4,000	
Charitable contributions ($10,000 less $2,000 allocated to tax-exempt interests).	8,000	
		17,000
Distributable net income (section 643(a))		30,000

(d) The character of the amounts distributed under section 661(a), determined in accordance with the rules prescribed in §§ 1.661(b)-1 and 1.661(b)-2 is shown by the following table (for the purpose of this allocation, it is assumed that the trustee elected to allocate the trustee's commissions to rental income except for the amount required to be allocated to tax-exempt interest):

	Rental income	Taxable dividends	Excluded dividends	Partially Tax-exempt interest	Tax-exempt interest	Total
Trust income	$20,000	$9,950	$50	$10,000	$10,000	$50,000
Less:						
Charitable contributions	4,000	2,000	——	2,000	2,000	10,000
Rental expenses	2,000	——	——	——	——	2,000
Depreciation	3,000	——	——	——	——	3,000
Trustee's commissions	4,000	——	——	——	1,000	5,000
Total deductions	13,000	2,000	0	2,000	3,000	20,000
Distributable net income	7,000	7,950	50	8,000	7,000	30,000
Amounts deemed distributed under section 661(a) before applying the limitation of section 661(c)	3,500	3,975	25	4,000	3,500	15,000

In the absence of specific provisions in the trust instrument for the allocation of different classes of income, the charitable contribution is deemed to consist of a pro rata portion of the gross amount of each items of income of the trust (except dividends excluded under section 116) and the trust is deemed to have distributed to A a pro rata portion (one-half) of each item of income included in distributable net income.

(e) The taxable income of the trust is $11,375 computed as follows:

Rental income		$20,000
Dividends ($10,000 less $50 exclusion)		9,950
Partially tax-exempt interest		10,000
Gross income		39,950
Deductions:		
Rental expenses	$ 2,000	
Depreciation of rental property	3,000	
Trustee's commissions	4,000	
Charitable contributions	8,000	
Distributions to A	11,475	
Personal exemption	100	
		28,575
Taxable income		11,375

In computing the taxable income of the trust no deduction is allowable for the portions of the charitable contributions deduction ($2,000) and trustee's commissions ($1,000) which are treated under section 661(b) as attributable to the tax-exempt interest excludable from gross income. Also, of the dividends of $4,000 deemed to have been distributed to A under section 661(a), $25 (25/50ths of $50) is deemed to have been distributed from the excluded dividends and is not an allowable deduction to the trust. Accordingly, the deduction allowable under section 661 is deemed to be composed of $3,500 rental income, $3,975 of dividends, and $4,000 partially tax-exempt interest. No deduction is allowable for the portion of tax-exempt interest or for the portion of the excluded dividends deemed to have been distributed to the beneficiary.

(f) The trust is entitled to the credit allowed by section 34 with respect to dividends of $5,975 ($9,950 less $3,975 distributed to A) included in gross income. Also, the trust is allowed the credit provided by section 35 with respect to partially tax-exempt interest of $6,000 ($10,000 less $4,000 deemed distributed to A) included in gross income.

(g) Dividends of $4,000 allocable to A are to be aggregated with his other dividends (if any) for purposes of the dividend exclusion under section 116 and the dividend received credit under section 84.

[T.D. 6217, Dec. 19, 1956]

§ 1.662(a)-1 Inclusion of amounts in gross income of beneficiaries of estates and complex trusts; general.

There is included in the gross income of a beneficiary of an estate or complex trust the sum of:

(1) Amounts of income required to be distributed currently to him, and

(2) All other amounts properly paid, credited, or required to be distributed to him

by the estate or trust. The preceding sentence is subject to the rules contained in § 1.662(a)-2 (relating to currently distributable income), § 1.662(a)-3 (relating to other amounts distributed), and §§ 1.662(b)-1 and 1.662(b)-2 (relating to character of amounts). Section 662 has no application to amounts excluded under section 663(a).

[T.D. 6217, Dec. 19, 1956]

§ 1.662(a)-2 Currently distributable income.

(a) There is first included in the gross income of each beneficiary under section 662(a)(1) the amount of income for the taxable year of the estate or trust required to be distributed currently to him, subject to the provisions of paragraph (b) of this section. Such amount is included in the beneficiary's gross income whether or not it is actually distributed.

(b) If the amount of income required to be distributed currently to all beneficiaries exceeds the distributable net income (as defined in section 643(a) but computed without taking into account the payment, crediting, or setting aside of an amount for which a charitable contributions deduction is allowable under section 642(c)) of the estate or trust, then there is included in the gross income of each beneficiary an amount which bears the same ratio to distributable net income (as so computed) as the amount of income required to be distributed currently to the beneficiary bears to the amount required to be distributed currently to all beneficiaries.

(c) The phrase "the amount of income for the taxable year required to be distributed currently" includes any amount required to be paid out of income or corpus to the extent the amount is satisfied out of income for the taxable year. Thus, an annuity required to be paid in all events (either out of income or corpus) would qualify as income required to be distributed currently to the extent there is income (as defined in section 643(b)) not paid, credited, or required to be distributed to other beneficiaries for the taxable year. If an annuity or a portion of an annuity is deemed under this paragraph to be income required to be distributed currently, it is treated in all respects in the same manner as an amount of income actually required to be distributed currently. The phrase "the amount of income for the taxable year required to be distributed currently" also includes any amount required to be paid during the taxable year in all events (either out of income or corpus) pursuant to a court order or decree or under local law, by a decedent's estate as an allowance or award for the support of the decedent's widow or other dependent for a limited period during the administration of the estate to the extent there is income (as defined in section 643(b)) of the estate for the taxable year not paid, credited, or required to be distributed to other beneficiaries.

(d) If an annuity is paid, credited, or required to be distributed tax free, that is, under a provision whereby the executor or trustee will pay the income tax of the annuitant resulting from the receipt of the annuity, the payment of or for the tax by the executor or trustee will be treated as income paid, credited, or required to be distributed currently to the extent it is made out of income.

(e) The application of the rules stated in this section may be illustrated by the following examples:

Example (1). (1) Assume that under the terms of the trust instrument $5,000 is to be paid to X charity out of income each year; that $20,000 of income is currently distributable to A; and that an annuity of $12,000 is to be paid to B out of income or corpus. All expenses are charges against income and capital gains are allocable to corpus. During the taxable year the trust had income of $30,000 (after the payment of expenses) derived from taxable interest and made the payments to X charity and distributions to A and B as required by the governing instrument.

(2) The amounts treated as distributed currently under section 662(a)(1) total $25,000 ($20,000 to A and $5,000 to B). Since the charitable contribution is out of income the amount of income available for B's annuity is only $5,000. The distributable net income of the trust computed under section 643(a) without taking into consideration the charitable contributions deduction of $5,000 as provided by section 661(a)(1), is $30,000. Since the amounts treated as distributed currently of $25,000 do not exceed the distributable net income (as modified) of $30,000, A is required to include $20,000 in his gross income and B is required to include $5,000 in his gross income under section 662(a)(1).

Example (2). Assume the same facts as in paragraph (1) of example (1), except that the trust has, in addition, $10,000 of administration expenses, commissions, etc., chargeable to corpus. The amounts treated as distributed currently under section 662(a)(1) total $25,000 ($20,000 to A and $5,000 to B), since trust income under section 643(b) remains the same as in example (1). Distributable net income of the trust computed under section 643(a) but without taking into account the charitable contributions deduction of $5,000 as provided by section 662(a)(1) is only $20,000. Since the amounts treated as distributed currently of $25,000 exceed the distributable net income (as so computed) of $20,000, A is required to include $16,000 (20,000/25,000 of $20,000) in his gross income and B is required to include $4,000 (5,000/25,000 of $20,000) in his gross income under section 662(a)(1). Because A and B are beneficiaries of amounts of income required to be distributed currently, they do not benefit from the reduction of distributable net income by the charitable contributions deduction.

[T.D. 6217, Dec. 19, 1956, as amended by T.D. 7287, Sept. 26, 1973]

§ 1.662(a)–3 Other amounts distributed.

(a) There is included in the gross income of a beneficiary under section 662(a)(2) any amount properly paid, credited, or required to be distributed to the beneficiary for the taxable year, other than (1) income required to be distributed currently, as determined under § 1.662(a)–2, (2) amounts excluded under section 663(a) and the regulations thereunder, and (3) amounts in excess of distributable net income (see paragraph (c) of this section). An amount which is credited or required to be distributed is included in the gross income of a beneficiary whether or not it is actually distributed.

(b) Some of the payments to be included under paragraph (a) of this section are: (1) A distribution made to a beneficiary in the discretion of the fiduciary; (2) a distribution required by the terms of the governing instrument upon the happening of a specified event; (3) an annuity which is required to be paid in all events but which is payable only out of corpus; (4) a distribution of property in kind (see paragraph (f) of § 1.661(a)–2); (5) an amount applied or distributed for the support of a dependent of a grantor or a trustee or cotrustee under the circumstances specified in section 677(b) or section 678(c) out of corpus or out of other than income for the taxable year; and (6) an amount required to be paid during the taxable year pursuant to a court order or decree or under local law, by a decedent's estate as an allowance or award for the support of the decedent's widow or other dependent for a limited period during the administration of the estate which is payable only out of corpus of the estate under the order or decree or local law.

(c) If the sum of the amounts of income required to be distributed currently (as determined under § 1.662(a)–2) and other amounts properly paid, credited, or required to be distributed (as determined under paragraph (a) of this section) exceeds distributable net income (as defined in section 643(a)), then such other amounts properly paid, credited, or required to be distributed are included in gross income of the beneficiary but only to the extent of the excess of such distributable net income over the amounts of income required to be distributed currently. If the other amounts are paid, credited, or required to be distributed to more than one beneficiary, each beneficiary includes in gross income his proportionate share of the amount includible in gross income pursuant to the preceding sentence. The proportionate share is an amount which bears the same ratio to distributable net income (reduced by amounts of income required to be distributed currently) as the other amounts (as determined under paragraphs (a) and (d) of this section) distributed to the beneficiary bear to the other amounts distributed to all beneficiaries. For treatment of excess distributions by trusts, see sections 665 to 668, inclusive, and the regulations thereunder.

(d) The application of the rules stated in this section may be illustrated by the following example:

Example. The terms of a trust require the distribution annually of $10,000 of income to A. If any income remains, it may be accumulated or distributed to B, C, and D in amounts in the trustee's discretion. He may also invade corpus for the benefit of A, B, C, or D. In the taxable year, the trust has $20,000 of income after the deduction of all expenses. Distributable net income is $20,000. The trustee distributes $10,000 of income to A. Of the remaining $10,000 of income, he distributes $3,000 each to B, C, and D, and also distributes an additional $5,000 to A. A includes $10,000 in income under section 662(a)(1). The "other amounts distributed" amount of $14,000, includible in the income of the recipients to the extent of $10,000, distributable net income less the income currently distributable to A. A will include an additional $3,571 (5,000/14,000×$10,000) in income under this section, and B, C, and D will each include $2,143 (3,000/14,000×$10,000).

[T.D. 6217, Dec. 19, 1956, as amended by T.D. 7287, Sept. 26, 1973]

§ 1.662(a)-4 Amounts used in discharge of a legal obligation.

Any amount which, pursuant to the terms of a will or trust instrument, is used in full or partial discharge or satisfaction of a legal obligation of any person is included in the gross income of such person under section 662(a)(1) or (2), whichever is applicable, as though directly distributed to him as a beneficiary, except in cases to which section 71 (relating to alimony payments) or section 682 (relating to income of a trust in case of divorce, etc.) applies. The term "legal obligation" includes a legal obligation to support another person if, and only if, the obligation is not affected by the adequacy of the dependent's own resources. For example, a parent has a "legal obligation" within the meaning of the preceding sentence to support his minor child if under local law property or income from property owned by the child cannot be used for his support so long as his parent is able to support him. On the other hand, if under local law a mother may use the resources of a child for the child's support in lieu of supporting him herself, no obligation of support exists within the meaning of this paragraph, whether or not income is actually used for support. Similarly, since under local law a child ordinarily is obligated to support his parent only if the parent's earnings and resources are insufficient for the purpose, no obligation exists whether or not the parent's earnings and resources are sufficient. In any event the amount of trust income which is included in the gross income of a person obligated to support a dependent is limited by the extent of his legal obligation under local law. In the case of a parent's obligation to support his child, to the extent that the parent's legal obligation of support, including education, is determined under local law by the family's station in life and by the means of the parent, it is to be determined without consideration of the trust income in question.

[T.D. 6217, Dec. 19, 1956]

§ 1.662(b)-1 Character of amounts; when no charitable contributions are made.

In determining the amount includible in the gross income of a beneficiary, the amounts which are determined under section 662(a) and §§ 1.662(a)-1 through 1.662(a)-4 shall have the same character in the hands of the beneficiary as in the hands of the estate or trust. The amounts are treated as consisting of the same proportion of each class of items entering into the computation of distributable net income as the total of each class bears to the total distributable net income of the estate or trust unless the terms of the governing instrument specifically allocate different classes of income to different beneficiaries, or unless local law requires such an allocation. For this purpose, the principles contained in § 1.652(b)-1 shall apply.

[T.D. 6217, Dec. 19, 1956]

§ 1.662(c)-1 Different taxable years.

If a beneficiary has a different taxable year (as defined in section 441 or 442) from the taxable year of an estate or trust, the amount he is required to include in gross income in accordance with section 662(a) and (b) is based upon the distributable net income of the estate or trust and the amounts properly paid, credited, or required to be distributed to the beneficiary for any taxable year or years of the estate or trust ending with or within his taxable year. This rule applies as to so-called short taxable years as well as taxable years of normal duration. Income of an estate or trust for its taxable year or years is determined in accordance with its method of accounting and without regard to that of the beneficiary.

[T.D. 6217, Dec. 19, 1956]

§ 1.662(c)–2 Death of individual beneficiary.

If an amount specified in section 662(a)(1) or (2) is paid, credited, or required to be distributed by an estate or trust for a taxable year which does not end with or within the last taxable year of a beneficiary (because of the beneficiary's death), the extent to which the amount is included in the gross income of the beneficiary for his last taxable year or in the gross income of his estate is determined by the computations under section 662 for the taxable year of the estate or trust in which his last taxable year ends. Thus, the distributable net income and the amounts paid, credited, or required to be distributed for the taxable year of the estate or trust, determine the extent to which the amounts paid, credited, or required to be distributed to the beneficiary are included in his gross income for his last taxable year or in the gross income of his estate. (Section 662(c) does not apply to such amounts.) The gross income for the last taxable year of a beneficiary on the cash basis includes only income actually distributed to the beneficiary before his death. Income required to be distributed, but in fact distributed to his estate, is included in the gross income of the estate as income in respect of a decedent under section 691. See paragraph (e) of § 1.663(c)–3 with respect to separate share treatment for the periods before and after the death of a trust's beneficiary.

[T.D. 6217, Dec. 19, 1956]

§ 1.662(c)–3 Termination of existence of other beneficiaries.

If the existence of a beneficiary which is not an individual terminates, the amount to be included under section 662(a) in its gross income for the last taxable year is computed with reference to §§ 1.662(c)–1 and 1.662(c)–2 as if the beneficiary were a deceased individual, except that income required to be distributed prior to the termination but actually distributed to the beneficiary's successor in interest is included in the beneficiary's income for its last taxable year.

[T.D. 6217, Dec. 19, 1956]

§ 1.662(c)–4 Illustration of the provisions of sections 661 and 662.

The provisions of sections 661 and 662 may be illustrated in general by the following example:

Example. (a) Under the terms of a testamentary trust one-half of the trust income is to be distributed currently to W, the decedent's wife, for her life. The remaining trust income may, in the trustee's discretion, either be paid to D, the grantor's daughter, paid to designated charities, or accumulated. The trust is to terminate at the death of W and the principal will then be payable to D. No provision is made in the trust instrument with respect to depreciation of rental property. Capital gains are allocable to the principal account under the applicable local law. The trust and both beneficiaries file returns on the calendar year basis. The records of the fiduciary show the following items of income and deduction for the taxable year 1955:

Rents	$50,000
Dividends of domestic corporations	50,000
Tax-exempt interest	20,000
Partially tax-exempt interest	10,000
Capital gains (long term)	20,000
Depreciation of rental property	10,000
Expenses attributable to rental income	15,400
Trustee's commissions allocable to income account	2,800
Trustee's commissions allocable to principal account	1,100

(b) The income for trust accounting purposes is $111,800, and the trustee distributes one-half ($55,900) to W and in his discretion makes a contribution of one-quarter ($27,950) to charity X and distributes the remaining one-quarter ($27,950) to D. The total of the distributions to beneficiaries is $83,850, consisting of (1) income required to be distributed currently to W of $55,900 and (2) other amounts properly paid or credited to D of $27,950. The income for trust accounting purposes of $111,800 is determined as follows:

Rents		$50,000
Dividends		50,000
Tax-exempt interest		20,000
Partially tax-exempt interest		10,000
Total		130,000
Less:		
Rental expenses	$15,400	
Trustee's commissions allocable to income account	2,800	
		18,200
Income as computed under section 643(b)		111,800

(c) The distributable net income of the trust as computed under section 643(a) is $82,750, determined as follows:

Rents			$50,000
Dividends			50,000
Partially tax-exempt interest			10,000
Tax-exempt interest		$20,000	
Less:			
Trustee's commissions allocable thereto (20,000/130,000 of $3,900)	$ 600		
Charitable contributions allocable thereto (20,000/130,000 of $27,950)	$4,300		
		4,900	
			15,100
Total			125,100
Deductions:			
Rental expenses		15,400	
Trustee's commissions ($3,900 less $600 allocated to tax-exempt interest)		3,300	
Charitable deduction ($27,950 less $4,300 attributable to tax-exempt interest)		23,650	
			42,350
Distributable net income			82,750

In computing the distributable net income of $82,750, the taxable income of the trust was computed with the following modifications: No deductions were allowed for distributions to beneficiaries and for personal exemption of the trust (section 643(a)(1) and (2)); capital gains were excluded and no deduction under section 1202 (relating to the 50 percent deduction for long-term capital gains) was taken into account (section 643(a)(3)); and the tax-exempt interest (as adjusted for expenses and charitable contributions) and the dividend exclusion of $50 were included (section 643(a)(5) and (7)).

(d) Inasmuch as the distributable net income of $82,750 as determined under section 643(a) is less than the sum of the amounts distributed to W and D of $83,850, the deduction allowable to the trust under section 661(a) is such distributable net income as modified under section 661(c) to exclude therefrom the items of income not included in the gross income of the trust, as follows:

Distributable net income		$82,750
Less:		
Tax-exempt interest (as adjusted for expenses and the charitable contributions)	$15,100	
Dividend exclusion allowable under section 116	50	
		15,150
Deduction allowable under section 661(a)		67,600

(e) For the purpose of determining the character of the amounts deductible under section 642(c) and section 661(a), the trustee elected to offset the trustee's commissions (other than the portion required to be allocated to tax-exempt interest) against the rental income. The following table shows the determination of the character of the amounts deemed distributed to beneficiaries and contributed to charity.

	Rents	Taxable dividends	Excluded dividends	Tax-exempt interest	Partially tax-exempt interest	Total
Trust income	$50,000	$49,950	$50	$20,000	$10,000	$130,000
Less:						
Charitable contribution	10,750	10,750	———	4,300	2,150	27,950
Rental expenses	15,400	———	———	———	———	15,400
Trustee's commissions	3,300	———	———	600	———	3,900
Total deductions	29,450	10,750	0	4,900	2,150	47,250
Amounts distributable to beneficiaries	20,550	39,200	50	15,100	7,850	82,750

The character of the charitable contribution is determined by multiplying the total charitable contribution ($27,950) by a fraction consisting of each item of trust income, respectively, over the total trust income, except that no part of the dividends excluded from gross income are deemed included in the charitable contribution. For example, the charitable contribution is deemed to consist of rents of $10,750 (50,000/130,000×$27,950).

(f) The taxable income of the trust is $9,900 determined as follows:

Rental income	$ 50,000
Dividends ($50,000 less $50 exclusion)	49,950
Partially tax-exempt interest	10,000
Capital gains	20,000
Gross income	129,950

Deductions:

Rental expenses	$15,400	
Trustee's commissions	3,300	
Charitable contributions	23,650	
Capital gain deductions	10,000	
Distributions to beneficiaries	67,600	
Personal exemption	100	
		120,050
Taxable income		9,900

(g) In computing the amount includible in W's gross income under section 662(a)(1), the $55,900 distribution to her is deemed to be composed of the following proportions of the items of income deemed to have been distributed to the beneficiaries by the trust (see paragraph (e) of this example):

Rents (20,550/82,750 × $55,900)	$13,882
Dividends (39,250/82,750 × $55,900)	26,515
Partially tax-exempt interest (7,850/82,750 × $55,900)	5,303
Tax-exempt interest (15,100/82,750 × $55,900)	10,200
Total	55,900

Accordingly, W will exclude $10,200 of tax-exempt interest from gross income and will receive the credits and exclusion for dividends received and for partially tax-exempt interest provided in sections 34, 116, and 35, respectively, with respect to the dividends and partially tax-exempt interest deemed to have been distributed to her, her share of the dividends being aggregated with other dividends received by her for purposes of the dividend credit and exclusion. In addition, she may deduct a share of the depreciation deduction proportionate to the trust income allocable to her; that is, one-half of the total depreciation deduction, or $5,000.

(h) Inasmuch as the sum of the amount of income required to be distributed currently to W ($55,900) and the other amounts properly paid, credited, or required to be distributed to D ($27,950) exceeds the distributable net income ($82,750) of the trust as determined under section 643(a), D is deemed to have received $26,850 ($82,750 less $55,900) for income tax purposes. The character of the amounts deemed distributed to her is determined as follows:

Rents (20,550/82,750 × $26,850)	$ 6,668
Dividends (39,250/82,750 × $26,850)	12,735
Partially tax-exempt interest (7,850/82,750 × $26,850)	2,547
Tax-exempt interest (15,100/82,750 × $26,850)	4,900
Total	26,850

Accordingly, D will exclude $4,900 of tax-exempt interest from gross income and will receive the credits and exclusion for dividends received and for partially tax-exempt interest provided in sections 34, 116, and 35, respectively, with respect to the dividends and partially tax-exempt interest deemed to have been distributed to her, her share of the dividends being aggregated with other dividends received by her for purposes of the dividend credit and exclusion. In addition, she may deduct a share of the depreciation deduction proportionate to the trust income allocable to her; that is, one-fourth of the total depreciation deduction, or $2,500.

(j) The remaining $2,500 of the depreciation deduction is allocated to the amount distributed to charity X and is hence nondeductible by the trust, W, or D. (See § 1.642(e)-1.)

[T.D. 6217, Dec. 19, 1956]

§ 1.663(a)-1 Special rules applicable to sections 661 and 662; exclusions; gifts, bequests, etc.

(a) **In general.** A gift or bequest of a specific sum of money or of specific property, which is required by the specific terms of the will or trust instrument and is properly paid or credited to a beneficiary, is not allowed as a deduction to an estate or trust under section 661 and is not included in the gross income of a beneficiary under section 662, unless under the terms of the will or trust instrument the gift or bequest is to be paid or credited to the recipient in more than three installments. Thus, in order for a gift or bequest to be excludable from the gross income of the recipient, (1) it must qualify as a gift or bequest of a specific sum of money or of specific property (see paragraph (b) of this section), and (2) the terms of the governing instrument must not provide for its payment in more than three installments (see paragraph (c) of this section). The date when the estate came into existence or the date when the trust was created is immaterial.

(b) **Definition of a gift or bequest of a specific sum of money or of specific property.** (1) In order to qualify as a gift or bequest of a specific sum of money or of specific property under section 663(a), the amount of money or the identity of the specific property must be ascertainable under the terms of a testator's will as of the date of his death, or under the terms of an inter vivos trust instrument as of the date of the inception of the trust. For example, bequests to a decedent's son of the decedent's interest in a partnership and to his daughter of a sum of money equal to the value of the partnership interest are bequests of specific property and of a specific sum of money, respectively. On the other hand, a bequest to the decedent's spouse of money or property, to be selected by the decedent's executor, equal in value to a fraction of the decedent's "adjusted gross estate" is neither a bequest of a specific sum of money or of specific property. The identity of the property and the amount of money specified in the preceding sentence are dependent both on the exercise of the executor's discretion and on the payment of administration expenses and other charges, neither of which are facts existing on the date of the decedent's death. It is immaterial that the value of the bequest is determinable after the decedent's death before the bequest is satisfied (so that gain or loss may be realized by the estate in the transfer of property in satisfaction of it).

(2) The following amounts are not considered as gifts or bequests of a sum of money or of specific property within the meaning of this paragraph:

(i) An amount which can be paid or credited only from the income of an estate or trust, whether from the income for the year of payment or crediting, or from the income accumulated from a prior year;

(ii) An annuity, or periodic gifts of specific property in lieu of or having the effect of an annuity;

(iii) A residuary estate or the corpus of a trust; or

(iv) A gift or bequest paid in a lump sum or in not more than three installments, if the gift or bequest is required to be paid in more than three installments under the terms of the governing instrument.

(3) The provisions of subparagraphs (1) and (2) of this paragraph may be illustrated by the following examples, in which it is assumed that the gift or bequest is not required to be made in more than three installments (see paragraph (c)):

Example (1). Under the terms of a will, a legacy of $5,000 was left to A, 1,000 shares of X company stock was left to W, and the balance of the estate was to be divided equally between W and X. No provision was made in the will for the disposition of income of the estate during the period of administration. The estate had income of $25,000 during the taxable year 1954, which was accumulated and added to corpus for estate accounting purposes. During the taxable year, the executor paid the legacy of $5,000 in a lump sum to A and transferred the X company stock to W. No other distributions to beneficiaries were made during the taxable year. The distributions to A and W qualify as exclusions within the meaning of section 663(a)(1).

Example (2). Under the terms of a will, the testator's estate was to be divided equally between A and B. No provision was made in the will for the disposition of income of the estate during the period of administration. The estate had income of $50,000 for the taxable year 1954. In accordance with an agreement among the beneficiaries that part of the assets of the estate would be distributed in kind to the beneficiaries, stock in corporation X was distributed to A during 1954. The fair market value of the stock was $40,000 on the date of distribution. No other distribution was made during the year. The distribution does not qualify as an exclusion within the meaning of section 663(a)(1), since it is not a specific gift to A required by the terms of the will. Accordingly, the fair market value of the property ($40,000) represents a distribution within the meaning of section 661(a) and section 662(a) (see paragraph (c) of § 1.661(a)-2).

Example (3). Under the terms of a trust instrument, income is to be accumulated during the minority of A. Upon A's reaching the age of 21, $10,000 is to be distributed to B out of income or corpus. Also at that time, $10,000 is to be distributed to C out of the accumulated income and the remainder of the accumulations are to be paid to A. A is then to receive all the income until he is 25, when the trust is to terminate. Only the distribution to B would qualify for exclusion under section 663(a)(1).

(4) A gift or bequest of a specific sum of money or of specific property is not disqualified under this paragraph solely because its payment is subject to a condition. For example, provision for a payment by a trust to beneficiary A of $10,000 when he reaches age 25, and $10,000 when he reaches age 30, with payment over to B of any amount not paid to A because of his death, is a gift to A of a specific sum of money payable in two installments, within the meaning of this paragraph, even though the exact amount payable to A cannot be ascertained with certainty under the terms of the trust instrument.

(c) **Installment payments.** (1) In determining whether a gift or bequest of a specific sum of money or of specific property, as defined in paragraph (b) of this section, is required to be paid or credited to a particular beneficiary in more than three installments—

(i) Gifts or bequests of articles for personal use (such as personal and household effects, automobiles, and the like) are disregarded.

(ii) Specifically devised real property, the title to which passes directly from the decedent to the devisee under local law, is not taken into account, since it would not constitute an amount paid, credited, or required to be distributed under section 661 (see paragraph (e) of § 1.661(a)-2).

(iii) All gifts and bequests under a decedent's will (which are not disregarded pursuant to subdivisions (i) and (ii) of this subparagraph) for which no time of payment or crediting is specified, and which are to be paid or credited in the ordinary course of administration of the decedent's estate, are considered as required to be paid or credited in a single installment.

(iv) All gifts and bequests (which are not disregarded pursuant to subdivisions (i) and (ii) of this subparagraph) payable at any one specified time under the terms of the governing instrument are taken into account as a single installment.

For purposes of determining the number of installments paid or credited to a particular beneficiary, a decedent's estate and a testamentary trust shall each be treated as a separate entity.

(2) The application of the rules stated in subparagraph (1) of this paragraph may be illustrated by the following examples:

Example (1). (i) Under the terms of a decedent's will, $10,000 in cash, household furniture, a watch, an automobile, 100 shares of X company stock, 1,000 bushels of grain, 500 head of cattle, and a farm (title to which passed directly to A under local law) are bequeathed or devised outright to A. The will also provides for the creation of a trust for the benefit of A, under the terms of which there are required to be distributed to A, $10,000 in cash and 100 shares of Y company stock when he reaches 25 years of age, $25,000 in cash and 200 shares of Y company stock when he reaches 30 years of age, and $50,000 in cash and 300 shares of Y company stock when he reaches 35 years of age.

(ii) The furniture, watch, automobile, and the farm are excluded in determining whether any gift or bequest is required to be paid or credited to A in more than three installments. These items qualify for the exclusion under section 663(a)(1) regardless of the treatment of the other items of property bequeathed to A.

(iii) The $10,000 in cash, the shares of X company stock, the grain, the cattle and the assets required to create the trust, to be paid or credited by the estate to A and the trust are considered as required to be paid or credited in a single installment to each, regardless of the manner of payment or distribution by the executor, since no time of payment or crediting is specified in the will. The $10,000 in cash and shares of Y company stock required to be distributed by the trust to A when he is 25 years old are considered as required to be paid or distributed as one installment under the trust. Likewise, the distributions to be made by the trust to A when he is 30 and 35 years old are each considered as one installment under the trust. Since the total number of installments to be made by the estate does not exceed three, all of the items of money and property distributed by the estate qualify for the exclusion under section 663(a)(1). Similarly, the three distributions by the trust qualify.

Example (2). Assume the same facts as in example (1), except that another distribution of a specified sum of money is required to be made by the trust to A when he becomes 40 years old. This distribution would also qualify as an installment, thus making four installments in all under the trust. None of the gifts to A under the trust would qualify for the exclusion under section 663(a)(1). The situation as to the estate, however, would not be changed.

Example (3). A trust instrument provides that A and B are each to receive $75,000 in installments of $25,000, to be paid in alternate years. The trustee distributes $25,000 to A in 1954, 1956, and 1958, and to B in 1955, 1957, and 1959. The gifts to A and B qualify for exclusion under section 663(a)(1), although a total of six payments is made. The gifts of $75,000 to each beneficiary are to be separately treated.

[T.D. 6217, Dec. 19, 1956]

§ 1.663(a)–2 Charitable, etc., distributions.

Any amount paid, permanently set aside, or to be used for the charitable, etc., purposes specified in section 642(c) and which is allowable as a deduction under that section is not allowed as a deduction to an estate or trust under section 661 or treated as an amount distributed for purposes of determining the amounts includible in gross income of beneficiaries under section 662. Amounts paid, permanently set aside, or to be used for charitable, etc., purposes are deductible by estates or trusts only as provided in section 642(c). For purposes of this section, the deduction provided in section 642(c) is computed without regard to the provisions of section 508(d), section 681, or section 4948(c)(4) (concerning unrelated business income and private foundations).

[T.D. 6217, Dec. 19, 1956, as amended by T.D. 7428, Aug. 13, 1976]

§ 1.663(b)–1 Distributions in first sixty-five days of taxable year; scope.

(a) **Taxable years beginning after December 31, 1968—(1) General rule.** With respect to taxable years beginning after December 31, 1968, the fiduciary of a trust may elect under section 663(b) to treat any amount or portion thereof that is properly paid or credited to a beneficiary within the first 65 days following the close of the taxable year as an amount that was properly paid or credited on the last day of such taxable year.

(2) **Effect of election.** (i) An election is effective only with respect to the taxable year for which the election is made. In the case of distributions made after May 8, 1972, the amount to which the election applies shall not exceed—

(a) The amount of income of the trust (as defined in § 1.643(b)–1) for the taxable year for which the election is made, or

(b) The amount of distributable net income of the trust (as defined in §§ 1.643(a)–1 through 1.643(a)–7) for such taxable year, if greater,

reduced by any amounts paid, credited, or required to be distributed in such taxable year other than those amounts considered paid or credited in a preceding taxable year by reason of section 663(b) and this section. An election shall be made for each taxable year for which the treatment is desired. The application of this paragraph may be illustrated by the following example:

Example. X Trust, a calendar year trust, has $1,000 of income (as defined in § 1.643(b)–1) and $800 of distributable net income (as defined in §§ 1.643(a)–1 through 1.643(a)–7) in 1972. The trust properly pays $550 to A, a beneficiary, on January 15, 1972, which the trustee elects to treat under section 663(b) as paid on December 31, 1971. The trust also properly pays to A $600 on July 19, 1972, and $450 on January 17, 1973. For 1972, the maximum amount that may be elected under this subdivision to be treated as properly paid or credited on the last day of 1972 is $400 ($1,000 – $600). The $550 paid on January 15, 1972, does not reduce the maximum amount to which the election may apply, because that amount is treated as properly paid on December 31, 1971.

(ii) If an election is made with respect to a taxable year of a trust, this section shall apply only to those amounts which are properly paid or credited within the first 65 days following such year and which are so designated by the fiduciary in his election. Any amount considered under section 663(b) as having been distributed in the preceding taxable year shall be so treated for all purposes. For example, in determining the beneficiary's tax liability, such amount shall be considered as having been received by the beneficiary in his taxable year in which or with which the last day of the preceding taxable year of the trust ends.

(b) Taxable years beginning before January 1, 1969. With respect to taxable years of a trust beginning before January 1, 1969, the fiduciary of the trust may elect under section 663(b) to treat distributions within the first 65 days following such taxable year as amounts which were paid or credited on the last day of such taxable year, if:

(1) The trust was in existence prior to January 1, 1954;

(2) An amount in excess of the income of the immediately preceding taxable year may not (under the terms of the governing instrument) be distributed in any taxable year; and

(3) The fiduciary elects (as provided in § 1.663(b)-2) to have section 663(b) apply.

[T.D. 6217, Dec. 19, 1956, as amended by T.D. 7204, Aug. 24, 1972]

§ 1.663(b)-2 Election.

(a) Manner and time of election; irrevocability—(1) When return is required to be filed. If a trust return is required to be filed for the taxable year of the trust for which the election is made, the election shall be made in the appropriate place on such return. The election under this subparagraph shall be made not later than the time prescribed by law for filing such return (including extensions thereof). Such election shall become irrevocable after the last day prescribed for making it.

(2) When no return is required to be filed. If no return is required to be filed for the taxable year of the trust for which the election is made, the election shall be made in a statement filed with the internal revenue office with which a return by such trust would be filed if such trust were required to file a return for such taxable year. See section 6091 and the regulations thereunder for place for filing returns. The election under this subparagraph shall be made not later than the time prescribed by law for filing a return if such trust were required to file a return for such taxable year. Such election shall become irrevocable after the last day prescribed for making it.

(b) Elections under prior law. Elections made pursuant to section 663(b) prior to its amendment by section 331(b) of the Tax Reform Act of 1969 (83 Stat. 598), which, under prior law, were irrevocable for the taxable year for which the election was made and all subsequent years, are not effective for taxable years beginning after December 31, 1968. In the case of a trust for which an election was made under prior law, the fiduciary shall make the election for each taxable year beginning after December 31, 1968, for which the treatment provided by section 663(b) is desired.

[T.D. 6217, Dec. 19, 1956. Amended by T.D. 7204, Aug. 24, 1972]

§ 1.663(c)-1 Separate shares treated as separate trusts; in general.

(a) If a single trust has more than one beneficiary, and if different beneficiaries have substantially separate and independent shares, their shares are treated as separate trusts for the sole purpose of determining the amount of distributable net income allocable to the respective beneficiaries under sections 661 and 662. Application of this rule will be significant in, for example, situations in which income is accumulated for beneficiary A but a distribution is made to beneficiary B of both income and corpus in an amount exceeding the share of income that would be distributable to B had there been separate trusts. In the absence of a separate share rule B would be taxed on income which is accumulated for A. The division of distributable net income into separate shares will limit the tax liability of B. Section 663(c) does not affect the principles of applicable law in situations in which a single trust instrument creates not one but several separate trusts, as opposed to separate shares in the same trust within the meaning of this section.

(b) The separate share rule does not permit the treatment of separate shares as separate trusts for any purpose other than the application of distributable net income. It does not, for instance, permit the treatment of separate shares as separate trusts for purposes of:

(1) The filing of returns and payment of tax,

(2) The exclusion of dividends under section 116,

(3) The deduction of personal exemption under section 642(b), and

(4) The allowance to beneficiaries succeeding to the trust property of excess deductions and unused net operating loss and capital loss carryovers on termination of the trust under section 642(h).

(c) The separate share rule may be applicable even though separate and independent accounts are not maintained and are not required to be maintained for each share on the books of account of the trust, and even though no physical segregation of assets is made or required.

(d) Separate share treatment is not elective. Thus, if a trust is properly treated as having separate and independent shares, such treatment must prevail in all taxable years of the trust unless an event occurs as a result of which the terms of the trust instrument and the requirements of proper administration require different treatment.

[T.D. 6217, Dec. 19, 1956]

§ 1.663(c)-2 Computation of distributable net income.

The amount of distributable net income for any share under section 663(c) is computed for each share as if each share constituted a separate trust. Accordingly, any deduction or any loss which is applicable solely to one separate share of the trust is not available to any other share of the same trust.

[T.D. 6217, Dec. 19, 1956]

§ 1.663(c)-3 Applicability of separate share rule.

(a) The applicability of the separate share rule provided by section 663(c) will generally depend upon whether distributions of the trust are to be made in substantially the same manner as if separate trusts had been created. Thus, if an instrument directs a trustee to divide the testator's residuary estate into separate shares (which under applicable law do not constitute separate trusts) for each of the testator's children and the trustee is given discretion, with respect to each share, to distribute or accumulate income or to distribute principal or accumulated income, or to do both, separate shares will exist under section 663(c). In determining whether separate shares exist, it is immaterial whether the principal and any accumulated income of each share is ultimately distributable to the beneficiary of such share, to his descendants, to his appointees under a general or special power of appointment, or to any other beneficiaries (including a charitable organization) designated to receive his share of the trust and accumulated income upon termination of the beneficiary's interest in the share. Thus, a separate share may exist if the instrument provides that upon the death of the beneficiary of the share, the share will be added to the shares of the other beneficiaries of the trust.

(b) Separate share treatment will not be applied to a trust or portion of a trust subject to a power to:

(1) Distribute, apportion, or accumulate income, or

(2) Distribute corpus

to or for one or more beneficiaries within a group or class of beneficiaries, unless payment of income, accumulated income, or corpus of a share of one beneficiary cannot affect the proportionate share of income, accumulated income, or corpus of any shares of the other beneficiaries, or unless substantially proper adjustment must thereafter be made (under the governing instrument) so that substantially separate and independent shares exist.

(c) A share may be considered as separate even though more than one beneficiary has an interest in it. For example, two beneficiaries may have equal, disproportionate, or indeterminate interests in one share which is separate and independent from another share in which one or more beneficiaries have an interest. Likewise, the same person may be a beneficiary of more than one separate share.

(d) Separate share treatment may be given to a trust or portion of a trust otherwise qualifying under this section if the trust or portion of a trust is subject to a power to pay out to a beneficiary of a share (of such trust or portion) an amount of corpus in excess of his proportionate share of the corpus of the trust if the possibility of exercise of the power is remote. For example, if the trust is subject to a power to invade the entire corpus for the health, education, support, or maintenance of A, separate share treatment is applied if exercise of the power requires consideration of A's other income which is so substantial as to make the possibility of exercise of the power remote. If instead it appears that A and B have separate shares in a trust, subject to a power to invade the entire corpus for the comfort, pleasure, desire, or happiness of A, separate share treatment shall not be applied.

(e) For taxable years ending before December 31, 1978, the separate share rule may also be applicable to successive interests in point of time, as for instance in the case of a trust providing for a life estate to A and a second life estate or outright remainder to B. In such a case, in the taxable year of a trust in which a beneficiary dies items of income and deduction properly allocable under trust accounting principles to the period before a beneficiary's death are attributed to one share, and those allocable to the period after the beneficiary's death are attributed to the other share. Separate share treatment is not available to a succeeding interest, however, with respect to distributions which would otherwise be deemed distributed in a taxable year of the earlier interest under the throwback provisions of subpart D (section 665 and following), part 1, subchapter J, chapter 1 of the Code. The application of this paragraph may be illustrated by the following example:

Example. A trust instrument directs that the income of a trust is to be paid to A for her life. After her death income may be distributed to B or accumulated. A dies on June 1, 1956. The trust keeps its books on the basis of the calendar year. The trust instrument permits invasions of corpus for the benefit of A and B, and an invasion of corpus was in fact made for A's benefit in 1956. In determining the distributable net income of the trust for the purpose of determining the amounts includible in A's income, income and deductions properly allocable to the period before A's death are treated as income and deductions of a separate share; and for that purpose no account is taken of income and deductions allocable to the period after A's death.

(f) Separate share treatment is not applicable to an estate.

[T.D. 6217, Dec. 19, 1956, as amended by T.D. 7633, July 19, 1979]

§ 1.663(c)–4 Example.

Section 663(c) may be illustrated by the following example:

Example. (a) A single trust was created in 1940 for the benefit of A, B, and C, who were aged 6, 4, and 2, respectively. Under the terms of the instrument, the trust income is required to be divided into three equal shares. Each beneficiary's share of the income is to be accumulated until he becomes 21 years of age. When a beneficiary reaches the age of 21, his share of the income may thereafter be either accumulated or distributed to him in the discretion of the trustee. The trustee also has discretion to invade corpus for the benefit of any beneficiary to the extent of his share of the trust estate, and the trust instrument requires that the beneficiary's right to future income and corpus will be proportionately reduced. When each beneficiary reaches 35 years of age, his share of the trust estate shall be paid over to him. The interest in the trust estate of any beneficiary dying without issue and before he has attained the age of 35 is to be equally divided between the other beneficiaries of the trust. All expenses of the trust are allocable to income under the terms of the trust instrument.

(b) No distributions of income or corpus were made by the trustee prior to 1955, although A became 21 years of age on June 30, 1954. During the taxable year of 1955, the trust has income from royalties of $20,000 and expenses of $5,000. The trustee in his discretion distributes $12,000 to A. Both A and the trust report on the calendar year basis.

(c) The trust qualifies for the separate share treatment under section 663(c) and the distributable net income must be divided into three parts for the purpose of determining the amount deductible by the trust under section 661 and the amount includible in A's gross income under section 662.

(d) The distributable net income of each share of the trust is $5,000 ($6,667 less $1,667). Since the amount ($12,000) distributed to A during 1955 exceeds the distributable net income of $5,000 allocated to his share, the trust is deemed to have distributed to him $5,000 of 1955 income and $7,000 of amounts other than 1955 income. Accordingly, the trust is allowed a deduction of $5,000 under section 661. The taxable income of the trust for 1955 is $9,900, computed as follows:

Royalties		$20,000
Deductions:		
Expenses	$5,000	
Distribution to A	5,000	
Personal exemption	100	
		10,100
Taxable income		9,900

(e) In accordance with section 662, A must include in his gross income for 1955 an amount equal to the portion ($5,000) of the distributable net income of the trust allocated to his share. Also, the excess distribution of $7,000 made by the trust is subject to the throwback provisions of subpart D (section 665 and following), part I, subchapter J, chapter 1 of the Code, and the regulations thereunder.

[T.D. 6217, Dec. 19, 1956]

§ 1.664-1 Charitable remainder trusts.

(a) In general—(1) Introduction—(i) General description of a charitable remainder trust. Generally, a charitable remainder trust is a trust which provides for a specified distribution, at least annually, to one or more beneficiaries, at least one of which is not a charity, for life or for a term of years, with an irrevocable remainder interest to be held for the benefit of, or paid over to, charity. The specified distribution to be paid at least annually must be a sum certain which is not less than 5 percent of the initial net fair market value of all property placed in trust (in the case of a charitable remainder annuity trust) or a fixed percentage which is not less than 5 percent of the net fair market value of the trust assets, valued annually (in the case of a charitable remainder unitrust). A trust created after July 31, 1969, which is a charitable remainder trust is exempt from all of the taxes imposed by subtitle A of the Code for any taxable year of the trust except a taxable year in which it has unrelated business taxable income.

(ii) Scope. This section provides definitions, general rules governing the creation and administration of a charitable remainder trust, and rules governing the taxation of the trust and its beneficiaries. For the application of certain foundation rules to charitable remainder trusts, see paragraph (b) of this section. If the trust has unrelated business taxable income, see paragraph (c) of this section. For the treatment of distributions to recipients, see paragraph (d) of this section. For the treatment of distributions to charity, see paragraph (e) of this section. For the time limitations for amendment of governing instruments, see paragraph (f) of this section. For transitional rules under which particular requirements are inapplicable to certain trusts, see paragraph (g) of this section. Section 1.664-2 provides rules relating solely to a charitable remainder annuity trust. Section 1.664-3 provides rules relating solely to a charitable remainder unitrust. Section 1.664-4 provides rules governing the calculation of the fair market value of the remainder interest in a charitable remainder unitrust. For rules relating to the filing of returns for a charitable remainder trust, see paragraph (a)(6) of § 1.6012-3 and section 6034 and the regulations thereunder.

(iii) Definitions. As used in this section and §§ 1.664–2, 1.664–3, and 1.664–4:

(a) Charitable remainder trust. The term "charitable remainder trust" means a trust with respect to which a deduction is allowable under section 170, 2055, 2106, or 2522 and which meets the description of a charitable remainder annuity trust (as described in § 1.664–2) or a charitable remainder unitrust (as described in § 1.664–3).

(b) Annuity amount. The term "annuity amount" means the amount described in paragraph (a)(1) of § 1.664–2 which is payable, at least annually, to the beneficiary of a charitable remainder annuity trust.

(c) Unitrust amount. The term "unitrust amount" means the amount described in paragraph (a)(1) of § 1.664–3 which is payable, at least annually, to the beneficiary of a charitable remainder unitrust.

(d) Recipient. The term "recipient" means the beneficiary who receives the possession or beneficial enjoyment of the annuity amount or unitrust amount.

(e) Governing instrument. The term "governing instrument" has the same meaning as in section 508(e) and the regulations thereunder.

(2) Requirement that the trust must be either a charitable remainder annuity trust or a charitable remainder unitrust. A trust is a charitable remainder trust only if it is either a charitable remainder annuity trust in every respect or a charitable remainder unitrust in every respect. For example, a trust which provides for the payment each year to a noncharitable beneficiary of the greater of a sum certain or a fixed percentage of the annual value of the trust assets is not a charitable remainder trust inasmuch as the trust is neither a charitable remainder annuity trust (for the reason that the payment for the year may be a fixed percentage of the annual value of the trust assets which is not a "sum certain") nor a charitable remainder unitrust (for the reason that the payment for the year may be a sum certain which is not a "fixed percentage" of the annual value of the trust assets).

(3) Restrictions on investments. A trust is not a charitable remainder trust if the provisions of the trust include a provision which restricts the trustee from investing the trust assets in a manner which could result in the annual realization of a reasonable amount of income or gain from the sale or disposition of trust assets. In the case of transactions with, or for the benefit of, a disqualified person, see section 4941(d) and the regulations thereunder for rules relating to the definition of self-dealing.

(4) Requirement that trust must meet definition of and function exclusively as a charitable remainder trust from its creation. In order for a trust to be a charitable remainder trust, it must meet the definition of and function exclusively as a charitable remainder trust from the creation of the trust. Solely for the purposes of section 664 and the regulations thereunder, the trust will be deemed to be created at the earliest time that neither the grantor nor any other person is treated as the owner of the entire trust under subpart E, part 1, subchapter J, chapter 1, subtitle A of the Code (relating to grantors and others treated as substantial owners), but in no event prior to the time property is first transferred to the trust. For purposes of the preceding sentence, neither the grantor nor his spouse shall be treated as the owner of the trust under such subpart E merely because the grantor or his spouse is named as a recipient. See examples 1 through 3 of subparagraph (6) of this paragraph for illustrations of the foregoing rule.

(5) Rules applicable to testamentary transfers—(i) Deferral of annuity or unitrust amount. Notwithstanding subparagraph (4) of this paragraph and §§ 1.664-2 and 1.664-3, for purposes of sections 2055 and 2106 a charitable remainder trust shall be deemed created at the date of death of the decedent (even though the trust is not funded until the end of a reasonable period of administration or settlement) if the obligation to pay the annuity or unitrust amount with respect to the property passing in trust at the death of the decedent begins as of the date of death of the decedent, even though the requirement to pay such amount is deferred in accordance with the rules provided in this subparagraph. If permitted by applicable local law or authorized by the provisions of the governing instrument, the requirement to pay such amount may be deferred until the end of the taxable year of the trust in which occurs the complete funding of the trust. Within a reasonable period after such time, the trust must pay (in the case of an underpayment) or must receive from the recipient (in the case of an overpayment) the difference between—

(a) Any annuity or unitrust amounts actually paid, plus interest on such amounts computed at the rate of interest specified in paragraph (a)(5)(iv) of this section, compounded annually, and

(b) The annuity or unitrust amounts payable, plus interest on such amounts computed at the rate of interest specified in paragraph (a)(5)(iv) of this section, compounded annually.

The amounts payable shall be retroactively determined by using the taxable year, valuation method, and valuation dates which are ultimately adopted by the charitable remainder trust. See subdivision (ii) of this subparagraph for rules relating to retroactive determination of the amount payable under a charitable remainder unitrust. See paragraph (d)(4) of this section for rules relating to the year of inclusion in the case of an underpayment to a recipient and the allowance of a deduction in the case of an overpayment to a recipient.

(ii) For purposes of retroactively determining the amount under subdivision (i)(b) of this subparagraph, the governing instrument of a charitable remainder unitrust may provide that the amount described in subdivision (i)(b) of this subparagraph with respect to property passing in trust at the death of the decedent for the period which begins on the date of death of the decedent and ends on the earlier of the date of death of the last recipient or the end of the taxable year of the trust in which occurs the complete funding of the trust shall be computed by multiplying—

(a) The sum of *(1)* the value, on the earlier of the date of death of the last recipient or the last day in such taxable year, of the property held in trust which is attributable to property passing to the trust at the death of the decedent, *(2)* any distributions in respect of unitrust amounts made by the trust or estate before such date, and *(3)* interest on such distributions computed at the rate of interest specified in paragraph (a)(5)(iv) of this section, compounded annually, from the date of distribution to such date by—

(b) A factor equal to 1.0 less the factor under the appropriate payout rate in column 2 of Table D in § 1.664-4(b)(5) opposite the number of years in column 1 between the date of death of the decedent and the date of the earlier of the death of the last recipient or the last day in such taxable year.

If the number of years between the date of death and the date of the earlier of the death of the last recipient or end of such taxable year is between periods for which factors are provided in Table D, a linear interpolation must be made.

(iii) Treatment of distributions. The treatment of a distribution to a charitable remainder trust, or to a recipient in respect of an annuity or unitrust amount, paid, credited, or required to be distributed by an estate, or by a trust which is not a charitable remainder trust, shall be governed by the rules of subchapter J, chapter 1, subtitle A of the Code other than section 664. In the case of a charitable remainder trust which is partially or fully funded during the period of administration of an estate or settlement of a trust (which is not a charitable remainder trust), the treatment of any amount paid, credited, or required to be distributed by the charitable remainder trust shall be governed by the rules of section 664.

(iv) Rate of interest. The following rates of interest shall apply for purposes of paragraphs (a)(5)(i) through (iii) of this section:

(a) 10 percent for instruments executed or amended on or after August 9, 1984;

(b) 6 percent or 10 percent for instruments executed or amended after October 24, 1983, and before August 9, 1984; and

(c) 6 percent for instruments executed before October 25, 1983, and not subsequently amended.

(6) Examples. The application of the rules in subparagraphs (4) and (5) of this paragraph may be illustrated by the following examples:

Example (1). On September 19, 1971, H transfers property to a trust over which he retains an inter vivos power of revocation. The trust is to pay W 5 percent of the value of the trust assets, valued annually, for her life, remainder to charity. The trust would satisfy all of the requirements of section 664 if it were irrevocable. For purposes of section 664, the trust is not deemed created in 1971 because H is treated as the owner of the entire trust under subpart E. On May 26, 1975, H predeceases W at which time the trust becomes irrevocable. For purposes of section 664, the trust is deemed created on May 26, 1975, because that is the earliest date on which H is not treated as the owner of the entire trust under subpart E. The trust becomes a charitable remainder trust on May 26, 1975, because it meets the definition of a charitable remainder trust from its creation.

Example (2). The facts are the same as in example (1), except that H retains the inter vivos power to revoke only one-half of the trust. For purposes of section 664, the trust is deemed created on September 19, 1971, because on that date the grantor is not treated as the owner of the entire trust under subpart E. Consequently, a charitable deduction is not allowable either at the creation of the trust or at H's death because the trust does not meet the definition of a charitable remainder trust from the date of its creation. The trust does not meet the definition of a charitable remainder trust from the date of its creation because the trust is subject to a partial power to revoke on such date.

Example (3). The facts are the same as in example (1), except that the residue of H's estate is to be paid to the trust and the trust is required to pay H's debts. The trust is not a charitable remainder trust at H's death because it does not function exclusively as a charitable remainder trust from the date of its creation which, in this case, is the date it becomes irrevocable.

Example (4). (i) In 1971, H transfers property to Trust A over which he retains an inter vivos power of revocation. Trust A, which is not a charitable remainder trust, is to provide income or corpus to W until the death of H. Upon H's death the trust is required by its governing instrument to pay the debts and administration expenses of H's estate, and then to terminate and distribute all of the remaining assets to a separate Trust B which meets the definition of a charitable remainder annuity trust.

(ii) Trust B will be charitable remainder trust from the date of its funding because it will function exclusively as a charitable remainder trust from its creation. For purposes of section 2055, Trust B will be deemed created at H's death if the obligation to pay the annuity amount begins on the date of H's death. For purposes of section 664, Trust B becomes a charitable remainder trust as soon as it is partially or completely funded. Consequently, unless Trust B has unrelated business taxable income, the income of the trust is exempt from all taxes imposed by subtitle A of the Code, and any distributions by the trust, even before it is completely funded, are governed by the rules of section 664. Any distributions made by Trust A, including distributions to a recipient in respect of annuity amounts, are governed by the rules of subchapter J, chapter 1, subtitle A of the Code other than section 664.

Example (5). In 1973, H dies testate leaving the net residue of his estate (after payment by the estate of all debts and administration expenses) to a trust which meets the definition of a charitable remainder unitrust. For purposes of section 2055, the trust is deemed created at H's death if the requirement to pay the unitrust amount begins on H's death and is a charitable remainder trust even though the estate is obligated to pay debts and administration expenses.

For purposes of section 664, the trust becomes a charitable remainder trust as soon as it is partially or completely funded. Consequently, unless the trust has unrelated business taxable income, the income of the trust is exempt from all taxes imposed by subtitle A of the Code, and any distributions by the trust, even before it is completely funded, are governed by the rules of section 664. Any distributions made by H's estate, including distributions to a recipient in respect of unitrust amounts, are governed by the rules of subchapter J, chapter 1, subtitle A of the Code other than section 664.

Example (6). (i) On January 1, 1974, H dies testate leaving the residue of his estate to a charitable remainder unitrust. The governing instrument provides that, beginning at H's death, the trustee is to make annual payments to W, on December 31 of each year of 5 percent of the net fair market value of the trust assets, valued as of December 31 of each year, for W's life and to pay the remainder to charity at the death of W. The governing instrument also provides that the actual payment of the unitrust amount need not be made until the end of the taxable year of the trust in which occurs the complete funding of the trust. The governing instrument also provides that the amount payable with respect to the period between the date of death and the end of such taxable year shall be computed under the special method provided in subparagraph (5)(ii) of this paragraph. The governing instrument provides that, within a reasonable period after the end of the taxable year of the trust in which occurs the complete funding of the trust, the trustee shall pay (in the case of an underpayment) or shall receive from the recipient (in the case of an overpayment) the difference between the unitrust amounts paid (plus interest at 6 percentage compounded annually) and the amount computed under the special method. The trust is completely funded on September 20, 1976. No amounts were paid before June 30, 1977. The trust adopts a fiscal year of July 1 to June 30. The net fair market value of the trust assets on June 30, 1977, is $100,000.

(ii) Because no amounts were paid prior to the end of the taxable year in which the trust was completely funded, the amount payable at the end of such taxable year is equal to the net fair market value of the trust assets on the last day of such taxable year (June 30, 1977) multiplied by a factor equal to 1.0 minus the factor in Table D corresponding to the number of years in the period between the date of death and the end of such taxable year. The adjusted payout rate (determined under § 1.664–4(b)(2)) is 5 percent. Because the last day of the taxable year in which the trust is completely funded is June 30, 1977, there are 3 181/365 years in such period. Because there is no factor given in Table D for such a period, a linear interpolation must be made:

1.0 minus 0.814506 (factor at 5 percent for 4 years)	0.185494
1.0 minus .857375 (factor at 5 percent for 3 years)	.142625
Difference	.042869

$$\frac{181}{365} = \frac{X}{.042869} \qquad X = 0.021258$$

1.0 minus 0.857375 (factor at 5 percent for 3 years)	0.142625
Plus: X	.021258
Interpolated factor	.163883

Thus, the amount payable for the period from January 1, 1974, to June 30, 1977, is $16,388.30 ($100,000 × 0.163883). Thereafter, the trust assets must be valued on December 31 of each year and 5 percent of such value paid annually to W for her life.

(b) Application of certain foundation rules to charitable remainder trusts. See section 4947(a)(2) and section 4947(b)(3)(B) and the regulations thereunder for the application to charitable remainder trusts of certain provisions relating to private foundations. See section 508(e) for rules relating to required provisions in governing instruments prohibiting certain activities specified in section 4947(a)(2).

(c) Taxation of nonexempt charitable remainder trusts. If the charitable remainder trust has any unrelated business taxable income (within the meaning of section 512 and the regulations thereunder, determined as if part III, subchapter F, chapter 1, subtitle A of the Code applied to such trust) for any taxable year, the trust is subject to all of the taxes imposed by subtitle A of the Code for such taxable year. For taxable years beginning after December 31, 1969, unrelated business taxable income includes debt-financed income. The taxes imposed by subtitle A of the Code upon a nonexempt charitable remainder trust shall be computed under the rules prescribed by subparts A and C, part 1, subchapter J, chapter 1, subtitle A of the Code for trusts which may accumulate income or which distribute corpus. The provisions of subpart E, part 1 of such subchapter J are not applicable with respect to a nonexempt charitable remainder trust. The application of the above rules may be illustrated by the following example:

Example. In 1975, a charitable remainder trust which has a calendar year as its taxable year has $1,000 of ordinary income, including $100 of unrelated business taxable income, and no deductions other than under sections 642(b) and 661(a). The trust is required to pay out $700 for 1975 to a noncharitable recipient. Because the trust has some unrelated business taxable income in 1975, it is not exempt for such year. Consequently, the trust is taxable on all of its income as a complex trust. Under section 661(a) of the Code, the trust is allowed a deduction of $700. Under section 642(b) of the Code, the trust is allowed a deduction of $100. Consequently, the taxable income of the trust for 1975 is $200 ($1,000–$700–$100).

(d) Treatment of annual distributions to recipients—(1) Character of distributions—(i) Order of distributions. Annuity and unitrust amounts shall be treated as having the following characteristics in the hands of the recipients (whether or not the trust is exempt) without credit for any taxes which are imposed by subtitle A of the Code on the trust:

(a) Ordinary income. First, as ordinary income to the extent of the sum of the trust's ordinary income for the taxable year of the trust and its undistributed ordinary income for prior years. An ordinary loss for the current year shall be used to reduce undistributed ordinary income for prior years and any excess shall be carried forward indefinitely to reduce ordinary income for future years. For purposes of this section, the amount of current and prior years' income shall be computed without regard to the deduction for net operating losses provided by section 172 or 642(d).

(b) Capital gain. Second, as capital gain to the extent of the trust's undistributed capital gains. Undistributed capital gains of the trust are determined on a cumulative net basis under the rules of this subdivision without regard to the provisions of section 1212.

(1) Long- and short-term capital gains. If, in any taxable year of the trust, the trust has both undistributed short-term capital gain and undistributed long-term capital gain, then the short-term capital gain shall be deemed distributed prior to any long-term capital gain.

(2) Capital losses in excess of capital gains. If the trust has for any taxable year capital losses in excess of capital gains, any excess of the net short-term capital loss over the net long-term capital gain for such year shall be a short-term capital loss in the succeeding taxable year and any excess of the net long-term capital loss over the net short-term capital gain for such year shall be a long-term capital loss in the succeeding taxable year.

(3) Capital gains in excess of capital losses. If the trust has for any taxable year capital gains in excess of capital losses, any excess of the net short-term capital gain over the net long-term capital loss for such year shall be, to the extent not deemed distributed, a short-term capital gain in the succeeding taxable year and any excess of the net long-term capital gain over the net short-term capital loss for such year shall be, to the extent not deemed distributed, a long-term capital gain in the succeeding taxable year.

The application of the rules in this subdivision (b) may be illustrated by the following example:

Example. (i) The X Trust is a charitable remainder trust created on January 1, 1975, and has the calendar year as its taxable year. During the years indicated, it has the following capital transactions:

1975:	
Long-term capital loss	$ 10
Short-term capital gain	5
1976:	
Short-term capital gain	20
Short-term capital loss	5
1977:	
Long-term capital gain	15

Distributions for 1975 and 1976 were not in excess of current and accumulated ordinary income for those years. In 1977, distributions exceeded current and accumulated ordinary income by $5.

(ii) The treatment of the 1975 and 1976 transactions is as follows:

1975:	
Long-term capital loss recognized	$ (10)
Short-term capital gain recognized	5
Net long-term capital loss carried forward to 1976	(5)
1976:	
Short-term capital gain recognized	20
Short-term capital loss recognized	(5)
Long-term capital loss carried forward from 1975	(5)
Net short-term capital gain carried forward to 1977	$ 10
1977:	
Long-term capital gain recognized	15
Net short-term capital gain carried forward from 1976	10

(iii) In 1977, the trust has long-term capital gain of $15 and short-term capital gain of $10. If the trust has both short-term capital gain and long-term capital gain for the same taxable year, the short-term capital gain is deemed distributed prior to the long-term capital gain. Therefore, the distribution of $5 in 1977 is deemed to be short-term capital gain. The undistributed net short-term capital gain of $5 is a short-term capital gain carried forward to 1978. The undistributed net long-term capital gain of $15 is a long-term capital gain carried forward to 1978.

(c) **Other income.** Third, as other income (including income excluded under part III, subchapter B, chapter 1, subtitle A of the Code) to the extent of the sum of the trust's other income for the taxable year and its undistributed other income for prior years. A loss in this category for the current year shall be used to reduce undistributed income in such category for prior years and any excess shall be carried forward indefinitely to reduce such income for future years.

(d) **Corpus.** Finally, as a distribution of trust corpus. For purposes of this section, the term "corpus" means the net fair market value of the trust assets less the total undistributed income (but not loss) in each of the above categories.

(ii) **Rules relating to character of distributions.** The determination of the character of amounts distributed shall be made as of the end of the taxable year of the trust. Amounts treated as paid from one of the categories of income described in (a), (b) or (c) of subdivision (i) of this subparagraph shall be treated as consisting of the same proportion of each class of items included in such category as the total of the current and accumulated income of each class of items bears to the total of the current and accumulated income for that category. A loss in one of such categories may not be used to reduce a gain in any other category. The provisions of subparts D and E, part 1, subchapter J, chapter 1, subtitle A of the Code are not applicable with respect to a charitable remainder trust (regardless of whether the trust is exempt).

(2) **Allocation of deductions.** Items of deduction of the trust for a taxable year of the trust which are deductible in determining taxable income (other than the deductions permitted by sections 642(b), 642(c), 661, and 1202) which are directly attributable to one or more classes of items within a category of income or to corpus (determined under subparagraph (1)(i) of this paragraph) shall be allocated to such classes of items or to corpus. All other allowable deductions for such taxable year which are not directly attributable to one or more classes of items within a category of income or to corpus (other than the deductions permitted by sections 642(b), 642(c), 661, and 1202) shall be allocated among the classes of items within the category (excluding classes of items with net losses) on the basis of the gross income of such classes for such taxable year reduced by the deductions allocated thereto under the first sentence of this subparagraph, but in no event shall the amount of expenses allocated to any class of items exceed such income of such class for the taxable year. Items of deduction which are not allocable under the above two sentences (other than the deductions permitted by sections 642(b), 642(c), 661, and 1202) may be allocated in any manner. All taxes imposed by subtitle A of the Code for which the trust is liable because it has unrelated business taxable income and all taxes imposed by chapter 42 of the Code shall be allocated to corpus. Any expense which is not deductible in determining taxable income and which is not allocable to any class of items described in subparagraph (1)(i)(c) of this paragraph shall be allocated to corpus. The deductions allowable to a trust under sections 642(b), 642(c), 661, and 1202 are not allowed in determining the amount or character of any class of items within a category of income or corpus in the categories described in subparagraph (1) of this paragraph.

(3) **Allocation of income among recipients.** If there are two or more recipients, each will be treated as receiving his pro rata portion of the categories of income and corpus. The application of this rule may be illustrated by the following example:

Example. X transfers $40,000 to a charitable remainder annuity trust which is to pay $3,000 per year to X and $2,000 per year to Y for a term of 5 years. During the first taxable year the trust has $3,000 of ordinary income, $500 of capital gain, and $500 of tax-exempt income after allocation of all expenses. X is treated as receiving ordinary income of $1,800 ($3,000/$5,000 × $3,000), capital gain of $300 ($3,000/$5,000 × $500), tax-exempt income of $300 ($3,000/$5,000 × $500), and corpus of $600 ($3,000/$5,000 × [$5,000 − $4,000]). Y is treated as receiving ordinary income of $1,200 ($2,000/$5,000 × $3,000), capital gain of $200 ($2,000/$5,000 × $500), tax-exempt income of $200 ($2,000/$5,000 × $500), and corpus of $400 ($2,000/$5,000 × [$5,000 − $4,000]).

(4) Year of inclusion—(i) General rule. To the extent required by this paragraph, the annuity or unitrust amount is includible in the recipient's gross income for the taxable year in which the annuity or unitrust amount is required to be distributed even though the annuity or unitrust amount is not distributed until after the close of the taxable year of the trust. If a recipient has a different taxable year (as defined in section 441 or 442) from the taxable year of the trust, the amount he is required to include in gross income to the extent required by this paragraph shall be included in his taxable year in which or with which ends the taxable year of the trust in which such amount is required to be distributed.

(ii) Payments resulting from incorrect valuations. Notwithstanding subdivision (i) of this subparagraph, any payments which are made or required to be distributed by a charitable remainder trust pursuant to paragraph (a)(5) of this section, under paragraph (f)(3) of this section because of an amendment to the governing instrument, or under paragraphs (a)(1) of §§ 1.664-2 and 1.664-3 because of an incorrect valuation, shall, to the extent required by this paragraph, be included in the gross income of the recipient in his taxable year in which or with which ends the taxable year of the trust in which the amount is paid, credited, or required to be distributed. For rules relating to required adjustments of underpayments and overpayments of the annuity or unitrust amounts in respect of payments made prior to the amendment of a governing instrument, see paragraph (f)(3) of this section. There is allowable to a recipient a deduction from gross income for any amounts repaid to the trust because of an overpayment during the reasonable period of administration or settlement or until the trust is fully funded, because of an amendment, or because of an incorrect valuation, to the extent such amounts were included in his gross income. See section 1341 and the regulations thereunder for rules relating to the computation of tax where a taxpayer restores substantial amounts held under a claim of right.

(iii) Rules applicable to year of recipient's death. If the taxable year of the trust does not end with or within the last taxable year of the recipient because of the recipient's death, the extent to which the annuity or unitrust amount required to be distributed to him is included in the gross income of the recipient for his last taxable year, or in the gross income of his estate, is determined by making the computations required under this paragraph for the taxable year of the trust in which his last taxable year ends. (The last sentence of subdivision (i) of this subparagraph does not apply to such amounts.) The gross income for the last taxable year of a recipient on the cash basis includes (to the extent required by this paragraph) amounts actually distributed to the recipient before his death. Amounts required to be distributed which are distributed to his estate are included (to the extent required by this paragraph) in the gross income of the estate as income in respect of a decedent under section 691.

(5) Distributions in kind. The annuity or unitrust amount may be paid in cash or in other property. In the case of a distribution made in other property, the amount paid, credited, or required to be distributed shall be considered as an amount realized by the trust from the sale or other disposition of property. The basis of the property in the hands of the recipient is its fair market value at the time it was paid, credited, or required to be distributed. The application of these rules may be illustrated by the following example:

Example. On January 1, 1971, X creates a charitable remainder annuity trust, whose taxable year is the calendar year, under which X is to receive $5,000 per year. During 1971, the trust receives $500 of ordinary income. On December 31, 1971, the trust distributed cash of $500 and a capital asset of the trust having a fair market value of $4,500 and a basis of $2,200. The trust is deemed to have realized a capital gain of $2,300. X treats the distribution of $5,000 as being ordinary income of $500, capital gain of $2,300 and trust corpus of $2,200. The basis of the distributed property is $4,500 in the hands of X.

(e) Other distributions—(1) Character of distributions. An amount distributed by the trust to an organization described in section 170(c) other than the annuity or unitrust amount shall be considered as a distribution of corpus and of those categories of income specified in paragraph (d)(1) of this section in an order inverse to that prescribed in such paragraph. The character of such amount shall be determined as of the end of the taxable year of the trust in which the distribution is made after the character of the annuity or unitrust amount has been determined.

(2) Distributions in kind. In the case of a distribution of an amount to which subparagraph (1) of this paragraph applies, no gain or loss is realized by the trust by reason of a distribution in kind unless such distribution is in satisfaction of a right to receive a distribution of a specific dollar amount or in specific property other than that distributed.

(f) Effective date—(1) General rule. The provisions of this section are effective with respect to transfers in trust made after July 31, 1969. Any trust created (within the meaning of applicable local law) prior to August 1, 1969, is not a charitable remainder trust even if it otherwise satisfies the definition of a charitable remainder trust.

(2) Transfers to pre-1970 trusts. Property transferred to a trust created (within the meaning of applicable local law) before August 1, 1969, whose governing instrument provides that an organization described in section 170(c) receives an irrevocable remainder interest in such trust, shall, for purposes of subparagraphs (1) and (3) of this paragraph, be deemed transferred to a trust created on the date of such transfer provided that the transfer occurs after July 31, 1969, and prior to October 18, 1971, and the transferred property and any undistributed income therefrom is severed and placed in a separate trust before December 31, 1972, or if later, on or before the 30th day after the date on which any judicial proceedings begun before December 31, 1972, which are required to sever such property, become final.

(3) Amendment of post-1969 trusts. A trust created (within the meaning of applicable local law) subsequent to July 31, 1969, and prior to December 31, 1972, which is not a charitable remainder trust at the date of its creation, may be treated as a charitable remainder trust from the date it would be deemed created under § 1.664-1(a)(4) and (5)(i) for all purposes: *Provided,* That all the following requirements are met:

(i) At the time of the creation of the trust, the governing instrument provides that an organization described in section 170(c) receives an irrevocable remainder interest in such trust.

(ii) The governing instrument of the trust is amended so that the trust will meet the definition of a charitable remainder trust and, if applicable, will meet the requirement of paragraph (a)(5)(i) of this section that obligation to make payment of the annuity or unitrust amount with respect to property passing at death begin as of the date of death, before December 31, 1972, or if later, on or before the 30th day after the date on which any judicial proceedings which are begun before December 31, 1972, and which are required to amend its governing instrument, become final. In the case of a trust created (within the meaning of applicable local law) subsequent to July 31, 1969, and prior to December 31, 1972, the provisions of section 508(d)(2)(A) shall not apply if the governing instrument of the trust is amended so as to comply with the requirements of section 508(e) before December 31, 1972, or if later, on or before the 30th day after the date on which any judicial proceedings which are begun before December 31, 1972, and which are required to amend its governing instrument, become final. Notwithstanding the provisions of paragraphs (a)(3) and (a)(4) of §§ 1.664-2 and 1.664-3, the governing instrument may grant to the trustee a power to amend the governing instrument for the sole purpose of complying with the requirements of this section and § 1.664-2 or § 1.664-3: *Provided,* That at the creation of the trust, the governing instrument *(a)* provides for the payment of a unitrust amount described in § 1.664-3(a)(1)(i) or an annuity which meets the requirements of paragraph (a)(2) of § 1.664-2 or § 1.664-3, *(b)* designates the recipients of the trust and the period for which the amount described in (a) of this subdivision (ii) is to be paid, and *(c)* provides that an organization described in section 170(c) receives an irrevocable remainder interest in such trust. The mere granting of such a power is not sufficient to meet the requirements of this subparagraph that the governing instrument be amended in the manner and within the time limitations of this subparagraph.

(iii)(a) Where the amount of the distributions which would have been made by the trust to a recipient if the amended provisions of such trust had been in effect from the time of creation of such trust exceeds the amount of the distributions made by the trust prior to its amendment, the trust pays an amount equal to such excess to the recipient.

(b) Where the amount of distributions made to the recipient prior to the amendment of the trust exceeds the amount of the distributions which would have been made by such trust if the amended provisions of such trust had been in effect from the time of creation of such trust, such excess is repaid to the trust by the recipient. See paragraph (d)(4) of this section for rules relating to the year of inclusion in the case of an underpayment to a recipient and the allowance of a deduction in the case of an overpayment to a recipient. A deduction for a transfer to a charitable remainder trust shall not be allowed until the requirements of this paragraph are met and then only if the deduction is claimed on a timely-filed return (including extensions) or on a claim for refund filed within the period of limitations prescribed by section 6511(a).

(g) Transitional effective date. Notwithstanding any other provision of this section, § 1.664-2 or § 1.664-3, the requirement of paragraph (a)(5)(i) of this section that interest accrue on overpayments and underpayments, the requirement of paragraph (a)(5)(ii) of this section that the unitrust amount accruing under the formula provided therein cease with the death of the last recipient, and the requirement that the governing instrument of the trust contain the provisions specified in paragraph (a)(1)(iv) of § 1.664-2 (relating to computation of the annuity amount in certain circumstances), paragraph (a)(1)(v) of § 1.664–3 (relating to computation of the unitrust amount in certain circumstances), paragraphs (b) of §§ 1.664–2 and 1.664–3 (relating to additional contributions), and paragraph (a)(1)(iii) of § 1.664–3 (relating to incorrect valuations), paragraphs (a)(6)(iv) of §§ 1.664–2 and 1.664–3 (relating to alternative remaindermen) shall not apply to:

(1) A will executed on or before December 31, 1972, if:

(i) The testator dies before December 31, 1975, without having republished the will after December 31, 1972, by codicil or otherwise,

(ii) The testator at no time after December 31, 1972, had the right to change the provisions of the will which pertain to the trust, or

(iii) The will is not republished by codicil or otherwise before December 31, 1975, and the testator is on such date and at all times thereafter under a mental disability to republish the will by codicil or otherwise, or

(2) A trust executed on or before December 31, 1972, if:

(i) The grantor dies before December 31, 1975, without having amended the trust after December 31, 1972,

(ii) The trust is irrevocable on December 31, 1972, or

(iii) The trust is not amended before December 31, 1975, and the grantor is on such date and at all times thereafter under a mental disability to change the terms of the trust.

[T.D. 7202, Aug. 22, 1972, as amended by T.D. 7955, May 10, 1984]

§ 8.1 Charitable remainder trusts.

(a) Certain wills and trusts in existence on September 21, 1974. In the case of a will executed before September 21, 1974, or a trust created (within the meaning of applicable local law) after July 31, 1969, and before September 21, 1974, which is amended pursuant to section 2055(e)(3) and § 24.1 of this Chapter (Temporary Estate Tax Regulations), a charitable remainder trust resulting from such amendment will be treated as a charitable remainder trust from the date it would be deemed created under § 1.664–1(a)(4) and (5) of this chapter (Income Tax Regulations), whether or not such date is after September 20, 1974.

(b) Certain transfers to trusts created before August 1, 1969. Property transferred to a trust created (within the meaning of applicable local law) before August 1, 1969, whose governing instrument provides that an organization described in section 170(c) receives an irrevocable remainder interest in such trust shall be deemed transferred to a trust created on the date of such transfer, provided that the transfer occurs after July 31, 1969 and prior to October 18, 1971, and pursuant to an amendment provided in § 24.1 of this chapter (Temporary Estate Tax Regulations), the transferred property and any undistributed income therefrom is severed and placed in a separate trust as of the date of the amendment.

[T.D. 7393, Dec. 16, 1975]

§ 1.664–2 Charitable remainder annuity trust.

(a) Description. A charitable remainder annuity trust is a trust which complies with the applicable provisions of § 1.664–1 and meets all of the following requirements:

(1) **Required payment of annuity amount—(i) Payment of sum certain at least annually.** The governing instrument provides that the trust shall pay a sum certain not less often than annually to a person or persons described in subparagraph (3) of this paragraph for each taxable year of the period specified in subparagraph (5) of this paragraph. The trust will not be deemed to have engaged in an act of self-dealing (within the meaning of section 4941), to have unrelated debt-financed income (within the meaning of section 514), to have received an additional contribution (within the meaning of § 1.664–2(b)), or to have failed to function exclusively as a charitable remainder trust (within the meaning of § 1.664–4(a)(4)) merely because payment of the annuity amount is made after the close of the taxable year: Provided, That such payment is made within a reasonable time after the close of such taxable year. For purposes of the preceding sentence, a reasonable time will not ordinarily extend beyond the date by which the trustee is required to file Form 1041–B (including extensions) for such year.

(ii) **Definition of sum certain.** A sum certain is a stated dollar amount which is the same either as to each recipient or as to the total amount payable for each year of such period. For example, a provision for an amount which is the same every year to A until his death and concurrently an amount which is the same every year to B until his death, with the amount to each recipient to terminate at his death, would satisfy the above rule. Similarly, provisions for an amount to A and B for their joint lives and then to the survivor would satisfy the above rule. In the case of a distribution to an organization described in section 170(c) at the death of a recipient or the expiration of a term of years, the governing instrument may provide for a reduction of the stated amount payable after such a distribution provided that:

(a) The reduced amount payable is the same either as to each recipient or as to the total amount payable for each year of the balance of such period, and

(b) The requirements of subparagraph (2)(ii) of this paragraph are met.

(iii) **Sum certain stated as a fraction or percentage.** The stated dollar amount may be expressed as a fraction or a percentage of the initial net fair market value of the property irrevocably passing in trust as finally determined for Federal tax purposes. If the stated dollar amount is so expressed and such market value is incorrectly determined by the fiduciary, the requirement of this subparagraph will be satisfied if the governing instrument provides that in such event the trust shall pay to the recipient (in the case of an undervaluation) or be repaid by the recipient (in the case of an overvaluation) an amount equal to the difference between the amount which the trust should have paid the recipient if the correct value were used and the amount which the trust actually paid the recipient. Such payments or repayments must be made within a reasonable period after the final determination of such value. Any payment due to a recipient by reason of such incorrect valuation shall be considered to be a payment required to be distributed at the time of such final determination for purposes of paragraph (d)(4)(ii) of § 1.664–1. See paragraph (d)(4) of § 1.664–1 for rules relating to the year of inclusion of such payments and the allowance of a deduction for such repayments. See paragraph (b) of this section for rules relating to future contributions. For rules relating to required adjustments for underpayments or overpayments of the amount described in this paragraph in respect of payments made during a reasonable period of administration, see paragraph (a)(5) of § 1.664-1. The application of the rule permitting the stated dollar amount to be expressed as a fraction or a percentage of the initial net fair market value of the property irrevocably passing in trust as finally determined for Federal tax purposes may be illustrated by the following example:

Example. The will of X provides for the transfer of one-half of his residuary estate to a charitable remainder annuity trust which is required to pay to W for life an annuity equal to 5 percent of the initial net fair market value of the interest passing in trust as finally determined for Federal tax purposes. The annuity is to be paid on December 31 of each year computed from the date of X's death. The will also provides that if such initial net fair market value is incorrectly determined, the trust shall pay to W, in the case of an undervaluation, or be repaid by W, in the case of an overvaluation, an amount equal to the difference between the amount which the trust should have paid if the correct value were used and the amount which the trust actually paid. X dies on March 1, 1971. The executor files an estate tax return showing the value of the residuary estate as $250,000 before reduction for taxes and expenses of $50,000. The executor paid to W $4,192 ([$250,000–$50,000]×½×5 percent×306/365) on December 31, 1971. On January 1, 1972, the executor transfers one-half of the residue of the estate to the trust. The trust adopts the calendar year as its taxable year. The value of the residuary estate is finally determined for Federal tax purposes to be $240,000 ($290,000–$50,000). Accordingly, the amount which the executor should have paid to W is $5,030 ([$290,000–$50,000]×½×5 percent×306/365). Consequently, an additional amount of $838 ($5,030–$4,192) must be paid to W within a reasonable period after the final determination of value for Federal tax purposes.

* * *

(2) **Minimum annuity amount—(i) General rule.** The total amount payable under subparagraph (1) of this paragraph is not less than 5 percent of the initial net fair market value of the property placed in trust as finally determined for Federal tax purposes.

(ii) **Reduction of annuity amount in certain cases.** A trust will not fail to meet the requirements of this subparagraph by reason of the fact that it provides for a reduction of the stated amount payable upon the death of a recipient or the expiration of a term of years provided that:

(a) A distribution is made to an organization described in section 170(c) at the death of such recipient or the expiration of such term of years, and

(b) The total amounts payable each year under subparagraph (1) of this paragraph after such distribution are not less than a stated dollar amount which bears the same ratio to 5 percent of the initial net fair market value of the trust assets as the net fair market value of the trust assets immediately after such distribution bears to the net fair market value of the trust assets immediately before such distribution.

(iii) **Rule applicable to inter vivos trust which does not provide for payment of minimum annuity amount.** In the case where the grantor of an inter vivos trust underestimates in good faith the initial net fair market value of the property placed in trust as finally determined for Federal tax purposes and specifies a fixed dollar amount for the annuity which is less than 5 percent of the initial net fair market value of the property placed in trust as finally determined for Federal tax purposes, the trust will be deemed to have met the 5 percent requirement if the grantor or his representative consents, by appropriate agreement with the District Director, to accept an amount equal to 20 times the annuity as the fair market value of the property placed in trust for purposes of determining the appropriate charitable contributions deduction.

(3) **Permissible recipients—(i) General rule.** The amount described in subparagraph (1) of this paragraph is payable to or for the use of a named person or persons, at least one of which is not an organization described in section 170(c). If the amount described in subparagraph (1) of this paragraph is to be paid to an individual or individuals, all such individuals must be living at the time of the creation of the trust. A named person or persons may include members of a named class provided that, in the case of a class which includes any individual, all such individuals must be alive and ascertainable at the time of the creation of the trust unless the period for which the annuity amount is to be paid to such class consists solely of a term of years. For example, in the case of a testamentary trust, the testator's will may provide that an amount shall be paid to his children living at his death.

(ii) Power to alter amount paid to recipients. A trust is not a charitable remainder annuity trust if any person has the power to alter the amount to be paid to any named person other than an organization described in section 170(c) if such power would cause any person to be treated as the owner of the trust, or any portion thereof, if subpart E, Part 1, subchapter J, chapter 1, Subtitle A of the Code were applicable to such trust. See paragraph (a)(4) of this section for a rule permitting the retention by a grantor of a testamentary power to revoke or terminate the interest of any recipient other than an organization described in section 170(c). For example, the governing instrument may not grant the trustee the power to allocate the annuity among members of a class unless such power falls within one of the exceptions to section 674(a).

(4) **Other payments.** No amount other than the amount described in subparagraph (1) of this paragraph may be paid to or for the use of any person other than an organization described in section 170(c). An amount is not paid to or for the use of any person other than an organization described in section 170(c) if the amount is transferred for full and adequate consideration. The trust may not be subject to a power to invade, alter, amend, or revoke for the beneficial use of a person other than an organization described in section 170(c). Notwithstanding the preceding sentence, the grantor may retain the power exercisable only by will to revoke or terminate the interest of any recipient other than an organization described in section 170(c). The governing instrument may provide that any amount other than the amount described in subparagraph (1) of this paragraph shall be paid (or may be paid in the discretion of the trustee) to an organization described in section 170(c) provided that in the case of distributions in kind, the adjusted basis of the property distributed is fairly representative of the adjusted basis of the property available for

payment on the date of payment. For example, the governing instrument may provide that a portion of the trust assets may be distributed currently, or upon the death of one or more recipients, to an organization described in section 170(c).

(5) Period of payment of annuity amount—(i) General rules. The period for which an amount described in subparagraph (1) of this paragraph is payable begins with the first year of the charitable remainder trust and continues either for the life or lives of a named individual or individuals or for a term of years not to exceed 20 years. Only an individual or an organization described in section 170(c) may receive an amount for the life of an individual. If an individual receives an amount for life, it must be solely for his life. Payment of the amount described in subparagraph (1) of this paragraph may terminate with the regular payment next preceding the termination of the period described in this subparagraph. The fact that the recipient may not receive such last payment shall not be taken into account for purposes of determining the present value of the remainder interest. In the case of an amount payable for a term of years, the length of the term of years shall be ascertainable with certainty at the time of the creation of the trust, except that the term may be terminated by the death of the recipient or by the grantor's exercise by will of a retained power to revoke or terminate the interest of any recipient other than an organization described in section 170(c). In any event, the period may not extend beyond either the life or lives of a named individual or individuals or a term of years not to exceed 20 years. For example, the governing instrument may not provide for the payment of an annuity amount to A for his life and then to B for a term of years because it is possible for the period to last longer than either the lives of recipients in being at the creation of the trust or a term of years not to exceed 20 years. On the other hand, the governing instrument may provide for the payment of an annuity amount to A for his life and then to B for his life or a term of years (not to exceed 20 years), whichever is shorter (but not longer), if both A and B are in being at the creation of the trust because it is not possible for the period to last longer than the lives of recipients in being at the creation of the trust.

(ii) Relationship to 5 percent requirement. The 5 percent requirement provided in subparagraph (2) of this paragraph must be met until the termination of all of the payments described in subparagraph (1) of this paragraph. For example, the following provisions would satisfy the above rules:

(a) An amount equal to at least 5 percent of the initial net fair market value of the property placed in trust to A and B for their joint lives and then to the survivor for his life;

(b) An amount equal to at least 5 percent of the initial net fair market value of the property placed in trust to A for life or for a term of years not longer than 20 years, whichever is longer (or shorter);

(c) An amount equal to at least 5 percent of the initial net fair market value of the property placed in trust to A for a term of years not longer than 20 years and then to B for life (provided B was living at the date of creation of the trust);

(d) An amount to A for his life and concurrently an amount to B for his life (the amount to each recipient to terminate at his death) if the amount given to each individual is not less than 5 percent of the initial net fair market value of the property placed in trust; or

(e) An amount to A for his life and concurrently an equal amount to B for his life, and at the death of the first to die, the trust to distribute one-half of the then value of its assets to an organization described in section 170(c), if the total of the amounts given to A and B is not less than 5 percent of the initial net fair market value of the property placed in trust.

(6) Permissible remaindermen—(i) General rule. At the end of the period specified in subparagraph (5) of this paragraph the entire corpus of the trust is required to be irrevocably transferred, in whole or in part, to or for the use of one or more organizations described in section 170(c) or retained, in whole or in part, for such use.

(ii) Treatment of trust. If all of the trust corpus is to be retained for such use, the taxable year of the trust shall terminate at the end of the period specified in subparagraph (5) of this paragraph and the trust shall cease to be treated as a charitable remainder trust for all purposes. If all or any portion of the trust corpus is to be transferred to or for the use of such organization or organizations, the trustee shall have a reasonable time after the period specified in subparagraph (5) of this paragraph to complete the settlement of the trust. During such time, the trust shall continue to be treated as a charitable remainder trust for all purposes, such as sections 664, 4947(a)(2), and 4947(b)(3)(B). Upon the expiration of such period, the taxable year of the trust shall terminate and the trust shall cease to be treated as a charitable remainder trust for all purposes. If the trust continues in existence, it will be subject to the provisions of section 4947(a)(1) unless the trust is exempt from taxation under section 501(a). For purposes of determining whether the trust is exempt under section 501(a) as an organization described in section 501(c)(3), the trust shall be deemed to have been created at the time it ceases to be treated as a charitable remainder trust.

(iii) Concurrent or successive remaindermen. Where interests in the corpus of the trust are given to more than one organization described in section 170(c) such interests may be enjoyed by them either concurrently or successively.

(iv) Alternative remaindermen. The governing instrument shall provide that if an organization to or for the use of which the trust corpus is to be transferred or for the use of which the trust corpus is to be retained is not an organization described in section 170(c) at the time any amount is to be irrevocably transferred to or for the use of such organization, such amount shall be transferred to or for the use of one or more alternative organizations which are described in section 170(c) at such time or retained for such use. Such alternative organization or organizations may be selected in any manner provided by the terms of the governing instrument.

(b) Additional contributions. A trust is not a charitable remainder annuity trust unless its governing instrument provides that no additional contributions may be made to the charitable remainder annuity trust after the initial contribution. For purposes of this section, all property passing to a charitable remainder annuity trust by reason of death of the grantor shall be considered one contribution.

(c) **Calculation of the fair market value of the remainder interest of a charitable remainder annuity trust.** For purposes of sections 170, 2055, 2106, and 2522, the fair market value of the remainder interest of a charitable remainder annuity trust (as described in this section) is the net fair market value (as of the appropriate valuation date) of the property placed in trust less the present value of the annuity. For purposes of this section, the term "appropriate valuation date" means the date on which the property is transferred to the trust by the donor except that, for purposes of section 2055 or 2106, it means the date of death unless the alternate valuation date is elected in accordance with section 2032 and the regulations thereunder in which event it means the alternate valuation date. The present value of an annuity is computed under § 20.2031–7 or 20.2031–10, whichever is appropriate, of the Estate Tax Regulations regardless of when the trust was created.

(d) **Deduction for transfers to a charitable remainder annuity trust.** For rules relating to a deduction for transfers to a charitable remainder annuity trust, see sections 170, 2055, 2106, or 2522 and the regulations thereunder. Any claim for deduction on any return for the value of a remainder interest in a charitable remainder annuity trust must be supported by a full statement attached to the return showing the computation of the present value of such interest. The deduction allowed by section 170 is limited to the fair market value of the remainder interest of a charitable remainder annuity trust regardless of whether an organization described in section 170(c) also receives a portion of the annuity. For a special rule relating to the reduction of the amount of a charitable contribution deduction with respect to a contribution of certain ordinary income property or capital gain property, see sections 170(e)(1)(A) or 170(e)(1)(B)(i) and the regulations thereunder. For rules for postponing the time for deduction of a charitable contribution of a future interest in tangible personal property, see section 170(a)(3) and the regulations thereunder.

[T.D. 7202, Aug. 22, 1972, as amended by T.D. 7955, May 10, 1984]

§ 1.664–3 Charitable remainder unitrust.

(a) **Description.** A charitable remainder unitrust is a trust which complies with the applicable provisions of § 1.664–1 and meets all of the following requirements:

(1) **Required payment of unitrust amount—(i) Payment of fixed percentage at least annually**—(a) General rule. The governing instrument provides that the trust shall pay not less often than annually a fixed percentage of the net fair market value of the trust assets determined annually to a person or persons described in subparagraph (3) of this paragraph for each taxable year of the period specified in subparagraph (5) of this paragraph. The trust will not be deemed to have engaged in an act of self-dealing (within the meaning of section 4941), to have unrelated debt-financed income (within the meaning of section 4941), to have received an additional contribution (within the meaning of § 1.664–3(b)), or to have failed to function exclusively as a charitable remainder trust (within the meaning of § 1.664–1(a)(4)) merely because payment of the unitrust amount is made after the close of the taxable year: *Provided,* That such payment is

made within a reasonable time after the close of such taxable year. For purposes of the preceding sentence, a reasonable time will not ordinarily extend beyond the date by which the trustee is required to file Form 1041–B (including extensions) for such year.

(b) Income exception. Instead of the amount described in (a) of this subdivision (i), the governing instrument may provide that the trust shall pay for any year either the amount described in (1) or the total of the amounts described in (1) and (2) of this subdivision (b).

(1) The amount of trust income (as defined in section 643(b) and the regulations thereunder), for a taxable year to the extent that such amount is not more than the amount required to be distributed under (a) of this subdivision (i).

(2) An amount of trust income for a taxable year which is in excess of the amount required to be distributed under (a) of this subdivision (i) for such year, to the extent that (by reason of (1)) the aggregate of the amounts paid in prior years was less than the aggregate of such required amounts.

(ii) Definition of fixed percentage. The fixed percentage may be expressed either as a fraction or as a percentage and must be payable each year in the period specified in subparagraph (5) of this paragraph. A percentage is fixed if the percentage is the same either as to each recipient or as to the total percentage payable each year of such period. For example, provision for a fixed percentage which is the same every year to A until his death and concurrently a fixed percentage which is the same every year to B until his death, the fixed percentage to each recipient to terminate at his death, would satisfy the rule. Similarly, provision for a fixed percentage to A and B for their joint lives and then to the survivor would satisfy the rule. In the case of a distribution to an organization described in section 170(c) at the death of a recipient or the expiration of a term of years, the governing instrument may provide for a reduction of the fixed percentage payable after such distribution provided that:

(a) The reduced fixed percentage is the same either as to each recipient or as to the total amount payable for each year of the balance of such period, and

(b) The requirements of subparagraph (2)(ii) of this paragraph are met.

(iii) Rules applicable to incorrect valuations. The governing instrument provides that in the case where the net fair market value of the trust assets is incorrectly determined by the fiduciary, the trust shall pay to the recipient (in the case of an undervaluation) or be repaid by the recipient (in the case of an overvaluation) an amount equal to the difference between the amount which the trust should have paid the recipient if the correct value were used and the amount which the trust actually paid the recipient. Such payments or repayments must be made within a reasonable period after the final determination of such value. Any payment due to a recipient by reason of such incorrect valuation shall be considered to be a payment required to be distributed at the time of such final determination for purposes of paragraph (d)(4)(ii) of § 1.664–1. See paragraph (d)(4) of § 1.664–1 for rules relating to the year of inclusion of such payments and the allowance of a deduction for such repayments. See paragraph (b), of this section for rules relating to additional contributions.

(iv) **Rules applicable to valuation.** In computing the net fair market value of the trust assets there shall be taken into account all assets and liabilities without regard to whether particular items are taken into account in determining the income of the trust. The net fair market value of the trust assets may be determined on any one date during the taxable year of the trust, or by taking the average of valuations made on more than one date during the taxable year of the trust, so long as the same valuation date or dates and valuation methods are used each year. If the governing instrument does not specify the valuation date or dates, the trustee shall select such date or dates and shall indicate his selection on the first return on Form 1041–B which the trust is required to file. The amount described in subdivision (i)(a) of this subparagraph which must be paid each year must be based upon the valuation for such year.

(v) **Computation of unitrust amount in certain circumstances—(a) Short taxable years.** The governing instrument provides that, in the case of a taxable year which is for a period of less than 12 months other than the taxable year in which occurs the end of the period specified in subparagraph (5) of this paragraph:

(1) The amount determined under subdivision (i)(a) of this subparagraph shall be the amount otherwise determined under that subdivision multiplied by a fraction the numerator of which is the number of days in the taxable year of the trust and the denominator of which is 365 (366 if February 29 is a day included in the numerator),

(2) The amount determined under subdivision (i)(b) of this subparagraph shall be computed by using the amount determined under subdivision (a)(1) of this subdivision (v), and

(3) If no valuation date occurs before the end of the taxable year of the trust, the trust assets shall be valued as of the last day of the taxable year of the trust.

(b) Last taxable year of period. (1) The governing instrument provides that, in the case of the taxable year in which occurs the end of the period specified in subparagraph (5) of this paragraph:

(i) The unitrust amount which must be distributed under subdivision (i)(a) of this subparagraph shall be the amount otherwise determined under that subdivision multiplied by a fraction the numerator of which is the number of days in the period beginning on the first day of such taxable year and ending on the last day of the period specified in subparagraph (5) of this paragraph and the denominator of which is 365 (366 if February 29 is a day included in the numerator),

(ii) The amount determined under subdivision (i)(b) of this subparagraph shall be computed by using the amount determined under (b)(1)(i) of this subdivision (v), and

(iii) If no valuation date occurs before the end of such period, the trust assets shall be valued as of the last day of such period.

(2) See subparagraph (5) of this paragraph for a special rule allowing termination of payment of the unitrust amount with the regular payment next preceding the termination of the period specified therein.

(2) **Minimum unitrust amount—(i) General rule.** The fixed percentage described in subparagraph (1)(i) of this paragraph with respect to all beneficiaries taken together is not less than 5 percent.

(ii) Reduction of unitrust amount in certain cases. A trust will not fail to meet the requirements of this subparagraph by reason of the fact that it provides for a reduction of the fixed percentage payable upon the death of a recipient or the expiration of a term of years provided that:

(a) A distribution is made to an organization described in section 170(c) at the death of such recipient or the expiration of such term of years, and

(b) The total of the percentage payable under subparagraph (1) of this paragraph after such distribution is not less than 5 percent.

(3) Permissible recipients—(i) General rule. The amount described in subparagraph (1) of this paragraph is payable to or for the use of a named person or persons, at least one of which is not an organization described in section 170(c). If the amount described in subparagraph (1) of this paragraph is to be paid to an individual or individuals, all such individuals must be living at the time of creation of the trust. A named person or persons may include members of a named class except in the case of a class which includes any individual, all such individuals must be alive and ascertainable at the time of the creation of the trust unless the period for which the unitrust amount is to be paid to such class consists solely of a term of years. For example, in the case of a testamentary trust, the testator's will may provide that the required amount shall be paid to his children living at his death.

(ii) Power to alter amount paid to recipients. A trust is not a charitable remainder unitrust if any person has the power to alter the amount to be paid to any named person other than an organization described in section 170(c) if such power would cause any person to be treated as the owner of the trust, or any portion thereof, if subpart E, part 1, subchapter J, chapter 1, subtitle A of the Code were applicable to such trust. See paragraph (a)(4) of this section for a rule permitting the retention by a grantor of a testamentary power to revoke or terminate the interest of any recipient other than an organization described in section 170(c). For example, the governing instrument may not grant the trustee the power to allocate the fixed percentage among members of a class unless such power falls within one of the exceptions to section 674(a).

(4) Other payments. No amount other than the amount described in subparagraph (1) of this paragraph may be paid to or for the use of any person other than an organization described in section 170(c). An amount is not paid to or for the use of any person other than an organization described in section 170(c) if the amount is transferred for full and adequate consideration. The trust may not be subject to a power to invade, alter, amend, or revoke for the beneficial use of a person other than an organization described in section 170(c). Notwithstanding the preceding sentence, the grantor may retain the power exercisable only by will to revoke or terminate the interest of any recipient other than an organization described in section 170(c). The governing instrument may provide that any amount other than the amount described in subparagraph (1) of this paragraph shall be paid (or may be paid in the discretion of the trustee) to an organization described in section 170(c) provided that, in the case of distributions in kind, the adjusted basis of the property distributed is fairly representative of the adjusted basis of the property available for payment on the date of payment. For example, the governing instrument may provide that a portion of the trust assets may be distributed currently, or upon the death of one or more recipients, to an organization described in section 170(c).

(5) Period of payment of unitrust amount—(i) General rules. The period for which an amount described in subparagraph (1) of this paragraph is payable begins with the first year of the charitable remainder trust and continues either for the life or lives of a named individual or individuals or for a term of years not to exceed 20 years. Only an individual or an organization described in section 170(c) may receive an amount for the life of an individual. If an individual receives an amount for life, it must be solely for his life. Payment of the amount described in subparagraph (1) of this paragraph may terminate with the regular payment next preceding the termination of the period described in this subparagraph. The fact that the recipient may not receive such last payment shall not be taken into account for purposes of determining the present value of the remainder interest. In the case of an amount payable for a term of years, the length of the term of years shall be ascertainable with certainty at the time of the creation of the trust, except that the term may be terminated by the death of the recipient or by the grantor's exercise by will of a retained power to revoke or terminate the interest of any recipient other than an organization described in section 170(c). In any event, the period may not extend beyond either the life or lives of a named individual or individuals or a term of years not to exceed 20 years. For example, the governing instrument may not provide for the payment of a unitrust amount to A for his life and then to B for a term of years because it is possible for the period to last longer than either the lives of recipients in being at the creation of the trust or a term of years not to exceed 20 years. On the other hand, the governing instrument may provide for the payment of a unitrust amount to A for his life and then to B for his life or a term of years (not to exceed 20 years), whichever is shorter (but not longer), if both A and B are in being at the creation of the trust because it is not possible for the period to last longer than the lives of recipients in being at the creation of the trust.

(ii) Relationship to 5 percent requirement. The 5 percent requirement provided in subparagraph (2) of this paragraph must be met until the termination of all of the payments described in subparagraph (1) of this paragraph. For example, the following provisions would satisfy the above rules:

(a) A fixed percentage of at least 5 percent to A and B for their joint lives and then to the survivor for his life;

(b) A fixed percentage of at least 5 percent to A for life or for a term of years not longer than 20 years, whichever is longer (or shorter);

(c) A fixed percentage of at least 5 percent to A for a term of years not longer than 20 years and then to B for life (provided B was living at the creation of the trust);

(d) A fixed percentage to A for his life and concurrently a fixed percentage to B for his life (the percentage to each recipient to terminate at his death) if the percentage given to each individual is not less than 5 percent;

(e) A fixed percentage to A for his life and concurrently an equal percentage to B for his life, and at the death of the first to die, the trust to distribute one-half of the then value of its assets to an organization described in section 170(c) if the total of the percentages is not less than 5 percent for the entire period described in this subparagraph.

(6) Permissible remaindermen—(i) General rule. At the end of the period specified in subparagraph (5) of this paragraph, the entire corpus of the trust is required to be irrevocably transferred, in whole or in part, to or for the use of one or more organizations described in section 170(c) or retained, in whole or in part, for such use.

(ii) Treatment of trust. If all of the trust corpus is to be retained for such use, the taxable year of the trust shall terminate at the end of the period specified in subparagraph (5) of this paragraph and the trust shall cease to be treated as a charitable remainder trust for all purposes. If all or any portion of the trust corpus is to be transferred to or for the use of such organization or organizations, the trustee shall have a reasonable time after the period specified in subparagraph (5) of this paragraph to complete the settlement of the trust. During such time, the trust shall continue to be treated as a charitable remainder trust for all purposes, such as sections 664, 4947(a)(2), and 4947(b)(3)(B). Upon the expiration of such period, the taxable year of the trust shall terminate and the trust shall cease to be treated as a charitable remainder trust for all purposes. If the trust continues in existence, it will be subject to the provisions of section 4947(a)(1) unless the trust is exempt from taxation under section 501(a). For purposes of determining whether the trust is exempt under section 501(a) as an organization described in section 501(c)(3), the trust shall be deemed to have been created at the time it ceases to be treated as a charitable remainder trust.

(iii) Concurrent or successive remaindermen. Where interests in the corpus of the trust are given to more than one organization described in section 170(c) such interests may be enjoyed by them either concurrently or successively.

(iv) Alternative remaindermen. The governing instrument shall provide that if an organization to or for the use of which the trust corpus is to be transferred or for the use of which the trust corpus is to be retained is not an organization described in section 170(c) at the time any amount is to be irrevocably transferred to or for the use of such organization, such amount shall be transferred to or for the use of or retained for the use of one or more alternative organizations which are described in section 170(c) at such time. Such alternative organization or organizations may be selected in any manner provided by the terms of the governing instrument.

(b) Additional contributions. A trust is not a charitable remainder unitrust unless its governing instrument either prohibits additional contributions to the trust after the initial contribution or provides that for the taxable year of the trust in which the additional contribution is made:

(1) Where no valuation date occurs after the time of the contribution and during the taxable year in which the contribution is made, the additional property shall be valued as of the time of contribution; and

(2) The amount described in paragraph (a)(1)(i)(a) of this section shall be computed by multiplying the fixed percentage by the sum of (i) the net fair market value of the trust assets (excluding the value of the additional property and any earned income from and any appreciation on such property after its contribution), and (ii) that proportion of the value of the additional property (that was excluded under subdivision (i) of this paragraph), which the number of days in the period which begins with the date of contribution and ends with the earlier of the last day of such taxable year or the last day of the period described in paragraph (a)(5) of this section bears to the number of days in the period which begins with the first day of such taxable year and ends with the earlier of the last day of such taxable year or the last day of the period prescribed in paragraph (a)(5) of this section.

For purposes of this section, all property passing to a charitable remainder unitrust by reason of death of the grantor shall be considered one contribution. The application of the preceding rules may be illustrated by the following examples:

Example (1). On March 2, 1971, X makes an additional contribution of property to a charitable remainder unitrust. The taxable year of the trust is the calendar year and the regular valuation date is January 1 of each year. For purposes of computing the required payout with respect to the additional contribution for the year of contribution, the additional contribution is valued on March 2, 1971, the time of contribution. The property had a value on that date of $5,000. Income from such property in the amount of $250 was received on December 31, 1971. The required payout with respect to the additional contribution for the year of contribution is $208 (5 percent × $5,000 × 305/365). The income earned after the date of the contribution and after the regular valuation date does not enter into the computation.

Example (2). On July 1, 1971, X makes an additional contribution of $10,000 to a charitable remainder unitrust. The taxable year of the trust is the calendar year and the regular valuation date is December 31 of each year. The fixed percentage is 5 percent. Between July 1, 1971, and December 31, 1971, the additional property appreciates in value to $12,500 and earns $500 of income. Because the regular valuation date for the year of contribution occurs after the date of the additional contribution, the additional contribution including income earned by it is valued on the regular valuation date. Thus, the required payout with respect to the additional contribution is $325.87 (5 percent × [$12,500 + $500] × 183/365).

(c) **Calculation of the fair market value of the remainder interest of a charitable remainder unitrust.** See § 1.664–4 for rules relating to the calculation of the fair market value of the remainder interest of a charitable remainder unitrust.

(d) **Deduction for transfers to a charitable remainder unitrust.** For rules relating to a deduction for transfers to a charitable remainder unitrust, see sections 170, 2055, 2106, or 2522 and the regulations thereunder. The deduction allowed by section 170 for transfers to charity is limited to the fair market value of the remainder interest of a charitable remainder unitrust regardless of whether an organization described in section 170(c) also receives a portion of the amount described in § 1.664–3(a)(1). For a special rule relating to the reduction of the amount of a charitable contribution deduction with respect to a contribution of certain ordinary income property or capital gain property, see section 170(e)(1)(A) or (B)(i) and the regulations thereunder. For rules for postponing the time for deduction of a charitable contribution of a future interest in tangible personal property, see section 170(a)(3) and the regulations thereunder.

[T.D. 7202, Aug. 22, 1972]

Treatment of Excess Distribution By Trusts

§ 1.665(a)–0A Excess distributions by trusts; scope of subpart D.

(a) **In general.** (1) Subpart D (section 665 and following), part I, subchapter J, chapter 1 of the Code as amended by the Tax Reform Act of 1969, is designed to tax the beneficiary of a trust that accumulates, rather than distributes, all or part of its income currently (i.e., an accumulation trust), in most cases, as if the income had been currently distributed to the beneficiary instead of accumulated by the trusts. Accordingly, subpart D provides special rules for the treatment of amounts paid, credited, or required to be distributed by a complex trust (one that is subject to subpart C (section 661 and following) of such part I) in any year in excess of "distributable net income" (as defined in section 643(a)) for that year. Such an excess distribution is an "accumulation distribution" (as defined in section 665(b)). The special rules of subpart D are generally inapplicable to amounts paid, credited, or required to be distributed by a trust in a taxable year in which it qualifies as a simple trust (one that is subject to subpart B (section 651 and following) of such part I). However, see § 1.665(e)-1A(b) for rules relating to the treatment of a simple trust as a complex trust.

(2) An accumulation distribution is deemed to consist of, first, "undistributed net income" (as defined in section 665(a)) of the trust from preceding taxable years, and, after all the undistributed net income for all preceding taxable years has been deemed distributed, "undistributed capital gain" (as defined in section 665(f)) of the trust for all preceding taxable years commencing with the first year such amounts were accumulated. An accumulation distribution of undistributed capital gain is a "capital gain distribution" (as defined in section 665(g)). To the extent an accumulation distribution exceeds the "undistributed net income" and "undistributed capital gain" so determined, it is deemed to consist of corpus.

(3) The accumulation distribution is "thrown back" to the earliest "preceding taxable year" of the trust, which, in the case of distributions made for a taxable year beginning after December 31, 1973, from a trust (other than a foreign trust created by a U.S. person), is any taxable year beginning after December 31, 1968. Special transitional rules apply for distributions made in taxable years beginning before January 1, 1974. In the case of a foreign trust created by a U.S. person, a "preceding taxable year" is any year of the trust to which the Code applies.

(4) A distribution of undistributed net income (included in an accumulation distribution) and a capital gain distribution will be included in the income of the beneficiary in the year they are actually paid, credited, or required to be distributed to him. The tax on the distribution will be approximately the amount of tax the beneficiary would have paid with respect to the distribution had the income and capital gain been distributed to the beneficiary in the year earned by the trust. An additional amount equal to the "taxes imposed on the trust" for the preceding year is also deemed distributed. To prevent double taxation, however, the beneficiary receives a credit for such taxes.

(b) **Effective dates.** All regulations sections under subpart D (sections 665 through 669) which have an "A" suffix (such as §§ 1.665(a)A and 1.666(b)-1A) are applicable to taxable years beginning on or after January 1, 1969, and all references therein to sections 665 through 669 are references to such sections as amended by the Tax Reform Act of 1969. Sections without the "A" suffix (such as §§ 1.665(a) and 1.666(b)-1) are applicable only to taxable years beginning before January 1, 1969, and all references therein to sections 665 through 669 are references to such sections before amendment by the Tax Reform Act of 1969.

(c) **Examples.** Where examples contained in the regulations under subpart D refer to tax rates for years after 1968, such tax rates are not necessarily the actual rates for such years, but are only used for example purposes.

(d) Applicability to estates. Subpart D does not apply to any estate. [T.D. 7204, Aug. 24, 1972]

§ 1.665(a)-1A Undistributed net income.

(a) Domestic trusts. The term "undistributed net income", in the case of a trust (other than a foreign trust created by a U.S. person) means, for any taxable year beginning after December 31, 1968, the distributable net income of the trust for that year (as determined under section 643(a)), less:

(1) The amount of income required to be distributed currently and any other amounts properly paid or credited or required to be distributed to beneficiaries in the taxable year as specified in section 661(a), and

(2) The amount of taxes imposed on the trust attributable to such distributable net income, as defined in § 1.665(d)-1A. The application of the rule in this paragraph to a taxable year of a trust in which income is accumulated may be illustrated by the following example:

Example. Under the terms of the trust, $10,000 of income is required to be distributed currently to A and the trustee has discretion to make additional distributions to A. During the taxable year 1971 the trust had distributable net income of $30,100 derived from royalties and the trustee made distributions of $20,000 to A. The taxable income of the trust is $10,000 on which a tax of $2,190 is paid. The undistributed net income of the trust for the taxable year 1971 is $7,910, computed as follows:

Distributable net income		$30,100
Less:		
Income currently distributable to A	$10,000	
Other amounts distributed to A	10,000	
Taxes imposed on the trust attributable to the undistributed net income (see § 1.665(d)-1A)	2,190	
Total		22,190
Undistributed net income		7,910

* * *

[T.D. 7204, Aug. 24, 1972]

§ 1.665(b)-1A Accumulation distributions.

(a) In General. (1) For any taxable year of a trust the term "accumulation distribution" means an amount by which the amounts properly paid, credited, or required to be distributed within the meaning of section 661(a)(2) (*i.e.,* all amounts properly paid, credited, or required to be distributed to the beneficiary other than income required to be distributed currently within the meaning of section 661(a)(1)) for that year exceed the distributable net income (determined under section 643(a)) of the trust, reduced (but not below zero) by the amount of income required to be distributed currently. To the extent provided in section 663(b) and the regulations thereunder, distributions made within the first 65 days following a taxable year may be treated as having been distributed on the last day of such taxable year.

(2) An accumulation distribution also includes, for a taxable year of the trust, any amount to which section 661(a)(2) and the preceding paragraph are inapplicable and which is paid, credited, or required to be distributed during the taxable year of the trust by reason of the exercise of a power to appoint, distribute, consume, or withdraw corpus of the trust or income of the trust

accumulated in a preceding taxable year. No accumulation distribution is deemed to be made solely because the grantor or any other person is treated as owner of a portion of the trust by reason of an unexercised power to appoint, distributed, consume, or withdraw corpus or accumulated income of the trust. Nor will an accumulation distribution be deemed to have been made by reason of the exercise of a power that may affect only taxable income previously attributed to the holders of such power under subpart E (section 671 and following). See example 4 of paragraph (d) of this section for an example of an accumulation distribution occurring as a result of the exercise of a power of withdrawal.

(3) Although amounts properly paid or credited under section 661(a) do not exceed the income of the trust during the taxable year, an accumulation distribution may result if the amounts properly paid or credited under section 661(a)(2) exceed distributable net income reduced (but not below zero) by the amount required to be distributed currently under section 661(a)(1). This may occur, for example, when expenses, interest, taxes, or other items allocable to corpus are taken into account in determining taxable income and hence causing distributable net income to be less than the trust's income.

(b) Payments that are accumulation distributions. The following are some instances in which an accumulation distribution may arise:

(1) One trust to another. A distribution from one trust to another trust is generally an accumulation distribution. See § 1.643(c)–1. This general rule will apply regardless of whether the distribution is to an existing trust or to a newly created trust and regardless of whether the trust to which the distribution is made was created by the same person who created the trust from which the distribution is made or a different person. However, a distribution made from one trust to a second trust will be deemed an accumulation distribution by the first trust to an ultimate beneficiary of the second trust if the primary purpose of the distribution to the second trust is to avoid the capital gain distribution provisions (see section 669 and the regulations thereunder). An amount passing from one separate share of a trust to another separate share of the same trust is not an accumulation distribution. See § 1.665(g)–2A. For rules relating to the computation of the beneficiary's tax under section 668 by reason of an accumulation distribution from the second trust, see paragraphs (b)(1) and (c)(1)(i) of § 1.668(b)–1A and paragraphs (b)(1) and (c)(1)(i) of § 1.669(b)–1A.

(2) Income accumulated during minority. A distribution of income accumulated during the minority of the beneficiary is generally an accumulation distribution. For example, if a trust accumulates income until the beneficiary's 21st birthday, and then distributes the income to the beneficiary, such a distribution is an accumulation distribution. However, see § 1.665(b)–2A for rules governing income accumulated in taxable years beginning before January 1, 1969.

(3) Amounts paid for support. To the extent that amounts forming all or part of an accumulation distribution are applied or distributed for the support of a dependent under the circumstances specified in section 677(b) or section 678(c) or are used to discharge or satisfy any person's legal obligation as that term is used in § 1.662(a)–4, such amounts will be considered as having been distributed directly to the person whose obligation is being satisfied.

(c) Payments that are not accumulation distributions—(1) Gifts, bequests, etc., described in section 663(a)(1). A gift or bequest of a specific sum of money or of specific property described in section 663(a)(1) is not an accumulation distribution.

(2) Charitable payments. Any amount paid, permanently set aside, or used for the purposes specified in section 642(c) is not an accumulation distribution, even though no charitable deduction is allowed under such section with respect to such payment.

(3) Income required to be distributed currently. No accumulation distribution will arise by reason of a payment of income required to be distributed currently even though such income exceeds the distributable net income of the trust because the payment is an amount specified in section 661(a)(1).

(d) Examples. The provisions of this section may be illustrated by the following examples:

Example (1). A trustee properly makes a distribution to a beneficiary of $20,000 during the taxable year 1976, of which $10,000 is income required to be distributed currently to the beneficiary. The distributable net income of the trust is $15,000. There is an accumulation distribution of $5,000 computed as follows:

Total distribution		$20,000
Less: Income required to be distributed currently (section 661(a)(1))		10,000
Other amounts distributed (section 661(a)(2))		10,000
Distributable net income	$15,000	
Less: Income required to be distributed currently	10,000	
Balance of distributable net income		5,000
Accumulation distribution		5,000

Example (2). Under the terms of the trust instrument, an annuity of $15,000 is required to be paid to A out of income each year and the trustee may in his discretion make distributions out of income or corpus to B. During the taxable year the trust had income of $18,000, as defined in section 643(b), and expenses allocable to corpus of $5,000. Distributable net income amounted to $13,000. The trustee distributed $15,000 of income to A and, in the exercise of his discretion, paid $5,000 to B. There is an accumulation distribution of $5,000 computed as follows:

Total distribution		$20,000
Less: Income required to be distributed currently to A (section 661(a)(1))		15,000
Other amounts distributed (section 661(a)(2))		5,000
Distributable net income	$13,000	
Less: Income required to be distributed currently to A	15,000	
Balance of distributable net income		0
Accumulation distribution to B		5,000

Example (3). Under the terms of a trust instrument, the trustee may either accumulate the trust income or make distributions to A and B. The trustee may also invade corpus for the benefit of A and B. During the taxable year, the trust had income as defined in section 643(b) of $22,000 and expenses of $5,000 allocable to corpus. Distributable net income amounts to $17,000.

The trustee distributed $10,00 each to A and B during the taxable year. There is an accumulation distribution of $3,000 computed as follows:

Total distribution		$20,000
Less: Income required to be distributed currently		0
Other amounts distributed (section 661(a)(2))		20,000
Distributable net income	$17,000	
Less: Income required to be distributed currently	0	
Balance of distributable net income		17,000
Accumulation distribution		3,000

Example (4). A dies in 1974 and bequeaths one-half the residue of his estate in trust. His widow, W, is given a power, exercisable solely by her, to require the trustee to pay her each year of the trust $5,000 from corpus. W's right to exercise such power was exercisable at any time during the year but was not cumulative, so that, upon her failure to exercise it before the end of any taxable year of the trust, her right as to that year lapsed. The trust's taxable year is the calendar year. During the calendar years 1975 and 1976, W did not exercise her right and it lapsed as to those years. In the calendar years 1977 and 1978, in which years the trust had no distributable net income, she exercised her right and withdrew $4,000 in 1977 and $5,000 in 1978. No accumulation distribution was made by the trust in the calendar years 1975 and 1976. An accumulation distribution of $4,000 was made in 1977 and an accumulation distribution of $5,000 was made in 1978. The accumulation distribution for the years 1977 and 1978 is not reduced by any amount of income of the trust attributable to her under section 678 by reason of her power of withdrawal.

[T.D. 7204, Aug. 24, 1972]

§ 1.665(d)–1A Taxes imposed on the trust.

(a) In general. (1) For purposes of subpart D, the term "taxes imposed on the trust" means the amount of Federal income taxes properly imposed for any taxable year on the trust that are attributable to the undistributed portions of distributable net income and gains in excess of losses from the sales or exchanges of capital assets. Except as provided in paragraph (c)(2) of this section, the minimum tax for tax preferences imposed by section 56 is not a tax attributable to the undistributed portions of distributable net income and gains in excess of losses from the sales or exchanges of capital assets. See section 56 and the regulations thereunder.

(2) In the case of a trust that has received an accumulation distribution from another trust, the term "taxes imposed on the trust" also includes the amount of taxes deemed distributed under §§ 1.666(b)–1A, 1.666(c)–1A, 1.669(d)–1A, and 1.669(e)–1A (whichever are applicable) as a result of such accumulation distribution, to the extent that they were taken into account under paragraphs (b)(2) or (c)(1)(vi) of § 1.668(b)–1A and (b)(2) or (c)(1)(vi) of § 1.669(b)–1A in computing the partial tax on such accumulation distribution. For example, assume that trust A, a calendar year trust, makes an accumulation distribution in 1975 to trust B, also on the calendar year basis, in connection with which $500 of taxes are deemed under § 1.666(b)–1A to be distributed to trust B. The partial tax on the accumulation distribution is computed under paragraph (b) of § 1.668(b)–1A (the exact method) to be $600 and all of the $500 is used under paragraph (b)(2) of § 1.668(b)–1A to reduce the partial tax to $100. The taxes imposed on trust B for 1975 will, in addition to the $100 partial tax, also include the $500 used to reduce the partial tax.

(b) Taxes imposed on the trust attributable to undistributed net income. (1) For the purpose of subpart D, the term "taxes imposed on the trust attributable to the undistributed net income" means the amount of Federal income taxes for the taxable year properly allocable to the undistributed portion of the distributable net income for such taxable year. This amount is (i) an amount that bears the same relationship to the total taxes of the trust for the year (other than the minimum tax for tax preferences imposed by section 56), computed after the allowance of credits under section 642(a), as (a) the taxable income of the trust, other than the capital gains not included in distributable net income less their share of section 1202 deduction, bears to (b) the total taxable income of the trust for such year or, (ii) if the alternative tax computation under section 1201(b) is used and there are no net short-term gains, an amount equal to such total taxes less the amount of the alternative tax imposed on the trust and attributable to the capital gain. Thus, for the purposes of subpart D, in determining the amount of taxes imposed on the trust attributable to the undistributed net income, that portion of the taxes paid by the trust attributable to capital gain allocable to corpus is excluded. The rule stated in this subparagraph may be illustrated by the following example, which assumes that the alternative tax computation is not used:

Example. (1) Under the terms of a trust, which reports on the calendar year basis, the income may be accumulated or distributed to A in the discretion of the trustee and capital gains are allocable to corpus. During the taxable year 1974, the trust had income of $20,000 from royalties, long-term capital gains of $10,000, and expenses of $2,000. The trustee in his discretion made a distribution of $10,000 to A. The taxes imposed on the trust for such year attributable to the undistributed net income are $2,319, determined as shown below.

(2) The distributable net income of the trust computed under section 643(a) is $18,000 (royalties of $20,000 less expenses of $2,000). The total taxes paid by the trust are $3,787, computed as follows:

Royalties		$20,000
Capital gain allocable to corpus		10,000
Gross income		30,000
Deductions:		
Expenses	$ 2,000	
Distributions to A	10,000	
Capital gain deduction	5,000	
Personal exemption	100	
		17,100
Taxable income		12,900
Total income taxes		3,787

(3) Taxable income other than capital gains less the section 1202 deduction is $7,900 ($12,900–($10,000–$5,000)). Therefore, the amount of taxes imposed on the trust attributable to the undistributed net income is $2,319, computed as follows:

$3,787 (total taxes) × $7,900 (taxable income other than capital gains not included in d.n.i. less the 1202 deduction) divided by $12,900 (taxable income)	$2,319

(4) If in any taxable year an accumulation distribution of undistributed net income is made by the trust which results in a throwback to a prior year, the taxes of the prior year imposed on the trust attributable to any remaining undistributed net income of such prior year are the taxes prescribed in subparagraph (1) of this paragraph reduced by the taxes of the prior year deemed distributed under section 666(b) or (c). The provisions of this subparagraph may be illustrated by the following example:

Example. Assume the same facts as in the example in subparagraph (1) of this paragraph. In 1975 the trust makes an accumulation distribution, of which an amount of undistributed net income is deemed distributed in 1974. Taxes imposed on the trust (in the amount of $1,000) attributable to the undistributed net income are therefore deemed distributed in such year. Consequently, the taxes imposed on the trust subsequent to the 1975 distribution attributable to the remaining undistributed net income are $1,319 ($2,319 less $1,000).

(c) Taxes imposed on the trust attributable to undistributed capital gain—(1) Regular tax. For the purpose of subpart D the term "taxes imposed on the trust attributable to undistributed capital gain" means the amount of Federal income taxes for the taxable year properly attributable to that portion of the excess of capital gains over capital losses of the trust that is allocable to corpus for such taxable year. Such amount is the total of—

(i) The amount computed under subparagraph (2) of this paragraph (the minimum tax), plus

(ii) The amount that bears the same relationship to the total taxes of the trust for the year (other than the minimum tax), computed after the allowance of credits under section 642(a), as (*a*) the excess of capital gains over capital losses for such year that are not included in distributable net income, computed after its share of the deduction under section 1202 (relating to the deduction for capital gains) has been taken into account, bears to the greater of (*b*) the total taxable income of the trust for such year, or (*c*) the amount of capital gains computed under (a) of this subdivision.

However, if the alternative tax computation under section 1201(b) is used and there are no net short-term gains, the amount is the amount of the alternative tax imposed on the trust and attributable to the capital gain. The application of this subparagraph may be illustrated by the following example, which assumes that the alternative tax computation is not used:

Example. Assume the same facts as in the example in paragraph (b)(1). The capital gains not included in d.n.i. are $10,000, and the deduction under section 1202 is $5,000. The amount of taxes imposed on the trust attributable to undistributed capital gain is $1,468, computed as follows:

$3,787 (total taxes) × $5,000 (capital gains not included in d.n.i. less section 1202 deductions) divided by $12,900 (taxable income)	$1,468

(2) Minimum tax. The term "taxes imposed on the trust attributable to the undistributed capital gain" also includes the minimum tax for tax preferences imposed on the trust by section 56 with respect to the undistributed capital gain. The amount of such minimum tax so included bears the same relation to the total amount of minimum tax imposed on the trust by section 56 for the taxable year as one-half the net capital gain (net section 1201 gain for taxable years beginning before January 1, 1977) (as defined in section 1222(11)) from such taxable year bears to the sum of the items of tax preference of the trust for such taxable year which are apportioned to the trust in accordance with § 1.58-3(a)(1).

(3) Reduction for prior distribution. If in any taxable year a capital gain distribution is made by the trust which results in a throwback to a prior year, the taxes of the prior year imposed on the trust attributable to any remaining undistributed capital gain of the prior year are the taxes prescribed in subparagraph (1) of this paragraph reduced by the taxes of the prior year deemed distributed under section 669(d) or (e). The provisions of this subparagraph may be illustrated by the following example:

Example. Assume the same facts as in the example in subparagraph (1) of this paragraph. In 1976, the trust makes a capital gain distribution, of which an amount of undistributed capital gain is deemed distributed in 1974. Taxes imposed on the trust (in the amount of $500) attributable to the undistributed capital gain are therefore deemed distributed in such year. Consequently, the taxes imposed on the trust attributable to the remaining undistributed capital gain are $968 ($1,468 less $500).

[T.D. 7204, Aug. 24, 1972, as amended by T.D. 7728, Oct. 31, 1980]

§ 1.665(e)-1A Preceding taxable year.

(a) Definition—(1) Domestic trusts—(i) In general. For purposes of subpart D, in the case of a trust other than a foreign trust created by a U.S. person, the term "preceding taxable year" serves to identify and limit the taxable years of a trust to which an accumulation distribution consisting of undistributed net income or undistributed capital gain may be allocated (or "thrown back") under sections 666(a) and 669(a). An accumulation distribution consisting of undistributed net income or undistributed capital gain may not be allocated or "thrown back" to a taxable year of a trust if such year is not a "preceding taxable year."

(ii) Accumulation distributions. In the case of an accumulation distribution consisting of undistributed net income made in a taxable year beginning before January 1, 1974, any taxable year of the trust that precedes by more than five years the taxable year of the trust in which such accumulation distribution was made is not a "preceding taxable year." Thus, for a domestic trust on a calendar year basis, calendar year 1967 is not a "preceding taxable year" with respect to an accumulation distribution made in calendar year 1973, whereas calendar year 1968 is a "preceding taxable year." In the case of an accumulation distribution made during a taxable year beginning after December 31, 1973, any taxable year of the trust that begins before January 1, 1969, is not a "preceding taxable year." Thus, for a domestic trust on a calendar year basis, calendar year 1968 is not a "preceding taxable year" with respect to an accumulation distribution made in calendar year 1975, whereas calendar year 1969 is a "preceding taxable year."

(iii) Capital gain distributions. In the case of an accumulation distribution that is a capital gain distribution, any taxable year of the trust that (*a*) begins before January 1, 1969, or (*b*) is prior to the first year in which income is accumulated, whichever occurs later, is not a "preceding taxable year." Thus, for the purpose of capital gain distributions and section 669, only taxable years beginning after December 31, 1968, can be "preceding taxable years." See § 1.688(a)-1A(c).

(2) **Foreign trusts created by United States persons.** For purposes of subpart D, in the case of a foreign trust created by a U.S. person, the term "preceding taxable year" does not include any taxable year to which part I of subchapter J does not apply. See section 683 and regulations thereunder. Accordingly, the provisions of subpart D may not, in the case of a foreign trust created by a U.S. person, be applied to any taxable year which begins before 1954 or ends before August 17, 1954. For example, if a foreign trust created by a U.S. person (reporting on the calendar year basis) makes a distribution during the calendar year 1970 of income accumulated during prior years, the earliest year of the trust to which the accumulation distribution may be allocated under such subpart D is 1954, but it may not be allocated to 1953 and prior years, since the Internal Revenue Code of 1939 applies to those years.

(b) **Simple trusts.** A taxable year of a trust during which the trust was a simple trust (that is, was subject to subpart B) for the entire year shall not be considered a "preceding taxable year" unless during such year the trust received "outside income" or unless the trustee did not distribute all of the income of the trust that was required to be distributed currently for such year. In such event, undistributed net income for such year shall not exceed the greater of the "outside income" or income not distributed during such year. For purposes of this paragraph, the term "outside income" means amounts that are included in distributable net income of the trust for the year but that are not "income" of the trust as that term is defined in § 1.643(b)-1. Some examples of "outside income" are:

(1) Income taxable to the trust under section 691;

(2) Unrealized accounts receivable that were assigned to the trust; and

(3) Distributions from another trust that include distributable net income or undistributed net income of such other trust.

The term "outside income," however, does not include amounts received as distributions from an estate, other than income specified in (1) and (2), for which the estate was allowed a deduction under section 661(a). The application of this paragraph may be illustrated by the following examples:

Example (1). By his will D creates a trust for his widow W. The terms of the trust require that the income be distributed currently (*i.e.*, it is a simple trust), and authorize the trustee to make discretionary payments of corpus to W. Upon W's death the trust corpus is to be distributed to D's then living issue. The executor of D's will makes a $10,000 distribution of corpus to the trust that carries out estate income consisting of dividends and interest to the trust under section 662(a)(2). The trust reports this income as its only income on its income tax return for its taxable year in which ends the taxable year of the estate in which the $10,000 distribution was made, and pays a tax thereon of $2,106. Thus, the trust has undistributed net income of $7,894 ($10,000–$2,106). Several years later the trustee makes a discretionary corpus payment of $15,000 to W. This payment is an accumulation distribution under section 665(b). However, since the trust had no "outside income" in the year of the estate distribution, such year is not a preceding taxable year. Thus, W is not treated as receiving undistributed net income of $7,894 and taxes thereon of $2,106 for the purpose of including the same in her gross income under section 668. The result would be the same if the invasion power were not exercised and the accumulation distribution occurred as a result of the distribution of the corpus to D's issue upon the death of W.

Example (2). Trust A, a simple trust on the calendar year basis, received in 1972 extraordinary dividends or taxable stock dividends that the trustee in good faith allocated to corpus, but that are determined in 1974 to have been currently distributable to the beneficiary. See section 643(a)(4) and § 1.643(a)-4. Trust A would qualify for treatment under subpart C for 1974, the year of distribution of the extraordinary dividends or taxable stock dividends, because the distribution is not out of income of the current taxable year and is treated as another amount properly paid or credited or required to be distributed for such taxable year within the meaning of section 661(a)(2). Also, the distribution in 1974 qualifies as an accumulation distribution for the purposes of subpart D. For purposes only of such subpart D, trust A would be treated as subject to the provisions of such subpart C for 1972, the preceding taxable year in which the extraordinary or taxable stock dividends were received, and, in computing undistributed net income for 1972, the extraordinary or taxable stock dividends would be included in distributable net income under section 643(a). The rule stated in the preceding sentence would also apply if the distribution in 1974 was made out of corpus without regard to a determination that the extraordinary dividends or taxable stock dividends in question were currently distributable to the beneficiary.

[T.D. 7204, Aug. 24, 1972]

§ 1.665(f)-1A Undistributed capital gain.

(a) Domestic trusts. (1) The term "undistributed capital gain" means (in the case of a trust other than a foreign trust created by a U.S. person), for any taxable year of the trust beginning after December 31, 1968, the gains in excess of losses for that year from the sale or exchange of capital assets of the trust less:

(i) The amount of such gains that are included in distributable net income under section 643(a)(3) and § 1.643(a)-3,

(ii) The amount of taxes imposed on the trust for such year attributable to such gains, as defined in § 1.665(d)-1A, and

(iii) In the case of a trust that does not use the alternative method for computing taxes on capital gains of the taxable year, the excess of deductions (other than deductions allowed under section 642(b) relating to personal exemption or section 642(c) relating to charitable contributions) over distributable net income for such year to the extent such excess deductions are properly allowable in determining taxable income for such year.

For purposes of computing the amount of capital gain under this paragraph, no deduction under section 1202, relating to deduction for excess of capital gains over capital losses, shall be taken into account. The application of this subparagraph may be illustrated by the following example:

Example. Under the terms of the trust, the trustee must distribute all income currently and has discretion to distribute capital gain to A or to allocate it to corpus. During the taxable year 1971 the trust recognized capital gain in the amount of $15,000, and capital losses of $5,000, and had interest income (after expenses) of $6,000. The trustee distributed $8,000 to A, consisting of $6,000 of interest and $2,000 of capital gain. The $2,000 of gain distributed to

A is included in the computation of distributable net income under § 1.643(a)–3. The balance of the capital gain is not included in distributable net income since it is allocated to corpus and not paid, credited, or required to be distributed to any beneficiary. The trust paid taxes of $671, all of which are attributable under § 1.665(d)–1A to the undistributed capital gain. The amount of undistributed capital gain of the trust for 1971 is therefore $7,329, computed as follows:

Total capital gains	$15,000	
Less:		
Capital losses	5,000	
Gains in excess of losses		$10,000
Less:		
Amount of capital gain included in distributable net income	2,000	
Taxes imposed on the trust attributable to the undistributed capital gain (see § 1.665(d)–1A)	671	
		2,671
Undistributed capital gain		7,329

(2) For purposes of subparagraph (1) of this paragraph, the term "losses for that year" includes losses of the trust from the sale or exchange of capital assets in preceding taxable years not included in the computation of distributable net income of any year, reduced by such losses taken into account in a subsequent preceding taxable year in computing undistributed capital gain but not reduced by such losses taken into account in determining the deduction under section 1211. See section 1212(b)(2) and the regulations thereunder. For example, assume that a trust had a net long-term capital loss in 1970 of $5,000. During the years 1971 through 1975, the trust had no capital gains or capital losses. In 1976, it has a long-term capital gain of $8,000, which it allocates to corpus and does not distribute to a beneficiary, but has no taxes attributable to such gain. The undistributed capital gain for 1976 is $8,000–$5,000, or $3,000, even though all or a part of the $5,000 loss was claimed under section 1211 as a deduction in years 1970 through 1975.

(b) Foreign trusts. Distributable net income for a taxable year of a foreign trust created by a U.S. person includes capital gains in excess of capital losses for such year (see § 1.643(a)–6(a)(3)). Thus, a foreign trust created by a U.S. person can never have any undistributed capital gain.

[T.D. 7204, Aug. 24, 1972]

§ 1.665(g)–2A Application of separate share rule.

(a) In general. If the separate share rule of section 663(c) is applicable for any taxable year of a trust, subpart D is applied as if each share were a separate trust except as provided in paragraph (c) of this section and in § 1.668(a)–1A(c). Thus, the amounts of an "accumulation distribution", "undistributed net income", "undistributed capital gain", and "capital gain distribution" are computed separately for each share.

(b) Allocation of taxes—undistributed net income. The "taxes imposed on the trust attributable to the undistributed net income" are allocated as follows:

(1) There is first allocated to each separate share that portion of the "taxes imposed on the trust attributable to the undistributed net income" (as defined in § 1.665(d)–1A(b)), computed before the allowance of any

credits under section 642(a), that bears the same relation to the total of such taxes that the distributable net income of the separate share bears to the distributable net income of the trust, adjusted for this purpose as follows:

(i) There is excluded from distributable net income of the trust and of each separate share any tax-exempt interest, foreign income of a foreign trust, and excluded dividends, to the extent such amounts are included in distributable net income pursuant to section 643(a)(5), (6), and (7); and

(ii) The distributable net income of the trust is reduced by any deductions allowable under section 661 for amounts paid, credited, or required to be distributed during the taxable year, and the distributable net income of each separate share is reduced by any such deduction allocable to that share.

(2) The taxes so determined for each separate share are then reduced by that portion of the credits against tax allowable to the trust under section 642(a) in computing the "taxes imposed on the trust" that bears the same relation to the total of such credits that the items of distributable net income allocable to the separate share with respect to which the credit is allowed bear to the total of such items of the trust.

(c) **Allocation of taxes—undistributed capital gain.** The "taxes imposed on the trust attributable to undistributed capital gain" are allocated as follows:

(1) There is first allocated to each separate share that portion of the "taxes imposed on the trust attributable to undistributed capital gain" (as defined in § 1.665(d)–1A(c)), computed before the allowance of any credits under section 642(a), that bears the same relation to the total of such taxes that the undistributed capital gain (prior to the deduction of taxes under section 665(c)(2)) of the separate share bears to the total such undistributed capital gain of the trust.

(2) The taxes so determined for each separate share are then reduced by that portion of the credits against tax allowable to the trust under section 642(a) in computing the "taxes imposed on the trust" that bears the same relation to the total of such credits that the capital gain allocable to the separate share with respect to which the credit is allowed bear to the total of such capital gain of the trust.

(d) **Termination of a separate share.** (1) If upon termination of a separate share, an amount is properly paid, credited, or required to be distributed by the trust under section 661(a)(2) to a beneficiary from such share, an accumulation distribution will be deemed to have been made to the extent of such amount. In determining the distributable net income of such share, only those items of income and deduction for the taxable year of the trust in which such share terminates, properly allocable to such share, shall be taken into consideration.

(2) No accumulation distribution will be deemed to have been made upon the termination of a separate share to the extent that the property constituting such share, or a portion thereof, continues to be held as a part of the same trust. The undistributed net income, undistributed capital gain, and the taxes imposed on the trust attributable to such items, if any, for all preceding taxable years (reduced by any amounts deemed distributed under sections 666(a) and

669(a) by reason of any accumulation distribution of undistributed net income or undistributed capital gain in prior years or the current taxable year), which were allocable to the terminating share, shall be treated as being applicable to the trust itself. However, no adjustment will be made to the amounts deemed distributed under sections 666 and 669 by reason of an accumulation distribution of undistributed net income or undistributed capital gain from the surviving share or shares made in years prior to the year in which the terminating share was added to such surviving share or shares.

(3) The provisions of this paragraph may be illustrated by the following example:

Example. A trust was established under the will of X for the benefit of his wife and upon her death the property was to continue in the same trust for his two sons, Y and Z. The separate share rule is applicable to this trust. The trustee had discretion to pay or accumulate the income to the wife, and after her death was to pay each son's share to him after he attained the age of 25. When the wife died, Y was 23 and Z was 28.

(1) Upon the death of X's widow, there is no accumulation distribution. The entire trust is split into two equal shares, and therefore the undistributed net income and the undistributed capital gain of the trust are split into two shares.

(2) The distribution to Z of his share after his mother's death is an accumulation distribution of his separate share of one-half of the undistributed net income and undistributed capital gain.

[T.D. 7204, Aug. 24, 1972.]

§ 1.666(a)–1A Amount allocated.

(a) In general. In the case of a trust that is subject to subpart C of part I of subchapter J of chapter 1 of the Code (relating to estates and trusts that may accumulate income or that distribute corpus), section 666(a) prescribes rules for determining the taxable years from which an accumulation distribution will be deemed to have been made and the extent to which the accumulation distribution is considered to consist of undistributed net income. In general, an accumulation distribution made in taxable years after December 31, 1969, is deemed to have been made first from the earliest preceding taxable year of the trust for which there is undistributed net income. * * *

(b) Distributions by domestic trusts—(1) Taxable years beginning after December 31, 1973. An accumulation distribution made by a trust (other than a foreign trust created by a U.S. person) in any taxable year beginning after December 31, 1973, is allocated to the preceding taxable years of the trust (defined in § 1.665(e)–1A(a)(1)(ii) as those beginning after December 31, 1968) according to the amount of undistributed net income of the trust for such years. For this purpose, an accumulation distribution is first to be allocated to the earliest such preceding taxable year in which there is undistributed net income and shall then be allocated, beginning with the next earliest, to any remaining preceding taxable years of the trust. The portion of the accumulation distribution allocated to the earliest preceding taxable year is the amount of the undistributed net income for that preceding taxable year. The portion of the accumulation distribution allocated to any preceding taxable year subsequent to the earliest such preceding taxable year is the excess of the accumulation distribution over the aggregate of the undistributed net income for all earlier preceding taxable years. See paragraph (d) of this section for adjustments to undistributed net income for prior distributions. The provisions of this subparagraph may be illustrated by the following example:

Example. In 1977, a domestic trust reporting on the calendar year basis makes an accumulation distribution of $33,000. Therefore, years before 1969 are ignored. In 1969, the trust had $6,000 of undistributed net income; in 1970, $4,000; in 1971, none; in 1972, $7,000; in 1973, $5,000; in 1974, $8,000; in 1975, $6,000; and $4,000 in 1976. The accumulation distribution is deemed distributed $6,000 in 1969, $4,000 in 1970, none in 1971, $7,000 in 1972, $5,000 in 1973, $8,000 in 1974, and $3,000 in 1975.

* * *

(d) **Reduction of undistributed net income for prior accumulation distributions.** For the purposes of allocating to any preceding taxable year an accumulation distribution of the taxable year, the undistributed net income of such preceding taxable year is reduced by the amount from such year deemed distributed in any accumulation distribution of undistributed net income made in any taxable year intervening between such preceding taxable year and the taxable year. Accordingly, for example, if a trust has undistributed net income for 1974 and makes accumulation distributions during the taxable years 1978 and 1979, in determining that part of the 1979 accumulation distribution that is thrown back to 1974 the undistributed net income for 1974 is first reduced by the amount of the undistributed net income for 1974 deemed distributed in the 1978 accumulation distribution.

(e) **Rule when no undistributed net income.** If, before the application of the provisions of subpart D to an accumulation distribution for the taxable year, there is no undistributed net income for a preceding taxable year, then no portion of the accumulation distribution is undistributed net income deemed distributed on the last day of such preceding taxable year. Thus, if an accumulation distribution is made during the taxable year 1975 from a trust whose earliest preceding taxable year is taxable year 1970, and the trust had no undistributed net income for 1970, then no portion of the 1975 accumulation distribution is undistributed net income deemed distributed on the last day of 1970.

[T.D. 7204, Aug. 24, 1972]

§ 1.666(b)-1A Total taxes deemed distributed.

(a) If an accumulation distribution is deemed under § 1.666(a)-1A to be distributed on the last day of a preceding taxable year and the amount is not less than the undistributed net income for such preceding taxable year, then an additional amount equal to the "taxes imposed on the trust attributable to the undistributed net income" (as defined in § 1.665(d)-1A(b)) for such preceding taxable year is also deemed distributed under section 661(a)(2). For example, a trust has undistributed net income of $8,000 for the taxable year 1974. The taxes imposed on the trust attributable to the undistributed net income are $3,032. During the taxable year 1977, an accumulation distribution of $8,000 is made to the beneficiary, which is deemed under § 1.666(a)-1A to have been distributed on the last day of 1974. The 1977 accumulation distribution is not less than the 1974 undistributed net income. Accordingly, the taxes of $3,032 imposed on the trust attributable to the undistributed net income for 1974 are also deemed to have been distributed on the last day of 1974. Thus, a total of $11,032 will be deemed to have been distributed on the last day of 1974.

(b) For the purpose of paragraph (a) of this section, the undistributed net income of any preceding taxable year and the taxes imposed on the trust for such preceding taxable year attributable to such undistributed net income are computed after taking into account any accumulation distributions of taxable years intervening between such preceding taxable year and the taxable year. See paragraph (d) of § 1.666(a)–1A.

[T.D. 7204, Aug. 24, 1972]

§ 1.666(c)–1A Pro rata portion of taxes deemed distributed.

(a) If an accumulation distribution is deemed under § 1.666(a)–1A to be distributed on the last day of a preceding taxable year and the amount is less than the undistributed net income for such preceding taxable year, then an additional amount is also deemed distributed under section 661(a)(2). The additional amount is equal to the "taxes imposed on the trust attributable to the undistributed net income" (as defined in § 1.665(a)–1A(b)) for such preceding taxable year, multiplied by a fraction, the numerator of which is the amount of the accumulation distribution allocated to such preceding taxable year and the denominator of which is the undistributed net income for such preceding taxable year. * * *

(b) For the purpose of paragraph (a) of this section, the undistributed net income of any preceding taxable year and the taxes imposed on the trust for such preceding taxable year attributable to such undistributed net income are computed after taking into account any accumulation distributions of any taxable years intervening between such preceding taxable year and the taxable year. * * *

§ 1.666(c)–2A Illustration of the provisions of section 666(a), (b), and (c).

The application of the provisions of §§ 1.666(a)–1A, 1.666(b)–1A, and 1.666(c)–1A may be illustrated by the following examples:

Example (1). (a) A trust created on January 1, 1974, makes accumulation distributions as follows:

1979	$ 7,000
1980	26,000

For 1974 through 1978, the undistributed portion of distributable net income, taxes imposed on the trust attributable to the undistributed net income, and undistributed net income are as follows:

Year	Undistributed portion of distributable net income	Taxes imposed on the trust attributable to the undistributed net income	Undistributed net income
1974	$12,100	$3,400	$ 8,700
1975	16,100	5,200	10,900
1976	6,100	1,360	4,740
1977	None	None	None
1978	10,100	2,640	7,460

The trust has no undistributed capital gain.

(b) Since the entire amount of the accumulation distribution for 1979 ($7,000) is less than the undistributed net income for 1974 ($8,700), an additional amount of $2,736 ($7,000/$8,700 × $3,400) is deemed distributed under section 666(c).

(c) In allocating the accumulation distribution for 1980, the amount of undistributed net income for 1974 will reflect the accumulation distribution for 1979. The undistributed net income for 1974 will then be $1,700 and the taxes imposed on the trust for 1974 will be $664, determined as follows:

Undistributed net income as of the close of 1974	$8,700
Less:	
Accumulation distribution (1979)	7,000
Balance (undistributed net income as of the close of 1979)	$1,700
Taxes imposed on the trust attributable to the undistributed net income as of the close of 1979 ($1,700/$8,700 × $3,400)	664

(d) The accumulation distribution of $26,000 for 1980 is deemed to have been made on the last day of the preceding taxable years of the trust to the extent of $24,800, the total of the undistributed net income for such years, as shown in the tabulation below. In addition, $9,864, the total taxes imposed on the trust attributable to the undistributed net income for such years is also deemed to have been distributed on the last day of such years, as shown below:

Year	Undistributed net income	Taxes imposed on the trust
1974	$ 1,700	$ 664
1975	10,900	5,200
1976	4,740	1,360
1977	None	None
1978	7,460	2,640
1979	None	None

Example (2). (a) Under the terms of a trust instrument, the trustee has discretion to accumulate or distribute the income to X and to invade corpus for the benefit of X. The entire income of the trust is from royalties. Both X and the trust report on the calendar year basis. All of the income for 1974 was accumulated. The distributable net income of the trust for the taxable year 1974 is $20,100 and the income taxes paid by the trust for 1974 attributable to the undistributed net income are $7,260. All of the income for 1975 and 1976 was distributed and in addition the trustee made accumulation distributions within the meaning of section 665(b) of $5,420 for each year.

(b) The undistributed net income of the trust determined under section 665(a), as of the close of 1974, is $12,840, computed as follows:

Distributable net income	$20,100
Less: Taxes imposed on the trust attributable to the undistributed net income...	7,260
Undistributed net income as of the close of 1974	12,840

(c) The accumulation distribution of $5,420 made during the taxable year 1975 is deemed under section 666(a) to have been made on December 31, 1974. Since this accumulation distribution is less than the 1974 undistributed net income of $12,840, a portion of the taxes imposed on the trust for 1974 is also deemed under section 666(c) to have been distributed on December 31, 1974. The total amount deemed to have been distributed to X on December 31, 1974 is $8,484, computed as follows:

Accumulation distribution	$ 5,420
Taxes deemed distributed (5,420/12,840 × $7,260).............	3,064
Total	8,484

(d) After the application of the provisions of subpart D to the accumulation distribution of 1975, the undistributed net income of the trust for 1974 is $7,420, computed as follows:

Undistributed net income as of the close of 1974	$12,840
Less: 1975 accumulation distribution deemed distributed on December 31, 1974 (paragraph (c) of this example)	5,420
Undistributed net income for 1974 as of the close of 1975	7,420

(e) The taxes imposed on the trust attributable to the undistributed net income for the taxable year 1974, as adjusted to give effect to the 1975 accumulation distribution, amount to $4,196, computed as follows:

Taxes imposed on the trust attributable to undistributed net income as of the close of 1974	$ 7,260
Less: Taxes deemed distributed in 1974	3,064
Taxes attributable to the undistributed net income determined as of the close of 1975	4,196

(f) The accumulation distribution of $5,420 made during the taxable year 1976 is, under section 666(a), deemed a distribution to X on December 31, 1974, within the meaning of section 661(a)(2). Since the accumulation distribution is less than the 1974 adjusted undistributed net income of $7,420, the trust is deemed under section 666(c) also to have distributed on December 31, 1974, a portion of the taxes imposed on the trust for 1974. The total amount deemed to be distributed on December 31, 1974, with respect to the accumulation distribution made in 1976, is $8,484, computed as follows:

Accumulation distribution	$ 5,420
Taxes deemed distributed (5,420/7,420 × $4,196)	3,064
Total	8,484

(g) After the application of the provisions of subpart D to the accumulation distribution of 1976, the undistributed net income of the trust for 1974 is $2,000, computed as follows:

Undistributed net income for 1974 as of the close of 1975	$ 7,420
Less: 1976 accumulation distribution deemed distributed on December 31, 1974 (paragraph (f) of this example)	5,420
Undistributed net income for 1974 as of the close of 1976	2,000

(h) The taxes imposed on the trust attributable to the undistributed net income of the trust for the taxable year 1974, determined as of the close of the taxable year 1976, amount to $1,132 ($4,196 less $3,064).

[T.D. 7204, Aug. 24, 1972]

§ 1.666(d)–1A Information required from trusts.

(a) Adequate records required. For all taxable years of a trust, the trustee must retain copies of the trust's income tax return as well as information pertaining to any adjustments in the tax shown as due on the return. The trustee shall also keep the records of the trust required to be retained by section 6001 and the regulations thereunder for each taxable year as to which the period of limitations on assessment of tax under section 6501 has not expired. If the trustee fails to produce such copies and records, and such failure is due to circumstances beyond the reasonable control of the trustee or any predecessor trustee, the trustee may reconstruct the amount of corpus, accumulated income, etc., from competent sources (including, to the extent permissible, Internal Revenue Service records). To the extent that an accurate reconstruction can be made for a taxable year, the requirements of this paragraph shall be deemed satisfied for such year.

(b) Rule when information is not available—(1) Accumulation distributions. If adequate records (as required by paragraph (a) of this section) are not available to determine the proper application of subpart D to an accumulation distribution made in a taxable year by a trust, such accumulation distribution shall be deemed to consist of undistributed net income earned during the earliest preceding taxable year (as defined in § 1.665(e)–1A) of the trust in which it can be established that the trust was in existence. If adequate records are available for some years, but not for others, the accumulation distribution shall be allocated first to the earliest preceding taxable year of the trust for which there are adequate records and then to each subsequent preceding taxable year for which there are adequate records. To the extent that the distribution is not allocated in such manner to years for which adequate records are available, it will be deemed distributed on the last day of the earliest preceding taxable year of the trust in which it is established that the trust was in existence and for which the trust has no records. The provisions of this subparagraph may be illustrated by the following example:

Example. A trust makes a distribution in 1975 of $100,000. The trustee has adequate records for 1973, 1974, and 1975. The records show that the trust is on the calendar year basis, had distributable net income in 1975 of $20,000, and undistributed net income in 1974 of $15,000, and in 1973 of $16,000. The trustee has no other records of the trust except for a copy of the trust instrument showing that the trust was established on January 1, 1965. He establishes that the loss of the records was due to circumstances beyond his control. Since the distribution is made in 1975, the earliest "preceding taxable year", as defined in § 1.665(e)–1A, is 1969. Since $80,000 of the distribution is an accumulation distribution, and $31,000 thereof is allocated to 1974 and 1973, $49,000 is deemed to have been distributed on the last day of 1969.

(2) Taxes. (i) If an amount is deemed under this paragraph to be undistributed net income allocated to a preceding taxable year for which adequate records are not available, there shall be deemed to be "taxes imposed on the trust" for such preceding taxable year an amount equal to the taxes that the trust would have paid if the deemed undistributed net income were the amount remaining when the taxes were subtracted from taxable income of the trust for such year. For example, assume that an accumulation distribution in 1975 of $100,000 is deemed to be undistributed net income from 1971, and that the taxable income required to produce $100,000 after taxes in 1971 would be $284,966. Therefore the amount deemed to be "taxes imposed on the trust" for such preceding taxable year is $184,966.

(ii) The credit allowed by section 667(b) shall not be allowed for any amount deemed under this subparagraph to be "taxes imposed on the trust".

[T.D. 7204, Aug. 24, 1972]

§ 1.667(a)–1A Denial of refund to trusts.

If an amount is deemed under section 666 or 669 to be an amount paid, credited, or required to be distributed on the last day of a preceding taxable year, the trust is not allowed a refund or credit of the amount of "taxes imposed on the trust", as defined in § 1.665(d)–1A. However, such taxes imposed on the trust are allowed as a credit under section 667(b) against the tax of certain beneficiaries who are treated as having received the distributions in the preceding taxable year.

[T.D. 7204, Aug. 24, 1972]

Grantors and Others Treated as Substantial Owners

§ 1.671-1 Grantors and others treated as substantial owners; scope.

(a) Subpart E (section 671 and following), part I, subchapter J, chapter 1 of the Code, contains provisions taxing income of a trust to the grantor or another person under certain circumstances even though he is not treated as a beneficiary under subparts A through D (section 641 and following) of such part I. Sections 671 and 672 contain general provisions relating to the entire subpart. Sections 673 through 677 define the circumstances under which income of a trust is taxed to a grantor. These circumstances are in general as follows:

(1) If the grantor has retained a reversionary interest in the trust, within specified time limits (section 673);

(2) If the grantor or a nonadverse party has certain powers over the beneficial interests under the trust (section 674);

(3) If certain administrative powers over the trust exist under which the grantor can or does benefit (section 675).

(4) If the grantor or a nonadverse party has a power to revoke the trust or return the corpus to the grantor (section 676); or

(5) If the grantor or a nonadverse party has the power to distribute income to or for the benefit of the grantor or the grantor's spouse (section 677).

Under section 678, income of a trust is taxed to a person other than the grantor to the extent that he has the sole power to vest corpus or income in himself.

(b) Sections 671 through 677 do not apply if the income of a trust is taxable to a grantor's spouse under section 71 or 682 (relating respectively to alimony and separate maintenance payments, and the income of an estate or trust in the case of divorce, etc.).

(c) Except as provided in such subpart E, income of a trust is not included in computing the taxable income and credits of a grantor or another person solely on the grounds of his dominion and control over the trust. However, the provisions of subpart E do not apply in situations involving an assignment of future income, whether or not the assignment is to a trust. Thus, for example, a person who assigns his right to future income under an employment contract may be taxed on that income even though the assignment is to a trust over which the assignor has retained none of the controls specified in sections 671 through 677. Similarly, a bondholder who assigns his right to interest may be taxed on interest payments even though the assignment is to an uncontrolled trust. Nor are the rules as to family partnerships affected by the provisions of subpart E, even though a partnership interest is held in trust. Likewise, these sections have no application in determining the right of a grantor to deductions for payments to a trust under a transfer and leaseback arrangement. In addition, the limitation of the last sentence of section 671 does not prevent any person from being taxed on the income of a trust when it is used to discharge his legal obligation. See § 1.662(a)-4. He is then treated as a beneficiary under subparts A through D or treated as an owner under section 677 because the income is distributed for his benefit, and not because of his dominion or control over the trust.

(d) The provisions of subpart E are not applicable with respect to a pooled income fund as defined in paragraph (5) of section 642(c) and the regulations thereunder, a charitable remainder annuity trust as defined in paragraph (1) of section 664(d) and the regulations thereunder, or a charitable remainder unitrust as defined in paragraph (2) of section 664(d) and the regulations thereunder.

* * *

[T.D. 6217, Dec. 19, 1956, as amended by T.D. 7148, Oct. 28, 1971; T.D. 7741, Dec. 11, 1980]

§ 1.671-2 Applicable principles.

(a) Under section 671 a grantor or another person includes in computing his taxable income and credits those items of income, deduction, and credit against tax which are attributable to or included in any portion of a trust of which he is treated as the owner. Sections 673 through 678 set forth the rules for determining when the grantor or another person is treated as the owner of any portion of a trust. The rules for determining the items of income, deduction, and credit against tax that are attributable to or included in a portion of the trust are set forth in § 1.671-3.

(b) Since the principle underlying subpart E (section 671 and following), part I, subchapter J, chapter 1 of the Code, is in general that income of a trust over which the grantor or another person has retained substantial dominion or control should be taxed to the grantor or other person rather than to the trust which receives the income or to the beneficiary to whom the income may be distributed, it is ordinarily immaterial whether the income involved constitutes income or corpus for trust accounting purposes. Accordingly, when it is stated in the regulations under subpart E that "income" is attributed to the grantor or another person, the reference, unless specifically limited, is to income determined for tax purposes and not to income for trust accounting purposes. When it is intended to emphasize that income for trust accounting purposes (determined in accordance with the provisions set forth in § 1.643(b)-1 is meant, the phrase "ordinary income" is used.

(c) An item of income, deduction, or credit included in computing the taxable income and credits of a grantor or another person under section 671 is treated as if it had been received or paid directly by the grantor or other person (whether or not an individual). For example, a charitable contribution made by a trust which is attributed to the grantor (an individual) under sections 671 through 677 will be aggregated with his other charitable contributions to determine their deductibility under the limitations of section 170(b)(1). Likewise, dividends received by a trust from sources in a particular foreign country which are attributed to a grantor or another person under subpart E will be aggregated with his other income from sources within that country to determine whether the taxpayer is subject to the limitations of section 904 with respect to credit for the tax paid to that country.

(d) Items of income, deduction, and credit not attributed to or included in any portion of a trust of which the grantor or another person is treated as the owner under subpart E are subject to the provisions of subparts A through D (section 641 and following), of such part I.

(e) The term "grantor" as used in the regulations under subpart E includes a corporation.

[T.D. 6217, Dec. 19, 1956]

§ 1.671-3 Attribution or inclusion of income, deductions, and credits against tax.

(a) When a grantor or another person is treated under subpart E (section 671 and following) as the owner of any portion of a trust, there are included in computing his tax liability those items of income, deduction, and credit against tax attributable to or included in that portion. For example:

(1) If a grantor or another person is treated as the owner of an entire trust (corpus as well as ordinary income), he takes into account in computing his income tax liability all items of income, deduction, and credit (including capital gains and losses) to which he would have been entitled had the trust not been in existence during the period he is treated as owner.

(2) If the portion treated as owned consists of specific trust property and its income, all items directly related to that property are attributable to the portion. Items directly related to trust property not included in the portion treated as owned by the grantor or other person are governed by the provisions of subparts A through D (section 641 and following), part I, subchapter J, chapter 1 of the Code. Items that relate both to the portion treated as owned by the grantor and to the balance of the trust must be apportioned in a manner that is reasonable in the light of all the circumstances of each case, including the terms of the governing instrument, local law, and the practice of the trustee if it is reasonable and consistent.

(3) If the portion of a trust treated as owned by a grantor or another person consists of an undivided fractional interest in the trust, or of an interest represented by a dollar amount, a pro rata share of each item of income, deduction, and credit is normally allocated to the portion. Thus, where the portion owned consists of an interest in or a right to an amount of corpus only, a fraction of each item (including items allocated to corpus, such as capital gains) is attributed to the portion. The numerator of this fraction is the amount which is subject to the control of the grantor or other person and the denominator is normally the fair market value of the trust corpus at the beginning of the taxable year in question. The share not treated as owned by the grantor or other person is governed by the provisions of subparts A through D. See the last three sentences of paragraph (c) of this section for the principles applicable if the portion treated as owned consists of an interest in part of the ordinary income in contrast to an interest in corpus alone.

(b) If a grantor or another person is treated as the owner of a portion of a trust, that portion may or may not include both ordinary income and other income allocable to corpus. For example—

(1) Only ordinary income is included by reason of an interest in or a power over ordinary income alone. Thus, if a grantor is treated under section 673 as an owner by reason of a reversionary interest in ordinary income only, items of income allocable to corpus will not be included in the portion he is treated as owning. Similarly, if a grantor or another person is treated under sections 674–678 as an owner of a portion by reason of a power over ordinary income only, items of income allocable to corpus are

not included in that portion. (See paragraph (c) of this section to determine the treatment of deductions and credits when only ordinary income is included in the portion.)

(2) Only income allocable to corpus is included by reason of an interest in or a power over corpus alone, if satisfaction of the interest or an exercise of the power will not result in an interest in or the exercise of a power over ordinary income which would itself cause that income to be included. For example, if a grantor has a reversionary interest in a trust which is not such as to require that he be treated as an owner under section 673, he may nevertheless be treated as an owner under section 677(a)(2) since any income allocable to corpus is accumulated for future distribution to him, but items of income included in determining ordinary income are not included in the portion he is treated as owning. Similarly, he may have a power over corpus which is such that he is treated as an owner under section 674 or 676(a), but ordinary income will not be included in the portion he owns, if his power can only affect income received after a period of time such that he would not be treated as an owner of the income if the power were a reversionary interest. (See paragraph (c) of this section to determine the treatment of deductions and credits when only income allocated to corpus is included in the portion.)

(3) Both ordinary income and other income allocable to corpus are included by reason of an interest in or a power over both ordinary income and corpus, or an interest in or a power over corpus alone which does not come within the provisions of subparagraph (2) of this paragraph. For example, if a grantor is treated under section 673 as the owner of a portion of a trust by reason of a reversionary interest in corpus, both ordinary income and other income allocable to corpus are included in the portion. Further, a grantor includes both ordinary income and other income allocable to corpus in the portion he is treated as owning if he is treated under section 674 or 676 as an owner because of a power over corpus which can affect income received within a period such that he would be treated as an owner under section 673 if the power were a reversionary interest. Similarly, a grantor or another person includes both ordinary income and other income allocable to corpus in the portion he is treated as owning if he is treated as an owner under section 675 or 678 because of a power over corpus.

(c) If only income allocable to corpus is included in computing a grantor's tax liability, he will take into account in that computation only those items of income, deductions, and credit which would not be included under subparts A through D in the computation of the tax liability of the current income beneficiaries if all distributable net income had actually been distributed to those beneficiaries. On the other hand, if the grantor or another person is treated as an owner solely because of his interest in or power over ordinary income alone, he will take into account in computing his tax liability those items which would be included in computing the tax liability of a current income beneficiary, including expenses allocable to corpus which enter into the computation of distributable net income. If the grantor or other person is treated as an owner because of his power over or right to a dollar amount of ordinary income, he will first take into account a portion of those items of income and expense entering into the computation of ordinary income under the trust instrument or local law sufficient to produce income of the dollar amount required. There will then be attributable to him a pro rata portion of other items entering into the computation of distributable net income under subparts A through D, such as expenses allocable to corpus, and a pro rata portion of credits of the trust. For examples of computations under this paragraph, see paragraph (g) of § 1.677(a)-1.

[T.D. 6217, Dec. 19, 1956, as amended by T.D. 6989, Jan. 16, 1969]

§ 1.671-4 Method of reporting.

(a) Portion of trust income taxed to grantor. Except as provided in paragraphs (b)(1) and (2) of this section, items of income, deduction, and credit attributable to any portion of a trust which, under the provisions of subpart E (section 671 and following), part I, subchapter J, chapter 1 of the Code, are treated as owned by the grantor or another person should not be reported by the trust on Form 1041, but should be shown on a separate statement to be attached to that form.

(b) Trust income taxed entirely to grantor. **(1)** In the case of a trust when

(i) the same individual is both grantor and trustee (or co-trustee), and

(ii) that individual is treated as owner for the taxable year of all of the assets of the trust by the application of section 676,

a Form 1041 should not be filed. Instead, all items of income, deduction, and credit from the trust should be reported on the individual's Form 1040 in accordance with its instructions. For provisions dealing with taxpayer identifying numbers, see § 301.6109-1 (Regulations on Procedure and Administration).

(2) In the case of a trust when

(i) a husband and wife are the sole grantors, and

(ii) one spouse is trustee or co-trustee with a third party or both spouses are trustees or co-trustees with a third party, and

(iii) one or both spouses are treated as owners of all of the assets of the trust for the taxable year by the application of section 676, and

(iv) the husband and wife for the taxable year make a single return jointly of income taxes under section 6013,

a Form 1041 should not be filed. Instead, all items of income, deduction, and credit from the trust should be reported on the spouses' Form 1040 in accordance with its instructions.

(3) The grantor of a trust described in § 1.671-4(b)(1) or (2) who filed a Form 1041 on or before November 24, 1981, may continue to report income, deductions, and credits of the trust pursuant to § 1.671-4(a). Alternatively, the grantor of such a trust may file a final Form 1041 for the trust's current taxable year pursuant to § 1.671-4(a). In such a case, the grantor must write across the front of the Form 1041 a statement in substance saying "Pursuant to § 1.671-4(b), this is the final Form 1041 for this grantor trust." For the next taxable year, the grantor must furnish payers of income with his or her social security number, pursuant to § 301.6109-1(a)(2), and must follow the rule of § 1.671-4(b)(1) or (2), as the case may be.

(4) This paragraph (b) of this section shall not apply to a trust if the situs of the trust or any of the assets of the trust are not in the United States.

(c) Effective date. Paragraphs (b)(1) and (2) of this section apply to trusts created in tax years beginning on or after January 1, 1981. Paragraph (b)(3) of this section is effective immediately.

[T.D. 6217, Dec. 19, 1956, as amended by T.D. 7796, Nov. 23, 1981]

§ 1.672(a)-1 Definition of adverse party.

(a) Under section 672(a) an adverse party is defined as any person having a substantial beneficial interest in a trust which would be adversely affected by the exercise or nonexercise of a power which he possesses respecting the trust. A trustee is not an adverse party merely because of his interest as trustee. A person having a general power of appointment over the trust property is deemed to have a beneficial interest in the trust. An interest is a substantial interest if its value in relation to the total value of the property subject to the power is not insignificant.

(b) Ordinarily, a beneficiary will be an adverse party, but if his right to share in the income or corpus of a trust is limited to only a part, he may be an adverse party only as to that part. Thus, if A, B, C, and D are equal income beneficiaries of a trust and the grantor can revoke with A's consent, the grantor is treated as the owner of a portion which represents three-fourths of the trust; and items of income, deduction, and credit attributable to that portion are included in determining the tax of the grantor.

(c) The interest of an ordinary income beneficiary of a trust may or may not be adverse with respect to the exercise of a power over corpus. Thus, if the income of a trust is payable to A for life, with a power (which is not a general power of appointment) in A to appoint the corpus to the grantor either during his life or by will, A's interest is adverse to the return of the corpus to the grantor during A's life, but is not adverse to a return of the corpus after A's death. In other words, A's interest is adverse as to ordinary income but is not adverse as to income allocable to corpus. Therefore, assuming no other relevant facts exist, the grantor would not be taxable on the ordinary income of the trust under section 674, 676, or 677, but would be taxable under section 677 on income allocable to corpus (such as capital gains), since it may in the discretion of a nonadverse party be accumulated for future distribution to the grantor. Similarly, the interest of a contingent income beneficiary is adverse to a return of corpus to the grantor before the termination of his interest but not to a return of corpus after the termination of his interest.

(d) The interest of a remainderman is adverse to the exercise of any power over the corpus of a trust, but not to the exercise of a power over any income interest preceding his remainder. For example, if the grantor creates a trust which provides for income to be distributed to A for 10 years and then for the corpus to go to X if he is then living, a power exercisable by X to revest corpus in the grantor is a power exercisable by an adverse party; however, a power exercisable by X to distribute part or all of the ordinary income to the grantor may be a power exercisable by a nonadverse party (which would cause the ordinary income to be taxed to the grantor).

[T.D. 6217, Dec. 19, 1956]

§ 1.672(b)-1 Nonadverse party.

A "nonadverse party" is any person who is not an adverse party.

[T.D. 6217, Dec. 19, 1956]

§ 1.672(c)-1 Related or subordinate party.

Section 672(c) defines the term "related or subordinate party". The term, as used in sections 674(c) and 675(3), means any nonadverse party who is the grantor's spouse if living with the grantor; the grantor's father, mother, issue, brother or sister; an employee of the grantor; a corporation or any employee of a corporation in which the stock holdings of the grantor and the trust are significant from the viewpoint of voting control; or a subordinate employee of a corporation in which the grantor is an executive. For purposes of sections 674(c) and 675(3), these persons are presumed to be subservient to the grantor in respect of the exercise or nonexercise of the powers conferred on them unless shown not to be subservient by a preponderance of the evidence.

[T.D. 6217, Dec. 19, 1956]

§ 1.672(d)-1 Power subject to condition precedent.

Section 672(d) provides that a person is considered to have a power described in subpart E (section 671 and following), part I, subchapter J, chapter 1 of the Code, even though the exercise of the power is subject to a precedent giving of notice or takes effect only after the expiration of a certain period of time. However, although a person may be considered to have such a power, the grantor will nevertheless not be treated as an owner by reason of the power if its exercise can only affect beneficial enjoyment of income received after the expiration of a period of time such that, if the power were a reversionary interest, he would not be treated as an owner under section 673. See sections 674(b)(2), 676(b), and the last sentence of section 677(a). Thus, for example, if a grantor creates a trust for the benefit of his son and retains a power to revoke which takes effect only after the expiration of 2 years from the date of exercise, he is treated as an owner from the inception of the trust. However, if the grantor retains a power to revoke, exercisable at any time, which can only affect the beneficial enjoyment of the ordinary income of a trust received after the expiration of 10 years commencing with the date of the transfer in trust, or after the death of the income beneficiary, the power does not cause him to be treated as an owner with respect to ordinary income during the first 10 years of the trust or during the income beneficiary's life, as the case may be. See section 676(b).

[T.D. 6217, Dec. 19, 1956]

§ 1.673(a)-1 Reversionary interests; income payable to beneficiaries other than certain charitable organizations; general rule.

(a) Under section 673(a), a grantor, in general, is treated as the owner of any portion of a trust in which he has a reversionary interest in either the corpus or income if, as of the inception of that portion of the trust, the grantor's interest will or may reasonably be expected to take effect in possession or enjoyment within 10 years commencing with the date of transfer of that portion of the trust. However, the following types of reversionary interests are excepted from the general rule of the preceding sentence:

(1) A reversionary interest after the death of the income beneficiary of a trust (see paragraph (b) of this section).

* * *

Even though the duration of the trust may be such that the grantor is not treated as its owner under section 673, and therefore is not taxed on the ordinary income, he may nevertheless be treated as an owner under section 677(a)(2) if he has a reversionary interest in the corpus. In the latter case, items of income, deduction, and credit allocable to corpus, such as capital gains and losses, will be included in the portion he owns. See § 1.671–3 and the regulations under section 677. See § 1.673(d)–1 with respect to a postponement of the date specified for reacquisition of a reversionary interest.

(b) Section 673(c) provides that a grantor is not treated as the owner of any portion of a trust by reason of section 673 if his reversionary interest in the portion is not to take effect in possession or enjoyment until the death of the person or persons to whom the income of the portion is regardless of the life expectancies of the income beneficiaries. If his reversionary interest is to take effect on or after the death of an income beneficiary or upon the expiration of a specific term of years, whichever is earlier, the grantor is treated as the owner if the specific term of years is less than 10 years (but not if the term is 10 years or longer).

(c) Where the grantor's reversionary interest in a portion of a trust is to take effect in possession or enjoyment by reason of some event other than the expiration of a specific term of years or the death of the income beneficiary, the grantor is treated as the owner of the portion if the event may reasonably be expected to occur within 10 years from the date of transfer of that portion, but he is not treated as the owner under section 673 if the event may not reasonably be expected to occur within 10 years from that date. For example, if the reversionary interest in any portion of a trust is to take effect on or after the death of the grantor (or any person other than the person to whom the income is payable) the grantor is treated under section 673 as the owner of the portion if the life expectancy of the grantor (or other person) is less than 10 years on the date of transfer of the portion, but not if the life expectancy is 10 years or longer. If the reversionary interest in any portion is to take effect on or after the death of the grantor (or any person other than the person to whom the income is payable) or upon the expiration of a specific term of years, whichever is earlier, the grantor is treated as the owner of the portion if on the date of transfer of the portion either the life expectancy of the grantor (or other person) or the specific term is less than 10 years; however, if both the life expectancy and the specific term are 10 years or longer the grantor is not treated as the owner of the portion under section 673. Similarly, if the grantor has a reversionary interest in any portion which will take effect at the death of the income beneficiary or the grantor, whichever is earlier, the grantor is not treated as an owner of the portion unless his life expectancy is less than 10 years.

(d) It is immaterial that a reversionary interest in corpus or income is subject to a contingency if the reversionary interest may, taking the contingency into consideration, reasonably be expected to take effect in possession or enjoyment within 10 years. For example, the grantor is taxable where the trust income is to be paid to the grantor's son for 3 years, and the corpus is then to be returned to the grantor if he survives that period, or to be paid to the grantor's son if he is already deceased.

(e) See section 671 and §§ 1.671–2 and 1.671–3 for rules for treatment of items of income, deduction, and credit when a person is treated as the owner of all or only a portion of a trust.

[T.D. 6217, Dec. 19, 1956, as amended by T.D. 7357, May 30, 1975]

§ 1.673(d)-1 Postponement of date specified for reacquisition.

Any postponement of the date specified for the reacquisition of possession or enjoyment of any reversionary interest is considered a new transfer in trust commencing with the date on which the postponement is effected and terminating with the date prescribed by the postponement. However, the grantor will not be treated as the owner of any portion of a trust for any taxable year by reason of the foregoing sentence if he would not be so treated in the absence of any postponement. The rules contained in this section may be illustrated by the following example:

Example. G places property in trust for the benefit of his son B. Upon the expiration of 12 years or the earlier death of B the property is to be paid over to G or his estate. After the expiration of 9 years G extends the term of the trust for an additional 2 years. G is considered to have made a new transfer in trust for a term of 5 years (the remaining 3 years of the original transfer plus the 2-year extension). However, he is not treated as the owner of the trust under section 673 for the first 3 years of the new term because he would not be so treated if the term of the trust had not been extended. G is treated as the owner of the trust, however, for the remaining 2 years.

[T.D. 6217, Dec. 19, 1956]

§ 1.674(a)-1 Power to control beneficial enjoyment; scope of section 674.

(a) Under section 674, the grantor is treated as the owner of a portion of trust if the grantor or a nonadverse party has a power, beyond specified limits, to dispose of the beneficial enjoyment of the income or corpus, whether the power is a fiduciary power, a power of appointment, or any other power. Section 674(a) states in general terms that the grantor is treated as the owner in every case in which he or a nonadverse party can affect the beneficial enjoyment of a portion of a trust, the limitations being set forth as exceptions in subsections (b), (c), and (d) of section 674. These exceptions are discussed in detail in §§ 1.674(b)-1 through 1.674(d)-1. Certain limitations applicable to section 674(b), (c), and (d) are set forth in § 1.674(d)-2. Section 674(b) describes powers which are excepted regardless of who holds them. Section 674(c) describes additional powers of trustees which are excepted if at least half the trustees are independent, and if the grantor is not a trustee. Section 674(d) describes a further power which is excepted if it is held by trustees other than the grantor or his spouse (if living with the grantor).

(b) In general terms the grantor is treated as the owner of a portion of a trust if he or a nonadverse party or both has a power to dispose of the beneficial enjoyment of the corpus or income unless the power is one of the following:

(1) **Miscellaneous powers over either ordinary income or corpus.** (i) A power that can only affect the beneficial enjoyment of income (including capital gains) received after a period of time such that the grantor would not be treated as an owner under section 673 if the power were a reversionary interest (section 674(b)(2));

(ii) A testamentary power held by anyone (other than a testamentary power held by the grantor over accumulated income) (section 674(b)(3));

(iii) A power to choose between charitable beneficiaries or to affect the manner of their enjoyment of a beneficial interest (section 674(b)(4));

(iv) A power to allocate receipts and disbursements between income and corpus (section 674(b)(8)).

(2) **Powers of distribution primarily affecting only one beneficiary.** (i) A power to distribute corpus to or for a current income beneficiary, if the distribution must be charged against the share of corpus from which the beneficiary may receive income (section 674(b)(5)(B));

(ii) A power to distribute income to or for a current income beneficiary or to accumulate it either (a) if accumulated income must either be payable to the beneficiary from whom it was withheld or as described in paragraph (b)(6) of § 1.674(b)-1 (section 674(b)(6)); (b) if the power is to apply income to the support of a dependent of the grantor, and the income is not so applied (section 674(b)(1)); or (c) if the beneficiary is under 21 or under a legal disability and accumulated income is added to corpus (section 674(b)(7)).

(3) **Powers of distribution affecting more than one beneficiary.** A power to distribute corpus or income to or among one or more beneficiaries or to accumulate income, either (i) if the power is held by a trustee or trustees other than the grantor, at least half of whom are independent (section 674(c)), or (ii) if the power is limited by a reasonably definite standard in the trust instrument, and in the case of a power over income, if in addition the power is held by a trustee or trustees other than the grantor and the grantor's spouse living with the grantor (section 674(b)(5)(A) and (d)). (These powers include both powers to "sprinkle" income or corpus among current beneficiaries, and powers to shift income or corpus between current beneficiaries and remaindermen; however, certain of the powers described under subparagraph (2) of this paragraph can have the latter effect incidentally.)

(c) See section 671 and §§ 1.671–2 and 1.671–3 for rules for the treatment of income, deductions, and credits when a person is treated as the owner of all or only a portion of a trust.

[T.D. 6217, Dec. 19, 1956]

§ 1.674(b)–1 Excepted powers exercisable by any person.

(a) Paragraph (b)(1) through (8) of this section sets forth a number of powers which may be exercisable by any person without causing the grantor to be treated as an owner of a trust under section 674(a). Further, with the exception of powers described in paragraph (b)(1) of this section, it is immaterial whether these powers are held in the capacity of trustee. It makes no difference under section 674(b) that the person holding the power is the grantor, or a related or subordinate party (with the qualifications noted in paragraph (b)(1) and (3) of this section).

(b) The exceptions referred to in paragraph (a) of this section are as follows (see, however, the limitations set forth in § 1.674(d)–2):

(1) **Powers to apply income to support of a dependent.** Section 674(b)(1) provides, in effect, that regardless of the general rule of section 674(a), the income of a trust will not be considered as taxable to the grantor merely because in the discretion of any person (other than a grantor who is not acting as a trustee or cotrustee) it may be used for the support of a beneficiary whom the grantor is legally obligated to support, except to the

extent that it is in fact used for that purpose. See section 677(b) and the regulations thereunder.

(2) **Powers affecting beneficial enjoyment only after a period.** Section 674(b)(2) provides an exception to section 674(a) if the exercise of a power can only affect the beneficial enjoyment of the income of a trust received after a period of time which is such that a grantor would not be treated as an owner under section 673 if the power were a reversionary interest. See §§ 1.673(a)-1 and 1.673(b)-1. For example, if a trust created on January 1, 1955, provides for the payment of income to the grantor's son, and the grantor reserves the power to substitute other beneficiaries of income or corpus in lieu of his son on or after January 1, 1965, the grantor is not treated under section 674 as the owner of the trust with respect to ordinary income received before January 1, 1965. But the grantor will be treated as an owner on and after that date unless the power is relinquished. If the beginning of the period during which the grantor may substitute beneficiaries is postponed, the rules set forth in § 1.673(d)-1 are applicable in order to determine whether the grantor should be treated as an owner during the period following the postponement.

(3) **Testamentary powers.** Under paragraph (3) of section 674(b) a power in any person to control beneficial enjoyment exercisable only by will does not cause a grantor to be treated as an owner under section 674(a). However, this exception does not apply to income accumulated for testamentary disposition by the grantor or to income which may be accumulated for such distribution in the discretion of the grantor or a nonadverse party, or both, without the approval or consent of any adverse party. For example, if a trust instrument provides that the income is to be accumulated during the grantor's life and that the grantor may appoint the accumulated income by will, the grantor is treated as the owner of the trust. Moreover, if a trust instrument provides that the income is payable to another person for his life, but the grantor has a testamentary power of appointment over the remainder, and under the trust instrument and local law capital gains are added to corpus, the grantor is treated as the owner of a portion of the trust and capital gains and losses are included in that portion. (See § 1.671-3.)

* * *

(5) **Powers to distribute corpus.** Paragraph (5) of section 674(b) provides an exception to section 674(a) for powers to distribute corpus, subject to certain limitations, as follows:

(i) If the power is limited by a reasonably definite standard which is set forth in the trust instrument, it may extend to corpus distributions to any beneficiary or beneficiaries or class of beneficiaries (whether income beneficiaries or remaindermen) without causing the grantor to be treated as an owner under section 674. See section 674(b)(5)(A). It is not required that the standard consist of the needs and circumstances of the beneficiary. A clearly measurable standard under which the holder of a power is legally accountable is deemed a reasonably definite standard for this purpose. For instance, a power to distribute corpus for the education, support, maintenance, or health of the beneficiary; for his reasonable support and comfort; or to enable him to maintain his accustomed standard of living; or to meet an emergency, would be limited by a reasonably definite standard. However, a power to distribute corpus for the pleasure, desire, or happiness of a beneficiary is not limited by a reasonably definite standard. The entire context of a provision of a trust instrument granting a power must be considered in determining whether the power is limited by a reasonably definite standard. For example, if a trust instrument provides that the determination of the trustee shall be conclusive with respect to the exercise or nonexercise of a power, the power is not limited by a reasonably definite standard. However, the fact that the governing instrument is phrased in discretionary terms is not in itself an indication that no reasonably definite standard exists.

(ii) If the power is not limited by a reasonably definite standard set forth in the trust instrument, the exception applies only if distributions of corpus may be made solely in favor of current income beneficiaries, and any corpus distribution to the current income beneficiary must be chargeable against the proportionate part of corpus held in trust for payment of income to that beneficiary as if it constituted a separate trust (whether or not physically segregated). See section 674(b)(5)(B).

(iii) This subparagraph may be illustrated by the following examples:

Example (1). A trust instrument provides for payment of the income to the grantor's two brothers for life, and for payment of the corpus to the grantor's nephews in equal shares. The grantor reserves the power to distribute corpus to pay medical expenses that may be incurred by his brothers or nephews. The grantor is not treated as an owner by reason of this power because section 674(b)(5)(A) excepts a power, exercisable by any person, to invade corpus for any beneficiary, including a remainderman, if the power is limited by a reasonably definite standard which is set forth in the trust instrument. However, if the power were also exercisable in favor of a person (for example, a sister) who was not otherwise a beneficiary of the trust, section 674(b)(5)(A) would not be applicable.

Example (2). The facts are the same as in example (1) except that the grantor reserves the power to distribute any part of the corpus to his brothers or to his nephews for their happiness. The grantor is treated as the owner of the trust. Paragraph (5)(A) of section 674(b) is inapplicable because the power is not limited by a reasonably definite standard. Paragraph (5)(B) is inapplicable because the power to distribute corpus permits a distribution of corpus to persons other than current income beneficiaries.

Example (3). A trust instrument provides for payment of the income to the grantor's two adult sons in equal shares for 10 years, after which the corpus is to be distributed to his grandchildren in equal shares. The grantor reserves the power to pay over to each son up to one-half of the corpus during the 10-year period, but any such payment shall proportionately reduce subsequent income and corpus payments made to the son receiving the corpus. Thus, if one-half of the corpus is paid to one son, all the income from the remaining half is thereafter payable to the other son. The grantor is not treated as an owner under section 674(a) by reason of this power because it qualifies under the exception of section 674(b)(5)(B).

(6) Powers to withhold income temporarily. **(i)** Section 674(b)(6) excepts a power which, in general, enables the holder merely to effect a postponement in the time when the ordinary income is enjoyed by a current income beneficiary. Specifically, there is excepted a power to distribute or apply ordinary income to or for a current income beneficiary or to accumulate the income, if the accumulated income must ultimately be payable either:

(a) To the beneficiary from whom it was withheld, his estate, or his appointees (or persons designated by name, as a class, or otherwise as alternate takers in default of appointment) under a power of appointment held by the beneficiary which does not exclude from the class of possible appointees any person other than the beneficiary, his estate, his creditors, or the creditors of his estate (section 674(b)(6)(A));

(b) To the beneficiary from whom it was withheld, or if he does not survive a date of distribution which could reasonably be expected to occur within his lifetime, to his appointees (or alternate takers in default of appointment) under any power of appointment, general or special, or if he has no power of appointment to one or more designated alternate takers (other than the grantor of the grantor's estate) whose shares have been irrevocably specified in the trust instrument (section 674(b)(6)(A) and the flush material following); or

(c) On termination of the trust, or in conjunction with a distribution of corpus which is augmented by the accumulated income, to the current income beneficiaries in shares which have been irrevocably specified in the trust instrument, or if any beneficiary does not survive a date of distribution which would reasonably be expected to occur within his lifetime, to his appointees (or alternate takers in default of appointment) under any power of appointment, general or special, or if he has no power of appointment to one or more designated alternate takers (other than the grantor or the grantor's estate) whose shares have been irrevocably specified in the trust instrument (section 674(b)(6)(B) and the flush material following).

(In the application of (a) of this subdivision, if the accumulated income of a trust is ultimately payable to the estate of the current income beneficiary or is ultimately payable to his appointees or takers in default of appointment, under a power of the type described in (a) of this subdivision, it need not be payable to the beneficiary from whom it was withheld under any circumstances. Furthermore, if a trust otherwise qualifies for the exception in (a) of this subdivision the trust income will not be considered to be taxable to the grantor under section 677 by reason of the existence of the power of appointment referred to in (a) of this subdivision.) In general, the exception in section 674(b)(6) is not applicable if the power is in substance one to shift ordinary income from one beneficiary to another. Thus, a power will not qualify for this exception if ordinary income may be distributed to beneficiary A, or may be added to corpus which is ultimately payable to beneficiary B, a remainderman who is not a current income beneficiary. However, section 674(b)(6)(B), and (c) of this subdivision, permit a limited power to shift ordinary income among current income beneficiaries, as illustrated in example (1) of this subparagraph.

(ii) The application of section 674(b)(6) may be illustrated by the following examples:

Example (1). A trust instrument provides that the income shall be paid in equal shares to the grantor's two adult daughters but the grantor reserves the power to withhold from either beneficiary any part of that beneficiary's share of income and to add it to the corpus of the trust until the younger daughter reaches the age of 30 years. When the younger daughter reaches the age of 30, the trust is to terminate and the corpus is to be divided equally between the two daughters or their estates. Although exercise of this power may permit the shifting of accumulated income from one beneficiary to the other (since the corpus with the accumulations is to be divided equally) the power is excepted under section 674(b)(6)(B) and subdivision (i)(c) of this subparagraph.

Example (2). The facts are the same as in example (1), except that the grantor of the trust reserves the power to distribute accumulated income to the beneficiaries in such shares as he chooses. The combined powers are not excepted by section 674(b)(6)(B) since income accumulated pursuant to the first power is neither required to be payable only in conjunction with a corpus distribution nor required to be payable in shares specified in the trust instrument. See, however, section 674(c) and § 1.674(c)-1 for the effect of such a power if it is exercisable only by independent trustees.

Example (3). A trust provides for payment of income to the grantor's adult son with the grantor retaining the power to accumulate the income until the grantor's death, when all accumulations are to be paid to the son. If the son predeceases the grantor, all accumulations are, at the death of the grantor, to be paid to his daughter, or if she is not living, to alternate takers (which do not include the grantor's estate) in specified shares. The power is excepted under section 674(b)(6)(A) since the date of distribution (the date of the grantor's death) may, in the usual case, reasonably be expected to occur during the beneficiary's (the son's) lifetime. It is not necessary that the accumulations be payable to the son's estate or his appointees if he should predecease the grantor for this exception to apply.

(7) **Power to withhold income during disability.** Section 674(b)(7) provides an exception for a power which, in general, will permit ordinary income to be withheld during the legal disability of an income beneficiary or while he is under 21. Specifically, there is excepted a power, exercisable only during the existence of a legal disability of any current income beneficiary or the period during which any income beneficiary is under the age of 21 years, to distribute or apply ordinary income to or for that beneficiary or to accumulate the income and add it to corpus. To qualify under this exception it is not necessary that the income ultimately be payable to the income beneficiary from whom it was withheld, his estate, or his appointees; that is, the accumulated income may be added to corpus and ultimately distributed to others. For example, the grantor is not treated as an owner under section 674 if the income of a trust is payable to his son for life, remainder to his grandchildren, although he reserves the power to accumulate income and add it to corpus while his son is under 21.

(8) **Powers to allocate between corpus and income.** Paragraph (8) of section 674(b) provides that a power to allocate receipts and disbursements between corpus and income, even though expressed in broad language, will not cause the grantor to be treated as an owner under the general rule of section 674(a).

[T.D. 6217, Dec. 19, 1956]

§ 1.674(c)-1 Excepted powers exercisable only by independent trustees.

Section 674(c) provides an exception to the general rule of section 674(a) for certain powers that are exercisable by independent trustees. This exception is in addition to those provided for under section 674(b) which may be held by any person including an independent trustee. The powers to which section 674(c) apply are powers (a) to distribute, apportion, or accumulate income to or for a beneficiary or beneficiaries, or to, for, or within a class of beneficiaries, or (b) to pay out corpus to or for a beneficiary or beneficiaries or to or for a class of beneficiaries (whether or not income beneficiaries). In order for such a power to fall within the exception of section 674(c) it must be exercisable solely (without the approval or consent of any other person) by a trustee or trustees none of whom is the grantor and no more than half of whom are related or subordinate parties who are subservient to the wishes of the grantor. (See section 672(c) for definitions of these terms.) An example of the application of section 674(c) is a trust whose income is payable to the grantor's three adult sons with power in an independent trustee to allocate without restriction the amounts of income to be paid to each son each year. Such a power does not cause the grantor to be treated as the owner of the trust. See however, the limitations set forth in § 1.674(d)-2.

[T.D. 6217, Dec. 19, 1956]

§ 1.674(d)-1 Excepted powers exercisable by any trustee other than grantor or spouse.

Section 674(d) provides an additional exception to the general rule of section 674(a) for a power to distribute, apportion, or accumulate income to or for a beneficiary or beneficiaries or to, for, or within a class of beneficiaries, whether or not the conditions of section 674(b)(6) or (7) are satisfied, if the power is solely exercisable (without the approval or consent of any other person) by a trustee or trustees none of whom is the grantor or spouse living with the grantor, and if the power is limited by a reasonably definite external standard set forth in the trust instrument (see paragraph (b)(5) of § 1.674(b)-1 with respect to what constitutes a reasonably definite standard). See, however, the limitations set forth in § 1.674(d)-2.

[T.D. 6217, Dec. 19, 1956]

§ 1.674(d)-2 Limitations on exceptions in section 674(b), (c), and (d).

(a) Power to remove trustee. A power in the grantor to remove, substitute, or add trustees (other than a power exercisable only upon limited conditions which do not exist during the taxable year, such as the death or resignation of, or breach of fiduciary duty by, an existing trustee) may prevent a trust from qualifying under section 674(c) or (d). For example, if a grantor has an unrestricted power to remove an independent trustee and substitute any person including himself as trustee, the trust will not qualify under section 674(c) or (d). On the other hand if the grantor's power to remove, substitute, or add trustees is limited so that its exercise could not alter the trust in a manner that would disqualify it under section 674(c) or (d), as the case may be, the power itself does not disqualify the trust. Thus, for example, a power in the grantor to remove or discharge an independent trustee on the condition that he substitute another independent trustee will not prevent a trust from qualifying under section 674(c).

(b) Power to add beneficiaries. The exceptions described in section 674(b)(5), (6), and (7), (c), and (d), are not applicable if any person has a power to add to the beneficiary or beneficiaries or to a class of beneficiaries designated to receive the income or corpus, except where the action is to provide for after-born or after-adopted children. This limitation does not apply to a power held by a beneficiary to substitute other beneficiaries to succeed to his interest in the trust (so that he would be an adverse party as to the exercise or nonexercise of that power). For example, the limitation does not apply to a power in a beneficiary of a nonspendthrift trust to assign his interest. Nor does the limitation apply to a power held by any person which would qualify as an exception under section 674(b)(3) (relating to testamentary powers).

[T.D. 6217, Dec. 19, 1956]

§ 1.675–1 Administrative powers.

(a) General rule. Section 675 provides in effect that the grantor is treated as the owner of any portion of a trust if under the terms of the trust instrument or circumstances attendant on its operation administrative control is exercisable primarily for the benefit of the grantor rather than the beneficiaries of the trust. If a grantor retains a power to amend the administrative provisions of a trust instrument which is broad enough to permit an amendment causing the grantor to be treated as the owner of a portion of the trust under section 675, he will be treated as the owner of the portion from its inception. See section 671 and §§ 1.671–2 and 1.671–3 for rules for treatment of items of income, deduction, and credit when a person is treated as the owner of all or only a portion of a trust.

(b) Prohibited controls. The circumstances which cause administrative controls to be considered exercisable primarily for the benefit of the grantor are specifically described in paragraphs (1) through (4) of section 675 as follows:

(1) The existence of a power, exercisable by the grantor or a nonadverse party, or both, without the approval or consent of any adverse party, which enables the grantor or any other person to purchase, exchange, or otherwise deal with or dispose of the corpus or the income of the trust for less than adequate consideration in money or money's worth. Whether the existence of the power itself will constitute the holder an adverse party will depend on the particular circumstances.

(2) The existence of a power exercisable by the grantor or a nonadverse party, or both, which enables the grantor to borrow the corpus or income of the trust, directly or indirectly, without adequate interest or adequate security. However, this paragraph does not apply where a trustee (other than the grantor acting alone) is authorized under a general lending power to make loans to any person without regard to interest or security. A general lending power in the grantor, acting alone as trustee, under which he has power to determine interest rates and the adequacy of security is not in itself an indication that the grantor has power to borrow the corpus or income without adequate interest or security.

(3) The circumstance that the grantor has directly or indirectly borrowed the corpus or income of the trust and has not completely repaid the loan, including any interest, before the beginning of the taxable year. The preceding sentence does not apply to a loan which provides for adequate interest and adequate security, if it is made by a trustee other than the grantor or a related or subordinate trustee subservient to the grantor. See section 672(c) for definition of "a related or subordinate party".

(4) The existence of certain powers of administration exercisable in a nonfiduciary capacity by any nonadverse party without the approval or consent of any person in a fiduciary capacity. The term "powers of administration" means one or more of the following powers:

(i) A power to vote or direct the voting of stock or other securities of a corporation in which the holdings of the grantor and the trust are significant from the viewpoint of voting control;

(ii) A power to control the investment of the trust funds either by directing investments or reinvestments, or by vetoing proposed investments or reinvestments, to the extent that the trust funds consist of stocks or securities of corporations in which the holdings of the grantor and the trust are significant from the viewpoint of voting control; or

(iii) A power to reacquire the trust corpus by substituting other property of an equivalent value.

If a power is exercisable by a person as trustee, it is presumed that the power is exercisable in a fiduciary capacity primarily in the interests of the beneficiaries. This presumption may be rebutted only by clear and convincing proof that the power is not exercisable primarily in the interests of the beneficiaries. If a power is not exercisable by a person as trustee, the determination of whether the power is exercisable in a fiduciary or a nonfiduciary capacity depends on all the terms of the trust and the circumstances surrounding its creation and administration.

(c) **Authority of trustee.** The mere fact that a power exercisable by a trustee is described in broad language does not indicate that the trustee is authorized to purchase, exchange, or otherwise deal with or dispose of the trust property or income for less than an adequate and full consideration in money or money's worth, or is authorized to lend the trust property or income to the grantor without adequate interest. On the other hand, such authority may be indicated by the actual administration of the trust.

[T.D. 6217, Dec. 19, 1956]

§ 1.676(a)-1 Power to revest title to portion of trust property in grantor; general rule.

If a power to revest in the grantor title to any portion of a trust is exercisable by the grantor or a nonadverse party, or both, without the approval or consent of an adverse party, the grantor is treated as the owner of that portion, except as provided in section 676(b) (relating to powers affecting beneficial enjoyment of income only after the expiration of certain periods of time). If the title to a portion of the trust will revest in the grantor upon the exercise of a power by the grantor or a nonadverse party, or both, the grantor is treated as the owner of that portion regardless of whether the power is a power to revoke, to terminate, to alter or amend, or to appoint. See section 671 and §§ 1.671-2 and 1.671-3 for rules for treatment of items of income, deduction, and credit when a person is treated as the owner of all or only a portion of a trust.

[T.D. 6217, Dec. 19, 1956]

§ 1.676(b)-1 Powers exercisable only after a period of time.

Section 676(b) provides an exception to the general rule of section 676(a) when the exercise of a power can only affect the beneficial enjoyment of the income of a trust received after the expiration of a period of time which is such that a grantor would not be treated as the owner of that portion, except as power were a reversionary interest. See §§ 1.673(a)-1 and 1.673(b)-1. Thus, for example, a grantor is excepted from the general rule of section 676(a) with respect to ordinary income if exercise of a power to revest corpus in him cannot affect the beneficial enjoyment of the income received within 10 years after the date of transfer of that portion of the trust. It is immaterial for this purpose that the power is vested at the time of the transfer. However, the grantor is subject to the general rule of section 676(a) after the expiration of the period unless the power is relinquished. Thus, in the above example, the grantor may be treated as the owner and be taxed on all income in the eleventh and succeeding years if exercise of the power can affect beneficial enjoyment of income received in those years. If the beginning of the period during which the grantor may revest is postponed, the rules set forth in § 1.673(d)-1 are applicable to determine whether the grantor should be treated as an owner during the period following the postponement.

[T.D. 6217, Dec. 19, 1956]

§ 1.677(a)-1 Income for benefit of grantor; general rule.

(a)(1) Scope. Section 677 deals with the treatment of the grantor of a trust as the owner of a portion of the trust because he has retained an interest in the income from that portion. For convenience, "grantor" and "spouse" are generally referred to in the masculine and feminine genders, respectively, but if the grantor is a woman the reference to "grantor" is to her and the reference to "spouse" is to her husband. Section 677 also deals with the treatment of the grantor of a trust as the owner of a portion of the trust because the income from property transferred in trust after October 9, 1969, is, or may be, distributed to his spouse or applied to the payment of premiums on policies of insurance on the life of his spouse. However, section 677 does not apply when the income of a trust is taxable to a grantor's spouse under section 71 (relating to alimony and separate maintenance payments) or section 682 (relating to income of an estate or trust in case of divorce, etc.). See section 671-1(b).

* * *

(b) Income for benefit of grantor or his spouse; general rule—

* * *

(2) Property transferred in trust after October 9, 1969. With respect to property transferred in trust after October 9, 1969, the grantor is treated, under section 677, in any taxable year as the owner (whether or not he is treated as an owner under section 674) of a portion of a trust of which the income for the taxable year or for a period not within the exception described in paragraph (e) of this section is, or in the discretion of the grantor, or his spouse, or a nonadverse party, or any combination thereof (without the approval or consent of any adverse party other than the grantor's spouse) may be:

(i) Distributed to the grantor or the grantor's spouse;

(ii) Held or accumulated for future distribution to the grantor or the grantor's spouse; or

(iii) Applied to the payment of premiums on policies of insurance on the life of the grantor or the grantor's spouse, except policies of insurance irrevocably payable for a charitable purpose specified in section 170(c).

With respect to the treatment of a grantor as the owner of a portion of a trust solely because its income is, or may be, distributed or held or accumulated for future distribution to a beneficiary who is his spouse or applied to the payment of premiums for insurance on the spouse's life, section 677(a) applies to the income of a trust solely during the period of the marriage of the grantor to a beneficiary. In the case of divorce or separation, see sections 71 and 682 and the regulations thereunder.

(c) **Constructive distribution; cessation of interest.** Under section 677 the grantor is treated as the owner of a portion of a trust if he has retained any interest which might, without the approval or consent of an adverse party, enable him to have the income from that portion distributed to him at some time either actually or constructively (subject to the exception described in paragraph (e) of this section). In the case of a transfer in trust after October 9, 1969, the grantor is also treated as the owner of a portion of a trust if he has granted or retained any interest which might, without the approval or consent of an adverse party (other than the grantor's spouse), enable his spouse to have the income from the portion at some time, whether or not within the grantor's lifetime, distributed to the spouse either actually or constructively. See paragraph (b)(2) of this section for additional rules relating to the income of a trust prior to the grantor's marriage to a beneficiary. Constructive distribution to the grantor or to his spouse includes payment on behalf of the grantor or his spouse to another in obedience to his or her direction and payment of premiums upon policies of insurance on the grantor's, or his spouse's, life (other than policies of insurance irrevocably payable for charitable purposes specified in section 170(c)). If the grantor (in the case of property transferred prior to Oct. 10, 1969) or the grantor and his spouse (in the case of property transferred after Oct. 9, 1969) are divested permanently and completely of every interest described in this paragraph, the grantor is not treated as an owner under section 677 after that divesting. The word "interest" as used in this paragraph does not include the possibility that the grantor or his spouse might receive back from a beneficiary an interest in a trust by inheritance. Further, with respect to transfers in trust prior to October 10, 1969, the word "interest" does not include the possibility that the grantor might receive back from a beneficiary an interest in a trust as a surviving spouse under a statutory right of election or a similar right.

(d) **Discharge of legal obligation of grantor or his spouse.** Under section 677 a grantor is, in general, treated as the owner of a portion of a trust whose income is, or in the discretion of the grantor or a nonadverse party, or both, may be applied in discharge of a legal obligation of the grantor (or his spouse in the case of property transferred in trust by the grantor after October 9, 1969). However, see § 1.677(b)–1 for special rules for trusts whose income may not be applied for the discharge of any legal obligation of the grantor or the grantor's spouse other than the support or maintenance of a beneficiary (other than the grantor's spouse) whom the grantor or grantor's spouse is legally obligated to support.

(e) **Exception for certain discretionary rights affecting income.** The last sentence of section 677(a) provides that a grantor shall not be treated as the owner when a discretionary right can only affect the beneficial enjoyment of the income of a trust received after a period of time during which a grantor would not be treated as an owner under section 673 if the power were a reversionary interest. See §§ 1.673(a)–1 and 1.673(b)–1. For example, if the ordinary income of a trust is payable to B for 10 years and then in the grantor's discretion income or corpus may be paid to B or to the grantor (or his spouse in the case of property transferred in trust by the grantor after October 9, 1969), the grantor is not treated as an owner with respect to the ordinary income under section 677 during the first 10 years. He will be treated as an owner under section 677 after the expiration of the 10-year period unless the power is relinquished. If the beginning of the period during which the grantor may substitute beneficiaries is postponed, the rules set forth in § 1.673(d)–1 are applicable in determining whether the grantor should be treated as an owner during the period following the postponement.

(f) Accumulation of income. If income is accumulated in any taxable year for future distribution to the grantor (or his spouse in the case of property transferred in trust by the grantor after Oct. 9, 1969), section 677(a)(2) treats the grantor as an owner for that taxable year. The exception set forth in the last sentence of section 677(a) does not apply merely because the grantor (or his spouse in the case of property transferred in trust by the grantor after Oct. 9, 1969) must await the expiration of a period of time before he or she can receive or exercise discretion over previously accumulated income of the trust, even though the period is such that the grantor would not be treated as an owner under section 673 if a reversionary interest were involved. Thus, if income (including capital gains) of a trust is to be accumulated for 10 years and then will be, or at the discretion of the grantor, or his spouse in the case of property transferred in trust after October 9, 1969, or a nonadverse party, may be, distributed to the grantor (or his spouse in the case of property transferred in trust after Oct. 9, 1969), the grantor is treated as the owner of the trust from its inception. If income attributable to transfers after October 9, 1969 is accumulated in any taxable year during the grantor's lifetime for future distribution to his spouse, section 677(a)(2) treats the grantor as an owner for that taxable year even though his spouse may not receive or exercise discretion over such income prior to the grantor's death.

(g) Examples. The application of section 677(a) may be illustrated by the following examples:

Example (1). G creates an irrevocable trust which provides that the ordinary income is to be payable to him for life and that on his death the corpus shall be distributed to B, an unrelated person. Except for the right to receive income, G retains no right or power which would cause him to be treated as an owner under sections 671 through 677. Under the applicable local law capital gains must be applied to corpus. During the taxable year 1970 the trust has the following items of gross income and deductions:

Dividends	$5,000
Capital gain	1,000
Expenses allocable to income	200
Expenses allocable to corpus	100

Since G has a right to receive income he is treated as an owner of a portion of the trust under section 677. Accordingly, he should include the $5,000 of dividends, $200 income expense, and $100 corpus expense in the computation of his taxable income for 1970. He should not include the $1,000 capital gain since that is not attributable to the portion of the trust that he owns. See § 1.671-3(b). The tax consequences of the capital gain are governed by the provisions of subparts A, B, C, and D (section 641 and following), part I, subchapter J, chapter 1 of the Code. Had the trust sustained a capital loss in any amount the loss would likewise not be included in the computation of G's taxable income, but would also be governed by the provisions of such subparts.

Example (2). G creates a trust which provides that the ordinary income is payable to his adult son. Ten years and one day from the date of transfer or on the death of his son, whichever is earlier, corpus is to revert to G. In addition, G retains a discretionary right to receive $5,000 of ordinary income each year. (Absent the exercise of this right all the ordinary income is to be distributed to his son.) G retained no other right or power which would cause him to be treated as an owner under subpart E (section 671 and following). Under the terms of the trust instrument and applicable local law capital gains must be applied to corpus. During the taxable year 1970 the trust had the following items of income and deductions:

Dividends	$10,000
Capital gain	2,000
Expenses allocable to income	400
Expenses allocable to corpus	200

Since the capital gain is held or accumulated for future distributions to G, he is treated under section 677(a)(2) as an owner of a portion of the trust to which the gain is attributable. See § 1.671-3(b).

Therefore, he must include the capital gain in the computation of his taxable income. (Had the trust sustained a capital loss in any amount, G would likewise include that loss in the computation of his taxable income.) In addition, because of G's discretionary right (whether exercised or not) he is treated as the owner of a portion of the trust which will permit a distribution of income to him of $5,000. Accordingly, G includes dividends of $5,208.33 and income expenses of $208.33 in computing his taxable income, determined in the following manner:

Total dividends	$10,000.00
Less: Expenses allocable to income	400.00
Distributable income of the trust	9,600.00
Portion of dividends attributable to G (5,000/9,600 × $10,000)	5,208.33
Portion of income expenses attributable to G (5,000/9,600 × $400)	208.33
Amount of income subject to discretionary right	5,000.00

In accordance with § 1.671-3(c), G also takes into account $104.17 (5,000/9,600 × $200) of corpus expenses in computing his tax liability. The portion of the dividends and expenses of the trust not attributable to G are governed by the provisions of Subparts A through D.

[T.D. 6217, Dec. 19, 1956, as amended by T.D. 7148, Oct. 28, 1971]

§ 1.677(b)-1 Trusts for support.

(a) Section 677(b) provides that a grantor is not treated as the owner of a trust merely because its income may in the discretion of any person other than the grantor (except when he is acting as trustee or cotrustee) be applied or distributed for the support or maintenance of a beneficiary (other than the grantor's spouse in the case of income from property transferred in trust after October 9, 1969), such as the child of the grantor, whom the grantor or his spouse is legally obligated to support. If income of the current year of the trust is actually so applied or distributed the grantor may be treated as the owner of any portion of the trust under section 677 to that extent, even though it might have been applied or distributed for other purposes. In the case of property transferred to a trust before October 10, 1969, for the benefit of the grantor's spouse, the grantor may be treated as the owner to the extent income of the current year is actually applied for the support or maintenance of his spouse.

(b) If any amount applied or distributed for the support of a beneficiary, including the grantor's spouse in the case of property transferred in trust before October 10, 1969, whom the grantor is legally obligated to support is paid out of corpus or out of income other than income of the current year, the grantor is treated as a beneficiary of the trust, and the amount applied or distributed is considered to be an amount paid within the meaning of section 661(a)(2), taxable to the grantor under section 662. Thus, he is subject to the other relevant portions of subparts A through D (section 641 and following), part I, subchapter J, chapter 1 of the Code. Accordingly, the grantor may be taxed on an accumulation distribution or a capital gain distribution under subpart D (section 665 and following) of such part I. Those provisions are applied on the basis that the grantor is the beneficiary.

(c) For the purpose of determining the items of income, deduction, and credit of a trust to be included under this section in computing the grantor's tax liability, the income of the trust for the taxable year of distribution will be deemed to have been first distributed. For example, in the case of a trust reporting on the calendar year basis, a distribution made on January 1, 1956, will be deemed to have been made out of ordinary income of the trust for the calendar year 1956 to the extent of the income for that year even though the trust had received no income as of January 1, 1956. Thus, if a distribution of $10,000 is made on January 1, 1956, for the support of the grantor's dependent, the grantor will be treated as the owner of the trust for 1956 to that extent. If the trust received dividends of $5,000 and incurred expenses of $1,000 during that year but subsequent to January 1, he will take into account dividends of $5,000 and expenses of $1,000 in computing his tax liability for 1956. In addition, the grantor will be treated as a beneficiary of the trust with respect to the $6,000 ($10,000 less distributable income of $4,000 (dividends of $5,000 less expenses of $1,000)) paid out of corpus or out of other than income of the current year. See paragraph (b) of this section.

(d) The exception provided in section 677(b) relates solely to the satisfaction of the grantor's legal obligation to support or maintain a beneficiary. Consequently, the general rule of section 677(a) is applicable when in the discretion of the grantor or nonadverse parties income of a trust may be applied in discharge of a grantor's obligations other than his obligation of support or maintenance falling within section 677(b). Thus, if the grantor creates a trust the income of which may in the discretion of a nonadverse party be applied in the payment of the grantor's debts, such as the payment of his rent or other household expenses, he is treated as an owner of the trust regardless of whether the income is actually so applied.

(e) The general rule of section 677(a), and not section 677(b), is applicable if discretion to apply or distribute income of a trust rests solely in the grantor, or in the grantor in conjunction with other persons, unless in either case the grantor has such discretion as trustee or cotrustee.

(f) The general rule of section 677(a), and not section 677(b), is applicable to the extent that income is required, without any discretionary determination, to be applied to the support of a beneficiary whom the grantor is legally obligated to support.

[T.D. 6217, Dec. 19, 1956, as amended by T.D. 7148, Oct. 28, 1971]

§ 1.678(a)–1 Person other than grantor treated as substantial owner; general rule.

(a) Where a person other than the grantor of a trust has a power exercisable solely by himself to vest the corpus or the income of any portion of a testamentary or inter vivos trust in himself, he is treated under section 678(a) as the owner of that portion, except as provided in section 678(b) (involving taxation of the grantor) and section 678(c) (involving an obligation of support). The holder of such a power also is treated as an owner of the trust even though he has partially released or otherwise modified the power so that he can no longer vest the corpus or income in himself, if he has retained such control of the trust as would, if retained by a grantor, subject the grantor to treatment as the owner under sections 671 to 677, inclusive. See section 671 and §§ 1.671-2 and 1.671-3 for rules for treatment of items of income, deduction, and credit where a person is treated as the owner of all or only a portion of a trust.

(b) Section 678(a) treats a person as an owner of a trust if he has a power exercisable solely by himself to apply the income or corpus for the satisfaction of his legal obligations, other than an obligation to support a dependent (see § 1.678(c)-1 subject to the limitation of section 678(b)). Section 678 does not apply if the power is not exercisable solely by himself. However, see § 1.662(a)-4 for principles applicable to income of a trust which, pursuant to the terms of the trust instrument, is used to satisfy the obligations of a person other than the grantor.

[T.D. 6217, Dec. 19, 1956]

§ 1.678(b)-1 If grantor is treated as the owner.

Section 678(a) does not apply with respect to a power over income, as originally granted or thereafter modified, if the grantor of the trust is treated as the owner under sections 671 to 677, inclusive.

[T.D. 6217, Dec. 19, 1956]

§ 1.678(c)-1 Trusts for support.

(a) Section 678(a) does not apply to a power which enables the holder, in the capacity of trustee or cotrustee, to apply the income of the trust to the support or maintenance of a person whom the holder is obligated to support, except to the extent the income is so applied. See paragraphs (a), (b), and (c) of § 1.677(b)-1 for applicable principles where any amount is applied for the support or maintenance of a person whom the holder is obligated to support.

(b) The general rule in section 678(a) (and not the exception in section 678(c)) is applicable in any case in which the holder of a power exercisable solely by himself is able, in any capacity other than that of trustee or cotrustee, to apply the income in discharge of his obligation of support or maintenance.

(c) Section 678(c) is concerned with the taxability of income subject to a power described in section 678(a). It has no application to the taxability of income which is either required to be applied pursuant to the terms of the trust instrument or is applied pursuant to a power which is not described in section 678(a), the taxability of such income being governed by other provisions of the Code. See § 1.662(a)-4.

[T.D. 6217, Dec. 19, 1956]

§ 1.678(d)-1 Renunciation of power.

Section 678(a) does not apply to a power which has been renounced or disclaimed within a reasonable time after the holder of the power first became aware of its existence.

[T.D. 6217, Dec. 19, 1956]

Income in Respect of Decedents

§ 1.691(a)–1 Income in respect of a decedent.

(a) **Scope of section 691.** In general, the regulations under section 691 cover: (1) The provisions requiring that amounts which are not includible in gross income for the decedent's last taxable year or for a prior taxable year be included in the gross income of the estate or persons receiving such income to the extent that such amounts constitute "income in respect of a decedent"; (2) the taxable effect of a transfer of the right to such income; (3) the treatment of certain deductions and credit in respect of a decedent which are not allowable to the decedent for the taxable period ending with his death or for a prior taxable year; (4) the allowance to a recipient of income in respect of a decedent of a deduction for estate taxes attributable to the inclusion of the value of the right to such income in the decedent's estate; (5) special provisions with respect to installment obligations acquired from a decedent and with respect to the allowance of a deduction for estate taxes to a surviving annuitant under a joint and survivor annuity contract; and (6) special provisions relating to installment obligations transmitted at death when prior law applied to the transmission.

(b) **General definition.** In general, the term "income in respect of a decedent" refers to those amounts to which a decedent was entitled as gross income but which were not properly includible in computing his taxable income for the taxable year ending with the date of his death or for a previous taxable year under the method of accounting employed by the decedent. See the regulations under section 451. Thus, the term includes—

(1) All accrued income of a decedent who reported his income by use of the cash receipts and disbursements method;

(2) Income accrued solely by reason of the decedent's death in case of a decedent who reports his income by use of an accrual method of accounting; and

(3) Income to which the decedent had a contingent claim at the time of his death.

See sections 736 and 753 and the regulations thereunder for "income in respect of a decedent" in the case of a deceased partner.

(c) **Prior decedent.** The term "income in respect of a decedent" also includes the amount of all items of gross income in respect of a prior decedent, if (1) the right to receive such amount was acquired by the decedent by reason of the death of the prior decedent or by bequest, devise, or inheritance from the prior decedent and if (2) the amount of gross income in respect of the prior decedent was not properly includible in computing the decedent's taxable income for the taxable year ending with the date of his death or for a previous taxable year. See example (2) of paragraph (b) of § 1.691(a)–2.

(d) **Items excluded from gross income.** Section 691 applies only to the amount of items of gross income in respect of a decedent, and items which are excluded from gross income under subtitle A of the Code are not within the provisions of section 691.

* * *

[T.D. 6217, Dec. 19, 1956, as amended by T.D. 6808, March 15, 1965]

§ 1.691(a)–2 Inclusion in gross income by recipients.

(a) Under section 691(a)(1), income in respect of a decedent shall be included in the gross income, for the taxable year when received, of—

(1) The estate of the decedent, if the right to receive the amount is acquired by the decedent's estate from the decedent;

(2) The person who, by reason of the death of the decedent, acquires the right to receive the amount, if the right to receive the amount is not acquired by the decedent's estate from the decedent; or

(3) The person who acquires from the decedent the right to receive the amount by bequest, devise, or inheritance, if the amount is received after a distribution by the decedent's estate of such right.

These amounts are included in the income of the estate or of such persons when received by them whether or not they report income by use of the cash receipts and disbursements methods.

(b) The application of paragraph (a) of this section may be illustrated by the following examples, in each of which it is assumed that the decedent kept his books by use of the cash receipts and disbursements method.

Example (1). The decedent was entitled at the date of his death to a large salary payment to be made in equal annual installments over five years. His estate, after collecting two installments, distributed the right to the remaining installment payments to the residuary legatee of the estate. The estate must include in its gross income the two installments received by it, and the legatee must include in his gross income each of the three installments received by him.

Example (2). A widow acquired, by bequest from her husband, the right to receive renewal commissions on life insurance sold by him in his lifetime, which commissions were payable over a period of years. The widow died before having received all of such commissions, and her son inherited the right to receive the rest of the commissions. The commissions received by the widow were includible in her gross income. The commissions received by the son were not includible in the widow's gross income but must be included in the gross income of the son.

Example (3). The decedent owned a Series E United States savings bond, with his wife as co-owner or beneficiary, but died before the payment of such bond. The entire amount of interest accruing on the bond and not includible in income by the decedent, not just the amount accruing after the death of the decedent, would be treated as income to his wife when the bond is paid.

Example (4). A, prior to his death, acquired 10,000 shares of the capital stock of the X Corporation at a cost of $100 per share. During his lifetime, A had entered into an agreement with X Corporation whereby X Corporation agreed to purchase and the decedent agreed that his executor would sell the 10,000 shares of X Corporation stock owned by him at the book value of the stock at the date of A's death. Upon A's death, the shares are sold by A's executor for $500 a share pursuant to the agreement. Since the sale of stock is consummated after A's death, there is no income in respect of a decedent with respect to the appreciation in value of A's stock to the date of his death. If, in this example, A had in fact sold the stock during his lifetime but payment had not been received before his death, any gain on the sale would constitute income in respect of a decedent when the proceeds were received.

Example (5). (1) A owned and operated an apple orchard. During his lifetime, A sold and delivered 1,000 bushels of apples to X, a canning factory, but did not receive payment before his death. A also entered into negotiations to sell 3,000 bushels of apples to Y, a canning factory, but did not complete the sale before his death. After A's death, the executor received payment from X. He also completed the sale to Y and transferred to Y 1,200 bushels of apples on hand at A's death and harvested and transferred an additional 1,800 bushels. The gain from the sale of apples by A to X constitutes income in respect of a decedent when received. On the other hand, the gain from the sale of apples by the executor to Y does not.

(2) Assume that, instead of the transaction entered into with Y, A had disposed of the 1,200 bushels of harvested apples by delivering them to Z, a cooperative association, for processing and sale. Each year the association commingles the fruit received from all of its members into a pool and assigns to each member a percentage interest in the pool based on the fruit delivered by him. After the fruit is processed and the products are sold, the association distributes the net proceeds from the pool to its members in proportion to their interests in the pool. After A's death, the association made distributions to the executor with respect to A's share of the proceeds from the pool in which A had an interest. Under such circumstances, the proceeds from the disposition of the 1,200 bushels of apples constitute income in respect of a decedent.

[T.D. 6257, Oct. 7, 1957]

§ 1.691(a)–3 Character of gross income.

(a) The right to receive an amount of income in respect of a decedent shall be treated in the hands of the estate, or by the person entitled to receive such amount by bequest, devise, or inheritance from the decedent or by reason of his death, as if it had been acquired in the transaction by which the decedent (or a prior decedent) acquired such right, and shall be considered as having the same character it would have had if the decedent (or a prior decedent) had lived and received such amount. The provisions of section 1014(a), relating to the basis of property acquired from a decedent, do not apply to these amounts in the hands of the estate and such persons. See section 1014(c).

* * *

[T.D. 6217, Dec. 19, 1956, as amended by T.D. 6885, June 1, 1966; T.D. 7728, Oct. 31, 1980]

§ 1.691(a)–4 Transfer of right to income in respect of a decedent.

(a) Section 691(a)(2) provides the rules governing the treatment of income in respect of a decedent (or a prior decedent) in the event a right to receive such income is transferred by the estate or person entitled thereto by bequest, devise, or inheritance, or by reason of the death of the decedent. In general, the transferor must include in his gross income for the taxable period in which the transfer occurs the amount of the consideration, if any, received for the right or the fair market value of the right at the time of the transfer, whichever is greater. Thus, upon a sale of such right by the estate or person entitled to receive it, the fair market value of the right or the amount received upon the sale, whichever is greater, is included in the gross income of the vendor. Similarly, if such right is disposed of by gift, the fair market value of the right at the time of the gift must be included in the gross income of the donor. In the case of a satisfaction of an installment obligation at other than face value, which is likewise considered a transfer under section 691(a)(2), see § 1.691(a)–5.

(b) If the estate of a decedent or any person transmits the right to income in respect of a decedent to another who would be required by section 691(a)(1) to include such income when received in his gross income, only the transferee will include such income when received in his gross income. In this situation, a transfer within the meaning of section 691(a)(2) has not occurred. This paragraph may be illustrated by the following:

> **(1)** If a person entitled to income in respect of a decedent dies before receiving such income, only his estate or other person entitled to such income by bequest, devise, or inheritance from the latter decedent, or by reason of the death of the latter decedent, must include such amount in gross income when received.
>
> **(2)** If a right to income in respect of a decedent is transferred by an estate to a specific or residuary legatee, only the specific or residuary legatee must include such income in gross income when received.
>
> **(3)** If a trust to which is bequeathed a right of a decedent to certain payments of income terminates and transfers the right to a beneficiary, only the beneficiary must include such income in gross income when received.

If the transferee described in subparagraphs (1), (2), and (3) of this paragraph transfers his right to receive the amounts in the manner described in paragraph (a) of this section, the principles contained in paragraph (a) are applied to such transfer. On the other hand, if the transferee transmits his right in the manner described in this paragraph, the principles of this paragraph are again applied to such transfer.

[T.D. 6217, Dec. 19, 1956]

§ 1.691(a)–5 Installment obligations acquired from decedent.

(a) Section 691(a)(4) has reference to an installment obligation which remains uncollected by a decedent (or a prior decedent) and which was originally acquired in a transaction the income from which was properly reportable by the decedent on the installment method under section 453. Under the provisions of section 691(a)(4), an amount equal to the excess of the face value of the obligation over its basis in the hands of the decedent (determined under section 453(d)(2) and the regulations thereunder) shall be considered an amount of income in respect of a decedent and shall be treated as such. The decedent's estate (or the person entitled to receive such income by bequest or inheritance from the decedent or by reason of the decedent's death) shall include in its gross income when received the same proportion of any payment in satisfaction of such obligations as would be returnable as income by the decedent if he had lived and received such payment. No gain on account of the transmission of such obligations by the decedent's death is required to be reported as income in the return of the decedent for the year of his death. See § 1.691(e)–1 for special provisions relating to the filing of an election to have the provisions of section 691(a)(4) apply in the case of installment obligations in respect of which section 44(d) of the Internal Revenue Code of 1939 (or corresponding provisions of prior law) would have applied but for the filing of a bond referred to therein.

(b) If an installment obligation described in paragraph (a) of this section is transferred within the meaning of section 691(a)(2) and paragraph (a) of

§ 1.691(a)-4, the entire installment obligation transferred shall be considered a right to income in respect of a decedent but the amount includible in the gross income of the transferor shall be reduced by an amount equal to the basis of the obligation in the hands of the decedent (determined under section 453(d)(2) and the regulations thereunder) adjusted, however, to take into account the receipt of any installment payments after the decedent's death and before such transfer. Thus, the amount includible in the gross income of the transferor shall be the fair market value of such obligation at the time of the transfer or the consideration received for the transfer of the installment obligation, whichever is greater, reduced by the basis of the obligation as described in the preceding sentence. For purposes of this paragraph, the term "transfer" in section 691(a)(2) and paragraph (a) of § 1.691(a)-4 includes the satisfaction of an installment obligation at other than face value.

(c) The application of this section may be illustrated by the following example:

Example. An heir of a decedent is entitled to collect an installment obligation with a face value of $100, a fair market value of $80, and a basis in the hands of the decedent of $60. If the heir collects the obligation at face value, the excess of the amount collected over the basis is considered income in respect of a decedent and includible in the gross income of the heir under section 691(a)(1). In this case, the amount includible would be $40 ($100 less $60). If the heir collects the obligation at $90, an amount other than face value, the entire obligation is considered a right to receive income in respect of a decedent but the amount ordinarily required to be included in the heir's gross income under section 691(a)(2) (namely, the consideration received in satisfaction of the installment obligation or its fair market value, whichever is greater) shall be reduced by the amount of the basis of the obligation in the hands of the decedent. In this case, the amount includible would be $30 ($90 less $60).

[T.D. 6257, Oct. 7, 1957, as amended by T.D. 6808, Mar. 15, 1965]

§ 1.691(b)-1 Allowance of deductions and credit in respect to decedents.

(a) Under section 691(b) the expenses, interest, and taxes described in sections 162, 163, 164, and 212 for which the decedent (or a prior decedent) was liable, which were not properly allowable as a deduction in his last taxable year or any prior taxable year, are allowed when paid—

(1) As a deduction by the estate; or

(2) If the estate was not liable to pay such obligation, as a deduction by the person who by bequest, devise, or inheritance from the decedent or by reason of the death of the decedent acquires, subject to such obligation, an interest in property of the decedent (or the prior decedent).

Similar treatment is given to the foreign tax credit provided by section 33. For the purposes of subparagraph (2) of this paragraph, the right to receive an amount of gross income in respect of a decedent is considered property of the decedent; on the other hand, it is not necessary for a person, otherwise within the provisions of subparagraph (2) of this paragraph, to receive the right to any income in respect of a decedent. Thus, an heir who receives a right to income in respect of a decedent (by reason of the death of the decedent) subject to any income tax imposed by a foreign country during the decedent's life, which tax must be satisfied out of such income, is entitled to the credit provided by section 33 when he pays the tax. If a decedent who reported income by use of the cash receipts and disbursements method owned real property on which accrued taxes had become a lien, and if such property passed directly to the heir of the decedent in a jurisdiction in which real property does not become a part of a decedent's estate, the heir, upon paying such taxes, may take the same deduction under section 164 that would be allowed to the decedent if, while alive, he had made such payment.

(b) The deduction for percentage depletion is allowable only to the person (described in section 691(a)(1)) who receives the income in respect of the decedent to which the deduction relates, whether or not such person receives the property from which such income is derived. Thus, an heir who (by reason of the decedent's death) receives income derived from sales of units of mineral by the decedent (who reported income by use of the cash receipts and disbursements method) shall be allowed the deduction for percentage depletion, computed on the gross income from such number of units as if the heir had the same economic interest in the property as the decedent. Such heir need not also receive any interest in the mineral property other than such income. If the decedent did not compute his deduction for depletion on the basis of percentage depletion, any deduction for depletion to which the decedent was entitled at the date of his death would be allowable in computing his taxable income for his last taxable year, and there can be no deduction in respect of the decedent by any other person for such depletion.

[T.D. 6217, Dec. 19, 1956]

§ 1.691(c)-1 Deduction for estate tax attributable to income in respect of a decedent.

(a) In general. A person who is required to include in gross income for any taxable year an amount of income in respect of a decedent may deduct for the same taxable year that portion of the estate tax imposed upon the decedent's estate which is attributable to the inclusion in the decedent's estate of the right to receive such amount. The deduction is determined as follows:

(1) Ascertain the net value in the decedent's estate of the items which are included under section 691 in computing gross income. This is the excess of the value included in the gross estate on account of the items of gross income in respect of the decedent (see § 1.691(a)-1 and paragraph (c) of this section) over the deductions from the gross estate for claims which represent the deductions and credit in respect of the decedent (see § 1.691(b)-1). But see section 691(d) and paragraph (b) of § 1.691(d)-1 for computation of the special value of a survivor's annuity to be used in computing the net value for estate tax purposes in cases involving joint and survivor annuities.

(2) Ascertain the portion of the estate tax attributable to the inclusion in the gross estate of such net value. This is the excess of the estate tax over the estate tax computed without including such net value in the gross estate. In computing the estate tax without including such net value in the gross estate, any estate tax deduction (such as the marital deduction) which may be based upon the gross estate shall be recomputed so as to take into account the exclusion of such net value from the gross estate. See example (2), paragraph (e) of § 1.691(d)-1. For purposes of this section, the term "estate tax" means the tax imposed under section 2001 or 2101 (or the corresponding provisions of the Internal Revenue Code of 1939), reduced by the credits against such tax. Each person including in gross income an amount of income in respect of a decedent may deduct as his share of the portion of the estate tax (computed under subparagraph (2) of this paragraph) an amount which bears the same ratio to such portion as the value in the gross estate of the right to the income included by such person in gross income (or the amount included in gross income if lower) bears to the value in the gross estate of all the items of gross income in respect of the decedent.

(b) Prior decedent. If a person is required to include in gross income an amount of income in respect of a prior decedent, such person may deduct for the same taxable year that portion of the estate tax imposed upon the prior decedent's estate which is attributable to the inclusion in the prior decedent's estate of the value of the right to receive such amount. This deduction is computed in the same manner as provided in paragraph (a) of this section and is in addition to the deduction of estate tax imposed upon the decedent's estate which is attributable to the inclusion in the decedent's estate of the right to receive such amount.

(c) Amounts deemed to be income in respect of a decedent. For purposes of allowing the deduction under section 691(c), the following items are also considered to be income in respect of a decedent under section 691(a):

(1) The value for estate tax purposes of stock options in respect of which amounts are includible in gross income under section 421(b) (prior to amendment by section 221(a) of the Revenue Act of 1964), in the case of taxable years ending before January 1, 1964, or under section 422(c)(1), 423(c), or 424(c)(1), whichever is applicable, in the case of taxable years ending after December 31, 1963. See section 421(d)(6) (prior to amendment by sec. 221(a) of the Revenue Act of 1964), in the case of taxable years ending before January 1, 1964, and section 421(c)(2), in the case of taxable years ending after December 31, 1963.

(2) Amounts received by a surviving annuitant during his life expectancy period as an annuity under a joint and survivor annuity contract to the extent included in gross income under section 72. See section 691(d).

(d) Examples. Paragraphs (a) and (b) of this section may be illustrated by the following examples:

Example (1). X, an attorney who kept his books by use of the cash receipts and disbursements method, was entitled at the date of his death to a fee for services rendered in a case not completed at the time of his death, which fee was valued in his estate at $1,000, and to accrued bond interest, which was valued in his estate at $500. In all, $1,500 was included in his gross estate in respect of income described in section 691(a)(1). There were deducted as claims against his estate $150 for business expenses for which his estate was liable and $50 for taxes accrued on certain property which he owned. In all, $200 was deducted for claims which represent amounts described in section 691(b) which are allowable as deductions to his estate or to the beneficiaries of his estate. His gross estate was $185,000 and, considering deductions of $15,000 and an exemption of $60,000, his taxable estate amounted to $110,000. The estate tax on this amount is $23,700 from which is subtracted a $75 credit for State death taxes leaving an estate tax liability of $23,625. In the year following the closing of X's estate, the fee in the amount of $1,200 was collected by X's son, who was the sole beneficiary of the estate. This amount was included under section 691(a)(1)(C) in the son's gross income. The son may deduct, in computing his taxable income for such year, $260 on account of the estate tax attributable to such income, computed as follows:

(1)	(i) Value of income described in section 691(a)(1) included in computing gross estate	$ 1,500
	(ii) Deductions in computing gross estate for claims representing deductions described in section 691(b)	200
	(iii) Net value of items described in section 691(a)(1)	1,300
(2)	(i) Estate tax	23,625
	(ii) Less: Estate tax computed without including $1,300 (item (1)(iii)) in gross estate	23,235
	(iii) Portion of estate tax attributable to net value of items described in section 691(a)(1)	390
(3)	(i) Value in gross estate of items described in section 691(a)(1) received in taxable year (fee)	1,000
	(ii) Value in gross estate of all income items described in section 691(a)(1) (item (1)(i))	1,500
	(iii) Part of estate tax deductible on account of receipt of $1,200 fee (1,000/1,500 of $390)	260

Although $1,200 was later collected as the fee, only the $1,000 actually included in the gross estate is used in the above computations. However, to avoid distortion, section 691(c) provides that if the value included in the gross estate is greater than the amount finally collected, only the amount collected shall be used in the above computations. Thus, if the amount collected as the fee were only $500, the estate tax deductible on the receipt of such amount would be 500/1,500 of $390, or $130. With respect taxable years ending before January 1, 1964, see paragraph (d)(3) of § 1.421–5 for a similar example involving a restricted stock option. With respect to taxable years ending after December 31, 1963, see paragraph (c)(3) of § 1.421–8 for a similar example involving a stock option subject to the provisions of part II of subchapter D.

Example (2). Assume that in example (1) the fee valued at $1,000 had been earned by prior decedent Y and had been inherited by X who died before collecting it. With regard to the son, the fee would be considered income in respect of a prior decedent. Assume further that the fee was valued at $1,000 in Y's estate, that the net value in Y's estate of items described in section 691(a)(1) was $5,000 and that the estate tax imposed on Y's estate attributable to such net value was $550. In such case, the portion of such estate tax attributable to the fee would be 1,000/5,000 of $550, or $110. When the son collects the $1,200 fee, he will receive for the same taxable year a deduction of $110 with respect to the estate tax imposed on the estate of prior decedent Y as well as the deduction of $260 (as computed in example (1)) with respect to the estate tax imposed on the estate of decedent X.

[T.D. 6257, Oct. 7, 1967, as amended by T.D. 6887, June 23, 1966]

§ 1.691(c)–2 Estates and trusts.

(a) In the case of an estate or trust, the deduction prescribed in section 691(c) is determined in the same manner as described in § 1.691(c)–1, with the following exceptions:

(1) If any amount properly paid, credited, or required to be distributed by an estate or trust to a beneficiary consists of income in respect of a decedent received by the estate or trust during the taxable year—

(i) Such income shall be excluded in determining the income in respect of the decedent with respect to which the estate or trust is entitled to a deduction under section 691(c), and

(ii) Such income shall be considered income in respect of a decedent to such beneficiary for purposes of allowing the deduction under section 691(c) to such beneficiary.

(2) For determination of the amount of income in respect of a decedent received by the beneficiary, see sections 652 and 662, and §§ 1.652(b)-2 and 1.662(b)-2. However, for this purpose, distributable net income as defined in section 643(a) and the regulations thereunder shall be computed without taking into account the estate tax deduction provided in section 691(c) and this section. Distributable net income as modified under the preceding sentence shall be applied for other relevant purposes of subchapter J, chapter 1 of the Code, such as the deduction provided by section 651 or 661, or subpart D, part I of subchapter J, relating to excess distributions by trusts.

(3) The rule stated in subparagraph (1) of this paragraph does not apply to income in respect of a decedent which is properly allocable to corpus by the fiduciary during the taxable year but which is distributed to a beneficiary in a subsequent year. The deduction provided by section 691(c) in such a case is allowable only to the estate or trust. If any amount properly paid, credited, or required to be distributed by a trust qualifies as a distribution under section 666, the fact that a portion thereof constitutes income in respect of a decedent shall be disregarded for the purposes of determining the deduction of the trust and of the beneficiaries under section 691(c) since the deduction for estate taxes was taken into consideration in computing the undistributed net income of the trust for the preceding taxable year.

(b) This section shall apply only to amounts properly paid, credited, or required to be distributed in taxable years of an estate or trust beginning after December 31, 1953, and ending after August 16, 1954, except as otherwise provided in paragraph (c) of this section.

* * *

(d) The provisions of this section may be illustrated by the following example, in which it is assumed that the estate and the beneficiary make their returns on the calendar year basis:

Example (1) The fiduciary of an estate receives taxable interest of $5,500 and income in respect of a decedent of $4,500 during the taxable year. Neither the will of the decedent nor local law requires the allocation to corpus of income in respect of a decedent. The estate tax attributable to the income in respect of a decedent is $1,500. In his discretion, the fiduciary distributes $2,000 (falling within sections 661(a) and 662(a)) to a beneficiary during that year. On these facts the fiduciary and beneficiary are respectively entitled to estate tax deductions of $1,200 and $300, computed as follows:

(2) Distributable net income computed under section 643(a) without regard to the estate tax deduction under section 691(c) is $10,000, computed as follows:

Taxable interest	$ 5,500
Income in respect of a decedent	4,500
Total	10,000

(3) Inasmuch as the distributable net income of $10,000 exceeds the amount of $2,000 distributed to the beneficiary, the deduction allowable to the estate under section 661(a), and the amount taxable to the beneficiary under section 662(a), is $2,000.

(4) The character of the amounts distributed to the beneficiary under section 662(b) is shown in the following table:

	Taxable interest	Income in respect of a decedent	Total
Distributable net income	$5,000	$4,500	$10,000
Amount deemed distributed under section 662(b)	1,100	900	2,000

(5) Accordingly, the beneficiary will be entitled to an estate tax deduction of $300 (900/4,500 × $1,500) and the estate will be entitled to an estate tax deduction of $1,200 (3,600/4,500 × $1,500).

(6) The taxable income of the estate is $6,200, computed as follows:

Gross income		$10,000
Less:		
Distributions to the beneficiary	$2,000	
Estate tax deduction under section 691(c)	1,200	
Personal exemption	600	3,800
Taxable income		6,200

[T.D. 6257, Oct. 7, 1957]

§ 1.691(d)-1 Amounts received by surviving annuitant under joint and survivor annuity contract.

(a) In general. Under section 691(d), annuity payments received by a surviving annuitant under a joint and survivor annuity contract (to the extent indicated in paragraph (b) of this section) are treated as income in respect of a decedent under section 691(a) for the purpose of allowing the deduction for estate tax provided for in section 691(c)(1)(A). This section applies only if the deceased annuitant died after December 31, 1953, and after the annuity starting date as defined in section 72(c)(4).

(b) Special value for surviving annuitant's payments. Section 691(d) provides a special value for the surviving annuitant's payments to determine the amount of the estate tax deduction provided for in section 691(c)(1)(A). This special value is determined by multiplying—

(1) The excess of the value of the annuity at the date of death of the deceased annuitant over the total amount excludable from the gross income of the surviving annuitant under section 72 during his life expectancy period (see paragraph (d)(1)(i) of this section) by

(2) A fraction consisting of the value of the annuity for estate tax purposes over the value of the annuity at the date of death of the deceased annuitant.

This special value is used for the purpose of determining the net value for estate tax purposes (see section 691(c)(2)(B) and paragraph (a)(1) of § 1.691(c)-1) and for the purpose of determining the portion of estate tax attributable to the survivor's annuity (see paragraph (a) of § 1.691(c)-1).

(c) **Amount of deduction.** The portion of estate tax attributable to the survivor's annuity (see paragraph (a) of § 1.691(c)–1) is allowable as a deduction to the surviving annuitant over his life expectancy period. If the surviving annuitant continues to receive annuity payments beyond this period, there is no further deduction under section 691(d). If the surviving annuitant dies before expiration of such period, there is no compensating adjustment for the unused deduction.

(d) **Definitions.** (1) For purposes of section 691(d) and this section:

(i) The term "life expectancy period" means the period beginning with the first day of the first period for which an amount is received by the surviving annuitant under the contract and ending with the close of the taxable year with or in which falls the termination of the life expectancy of the surviving annuitant.

(ii) The life expectancy of the surviving annuitant shall be determined as of the date of death of the deceased annuitant, with reference to actuarial Table I set forth in § 1.72–9 (but without making any adjustment under paragraph (a)(2) of § 1.72–5).

(iii) The value of the annuity at the date of death of the deceased annuitant shall be the entire value of the survivor's annuity determined by reference to the principles set forth in section 2031 and the regulations thereunder, relating to the valuation of annuities for estate tax purposes.

(iv) The value of the annuity for estate tax purposes shall be that portion of the value determined under subdivision (iii) of this subparagraph which was includible in the deceased annuitant's gross estate.

(2) The determination of the "life expectancy period" of the survivor for purposes of section 691(d) may be illustrated by the following example:

Example. H and W file their income tax returns on the calendar year basis. H dies on July 15, 1955, on which date W is 70 years of age. On August 1, 1955, W receives a monthly payment under a joint and survivor annuity contract. W's life expectancy determined as of the date of H's death is 15 years as determined from Table I in § 1.72–9; thus her life expectancy ends on July 14, 1970. Under the provisions of section 691(d), her life expectancy period begins as of July 1, 1955, and ends as of December 31, 1970, thus giving her a life expectancy period of 15½ years.

(e) **Examples.** The application of section 691(d) and this section may be illustrated by the following examples:

Example (1). (1) H and W, husband and wife, purchased a joint and survivor annuity contract for $203,800 providing for monthly payments of $1,000 starting January 28, 1954, and continuing for their joint lives and for the remaining life of the survivor. H contributed $152,850 and W contributed $50,950 to the cost of the annuity. As of the annuity starting date, January 1, 1954, H's age at his nearest birthday was 70 and W's age at her nearest birthday was 67. H dies on January 1, 1957, and beginning on January 28, 1957, W receives her monthly payments of $1,000. The value of the annuity at the date of H's death is $159,000 (see paragraph (d)(1)(iii) of this section), and the value of the annuity for estate tax purposes (see paragraph (d)(1)(iv) of this section) is $119,250 (152,850/203,800 of $159,000). As of the date of H's death, W's age is 70 and her life expectancy period is 15 years (see paragraph (d) of this section for method of computation). Both H and W reported income by use of the cash receipts and disbursements method and filed income tax returns on the calendar year basis.

(2) The following computations illustrate the application of section 72 in determining the excludable portions of the annuity payments to W during her life expectancy period:

Amount of annuity payments per year (12 × $1,000)	$ 12,000
Life expectancy of H and W as of the annuity starting date (see section 72(c)(3)(A) and Table II of § 1.72–9 (male, age 70; female, age 67))	19.7
Expected return as of the annuity starting date, January 1, 1954 ($12,000 × 19.7 as determined under section 72(c)(3)(A) and paragraph (b) of § 1.72–5)	236,400
Investment in the contract as of the annuity starting date, January 1, 1954 (see section 72(c)(1) and paragraph (a) of § 1.72–6)	203,800
Exclusion ratio (203,800/236,400 as determined under section 72(b) and § 1.72–4) (percent)	86.2
Exclusion per year under section 72 ($12,000 × 86.2 percent)	10,344
Excludable during W's life expectancy period ($10,344 × 15)	155,160

(3) For the purpose of computing the deduction for estate tax under section 691(c), the value for estate tax purposes of the amounts includible in W's gross income and considered income in respect of a decedent by virtue of section 691(d)(1) is $2,880. This amount is arrived at in accordance with the formula contained in section 691(d)(2), as follows:

Value of annuity at date of H's death	$159,000
Total amount excludable from W's gross income under section 72 during W's life expectancy period (see subparagraph (2) of this example)	155,160
Excess	3,840
Ratio which value of annuity for estate tax purposes bears to value of annuity at date of H's death (119,250/159,000) (percent)	75
Value for estate tax purposes (75 percent of $3,840)	2,880

This amount ($2,880) is included in the items of income under section 691(a)(1) for the purpose of determining the estate tax attributable to each item under section 691(c)(1)(A). The estate tax determined to be attributable to the item of $2,880 is then allowed as a deduction to W over her 15–year life expectancy period (see example (2) of this paragraph).

Example (2). Assume, in addition to the facts contained in example (1) of this paragraph, that H was an attorney and was entitled at the date of his death to a fee for services rendered in a case not completed at the time of his death, which fee was valued at $1,000, and to accrued bond interest, which was valued at $500. Taking into consideration the annuity payments of example (1), valued at $2,880, a total of $4,380 was included in his gross estate in respect of income described in section 691(a)(1). There were deducted as claims against his estate $280 for business expenses for which his estate was liable and $100 for taxes accrued on certain property which he owned. In all, $380 was deducted for claims which represent amounts described in section 691(b) which are allowable as deductions to his estate or to the beneficiaries of his estate. His gross estate was $404,250 and considering deductions of $15,000, a marital deduction of $119,250 (assuming the annuity to be the only qualifying gift) and an exemption of $60,000, his taxable estate amounted to $210,000. The estate tax on this amount is $53,700 from which is subtracted a $175 credit for State death taxes, leaving an estate tax liability of $53,525. W may deduct, in computing her taxable income during each year of her 15–year life expectancy period, $14.73 on account of the estate tax attributable to the value for estate tax purposes of that portion of the annuity payments considered income in respect of a decedent, computed as follows:

(1)	(i) Value of income described in section 691(a)(1) included in computing gross estate	$ 4,380.00
	(ii) Deductions in computing gross estate for claims representing deductions described in section 691(b)	380.00
	(iii) Net value of items described in section 691(a)(1)	4,000.00
(2)	(i) Estate tax	53,525.00
	(ii) Less: Estate tax computed without including $4,000 (item (1)(iii)) in gross estate and by reducing marital deduction by $2,880 (portion of item (1)(iii) allowed as a marital deduction)	53,189.00
	(iii) Portion of estate tax attributable to net value of income items	336.00
(3)	(i) Value in gross estate of income attributable to annuity payments	2,880.00
	(ii) Value in gross estate of all income items described in section 691(a)(1) (item (1)(i))	4,380.00
	(iii) Part of estate attributable to annuity income (2,880/4,380 of $336)	220.93
	(iv) Deduction each year on account of estate tax attributable to annuity income (220.93 ÷ 15 (life expectancy period))	14.73

[T.D. 6257, Oct. 7, 1957]

*

Index

References are to Pages

References are to Pages

†

0-314-42565-9

9 780314 425652 90000